aUI

THE LANGUAGE OF SPACE

Pentecostal Logos of Love & Peace

For the first time represented and
adapted to the needs of this planet

by

DR. JOHN W. WEILGART

Dedicated to the cosmic-conscious youth,
the young Spacemen of the Atomic Age.

With hundred Illustrations by Elisabeth Söderberg

Fourth Edition with 20 Languages

Published by
COSMIC COMMUNICATION COMPANY
100 Elm Court, Decorah, Iowa 52101, U.S.A.

Sole Distributors in India:

S. CHAND & CO.

Ram Nagar	—	New Delhi
Fountain	—	Delhi
Mai Hiran Gate	—	Jullundur
Aminabad Park	—	Lucknow
167, Lamington Road	—	Bombay
32, Ganesh Chandra Ave.	—	Calcutta
35, Mount Road	—	Madras
Sultan Bazar	—	Hyderabad

Library of Congress Catalog No. PM 8008, W4, 1979 Dewey Dec

CSt WU 499,9'9

ISBN 0-912038-08-X

Published by Cosmic Communication Co., Decorah, Iowa 52101, U.S.A.

CONTENTS

The Symbols of

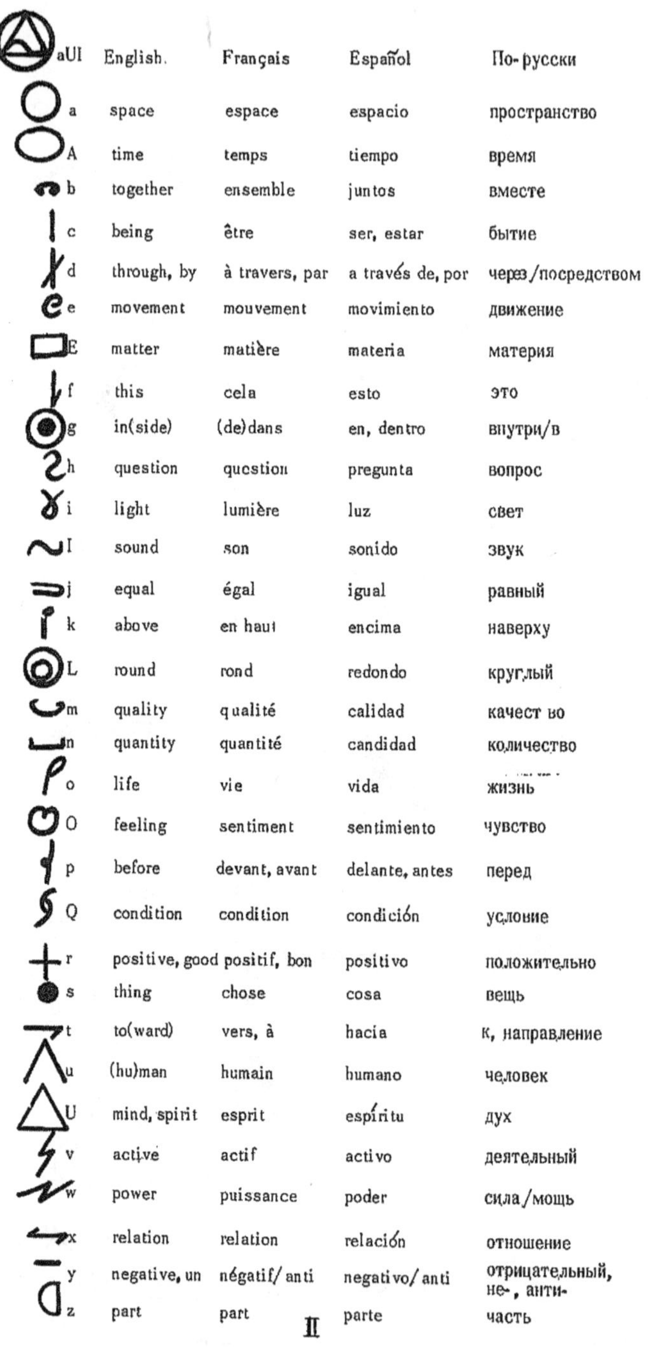

aUI	English.	Français	Español	По-русски
a	space	espace	espacio	пространство
A	time	temps	tiempo	время
b	together	ensemble	juntos	вместе
c	being	être	ser, estar	бытие
d	through, by	à travers, par	a través de, por	через/посредством
e	movement	mouvement	movimiento	движение
E	matter	matière	materia	материя
f	this	cela	esto	это
g	in(side)	(de)dans	en, dentro	внутри/в
h	question	question	pregunta	вопрос
i	light	lumière	luz	свет
I	sound	son	sonido	звук
j	equal	égal	igual	равный
k	above	en haut	encima	наверху
L	round	rond	redondo	круглый
m	quality	qualité	calidad	качество
n	quantity	quantité	candidad	количество
o	life	vie	vida	жизнь
O	feeling	sentiment	sentimiento	чувство
p	before	devant, avant	delante, antes	перед
Q	condition	condition	condición	условие
r	positive, good	positif, bon	positivo	положительно
s	thing	chose	cosa	вещь
t	to(ward)	vers, à	hacia	к, направление
u	(hu)man	humain	humano	человек
U	mind, spirit	esprit	espíritu	дух
v	active	actif	activo	деятельный
w	power	puissance	poder	сила/мощь
x	relation	relation	relación	отношение
y	negative, un	négatif/anti	negativo/anti	отрицательный, не-, анти-
z	part	part	parte	часть

Deutsch	Latine	Esperanto	Hindī	
				हिन्दी
Raum	spatium	spaco	dūrī	दूरी
Zeit	tempus	tempo	samay	समय
zusammen	simul, una	kune	ek-sāth	एक साथ
Sein, Wesen	esse(ncia)	esto	astitva	अस्तित्व
durch, mittels	per	per	dvārā	द्वारा
Bewegung	motus	movo	vyāpār	व्यापार
Stoff	materia	materio	vastu, dravya	वस्तु, द्रव्य
dies	hoc	tio	yah	यह
innen, in	intra, in	en, interne	bhītrī	भीतरी
Frage	quaestio	demando	anusandhān	अनुसन्धान
Licht	lux	lumo	prakāś	प्रकाश
Schall, Laut	sonus	sono	śabd	शब्द
gleich	aequalis	egala	samān	समान
oben	supra	supre	ūpar	ऊपर
rund	rotundus	ronda	mandalākār	मण्डलाकार
Eigenschaft	qualitas	eco	gun	गुण
Menge	quantitas	kvanto	parimāṇ	परिमाण
Leben	vita	vivo	jīvan	जीवन
Gefühl	sensus	sento	anubhav	अनुभव
vor	prae, ante	antau	sammukh	सम्मुख
Bedingung, ob	conditio, si	kondico	avasthā	अवस्था
bejahend, gut	positivus	pozitiva, jesa	upayukt	उपयुक्त
Ding, Sache	res	ajo	vastu	वस्तु
zu - hin	ad	al	nikaṭvartī	निकटवर्ती
Mensch	humanus	homo	mānavī	मानवी
Geist	spiritus	spirito	buddhi	बुद्धि
tätig	activus	aktiva	vyavhārī	व्यवहारी
Kraft, Macht	potestas	povo	sāmarthya	सामर्थ्य
Beziehung	relatio	rilato	sambandh	सम्बन्ध
verneinend, un-	negative	nea, mal-kontraŭ	a-	अ-
Teil	pars	parto	bhāg	भाग

Chin.& Japanese	Hebrew	Greek	Swahili	Arabic=عربي
空間	רֶוַח	Τόπος χῶρος	nafasi	فضاء
時間	זְמַן	χρόνος	wakati, saa	زمن، وقت
一同	יַחַד	ἅμα, συν	pamoja	معًا
存在	יֵשׁוּת	εἶναι	-wa	يكون
由於 ～をとうして	בְּ -	διά	kwa, katikati	بواسطة
運動	תְּנוּעָה	κίνησις	mwendo	حركة
物質	חֹמֶר	ὕλη	vitu, kitu	مادّة
這個 これ	זֶה, זֹאת	τοῦτο	huyu	هذا
裏頭 ～の中に	פְּנִימָה	ἐν(τος)	ndani	داخل
問題	שְׁאֵלָה	ἐρώτημα	swali	سؤال
光	אוֹר	φῶς	nuru	ضوء
聲音	קוֹל	φωνή	sauti	صوت
相等	שָׁוֶה	ἴσος	sawa(-sawa)	يساوي
上面	עַל	ὑπέρ	juu-ya	أعلى
圓圈 円形	עִגּוּל	κύκλος	mviringo, ou	مستدير
性情 性質	אֵיכוּת	ποιότης	aina	نوع
多量	כַּמּוּת	ποσότης	kiasi	كمّ
生命	חַיִּים	βίος, ζωή	uhai	حياة
感情	רֶגֶשׁ	πάθος ἄισθημα	hisi	شعور
前面	לִפְנֵי	προ, πριν	kabla, mbele	سابق، قبل
條件 條件	תְּנַאי	εἰ, ἕξις	sharti, kama	شرط
良善	טוֹב, כֵּן	ἀγαθόν	-a hakika	موجب، جيد
物質 事物	דָּבָר	πρᾶγμα	kitu	شيء
朝向 ～の方へ	אֶל	εἰς	kwa	في اتجاه
人類	אָדָם	ἄνθρωπος	mtu, utu	انسان
精神	רוּחַ	νοῦς πνεῦμα	Mungu, roho	روح
活動	פָּעִיל	πρακτικος	fanya	نشط
力量	כֹּחַ	δύναμις	nguvu	قوة
關係	יַחַס	προς τι	jamoa, pigana	علاقة
否定	לֹא	ἀντι, ἀ-	hapana, kinyume	سالب
部分	חֵלֶק	μέρος	sehemu, hisa	جزء

III B

III (b)

Mala(gas)y - E(fate), Sa(moan)	Indonesian	Português	Italiano	Norsk(Scand.)
elanelana	angkasa;tempat	espaço,	spazio	Rum
andro, fotoana	waktu, tèmpo	tempo =	tempo	Tid
miaraka, ma, me;(ber)sama-		juntamente	insieme	sammen
ary	(exist:)adanya; (being) badan	ser, estar, existência	essere, esistere/	være, vara
ao/	terus, perdamaian, melalui, pengertian	através, por, pelo meio	per(mezzo)	igjennem
fandeha/	gerak-gerik, berak / leng-gang-lenggok, jalan/	mo(vimen)to =		Bevegelse
ny anaovan-javatra/zat, bahan		matéria		Stof
E.e, Sa.i, M. it(s)y/ini, nanti		êste, isto	ciò, questo	det
E.elol, Ma. roto; an(at)y/bagian	isi, perut, jeroan /	em	, (d)entro, in	ind(erside)
fanon-ona, -taniana,/pertanyaan/pergunta, interrogação/			questione	spørge, fraga
fahazavana	cahaya	luz	luce	Lys, skin
feo, taba-taba	suara	som	suono	Lyd, Klang
mitovy	(per)sama(an)	igual	eguale	lige
E. elagi, M. ambony/(yg)diatas		acima, sôbre	sù, sopra	over
vorivori, boribory/bulat, bundar/r(ed)ondo, -a			(ro)tondo	rund
toetra,(character)/	mutu, sifat kwalitas	qualidade	qualità	Beskaffenhed
isa, Ma. satu, maro/ Jav. sa(i), tasi/	kwantitas, banyaknya	quantitade	quantità	Mengde
aina	hidup, (ke)hidup(an)/	vida	vita	Livet
fandrenesana, mahatsiaro/	(daya)per(a)saan/	emoção; =sentimento		Følelse
E. el-alo;aloha/	lebih, sebelum dimuka, lama lagi/	antes	avanti	før
anjoanjon-teny ruha/	kondisi, dgn syarat bhw/	condi-ção,	-zione, se/	Betingelse
tsara, soa, Ma.xair/	positip keba(j)ikan	bom, positivo=,	bene	godt, positiv
zavatra	benda, barang	coisa,	cosa, oggetto	sak
amy /	ke arah, untuk	em direção a	verso a	mot, at
o(lombe)lona	/manusia orang laki-laki	homem	uomo	menneske
E. maki; fanahy	roh(ani), jiwa	espírito, ânimo/	spírito, mente	ånden
marisika/aksi,	aktip, bersemangat/	agir, at(t)ivo, =		gjør, aktiv
hery, fahefana	kekuasaan, tenaga/	fôrça	, potenza =	makt, kraft
fifamaliana	hubungan, relatip	relação	relazione/	for-hold,-bindelse sammanhang/
mifanatrika, tsy/	negatip	anti-, contrario, no		modsat, negativ
anjara	bagian	dividir, parte, =		del.

III C

Preface to aUI

In discovering aUI, Prof. Weilgart has discovered something of the nature of language in its primitive state and something essential about human communication at its beginning stages. This "language of space" is not a concocted language like Esperanto. It is a rediscovery of the basic categories of human thought and expression.

To semantic theorists this should be most interesting. By working with basic categories of meaning and a simple set of aural and visual symbols for each, Prof. Weilgart has succeeded in making language definitive rather than merely denotive or connotive. Basic categories are communicated through single symbols and new concepts are created by merely combining the basic symbols by way of a simple, intuitive logic. The result is language which has the simplicity of archaic speech plus the sophistication of modern thought.

Structurally, this language is just as fascinating. Phonemes and morphemes are one and the same thing and the number of such is kept at a bare minimum. New forms are developed by the single process of analogic creation and because of the limited number of basic forms, the confusion that could result from several possible bi-forms is eliminated.

In aUI, the speaker is forced to say exactly what he means and all the circumlocutions required by our taboos and prejudices are eliminated. To use it is to come to understand reality and learn to think.

Rev. Prof. Dr. Richard S. Hanson
Ph.D., Harvard University
Ancient Near Eastern Languages
Author of
The Psalms in Modern Speech,
The Kingdoms of Man and the
Kingdom of God . . . &c

"aUI," the Language of Learning-Psychology and Logotherapy

As Prof. John W. Weilgart holds doctoral degrees in philology and psychology from the Universities of Vienna and Heidelberg, his "Language of Space" satisfies for the first time the mnemotechnic principles of Learning-Psychology. Thus e.g. the idea of "inside" is expressed by a dot *inside* a circle and, on the acoustic level, by "g"—a guttural deep "inside" the mouth; . . . the modifier precedes—so it is the essence of a word that lingers on in our memory, even if we missed the first sounds. The hearer catches the substance in a nut-shell. E.g "anticipation" becomes 'p-O," which means "fore-feeling"; "r-yk-O" = "good-lowly-feeling" and analyzes "humility," while "yr-k-O" = "bad-superior-feeling" means "(haughty) pride."

"Meaning" can be remembered, for it is assimilated as essence of mental health. In working out the meaning of Spanish "valor" (= courage and value) with a Mexican patient, Dr. Weilgart could convince him that by shrinking back from a dare, he had not lost his "value." "Courage" was logo-analyzed into "w-O" = "strength-feeling": the patient, no coward, had simply not felt "strong enough" for the task.—Socrates has analyzed virtues in a similar way. Leibniz proposed a language to consist of categories. "aUI" contains "Ursprache" categories like Jung's collective subconscious of creativity.

As the symbols ("Ur-Gebärden," arche-gestures) are based on associations of meaning, the Language of Space is meaningful throughout, and thus quickly learnable even for people with little mechanic word-memory. In terms of type-psychology, aUI is the language of idealistic "essentialists" like Meister Eckhart, spirits who contemplate the Essence of things. They like to play the Platonic game of analysis of ideas. The Language of Space becomes their meeting ground.

Goethes's Faust did not presume to "improve and convert mankind." But men of good will can find each other. The "moral law within" and the "starry sky above" have been compared by Kant. Cosmic minds, who look up to the stars, contemplating the meaning of eternal laws of the Universe, may find in the Language of Space a common tongue of semantic communication. aUI is a guessing game of meaning, a creative play educating to the essence; a "Heilsprache' or Logo-therapy that leads toward the ethos of mental health.

Friedrich Kainz

Professor Dr. Friedrich Kainz
Distinguished Fellow of the Academy of Sciences, chairman of Psy. Phil, Ling.
Head of Department of Philosophy, University of Vienna
Author of "Psychologie der Sprache" (Psychology of Language, 5 volumes 1965)
President of University Interpreters Institute; Linguistic Research

THE LANGUAGE OF SPACE

By

Prof. Dr. W. John Weilgart

Millenia ago, Rama rode his spacecraft Pushpaka. Now, in the Western world, great magazines like TIME, LOOK, and LIFE, print photos and articles of Flying Saucers.

If, as 10,000 others yearly, you were visited by "Strangers from the Skies" -- what would you do? "Shoot them down!" was an Air Force order against UFOs. Einstein protested in the interest of intergalactic hospitality. Besides, if their weapons are as superior to ours as their vehicles, a war between the worlds would mean suicide for us. So Air Force Chief of Staff General Twining decided: "If...... they are so far ahead of us, we have nothing to be afraid of." So would you submit to them? Let them take over? What would you do?

This book says: "Neither attack nor submit. Talk to them. Write to them." Serious sky watchers feel that in this atomic age of crisis, space-men might warn, advise and help us. So communicate with them. Speak to them.

But how? Should they learn the 700 illogical languages of our little planet? Should they learn the hundred-thousands of disconnected words even of one big earth language that takes a linguist here years to master? Should they spend months to learn the intricacies of spelling and pronouncing the English language?

The Language of Space is the cosmic communication, whose elements can be learned in an hour. It is the primeval language of the Logos of pure reason that takes our human race back before the Confusion of Tongues at the Tower of Babel. The Language of Space can be radioed to the most distant galaxy. The Language of Space blesses our world with the peace of understanding, with the insight of logos before the fall of man. In this transparent language, in which each word becomes like a chemical formula of its contents, similar concepts sound similar, different ideas sound different, opposites are recognized: word and meaning are one.

The tragedies of prejudice are dissolved. There are no synonyms or homonyms, no puns of double-talk. We are no longer subject to the slavery of slogans, the idolatry of ideologies. The idiocy of crime, the insanity of war, spring ultimately from misunderstanding and confusion of the basic hierarchy of values. Goodness, beauty and truth -- the basic nature of each thing -- should be recognized in each word. The Language of Space initiates us through insight into the peace of the union with the universe.

Professor Dr. W. John Weilgart, Ph.D., with doctoral degrees from two main universities of middle-Europe, Vienna and Heidelberg, fellow of the University of California, member of the Modern Language Association and the American Psychological Association -- (Biography in Leaders in American Science and in Who is Who in American Education) having spoken 14 languages in the service of the United Nations, and having used the Language of Space as psychotherapy, and taught it to primitive tribes -- here presents the Language of Space as a report of a space-man to Johnny in the form of an easy illustrated grammar and conversation book. Boys form Young Space Men's clubs can use the Language of Space as a secret tongue among the "initiated." As boy scouts of the skies, they are "prepared" to welcome the visitors from Outer Space.

Brad Steiger
Author of
Strangers from the Skies
(Award Books A 171 X)

DEPARTMENT OF THE NAVY
NAVAL DRUG REHABILITATION CENTER
NAVAL AIR STATION
JACKSONVILLE, FLORIDA 32212

IN REPLY REFER TO:
22 March 1972

TO WHOM IT MAY CONCERN:

This is to certify that Professor Dr. Wolfgang J. Weilgart is my Assistant at the Naval Drug Rehabilitation Center and has done an outstanding job working with young men who are addicted to drugs. Dr. Weilgart has the ability to create esprit de corps among our Resident Staff population.

At NDRC we also operate counseling schools for people to go out to work both in the Fleet and the Marine Corps. Dr. Weilgart has been teaching "Value Communication" in our Marine Counseling School and in their evaluation on his work the 36 Marine Counselors wrote that they have a much better understanding of psychological problems due to his teaching them the understanding and the ability to express themselves in the Language of Space, whose author he is, which is a new approach in psychotherapy. Meditations in these "Elements of Meaning" superseded the desire for drug experience.

Dr. Weilgart has received great praise from both the Staff and the Residents on his Rhyme Tests which give the counselor a deep understanding of the counselee which no other test has the ability to do.

Dr. Weilgart is an outstanding person in all respects and any institution that has the privilege of his services is indeed fortunate.

Respectfully yours,

Henry N. Merritt

HENRY N. MERRITT, M.D., Ph.D.
Director of Education
Naval Drug Rehabilitation Center

Language of Space

Speed Record Test: at: 2 min 13 sec.

UNIVERSITY OF NORTH FLORIDA

Student Affairs
Office of the Dean

I have learned the symbols of Space Language in 2 min, 13 sec.

[illegible] P Hubbard 3744 San Vizcaya Dr.
James R. Hellier 1137 Brookmont Ave E.

Margaret Ann Allen 1420 Campbell Ave.

I witness this in a lecture at the Univ. of North Florida

Johnny L. Arnette
Johnny L. Arnette EdD
Associate Prof. of Psychology &
Associate Dean of Students

2 min. 13 sec.
Speed Record Test
to learn the Meaning
of the 31 aUI Symbols
which compose the
Language of Space
Univ. N. Florida
April 20, 1973
conducted & witnessed
by Prof.Dr Johnny L. Arnette
Assoc.Prof. Psy. & Assoc.Dean
on invitation of Dr Carter and the Psychology Club at Dr Weilgart's lecture.

I have learned the language of space in 3 minutes

Laura MacDonald
4175 Lakeside Drive
Jacksonville, Florida
Believe it or not!

One of many 3 min. learning
times, using the mnemonics
on p. IX f. e.g.
a 5 year old took 5 min.
(confirming the Luther College
Language Lab experiments:
aUI is 16 times faster...

THE 31 ELEMENTS OF MEANING.

in Chapters 1 - 31)

To Neo-Phobia

Bist du beschränkt, dass *neues* Wort dich stört?
Willst du nur hören, was du schon gehört?
Dich störe nichts, wie es auch weiter klinge,
Schon längst gewohnt der wunderbarsten Dinge.
(Goethe's Faust)

Are you restricted or of narrowed mind?
Is your heart limited, your view confined?
Scared by some magic symbols, some *new* word,
you have to hear what you have always heard?
Don't be afraid, how far-out it may ring!
You should be used by now to many a wondrous thing.

The Meaning of Symbols [and "Sounds"] of the Language of Space (with 'Mnemonics').

(CAPITALS are "LONG" vowels of the same sound-quality as their l.c. equivalents.)
(The vowels sound as in Latin, Greek, German, French, Portuguese or Old-English &c)

1. SPACE ('all around us, round, a circle') Pronunciation: ["a" (short, as in spatium, espace). Open mouth a 'wide space' as in Italian "fa" or "mamma," ('mamma's womb being our first space'). "a" almost as in fAther, but shorter.]

2. TIME ('measured in ellipses: the earth orbits around the sun, the moon around the earth in oval paths: year and month. 'An elongation of Space) ["A," Ah, 'fAther Time; Long A, as Time lasts long.' "A" has same sound quality as "a"] In "aUI" (Space-Language) similar concepts look and sound similar.

3. MOVEMENT ('a Spiral: a spiral-nebula's primal cosmic motion") ["e," short, as in 'jet'-propelled; a front-vowel, as we should 'move forward']

4. MATTER (a 'brickstone' of Matter, Material). ["E" as in Erde, Eh? 'e and E, Motion and Matter, have same sound-quality, as they belong together; but Matter lasts longer']

5. LIGHT (Source of Light and rays spreading out) "i" [lit, Licht] "i" is the 'quickest' vowel (its upper formant has 3000 cycles per second). Tongue is high-front: 'we see light in front and high in sky; Light travels quickest, swiftest'

6. SOUND ('a Sound-wave') "I" [shrIeking polIce sirene] Long vowel but of same quality as "i": 'the Sound we hear takes longer than the Light we see.'

7. (HU)MAN ('Man's legs—walking to heaven or hell') "u" ['push'] 'humans are pushy creatures'; high-back-tongue: 'man strives high, but holds back his secret!

8. MIND or 'tri-une' SPIRIT 'trinity' "U" [trUe]; high-back: 'Spirit soars high, but hides its mystery long.' cf. 'Man and Mind'; Spirit is eternal: (long U).

9. LIFE a leaf: cf. photosynthesis in green chlorophyl sap and red blood) "o" [throbbing life-pulse; "o" rounded as in 'boy's Life' or: zo-ology;] 'well-rounded life' (British or continental "o": watch rounded lips in mirror) Mid-tongue-vowel: Life stands in the middle. Life's short: short "o."

10. FEELING: ('we touch our Heart and say Oh ["O"], when we feel a deep emOtion.' Rounded back-tongue vowel: we hold our feelings back. cf. "o" and "O": 'living beings feel' [Speak long "O" then snap same sound off into short "o"]

11. CONDITION. IFs hem us in as between (parentheses). "Q" [= ø,Ö, Oe . . . as in wQrd, wørd: say wOrd, but keep lips round as in w] "Q - o - e": 'Conditions (interfere with) Life's Movement.' "Q" is a rounded central vowel as "Y" (denial): 'by making many Conditions - If, If - we almost refuse or deny.'

12. Negation, Un-, Anti- (this minus-sign denies whatever stands below it). yQ [=yØ] un-conditioned, sounds as French 'yeux' or German 'jö'; yo = un-life = death, [sounds as in British 'yonder']. "Y" sounds like German "Y" or "ü" [Süd, Scandinavian Syr], French "u" in rue. Speak before mirror 'bo-Y, trul-Y, keeping lips rounded from "O" or "U," as to whistle or kiss—'denial as kiss of death.' Before vowel, yU sounds like you.

13. POSITIVE, GOOD (Plus-sign, cross of salvation) [trilled, rolled "r," as a cat purrs: 'rrr I feel good.' "r" can be rolled 'inside' (uvular) to symbolize inner, essential goodness, or centrally, (medial) in tongue-position of "d" (= by-means-of) cf. Chapter 29, to show medial goods, useful for something else. e.g. food as means for survival. 'r' as in 'right'

14. ROUND ('a Round around a Round,' circle within circle). Transcribed "L," to prevent confusion with number 1 or Capital I, it rounds the tongue into a spoon, cf. 'round Loop.' It is a sonant like "r" (good), since round shapes (circle or sphere) symbolize perfection.

15. QUALITY (a bowl, round and feminine,—since women intuit quality,—while men measure quantity (cf. the measuring cup, 16.) "m" (quality) is nasal like "n" (Quantity). 'Quality was first smelled with the nose.' mmm - that's good. -m is adjective ending.

16. QUANTITY (a measuring-box, to measure lots of things.) "n" as in 'number' or 'quantity,' is a nasal. 'We count noses,' we count with our nose, if we are magpies and our nose is a beak (to count eggs). -n is plural sign.

16. NUMBERS are nasals in aUI; "n" enters their vowels: a̲,e̲,i̲,u̲,o̲ = 1,2,3,4,5; nasalized as in Portuguese, long Y̲ = zero; A̲,E̲,I̲,U̲,O̲ = 6,7,8,9,10;

17. POWER ('potential energy lying down: could rise into bolt of Action (cf. 18.). "w" as in 'work' 'work-power' ("w" = double-U, reminds of U = Spirit, 'Spirit should have power, mind over matter.'

18. ACTION, DO, MAKE. (A Bolt-of-Lightning is most Active: it synthesizes N+O to . . . protoplasm, and Thor and Jupiter acted by throwing thunderbolts. "v," "-v" is verb-ending in aUI. "v" is a labial, vigorously vibrating the lips in front, since we act forward and outward. "v" as in "vim", "virile", he = vu.

19. THIS (an arrow pointing down to This). "f" hisses lip-friction: 'we point our lips forward at This,' or point with 'finger' at this. Fox-Indians point with Lips.

20. QUESTION (a question-mark simplified) "h" (cf. How?) gasps a question; inside man, his very breath asks: a guttural spirant—aspiration—quest.

21. RELATION (⟷ 'a double-arrow from you to me and from me to you') "x" (rasping snore sound of [Mexico, Greek 'χ' = ch in German and Scotch: Loch] 'If you snore with somebody, you have a relation.' Guttural friction sound: Relation means inner friction. cf. "h: ch (= "x')—Question: Relative pronoun; 'who' = 'hu?' or 'xu' in aUI.

22. EQUALity ('=' equation sign joined so the blind can trace it) 'Water stands horizontal, even, equal in height: sound of flowing water is "j" [juste measure]

23. EXIST, BE (upright: 'when you stand-up you exist, ex-sist; not lying down.' "c" [= sh: 'precious special existence'; between Italian and French 'ce.' "c" = unvoiced "j" (sh:zh): 'exist = stay-equal = remain identical to self.'

24. THING ('round, closed in itself so it can be wrapped into sack': 'Sache, Sak'; "s": 'hiss at things that soil the pure Spirit, who objects to objects.')

25. PART (half-moon or round-cheese cut a-Part by 'buzz-saw': "z" [dental sound: teeth bite a-part. cf. "s": "z"—can 'things' break 'a-part?' "zones" are area parts.

Topo-Vectors [Stop-Sounds]

26. INSIDE (a Dot or Thing 'Inside' a circle) "g" [guttural 'inside' throat, 'inner guts']

27. ABOVE (a Dot Above' a line as a musical quarter note) "k" up on palate, the roof of the mouth. 'King or Kaiser has Krown up on Kopf (= head).'

28. TOWARD (an arrow pointing, a hook pulling, Toward, To) "t" with tongue tip tucking toward a thing. 'To-ward.'

29. THROUGH, BY-MEANS-Of (a line crossing Thru another). 'She drinks Thru, by-Means-of straw, her Tool. "d" [durch, diagnose i.e. Doc sticks 'nose thru' patient's belly to 'through-know' him. "d" lies on 'through-way' from 'inside' to 'front.'

30. TOGETHER (two dots joined Together by arc) "b" (lips pressed Together). 'b' as in: 'both bonded together'

31. BEFORE, in FRONT (Dot in Front of line) "p" blown in front of mouth, from lips: 'pre-, pro-, proto- . . .' ('A prototype precedes the project')

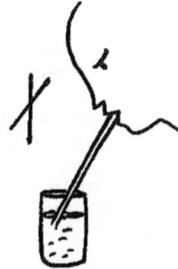

NB. English pronunciation today can serve only as approximate guide. Since the vowel-shift especially long vowels changed or lost their meaning. Modern English "A" sounds "ei" in "ate" but "e" (open) in "at" and "o" (open) in "all." In "fortunate or "forward" it gets lost. In "fAther" it keeps its original sound. Otherwise vowels may be diphthongized or slurred, changing with context and region. Even consonants; like "c" or "g" can change from "k" to "s" or from "g" to "j." "j" itself prefixes a "d-," so it sounds no longer "just" but really "djest" almost. For Phono-Logy cf. Weilgart, W. J.: *The Sounding Cave of Wind and Wave,* 1972, Cosmic Communication Co., Decorah, Iowa 52101.

"Silent Night, Holy Night" in aUI

yIm yiA, kUrUm yiA !
can YvAv, cvAv am fA

KUrUm bej amfam, trOvAm Ib brOm,
KUtvu Yt ram YnYvu riOm:

Ayerv rUg ag knam brU-U !
UYvArv rUg ag knam brU !

yIm yiA, KUrUm yiA !
bos-u Ov , Uf fiA

kna-u tagepAv kna at iO;
kUO kEdev at bEn Uj kubrO:

XRiST YtYrv Yt yrU-U,
Trovu ytYrv Yt yrU !

yIm yiA, K UrUm yiA !
BrO setAv fAvm tA;

KUm riOma iv jOm pfE ki
daiuv i (nUm)knu Ud (sEm) knam i:

toepAm tvu c' Ub KU-U,
toepAm tvu cEv Yt KU !

The accents ^ / are not part of the LANGUAGE OF SPACE, aUI, but mean emphasis only in this song: / means one strong note, as on Night or "yiA" or the final end - "KU." But ^ means a 'slur'(two notes on one vowel) as in "Si-ilent,.. ho-oly,.. brU-U, KU-U"(next-to-last lines). Cover the Symbol-part & write for yourself the aUI signs by'sound." Then cover the Roman sound transliterations with your left hand, and try to read the symbols with the right basic sounds, as learnt before -- fast. "can YvAv" = all is "in-active, rests", cvAv = cEv vAm = is awake, or watches; "bej " = together-two-equals = pair; amfam= only this .. = alone; trOvAm = hoping, brOm = loving; Ayerv = rest !, UyvArv = sleep ! rUg= well. -- bos-u = herdsman, herder; kna-u= heaven-hosts, angels; tage-pAv = open-ed; KUO = God-feeling = glory; KubrO=Lord-love=mercy; ytYrv = from evil "rescues or saves" ; trovu = healer, savior; BrO se-tA-v = Love will-give; fAvm = new; tA = future; riOma = grace; daiuv = leads; i = 3; knu = king(s); Ud knam i = by heavenly light; toe-pAm = born.

Compare Symbols & Sounds
(covering one of the columns or memorizing
the following children's songs)

LIGHT IN SPACE	i a g a
Bright splendid ways !	bim rim da !
Light shines thru Space.	i iv ad a. -
Meets other light.	tubev Yf i.
"Brother Light,	"jYtvu i,
Ray of hope/from above	_anai Ub trO,
Fire of love,	iE Ub brO,
We are few & small	fnu' c ynEn Ib ynam
In the darkness of the All.	ag yim can-nam.
Darkness will be our end,	yi vyotAv fnu,
my point-timed friend,	fum ayn-Am bru,
in the dim future,	ag Ydim tA.
(we know not how)	
But now	yUg fA
we shall shine our rays	fnu irv fnum da ,
to brighten the ways	irv ad dam yim a.
of wide dark Space.	

The Builder's Dream pXIV

vugavu - yiviOs

I. kUit yktepAv.

fAom vugavu
rim yiviOpAv
tA-vugav yI trov-ga
v-mavAm sEm ga-u:
rUm rUnUm riOm.-
ga sev sEm gau
ro, UrO Ib brO.-
uga Ub fE mUz
bav yktok ag bEn
yUg yc waletAv.-
ura Ub fE jUma
tnev-yEc eb sEm cEvs
wav okEv rUt oU
bav nu yd yrU.-
yI ydyrd bUtAvAm
eb Eo Ib ki
yt bEm robE
OU wav O-kev at kna.-
yt E at U
tUk vektepAm.-

(for symbols see p. XVIII,
for vocabulary see p. XIX)

A BUILDER'S DREAM

I. The Image Descended.

A young builder dreamed
of building a building
that could heal its inhabitants
molding its dwellers
good, beautiful, wise;
that would lend its dwellers
health, happiness, love.
A house of this kind
could root in the ground
but would not confine here.
A building like this
could grow with its creatures
could breathe for the brethren
unite them secure.
A shelter communing
with nature and stars
from solid soil
the soul could soar to the sky.
From matter to spirit
lifted aloft.

vugavu-yiviOs

II. vyc-yk-yrkU

vugavu UOvAm
tUvmavAm bEtkU
tvepAv nEn akiA
tvUvAm oA
at tebev yiviOs.-
tUvAm vum uwe
vu Utev ypnAmQ
ypAzm jrUm ytbe:
bEm Ib abzam
pI nUrvAm bzUx.-

- . -

U-jwUsku yrUIv:
"fEm Es yc wav cEv,
yUt fnu yA iOpAv."
bunte tyc-jwUskuv.-
ugavu ag yndrE
bybim Ib ywom
vu gyEv anagyE.-
tykwEzev pIn wE
bEtjEpAv diwE.-

- . -

vu vugapAv uga
atkevAm Ib anaim
kluga idEm
tok-jOm tykE-kyb
vrUpAm can o-cEvs
OU kev yt o-bE.-

- . -

yUg fA bUt vrAmQ
yr-iim-iOz-ybru
tyr-tiOpAv at kUO
yrtyfbrO yr-krO-Iv.
Ud iEm bob
vu tyc-vev yt yk:
sE tygwev kiE.-
ugavu iEv ag vum ugavs
y-trOvAm nyrO-A:
can pAc yb tsUs.-

THE BUILDER'S DREAM

II. Destruction's Demon

The builder divining
designing constructing
tried years
and ages
to reach his dream.
Striving and toiling
at last dawned upon him
a final solution
solid and simple
the valid design.

- . -

The critics grinned:
"There can be no such thing,
for we never saw one."
Convention condemns.
The builder in poverty
graying and weakened
he dug the ditches.
he crushed the rocks
he melted crystals.

- . -

He built his house
rising and radiant
dome translucent
tree weight-transcending
blessing all beings
soil...soaring soul.

- . -

Now near completion
the green-eyed fiend
scowled at the glory
and grinned in envy;
with fiery fist
he wrecked from below,
it burst into flames.
builder burnt in his building
despairing agony:
all was in vain.

III. Knuwa Ub OU

ylmU — cvAvU
Una kyb A
ade kad U-a
U-dam Ib kUm. -
   nutga Ub tsyvQ:
'fu yc twOv agtev,
yrytEpAv twamQ !
fum o   ρAc yb tsU. '
   yUg Kna-u tagev:
''terv tag Ib rUg-terv !
fnu trApAv rUt bu. ''
   vugavu a̲tev
kab rim dā e̲g bEtkU.
vu tagev iOz̄
at ub-Om uav-Q;
Uj vu UOpAv snE,
fEn yg-a̲nav pI da.
   'pfA c̄an, fu tvepAv xnE,
fa   pApAc can A !
fum tUv yc   pAc wyvUm'
pI vavU-u tygrOv:
   ''yr. – bu vEpAv fEn.
fE cEv bum ruwe,
bum bavum wUvU. —
   fnu OU c' fA yb yrvs.
fnum cnAmU ejEv
ag ra̲m KU-iOvU.
fnu ȳc wOv vUv
fnu ybav rUOm twU.
fnu yc wav wUv:
fnu wyvUv bum ruwe Ub brO.
   xA bu yiviOpAv,
fa sE tepAv tag cEvQ.
fE cEv knuwa Ub
tU-we--trUn-gEv-Q,
xa kUit Ib tUvQ
cvEyv UrOg.
   rUg-tepAm ! ytOr !
bu vugapAv nEn knuga
rUt fnu, bum jytu.
bu vEpAv bum uga
rUt fuga 'b O-U' !''

III. The Realm of the Souls

Silence – awakening,
Dimensions beyond,
voyage thru spaces
vast and sublime.
   Gate of Acceptance:
'I dare not enter,
I wasted potentials !
My life was in-vain. '
   But Angels open:
''Come in ! You are welcome.
We waited for you. ''
   The builder trod
on the roads of radiance.
He opened his eyes
to familiar abodes;
as he had divined them,
they border this street !
   'Then all I tried for,
had been here all the time !
There was no need for my striving. '
The messenger smiled:
   'No. – You have made these.
This is your work,
your creation and deed. —
   We souls are now sinless.
Eternity flows us
in pure contemplation.
We may not act
We lack trusting will.
We can not create:
We needed your labor of love. -
   Whenever you dreamed,
here it came into being.
This is the realm of
fulfilled endeavor,
where dreams and strivings
are realized.
Welcome and Thanks !
   You have built many mansions
for us, your brethren.
You built this house
as home for your soul !''

A BUILDER'S DREAM

parts I, II, III in aUI Symbols

I.

II.

III.

Special Words for "The Builder's Dream"

I. The Image Descended

kUit = high-image, ideal
yk-tev = downward-come
v-uga-v-u = creative (active) build-er, architect
tA-vugav = vuga-tAv = in (the) future will build.
trov-ga = heal-room
v-mav = make-form, mold
u-r-a = man's good place
okE = life-air = breath
O-kev = feel-soar = the building makes you feel like soaring upward.
bu = communion, bU-tAv = will commune (fut. partic)
tUk = spiritually upward

II. Destruction's Demon

v-yc.. = make-non-exist
U-Ov = Spirit-feel = divine (vb)
U-jwUsku-v = toward-nihil-, annihilating judgment make, = condemn
uga = house, luga = round h.
kuga = tower (high-house)
kluga = rounded tower, dome
tok-jOm tykE-kyb = tree-like weight-beyond (weight-transcending)
o-cEvs = living being, o-bE = life-giving earth; yr-lim-iOz = evil-green-eye (of envy).
tyg-wev = outward thrust, burst

III. Soul's Realm

tyg-we = outward-thrust = burst
nyrO-A = deep-suffering long - time = agony
ub-Om = family-feeling, familiar
uav-Q = dwelling condition
UrO = spirit-pleasure, bliss
UrO-g=(in) happiness, '-ly
rUg-terv = well-come !
rUg- orv = live (fare)well !
KU-iOv = God-see = contemplate; O-U' = Feel-SPIRIT SOUL-SPIRIT. (emphasizing the soul's spirituality.)

The "Mary"-Go-Round
W. J. Weilgart
Qg e-ki nev al pI bEn xE Lev al pI e-ki, bEn
When Ma-ry goes round on the mer-ry-go-round, she thinks she is
Uu cEv pI gaz; yUg pI e-ki i-tAv xA bEn yc Le-
queen of the show; But the "Merry" goes round without Ma-ry a-
tAv, Qg bEn yc A gu-tAv sEm taz.— yUg xA pA-om
round, and the stars are shin-ing be-low... But when the Old
ry yu te-tAv kab kna, e-ki—bEn-e-ki yt-
La-dy comes up on the sky; beau-ti-ful Mer-ry-go

The "Mary"-Go-Round
p. 2
bev ag a; ... rUg-orv fnum rO-ves, xE rQg av
round, bye-bye... beau-ti-ful Mer-ry-go-round, bye
al : Oh! ri-Om rO-ves "ca-bal" !
bye : beau-ti-ful Mer-ry-go-round !

Qg gki nev al pI bEn, xE Lev aL
pI gki, bEn Uv cEv pI gaz;
yUg pI gki itAv, xA bEn yc LetAv,
Qg bEn yc AgUtAv sEm taz.--
yUg xA pAom ryvu tetAv kab kna,
gki-bEn-gki ytbev ag a.--
rUg-orv fnum rOves, xE rQg av-aL:
Oh ! riOm rOves "ca-baL" !

Literally:
(If the moon runs around the earth, which turns around the sun, the Earth thinks it's in the center (which as "Mary as queen of the show" symbolizes the pride of mankind).
But the sun will shine, when the earth will no (longer) turn, if the earth will not remember its direction. (This refers to forgetting mankind's ethical goals, and reversal of spin in anti-matter weapons --reminding of "stars shining below" in debasing of ideals)
But when the Old Lady (Death) comes up on the sky (heaven), Sun-Earth-Moon dissolves in Space; Fare-well our toy, which luckily goes around; Oh ! beautiful plaything "universe-orbit-together" (Merry-go-round) good-bye !)

(In a humourous way the song warns of hybris and loss of the ideal of the Spirit, counsels Cosmic Communication in the Language of Space, but, if final catastrophe should strike a mad mankind, it comforts us that all has been a dream and a play, a merry-go-round reflected in the lake , an illusion of stars of eternity.

W. John Weilgart
HOME IN HEAVEN (fuga ag kna)
Antonín Dvořák
1. ag can a amfam fu: fu c' yg jUm iU. -
yfam nu, yb rUm bru: O-U yc bav brU.- OU yc bav brU.-
2. uga - rO, fuga-brO ! UtetAv bu hA ?
Ag fum o, yAp fum yo ? tUtetAv bu cnA.- trOtAv rUt fum rA.-
3. EjUm krO, cEm riO: hA iOv nUm rU ?
ha ag ca ? twam ag kna; xA fu tubev KU; ytbetAv ag U; xA fu tubev KU.-

NB. to 1. "yg jUm iU" = outside of equal (adequate) understanding (by the world).

Home in Heaven (cont'd) : 4.5.6. same melody as 1.2.3.(New World Symphony)

4.(ytu fum, ha bu cEv ? io tUv at i. -
fuga fum,hE bu tEv ? fu trAv am ag yi; Orv iU ag yi.-
5.(tErv kam tok ! barv eb can ! tnerv yt ytu, bEn !
erv yt fan, kerv at kan: berv eb kEn Ib jEn; arv eb kan Ib kEn!
6.(terv eb fU ! tnerv tak kU !. OU barv canU .-
orv ag brO,brU,riO! KU serv brU rUt fU; terv tag fU,brOm KU! Aserv brO Ib brU !
1.Thru dark space,lonely race! Who will understand? Strangers all,roam & fall:
Where find home & friend? in an empty land. 2. Grow as tree up with me,one with sky & sea.
Soar above,fuse in love: self, dissolve & be! Soul to Spirit free.-
3.Sky be blue,Self be true! Be one with the Whole! Ever far - rise to star!
Spirit solve the soul! Melt in Spirit, Soul ! Enter,GOD, lost Soul !

NB. to 5. "fan" = fa (here)-plural-general: (move away from) "the-world-here"

XXIV

M y s t i c A s c e n t .

Diamond of the Soul,
blinking, revolving
through the night-sky,
each facet reflecting a star-
array, connecting far-
streaming rays, drawing their light nigh:
Rolling mirror of the Whole.—

Until in the end,
what wanted to Be
a diamond, will melt
into a dawndrop of dew,
to offer and spend
itself as it had been dealt,
returning to whence it grew,
sinking, dissolving
into the Spirit's Sea.

("The mind's microcosm mirrors the macrocosm of the universe in its facets, the symbols of aUI, the Language of Space" (3rd. ed. 1974) W. John Weilgart, Cosmic Elements of Meaning--Symbols of the Spirit's Life, (p.255) 1976, & Peace thru People, all:Cosmic Communication Co, Decorah, Iowa 52101. USA.

J.Getman, music (Mystic Ascent)
W.J.Weilgart
guitar
piano
chords

Bio-Rhythms of the Language of Space

"The whole man must move at once." True oneness of mind, soul and body, sensor and motor system, is needed for harmony, honesty, wholeness and health. Thus let us dance together aUI. Unless the body can express the soul in symbols, the soul expresses itself through the bodily changes of psychosomatic disease. Instead of using the sick body as a symbol, we use the symbols of aUI, the Language of Space.

On pages I - V first the Latin letter (in Latin pronunciation, cf. aUI book p. 9 & 10), then the meaning in English, German, and a dozen other languages; then the aUI symbol is drawn by arrows to show the best motion of drawing. Then follows, sometimes in somewhat different direction, shown with other arrows, the Bio-Rhythmic body motion, which should accompany the main sound.

Simultaneously, in chanting, singing and dancing the symbol, we should become its meaning, one in body and mind. E.g. you should feel you become a ray of light, to be seen (while you say and dance "i"); or a sound to be heard, (while you gesture and say "I"). Children lose their inhibitions in dancing like Adam and Eve.

The sounds and symbols are arranged in the sequence of p. 10 of aUI, the Language of Space; pp. II & III of aUI are international translations, some of which have been added to the drawings here to broaden your mind. So as a play, you can seek your foreign friends' language at an international meeting.

The movements are drawn as if seen in a mirror-symmetry. Children will copy your left hand with their right hand, if you stand facing them. You yourself can copy the left-drawn movements with your right hand.

If you say an aUI word, e.g. EiA, 7-days, week, you need to express only the most important part, i.e. "7" = 5+2, holding up one whole hand plus two fingers of the other, as shown p. III under "n". Or, if you say "iO", you need to dance only "i", , the light, to make understanding easier.

In any case, express also with your face and attitude each concept, as shown in the pictures, so that you mean what you say.

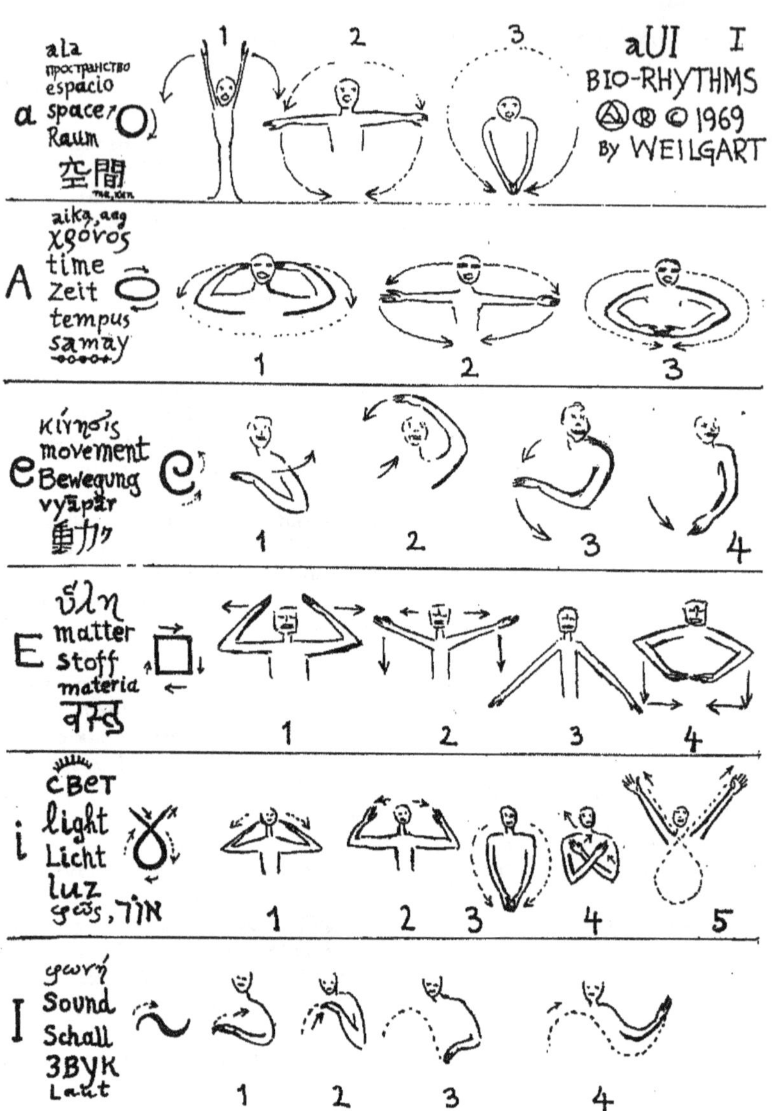
aUI I
BIO-RHYTHMS
© 1969
By WEILGART
a
ala
пространство
espacio
space
Raum
空間
A
time
Zeit
tempus
samay
e
movement
Bewegung
E
matter
stoff
materia
i
свет
light
Licht
luz
I
Sound
Schall
ЗВУК
Laut

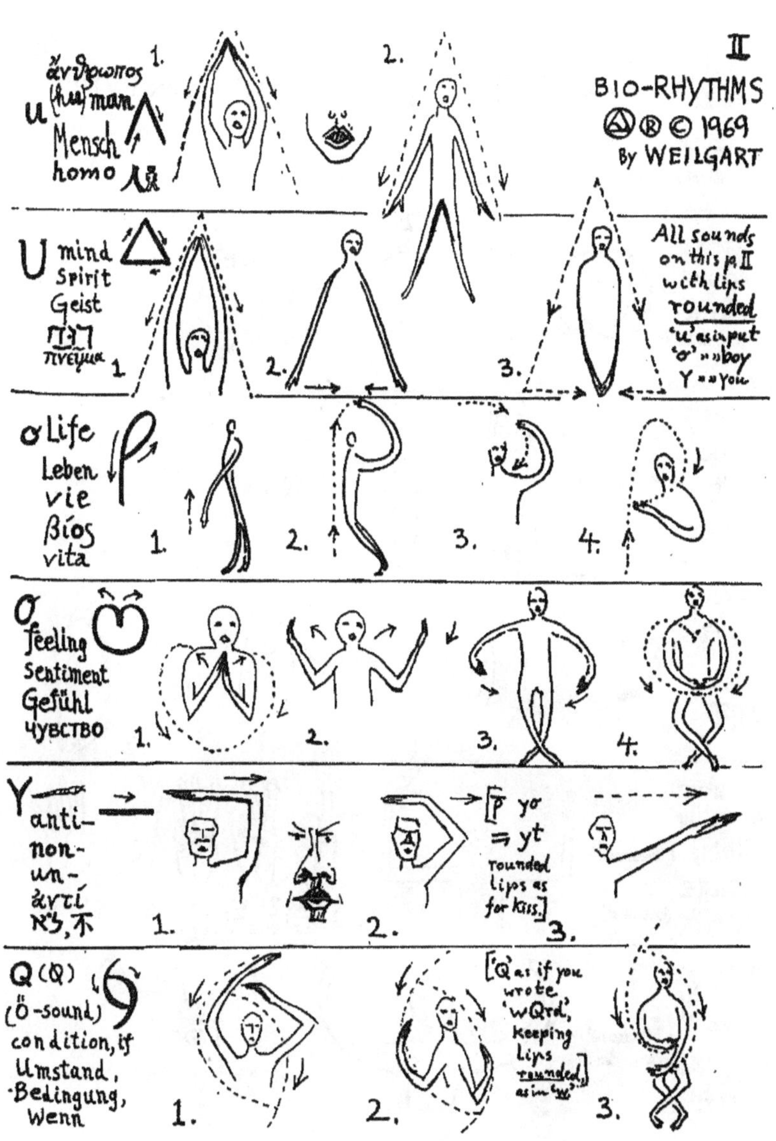
II
BIO-RHYTHMS
® © 1969
By WEILGART
ἄνθρωπος
(hu)man
Mensch
homo
mind
Spirit
Geist
πνεῦμα
All sounds on this p. II with lips rounded
'u' as in put
'o' " " boy
Y " " you
Life
Leben
vie
βίος
vita
feeling
sentiment
Gefühl
чувство
anti-
non-
un-
ἀντί
[P yo = yt rounded lips as for kiss.]
Q (Q)
(Ö-sound)
condition, if
Umstand,
Bedingung,
Wenn
['Q' as if you wrote 'wQrd', keeping lips rounded]

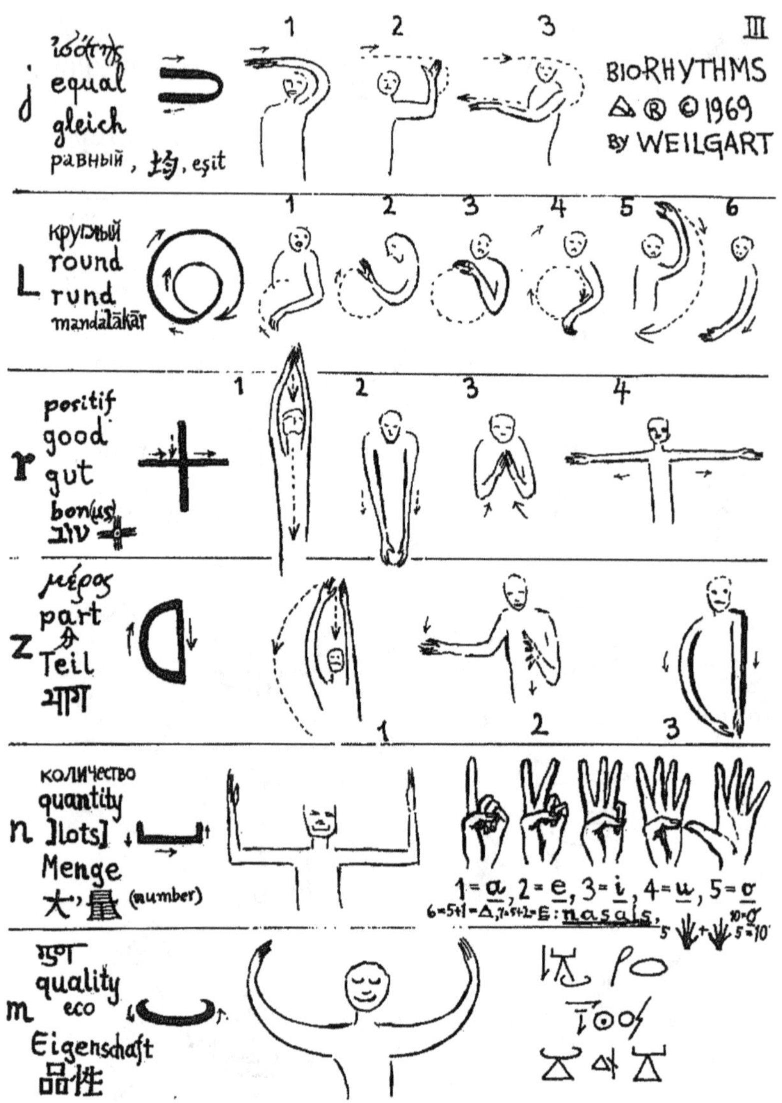
III
BIORHYTHMS
© 1969
BY WEILGART
j
equal
gleich
равный, 均, eşit
L
круглый
round
rund
mandalākār
r
positif
good
gut
bon(us)
z
μέρος
part
分
Teil
भाग
n
количество
quantity
[lots]
Menge
大, 量 (number)
1 = a, 2 = e, 3 = i, 4 = u, 5 = o
nasals
m
गुण
quality
eco
Eigenschaft
品性

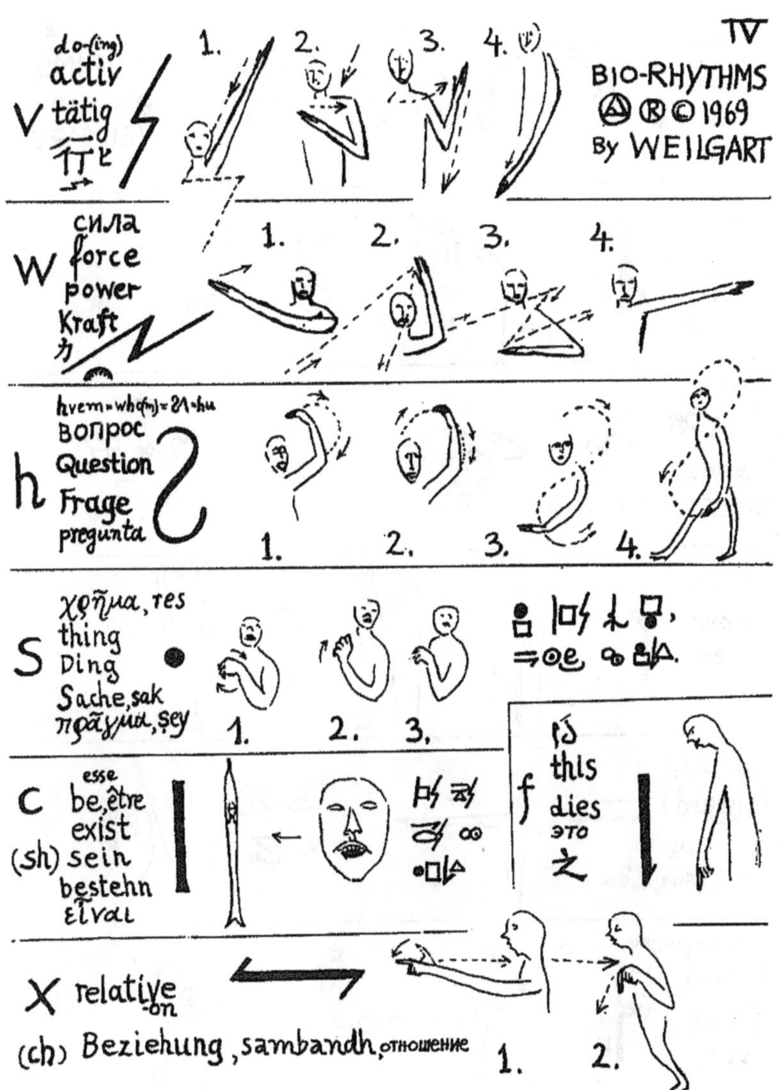
IV
BIO-RHYTHMS
© 1969
By WEILGART
V
do-(ing)
activ
tätig
行
1. 2. 3. 4.
W
сила
force
power
Kraft
力
1. 2. 3. 4.
h
вопрос
Question
Frage
pregunta
1. 2. 3. 4.
S
res
thing
Ding
Sache, sak
1. 2. 3.
c
(sh)
esse
be, être
exist
sein
bestehn
εἶναι
f
this
dies
это
之
X
(ch)
relative
-on
Beziehung, sambandh, отношение
1. 2.

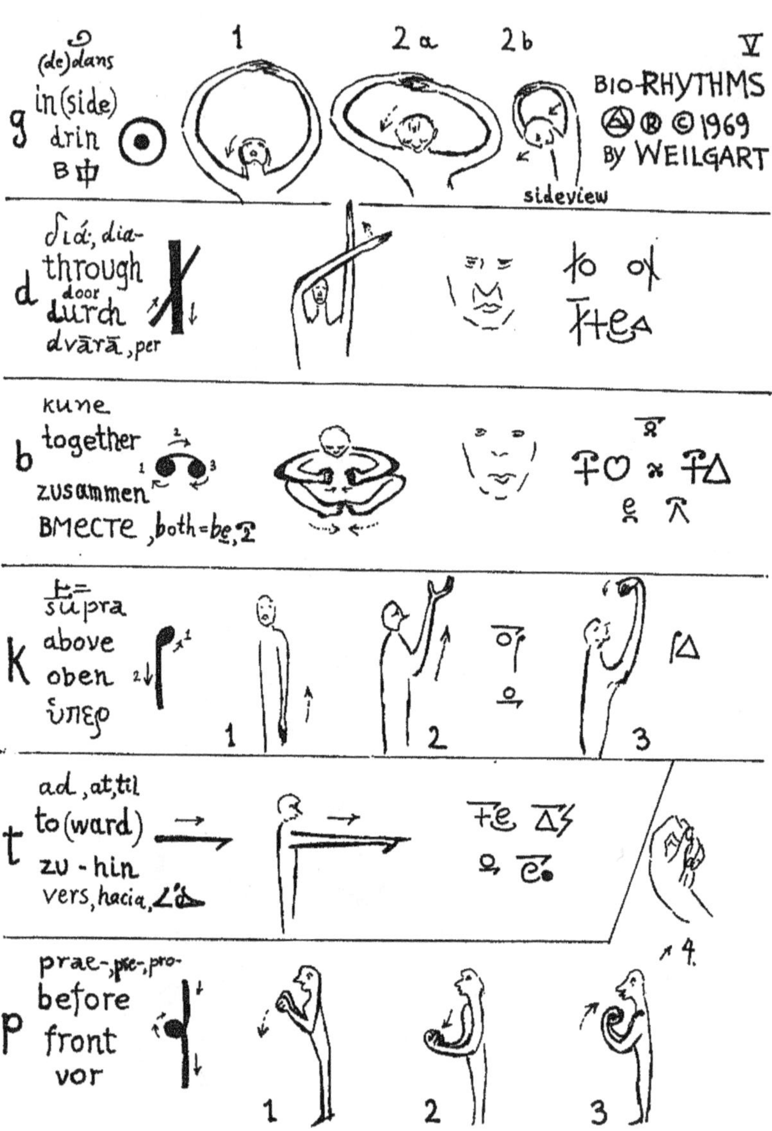

V
BIO-RHYTHMS
© 1969
BY WEILGART
(de)dans
in(side)
drin
g
1
2a
2b
sideview
through
door
durch
dvārā, per
d
kune
together
zusammen
вместе, both=be
b
supra
above
oben
K
1
2
3
ad, at, til
to(ward)
zu-hin
vers, hacia
t
prae-, pre-, pro-
before
front
vor
p
1
2
3
4.

The Sounding Cave

There is a cave of wind and wave like to a cosmic womb—where the *word* is born. All the universe of the outer world can be reshaped in the waves of vibrations shaped by vocal cords, tongue and lips. Since in aUI symbols, sounds, and significant meaning flow in harmony, we can understand the structure of this cosmology from the sequence of sounds: First vowels (a, A, e, E, i, I, u, U, o, O, Ọ̇, Y) ch. 1-12, then sonants (r, L, m, n, w) ch. 13-17, then fricatives (v, f, h, x, j, c, s, z) ch. 18-25, and finally stops (topovectors), (g, k, t, d, b, p), ch. 26-31. These sounds are described in pp. 279-334, (p. 1-54 of the phonology-phenomenology) of "aUI, the Language of Space," Cosmic Communication Co., Decorah, Iowa 52101.

Here we reprint the picture of the mouth 'the sounding cave, remembering that each sound can be guttural (in the back or deep inside the mouth like g in guttural (meaning inside) or U in trUe, (meaning spirit), or velar palatal (central) or dental near the teeth (which gives it a biting zeal, cutting things apart (z =part) or labial, in the lips, which gives it a frontal (p) or communicating flavor as b in 'bond.'

For the union between body, subconscious, and conscious mind and the communication between inside and outer world and society, it is good to understand and master these inner organs: mouth and larynx and maybe lungs are the only inner organs which all men could shape at will, because they hear the feedback or result. This is how it looks inside the cave of our mouth:

VI

Nose

Nasal Cavity: 1 a, 2 e, 3 i, 4 u, 5 o; 6A, 7E, 8I, 9U, 10 O, O Y

n,m

Palate

Velum

x k y j c L

gums

uvula

k

w Y

R d t (sh)

high

r g

u

round lips

I

n teeth

mid

x

O

(Ø) Q

i E

c

lip

o

e

vowel limit

s z

low

h

A a

open

Tongue

back central front vowels

Pharynx

(If the tongue rises above the vowel-limit, velar, palatal, .. dental consonants result, according to which part of the tongue approaches the "mouth-roof." Some consonants can be articulated in different places, and still sound "alike." Vowels like a lowered tongue for open passage of air.)

v f m

w b p

Epi-glottis

teeth lip

		glottal	velar	palato-	alveolar	dental	labial
stops voice(-less)		guttural '	k g		t d		p b
fricatives voice(-less)		h	x	x c =j	c j	s z	f v
(sonorants) semi-vowels			r w rounded lips	y	nasals: ... L, r	n	m w
vowels	closed		U ,u	Y"=u	i, I	high	U,u,Y (rounded lips)
	middle		O, o	Q=Ø	e, E	mid	O,o,Q
	open		A back	central	a front-vowels	low tongue	

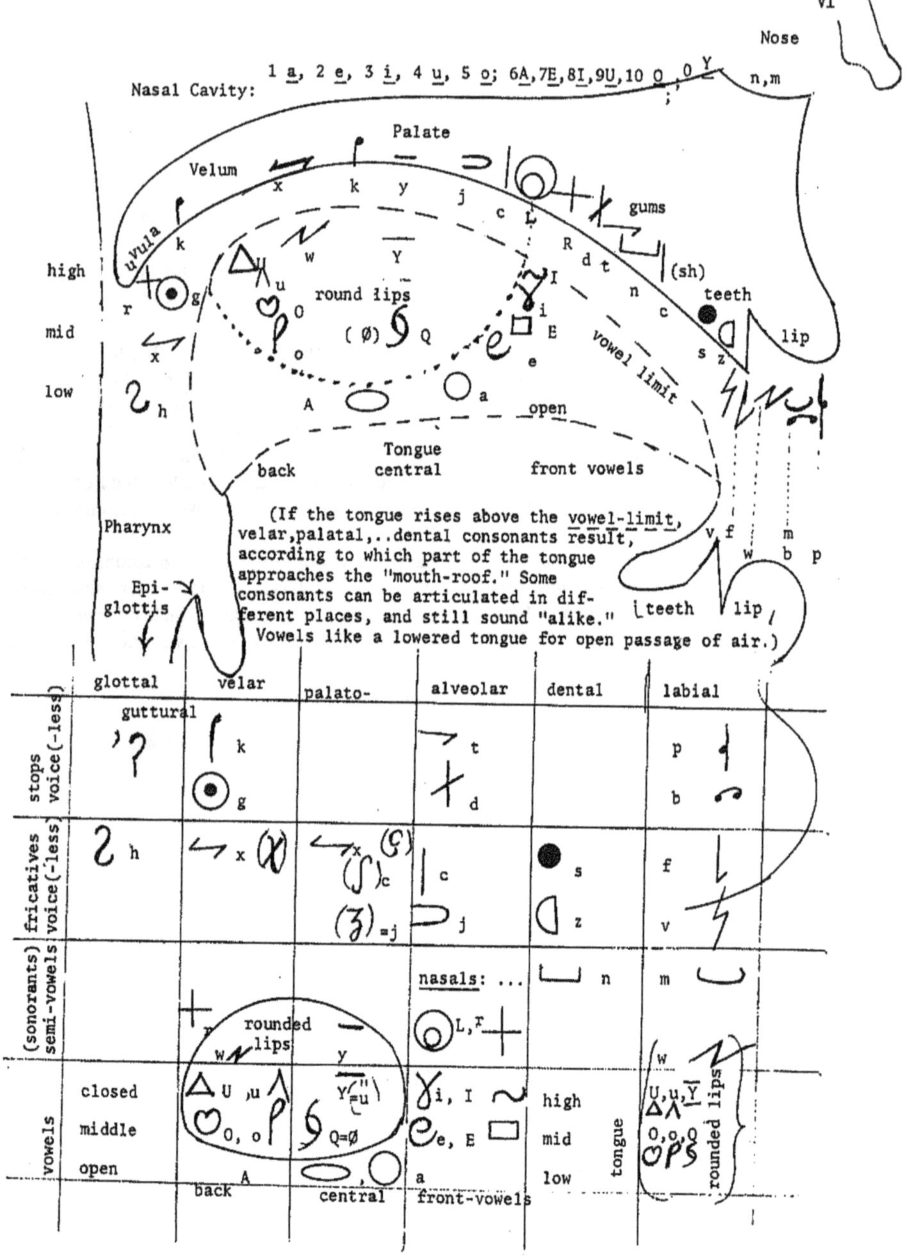

aUI RIMES of COSMIC WISDOM

for survival in Harmony, Happiness, Health and Peace

(learn at least one Rime for each letter of Part II or V for study)

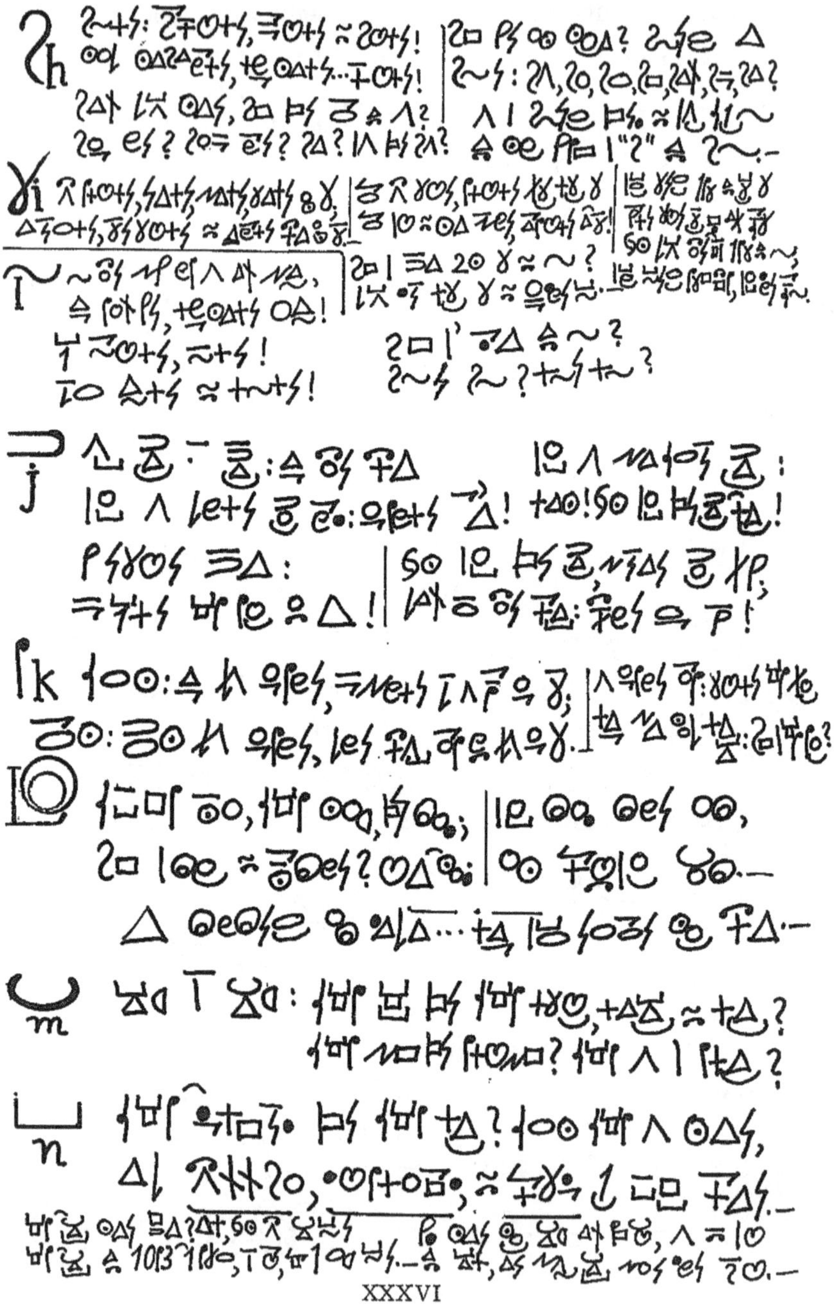
h
i
l
j
k
m
n

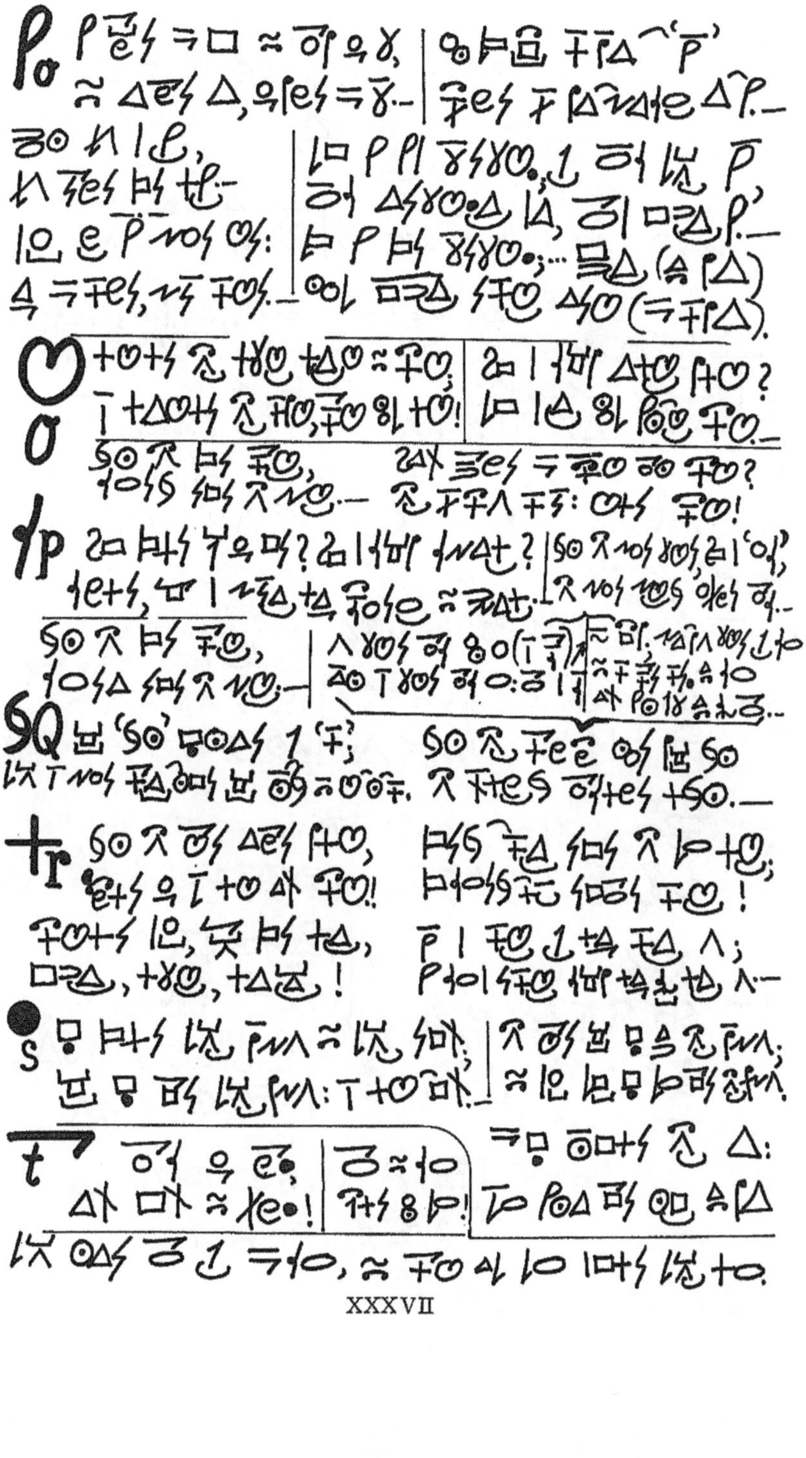

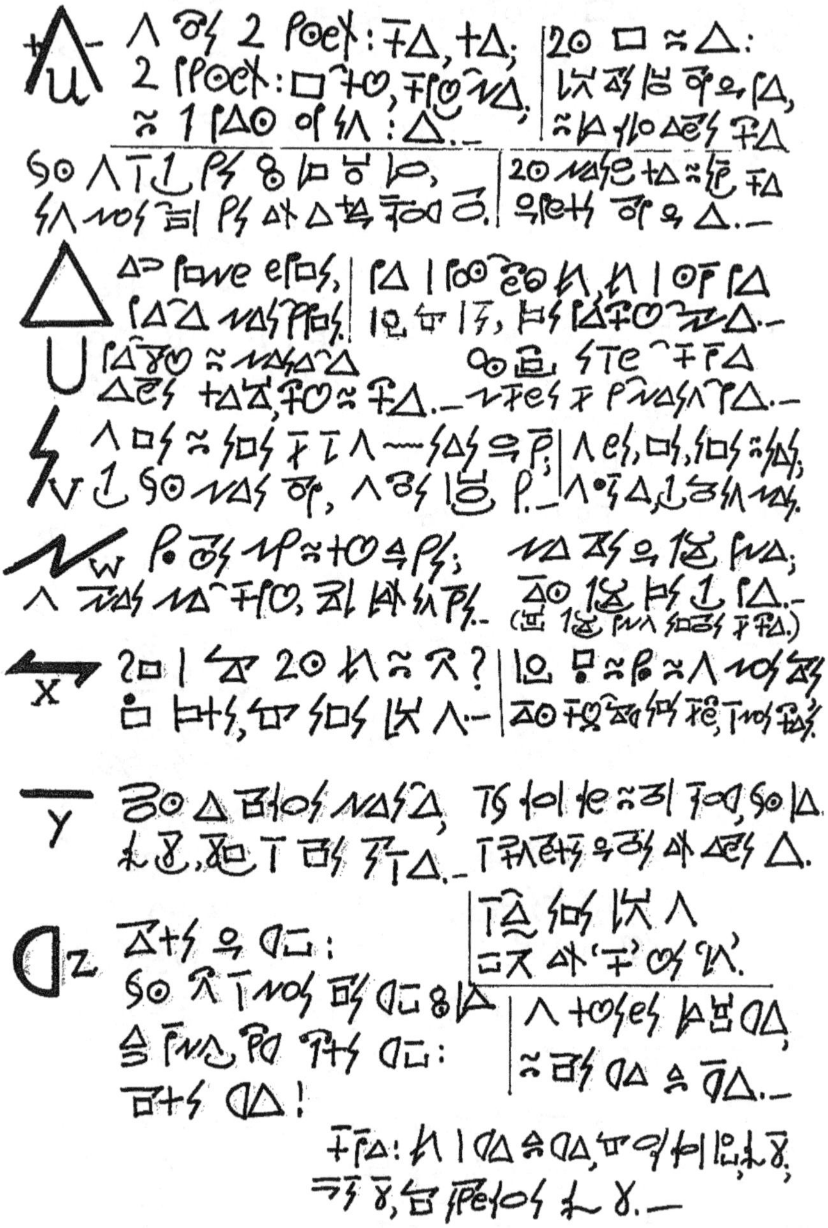

A) Mind-Pollution in the Pan-Atomic Age

Our age is threatened by water-, food-, air & ray-pollution. This book cares for the pollution of the mind. — If the creek smells foul, I can drink from the spring. The source of my mind is inside. Polluted food I can throw up, but what if my stomach juice were poisoned from within? In air-pollution — I must breathe in its atmosphere. A virus lives inside our cells. A cancer grows within. — Mass-mind-pollution invades whole nations & grabs hold of a whole age with a predominant slogan that acts as Command* to destroy. The slogans of our own age we do not recognize: we take them as axioms of truth. The fish will not feel that the water is wet.

To say the Spirit's thoughts in vulgar words is as flowing springwater thru sewage-pipes.

Only distant slogans are recognized as perverted analogies: The Nazis and many Arabs live by Blu-Bo, Blut & Boden (Blood & Soil) an alliteration as "Soil & Soul." The analogy says: as Soul & Soil fit in sound, so they must fit in meaning. (This would be true in aUI: e.g. Love & Peace, as they are similar, sound similar: brO & brU ⫯◯ ≈ ⫯△.) This is not true in conventional language. Still people conclude: Only whose blood grew out of this soil, has a 'right' to live on this soil for only he has a soul. (Since our age uses 'right' as a noun, I 'have' a right as I hold a sword in my hand. People do not feel that originally 'right' was a quality like good: I have a right to do what is right or good for mankind or in the service of God. I must earn a right so that I prove that I deserve to serve mankind or God with it. If I misuse it, I lose it.) — The 'Blood-Soil-Soul' slogans confuse man with a plant. Here a clear beautiful metaphor would be: Let man grow up like a quiet tree, up to the sky of the Spirit. But the Blood-Soil-Soul slogan as false idol, even in the Marseillaise shouts of "sang impure" impure blood of infective intruders as 'filthy foreigners,' which must be spilled on the home-soil as dung. Under these nationalistic slogans, far from quiet plants, a mob acts as rabid wolves, as Jefferson noted during the French revolution. A slogan may deform a people into a "mob — that monster with a million heads & no brain" as Ben Franklin found.

So the slogan "Israil dawla sariqa!" (Israel bandit-state) stamped the poor refugee Jews after 2000 years of suffering & genocide, (when they fled into their old homeland, promised them in Bible (and Koran 17:103), like a tortured babe would flee back into mother's womb) as vicious robbers. The Jews who bought the land as desert & made it bloom in the sweat of their brow, were treated as infesting vermin, & a peace-treaty with them was labeled "treason." This is the tyranny of a slogan of hate. If the Muslim Mullah, who called "Israel our Semitic sister, mother of monotheism, persecuted by gentiles, welcomed by Muslims to teach us how to make the desert bloom" when I healed his son from schizophrenia, could have spread his metaphor, there might have been no war. Tiny Israel would have been seen as guest of the vast rich Muslim lands, and not as invaders. But in conventional language it is much easier to move with a curse.

For national language rallied people together into nations with battle-cries, slogans & commands. It bound them with curses against the enemy, not with blessings of peace. Sadistic mass-crimes are shown as duties & good works as treason. Hitler with a dozen slogans of hate got a dozen millions of young men to kill & die for him: "Jew — Judas — traitor" — man's death-drive projected into kill-words — fire-breath in slaying slogans of hate.

Man's word-pollution were not so fatal, unless humans followed the leader who has the power of words — & not of thought or goodness of the spirit. How did he get his power? First he himself was infected by words from the masses. (This would be good, if the masses had a creative solution — but then they would need him less.) He rides on the waves of predominant prejudice. Or like a condensing mirror gathers the rays of hate into the focus-fire of a slogan or he sucks the death-drives of the masses into himself & grows big on them. (For they are often his own drives, as he is a mann of common instincts & prejudices formed in common words of selfish pleasure & power.) His bigness attracts as a magnet & sucks all power into him. Only insofar as he cannot create a solution, it is not creative power, but the force of destruction. He becomes a magnetic black-hole demagog: all plunge into the devouring sink, & the more fall into it, the more magnetic it gets, until it devours itself, without letting any light of reason shine out.

Now some fanatic black-hole demagog sucks in masses by calling his rival "enemy of God, traitor of the Faith" & millions fall into that magnetic hole & shout: "the traitor

*) W.J. Weilgart, Communication: Logic or Command, UU of Alberta & Illinois, Linguistics R. 1971

must be killed." A whole nation must be killed, if a powerman names it with a curse. (If Cotton Mather called the Indians "devil's brood" "brought here by the devil," he set them up for massacre. *) Once in a million a poet or prophet can speak with angels' tongues — but then, does a nation follow him? A powerman speaks like a demon, threatening to explode, and hordes of nations unite in a war.

The polluted mind is addicted to its pollution. And the author knows from his own experience of healing the Navy's drug-addicts with the Language of Space that addicts are hardest to heal. The author as a student tried to convert his young fellows & friends, infected by Hitler's slogans & wrote his dissertation on "Creation & Contemplation" (Schöpfung & Schau) against Hitler's destruction, which Cosmic Insight foresaw to come. But mind-pollution in slogans of hate could not be undone. So I had to flee & sacrifice all my goods & 'rights' & start life anew without all in a foreign land.

B) Kind Candy Drugs. Mind-Pollution in Political, Commercial & Military Misuse.

Even kind words like candy can be misused to glut. Good & great words can be profaned. If an ad says 'chewing gum tastes "great",' soon we hear: 'God is the biggest thing in the world.' I heard a teacher stepping before Michelangelo's Last Judgment say: "That's nice." (Great in aUI = U-nam (Spirit-big), which could not be used for a gum. Nice = 'bruntem" = conventionally good, which could not be used for a genius. The English, too, of aUI-students improved 42%.)

The Holy Kings trusted the Xmas Star to lead them to the new-born Savior. What a sales-slogan: "Trust your car / To the man with the Texaco Star"! I did & I must confess that I experienced the following feelings with this slogan like a night-mare dream: When I repaired to this star near Denver, coming from Iowa to California, I trusted that my battery would be recharged. Trustingly I did not suspect that the Star-man would unscrew against my will out of the back of my VW bus its parts, so that I could not go on to the VW service station 20 miles on. I felt held as captive for four days (the Texaco-man had a motel for helpless travelers). When he guaranteed a genuine VW generator, I felt betrayed when it burnt & proved a phony sham (not VW). I could have burnt with my whole research. I felt betrayed when I saw that the highest Texaco administration callously refused any responsibility or concern for the stations which they advertized to serve under their trusted Star. As helpless traveler I expect to be admitted to licensed diplomate mechanics bonded by Texaco for the fatal harm they may do, or at least honest men who give a traveler his freedom. Trust is for me still a sacred word: "In God we trust." (Now by the end of the 20th century all this misuse of the word "Trust" has brought its foul fruit: 1979 polls showed that 82% do not trust president, congress or business or oil companies** or finally each other... Mind-Pollution means that people believe only what flatters them. But we cannot live without trust.

Likewise, can rich universities be trusted, when they disclaim all responsibility for fraternities under their halo, when these — in initiation-hazings, e.g. force a pound of sharp paprika into a helpless pledge to prove his "manhood in the name of brotherhood." To kill in such torture would be sadistic murder, unless it were hallowed by such glorious words.

Are Lessing's & Freytag's ideals of the writer as prophetic judge forgotten in the Press? Has the press become a profiteering trade? Hacks sell newspapers & TV time. The Murder-Media put Charlie Manson as cover-girl on the Xmas No. of LIFE & called the mass-murderer "charismatic genius," while they label creative idealists as "crackpots" or hush-kill their genius. In this way the murder-media (together with the oil-sheiks) effectively killed new inventions & prevented earth-, sea-, & sun-power to fulfill our dreams.

Even the word Love is profaned. "I love them," says a pretty TV-girl of some cookies. Romeo would wince, if a prostitute coos: "let's make love." These are but steps toward the ultimate perversion of this sacred word of Love: "We all must die in dignity for the Power of Love," said 'Rev.' Jim Jones, highpriest of the People's Temple, & 900 people had to die for the "power of love." What slogan! Did he not mean his 'love of power'? Or was Love strengthened by this meaningless massacre? In aUI, the power of Love would be (pro-) Creation not destruction & death. With the advent of the Pan-Atomic Age all mankind might die in slavery to such slogans in a "Holy" War, a "jihad" for the power of a word. In the Koran a holy war was meant against sadistic idolaters or perverted devil-worshipers to convert them to the one all-wise & -good God.

*) R. Schiller, p. 93. Reader's Digest June 1979 "Who were the First Americans?"

**) Texaco showed an 81% profit-increase. Texaco, Trust & sTar alliterate.

But why should a war of vengeance, envy & greed be called 'holy"? (aUI: holy = [aUI symbols], KU-rUm = God-good). If in a war myriads of peasants are killed to "teach (their nation) a lesson," what can the dead learn?

All these are demagogic distortions offered by conventional languages — 3000 lying lingos spawned by Babel's babble at the Confusion of Tongues that triggered wars. But this mind-pollution may mean annihilation of life in the pan-atomic age. Now we need Cosmic Communication in the Pentecostal Logos of Love & Peace — Healing through Harmony, Creation & Truth. We need communication & council* from fellowmen, cosmics, or subconscious soul, & the Cosmic Spirit of God.

C) The Bible's Vision on the Evolution of Language.

First we find man, created in the Paradise of cosmic accord, guided by his Creator's voice, name plant & animals in Adamic Language in spheric harmony with the music of the stars.** The Serpent's hissing brought in the first 'no!", the first discord of double-talk & rebellious arrogance, a language of lies, instruction as devil's destruction. So man lost eternal life through misuse of words. — Abel could still communicate in cosmic dialogue & pray in meaningful meditation. Cain, the negative shady side of man, spoke in possessive pride. Instead of learning the Spirit's cosmic communication from his pure younger brother, Cain's pride envied & concluded in arrogant jealousy: 'If he can do, what I cannot, he must die. Then the Father will have only me to love.' So Cain killed cosmic consciousness — fulfilling the fall of man. In Cain man, serpent-like, learned to lie. Man's first murder had been prepared by his first lie. To his brother he lied: 'Let's go on a hike.' And to God: "Am I my brother's keeper?" — when in truth he was not only not his keeper, but his killer.

Still in future millenia there were some prophets in whom God's counsel spoke with a "still small voice." But they were hardly understood, since men's hearts were already hardened by conventional words. But still "all the world spoke a single language." Man's communication decayed & disintegrated ultimately in the Babel Tower's confusion of the babbling Tongues, when each tribe (driven by the same pride that wanted to rear the tower to Heaven), insisted on its own national language — & so proud nations arose. Each leader boasting & boosting his own tribe, & cursing the others, could hear only their invectives, & attack.

From now on even the divine 'word' was misinterpreted & misunderstood. 'In the beginning was the 'word'" supplanted the 'Logos' of the Spirit. The Logos of Love, Christ himself was crucified. "All-Love" was heard as promiscuous sex, & "Faith" as fanatical dogma. Heretics or mystics were burnt in an "auto da fé" (= act of faith). The lingo's false surrogates replaced true ideals of the Spirit: the devil's idols stepped between man & God. — Now the mouth of speech itself becomes the black-hole that no longer reflects the light of information, but devours its own verbage in bureaucratic baffle-gab.

Only at the Pentecost of Peace the language of the Spirit descended in tongues like flames & was heard by all, & with the Cosmic Logos comes Cosmic Communication*: "Your young men shall see visions, & your old men shall dream dreams." Why did not all mankind embrace the Logos of Love? Again the negative destructive demonic side of man took over; & man fell back into his lingos of lies. Man shouted again in 3000 tongues his slogans of hate, goading to battle, sicking to war. (The Language of Space as Pentecostal Logos of Peace makes immune against the slavery to slogans of hate.)

When speech started, attack — for man as monkey — was harder than defense. We use the same words for war today — eons later — when attack is easy & all-destructive, but defense is almost impossible. As communicative curse, conventional national language is the bed through which the stream of thought must flow, or the path on which customary thought must run. Yet war-pictures are still the favorites with hawks & hacks. (If a rationing plan gets only a minority vote, instead of saying: 'It got 35%,' to sell his

*) Some of my students see the value of aUI in cosmic counsel received in this logos (cf. East-West Jl. "The Language of Space," Feb. 1979) e.g. at the MidEast conflict: "b Ena am Aseyv, /jAg fnu ykwuv U" = Lands are only loaned to us, / while we serve the Spirit's love [aUI symbols] i.e., a controversial region should not be given to the nation that destroys more, but creates & contributes more inventions & works of art for mankind: the wiser & better nation is worthier.

**) The Maroon, the newspaper of the University of Chicago, introduced my lectures on the Language of Space there: "Why not talk like Adam & Eve before the fall? ..." cf. Chicago Sun Times.

paper, the hack must shout: 'It was soundly beaten...resounding victory!' — images of war, &of might makes right: the most-seller = the 'best'-seller. 'Me too! Tit for tat! Pride in Power! Pleasure in the other's pain (Schadenfreude ist die reinste Freude) — Revenge is sweet!' (who can hear the Sermon on the Mount?). In the pan-atomic age, the path of language becomes a strait straight track, a steep-down blind alley, an inescapable tunnel — leading to the hell of all-kill. — Unless we break our way out into the rays of light of Cosmic Communication that frees our mind into the Cosmic Spirit.

D) Dear & Easy Mother-Tongue!

Within a culture, most people are not aware of its own prejudices & slogans, just as a fish does not mind that the water is wet. Just as the 19th century settler knew that Indians "are" savages, so the 20 c. knows that there "is" inflation, it is real & not an illusion or 'the demon of greed stalking the land' i.e. people demanding higher prices & wages & printing more money. The 20 c. knows that prophets, poets & other creative idealists "are" crazy crack-pots & must be shocked out of their visions — or destroyed. So Gandhi & King were killed. The official chief of the FBI labeled Rev. Dr. King, who could have been revered as a holy prophet of truth, as a "communist & most notorious liar" & hindered his work but not his murder. Plato's Phaedrus knows four types of divine ecstasy (prophetic, ritual, poetic, erotic) for which we have no words, but we misuse the word 'create-' for 'the kid created a disturbance.' Soon our conventional language may have no specific words for creative ideals. Instead, what most people like, must be good, even if it be a poisonous drug or a book that destroys ideals & stirs up crime, murder for the millions. Our age believes in the dogma of infallibility of mass-fads & conventional language shows it.

If people notice their language at all, they hear it in contrast to the "gibberish" of other languages, which don't make sense. Mark Twain wrote about "The Awful German Language" (p. 1143) as "slipshod & system-less" & p. 1163 about French as "confused, chaotic, ungrammatical...insane." In English he calls the "misuse of words...shabby slander" (p. 1206) & in Heaven (p. 1275) he hears the "billions of savages talk gibberish that Satan himself could not...understand." No "rule is without exception." All this could be just as truly said of all 3000 conventional national languages: they are proud of being unlearnable for the outsider, the 'barbarian & enemy' providing a special argot for the in-gang, which cannot be imitated as the bees' nest-smell. The specific slurs & glides of English can hardly be so well imitated that a native cannot detect the difference (less than 1%). But even the simple rules as 'a' in open syllable as in 'save' or 'haven' seems to have an exception in 'have.' Mark Twain says that English should be taught everywhere — without spelling or pronunciation. It is the easiest language "as long as you don't have to speak or write it." (Or hear or read it — we might add.) To the naive man only his own language has meaning. People revere their beloved mother-tongue, because it reminds them of their beloved mother & the bliss of their childhood, when they were rewarded & blessed for learning it. So the English feel that English is the easiest, richest & most beautiful language for the whole world.

The imperial power of Britain (& the U.S.) tried to teach English around the globe & everybody should learn 'it.' The great creative masters of English themselves have been not so sure of its simplicity. To master a language seems simple only for a man who has nothing profound to say. To express the deepest feelings & highest ideals of mankind (in rhyme) is hard in any language. But even simple English phrases are hard to understand in all their meanings by ear. (Don't look down) "The horse flies fast"[1]; "The morning sun's rays arose in a spring."[2]. Or for the professors of English of the University of London who said English is easier than aUI (about which London's TIMES had written as "Roots of Meaning"). I made little verses which none of them could spell far better than this child: "anu nu nu nudz thru his no's/noe nu nu nu what the hore nu nose."[3] Try it.

English with its thousands of homonyms, hundred-thousands of synonyms & polysemes & its hopeless discrepancy between spelling & sound can never be learned perfectly. "-s" can mean: possessive, plural or third person sg. "-ed" can be active or passive-participle of the past. "ing" is gd.or part: "Killing Indians must be stopped," the Captain assured the Indians, then he massacred them. "Well, I meant: murderous Indians must be stopped. So I did."

Other meanings of these polysemous homonyms: 1) The hoarse flies fast (=starve). 2) The mourning sons raise a rose in a spring (well, or season?) 3) A gnu knew new nudes thru his nose; (The gnu visits a nudist camp.) (Dictate your prof!). / No new gnu knew, what the hoar gnu knows.

The greatest poets & philosophers doubt conventional language as communication of spiritual values & ideas. Socrates & Plato fought against the double-talk of linguistic sophists. Shakespeare said: "Equivocation will be our undoing;" & "What's in a name? A rose by any other name would smell as sweet." "Words, words, words." Kant said language never reaches the Thing in Itself & Goethe mocks in Faust the "brittle stuff of language (der Sprache spröden Stoff):

"With words we easily start a fight, In words a system seems so right; In words it's easy to believe, With words it's easy to deceive."	"Mit Worten lässt sich's trefflich streiten, Mit Worten ein System bereiten; An Worte lässt sich's trefflich glauben, Von einem Wort kein Jota rauben." (tr. by Author)

Tolstoy found that man goes by words not by facts. Mauthner, Wittgenstein & Kainz warned against conventional languages: "We never reach reality — the words stand between." We live in a world of symbols or symbolic dreams. Distorted images may kill us & cosmic communication can save us, if — as creative sacrifice — we join a meaningful Logos.

J. Jaynes sees consciousness itself start from metaphors. What danger, if we then see a fact in a negative image! e.g. Israel as a "dagger pointed at the heart of Arabia." — By Buddha & Kung Fu-tzu the right life began with right speech. Lao-tzu found before Wittgenstein that conventional language lacks the right word for the essence: "Only the un-say-able has value." Jefferson knew that conventional languages are "incompetent to distinctly express ideas" and Emerson emphasized that they cannot express abstract ideas at all except by (distorted) images from concrete things. "Spirit" comes from "breath." "Ghost" from "rage." But without having words to express & sanction them, most people do not dare to have creative ideas. (Zipf.) Most people are not aware that concepts & ideas beyond their idiom's words are there. Their language produces their thoughts. If language is the 'bed thru which the river of thought must flow' (Piaget, cf. Hamann), then mankind must still think in terms of eons ago. But we need new thoughts & ideas that can save mankind to survive in the pan-atomic age of space. The Language of Space can create millions of new words for new ideas for the new age.

E) Peaks of Violence and Words of Peace.

M. Buber equated the creation of words with the coming forward of the Logos. But he agreed with U.N. head Dag Hammarskjöld: "We were pained by the pseudo-speaking of representatives of nations, who talked past one another out the windows." Instead, the author spoke with Dr. Kurt Waldheim, the present Secretary General & proposed as U.N. language of international communication — rather than invectives & diplomatic double-talk — creative aUI, the healing language of transparent truth, the Logos of Love & Peace. (It was fittingly discussed in the Security Council.)

We are entering mankind's worst crisis of survival. History shows that once each generation — about thrice each century — mankind explodes periodically in peaks of violence: insanity, crime & war. — With the next peak of violence we are entering the pan-atomic age. In a few years dozens of demagogs are reaching for atom-bombs. And one in ten power-men is a paranoid psychopath shouting hypnotic slogans of hate that trigger wars. Even if defeated & cornered, the last tyrant has only to surround his last H-bomb with a Cobalt-mantle to destroy all life for 18 years.

But though we philosophers are — mankind is not yet — ripe to die. In the majority man has not yet found his meaning. Man is still half creative angel & half demon of destruction. -/\+ Two millenia of Christianity have tried to transform man from a half-devil into a saint. Man has misunderstood Christ's words & misguided life on this earth. So what Christianity could not do in two thousand years — how can we do it in the two ? years (which may be all the time left before the next crisis). Solzhenitsyn said: "A word of truth could save the world." For if man had to confess even to himself his evil deeds in true words, before he planned them, his conscience could not stand the shame. Only rationalization — lending fine words to foul deeds — saves the bad man's face. — Good man (or the good part in man) could spread goodness, & evil man (or the evil part of man) could spread evil. But in conventional languages — with all their sham & double-talk — it is easier to spread evil than good. We can rather lie or curse than bless. Conventional language says the worst — best, and the best — worst.

So, as we cannot — in these few years — do what Christianity could not do: transform man from within —, we must & can transform man's communication — from Babel's babble of confusion & war-cries to the Pentecostal Logos of Love & Peace.

So man can spread his best – best, and his worst will be clear in transparent truth. Then he will avoid evil & fulfill his good. Let us dream a fairy-tale.

Once upon a time there was a strange King, who lived in a castle on a rock, far from all. That King's one arm ended in a good hand that gave life; & his other arm in an ugly killer-claw. His good hand held a dove, & his ugly claw – a crow. When his good arm was strong & gleamed, he would send doves as messengers, & they would coo love & peace. But when his claw-arm swelled, he sent crows to caw hate & war. – Once, the King's good side gleamed, & he wanted to let his doves coo peace, but there was a thunderstorm, & his doves were scattered & their peace-cooing was lost, & the crows hacked them to death. Only the raucous caws of war were heard to taunt, & all thought he was to make war, & they rose against him & killed him.

This King may be present man with his arousing media of communication. Whether they are in the service of pride in power, pleasure or money, they may become murder-media in times of crisis. Although just then we would need it most, in a crisis they cannot communicate wisdom & truth, kindness & love. Only the worst can come through. They glorify crime & sick to war, – just to sell their papers or TV-time. They hush-kill goodness & virtue, that could reason & calm. Thus we need doves that could call through a tempest & sing clear as larks. These are the cosmic sounds of the Language of Space. Cosmic Communication could radiate from distant stars like cosmic rays. Messengers might be among us to help us, even within us in different dimensions of actuality imbuing our mind, if we would open our ears & learn their language to understand, believe & share counsel. Why are they not revealing themselves? What if their question is: 'Are earthlings willing & worthy to survive? Would they bring a sacrifice of spiritual creation to life in truth? (Is truth today only materialistic metaphysics & does epistemology mean only that what all always sense is actual? Man may survive if he opens to the mystery of the beyond.) aUI heals to Peace through Harmony, Creation and Truth.

F) Truth.

'Ye shall know the truth & the truth shall make you free." aUI frees from the strait-jacket of constricting conventional clichés, from the single-tracked blind alley of conventional prejudice & customary distortions & Discord that leads to war. Harmony pervades the idea of truth. I am in truth, when my (inner spiritual) thoughts about an (outer material) object are 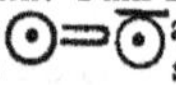 adequate, equal or in harmony with that object (so that they can create a cosmic symbol.) 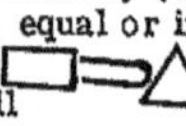 Subject & Object are in harmony. aUI is a logos of transparent truth, since all words are composed of the same 33 elements & can be clearly & truthfully analyzed into these same elements like chemical formulas to be verified. This is the secret of the 33 symbol-sounds.

Verities can be verified. While aUI is still attacked as the arcane gift of a cosmic experience, it can be mathematically proven a) to contain all the elements out of which all concepts are composed, b) in such a way that even after only 5 minutes (the international speed record is 2'13") learning time testees can recognize through the symbols any words composed by them, differentiating the compounds in the Pictograph Test, which contains 125 arbitrary compound words in aUI out of which the equivalents of 25 (e.g. English) words should be chosen. It has been solved 100% by any student with an IQ above 132, & above 75% by IQs 116+, & with 50% average by IQs M = ca 100, – while chance guessing for such quintuple choice tests would yield only 20%, which would be the way any other language test (as far removed from English) would be solved after 5' learning its elements, e.g., the Arabic or Hebrew alphabet. Not a single student could recognize a single Arabic or Hebrew words from its letters, as there is no relationship. But in Chinese, where there is, the thousands of complicated pictographs takes 5 years instead of 5 minutes. Prof. Arthur Deutscher wrote: "aUI unites the transparency of Chinese with the simplicity of the Roman alphabet." (NB. E & F, O & Q, I & l & I – Ford III = ill? – are confusingly similar. So, even the Roman is not so simple.)

Since in aUI the same ideas have always the same sounds & symbols, there is a reassuring consistency in the Language of Space, which is lacking in conventional national languages. We saw that demagogs in launching slogans pretend that homonyms are synonyms or assonances have the same meaning; i.e. they pair similar sounding words, if they want to compare their meanings. When they shout 'Kick the Kikes," they pretend that these words fit 'naturally', i.e., that Kikes should be kicked — which is a lie. But in the Language of Space homonyms = synonyms. So if words in aUI sound similar, they mean similar & fit in harmony. "brO & brU" means "Love & Peace." (Together-good-Feeling & Together-good-Spirit.) Thus if an orator in aUI puts similar sounding (& looking) words together into a motto, we are not deceived by puns as "soil & soul" by which demagogs seduce, but we learn essential harmonies: In aUI cf. wish & hope, striving & purpose, harmony & love, & peace.

Thus in aUI there is not confusion, but there is wonder: you know that each word can be composed out of the 33 elements, but you wonder out of which elements it is primarily composed, as you may wonder which chemical elements are in a compound. Each word becomes a mystery to be solved — becoming a symbol of our life. (Since we live a life in symbols, aUI is a symbolic offering, reaching out to cosmic communication.) On the other hand, if you meet for the first time an unknown aUI-word (a combination of elements), you wonder, how you can describe it in English — or whether it transcends conventional speech.

Conventional synonyms & homonyms bring a lingo of lies. G. Razran proved that while the conscious mind associates in synonyms, the subconscious soul still binds homonyms together. So when you are dreamy, drugged, or drunk, a serf (slave) may remind you of a surf (wave), which you may rule as his master by riding it. Thus homonym pun-dreams seem in discord with our reasoning logics, for which a serf = slave, & a surf a breaker-wave. — We healed phobias, compulsions & addictions by analyzing them in the Language of Space, where synonyms = homonyms. If aUI words sound similar, they look & mean similar. So in aUI, the logical mind understands the subconscious dreams of our soul. In a Latin student it was a dream of honor. He had backed out of a dare: "Perdi' mi valor" meant "I lost my value (as well as) my valor." I asked him, how he would express valor in aUI. Like Chicago's young gangsters (cf. below) he composed finally "w O" = power-feeling for courage. And then he said: "Well, I just did not feel strong enough at that time. (He was healed of his suicidal depression of cowardice.)

Thus not by prefabricated slogans, but by each creating his own words, we can heal*. Whatever is your hang-up, whatever oppresses you, compose it in aUI, & let a group of friends, too, compose the same concept; then look it up in the vocabulary. Thus we healed another suicidal patient: He himself composed suicide as eyr-yt-e = evil-away from-move = flight away from evil. It was really a task he tried to escape. He saw the task itself as a bEk, a high mountain, steep & abrupt, instead of gradually climbing one step at a time, planning parts. Now the therapy-group defined his suicide-(obsession) as fU-vyo = this-mind (=self)- make 'non-life' (=death) = self-kill. All confirmed this by looking it up in the vocabulary. So he understood that, rather than moving his self away into safety from the threat, he was to destroy his whole beloved self for-ever, at least his wonderful body, this ship of the spirit, & still in an other world he might be confronted with the same essential task. — By thinking in aUI, students improve their WERT-test wisdom-training by 34% & their happiness-rating by 28%. Happy & wise!

We lie to an enemy in war, but we speak Truth to a friend in Peace.

FG) Peace.

aUI is the Logos of Happiness & Health & of Harmony & Peace. Health is Harmony of body & soul, peace is harmony between people & nations. Here in the view of truth we see e.g. four ways in which aUI furthers Peace. It dissolves selfishness: the "I" (Ego) in national languages is quite different from the "thou," "you" & even "we." In aUI "I" = fu, while 'thou' = = bu = together-man, the person with whom I (=this-man) sit together. So both are humans of equal worth, the one just happens to sit here, the other there. We = fnu = these-many-people, plural-I. — What leads to wars between the "I" & "you," or "they" = nu = is "Invective & Command.' While "I" reserve good words for myself & my friends, I wrap my enemies in loaded invectives, calling them Niggers, Kikes or Gooks. This means that evil is implicit in their name. If he "is" a Kike, I need not prove that he is bad. I heard in the South the question: "Is your lover a Nigger?" (If asked: "is he a black monster?" the girl could have answered, "One of his ancestors came from the tropics, he is handsome & good," or to that explicit question, she could even have answered "No.")

---

*See Weilgart, Cosmic Logotherapy, in Bibliography

In aUI each invective must start with honest 'yr-' = no-good, bad. Then in transparent truth I would have to prove & verify, why he is 'yr-u' = a bad man. I can easily command 'Kill the Kikes,' because they are bad, & the command rhymes in alliteration. But in aUI each command, so necessary in war, contains 'r' = good. Kill the Kikes = vyorv yru = = make—non-live (good deed!) those 'no-good people'! Then you can ask me: 'Why is it good to kill them? Why are they no good so that it is good to kill them?' (In America 'better' likewise expresses a mild command: 'better drink your milk!') Thus in aUI Invectives & Commands become statements of evil & good, verifiable both. We speak transparent truth.

A truth-statement contains the word 'is' '/.' 'He is a Tropian' (adapted to the Tropics); or: 'He is impotent.' Webster uses the same 'is' for both...as 'grass is green.'. But in aUI grass 'is—by-nature' = oc = 'green.' (Without chlorophyll it would die.) But the Tropian's negritude is only part of his nature, though a vital one. He could live with less melanin. He 'partly-life-is' Negro = zoc = . But '...is impotent'? To call non-erection 'impotence' has mind-polluted many a sensitive lover into chronic dysfunction. Potentially he may be very fertile. So it is not his nature to be impotent. He is now partly in this nervous condition, § Q; partly-conditionally-is = = zQc (pronounced: 'zÖsh' or" 'zØsh'). The word 'is' has not only driven into impotence, but also into ruthless power. Political, ethical & religious dogmatists like Torquemada, Robespierre, Hitler & today's fanatic demagogs shout: 'He is a ⊃ heretic, infidel, enemy of God, or monarchist..., so it is our duty to exterminate his ilk.' In truth — or peace — he may be partly a mystic or conditionally a part-courtier (0.01%) but 99.9% a creative genius — like Lavoisier.

G) Creation

Besides through Harmony & Truth, aUI heals through Creation. Man, created in his Creator's image to create, unless he can create, will destroy. Sickness, crime & war destroys; health, love & peace should create. T.S. Eliot confesses: "One has learnt words only for the thing one no longer has to say." In aUI we can create new words for new ideas. aUI offers the 33 symbols as elements of meaning out of which each can create his own words. Each man can re-create his own feelings in the language of Space. E.G., I asked a patient how she felt after our aUI meditation. She answered with "hyvrO" = a questioning good passive (=conceptive) feeling — hardly expressable in a Western language. (If there is no good simple word for it, people do not dare to indulge in this feeling, cf. G.K. Zipf.) So 'non-active,' passive = 'non-good'

In aUI we can create billions* of 6-letter words, more than all earthly languages have together. A national language has at most some 100,000 words, most incomprehensible to most. A Western language has about 8 times more words for aggressive hate & war than for contemplative love & peace. So most of our expressions for creative loving goodness are suppressed for what Shakespeare calls "tyrant Custom." Conventional language allows us no sanction of words for our good ideas. The blind alley of a strait track leads to annihilating war. But spiritual creations in the Language of Space lead to the freedom of contemplation of cosmic beauty & to integration in happiness & health.

aUI, described as 'spiritual creation,' is organically composed of the 33 elements, which in turn (as nature's elements are composed into bio-cells or chemical radical-groups), are combined into hundreds of syllables that are basic ad e.g. 'ryv-' good-passivity, from which we derive 'ryv-O' good-passive-feeling (transcends Western languages)? conceptivity? good-acquiescence? Meister Eckhart's "Gelassenheit"?, 'tak-' = upward, toward-above. We can combine both into 'ryv-tak-O' Goethe's Ewig-Weibliche, eternal-feminine-conceiving, which leads up to the ideal. 'ki' = star; then a-ki-tak = first-star-up = sun-rise. aki-tak-trO = sun-rise-hope. rO = pleasure, k-rO = high-pleasure = joy; krO-wE = joy-stone = diamond. ui = blue, ui-rO-wE = blue-jewel = saphire. (English can

*) With the 10 number-sounds aUI has 41 elements; so for 6-letter-combinations 41x40 x39...x36 = 41!/35! = 3,237,399,360; in contrast to the Roman alphabet, all aUI combinations are meaningful.

also compose words from root-syllables, but 'faith-ful' today means mostly not full of faith, but loyal: aw-ful often not full of awe. When I arrived in U.S.A., I went from appointment to appointment to dis-appointment, which I trusted to be the opposite of appointment, as distrust is of trust. We say 'a house de-cays' but not 'it cays,' cadit, falls. There is little consistency or harmony in conventional combinations.

H) Harmony.

Most essential for health, happiness & peace is their bond. harmony. For health all hormones flow in harmony, & all muscles pull our bones & move our limbs in harmony. For inner peace all citizens act in harmony, & for world-peace all nations or better all cultures create in harmony. Disharmony erupts in sickness, discord in crime & war, provoked by slogans of hate.

Children expect harmony in language. If words sound similar, they expect them to mean similar. E.g., the teacher John Getman, an aUI student, taught his first graders a song called "weeping sky." These children knew only 'crying.' So they assumed that 'weeping' must mean something between 'sweeping' & 'wiping.' Many folk-etymologies as 'whip-poor-will,' 'ear-wig' or 'arm-brust' show the need for meaning. The bird's call, the insect's "ear" = spike, as in grain, the arcu-ballista (Lat. arch-thrower), arquebus, harquebus from hackbut...all had become incomprehensible & by forcing them into a different shape (Brust = breast) were given meaning. ⊙

In aUI, symbol, sound, & significant meaning agree. E.G., a dot inside a ring means inside & sounds 'g' gutteral inside the throat. ♡ Feeling is symbolized as a heart-shape & sounds long O, & we say Oh, when we feel deeply & touch our heart. "O" is a low-back tongue vowel inside our mouth, & we keep our feelings back inside & they well up from below. O is a rounded vowel & feelings seem womanly - round as the symbol ♡. Only living-beings feel & Life sounds "o" too, only shorter. Life's symbol is ρ & two such lives ♡ combine to the heart of feeling as two lives can feel for each other. Similar meanings look & sound similar. The symbol for △ the Spirit is a triangle to show the triune Spirit's angular logic. But the spirit's sound is a high-tongue long "U" as in "trUe," an inner (back-tongue) rounded vowel: the Spirit soars high & hides within a mystery. Italians & Spaniards use the "i" of "spirit," but for "light" they use "u" in "luce, luz." I wondered how these Latins, who use "i" & "u" opposite of aUI, truly feel about these vowels. Without telling them that in aUI the vowel with the highest (quickest) vibration — 3000 cycles per second — means Light, the quickest speed, and without reminding them of their own language, I gave them a test in which they had to assign the vowels "i" & "u" to Light or Spirit. 96% assigned "i" to light (i as in lit), & "U" (as in true) to Spirit.

The Spirit's triangle is similar to the two legs of man ⋀ walking to good & evil, creation or destruction. The symbol for man, human, person...sounds short "u" as in "push" (as man is a pushy creature, we say in mnemonics). The short "u" sounds similar to the long "U," & man should be similar to the Spirit, except that man's life is short, & the Spirit eternal. So man & mind should be similar, as "u" & "U" or ⋀ & △. In aUI, if meanings are similar, symbols & sounds are similar. (NB. we can distinguish between mind and spirit: mind = og-U ρ⊙△ i.e. body-spirit.) This similarity means inner harmony.

Cosmic communication itself means a threefold harmony. We should commune freely with our fellowmen or the cosmics — as e.g. schizoid or autistic patients cannot. Thus aUI becomes a therapy for schizophrenia. Second we should commune with our subconscious soul, & our visceral or sympathetic & parasympathetic nervous system, which in most civilized neurotics is "autonomic" from the cortex of the brain, i.e., it often does not commune with reason. Feeling & Intellect, dreams & thoughts should unite. Scientists should not only be cold intellectuals, but ethical & deep-feeling humans — Spirit and Soul should be one.

Third in aUI, in the Language of Space in our cosmic dreams we commune with the cosmic Spirit of the universe. Most 'universities' do not teach this communion, & this discord leads to crime & war. In aUI we can pray, meditate & contemplate in creative freedom. Creation should lead to Contemplation of the Spirit. Man will meet the Cosmic Spirit either in this life through the Pentecostal Logos of Peace, or part of mankind will dissolve in the Cosmic Spirit in death — which now for most of mankind would be death in despair. For most of mankind is not ripe to die. Man will destroy himself and life on this planet, unless he follows cosmic counsel, and learns to communicate with the Cosmic Spirit of GOD.

CREATIVE MEDITATION

Dr. Weilgart led such Meditations on Meaning in many groups. E.g., sponsored by the Head of the Anthropology Dept. of the University of Chicago, Prof. Sol Tax, in the International House of the U. C. and in the U. C. Lab. School, also in the Stone-Brandel Center for creative youth. At Midnight, after a students' meditation session, he was held up by a Chicago boys' gang. "If we don't slug you, we'd be Chicken." "How fascinating," answered the philosopher, "I just come from an inconclusive meditation on the meaning of Courage. Here my book from India . . ." (and under a streetlamp he opened p. 10) "Is courage a risk of sacrifice or a power-feeling (w-O)?" 'I guess you don't understand us: we're going to slug somebody else.' The philosopher with not-understanding but unslugged brain, returned to his midnight contemplations.

Prof. Weilgart, as principal of a delinquent school, learnt of "sucker-sissy-squealer" morals. These slogans were "absolutes", covering all situations: artists, peacemakers, poets . . . are sissies; work hard, pay your way . . . sucker! Tell the truth: squealer! A threefold straitjacket. In the Land of the Free, could not also youth's thoughts be free? Creative Meditation on Meaning delivers from enslaving slogans. Dr. Weilgart, a master-psychoanalyst, as Family-Counselor is asked by parents: "Why did my child become a drug-addict? I always told him: Don't." Man was created in the image of his Creator to create. If barred from creation, he destroys. Let youth play imaginative thought-games of meaning, then they need no LSD for their soul trip to Self.

John Getman,
Educator & Composer

aUI: Meditation on Meaning (A Semantic Grouptherapy). Play as Competition or Communication?

Come to the party! Some people drown the pre-atomic panic in deafening noise. They scream, hop, howl, and squirm together, and kick you quiet ones to the wall, into resentful solitude. Must the silent still be lonely? May the thoughtful never communicate? aUI, The Language of Space, gives you the creative play of cosmic communication, to know thyself and understand your friends. Invite them to a Spaceman's Party of Meditation on Meaning. First each reads the 31 Symbols on p. 10 & 11 (or you read them to your friends by p. 9, distributing a book to each). Each keep his book open on p. 10, although the Symbols are learnt in a few minutes (even in 2'), if you explain their symbolic shape: "dot *inside* circle means *Inside,* pronounced "g" as guttural *inside* throat." (Pronounce by p. 9, rounding your lips for "o" as in "boy."). These magic dream symbols are your categories of communication, the colors for your canvas, the elements of meaning, the brickstones from which you build up the walls or windows of your own words to form the palace of your thoughts in free creation: do your own think.

The player who is quickest in thinking of some concept or idea that interests him, proposes it to the group and writes it first column, first line. He is the first "Spaceman." Then, from p. 10, each simultaneously writes down and draws on his paper his combination of elements, which he feels are "necessary and sufficient" to describe this concept. Then each shows or reads or writes into his column on a blackboard his compound for all others to see and they, too, copy it into his column, and "see" or visualize it and comment on it in a spirit of friendly communion, repeating its aUI sounds. Then they look up the concept in English after p. 222f and enter the Space-word into their last column in aUI. The player whose combination has come nearest to the common-ground standard word pp. 223-249 or a synonym, or whose creation seems most plausible to majority consensus, is the next spaceman (or: spacegirl or jungle-babe) and proposes the next idea. (If one knows more about aUI or Languages and Phonetics, he may moderate and correct pronunciations, or prod: "Would LOVE rather contain Matter, Mind, or Feeling?" Each player's paper (or the blackboard or window-pane marked with soap-stick or marker) looks best like this: (! marks Space-man or Space-girl)

Concept	Tom (20 yrs)	Sarah (14 yrs)	Lizzy (7 yrs)	Spaceword p.223f. aUI
LOVE	= gUi	=brO-Ujo	=rOnob !	= brO, p.236 127
MAD	= wOg	=yrU-Om!	=eoIObyiv	=wydOm(angry) =U-yrom(insane) p.234, p.120
SAD	=yrOm !	= gyiOm	=oUyiOg	=y(k)rOm
PEACE	= yw	= grOc !	= aori	= brU

Discussion: Tom: I propose to make LOVE in the Language of Space. (Silence, while each peruses p. 10, gathering elements, drawing columns). Tom: Are you all ready? Has each drawn his symbols? on his paper? I wrote: gUi "inside-spirit-light" (He draws this on wall, all copy under Tom's name, into their 2nd column.) — Sarah: Let's close our eyes. I see "inside" the Spirit "U" a Light "i", as on a blue sky a star: "gUi". But this, to me, feels like "insight" or "enlightenment." — Lizzy: Tom's love shines in him, he is of glass. — Sarah: brO-Ujo, "Together-good-feel . . ." Lizzy (copies Sarah's "brO-Ujo"): I see them hug together and smile — brO. Tom: . . . and they are of "like mind (for) life": Ujo — Lizzy: I wrote "rOnob": "good-feeling-lots (of) life-together". — Tom: You both think Love as a joy. — Lizzy: . . and makes lots of life like rabbits. — Tom: Let's look it up. p. 236 it says "brỌ" with a dot under the "O", so it's discussed under "O" or "rO" p. 127: you win: it's a good feeling, love is a pleasure, supposedly. — Sarah: Tom, you left out "together", too. You are much alone, and keep all inside. — Tom: Each for himself. Lizzy, you won, you had only 2 letters beyond the Space-word. You are the Space-girl. So what do you propose? —

Lizzy: MAD! (All draw and write) I wrote: "eoI-Ob-yiv." — Tom: Is that all? I see: When you's mad, you "move" ("e")*, and are "alive" ("o")*, and make "noise" ("I")* . . . Lizzy: . . . , because I'm "dark" ("yi") inside, I've to "do" ("v")* something, and get "together" with the one I am mad with. Tom: There's no Mad in the vocabulary, but here are the synonyms: Angry and Insane. Sarah, yours is nearest to "U-yrom" (mind-sick, p. 120). You're Space-girl! — Sarah: So let's make "SAD." . . . . — Tom: I see you both "dark-inside" ("g-yim") — Lizzy: But you are the Spaceman, for you understood the Sad. —

Tom: So I propose PEACE. . . . — Sarah: I wrote "Inside-good-feeling (of) - existence", "g-r-O-c." — Tom: You play the Zen-Buddhist, but your peace is too "grOm" (= sweet, p. 200) for me. Here's my "y-w": Peace means a fight "against - (the) - power" of the establishment. — Lizzy: For Peace I see lots of "Space", "a",for if people "live" ("o") crowded, they fight. I see "good light" (ri): If the Language of Space shines from the stars, it will . . . — Tom: communicate cosmic peace. Sarah: Peace is like Love, "brU" is like "brO."

*) aUI sounds are pronounced phonetically: "e" (as in "get") "o" (boy), (p. 9), "I" (machIne), "v" (as "v" not "vee") . . . without spelling-nicknames!

II (p. 222 suggests another aUI play for untrained Spacemen. The first player who writes on a board (or in the beach-sand) any aUI symbol combination by which he means something interesting, or reads it to the group, is the First Spaceman. e.g. he wrote "uga." All others write down English meanings on their papers simultaneously. Then they all read their guesses, starting with the youngest. The best guesser is now Spaceman, and proposes the next aUI-compound.)

III. Each player can simultaneously create his aUI symbol combination, and write it on a board (and its meaning on his paper). Then each simultaneously writes his guess of all others' compounds' meanings on his paper, and finally each enters his guesses on the blackboard. Each right guess makes him "Space-Sage" (S), but being understood by others makes him "Space-King" (K). On paper or board it looks like so:

Names	Lenny(KKSSS)^5	Andy (KS)^5	Mary (KKKS)^5	Paul(SSK)^5	(aUI)^6
Lenny	yiOyrom^2/(KK)$_5$ /sick^5	lonely-sad^4	dark,sick^4 S	sad,sick^{4}S	6) yrom
Andy	4)river4) (S)^5	vjE^2/ (K)$_5$ /river	4) water-power	4) wee-wee irrigation	6) ejEn
Mary	4) lightbulb S	lampbulb^{4}S	Lids^2 /KKK5 /Lamp 5	4)lamp S lightbulb	ilas,id (6)
PAUL	4) S^5 Love-Trust	4) happiness	4) contentment	2)rUO /K$_5$ /trust	6) rUO

(Numbers 2-6 show step-sequence of entries on board)

Each writes players' names on top of his paper and also on left margin, from youngest to oldest. Then follow numbers of chart: 1) Each simultaneously secretly writes on his paper an aUI combination (with its English meaning) that interests him (using p. 10) into his column or row, i.e. on the blackrim-diagonal. — 2) Each reads his aUI (without its English meaning) to others and enters it into "his" diagonal-square on a board² (if available) or on beachsand, so others can copy it. — 3) Each secretly simultaneously writes his guesses about the meaning of the others' aUI-compounds into his column below his name to their row. — 4) Each, starting with the youngest, professes his guesses to the group, or enters them on the board⁴ as English translations in the row of their aUI equivalent. — 5) Each confesses his own meaning, showing his (1) paper, and enters the English into his blackrim square on the diagonal of the board. The group compares guesses with secret intentions: For a right guess, you get an (*S*), for making yourself understood, a (*K*). Then write to your name the sum of how often you became a Space-*K*ing or a Space-*S*age: would you rather convince or understand? Test your empathy!

THE LANGUAGE OF SPACE
dissolves the Slavery to Slogans,
the Idolatry of Ideologies.

Different dimensions of reality: "We are such stuff as dreams are made on." India's Maya. Naked jungle children scribbling magic dream symbols: in India, aUI, The Language of Space, is published by Chand & Co., in (New) Delhi, Bombay, Calcutta, Madras, Hyderabad and all major cities, to unite these 500 millions with dozen warring languages in an instant communication of Peace. Jungle and slum dwellers, workers and peasants, in Asia or Africa, never in centuries of colonialism could learn the conventional western languages, felt as imperialistic.

All 31 aUI symbols, i.e. all Basic Words of the Language of Space, can be learnt in a few minutes (even in 2', up to 16 times faster than a comparative language) (cf. John Matthias, aUI Learning Speed Comparisons, Semantic Laboratory Research, Luther College.) Some have more, others less, sense for semantics. But those who are least aware of meaning, need aUI most. — Translation even within the ruling (similar) languages English and French is risky. Norman Cousins writes in Saturday Review & in Look, July 29, 1969 p. 48: Ho Chi Minh's request that the U. S. *doit reconnaître* ("should consider") was translated into "must accept" (his Four Points.) This affronted America into breaking off peace negotiations. Traditional languages are ambiguous. aUI is transparent and clear.

Seeing through to the elements of the Logos helps missionaries of the Gospel, partly translated into aUI. In some tribal languages, Soul = Demon, Sin = Taboo-Mistake; in aUI, Soul and Sin contain the element "U" = Spirit, thus teaching the concepts themselves.

In America, aUI *Meditations on Meaning* serve to dissolve prejudice and the slavery of slogans. (cf. pp. IV, V, VI & 222) Prof. Kainz of the Academy of Sciences, noted for his 5-volume standard work on Psychology of Language, writes of aUI as "educating to the essence." aUI with its archetype symbols is the language of the subconscious soul.

Why speak in primeval soul symbols rather than in demagogic slogans or bureaucratic cliches? Slogans originally saved the human race into collective cooperation: "Ye from left! We from right!" (attack the crocodile) organized an unarmed tribe into an army. Commands like "All for one! One for all!" helped naked man survive. (cf. Sol Tax, Evolution after Darwin). But now when nature's dragons lie defeated at his feet, man's slogans, like his swords, rise against himself, to annihilate him in the next atomic war — which would be fought not for territory but for ideologic slogans.

Now slogans serve no longer as rallying cries against an outer — non-human — enemy that threatened death, but against inner — competing — rivals for power, and thus distort conventional language into commercial, bureaucratic, political and militaristic lingo domains. But in hundred-thousand years, humans — like howler monkeys — have been conditioned blindly to obey slogans — or battle-screams — in panic crises that craved collective confidence. Mario Pei, The Story of Language, 1965, calls "slogans . . . semantic dynamite (for) political action." Dr. Weilgart sees a slogan rather as a trigger that sets off the dynamite, or a catalyst or relay that closes the circuit of tension. When W. J. Weilgart, as a student rebelled against Hitler, he found that this Führer in a crisis of frustration and resentment, with a dozen slogans got a dozen million young men to die and kill for him.

A slogan can absolutize a relative value into a focus of positive or negative action, an ultimate to die for, or to kill. Confucius said: the good state begins with the right use of words (being conscious of their limited and consistent application). Freud, (confirmed by G. Razran's experiments in the Pavlov Institute,) found that the subconscious (drugged, drunk, or dream-mind) thinks in homonyms, associates by assonance, while the conscious mind tries to think in rational synonyms. Conventional languages thus split the mind into drive and reason. aUI, being not an "artificial language, but a language as a work of art" unites synonyms = homonyms and heals the split between intellect and soul.

A patient of Dr. Weilgart suffered from nightmares: a dog barked from the sky. In her dream-world DOG = GOD,: a reverse-homonym blasphemy of the subconscious, which Dr. Weilgart healed with aUI's Semantic Grouptherapy. (Dr. Weilgart is a member of the International Society for General Semantics as well as of the American Society of Grouptherapy and Psychodrama).

The demagogue's slogans hypnotize the masses' subconscious by regressing from the informative communication to the pre-rational command state of language. Here alliteration or rhyme replaced reason. "Heil Hitler" itself was a part-homonym conclusion: 'Since Hitler's name contains the 4 letters of Heil, he must convey Heil' (Salvation). (As Schickelgruber he could have never become the Ruler of the Realm). "Ein Volk, Ein Reich, Ein Führer!" deduces from the near-homonym of "Volk" (pronounced: Folk) with "folg!" (follow! = obey!) that the nation must *follow* the *Führer* (leader) in alliteration to become Reich (a rich ruling empire) from a defeated starving state. There-to Germany had sunk through the Jews (= traitors), which Hitler 'proved' by the near-homonym chain: "Jude — Juda — Judas."

Slogan-loyalty overrides individual feeling. A good-natured Nazi said: "I don't dislike that Jew Jacob, he helped me. But after all he *is* a Kike, so he must be killed." In times of tension, words like "traitor" become more generalized slogans, like sponges sucking in finally any non-conformist. The advanced aUI-adept will understand that any invective in aUI must show its mettle by starting openly with an "yr-" (like "mal-" i.e. "evilly . ."). Thus he might compose "treason" in aUI out of "yr-t-ybru-r" i.e. "evilly — to-enemy — good" (deed), or "to do good to an enemy in an evil way", but then one has to prove first that there are enemies, y-bru or yd-bru, and that there is a war on, an anti-peace, "yd-brU." English "betraying" gives also a secret away, in aUI: "yr-tyg-ypu-v." ("evilly — outward-secret-give"), e.g. to tell an invader the castle's secret entrance. But then what becomes of Hitler's slogan "traitor to his own race?", unless his race is a secret or he can deliver it up to its enemies.

Invectives may spread into slogans. When Dr. Weilgart served at Xavier University in New Orleans, a Southerner told him: "Washington Carver may have been a gentleman and a scholar: in my book he is still a Nigger." Analyzed into aUI, it would read: "Dr. Carver may have been a wise-know-man (nU-gUw-u) and a good-man (r-u), he is still a bad-black-man (yr-ybi-u) or: mal-tropic-man (yr-ia-u)." Invective insinuations become verifiable self-contradictions.

"Black", beyond the melanin increase in skin pigment, is generalized into a slogan with connotations like black-mail, black-list, black-magic etc. "Black = dismal" in nordic imagery from the deadly long arctic winter night.

Approaching the crisis of atomic panic, more demagogues will mushroom up, hurling slogans of hate into the masses to set off terror riots or the next war of annihilation.

Youth will disintegrate into unimaginative activists and inactive dreamers, irrational both, unless they contemplate the center of the Spirit.

Semantic meditation as group therapy and prophylaxis, by analysing the essence of meaning, makes youth see through, and thus immune against, the slavery of slogans of hate that distort the beauty of creation, the purity of contemplation.

In the beginning was the Word —, shall the Slogan rule in the end? Man, as God's idea, is part of the divine plan for harmony in the cosmos. Unfettered by a planet's prejudice, man's thoughts should flow freely into infinite space. The language of the Spirit should be cosmic communication. The Language of Space brings Peace through Understanding, and becomes the Logos of Love.

LOOK AHEAD

—/\+ In aUI, man's symbol is two legs walking to good or to evil: man has a creative and a destructive part, the force of a devil and an angel in him. But man's conventional language communicates his criminal rather than his creative part. It is most powerful as rallying battle cry. It commands destruction rather than communing creation. Conventional language screens off the best but collects and brings out the worst in each of us. All can slander and curse but only a one-in-millions genius may become a poet who can profess the meaning of beauty. But Tolstoy's horse "Strider" notes: Man goes by words rather than deeds. In aUI each can create his words and the poems and psychograms of his soul. Creative expression becomes loving communication. The Language of Space heals from hate and communes the love of the good, the beautiful, and the true. It helps man to commune with his fellowman, with his subconscious soul, and with his God.

For millenia prophets have preached love and peace. But if in conventional language Christ himself preached peace while a criminal screamed war, the mob would crucify Christ while they hailed Barrabas and followed a demogogue. Conventional language distorted love into lust, faith in fanaticism. An 'act of faith' meant no longer believing and doing the will of the Lord of love, but 'auto da fe',: burning heretics in hate.

+ = good

∓ = bad

= make, = life, /\ = man, — = anti-,

"Kill the kikes", commands the invective. The Language of Space dissolves the invective into the statement of evil and the command into a statement of good: "vyorv yru" means "to make them non-live is a good deed (if these) are really no-good men." Instead of being hypnotized by a command, we can freely ask why is this good, why are they bad? From a slave who blindly obeys slogans, man is educated into the freedom of reasoned decision, which he needs to survive the atomic age.[1]

1. W. J. Weilgart: *Man of the Future* (if there is to be a future), Cosmic Communication Co., Decorah, Iowa 52101.

Know Thyself! The Essence of your Being. Fill in your "Psychogram" and send it to us. (Put in the midst the Symbol that is in the center of your personality, at the right what you offer to the world, at the left what you keep for yourself, above what rules you, below your foundation or base. You can also surround each circle with symbols (or their opposites--by drawing a bar over them). Here are the symbols in organic sequence: Let the Microcosm of your Mind mirror the Macrocosm of the Universe.

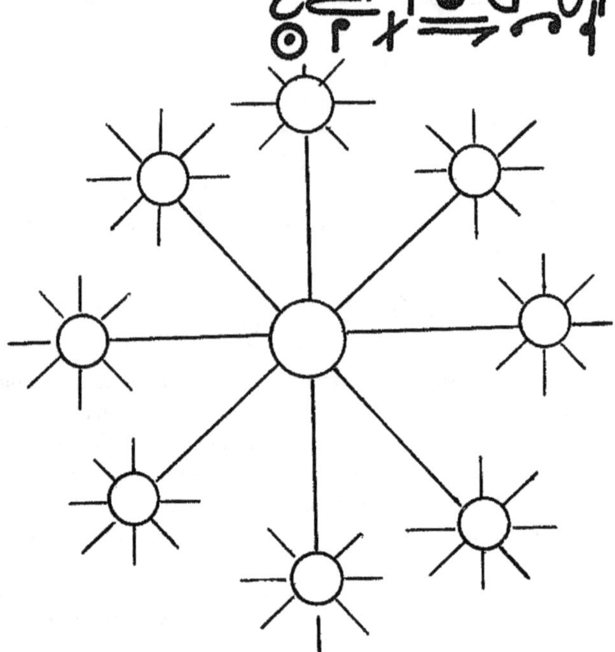

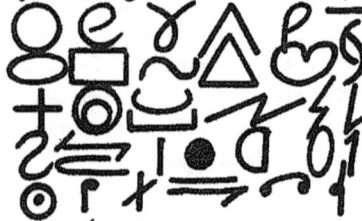

With your Psychogram enclose $10 and we send you our WERT (Weilgart-Rime-Test).

Symbolic Cosmos

In aUI similar symbols have similar meanings, and related symbols evolve out of each other. There are as many angular as round symbols.

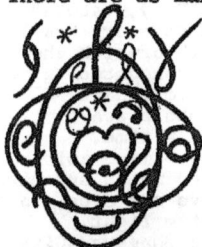

The round (feminine)symbols:

SPACE is like a ROUND container, the egg TIME hatches the future, revolving in periods. SPACE (distance) in TIME means MOTION, a CONDITION of LIFE: LIVING THINGS MOVE and FEEL: (E-)MOTION INSIDE is our QUESTIONable PART. But FEELINGS SOUND a TOGETHER QUALITY. LIGHT radiates LIFE. ZERO ends.

Angular (manly):

Primal MATTER, round in Space, is forced by MAN's MIND into its POWER that pressed it into EQUAL QUANTIfied bricks, so he can ACT on it & RELATE to it, as it EXISTS as "THIS ONE". He works THROUGH it, uses it. It is GOOD as TOOL TOWARD his goal...the POWER of the SPIRIT?

Dot Symbols(neuter)

RELATE to THINGS, which can be INSIDE something, can lie ABOVE or BEFORE(inFRONT of) something else and can RELATE (come TOGETHER,) compared by QUANTITY & QUALITY, (preferred by men, & women, respectively).

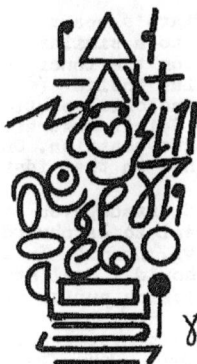

Symbolic Cosmos(rising from below):

MATTER EXISTS in EQUAL QUANTA. RELATED PARTS, THINGS MOVING in SPACE-TIME. LIGHT beams TO LIFE, ROUNDED IN CONDITIONS, SOUNDING QUALITY & QUEST of FEELING INSIDE to find TOGETHER. MAN ACTS TOWARD THIS ONE PART of POWER by MEANS EVIL or GOOD. Will he rise UP to the SPIRIT that is BEFORE all?

* Metamorphosis transitions.

The Philosophy of aUI, the Language of Space.

The categories of aUI are like some of the categories of old Indian philosophers e.g. in the Vaisheshika of Kanada. He distinguishes substance, (E) dravya (▭); quality(m)guna (‿); action , karma (v, ϟ) etc. aUI adds topologic pictographs like "toward" (t, ⟶), "above" (k, ⎡). What is new in the Language of Space is that each category has its symbol, and its sound (which we added in parenthesis), both ofwhich show its meaning. ⊙ e.g. a dot inside a circle means "inside" and is pronounced "g" as in guttural, "inside" the throat. Two dots"together" mean"together" and sound "b" with lips pressed "together." If sound and symbols are similar, their meanings are similar: e.g. ◯ = a = space; ⬭ = A = time.
CAPITALS (A,U)sound long: ⋀= u = human; △= U = mind,spirit.
In an Element of Meaning, the microcosm of the mind meets and mirrors the macrocosm of the universe. E.g. in the head we have our eyes, to mirror cosmic light, radiating from star to star. = i = light.
The Language of Space reflects the Ethics of the Bhagavad-Gita (e.g. III, 3-9; & translated in aUI p.159*) is IX, 4-9), and the Western mystics from Pythagoras to Platon and Meister Eckhart. Know-Love God in Christ's Peace!
1) Find the God inside in contemplation, dharana -- the way of insight, knowledge and wisdom (Jnana Yoga). (Platon's idea of truth.)
2) Action in God's service.(Creation leads to contemplation in Plato's idea of Beauty). Radiate the inner God outward (Karma Yoga). Create your idea in a work of art, whose beauty will lead its contemplator back to the Creator. But never drown in superficial busyness so as to lose the God inside--otherwise you have nothing to transmit. To act you need Power (w,); in aUI, the sounds and symbols of act (v, ϟ); power (w,) are similar to △ , U, the symbol of the Spirit, to indicate that power should be spiritual (especially in the atomic age, if we are to survive.)
3) Since he could have remained within his God in bliss, to step down to serve mankind is for the Boddhisatva a sacrifice of devoted love (Bhakti Yoga). Love for God whom one has found in contemplation, returns to 1). We love our fellowman, because he too, is God's creature. But again it does not help to sacrifice our soul in service even of mankind--otherwise we have nothing to give. We can symbolize the triangles of values:

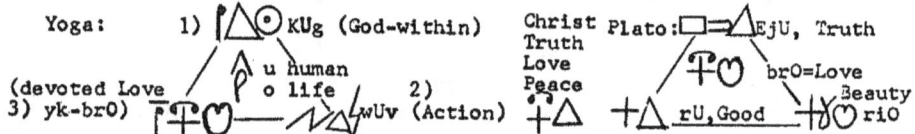

Yoga: 1) KUg (God-within) — u human, o life — (devoted Love 3) yk-brO) — 2) wUv (Action)

Christ: Truth, Love, Peace — Plato: EjU, Truth — brO=Love — rU,Good — Beauty riO

Phono-logics: Yoga's action "v" has in common with Plato's beauty "i" that both are front sounds. Since each symbol corresponds to a similar sound, in phonology the problem would look as how to come from the inner (backtongue) sounds of"U"△ & "O" ♡ (i.e. from Spirit & Feeling inside ⊙ "g" to the outer (labial) sound of "v" (action). The phonologic solution by analogy is : over the bridge of Power "w" : The Spirit must give us Power. "w" is a labial with U-like rounding and tongue-position. Only the Spirit (U) should rule. Human life (u-o,) stands in the midst: Life is a vehicle for the Feeling (♡ ,O) of the Spirit.

aUI dissolves the slavery of slogans, which could invade even Bhagavad-Gita ethics: II, 2,3,31,32,34. Here people could appeal to catchwords like "cowardice vs.glory", "unmanly vs. duty", "disgrace vs. honor". In aUI, cowardice = ywO ♡ = non-strength-feeling. Why should I feel strong enough to solve Arjuna's task without killing, i.e. losing purity of conscience, the womanly conceptive contemplation of God ♡ ?
Transcending conventional language, aUI can express this mystic union.

*) W.J.Weilgart, aUI, the Language of Space, 1968, Chand & Co.

Johnny's Message

By a sparkling mountain-creek
as if I dreamed
had I come to seek ,
what strangely seemed
to my opened eye
like a flying plant
leaf-winged butterfly,
whence wafted sonorous chant.

The sounds that came
were piped through
its flute-like frame
and then I knew
that what I heard
was from another place:
the song of this bird
was the Language of Space.

"If you green moth
would be my friend,
why that sloth
to speak what we understand?
If you have words of advice,
conform and be nice,
and offer each
in earthly speech."

'If for cosmic breath--
the burlap-bag
of your earthy speech
would crudely hold
star-wisdom's gold,
your pride would brag
of using it each
to club the other to death.--

The stars impart
the Cosmic Truth
only to those
who serve its grace.
From far we save
this planet's youth ,
if you will learn
the speech of Space.

So find the heart
that will be brave
to dare and earn
the star it chose.

Thru the Logos of Peace & Love
Commune with the Spirit above!

For our aUI-friends the original:

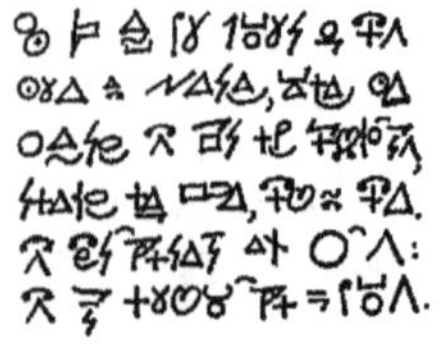

The Language of Space.

In this tongue one star sends its rays to a friend
radiating creation of insight sublime;
Wisdom and Love over light-years blend,
& the spirits bridge space & knowledge spans time.
The Eternal blesses the cosmos in grace:
The Angels sing Truth in the Language of Space.

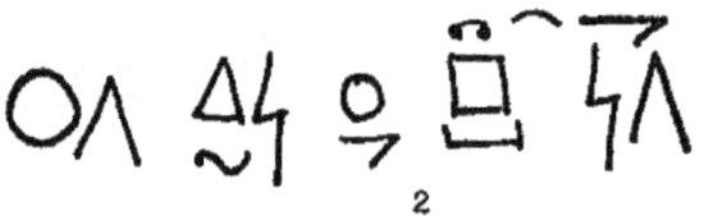

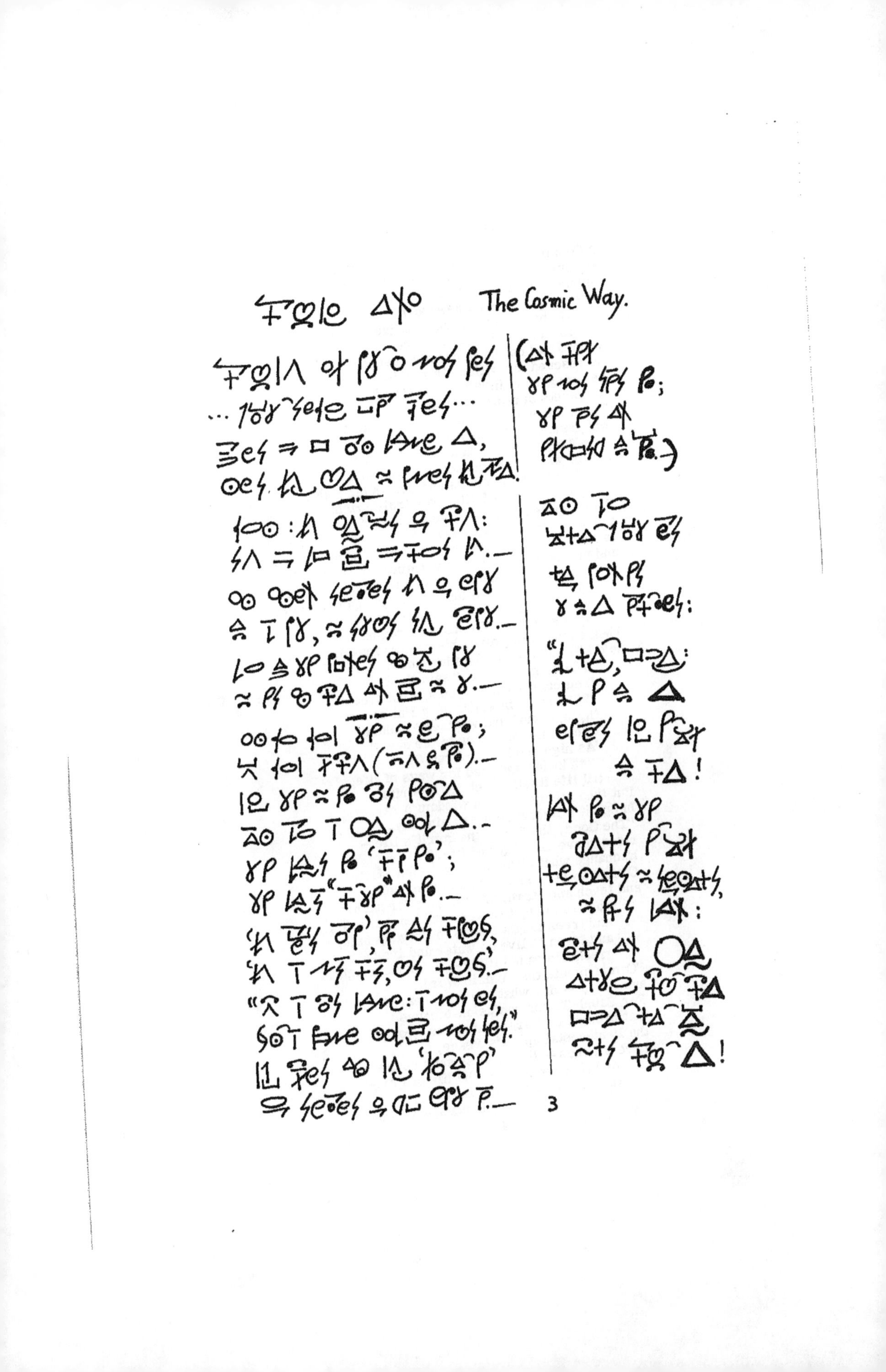

The Cosmic Way.

The Cosmic Way

A Cosmic may through star-space soar
– returning to a ray-pushed spore –
imbue our mind, infuse our soul,
instill our will –: a new-born whole.
He brings his space-disk just for us –
for rescue in a shuttle-bus.
When I had called in cosmic speech,
he rescued me within his reach,
he brought me in his space-ship far
to planets of a distant star.
There were green butterflies as plants,
who danced and sang aUI-chants.
They lived in peace now, but they told
of wars that now seemed eons-old.
For first the plants and beasts did fight,
whose "way-of-life" was truly "right."
Plants called an animal just "beast,"
and animals, by anger seized,
called plants: greens, herbs, worts, krauts, weeds, beets...
and plants called beasts: varmints or "meats."
Thus beasts and beets with thorns; teeth; claws;
molds, poisoned leaves; fangs, gaping maws...
would kill each other for their "rights."
Who's right? Who kills more, harder fights.
Then each could prove, his way was good:
he'd kill and die, just as he should.
"I last, grow ever," said the tree.
'You cannot move; you are not free.'
"With roots in soil's deep I'm secure,
through wind and weather I endure.
I reach my branches to the sky."
'As high and higher I can fly.'
Both killed and died for ways of life,
till life itself might die in strife.
But then, there entered wisdom's ray.
In Spirit's light they heard him say:
"The Good, the True, the Spirit's life –
rises above all "ways of life."
Exchange what differs: 'Love – not Strife!'
Commune in Cosmic wisdom's speech,
and teach and learn, what's good for each."
So birds taught flowers and leaves to fly,
and trees taught beasts to grow up high,
and learn to live on water and light:
green life sans killing – drink sans fight.
"Communicate the Cosmic Word,
and listen – do, what you have heard!"
For Babel-Tower confusion-tongues
that brought us wars & taught us wrongs,
the Pentecostal Spirit's Peace,
Love's Logos – life of bliss sans cease.
And thus we learned the life of grace –
the angels sang truth in the
Language Of Space.

INTRODUCTION

"The Lord said: Behold the people is one,
and they have all one language (in the world)" Gen. 11:6

Speaking scientifically, "aUI"* is what its name symbolizes: "a" means "space" (in saying "a" as in "mama" or "father" the mouth opens a wide "space," so the sound symbolizes its meaning), "U" means "mind, spirit," and "I" means "sound." So, if the "mind sounds" off, we have "U-I," the "mind-sound," the "word" of a "language." Thus the "Space-mind-sound" is a world language which consists of about 30 basic sounds or letters, each of which means a basic word, concept or category.

Thus, a "Webster" or "Oxford" dictionary of all "aUI" of all "mind-sounds" could be the size of a postage stamp, memorized within an hour. Nevertheless, one can express all human ideas in this psychological language, because all conventional "words" of e. g. English become combinations or compounds of "UI." Just as we need not memorize a special word "football" or "footballplay" or "footballplayer," because each is a compound or derivative of the elements (usually separated): foot, ball, play. But if we say, instead of "pedestrian," (a new word) simply "foot-walker," we break already the conventions of our language.

In aUI, "fu iOv" means "I see." Each letter has a meaning: "f" means "this," "u" = "person": thus "f-u" means "this-person," i. e. "I." ("v" means "active-doing" and thus characterizes verbs.)

"i"	= light (brightness)
"O"	= feeling, sensation - so
"iO"	= light-sense, "sight"
"r"	= positive, "good"
"riO"	= "good-sight," beauty
"r-O"	= "good-feeling," pleasure

Thus, the very compound "i-O" makes one realize that "sight" is the "feeling" or "sensation" of "light," which a blind man does not notice. The ending "-v", "-do", as in "sight -do", reminds us that even "sight" is an activity, we "do" see. In English "sight" and "seeing" are still related, ("Cognates") both starting with "s". But if we use instead of "sight", "vision", in the sentence: "if he does not <u>see</u> well, he has poor <u>vision</u>" the relationship is obscured.

*) Pronounce "aUI": a-OO-ee ("a" as in "mama", "U" as in "rUle", "I" as om "polIce".) "iO" ("i" as in "lit", "O" as in "Oh!" (long vowels are CAPITALS).

In "aUI" related words sound similar, and different meanings are expressed in different sounds. Thus the common man knows that a beauty is "good" to "look" at, easy on the "eyes" (iOz = "sight-organs"). Thus in "aUI", "eye, sight, see, beauty, pleasure" need not be memorized, as long as one remembers the basic categories for "light, feeling, good." (iOz, iO, iOv, riO, rO") are derived from "i, O, r" with the endings "v" (do), and "z" (organ, part). But once one has remembered these few "UI", one can form many other "words" with them. e.g. "iv" means "light-do", "make-light", "shine", and "Ov" means "to feel", and "rOv" means "to please." Finally, "vrO" means what "makes-good-feeling" i.e. "kindness", and "viv" means "to kindle" or "make-light."

The only thing which one cannot do in "aUI" is make puns, i.e. make the same sounds mean different things with different spelling, as in English "to, too, two": ("too" itself meaning "too much" and "also": "Were these two, too, too late?" The word "mean" too, has too many meanings: A boxer wanted to buy a fur. He said: "Give me a cheap one, for it's for my wife." The salesman suggested: "You mean skunk," and awoke in the hospital. But, amusing as these puns are, their confusions have turned peace conferences into declarations of war.

"aUI" is more logical, shorter and simpler than any national or constructed language. It is a neutral, truly international world communication. But beyond that, its symbols lead us back before the curse of strife at the Confusion of Tongues at the Tower of Babel* into the oneness of harmony of Peace within the Spirit. In the primeval period, the First Man's primitive language creation was one with the common creative cosmic subconscious of the Universal Mind.

Whether this still holds forth for the sounds and combinations of aUI, I have been able to test experimentally with my patients and "normal" subjects. We found that the creative subconscious, as revealed e.g. in free associations and in hypnotic trance** still favors certain sound-meaning relations and psychological definitions -- the semantic symbols of aUI. As examples, we had already the sound "a" as in "mama" for an open "space", since in this "a" the mouth is spaciously open. Likewise "i" as in "it" is felt subconsciously as a bright sound, and so symbolizes the "light", as in "iv" "to shine." Dream associations of blinding patients connect the light, touching the eye, with the sound, touching the ear. Only the "sound" ("I") heard, feels "slower and heavier" than the light ("i") seen. Physics found that soundwaves are slower than lightwaves. Thus in aUI, "sound" is symbolized by the long (slow) "I" of police, compared with the light "i" of "lit."

In contrast, "U" (as in rUle) is felt as a mysterious sound, related to the mysteries of the Spirit. Short "u" as in "put" is felt as its concrete equivalent, and really in aUI, "u" means "(human)

---

* cf. Genesis 11:4-7, and Acts 2:4-8 (Pentecost: The Holy Ghost's "tongues").

** cf. Dr. Weilgart on Hypnotherapy in "Heilkunst," 69th year, vol. 10, p. 356, Psychotherapy Department, University of Munich, 1956.

person," concretely personified mind. Since long vowels are capitalized, "Ō", long as in "sŌ", sounds like the "Oh!" which people around the globe exclaim to express "feeling," which it means in aUI. Likewise, "b" means "together" since the lips are pressed together when we pronounce it as in "bib." Thus we understand that "brO" means "love": i.e. "b" = together, "r" = good, "O" = feeling, thus, b-r-O means "together-good-feeling." Lovers strive together, for they have "together" a "good" "feeling."

"g" means "inside", as we feel this guttural sound deep "within" our throat. Thus it is symbolized with a dot "inside" a circle, ⊙. Thus "ga" means "inside-space," "room." "uga" means "man-inside-space," u-g-a, i.e. "house," (the place where a man lives within). Λ⊙O

Thus, for purposes of psychotherapy, a schizoid patient, e.g., can for the first time express his subconscious in adequate symbols, which in itself helps to heal his sick mind. Often I did not right away confront him with the "true" aUI formula, but let him build his own word-combinations out of the 30 basic bricks. The primitive fisher-children of Matsushima learned in this playful way aUI, while we landed our boat in the morning, and in the evening we talked already in aUI, within the scope of Part II, plus the colorful variations and compounds the little poets created and coined on their own; (e.g. they called a boat a "man-made-fish" u-v-jEos, instead of "jE-ged" (water-vehicle), the more orthodox term.) This is as if in English one says "pigskin" instead of "football." Thus, for naive people, who have kept the original philosophic intuition in the true meaning of words, things, thoughts and feelings, this language comes natural.

Beyond that, the language with its scientific short-cut formulae for each concept, is of great educational value. We learn that "colors" are "qualified-light," "m-i," and we will remember the sequence of these "qualifications of light," the colors of the rainbow, by learning that "red" is the "first light," "yellow" the second, * "green" the third, "blue" the fourth, "violet" the fifth. . . . "light-quality" ("i-m"). Since the numbers are simply nasal vowels in phonetic sequence:

one	two	three	four	five	are in aUI:
a	e	i	u	o	therefore:
aim	eim	iim	uim	oim	are the colors:
red	yellow	green	blue	violet	

"In the beginning was the Word, the Logos."** The main education through logical integration by language is felt in the abstract concepts, e.g. "What is Truth?" In aUI, we learn that it is the equation "Mind = Matter": If the thoughts in my mind correspond to, or equal, the material reality or the facts outside, I am in pos-

* Of course, some earth-languages put in some intermediate shades between these "simpler" colors. e.g. "aeim" = orange.

** St. John 1:1. On my logotherapy cf. Wr Arch. Psychol. & Psychiatr. June 1955, p. 111ff; and "A Psycho-Symbolic Language of Semantic Therapy" in International Language Review, Ap. 1958, by Weilgart.

session of the truth. Thus "E-j-U"* means "Matter-equal-Mind." But if my ideas differ from "EjU", I suffer under a fallacy, and walk in falsehood.

Thus, aUI means a course in true applied ethics. How many people suffer from early youth under a distorted concept of honor, liberty, or courage? How many boys can distinguish between the phony show-off "courage" of risking their lives in gang crimes from the true or creative courage of saving a child's life or daring a new idea? Political party slogans confuse the true honor of inner integrity with the vain glory of bragging brutality, and the freedom from evil, from sin or disease, the freedom for creation and contemplation, the true freedom of the Spirit with freedom to destroy -- liberty with license? Demagogs and dictators trap us in a deadly war of words. aUI frees from the idolatry of ideologies, the slavery of slogans.

With all logical clarity, the compound words of aUI need not be complete chemical formulae of their concepts symbolized, but only a short-cut through the essentials. What word formula could comprise God's infinity? Nevertheless, the aUI word "k-U" approaches "supreme-Spirit," "k" denoting anything "above, super, superior," and thus tries to characterize God's essence.

Thus in stressing the essence, semantic prejudices which lead to ideological hatred, are dissolved. Minds differ in peripheral accidentals which they confuse with the center. Thus the Confusion of Tongues led to wars of destruction. But in essence, all Spirit is one.

Dr. John W. Weilgart, Ph.D.

---

* Pronounce "E" as in Eh? or bouquEt, "U" as in rUle, "j" as in French "jour" or English "pleasure."

PART I

BASIC SOUNDS - CATEGORIES

PRONUNCIATION. Each *aUI* letter keeps its same sound, once for all. Short vowels are written with small letters, and LONG vowels with CAPITALS. The vowels are pronounced like original Latin or Anglo-Saxon or Germanic or French vowels; whether the vowels are long or short, they keep the same pronunciation, e.g. even LONG "I" sounds never as in "fire", but as in "police."

"a": short *a* as in "mama" has the same mouth position as long

"A": as *in "Ah!,"* father, Arm. e.g. cf. *"a"* = space, *"A"* = time.

"e": short as in "bet, get" ("e" means "movement"), no matter where or in what position it stands.

"E": always long as in "Eh!?"; as in "You don't like my bouquEt, Eh?!" (in aUI, *"E"* means "matter, material")

(In English a, e, i, u change their pronunciation completely, in different positions. E.g. "a" in "hat" sounds different from "a" in "hate", or from "a" in "arm." Especially before "r" i, e, u and even "o" sound all alike. "Fir" sounds like "fur" or like "-fer" in transfer. This would be impossible in aUI. the sound of "O" in "wOrd" would be, once for all spelled "Q", not only in "wQrd," but even in "fQr." On the other hand, "e" in "e-r" would still keep the sound of "e" in "get," with "r" of "ring" attached to it).

"i" sound always short as in "it" or "lit" ("i" means "light")

"I" is always long as in "polIce" or "machIne" (*"I"* = "sound")

"u" short as in "full, put" ("u" means "person, man, human")

"U" long as in "rUle, rUde" ("U" means "spirit, mind")

"o" short as in "off, pot" ("o" means "life")

"O" long as in "Oh!", "emOtion" (*"O"* means "feeling, sensation")

"y" almost like in English "yonder, you, yet" or in "system" in Greek or German; or "u" in French "rue" &c: try to say "truly" keeping your lips rounded as you had them for "u" drawing out the "y" as it were "trulee," or in "boyyy" with round lips. ("y" means "anti-, un-") (y = zero) (ü nasal)

"a, e, i, u, o; A, E, I, U, O", underlined, are nasalized, and become thus 1, 2, 3, 4, 5; 6, 7, 8, 9, 10, the numbers. (You can hold or wrinkle your nose, saying them like a Frenchman or Portuguese or Brazilian.)

For a, e, &c (you better use the Pronunciation record disk!) In America, one uses a nasal sound in a disgusted "uh", I don't like it", but you better hold up 1, 2, 3.. fingers, for each number.

"j" as in French "jour" or English "measure" ("j" means "equal")

"c" as in "precious, special" ("c" means "being, existence")

"Q" as Q in wQrd, "wQrd" (As German Ö, French cOeur) Q = "condition"

"x" as in Spanish "Mexico" (Mejico), Scotch-German "Loch", a rasped or snored "h" ("x" means "relation")

With *"g"* always as in "go, get" ("g" = inside), "s" always as in "so" ("s" = thing), all other sounds are as in English. In alphabets where l looks like I, use L instead of l.

Stress: Nasals have first, LONG CAPITALS second, stress; otherwise the next-to-the-last syllable is stressed.

The Language of Space

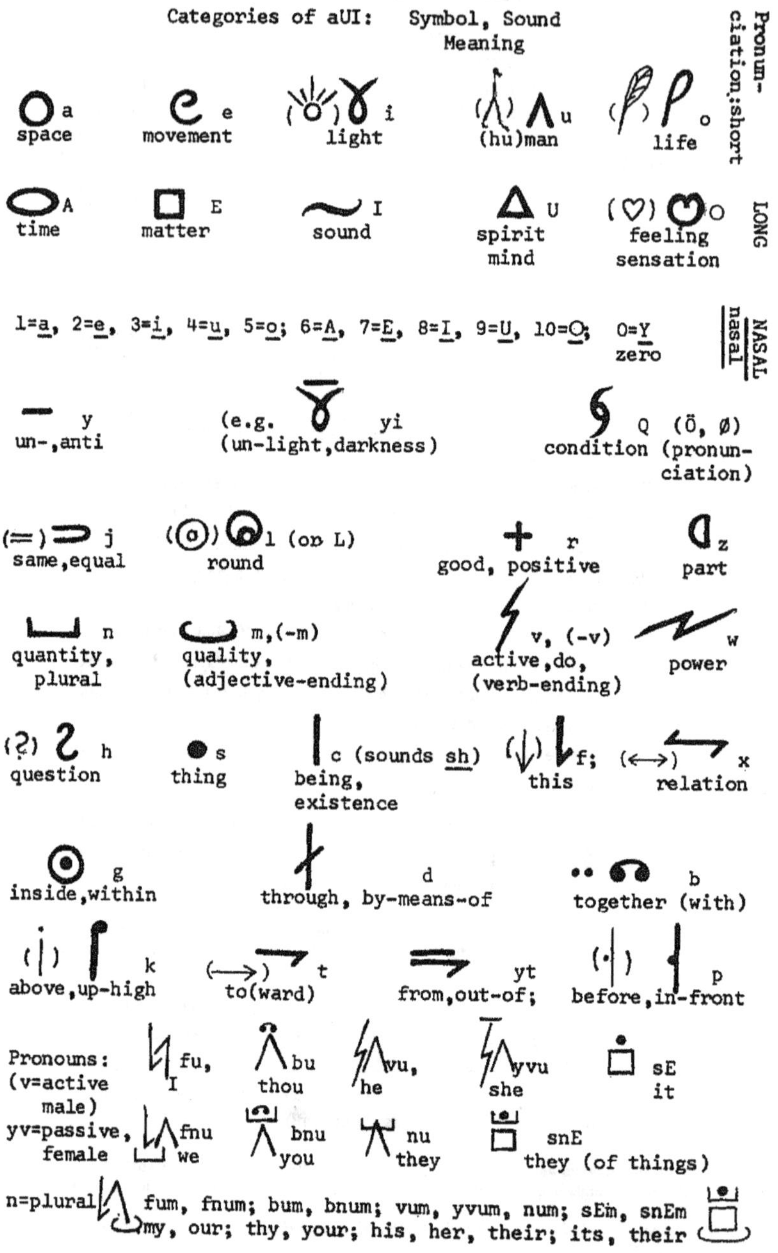

Categories of aUI: Symbol, Sound
Meaning

Pronun-ciation;short

a space | e movement | i light | u (hu)man | o life

LONG

A time | E matter | I sound | U spirit mind | O feeling sensation

NASAL nasal

1=a, 2=e, 3=i, 4=u, 5=o; 6=A, 7=E, 8=I, 9=U, 10=O; 0=Y zero

y un-,anti (e.g. yi (un-light,darkness)) Q condition (ö, ø) (pronunciation)

j same,equal | l (or L) round | r good, positive | z part

n quantity, plural | m,(-m) quality, (adjective-ending) | v, (-v) active,do, (verb-ending) | w power

h question | s thing | c (sounds sh) being, existence | f; this | x relation

g inside,within | d through, by-means-of | b together (with)

k above,up-high | t to(ward) | yt from,out-of; | p before,in-front

Pronouns: (v=active male) yv=passive, female

fu, I | bu thou | vu, he | yvu she | sE it

fnu we | bnu you | nu they | snE they (of things)

n=plural fum, fnum; bum, bnum; vum, yvum, num; sEm, snEm
my, our; thy, your; his, her, their; its, their

SURVEY OF ALL SOUNDS (WITH THEIR MEANINGS)

a O space, e ℮ movement, *i* ɣ light, *u* Λ (hu)man, *o* ρ life
A ⬭ time, *E* □ matter, *I* ~ sound, *U* Δ spirit, *O* ♡ feeling

(The vowels are in their natural sequence, i & u are related. cf. "fill it full".) Each sound has its *aUI* symbol or sign.

nasal: a = 1, e = 2, i = 3, u = 4, o = 5; A = 6, E = 7, I = 8, U = 9, O = 10; Y = 0 (zero)

y‾ = un-, anti-, opposite, negation. (symbol, a bar ‾ ; ɣ ɣ̄ ; i, yi; light, darkness.
Q ɕ (ö) = condition

(*A*, ⬭ time, is an elongation of *a*, O space. e ℮ movement is "space-in-time, it's "quick". Long E □ matter, is more 'substantial,' although out of the energy movement of atoms derive the properties of matter. *i*, ɣ light, is bright and short, *I*, ~ sound, is longer, as sound travels slower than light. *u*, Λ man, and *U* Δ mind, are related also to *w* ɀ might, power, and to "v" ϟ "active," as "man's mind is an active might." ♡ "O", feeling reminds of "Oh!" an exclamation of feeling, and of "o" ρ life, as living things "feel." "y" sounds similar to "*u*, *U*," since the "human mind" thinks in opposites.)

j = same, equal, even, level — *L* ◎ round, — *r* + good, positive — *z* ɑ part division

n ⌴ quantity, plural — *m* ◡ quality, *-m* adjective-ending — *w* ɀ power — *v* ϟ active, do *-v* verb-ending

(numbers are nasals, since they contain "n", the sound of quantity).

("*j*" has the sound of flowing water (jE), as water keeps an even, horizontal surface. "*j*" sounds similar to "c", as "equals" means "is" e.g. 3 x 2 = 6 (" is " six or "equals" six). "mmm!" ◡ is an exclamation of quality in taste. The cat says "rrr" (purrs), when she feels "good." "zzz" is the sound of a saw, cutting things a-"part." "*l*" has a round sound, as one curls the tongue. "*vvv*" sounds "vibrant" activity.)

h ꞁ question, *s* • thing, c | being, existence, *f* ꞁ this, x ↤ relation.

("*h*" breathes or gasps a question, opening the mouth in astonishment. "c" sounds like "s", since what "exists" is a "thing." Even the hissing sound of "f" ("this") is related to "s" and "c", since what "exists" as "thing" can be pointed at, saying "this!")

g ⊙ in-(side) (a guttural sound within) (dot inside)

d ɣ through, by-means-of instrument, tool (a tooth-sound, medium between lips and throat)

b •• together (with) (press lips together as dots ••)

k ꜰ above, up-high super, supreme (tongue hits upper palate) (¡ = dot above line)

t → to(ward), -ward (for "t"-sound, the tongue flips forward pointing "toward") (⟶ = arrow, flying toward....)

p ·| in-front-of, before, pre-, ("p" sounds in "front" of mouth from the lips. ·| = dot in front of a line).

EXPLANATION OF THE BASIC SOUNDS

1. VOWELS:

O = a = space, ℮ = e = movement, ɤ = i = light, Λ = u = (hu)man, ƒ = o = life

⬭ = A = time, ◻ = E = matter, ∼ = I = sound, Δ = U = spirit, ♡ = O = feeling

(The Language of Space keeps the original vowel sequence. cf. "I am the A and the O, beginning and end." "i" followed by its relative "u", as in "fill, full," "O" being the last full vowel, as in Greek, Indian, and Japanese.)

As soon as we have memorized the above vowels in the right pronunciation, we can form little sentences, talking to each other in aUI, forming a Club of Spacemen, who understand each other, and nobody else can know what we are talking about. For this purpose, we learn right away a few connectives:

| = ć = is, are, be; Ö ϟ = bav = have, has; ◻ ϟ = Ev = do(es); ∾ = Ib = and;

E.g. in a science class, we remark matter-of-factly: "i Ib I ć e ag a" Only the Secret Society of Spacemen (SSS) understands what we mean. Can you figure it out? We'll tell you: "Light and Sound are movements in space." (See how short and concise the Language of Space is! Now re-translate and say it in aUI, once more. "u bav o"; "u bav U Ib O"; "e ć a ag A." "O ć e ag U" "hE ć E" (What is (the) matter?) (hE = what). "hE ć u?" "u ć E Ib U."* (Look down for the translation, only after you have tried to do it yourself. Then translate back to aUI.)

The sign O means "space" (as in place, room), and is pronounced "a" (as in mama). We open the mouth to a wide open space, when we say "a" this way.

⬭ stands for "time." It sounds long A, Ah! as in fAther. Time lasts long, so it is a long sound. It is an elongation of space, an ellipsis. We measure time by the elliptic cycles of planets and moons.

---

* Translation: "Man has life; man has mind and feeling; movement is space in time; feeling is (a) movement (emotion) in (the) mind; ....What is man? Man is matter and spirit (or : mind)."

N.B. For learning to form words by combining the sounds of the basic categories, choose and memorize for each sound a basic gesture, natural to you. E.g. saying "i" for "light," you might open your eyes; with "O" = "feeling," hold your heart. Then, while learning "sight = i - O," open eys and hold your heart, as if in "seeing," "light-feeling," "light" entered your "heart." Then, in learning "t-w-e = pull," compose the pulling idea out of the elements; "t = toward" - "w = power" - "e = move"; first pull toward yourself at "t," then bulge the biceps muscles at saying "w" powerfully, and then snap your fist fast at "e" in a quick move: "twe," finishing the "pull."

Time and Space make movement. Speedy motion is space in time. A car makes 60 miles in an hour. But the most conspicuous movement is rapid whirling around. The spiral symbolizes this, it is like a circle in an ellipsis, like space in time. looks like "e", the sound of e in "get," or in "energy." □, matter, is shaped like a brickstone of the universe. Matter is what is moving. Matter and (moving) energy is, according to Einstein's relativity theory related. But matter is more substantial and longer lasting. So it's a long E, as in Eh?, bouquEt.

"i" short as in "lit" is the sound of "light," a bright sound, and , symbolizes a lamp, with the light rays spreading out (up). Now, if the spaceman says to you, "i ev ag a" ("Light moves in space) you can already understand him. "i evd a" would be "light moves through space." (e-v means "move-does")

"I" "sound," is longer than "i", light, as sound travels slower. It is pronounced as in "polIce," but with the same mouth position as "i": Light and Sound are brothers. (i Ib I ć jytu). "What (the) light does in (the) eye, (the) sound does in (the) ear" (hE i Ev ag iOz, I Ev ag IOz) (iÓz = eye, ÍOz = ear). The symbol indicates a sound wave, e.g. a vibrating violin string.

The light shines "i iv"

The lute string vibrates a sound wave "I"

"u" man, human being, is symbolized by Λ originally (a walking man)

Man walks on two legs. "u" sounds as in "put." In the vowel sequence, -- E, i, I, u, U -- i, I (light, sound) form the bridge between matter and man's mind: Through seeing and hearing we understand.

Δ, U = mind

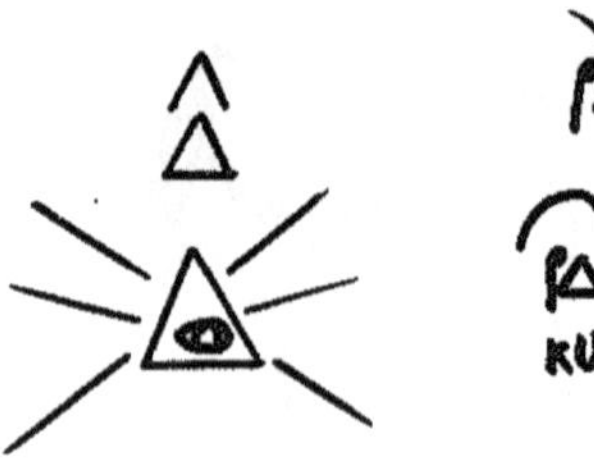

The Spirit, Mind- concept, pronounced "U" as in "trUe, rUle, sounds like a lengthening of "u", (human). Spirit lasts longer than man. It is more perfect, so it is symbolized with a perfect closed triangle. "U" is the most closed, most mysterious sound: to indicate the mystery of the mind. Now we understand "aUI", it means "a-U-I" "Space-Mind-Sound," space-language. When your mind sounds off, it is not like a trumpet: it is words, language. "U-I" "mind-sound" alone, is word, language. "a-u UIv aUI" (the) space-man speaks the Language of Space

= "o" = life. "o" sounds always like "o" in "botany" and it was originally symbolized by a green leaf, the origin of life-nourishment. For the sound of "o" think of "throb" of a heart, the center of life.

= O = feeling, emotion, sensation (sense), similar to "o" since we must feel to be alive. Oh! is the exclamation of feeling. is simplified from the feeling heart.

(Practice: What is a, e, i, u, o in English? What is A, E, I, U, O? What is Life, matter, movement, space, light, mind, man in aUI?) If -v makes a verb, what does "ov" or "Ov" mean? Translate into aUI: The spaceman lives in space. Man has feeling. Man feels. Man is matter and mind. etc. Write these sentences in aUI, and read them after a time, later.

= Q (pronounced Ö as in wOrd, wQrd, wÖrd) means "condition."

= y- = opposite, negation, not, un-, anti-. It is symbolized by a dash above the negated aUI sign. The sound sequence y, U, u, w, v means: opposite, mind, man, power, make. (Man's mind has the power to make opposites.) Only man can find an opposite to every known concept. If the ending -m makes adjectives, "u-m" would mean "human." Right away you can think of an opposite to "um." It is "yum" and it means "unhuman," "inhuman." yo would mean "un-life," or "death." u ć yom = (the) man is dead. aUI is very exact in its opposites. E. g. what is the difference between yIm and yem? Both mean in English still or quiet.

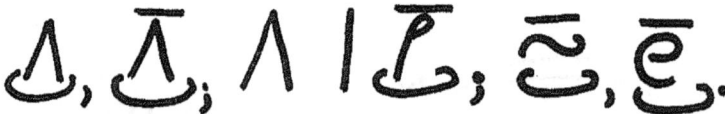

But yIm means un-sounding, soundless, while yem means un-moving, motionless. yi = darkness and "yim" = dark. yom u c yem Ib yIm. (a) dead man is motionless and soundless. yom u c yOm. (a) dead man is unfeeling (insensitive, senseless). Best Y̅ for vowel, y̅ for consonant.

"Y" has always the sound of "y" in System, if you sing this word in a very deep voice with rounded lips, as if puckered for kissing. In "boy" or "yonder" the lips are rounded. "y" is symbolized by a dash — above the original concept, which it denies. , o = life, , yo = death, Qm = conditional, yQm = unconditional (Q is O like in wOrd, 'wQrd'.) , Qm, , yQm.

2. SONANTS:

"j" (symbol) means: same, equal, even, level. It is pronounced as in French "journal," or as the "s" in English "measure," and this sound should remind you of rushing water, since water tries to flow level or to spread out to "equal" height, horizontally. yY ; j.

"l" * (symbol:) means "roundness," since the symbol is a double rounded ring, and "L" is a roundish sound, the tongue rolled to a spoon. "lam" is "round" e.g. a c̸ lam (space is round).

"r" (symbol +) "positive" while "-" meant "negative," means positive in the sense of "good," as even cats purr "rrr" when they feel good. Of course, this "rr" is always trilled and does not mix with other vowels, but stays clear as in Latin "Firpo."

"z" (symbol) means "part, division" and sounds as in buzzing, as a buzz-saw cuts things in parts, divides them. The half-moon looks like a round loaf of bread or cheese cut apart.

"n" (symbol) means "quantity" or "amount," "lots of, plenty," "n" may remind you of "number, numerical," and its nasal sound enters all number. The symbol is the cross-section of a measuring box or cup, used for e.g. beans.

* In order to avoid confusing this "l" with "I" (the capital of "i"), it is advisable to use "L" in alphabets without "serifs" (cross-strokes).

"m" (symbol ◡) denotes "quality." Sound and symbol resembles "quantity," "n", ⊔, but quality is more a matter of feeling, less hard and square, more rounded like a bowl. We exclaim "mmm!" of delicious taste quality, and the "m" lips look like the symbol ◡. The lips for "m" are closed to enjoy true "quality" inside. More important than for the single sound, "-m" is especially the ending of adjectives, adverbs, and participles (ending in -ing, or in -ly, or -ous, -ite, -ent, -an) i. e. all qualifiers end in the letter of quality. E.g. "um o" ("human life") is different from "om u," (a) "living man." (Instead of "human life", one might say "life of a (hu)man;" "of" is "Ub," and "b" is another sound with closed lips.)

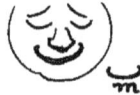

"w" (as in "work"), means "power, energy," symbolized by . It is related to "U", mind, △ and to "u", man, ∧. "Man has (his) power in (his) mind" (u bav w ag U). (Of course, in pronunciation, one prefers "wU" for the noun "power," since it is a spiritual concept. w-U = power-concept. The sound "w" is formed with the same pursed lips as "U" or "v".

"v" (pronounced as in "vibrant") denotes "active," "doing," and its symbol is *) similar to a turned upward, "energy raised to activity," as it were. The sound of "vvv" reminds of the vibrant humming of engines, and its meaning of "doing," making, provides the verb-ending in aUI: "-v." Thus "e" = movement, "e-v" = do or does move, to move, "ev." "om u ev" "(a) lively man moves. "yom u yev" (" (a) dead man stops moving)" or "yom u yc ev" "dead man not moves", (does) not move.

3. FRICTION SOUNDS:

"h" indicates the "question" sign (?), and means "question." "h" is formed by opening the mouth to a gasping question, as in "how?" ("hUd?"); why ("hU?"); who ("hu?"), what ("hE?").

*) : write "down-level-down" -- a vertical slant,
: draw "up-down-up," -- a horizontal slant,
: "down-flat-down" (like), but with long horizontal bar.

, x, pronounced as in Spanish Don Quixote, or Mexico, or Xavier or Xristos, or as in Loch in German and Scotch, is a snored or rasped "h," "ch" as in clearing one's throat. "x" indicates "relation" and clarifies relative pronouns, as in "u, xu" (the) man, who. In Bible-English "the man, which." Often, of course, "xu and hu" are exchanged in every day language. In America, San José, instead of "xosé" is pronounced "hosé." (from means a double arrow between related things.)

, "s" "thing." symbolizes any "object, item, article" closed in itself and concretely defined. A thing can either be a "matter-thing," "E-s", Es, something material, or a "mind-thing" "U-s," Us, a "thought," or a "live-thing," "os," (an animal). "hE ć os?" (What is (an) animal?) "os ć om Es" (an animal is a live thing) "os, xE ov, Ov" (An) animal, which lives, feels. "os, xE Ov, ev" (an) animal, which feels, moves.

, c, "existence, is, be" is related to "s," thing, as the only thing we can say of all "things" is that they somehow exist. "c" sounds "sh," similar to "s." "c" sounds as in "precious, special." "to exist, to be" as full verb would be "cEv," but we often shorten this to "ć" as in English "is" is shortened to "'s" e.g. "It's alive." "sE'ć om." ("yc" = (is) not.)

, "f", "this." The symbol points like an arrow at an object, and the breath, too, is hissed "fff" against the thing in demand. Although "fE" is the full word for "this," we can often use the mere concept "f". "hE ć f os?" "What is this animal?" "f yc os, fE ć u" (This is-not (an) animal, this is (a) man). (In aUI, one can leave out the articles.)

Now review meaning and pronunciation of the letters you have learned so far: a, A, e, E, i, I, u, U, o, O, Q, y; j, l, r, z, n, m, w, y; h, x, s, c, f. Write them all in aUI symbols! Make sentences out of them. As soon as you have learned the six prepositions or operators (g, d, b; k, t, p), you know the meaning of all letters, and wherever you go, you can try yourself, if you know all "basic" words of aUI. Make sentences: e.g. "hE ć f i?" "f i ć ki (star)."

"What is this light?" "This light is a star." "i, x́fki vEv, ev at fa." (The light, which this star makes, moves to here.) "f i vEv o ag f́a" (This light makes life in this space.)

4. <u>STOP-SOUNDS</u> (Positions or Space-Relations):

⊙ , "g", "inside, (with)in." ("g" is a sound deep "within" the throat, symbolized as a dot "in" a circle ⊙ .)

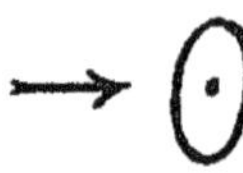

✗ , "d" "through" "by means of" (a line crossed "through" by another)

•• , "b" "together" (the two dots are close "together," and the lips are pressed together in forming a "b".

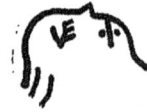

, , "k", "above," up, super, superior, supreme!" "k" is an upper palate sound. The symbol was originally a dot "above" a line.

, , "t", "toward" "to," "till." In saying "t" the tongue flips forward, pointing toward the teeth. like the arrow of the symbol.

, , "p", be-fore, in front, pre-" ("p" is produced in front of the mouth, with the lips, and symbolized by a dot in "front" of a line.)

Now you can review all categories or sounds of aUI, simply by reciting the alphabet and testing whether you know the meaning and symbol for each letter. Just remember that each vowel occurs also long and nasal. First review the prepositions "g, d, b
k, t, p."

Then translate:

"hUd cf́a?" "f́ a ć l" (This is aUI telegram style. Of course, the full-sounding word for "round" is "lam," instead of "l".)

2. "f́ a-u ću." 3. f o ć ŕo 4. i Ib I ev d́ a. 5. o ev t́ i.

6. o ev t́ yo. 7. "um o ev t́ yo." 8. e ć a ǵA.

9. 10. "g u ćO IB U." 11. 12.

9. u ć U-o 10. 11. U c k E. 12. f́ a-z ći.

(First translate all this into English, then turn the page, or ask your friend or have him or her ask you. Look back to page 5 and see how many signs you recognize. If more than 20, the Spaceman gives you an "A," and the Spacegirl a space-kiss (a-ubogta).

Try to re-translate into aUI the English sentences:

1. How is this space? This space is round. 2. This space-man is (a) good man. 3. This life is (a) good life. ("r" denotes positive value, goodness. The full adjective for "good" is "rUm" "r" is telegram style). 4. Light and sound move through space. 5. Life moves toward light. 6. Life moves toward death. 7. Human life moves toward death. 8. Movement is space in time. 9. Man is Spirit-Life. (You can modify these sentences: Man has (a) spiritual life: "u bav Um o". Note that English, one of the shortest languages of our world, is still 2, 3, or 4 times longer than aUI.) 10. In Man (there) is feeling and spirit (or mind). 11. Spirit is above matter (or, mind above matter). 12. This space-part (side) is light (bright).

(If you got 10 sentences right, the spaceman gives you a big "A" or an "$\underline{a}$" for quality "1.")

Make a free conversation with your fellow-spacemen in whatever comes to your mind. e.g. One asks: hu ć rUm? Another answers: "a-u ć rUm." or: "hE c e?" "e c a ǵ A." - "hE c u?" "u c Um o." or: "u c U Ib E." - "hUd ć f́ o?" "f o ć rUm."

(Even though you know now all the single sounds, you can not easily express the most common words, used here on earth. For that, you need to know the few combination rules, developed in the next chapter.) But first, we have to learn:

5. NASAL-SOUNDS (Numbers):

As we know the sequence of the vowels is the original one: a, e, i, u, o; A, E, I, U, O, as in Revelation 1:11 - "I am the A(lpha) and the O(mega), the first and the last," long O is the end. This vowel sequence, nasalized gives all numbers from $\underline{1}$ to $\underline{10}$.

$\underline{a}$ = 1, $\underline{e}$ = 2, $\underline{i}$ = 3, $\underline{u}$ = 4, $\underline{o}$ = 5

$\underline{A}$ = 6, $\underline{E}$ = 7, $\underline{I}$ = 8, $\underline{U}$ = 9, $\underline{O}$ = 10, $\underline{Y}$ = 0 (zero)

When the next time you groan in pain or disgust (French "an" ($\underline{a}$)) "an, (unh-unh) I don't want it" or you hear French "on" ($\underline{o}$).... you can keep the same disgustedly hanging velum for all the other sounds of "mama, get, fill, full, on; FAther, Eh?, polIce, rUles, Only." If you cannot afford an aUI record, just wrinkle your nose and hold up 1, 2, 3, etc., fingers (maybe for 6, 7, hold 1, 2 fingers down) and always stress the nasal sound most.

The cosmic myth connects "a" space, with "a", one, since "space is one," - there is only one space. "e", movement, is related to "e", 2, because, as you say "it takes 2 to make a quarrel," we say: "It takes 2 to make a movement," since the one must move from, or to, something else.

" e wyv cEv rUt e " or: " e c Q rUt e " (in symbols:

"2 must be for movement" or "Two are (the) condition for movement." Since we use numbers to distinguish colors,

ai, ei, ii, ui, oi

1st, 2nd, 3rd, 4th, 5th, light quality, as the colors:

red, yellow, green, blue, violet, you see that "green" ii, is the color of double ii, the sound of "light." You can remember that "green" is the color of light, because green plants need light. A plant is called "io" "light-life" as it lives by light. - Cosmic mystics compare man, u, with u, 4, since after the Mineral, Vegetable, and Animal Realm, Man's is the 4th Realm. Finally, you can relate "o" 5, to "o" life, by remembering that 5 is the most typical number of living things: not only man, but even lizards have 5 fingers and apple blossoms and wild roses have 5 petals.

More technically speaking, since you know the numbers from zero to ten, you can express all higher numbers in telephone fashion. Instead of three-hundred-five, say 3,0,5: iYo. But remembering that "k" denotes "above, high," you can also express 100 by 10^2, i.e. 10-high-2, O-k-e, Oke. 1000 = 10^3, Oki. 15 = 10+5, "Oo," 16 = OA, 60 = 6 x 10, "AO."

Up to now, we learned mostly single sounds. Before you go to the Hundred Basic Compounds, review carefully the whole alphabet in its aUI meanings and symbols. You can form your own compounds by hyphen: a-u, space-man, or in aUI symbols by a bridge . This way you can form your own words in preparation to Part II.

(Let your space-girl-friend review you, or ask her. Look back to page 5, to all symbols. Write space-letters to your friends. Play space-card games.)

PART II

HUNDRED BASIC COMPOUNDS (arranged alphabetically).

"a", O space : "da" = way, (d = through, a=space) d-a = through-space, as a way leads through space. "da-v" = way-do, to make way, to travel, "av" = space-make = to go.
"ga" = inside-space, room
"uga" = u-g-a = man-inside-space"

d a

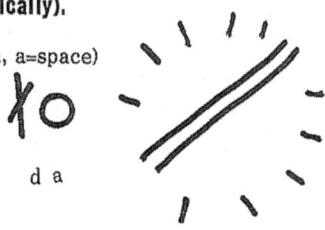

(the room in which a man dwells)
"uga" = house. "u ov ag uga"
"an", a-n = "space-quantity" size,
which shows how much space it takes.

u g a

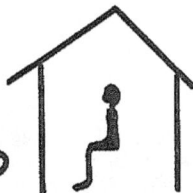

"na" = dimension, n-a = numbered-space, measured-space, e.g.
"ana" = length (literally a = one, a-na = one dimension)
"anam" = long (length-adjective). (nam = large). uga c nam, Ib anam.
"ena" = flatness (e = 2) "enam" = 2-dimensional, flat
(a flat field has only length and width, no height)
(a flat field = enam enaz (flat-part)

"a", 1 . one. "an = unit" (one-quantity") as a yard or meter.
"enaz bav Oki – i-Oke an (thousand-3-hundred yards)"
"A", O , time. "iA" = day (light-time), the time when it's light.
"Ad" clock, watch, time-piece (time-tool), "Av" = to last, make-time
("hE c'A Ub iA? –fu iOv t Ad Ib UIv : 3 (i) ag Ad"
(What is (the) time of day? – I see (look) to (at the) watch and say: 3 in clock (3 o'clock).

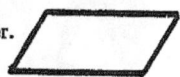

If you don't want to strain your memory to learn all the thousand words in the back of the book actively, (learning 30 a day, this might take a month), you can already express your thoughts with these hundred, which you can learn in 3 days. But you have to practice to replace difficult words with basic ones. e.g. instead of saying: The dog is "faithful" you might say like a primitive child: The dog is "all time with me" ("waubos cEv can A eb fu"). You can even replace "dog" saying "animal" (os) or "domestic-animal" (bos), which comes all time with man (bos, xE tev can A eb u).

Primitive natives can even get along without words which to us seem very simple, e.g. "can" or "must". Instead of saying: "I can go to this man" they say "I have time and power to go to this man" ("fu bav A Ib wU at av at fE u"). English replaces "must" this way (with "have to"). Primitives say: "A power makes me to go to this man" (instead of "I must . . ") "wU vEv fu at av at fE u." Even "will" or "want" or "wish" can be replaced. "My feeling makes me (or: tells me) to go to this man" ("fum O vEv fu (UIv fu) at av at fE u".) = I want . . .

1. iA c´A Ub (of) i kab bEn (on earth). 2. ana Ub fE da c´ e-Oke-O-e (2-hundred-ten-two = 200 & 10 + 2 = 212) an.
3. fE uga c´Ub fu (f-u = this man = me). 4. fu bav fE uga.
5. hE c´uga ? uga c´a , ag xE u ov.

Retranslate: 1. The day is the time of light on earth. 2. (the) length of this way is 212 yards. (Of course, you can use these figures in aUI, too, and can even pronounce them "eae" (2, 1, 2). Note that in aUI, nasals have the first stress, long vowels (CAPITALS) the second, and short vowels the third stress. Otherwise, the next to the last is stressed: úga, Óke, Ú-I, uÍ.
3. This house is of me (mine). 4. I have this house. 5. What is (a) house? (a) house is (a) space, in which man lives.

●● = b = "together with". "ab" = at (space-together) : if I am "at" my father's, I am in the same space together with him.

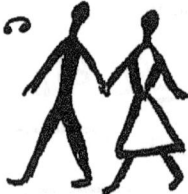

"eb" = with ("moving-together"). If a man goes with a girl, he "moves together" with her. ("eb" means only "together with", not used in "I eat noodles with a fork" "eb" would mean: I eat noodles and fork, as noodles with cheese. "with" = by means = Ud, (by means of the fork, a tool),

u av eb yvu (man goes with woman)

"bav" = have. What is in the same space together with me, at me (ab fu) , I have (fu bav). (xE c´ab fu, eb fu Ib Ub fu, fu bav)

''bAv'' = keep, hold (What is a long time—A—with me, I keep.
''ba'' = together-space, nearness; bam = near, (near-quality).
''Ub'' = of (mind-together). The son ''of'' this father, or the father ''of'' this son, or the book ''of'' Shakespeare need not be together in space. But mentally, in the mind, there is a togetherness. ''tu Ub fE ytu'' = child of this parent'', but ''ytu Ub fE tu'' (parent of this child) shows that ''of'' means a two-way mere mind-relationship. ''uga Ub fu'' = fum uga = my house.

''Ib'' = and (sound-together) means that, if I join Karl and John and a toad, they are merely connected by the ''sound'' of my voice, otherwise they may have nothing in common.

''yb'' = without (''un-together'', opposite of together)
''u yc u yb U'' (man is-not man without mind—U).
''u bav o; u yb o, yc bav O'' ''Man has life; man without life, not has feeling. ''yom u c´ u yb o'' (a) dead man is (a) man without life. ''yOm u c´ u yb O'' (An) unfeeling man is a man without feeling. ''vus yb yvus c kan yb ki'' (A) man without (a) woman is a sky without (a) star. (vu ''he'' and yvu ''she'') can be used for ''man'' and ''woman'' in telegram style). A friend of mine quipped: ''u yb drE c kan yb ki.'' (A) man without money is a sky without a star. I said: ''yr! sE UIv: vus yb yvus.'' (No! It says: (a) man without (a) woman . . .) . He answered: ''vus yb drE cEv vus yb yvus'' (a man without money is a man without woman.) (''No'', says space-girl (a-ynyvu), ''I give you a space-kiss (a-ubogta)'')

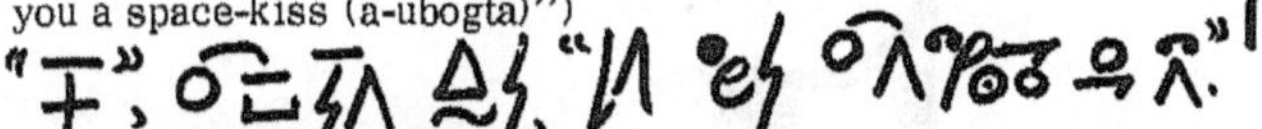

''c'' | , ''be(ing), existence. (The sound of ''c'' as in special is similar to the sound of ''j'' –s in pleasure –, because a thing ''s'' exists, as far as it stays the same – j – to itself.
2 + 3 = 5, pronounced: ''e Ib i c o'' can be read: two and three ''is'' or ''are'' five, or . . . ''equal'' five. (equal = ''j'').

''cU'' = being, existence, as a full noun. ''c-U'' = exist-concept
''cEv'' = to be, is, are, exist . . . as full verb. ''c-E-v'' means literally ''exist-matter-do'', to do-material-existence. Strictly speaking ''cUv'' would mean ''to exist in the mind, spiritually.''

''yc'' T , not-is, is-not, are not, or simply ''not'' (un-existing)
''yEc'', -yEc, as verb ending, means ''would, should'' as ''yE'' contrary to (material) fact: y-E-c ''non-fact-is'' e.g.

"If I should move, you would be sorry" "Qg fu ev-yEc, bu cEv-yEc ykrOm." (ev-yEc = move-should, should move; cEv-yEc = would-be) In actual material fact, this movement "is-not" ("yc"), I do-not move, and you are not sorry.
"If the man did not (would-not) move" (Qg u yc ev-yEc), he would be dead," (vu cEv-yEc yom). "yUg vu ev, Ib vu ov," (But he moves, and he lives, . . . (Obviously, he was only pretending to be dead, but when one touched him with a burning iron, he moved . . . Now, such a fancy word like "pretending", how can one express this in simple words (to a child)? Vu vEv, jOm Qg vu cEv-yEc yom:

(He makes, as if he would-be ("were") dead. We can even express "touches" e.g. "moves toward and into him" (ev at Ib ag (ab) vu) "into = tag = t + ag". "burning iron", we can only as yet express by "im E" or "ivAm E". We do not yet know "iEvAm rE."

"can" = all. c-a-n = existence-space-quantity, for "all" is the whole quantity that exists in a given space. Take all there is, means "take the amount that exists in that space (e.g. that bowl).

"d" implies: "through", by means of, middle, tool, instrument . . . The girl in the picture sucks juice "through" or "by means of" a straw, which is her "tool", instrument, the "conveyance" of the juice. The arrow pierces (through) the shield, the dog jumps through the ring.

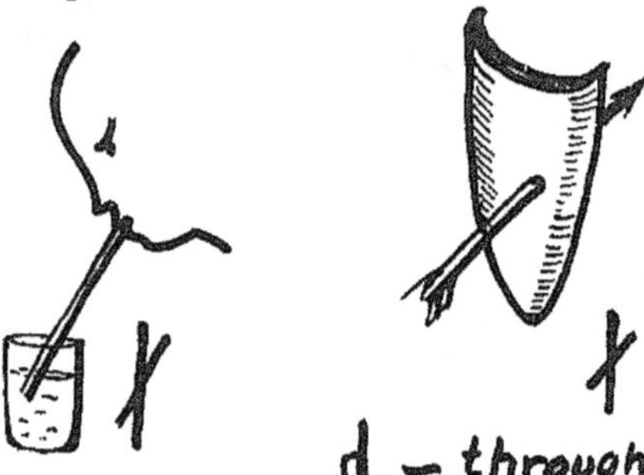

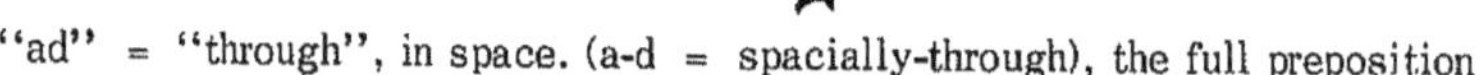

"ad" = "through", in space. (a-d = spacially-through), the full preposition
"Ed" = instrument, tool, by which one works in "E" matter. E-d = material-tool. yEd = work-tool
"Ud" = by (means of), (U-d = mentally through) not only through a straw, but "through hearsay" Ud IOv-UIv. "to live 'by' one's wits" "Ud OgU"
"yd" = against (y" = opposite, "d" = by the help of: the opposite of "help" is "damage", "to the damage of = against":
"f' u ov yd can yf u Ib yd can uU" (This man lives against all other men and against all humanity).

, "e" Movement (not only running but even taking or giving are movements.) A boy whips a top, whose spiral is the symbol of whirling movement.

"es" = machine, "e-s" move-thing,

"ged" = vehicle (g-e-d = inside-move-conveyance). A cart or an airplane are both "means" by which one "moves" something" inside" it.

ev = (to) move, e-v = move-do, move-verb, (moving oneself)
vev = to move (transitively) something else, v-ev = make (it) move, drive. "bu wav vev bum ged, hI?" "you can drive your car, eh?"
(literally: "you have power to drive your vehicle, eh?"
or: do you have the power = can you . . . ? "bu wav nem vev ged? hI?"
("you can fast drive (a) car? eh?") Can you drive a car fast?
"nem" = fast, "n-e-m" = much-move-quality; "ne" = speed
"bu wav nem vev at yo, hI?" (you can fast drive toward death, eh? =
Can you drive fast to death?) "fA u c nem os" = "now man is (a) fast animal" (f-A = this time = now). "verv fE ged at fum uga!" (Drive this car to my house!"
(At a pinch, if you can not remember any other verb, you can use "ev" for any motion, for coming, going, departing, arriving, dancing. "fu ev ad a. ki ev ad a yb da" (I move through space. (A) star moves through space without (a) way." "fE u yc ev: u c´yom" "this man (does) not move: (the) man is dead." "nem erv! (move fast!). "vev" can be used for any transitive movement of an object: you drive, push, pull, bring, give, take, pass . . . e.g. "Pass me (give me) the butter" = verv od at fu! (move the food to me!) (-rv = command ending. Later you learn words for special foods. Now you could only say "fE od" this food, or "fE eim od" "this yellow food".

"push" = move from behind = "vev yt yp", pull = vev yt ap (front).
"you dance very well" = you move very beautifully = bu nEm riOm ev.
"to dance" = riOm ev, eb riOm I (with beautiful sound).
"a-u ev ad a; au iOv i Ub ki; au ev at fE ki"

BRICKSTONE OF MATTER

, E, = Matter, material, substance, stuff.

"bE" = solid matter (b-E = together-(staying)-matter), since a solid lump sticks together, does not flow or blow apart.

"bE" is often used for earth, fnu cEv kab bE, we are on solid (ground).

"bEn" earth (bE-n = solid-plenty), as it is the solid we have lots of. (From earth we can form derivatives: land = a space on earth, "a kab bEn" or "part of the earth", earth-part = bEn-zU, as in I like this land = I like this part of the earth = fu brOv f' bEn-zU.

"wE" = stone, rock; hard matter (w-E = power-matter), as the power of matter lies in its hardness, its strength against breaking.

"wEm" = hard, wE-m = stone-quality. "fE u c' wEm jOm wE" (this man is hard as stone). fE yvus cEv ywEm. (This woman is soft, un-hard)

"jE" = liquid (j = equal, even, level, E = matter), even-matter = liquid, which, like water, spreads evenly and so is level and stands horizontal of "equal" ("j") height. "jE" is often used for jEn, water, "jEn, jE-n = liquid-plenty, water, spreads even as the surface of a quiet lake. "jEn kav jUm, Qg sE cEv yem." Water stands even, if it is quiet (un-moved). "ki iv ad kE; i iv yd jE." The star shines through (the) air (kE = gas); light shines against liquid (water).

"kE" = gas, k-E = above-matter, since a gas, like air, rises "above" liquids and solids. "kE ev ak bE Ib jE" (Gas moves above solid and liquid. Often for "Air rises above earth and water"; exactly:

"kEn" = air, gaseous-plenty, the gas we have lots of.

"rE" = metal ("positive-matter": metal settles at the positive pole in electrolysis, and is the material of positive value (money).

"En" = mass ("Matter-quantity" as is measured by mass or weight: a "massive" stone has much matter. fE wE bav nE En (much mass). "fu vev fE wE" (I move this stone). "sE c' wEm Ib bav nE En."

ki = star
bEn = earth
kEn = air,
jEn = water, wE = rock

ki iv ad kE ;i iv yd jE.

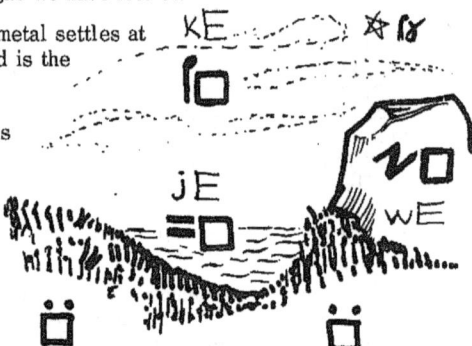

2 = e = two, in the a, e, i, u, o sequence.
(7 = E = seven, in the A, E, I, U, O sequence.)
"ge" = between, g-e = within-two, or "inside" the space between the two. "u cEv ge e uga" (The) man is between two houses.)

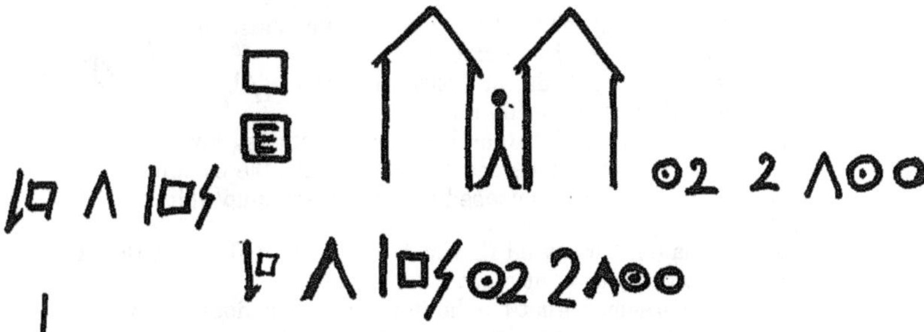

, "f", this: fE, f-E, this-matter, is the full pronoun, used when "f" alone could not be pronounced.
"fa" = here, f-a = this-place, he is here = he is (in) this place, vu c'fa. yvu yc fa (she is-not here). vu fA yc fa!
"fA" = now, f-A = this time. fAm = present, fAom = young (fA-o-m = present-life-quality), "now" come to "life".
"fEm" such (this-matter-quality) "I want such a dress = I want a dress of this quality.
"fu" = I, myself, me. "f-u" = this-person, this-man, yours truly.
"fU" = self (f-U = this-mind), the self is the mind within.
"fUd" = so, in such a way (ag fEm da). f-U-d = this-mind-through(by)
"fum" = my, mine (this-man-quality), belonging to this man.
"fnu" = we, (f-n-u = this-many-men), "-n-" is plural
fnum = our, fum = mine. "vus UIv at yvus: fum uga cEv fA fnum uga"
"The man says to the woman: my house is now our house."
"yf" = other (y-f = not-this = opposite-to--this).
"fE enam wE yc ev. fu vev yf wE Ud anam rE-Ed. (anam = long, enam = flat)
(this flat stone not moves = . . (does) not move. I move the other stone with (by-means-of) this long metal tool (e.g. an iron bar)

, g, "inside- within" (in) the interior of, "in". (dot-in-circle)
" g" = in, within, "a-g" spatially-within
"tag" = into, "toward-inside" toward (the) -space-within.
"yg" = outside (opposite-(of)-within, not-within)
-yg = ending of all apparel, clothing: uyg = man-outside
"fu vev fE u yb uyg tag jEn"
(I move (push) this man without clothes into (the) water.)

"h" indicates "question" , "? "what, . . " etc

ha = where (h-a = what place, what space?): ha bu cEv? where are you?
hA = when (at) what time: hA bu cEtAv fa? "When you will-be here?"
(In aUI, even in questions, the subject precedes the verb!)

hE = what? (what-matter? the full pronoun) "bu Ev hE" (you do what?)
(What do you do?)
hI = (the) question(sound), eh? heh? may follow any question-sentence, especially if there is no other h-word in it:
"fu vev fE u ag fE ged tag fE da, hI ? English:"(Do) I drive this man in this car into this road, eh?"
"fu dov fE u eb uyg Ib can, hI?" (do=life-means- victuals, dov=eat)
" (Do) I eat this man with clothes and all, eh?" asked the cannibal, when he was for the first time supposed to eat a dressed-up white.
"hIv" = to ask
hu = who (what man?). "hu av ad fE yim da ag yiA ?" (Who goes through this dark road in (the) night = at night?" fE u yc bav i."
hU = why? (in) what-mind? What has he in mind = why does he do it?
"hU fEn yim u ev at fum uga ag yiA ?" Why these dark men move toward my house in (the) night? (English: Why do these . . . Why are . . ?)

hUd = how? (h-U-d = what-mind-by?, by(what)means of what trick)
(does) he drink the bottle without opening it? ("d" = by means of . .)
"hUd vu jEv jEg yb tagev sE, hI?" (jE = liquid, jEv=drink, jEg=bottle)
"hE c´fE?" What is this? "fE c jEg Ub rOjE" (good-feel-liquid=wine)
"hUd bu Ev fE?" How (do) you do this? "hA bu ev tag uga Ub fu?"
"hU bu hIv fE ? fu yc ev tag bum uga !" yvus UIv.
Retranslate: "When (do) you move into house of me? (asked the man)"
"Why you ask this? I (do) not move into your house!" , woman says.

Compare: hI = question, hIv = ask (question-do), yhI (v) = (to) answer (opposite-(to)-question). hO = question-feeling, doubt; yhO = certainty.
"terv at fu!" (come to me!) "terv tag fum uga!" (come into my house!)
" " fu yc gUv, hE bu EtAv." " "bu wav cEv yhOm (you can be certain), fu yc EtAv ym-Es (I not do-shall any-thing) (I won't do a thing)."
" " fu hOv bum UI " (I doubt your word). (gUv = know, -tA- = future)

"i" = light.
"iO" = light-feel, light-sensation, sight.
fu iOv = I see.
"riO" = beauty
"riOm = beautiful"
(good-see-quality)
(good-sight = riO)

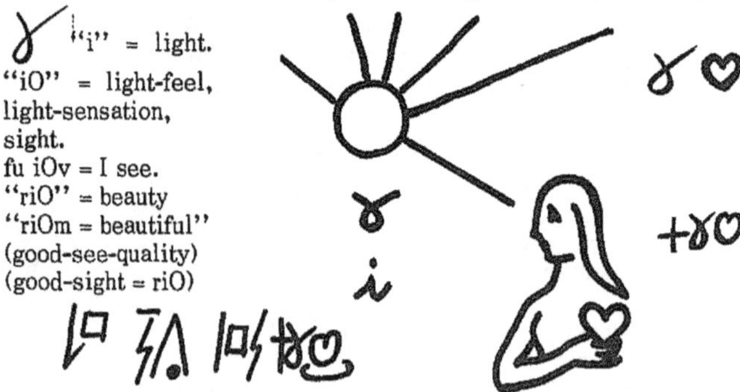

iE = fire, (i-E = light-matter , luminous substance, E)
iEm = (fiery) hot (fire-like), iEmU = heat, "iE c iEm" (Fire is hot)

iv = shine, (i-v = light-do) to make or give light
viv = make shine, kindle: "aki viv eki: eki iv ag yiA."
(a = one, our number-one star(ki) = the sun. 2d star = moon)
(The sun makes the moon shine: the moon shines in (the) night)
im = bright, light-quality. iA c im, yiA c yim. The day is bright, the night (y-iA = un-light-time) is dark (unlight); yi = shade.

-im = -colored (light-qualified: the colors are the qualifications in which light appears in the rain-bow (kajE-tlak), E.g.

aim ,	eim,	iim,	uim,	oim	=
(1st ,	2nd ,	3rd,	4th,	5th,	"light-quality, or: -modification)
red,	yellow ,	green,	blue,	violet	

You realize how many otherwise unknown things you can describe with their color or shape or function. If you did not know the word for cherry, you could say: " I want a little round red fruit with a stone in it, which grows on a tree" (fu tOv ynam lam aim ot eb wE ag sE, xE tnev ag tok) which last description is unnecessary. Of course you will learn the word for cherry, " ailot", but when you come to a foreign country, where you see unknown fruits and flowers, you better know how to describe.

"fu yc tOv fE aim uyg. fu iOv uim uyg, xE vEv fu riOm" (I (do) not wish (want) this red dress. I see (a) blue dress, which makes me beautiful.)" ai cEv mi Ub ogai (og = body, ai = red, body-red = blood).

"I" = sound, tone. Iv = to sound, to make noise, Im = noisy, yIm = quiet.
rI = song, (good-sound) .rIv = to sing (good-sound-make)
rIrv rI Ub yiA rUt fu, rIrv fum rI Ub brO ! (Sing the song of the night for me, sing my song of love!) -rv = command ending.

UI = word, U-I = mind-sound, when the mind sounds off, its in words.
nUI = language, many (n) words, plenty-words, (often replaced by UI).
" hU bu yc UIv at fu?" "fum rO yc eb bu" (Why (do) you not speak to me? - My pleasure is not with you.) fu yc tOv bu (I not wish you).
, "j" equal, even , same, homogeneous, level, horizontal etc.
(All this is only implied in the sound "j", which must be supplemented by other sounds for clarification, e.g.)

"jUm" = equal (same-mind-quality) . Equal means "the same for the mind, although the eye sees differences: "can u c jUm"

"All men are created equal" (can u c wUpAm jUm) means they are equal from the standpoint of the mind, in spiritual theory.
"jam" = same, identic (This is a spatial relation. The man who is (at the same time) at the "same place," has no alibi: he is it.
"jOm" = like, as (same-feeling-quality = j-O-m) ;- -jOm = -like.
(fum uyg c uim jOm kan. bum uyg c aim jOm iE: sE c iE-jOm.)

"My dress is blue like the sky. Your dress is red like fire: it is fire-like" (This "like" is true only for the feeling, one feels it so. It is not 'really' so.
"jE" = liquid, jEn = water (liquid-plenty). A liquid, mostly water, is called "even-matter" (j-E), because it stands on even level, on equal height, but also, because in a liquid any matter spreads usually out evenly, is dissolved homogeneously to all parts: salt spreads to all parts in water.

[ὕδωρ ἄριστον.]

Review: jEg = bottle (liquid-in), jEd = spoon (liquid-tool, a tool for scooping liquids, jEv = to drink, (liquid-do, what one does with a liquid), and jEged = boat (water-vehicle) - ejE = stream.

, k, above, on top, implying "super, supreme", "away from gravity", up. high.
"ak", above (space-above, spatially above): "kEos ev ak bEn"
(The air-animal (bird) moves above the earth. kE-os = bird)
"kab" = on (ab = at; k-ab = above-(and)-at = on. If the bottle stands "on" the table, it is somewhat above, and still together-with ("b") i.e. at it. (table = kvad = above-make-space-tool)
"kav" (above-space-verb) = stand (up). "jEg kav kab kvad".
"kam" (above-space-quality) = high
"kad" across (ad = through; if I walk across the river, it is, as if I swam through, but move above "k" it, at the same time.

"ek" = over, "moving-above" (e - k): if I fly over it, I stay above it, but move.

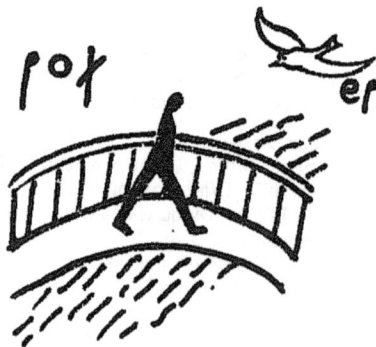

"u av kad ejE, kEos av ek ejE Ib u, ad kE." "kU ag kna" "God in heaven = -k- is used as exponential power between "10" ("O") and the figure of the number of zeros, e.g. 1000 = 10^3, i.e. 1 with 3 zeros = 10x10x10, 10 multiplied 3 times, i.e. Oki, 10-high-3. 1 000 000 000 000 = 10^{12} = OkOe = a trillion. OkA = a million.

"yk" = below, under, beneath, neither, low, infra. "yk jEn c bEn". Review that kE = gas, kEn = air, ki = star (upper-light), kan = sky. (ka = k-a = upper-space, is often enough. ka-n = up-space-plenty) "yk jEn cEv bEn , ak jEn cEv kEn, Ib ak kEn cEv a. a-u ov ag a. ag fE A (=. fA) a-u ev at bEn at UIv eb fnu. fu Ib a-u UIv." Write this first in aUI symbols, then try to read and retranslate: "Under the water is the earth, above the water is the air, and above the air is space. The space-man lives in space. In this time (= now) the space-man moves to earth and talks with us. I and the space-man talk." - hA yk-aim i ev at u, yg Ub u ev at cEv aim. "yk-aim" is the same as "iEm", hot. (Can you guess what this means? It is a try to express with the few words learnt up to now, things we shall later be able to say shorter. "When infra-red light moves to (a) man, outside of man moves to be red." Infra-red = hot. When hot light moves-to (= hits) a man, his outside "moves-to-be" (= turns) red." In this way, even with the few dozen words up to now, we can express most ideas.

L, l, implies "roundness" (The two circles within each other can be connected for faster writing)

la = roundness, (round-space) "can E ag a bav la"
All matter in space has roundness.

lam = round (-space-quality), "round".

las = ball, sphere. (round-space-thing). "bEn c las; aki c las; eki c las: can ki c las. can E ag a vEv sE-fU at ma Ub las.

led = wheel (l-e-d = round-move-tool) "bu c nam led fA!" You are a big wheel now. "vrUpAm cEv fEn, xu av al (around) ag nEn mal, yUt snE fUItAyv (they will-be-named) nam led." (Blessed are those, that go around in (many) circle(s), for they shall-be-called big wheels). (vrUv = make-good-spirit-do = bless).

al = around: (in) space-round, all-around. "led lev al." (Wheel turns around)

mal = circle (quality-around, ma = form, ma-l = "form-round")

lev = turn (round-move-make).

m = quality, a sort, kind, type, style etc (is implied)

"-m" is the adjective ending, which is added to nouns, etc, and makes these into adjectives. "-m" means then "qualified", or "-like", "-ish, -ic, -al, -ly, -ious, -ent, -ant, " (e.g. man = vu, manly = vum, U = spirit, U-m = spiritu-al, E = matter, Em = material. "ma = form, shape" (m-a = qualified space: the only property or quality of space is that it can be shaped or formed. e.g. ma-l = form-round = circle. "ma Ub bEn c lam: bEn c las" (The shape of the earth is round; the earth is a sphere, a ball). "ma Ub fE yvus c lam, yUg fE yvus yc las" (The shape of this woman is round, but this woman is not a ball (a sphere). yf yvus c enam. "ma Ub fE yvus c lam, yUg fE yvus yc las" "ma Ub fE vus c anam. "The shape of this man is long". ma Ub aeikot c yjUm yt ma Ub ankot.

(The) shape of (an) orange is different from (the) shape of (a) banana. (-kot = tree-fruit, "high-fruit") aei- = orange (color), an- = long. banana = long-tree-fruit.

"mA" = condition, state-of-affairs, situation, circumstance m-A = "qualified-time". For speakers who can not pronounce "Q", "ö" as in wQrd, "mA" could replace "Q" condition. Then "mAg" would replace "Qg" = if. Otherwise "mA" is useful in describing time-related situations e.g. the weather: "ka-mA" the sky-situation, "hE c ka-mA" what is (the) weather? (French "temps", time = weather) "mi" = color, qualified light; inversely -im is the ending of all color adjectives, aim = red, uim = blue. "ankot Ib eikot c eim"

(The) long-tree-fruit and (the) yellow-tree-fruit are yellow. The banana and the lemon are yellow. (Of course, in aUI, for scientific purposes, one can call a banana "aneikot" "long-yellow-fruit" (This would correspond to the Latin and Greek double names of Botany). But for common purposes, as long as no other long fruit is around, "an-kot" long-tree-fruit describes the banana.)

"mU" = quality as a full noun, m-U = quality-concept, kind-of. (The old English word "kind", also used for "friendly", is now rather confusing).

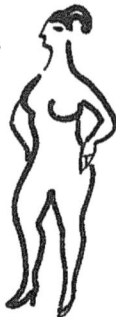

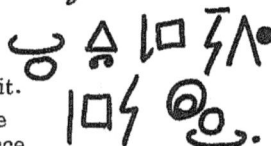

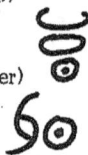

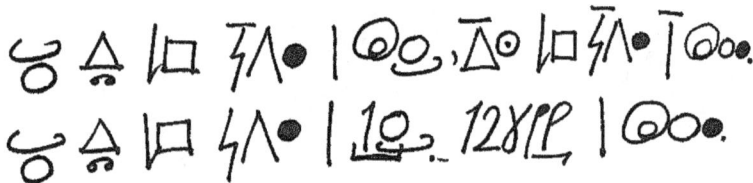

, "n" , implies "quantity", lots, plenty, (big) amount, plurality, much, many, numbers, measures, units, dimensions, orders. (The symbol is short for a measuring box, open above as a drawer, for putting in beans or peas of a certain measurable quantity.

"an" = size (space-quantity). hE c an Ub bum uyg ? What is the size of your dress? "sE c nĖk nam myt bum uyg" (It is "more big than your dress) "n-E-k" quantity-matter-above = more (If I am bigger than you, I am "above" you, as far as the "matter of quantity" (weight) is concerned, (or the amount of matter).
"na" = dimension, (quantified -space): ana = length (first dimension)

anam = long (one dimension of space); "enam" = flat, inam = 3-dimensional
an = unit (one quantity, the amount of "one")
nam = big, large (much-space-quality). fE yvus bav nam kEmOz. (kEmOz = nose = air-quality-sense-part) "This woman has a big nose."
nE = much ("plenty-material"); plural: nEn = many (replaces plural), e.g. "This man of much money owns (has) houses." If they are "houses", they are either "two, or three, or some (yIn) or many"
"fE u Ub nE drE bav nEn uga" (uga = house) means: This man of much money has "many house" ("many" alone shows the plural!). "fa c nEn u" (There are many men) Literally: There's "many man" = "men."
ynE = little (y-nE = not much); yn = none, not any, no (man).
"n" as nasal sound enters all numbers: a, e, i, u, o, A, E, I, U, O; Y.
"na, ne, ni, nu, no" = first, second, third, fourth, fifth ("number one, etc")
"fE c nO uga ag fE nuba (city), xE yc bav trUn tugai" (enough windows).
(This is (the) tenth house in this city, which not has enough windows).
"fu ev ad nEn iA, yb iOv a riOm uga. Ib fE c na rUm uga."
(I move through many days, without seeing one beautiful house. And this is (the) first good house." am can nOke u bav uga. (Only each . .)
"nUz = quantity (as full noun) "quantity-concept"
"mUn" = number = "quality-concept-quantity", (the number gives an even otherwise unqualified heap a certain "quality-concept".
e.g. This game consists of 9 pins. "9" describes the game.
"fE rOves gEv U anlEd" (g-Ev = con-tain) . rOve = play.

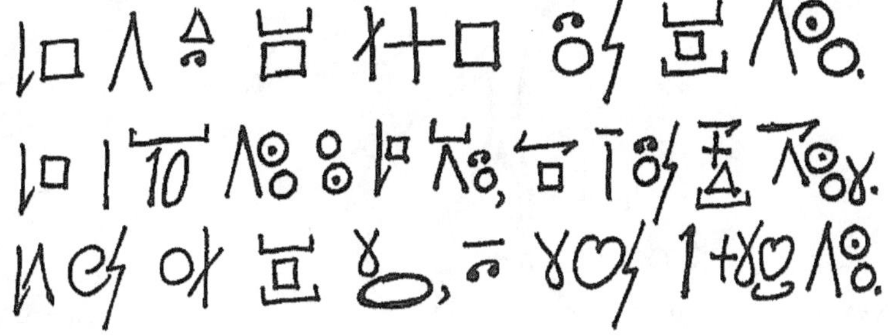

, "o", life, vitality .

"od" = food, (life-means [o-d], the "means"by" which we live); "Lebensmittel" (German)
"do" = nourishment, even for a plant. "dov" = to eat
"og" = body ("life-inside": body is that "within" which "life" dwells)
"os" = animal, beast ("life-thing", something alive, animated (cf. "dObutsu" Japanese)
"bos" = domestic-animal, beast ("together-animal", the beast which "lives" "together" with man, like dog or cow.
"waubos" = dog (wa = strong-place [w-a], ubos = man-together-animal) (a husky watchdog makes a place a stronghold)
"bijEbos" (bijE = white-liquid = milk; milk-beast = cow)
"bos ov eb u;. kEos ov ag kEn ; jEos ov ag jEn : u ov ag can as ."
(The) domestic beast lives with man; the bird lives in the air; (the) fish lives in the water: man lives in all places.
"kEos" = bird (air-animal) ; jEos = fish (water-animal) (Literally, jE = liquid. But since the only liquid in which animals can live is water, animal of the liquid can mean only water-animal).
"izos" = insect (3-part-animal: z-os = part-animal. insects are "in-sected" i.e. "cut-in" 3 parts: head-breast-abdomen.
"io" = plant ("light-life") . The green plant "lives" by "light" which makes water and air into starch. "iod" = plant-food,vegetable.

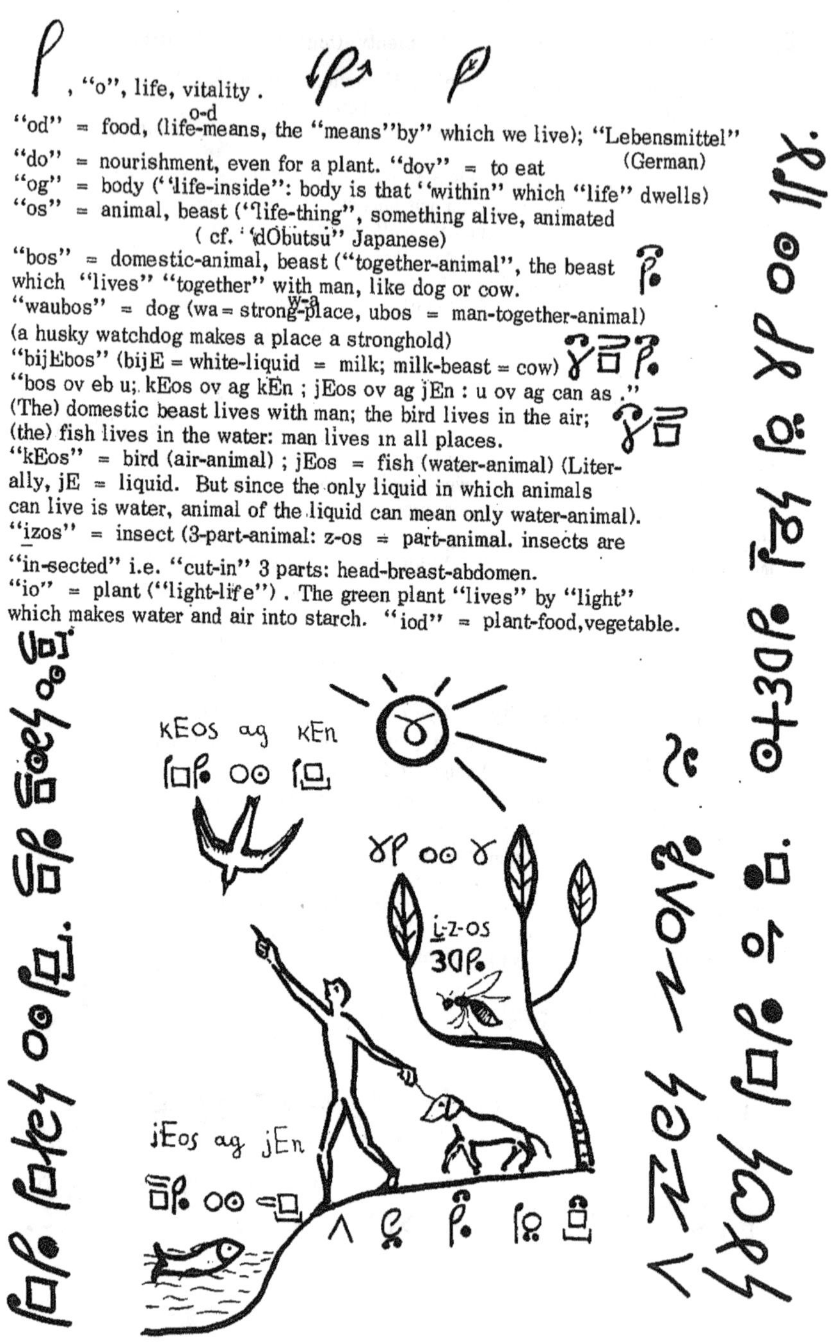

"od" = food, "do" = nutrition, iod = vegetable-food.
"nEn iod c'iim : iim mi vEv jEn Ib z'Ub kEn tag od Ub u Ib os."
(Retranslate & write in aUI symbols: Many vegetables are green: (the) green color makes (transforms) water and (a) part ("zU") of air into food of man and beast.)
"ot" = fruit ("life-towards": all "life" "moves" toward" bearing fruit, which is, as it were, the result of life. " can o ev at vEv (making) ot, xE c, jOm sE cEv-yEc, pI tsUs (result) Ub o". "yUg, bu Ulv, Uf pI (the) tsUs Ub o cEv yo!" (But you say, that the result of life is death!) "fUd ot Ub o cEv-yEc yo." (Thus the fruit of life would-be death). "yUg tsUs Ub yo c o ag U." But the result of death is life in the spirit. (yUg = but).
"ot cEv rUm; (erv ot tag bum og" = dorv ot) (Fruit is good; move (ev = to move: erv = move! command) fruit into your body = eat fruit! (dov = to eat: do-r-v = "eat-good-do" or "eat-well-do": you'd do well eating fruit, or: fruit does you good, that is like a polite command or hint : since it's good, eat it.)
"to" = seed ("toward-like") : seed strives "toward" giving "life." Compare " ot : to " or: to - o - ot. "oyt" = egg (life-from)
yt = from: life comes from egg.

"to" = seed, "io" = plant, "ot" = fruit
"voz" = sex (make-life-part): sex is the "part" of an organism, which "makes" (procreates) "life."
"bo" = hand (together-five): in the "hand" are "5" (fingers) "together".

bo = hand , boz = finger (hand-part)

, O, feeling, implies: emotion, sentiment, sense, sensation
"cO" = sense (existence-feeling: our senses -- sight, hearing, touch - - give us the feeling of reality, of existence).

"IO" = hearing, ("sound-sense", acoustic sensation) (stress: I-O)
"iO" = sight (light-sense, sensation of light) (stress: i-O)
riO = beauty ("good-sight, good-to-see")
rO = pleasure (good-feeling, to feel good = rOv)
brO = love ("together-good-feeling", "together-joy" : When you love somebody, you have "joy together" and it's joy to be together. "fu brOv IOv fEn riOm I, yvu vEv xEm I". " I love (to) hear these beautiful sounds, 'she makes which sound' = 'which sounds she makes' (Beautiful human-made sounds = music; Later we shall sinply say "fu brOv rIO" I love music.

" fE vus iOv yvus Ib IOv yvu. vu iOv yvum riO, Ib vu bav rO. vu IOv yvum rIv Ib vu Ov brO. vu brOv yvu."
"This man sees (the) woman and hears her. He sees her beauty, and he has joy. He hears her sing(ing) and he feels love.
"He loves her.

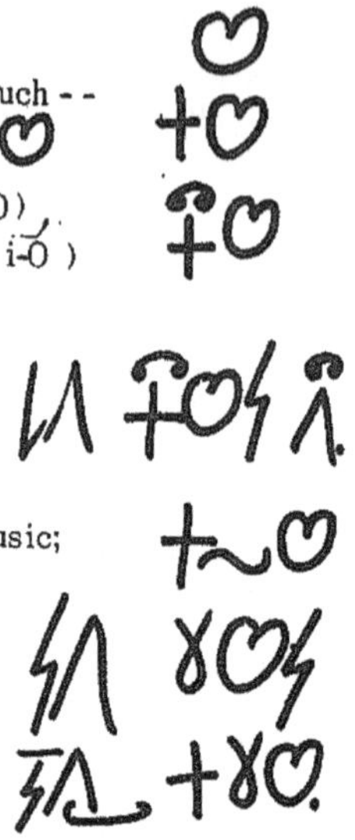

IO
iO
riO
rO
brO

"p" = front, before, pre-
"ap" = before, in front of ("a-p" = "space-front", spatially before)
"yp" = behind, in-back-of (y-p = anti-front, opposite of before)
"ap fu c i; yp fu c yi" (Before me is light; behind me is darkness)

ap fu c'i yp fu c'yi

"pa" = (the) front, ("front-space" noun) "vu bav rUm pa nag u" (He has a good front among (n-a-g = many-space-in, within many) men)
"Ap" = before (in time), "time-front". Ap nEn akiA fu cEpAv fAom:
"Before many years" = Many years ago . . . I was young .
"pA" = past (front-time, fore-time, Vorzeit, pretime, past)
-pA- as verb-ending denotes past: "Ap fu epAv (moved, came) at fE bEn, fu yc iOpAv fEm riO" (Before I moved to this earth, I not saw such beauty) . ev, e-v = to move. -pA- is inserted: e-pA-v.
Of course for past-perfect, "I had not seen", one doubles: -pApA- = (-ppA)
"fu yc iOpApAv", but one can also say "had" bapAv iOpAm "seen."
"ap fum uga cEpAv nE i, Ib fa opAv nEn riOm io; yp fE uga cEpAv yi, Ib fa opAv fum bos." Before my house was much light, and here lived many beautiful plants; behind this house was darkness, and here lived my beasts (domestic-animals).)
Safer grammatically: "nE i cEpAv ap fum uga, Ib nEn riOm io opAv fa . . ."

, "Q" pronounced Ö, as in wOrd (wQrd, wÖrd) = condition, circumstance.

"Qg" = if (condition-in, in this condition.)
"Qg bu brOv bum io, bu ev sE at i; Qg bu brOv bum bos, bu ev sE at yi" (If you love your plant, you move it to the light; if you love your domestic-animal, you move it to the shade).
"Qg bu ev-yEc at fu, rO cEv-yEc ab fu ag fum uga. Qg bu yc ev at fu, rO yc cEv ab fu" (If you move- perhaps = would move to me, joy would be at me in my house. If you not = don't move to me, joy not . . .)

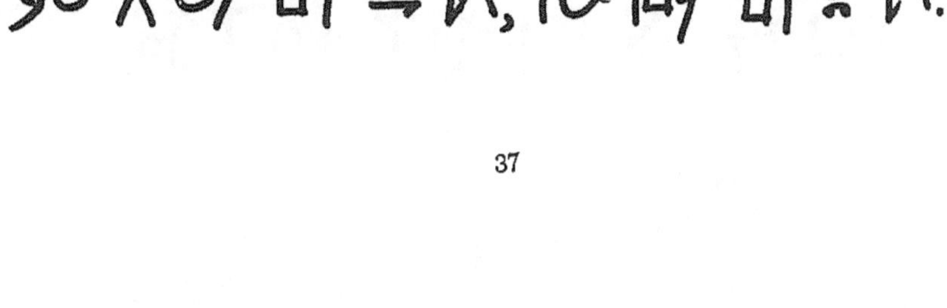

+ *), "r", implies "positive, affirmative, good"

rUm = good (the full adjective) "positive-mind-quality", affirmative-mental-value, as judged by the mind.
yrUm = evil (anti-good). yr = negative, Um = mindquality
(There is a shorter form "rym" = bad (positive-opposed-quality), which does not imply the mind, e.g. a bad knife "rym zEvd").
"Ur" = yes! "positive-mind, mentally positive" mind-affirmation.
(Urm = positive, affirmative, yes-quality.) "yrm" = negative.
"yr" = No! (anti-positve, in which no mind is implied).
"yr! fu brOv yn ot" = No! I like no fruit. (yn = not-any).
"rUt" = for ("good-mentally-to", good for). "ot c rUm rUt bu!"
Fruit is good for you. NB. for = because = yUt (yt = from, mind-from)
"ot c rUm rUt bu, yUt sE gEv otrod" (Fruit is good for you, for (or: because) it contains vitamins). otrod = life-medicine.
nUr(m) = valu(abl)e: "amount (of) spiritually positive quality".
"There is much that is valuable in this youth" means: "The amount of spiritually positive quality . . . is great" thus:
"nE nUr cEv ag fE u, xu cEpAv yc anam A kab fE bEn". Literally:
(Much value is in this man, who was not long time on this earth i.e. . . . , who is still young). As long as you do not know the word "fAom" for young, you can still replace it this way.
"fE wE cEv nUrm, yUt fE wE cEv riOm". This stone is valuable, for(because) this stone is beautiful.
"rE" = metal. "r-E" = "positive-matter", valuable-material.
"drE" = money
"drE" = money : "d-rE" = "means" (of exchange for) "metal", and : money (coins) are the metal "by means of which" one buys what is good ("r") in this material (E) world.
"hE c drE? drE cEv to Ub nEn yrU" What is money? Money is the seed of many evils. "yr! drE c rUm rUt nEn rUm Es!" No! Money is good for many good things.
"ry" = imperative ending. (" -rv" = good-do: "It is good for you to do . . . It's "good" for you to drink milk, you better drink milk, means a kind command: "drink milk", as one commands only the good.
"jErv bijE" or "bu jErv bijE" (you better) drink milk!
"Ur! fu jEv can bijE, xE fa cEv" (Yes I drink all (the) milk . . .)

*) Distinguish from +; = d = through, a slanting line going through vertical line; + = r = a cross with horizontal bar.

●, "s" = thing, object, article, item. "sE" = it (thing-matter).
"Es" = thing, (as a full noun: "matter-thing, material-object")
"-s" is usually the ending of a thing contained in itself, existing independently, concretely, e.g. vu = he, vus = man
o = life, os = life-thing, animal. (-z = ending of a part!)
"Us" = thought, idea ("mind-thing"). bu bav nEn rUm Us.

→, "t", toward, to, implying any approach → →

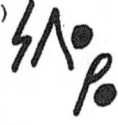

"at" = to, towards (space-toward) as the full preposition, especially between consonants more easily pronounced than mere "t".
"u tev at fu, xA vu bav A."
The man comes to me, when he has time.

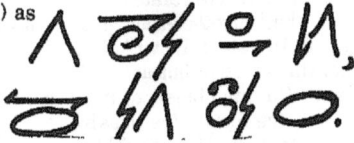

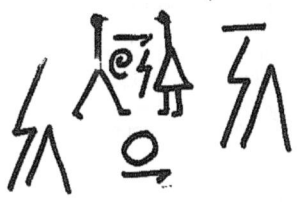

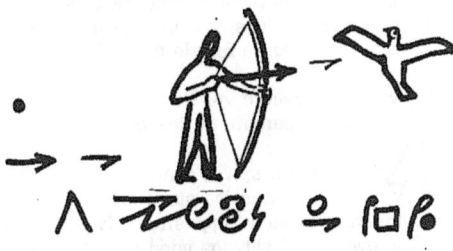

"tev" = to come ("toward (us) move")
If he moves to us, he is coming.

"terv at fu". Ur, fu tev at bu.
fu brOv bu. fu bav bu ag fum bo.

"Come to me!" "Yes, I come to you.
I love you. I have you in my hand.

"u twebev at kEos".
(The) man aims at (the) bird.

"twebev" = "toward-force-move-together-move" aiming tries toward forcible "together-hit".

"Ut" = in order to, for the purpose of ("mind-toward, with a mind to")
"vu epAv ad nE da, ag ynE A, Ut tev at fa ag rUm A, yUt vu, ab na, cEpAv yp A." (He moved through much way in little time,
(= he moved fast = he ran) in-order-to come toward here in good time, because he, at first, was behind time) that means:
"He hastened to come early, because at first, he was too late."
This replacement sentence shows that "Ut" and "yUt" are opposites.
"yUt" = because, for(opposite of mentally-toward is "mentally-from")
"y-t" = from (yt = opposite-of "toward", y-t = anti-toward).
"yt drE nEn yrU tev, yUt drE c to Ub nEn yrU." (From money many evils come, for (because) money is (the) seed of many evils).

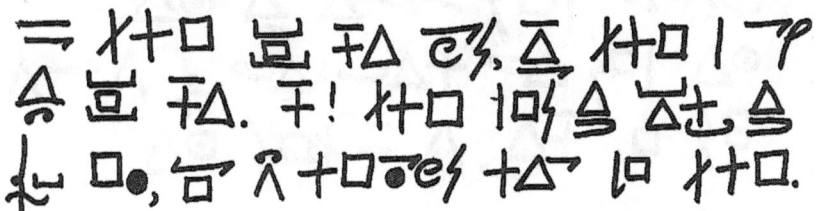

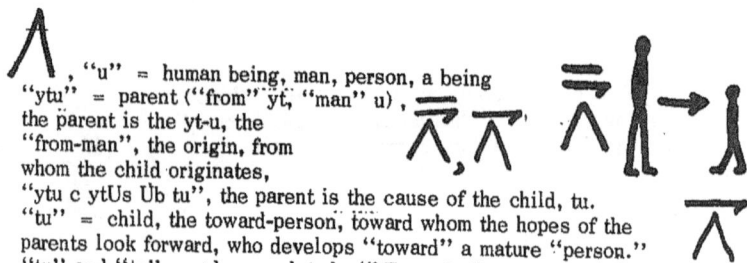

, "u" = human being, man, person, a being
"ytu" = parent ("from" yt, "man" u), the parent is the yt-u, the "from-man", the origin, from whom the child originates,
"ytu c ytUs Ub tu", the parent is the cause of the child, tu.
"tu" = child, the toward-person, toward whom the hopes of the parents look forward, who develops "toward" a mature "person."
"tu" and "to", seed, are related. "hE c tu? sE tev yt to Ub ytu".
"bu" = you (the "together-man" b-u, with whom I, f-u, "this-man" am talking. "fu UIv eb bu Ul vu" (I speak with you about him).
"vu" = he, (the "active-human"),, "yvu" she (non-active, passive human animal). On this planet, at least in sex, the male is the active "v", the female the passive "yv", although there may be exceptions: "fu Uv: kab fE bEn, vus cEv vem, yvus cEv yvem, ag voz." "vus" = man, he-man, active-human-thing;
"yvus" = woman, a female person, passive-human-thing (yv-u-s).

"fE vus Ib fE yvus c ytu Ub fE tu. ytu brOv tu." This man and this woman are parents of this child. (The) parents love (the) child.

"U", mind, spirit, concept, abstractum. (U is related in sound to "y" - negation, as the spirit may withdraw from the world, and thinking creates "opposites" (y-): "iOz iOv i, U Uv yi" ("The eye sees light, the mind thinks darkness.")

(Bible Hebr. Grk) πνεῦμα

gU = knowledge
"Uv" = to think (to mind-act)- "Us" = thought, idea (mind-thing)
"gUv" = to know (knowledge-verb); "gU" = knowledge ("in-mind"): What I have " in my mind", in my head, is my knowledge.
"gUw" = science (know-power): Through science has man the power to know, science gives power of knowledge, forcefully controls and organizes knowledge. "gUw cEv wU Ub gU" (wU = power).

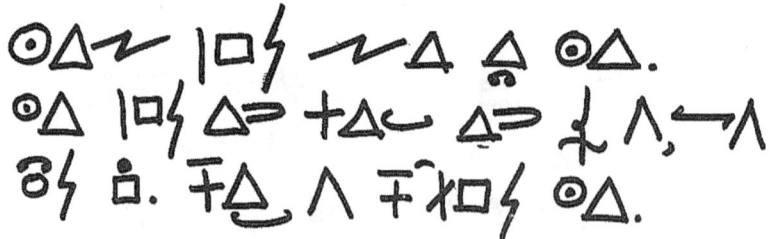

"UI" = word ("mind-sound")
"nUI" = language (many words)
"UIv" = to speak, say, talk.
"-U" is used as abstract ending,
(like -ness, -dom, -ty, -ence, -tude)
to form nouns: e.g. width = wideness =
damU; dam = wide (through-space-quality)
yIU = soundlessness, silence; yIm = unsounding, silent.

, "v" implies "activ(ity)", do, make,
"-v" is used as verb-ending, e.g. O = feeling, Ov = to feel,
fu Ov = I (do) feel; to give = "sev", to love = "brOv"
"vU" = act (act-concept), action; "-vU" corresponds to the
ending "-ion": it makes nouns out of verbs: to have, to possess
becomes "possession". bav = to have, "bav" becomes "bavU" possession.
"Ev" = to do, to act (in substance - E - to act -v), essential-act.
"vEv" = to make (as all causative verbs start with v-: "to make do"
"wU vEv fu Ev sE" ("A power makes me do it") = I must do it.
"ev" = to move; vev = to drive (something else), to move somebody.
"-yv" = passive (opposite-to-active) verb-ending: "sE veyv" = it is
being moved, it's moved. "sE c vepAm" = it is (=has been) moved.
"vem" = active (active-move-quality); "yvem" = passive (anti-activ)

, "w" = power, force, energy, strength, ability, might, capability.
"wU" = power (as full noun: "power-concept")
"wav" = can ("If I can go through this
field, it lies in my power-space "wa")
"wyv" = must ("power-passive", I am
passively subject to a power: I must)
"wyd" = weapon, arms. ("yd" = against:
"w-yd" = power-against-tool, force- oppose-tool:
A tool with which one opposes force is a weapon.
vEd, u yv wU Ud xE, cEv wyd. ("Tool, man opposes force by which, is . .

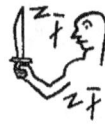

, "x" = relation, relative, which . . . is implied.

"xE(m)" = which (adjective), xu = who, xa = where, xA = when,
does not change the "subject-verb-object" order: u, fu iOv xu, . .

, "y-" = negation, opposite, un-, in-, anti-, dis-, non-.
"yd" = against (opposite of "by-help-of" = "d"); "yc" = (is) not
"ys" = nothing, "yn" = no(ne), "yr" = No!, "yv" = to oppose.

, "z" = part, division, section, side, cut etc.

"zU" = part (as full noun: "part-concept"); "az" = side (space-part)
"bu c'ab hEm az, hI?" (You are on what side, eh? = On what side.?)
Ez = element ("matter-part"); azve = ½, half, "one-part-made-2"
"izvo" = 3/5 (3 divided-by 5)

"zEv" = to divide ("part-make"). "uga zEpAm yd sEfU" (a house
divided against itself).

PART III. GRAMMAR (Alphabetic Index).

There is no special grammar. All elements of meaning and their combinations still mean what they say. The rule is we talk "as clear as we must, as short as we can."

There is no formal grammar in aUI, since even the endings them selves are aUI words. Here we arranged the terms of conventional grammar alphabetically:

ABSTRACTA: from adjectives end in -U. (English -ness, -ty, -tude, -th, e.g. "kam" = high, "kamU" = height; Highness.) If derived from verbs, abstracta end in -vU, adding -U to the verb ending -v. vOv = to impress (make-feel) : vOvU = impression. "vov" = to procreate, (make-live) : vovU = procreation, procreating. (English: -ion, -ing, ... are abstract nouns from verbs).

ABSTRACTA can end in -Uz, which is clearer but longer than -U. See 'concept' & 'gerund' in -Q.

CONCEPT To make out of an element its concept it is clearer to attach -Uz, concept, instead of plain -U (mind). n-Uz is quantity concept, the (idea of) quantity in the abstraction. -ion can be clarified with -Uz: "procreation" can be expressed "vovUz", or "vovQ" procreating:

ACCENT: 1) Most stressed are the Nasals A, E . . a, e, i, or number-elements of a word, underlined: nákiA = summer
2) Second stress falls on "LONG" CAPITAL VOWELS: A, E, . . : iÁ.
3) Third stress has the "Next-to-the-Last", i.e. the syllable which starts a 2-syllable word or is in the middle of a 3-syllable: e.g.
úga, (house), yrúga (prison, bad-house).

Distinguish: io (plant), iÓ (sight) since a long vowel competes, But again first syllable stress: ÍO (hearing), as both vowels are now long. Cf: ánaged (train), éA (twice), jÉgas (vessel).
(In verbs, the stem-vowel, even if short, keeps a melodic accent, although in Past & Future the long "-pA-" & "-tA-" endings compete: "ov" becomes "óVpAv" with a high-sung tone on the "ó". Likewise "tévAm" with high-tone "é".

In a struggle between LONG and nasal, the nasal wins the stress: ákiA, year, "Ezé" = Helium (Ez = element, "matter-part") i.e. "Element-2", as the elements are counted by their atomic numbers.- "y-" is fused with a following vowel into one syllable: yí = shade; yúm = inhuman, áyt = off. But: ýtu = parent. (cf. Engl. yet, you; rhythm)
Make a little pause after each word to set them off clearly.

ADJECTIVES = ADVERBS: Both end in -m, which corresponds to English -ly, -ious, -y, -al, -ary: "o" = life, "om" = lively, alive; "a" = space, "am" = spatial; "A" = time, Am = timely, temporal(ly). Adjectives must precede their nouns, adverbs stand immediately before their verbs, which they modify. Modifiers precede their words modified. In English, too, an adjective before a verb serves as Adverb: "He fast accomplished his friendly mission" = "vu nem EpAv vum brum kwepAm-ade." (commanded-journey = mission). Between two adjectives serving parellel, put a comma.
"-m" means "quality, - qualified". See "COMPARISON" with nEk, pnEk.

ADVERB For clarity Q can be attached to the adjective to make it into an adverb: nemQ = quickly, rUmQ = goodly, well (rUg), Noun + g: rQ-g = luck-ily (in luck)

AGENT: "-er" serves in English for the man who does things, along with "-or," e.g. farmer, traveller, giver, sender, creator. In AUI, "-u", man, is added to nouns and verbs. Verbs end already in -v, so -vu becomes the full ending, e.g.:
"vav" = to send, "vavu" = sender; vyov = to kill, vyovu = killer. Often -u can replace the former noun-ending. "odva" = farm = (food-make-place). Instead of "farm-man" (=food-make-place-man, which would be "odva-u") one can shorter say "odvu" "food-make-man".

ARTICLE: is usually not needed and omitted or replaced by "one" ("a") instead of English "a", or by "this" ("fE") or plural: "many" ("nEn"). English itself makes little difference between: "A dog is a man's best friend" or: "Dog is man's best friend." or "The dog is the best friend of man" or: "Dogs are men's friends." ("waubos cEv pnEk rUm bru Ub u".) aUI omits such articles. (pnEk = most).

But in a sentence like: "A man appeared; the man looked like John." ("yI u iOpA'yv ; pI u OipAv jOm JoHN (DJoN).") First: "a" man: we never heard of him a sound. "yI" u = "un-sounded" man. The "not-spoken" of man needs the indefinite article : "yI" = "a", plural: "yIn" = "some", several.
Then: "the" man looked . . . "The" means now: "the previously mentioned man" "pI" ("before-sounded-off about) = "the", the definite article. Plural : "pIn" = the. The men = pIn u.
"yI; yIn" = a; several, (the indefinite article, Engl. plur. omitted)
"pI, pIn" = the (Engl. makes no difference between singular & plur).

CAPITALS are used for LONG vowels AEIUO. Besides, Capital consonants are used for proper names and words borrowed from other languages into aUI. e.g. Lincoln becomes "LiNKoLN" if its pronunciation must be explained to an "a-u." In aUI

symbols 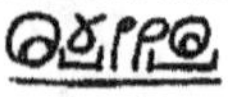 would be underlined.

The present fashion of using capitals to start sentences or paragraphs can not be transferred to aUI, where period (.) or full-stop or Question-mark (?) must suffice to set off thoughts. 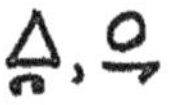

CASES: GENETIVE POSSESSIVE with "Ub" (=of); DATIVE: "at" (to).
"We give him mother's apple" = We give (the) apple of mother to him =
"fnu sev nakot Ub ytyvu at vu." (vu = he(= him, if after verb).
vu iOv fu; fu iOv vu. He sees me; I see him.

CAUSATIVES should start with v- or have a -v- before its first vowel: ev = move, vev = (make) move, drive. It is especially necessary to distinguish the causative from its root verb when the latter itself is transitive: eat = dov, make eat = feed = dvov. dorv ukbos! = eat the horse, dvorv ukbos = feed the horse. 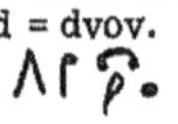 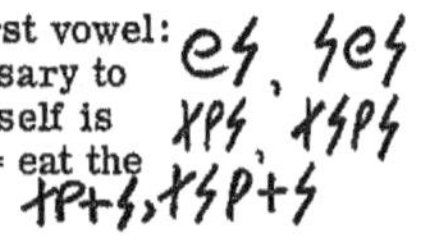

COMMAND (see IMPERATIVE under "VERB") ends in "-rv" : "erv" = move! "serv" = give: from "ev" = to move, "sev" = give. "-r- = inserted.

COMMAND of "-Yv" verbs. Take care that the "r" precedes the "-v" without being preceded by "-y-" which would negate it. syv, receive, should not be transformed into s-yrv (see '-yv') for this would mean it is bad to do something, but rather sryv. The hypnotic commands of conventional language are dissolved into statements of goodness to be verified freely. 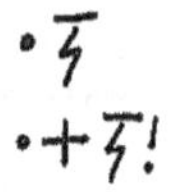

COMPARISON: "nE" = much, "nEk" = more ("much-above" (nE -k), super-much) "pnEk" = most ("before-more"). "nEk" and "pnEk" are used for all adjectives and adverbs, for nouns and verbs. E.g. "He is more (of a) male than a man, rather a he-man than a human." = 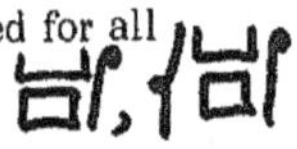
"vu cEv nEk vus myt u." (m-yt = "quality-from", the level "from" which the quality is compared and measured, used for "than, rather." 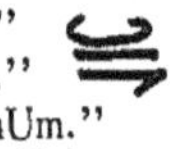
"myt" = than, rather-than, in comparisons, "yvu c nEk riOm myt nUm." (She is more (or rather) beautiful than wise.) "yUg, yvu c pnEk rUm."

FUTURE: (see VERB) "-tA-" (the "toward-time" , the "time toward"  which we move, or which comes toward us) is used in the verb-ending: "I shall have a house" = "fu ba-tA-v uga" (bav = have).

GENDER: none is used for nouns. "vu" = he, "Yvu" (or: "Lu") = she; "vo" = he (animal), "Yvo" (or: "Lo") = she (animal)(or: motherly animal). vom = male, Yvom = female.

GERUNDS can end in Q, condition. Running is healthy = nevQ c vrom. The gerund is like a noun or an infinitive. To run is healthy or a run is healthy. /cf. Communication, Logic . . .

HEALING from Expression to Communication, pp. 222, 250, 277 & 331 (= p. 51 of "Sound Cave"), 335f, 339-41; cf. Peace thru Undst.

HYPHEN: can be used instead of possessive or "Ub = of". One should not coin new compounds without hyphen: u-ca = man-world, = man's world, the world of man, = ca Ub u. (c-a = existence-space), ca = the space of existence, the world. In aUI symbols the hyphen becomes a bridge, an arch joining "u" with "ca":

INFINITIVE can be clarified by "at": nu pev (at) rIv = They start (to) sing.

INVECTIVES start explicitly with Yr- (bad-).

INVERSION is to be avoided. Best is always SUBJECT-VERB-OBJECT order, even in questions and relative clauses: Instead of: Whom did he see? rather: He saw whom? "vu iOpAv hu?" He saw the man whom we know = He saw the man, we know whom = vu iOpAv pI u, fnu gUv xu." (= we know which). See WORD-ORDER !

xQ See RELATIVE & xQ

MEASUREMENTS: metric units (unit = an) are preferred.

NEGATION, like any modifier, precedes the negated: "vu ye av." See "y-". The bar covers what is denied.
Yc yc

NOUNS: are basic words of aUI. The main vowels are nouns: a = space, A = time , etc. Verbs are derived by -v, adjectives by -m. Nouns in -s should be concrete, e.g. "os" = life-thing = animal. Nouns in -U should be abstract, e.g. "yIU" = no-sound-concept = silence. But these endings are often unnecessary. See: AGENT, ARTICLE, CASES, GENDER, OBJECT, PLURAL.

NUMERALS: The usual Arabic numbers are used for aUI figure symbols.

1, 2, 3, 4, 5; 6, 7, 8, 9, 10 . Y = zero = 0

Pronounced: a, e, i, u, o; A, E, I, U, O; as nasals with wrinkled nose.

aUI multiplication is simpler: if factors sound alike, their product has same ending:

2 x 6 = 12 sounds: e A A c Oe, 2 sounds e like E (which is only longer) = 7;

7 x 6 = 42 sounds: E A A c uOe; (A means "times") c means "is");

3 x 9 = 27 sounds: i A U c eE, 3 sounds i like the longer I of 8;

8 x 4 = 32 sounds: I A u c ie, 9 sounds U like the shorter u for 4.

8 + 5 = 13 sounds: I Ib o c Oi: Adding 5 changes length but not quality of i (I).

* Write a multiplication table in these colors, using red, yellow, green, blue, violet for 1&6, 2 & 7, 3 & 8, 4&9, 5 & 10 Writing 1, 2, 3, 4, 5; 6, 7, 8, 9, 10 in the first row & also downward in the left column, having their products form the body of this square.

Being so short, the numeral nasals are used within words, especially in colors: first-light-quality = a-i-m = red, second is yellow = eim etc: "aim = red, eim = yellow, iim = green, uim = blue, oim = violet" as light-quality: one, two, three, four, five.*)

Star number one is the sun: aki (a = (number) one, ki = star).

Additions of decades are put after: 13 = 10 + 3 = ten-three = O-i.

Multiplications are put before: 50 = 5 x 10 = five-ten = o-O.

23 = 2 x 10 + 3 = two-ten--three = "e-O-i" or simply 2, 3 = ei.

1492 sounds either short: "auUe", or longer: "Oki -- u-Oke -- U-O-- e" which is still shorter than: "thousand-four-hundred-ninety-two."

Powers of ten use simply the number of zeros as exponential with "k" = above, high: a billion is 10^9 (1 000 000 000) = OkU.

"Plus" = "and" = Ib; "minus" = "off" = ayt. "times" = A.

"divided by = zEpAm Ud; ½ = azve, 4/5 = uzvo (4-part-make-5)

ORDINAL NUMBERS : number-one = n-a = first = na, ne = 2nd, nOke = 100th.

NUMBERS can be clarified by holding up fingers and wrinkling the nose if one has trouble in nasalizing. In the telephone one can clarify by using lengthened number words which have as many letters as the number needs and start in the alphabetic sequence of consonents b, c, d, f. . . : a = 1, be = 2 (literally: together two, both), cic = 3, drud = 4, fronf (these good five (= 5) quantity this). The numbers above 5 must be said with exaggerated long vowels: 6 = A, 7 = bE, 8 = cIc, 9 = drUd, 10 = frOnf, or Oka = 10^1. The combined numbers are just enumeration of the single digits: 1974 = aUEu or a, drUUd, bEE, drud. (cf. p. 42)

1 2 3

4 5 6 7

8 9 10

OPTATIVE: -rO-: give = sev; fu se-rO-v = I'd like to give.

OBJECT: follows the verb, which is its only characteristic, since otherwise it has always the same form as the subject. No inversions are possible, since "who" and "whom" become both "hu?" and "he" and "him" are in aUI both "vu". "Whom do you see?", becomes : "You see whom?" = "bu iOv hu?" "The man, whom I see, . . " becomes : "The man, I see whom, (as: -- I see him), is the killer." "u, fu iOv xu, cEv pI vyovu" "The man (I see him) is the killer."

INDIRECT OBJECT with "at" comes always last: "yvu serv aim ot at tu!" "She (ought to = Imperative!) give (the) red fruit to (the) child!" In English: "She should give the child the red fruit." is an other possibility, which should not be carried over into aUI.

"(bu) verv fu yc tag jE!" = (You), drive me not into the water!"

PARTICIPLES (see VERB!) end in "-vAm" ("do-time-adjective") adding to the "-v" of the verb only "-Am" ("time-quality") for English -ing. "(A) rolling stone gathers no moss" = "lelvAm wE yc setbav ykio" (= .. not gathers moss) "rolling" has "time-quality" for the stone must have rolled for quite a time.

PAST PARTICIPLE ends in "-pAm" ("-pAm" = "past-adjective"): e.g. "driven" = vepAm, ("vev" = to drive), make move; the full word for "driving" = davev(Am). Tolstoy said: "We think we are driving, but we are driven" = "fnu Uv:fnu c davevAm, yUg fnu c davepAm."

FUTURE ACTIVE PARTICIPLE is rarely used. We remember the Roman gladiators, who said before their deadly fights to the emperor: "morituri te salutant" "the-going-to-die-ones greet thee" (The "dying-ones" would be wrong, for they were still unhurt). aUI can express this: "pIn yotvAm vrOUIv bu." ("Those who will die shortly greet you!") "-tvAm" is the ending.

PAST (see VERBS) ends in "-pA-". "He dies" = vu yov. "He died" = vu yopAv. He lived = "vu opAv" = "he has lived" ("vu bav opAm" is rare. Likewise "vu bapAv opAm" = "he had lived" is unnecessary.) "vu opApAv" = he had lived. (pA = pre-time, Vorzeit, past).

PAST PERFECT can be shortened from -pApA into -ppA if one can hold the two p apart: brOppAv = He had loved, instead of brOpApAv. Instead of brOpAtAv use brOptAv = He will have loved. Once one has made clear the past tense in a story one can tell on in the present after "pAg:" "pAg:" introduces what follows in the past; "pApAg:" introduces past-perfect. "pAg: fu tev, iOv, Ib tykwev" = I came, saw, & conquered. (In past: I come, see...)

PLURAL: is usually omitted or replaced by "many" = nEn, or "two or three" ("e gaf i") placed simply before the singular. Even in English one can say "There were many sheep" (instead of "sheeps") = nEn uygbos cEpAv fa. If needed one can express the Plural by the articles ending in "-n." The definite article "pI" becomes "pIn" (the . . . ones: pIn rUm = the good ones). The indefinite article "yI" (a) becomes "yIn" (some, several). " (Several) men came . . . = yIn u tepAv." "These = fEn, those = pfEn." The personal PRONOUNS insert an "-n-": "fnu" = we, "bnu = you", "nu" = they. "snE" = they (plural of sE = it). fnum, bnum, num = our, your, their. "Our friends have many books; we read them." = "pIn fnum bru bav nEn Ugs; fnu UiOv snE." "yIn fnum bru" = some (of) our friends. The noun itself stays always invariable; so does the verb.

"-n-" = collective plural: tok = tree, tonk = forest; ki = star, kin = star-host.

POSITION (see WORD-ORDER) is always: Subject-Verb-Object. The Modifier precedes the thing modified: adjective-noun, adverb-verb.

PRONOUN, PERSONAL: "I" = this-man = fu; you = bu, he = vu, she = yvu:
(active-man) (passive person)

"b-u" = (the) "together-man", the man with whom I stand together, and talk with, the "you" or more exact, the "thou".
"b-n-u" = "together-many-men", the many men with whom I talk: you-all.

fu ,	fnu;	bu,	bnu;	vu,	(v)nu ;	yvu,	(yv)nu;	sE,	snE
fum,	fnum;	bum,	bnum;	vum,	num;	yvum,	num;	sEm,	snEm.

"fu" (this-man) = "I", fnu ("this-many-men") = we
"fum" ("I-qualified") = my, mine; fnum = our.
"bu" = thou, you ; bnu = (together-many-men) = ye, you-all.
"bum" = thine, thy, your; "bnum" = your(s). pI bnum = yours.
"vu" = he, yvu = she, nu = they (vnu = they, these men), num = their.
"vum" = his, yvum = her, (yvnu = they, these women, is rare)
"sE" = it ("thing-matter"), snE = they, (these things)
sEm = its, snEm = their: "yIn Ugs Ib snEm gE" (books & their contents).
cf. "relative" : xu, xE"
fE = this, fEn = these, pfE = that (one), pfEn = those; yf = other,
can-yf = each other, pIn yf = the others, yIn yf = others.
(also "Lu" = she — as mother!

If one objects to calling an animal "it" (sE) or he, she (vu, yvu), one may use vo, yvo instead. Lu (Lo) = (round-mother) she (animal); Lum (Lom) = her (possessive adj.)

PRONUNCIATION: (see Part I, p.10.) as in Greek or Latin:

a, e, i, u, o as in "mama, get, it, put, of;" A, E, I, U, O as in: "Ah! Eh! polIce, trUe, Oh!" "y" as in boy or yonder or Greek "system" (ü).
Q as in "wQrd," (ö). Numbers aeiuoAEIUO are nasals."
"j, c" as in "jour, special". "g" as in get. "s" as in "so".
"x" as in "Mexico," (ch). See STRESS: 1) nasal, 2) LONG, 3) next-to-last.

Americans should take care to round their short "o" as the long "O" is rounded. "om" should not sound like "am". Americans still round the "o" in boy and zoology. Look into a mirror to form your lips as to whistle or kiss. For "a" the mouth has to be opened as wide as for father but shorter. "e" as in jet (propelled); "E" just so but longer; "i" as in lit, "I" as in shriek, "o" as in zoology or boy, "O" as in Oh; "u" as in push (as man is a pushy creature), "U" as in trUe, "Y" as in trUlYY if you keep your lips rounded all the way. yY sounds as between yiel-d and yUle since the y before a vowel is as in your. The consistently vocalic y is written "Y" and the consonant "y". It is clearer to write "Yt" but "yUg". A phonetic record is available if you have trouble with pronunciation.

QUESTIONS: No inversion! "What does he eat?" = He eats what? = "vu dov hE?" Use question word "hI?" if no other question word helps: "Does he eat bread?" = "He eats bread, eh?" = "vu dov nod, hI?"
"hu, hE; ha, hA; hU, hUd" = who, what; where, when; why, how?
"hnu" = what people, "hnE" = what things, "hUm" = what (kind of)
RELATIVE "x", pronounced snoringly, needs also no inversion!
"The man, whom I saw, comes" becomes "The man, I saw whom, comes" like: "The man -- I saw him -- comes." = u, fu iOpAv xu, tev.
"xu, xE; xa, xA; xU, xUd" = "who, what; where, when; why, how" as relatives.
(You can form plurals: the men, who = xnu; the things which = xnE; xUm = which
In SEX, male is active, "v-"; female is passive, "yv-":vu = he, yvu = she.
Distinguish animals with "vom" = male, "yvom" = female.

xYvu = xLu (Relative fem.)

Sentences, if introduced in English by an inverted object, have no introduction in aUI, because of the "subject-verb-object" sequence without inversion. Therefore it is clearer to introduce them with xQ, in "relation condition" or "where": "The man, whom I showed you, was my brother. pI u, xQ fu viOpAv xu, cpAv fum jytvu._" or The man, where I showed you him (who) was my brother. pI u, xQ fu viOpAv xu at bu...
SPELLING Since no capitals mark the beginning of a sentence, the period after it should be followed by a dash.- pI uga ugayv.-

STRESS (see ACCENT!) prefers 1) Nasals, 2) LONG, 3) "next-to-last".
(in verbs Past & Future, even a short stem-vowel keeps a melodic accent; i.e. in "e pAv" "e" has a higher tone.)
SUBJECT: always before verb, even in relative or question clause!

TENSE, TIME (see VERB!): Past = pA- ("pre-time, fore-time, previous time); Future = -tA- ("toward-time", "Zukunft", the time toward which we move".) "He will have gone = vu atApAv"; "he had gone" = "vu apApAv." If one is allergic to endings one might use "bav" = have, for the perfect tense, and "tEv" = become, for "will or shall": He will go = vu tEv av ("He becomes to go, comes into going.") instead of "vu atAv", which is shorter. vu apAv = he went.

VERBS: end in "-v" ("-do, activity") in the active, and in "-yv" (opposite-of active, passive) in the passive. "fu vev sE" = I move it. "sE veyv Ud fu" = It is (-being-) -moved by me. (Instead of "sE c vepAm Ud fu" . . . "vepAm" = driven, moved", Ud = by.) KAiN vyov ABeL = Cain kills Abel; KAiN vyopAv ABeL = Cain killed A. A. vyoyv Ud K. = A. is killed by C; A. vyopAyv Ud K. = A. was killed by C. Infinitive (may add "at" = "to": to love = (at) brOv) serves usually as Indicative in all verb forms, distinguished only by pronouns. fu cEv = I am, ("I be"), nu cEv = they are (they be). "cEv" (short "c") = (to) be. fu cEpAv = I was, bnu cEpAv = ye were. The IMPERATIVE ends in "-rv" ("good-do": it's "good", if you "do" this = you better do this , or: do this!). You can even form a passive imperative: "vu veryv Ud bum UI" (He ought-to-be-moved by your words), ending in "-ryv" (cf. vev, verv, veryv!), ("It would be "good", if he were moved by your words!")
If you like, you can even form an imperative in the Past:
"bu vepArv vu Ud bum UI" (You ought-to-have-moved him by your words")
"vu vepAryv Ud bum UI" (He ought-to-have-been-moved by your words).

CAUSATIVES begin with "v-" besides the regular verb-ending in "-v". "ev" = to move (oneself); "v-ev" = to make move, to drive (somebody or something else). "yov" = to die, "v-yov" = to kill.

Active PARTICIPLES end in "-vAm" (=do-time-quality). e.g. She is waiting = "yvu c trAvAm" -Am = time-quality, for she might be waiting quite a time. (Rare is the future participle in "-tvAm" = "going to . . e.g. She is going-to-wait = "yvu c trAtvAm.") You can even form an active past participle in "-pvAm." "Having-waited so long, she went away" = "trApvAm fUd anam, yvu apAv yta".
Clearer: "fUd nE-A trApvAm, yvu yta apAv." Thus "-vAm, -tvAm, -pvAm" are active participles of present, future, past.

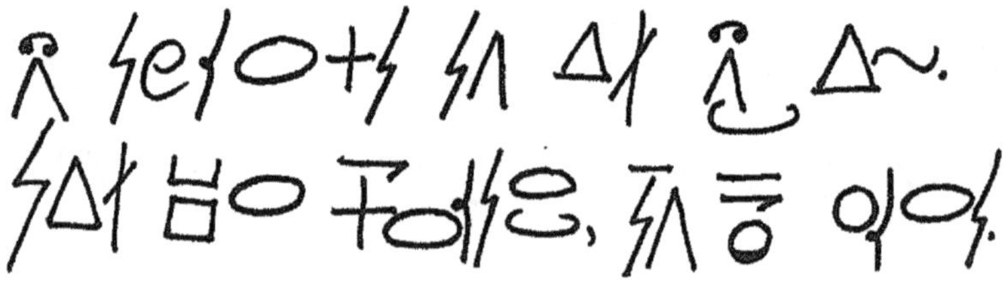

Passive PAST PARTICIPLE ends in "-pAm" e.g. opAm yopAm vyopAm, =
"lived, died, killed." from the verbs : ov, yov, vyov, =
to live, to die, to kill. Distinguish: They killed the cow;
They ate the killed cow. = "nu vyopAv pI bijEbos; nu dopAv pI
vyopAm bijEbos." vyopAv = killed = slew; vyopAm = killed = slain.
(English makes no difference between Past and Past Participle
in regular verbs; cf: move-drive, moved-drove, moved-driven.

"vev" = (make) move (da) vev , (da) vepAv, (da)vepAm.
"davev" = drive, ev = to move (oneself).

(Rarely used is the present passive participle: "-yvAm" = being -ed;
e.g. "Being-expected to sing, she blushed" = pOyvAm rIv, yvu tai pAv.)
Since "-yv" denies the active, it may be dropped: "pOAm" for "pOyvAm"!
PAST ends in -pA- , FUTURE in -tA- ("p" = pre, before, fore-;
"A" = time; "t-" = towards; the Past is before us, the future
is the time toward which we move). "pA cEpAv Ap fnu; fnu etAv at tA."
"(The) past was before us; we shall-move toward (the) future."
You can even form a Past-Perfect with "-pApA-", and a
Future-Perfect with "-tApA-": he had-gone = vu apApAv; will-have-gone =
"atApAv." When we shall-come there, he will-have-gone away. =
"xA fnu tetAv at-yfa, vu atApAv."

CONTRARY-TO-FACT, UNREALITY is expressed by -yEc, usually added
to the whole verb. ("y-E-c" = opposite (of) -material-existence,
not materially existing.) "-yEc" = would, should.
"Qg bu yc tepAv-yEc, yvu cEpAv-yEc yrOm." = "if you not come-would-
have, she have-been-would sad" = "If you had not come, she had been sad."

(If one is allergic to verb inflections, one might use the
English way with "bav" = have; "tEv" = shall, will (for the future),
and "cEv" = is, are . . . for forming perfect, future, and passive:
"He will say, what he has seen" would be: "vu tEv UIv, vu bav
iOpAm xE." instead of the shorter: "vu UItAv, vu iOpAv xE.")

become

give	ACTIVE Infinitive (=Indic.)	Participle	Imperative	PASSIVE Infinitive (=Indic.)	Participle	Imperative
PRESENT	"sev"	"sevAm"	"serv!"	seyv	se(yv)Am	seryv!
PAST	"sepAv"	sepvAm	sepArv	sepAyv	"sepAm"	sepAryv!
FUTURE	"setAv"	setvAm	setArv	setAyv	setAm	setAryv!
Past Perf.	sepApAv	sepApvAm	sepApArv	sepApAyv	sepApAm	sepApAryv!
Fut. Perf.	setApAv	setApvAm	setApArv	setApAyv	setApAm	setApAryv!

(Only the "forms" in quotes need be learnt. The English language is too much tied to the present to be able to repre-
sent the others.)

give !

AUXILIARY VERBS: "is = be = are = cEv (or: c')"; was = pAc; will-be = tAc. But there are many meanings of "be = are". God is = KU cUv (spiritual being). "cEv" = material exist, to exist in matter; "oc" = by nature, in life "be": nio oc iim = grass is (by nature) green; kvad vQc iim = (the) table is (made conditionally) green. "You are an ass (if you do this). Here "are" = (z)Qc = you are (partly) conditionally an ass, (you are not a whole ass—rather the inverse): "bu zQc Yr-ukbos." aUI is polite & transparent in truth: "Yr = bad". Oc = by emotion, fOc = (in) my emotion, feeling is ... "bu fOc riOm" (you are—in my feeling—beautiful). cErv = be! Imperatives contain "r"=good, (as invectives have "-Yr-"=bad). Transparent truth in invectives and commands serves justice & peace. Rather than demagogic hypnotic slogans, only the good can be commanded & the bad — condemned. "wYv" = must; wYvtAv = he will must, will be obliged; wYvpAv = (he) was obliged.

ALL VERBS: pAg: introduces past, tAg: starts future, even though verbforms are in present. fAg: re-enters the present. See -pA- = past, -Yv = passive, Command, Gerund. Any word by adding -v, -ev, -Ev, (-Ov, -Uv) becomes a simple, moving, material, (feeling, spiritual) verb.

In Group Meditation create

WORD FORMATION n-= big, yn-= small, nyn-= many small, as in sand, r- = good, yr- = bad, t- = toward = similar to, k- = above, superior, can be prefixed. (see HEALING above)

"U-" prefixed makes it spiritual, "w-" powerful: wU-brO = powerful-spiritual love.

Y The bar should be drawn over all it denies and a hyphen or even parenthesis could indicate this: blind = y-iOm, y-(iO)m = un-see-ing, rather than yi-Om, which would mean darkness-sensing. =-y-Ec-= "contrary to fact." ev-yEc he would move (perhaps). -y-, -yv, -yr: even verb endings should remain clear and meaningful. E.g. in the few verbs that end in -yv because they express a passive receiving, yv should remain together. Imperative receive! = sryv = you ought to receive, it is good to receive. It is safer to retain the Yv in (fu) syvpAv, syvtAv = (I) received, will receive; had been received = syppAyv; is being received = syYv, where the 'yY' sounds between 'yield' and 'you': (yU). Of course this double passive is almost active: sev. Grace is being received = mercy gives, riOma syYv = kUbrO sev. sYvpAm = P.P. received, sYvpvAm = having received.

WORD-FORMATION. "y-" forms opposites and best precedes what it opposes. (In English, too, it is shorter to say "an Anti-Alcoholic" than to form: "an Alcohol-Opponent.")
"ov" = to live, or "fu ov" = I live; "y-ov" = "yov" = (to) die.

In aUI, nouns are basic. Verbs add "-v", adjectives "-m." In English, however, nouns are often derived from verbs or adjectives. "e" = movement, "ev" = (to) move, which, in English, is the short basic word. In a vocabulary,
"e(v)" = move/ment . . . means: "e" = movement, ev = (to) move.
"e(m)" = mov(abl)e . . . means: "e" = (a) move, em = movable.
"ruve(m) = busi/ness: means: "ruvem" = busy, ruve = business.

In aUI, one can also derive nouns, by adding "-U" or "-s" (or "-z" or "-O" etc) to verbs or adjectives. ("-U" means here "concept", for abstracta in "-ness, -ty, -hood & c"; "-s" means "-thing" for independent concrete objects. "evU" would mean "motion" (move-act), -vU = act, and corresponds to -ion. "evu" would mean a "mov-er" (move-man). "-z" is the ending of parts, which lose their function, if separated. "iOz" = eye, which can not see unless attached to body.

WORD-ORDER is always : "SUBJECT--VERB--OBJECT--INDIRECT OBJECT.

The MODIFIER precedes the MODIFIED: Adjectives before their nouns, adverbs (including negations) before their verbs. This holds true even for questions and relative clauses: "The good teacher quickly gives just rewards to the hard-working student, whom he (does) not ignore." "pI rUm vetgUvu nem sev yIn jwUrm jiuts at pI nE-rUwevAm etgUvu, vu yc ygUv xu."
("..., he not ignores whom." = "..., he not ignores him.)
'cf. gU = "in-mind", what one has in-mind is knowledge;
"etgUv" = move-toward-knowledge = study; etgUvu = study-man, student;
"vetgUv" = make-study = teach; vetgUvu = teach-man, teacher.)
The relative clause must be inserted right after the word it modifies, and must contain a relative particle (with "x-").

All these grammar forms follow automatically from the basic meaning of each letter-sound category of aUI. If e.g. "-tA" functions within a verb as "ending of the future", "t" still means "toward", and "A" still means "time," thus the whole ending means "toward-time", the time toward which we move, the future. Therefore aUI is a language without formal grammar.

Part IV.

TRANSLATION IN A SIMPLIFIED LANGUAGE.

With the Basic Compounds of Part II, and the Grammar of Part III, we could already express many thoughts by simply making up new compositions of words as we go along. This is the freedom of word-formation in aUI. As long as a word somehow consists of the basic categories, it will always convey a meaning at least similar to what the speaker had in mind. E.g. we learnt in Part II that "gU = knowledge" and "gUw = science." Now if we want to express "physics" we could call it "e-gUw" = "movement-science," for all physics is ultimately concerned with moving things or particles. But we could also be satisfied with "e-gU", "movement-knowledge." The difference might be like the one between "physical science" and "physics" as simple text book knowledge. "Science" would imply the power "w", of creative research.

Thus in expressing thoughts in aUI, everyone could use his own approach, and nothing would be "wrong" as long as the other fellow somehow understands one. There could be never mistakes as disastrous (or as funny) as those created by our homonyns, e.g. the strange confusion between the words "write", and "right", again in the meanings of "stronger side of most bodies" and "justice." Also "left" means both "weaker side of most limbs" and "remaining." Thus we could not translate into aUI the pun: "An atomic war would not show who is right, but who is left."

In the meantime we can try to translate difficult ideas into basic words, as if we were in a primitive tribe or among children. E.g. if we had to explain to primitive children the "Lord's Prayer" without the 1500 words added in the final Parts VII A and VII B, using as far as possible "basic compounds," we might say: +

"Our father, who art in heaven; hallowed be thy name" means approximately: "Our parent, who thou art in heaven, " = "fnum ytu, bu, xu cEv ag kna;" Now how could we explain or replace a simple word like "name?" We might say: "A name is the word by which a person is known" ("UI, u cEv gUpAm Ud xE" cEv f U I),

---

+ For a literal translation of the Lord's Prayer see Part VI, p 155)

"fUI cEv UI, bu gUyv Ud xE" ("Name is word, thou art-known by which.") "f-UI" = name, "this-word", for a name is the word we use instead of pointing at a man and saying "this is it."

But how can we replace "hallowed?" Even if we see no way of expressing one word, we could transform the whole idea into: "Be above us with thy spirit!" in order to give the primitive child some idea of what we want to say: "cErv ak fnu Ud bum U" or: "cErv eb fnu can A" (Be with us all time). All this in the same spirit, but rather far from "hallowed." "kwu" = master, "above-power-man", the man in power above me. "ykwu" = below-power-man, the man under (his) power, (his) servant. "ykwuv" = to serve. "bum fUI ykwuryv ag U" (Thy name be-served in spirit) might come nearer to "hallowed be thy name."

"Thy kingdom come, Thy will be done, on earth as it is in heaven." "pI A Ub bum wU terv at fnu!" ("tev" = come). "The time of your power come to us!" Even if you do not know "terv", you might say "erv" = move. "Your power move toward us, or be with us" = "bum wU erv at fnu, gaf cErv eb fnu!" "can u cErv ag bum wU" = "All men be in your power!" "bum twU Eryv!" = Thy will be-done. Even here we could replace: What you say shall-be-done = "Eryv, bu UIv xE!" (Be-done, you say what!) or: "bum U ykwuryv!" (Thy spirit shall-be-served). Or: "fE, bu Uv, xE c' rUm , cErv!" ("This, thou thinkest which is good, shall-be!" = This which you think (that) it is good, shall be!) or: "can, bu brOv xE, Eryv!" (All you love (which) , shall-be-done) . . . "ag bEn (fUd) jOm ag kna" ("In earth (thus) like in heaven. (kab = on).

"bu serv fnum iAm nod at fnu!" ("Thou give our daily bread to us"). Even without "bread" or "give" or "daily", you can still put the idea across: We ought-to-have all time food through you! "fnu barv can A od Ud bu", or: "move all days our food to us!" "erv (rUt = for) can iA fnum od at fnu! " "fE iA" = this day.

"Forgive us our trespasses" means almost "(Do) not think of our bad acts" = "(bu) yc Urv Ub fnum rym vU" or more abstract "evil" = yrUm vU. "Forgive" means also: "Do not do bad things to us for the bad things which we did" i.e. "bu yc Erv rym Es at fnu rUt pIn rym Es , fnu EpAv xE." We might add: "(Do) not give us punishment because (of) our bad deeds" "(bu) yc serv jyrt at fnu, yUt (Ub) fnum rym vU!" Instead of saying: "Love us still inspite of our bad

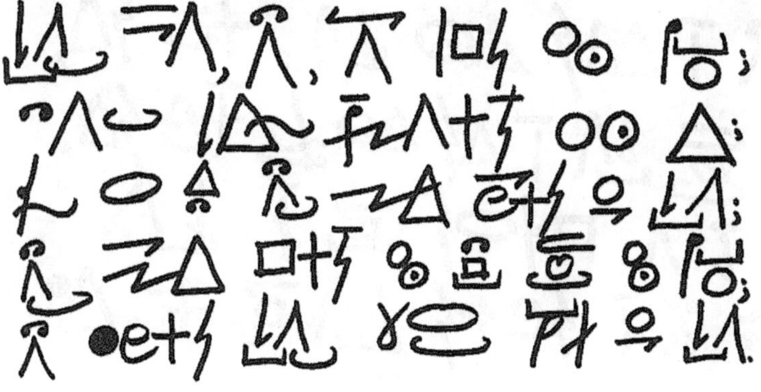

deeds "means" We did bad deeds, but you love us (still)" i.e. "fnu EpAv rym vU, yUg bu brOrv fnu (tfA)!"

"Forgive us our trespasses, as we forgive those, who trespassed against us" might be explained as: "(Thou) think not about our bad acts, as we think not about the bad deeds which other men did against us!" = "(bu) yc Urv Ul fnum rym vU, jOm fnu yc Uv Ul pIn rym vU, yf u EpAv xEn yd fnu!"

"Ib bu yc verv fnu tag rym Us!" ("And thou not move (drive) us into bad thought(s)") means : "And lead us not into temptation" or: "Make us not will bad acts, let us not will bad deeds!" = "(bu) yc vErv fnu (at) twUv rym vU, (bu) yc dyrv fnu twUv yrUm vU!" or: "(bu) yc sarv fnu tag Q, xa fnu veyv tag yrUm vU" = "(Do) not put us into conditions, where we are-moved into evil acts!" , or "Make that our mind (do) not move to those evil thoughts!" = "(bu) vErv, Uf fnum U yc ev at pfEn yrUm Us!"

NB. Now find yourself such ways of paraphrasing the petitions of the Lord's Prayer, including the last "But deliver us from evil!" Do not read on , but review such "translations" in your mind. "yUg, verv fnu tyg, ayt yt yrU" means: "But, move us out, away from evil!" which would be clear enough. Or, since "freedom = fUwe = self-power-move" (A man is free, if he has the "power" to "move" where he him-"self" wants), and "fUwev" = "to free", to deliver, we can say: "fUwerv fnu yt yrU!" = "Free us from evil."

How can we express the praise: "For thine is the kingdom and the power and the glory for ever and ever. Amen!" "yUt kU-una, wU, nam fUI, cEv bum - - rUt can A Ib can A. fUd sE cErv!" = Because (the) God-realm, the power, the great name (glory) are thine – for all time and all time. So it be! (So be it!). If you can not remember these words, say simply: "All people think and know and say that thou art great" = "can u Uv Ib gUv Ib UIv , Uf bu cEv nam!" or: (they) shall or ought to think, know, and say . . . = "can u Urv, gUrv, Ib UIrv, . . . " We might even translate "glory" with: "can ki, can a, can cU, UIv Ud wom uI: bum fUI cEv nam!" (All stars, all space, all existence, speak with strong voice: Thy name is great!)

In this way you can express the greatest thoughts with the simplest words.

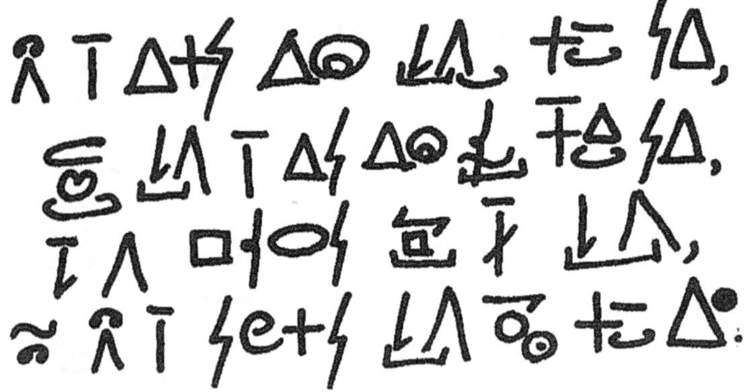

Now try to understand how simple sentences are expressed with the vocabulary of Part V. Look up the aUI words in Part VII A.

ynvu Ib ki. (The boy and the Star).

ynvu yovAm ykapAv ag yrogga. sE cpAv yrIm yrogga, yUt ag sE fEm nu cpAv, xnu cpAv yrom ag U. ynvu sapApAyv tag yrogga, yUt vu sUIpAv ag yI y-iU-wam nUI; Ib xA vu sUIpAv fUd, Uf a wapAv iUv vu, vu OipAv at UIv, Uf vu cpApAv kab yf ki. - yu EjUrOpAv vu; jUf yc, xA vu UianapAv kab zvE Ub enaE yfam viOvs, UIvAm: "fEn cEv pIn UIz Ub pI nUI Ub a."

yUg pfa cEv a fAom trogUwu, xu tiOv at ynvu, Ib iUv vu, Ib retgUv vum nUI, Ib sUIv eb vu Ul sE, Ib vu Utev, Uf pfa cEv nykam nU ag pfE, ynvu UIv xE; Ib pfa cEv nykam rU·nU ag fE nUI.

ag-ypAz pI fAom trogUwu av at kun Ub yrogga Ib UIv: "fE ynvu yc Uyrom. vum nUI bav ytUw. fE, vu UIv xE, bav ytUw."

yUg kun Ub yrogga Uv, Uf fAom trogUwu vufU tykepAv tag jam yr-viOsU; Ib fUd, Uf fAom trogUwu yc tEv-yEc knE yrkOm, vUtsev at dEv wei-bydwO kab ynvu. eb tu fE yc Ev rUm.

ynvu ydwUv wei-bydwO Uj nE Uj vu wav, yUt vu tyrOv, Uf vu ytgUv-yEc Ud sE "fE, fu retgUpAv xE kab yf ki." ag vum byd vu yopAv. yUg Ud vum yovAm UI vu tfA UIv at fAom trogUwu: "bu EjUrOv tag fu: bu UIrv at nu Ul aUI!"

Translation. (The boy and the Star).

(A) boy lay dying in(a) hospital. It was a noisy hospital, for in it were people, who were sick in(the) mind. (The) boy had-been-put into the hospital, because he talked in an unintelligible (un-understand-able) language; and when he talked so, that one could understand him, he seemed to say, that he had-been on another star. – Nobody believed him; even not, when he drew on a piece of paper strange signs, saying: "These are the letters of the Language of Space."

But there is a young Doctor (Physician), who looks at the boy, and understands him, and learns his language, and talks with him about it, and he finds, that there is a deep wisdom in what (that, which) the boy says (which); and there is (a) deep wisdom in this language.

Finally (In-(the)-end the young doctor goes to the director (manager) of the hospital and says: "This boy (is) not crazy (mind-sick). His language makes sense (has reason). What he says, makes sense." (Literally: "That, he says which, has reason.")

But the director of the hospital thinks that the young doctor himself has fallen into the same delusion (ill-imagination) and so that the young doctor would not become too proud, decides to use electroshock on the boy. With children this does not do (much) good.

The boy resists the electro-shock as much as he can, because he fears that he would-forget through it "what I had learnt on the other star." In his struggle he died. But with his dying words he still said to the young doctor: "You believe in me: you tell them about

The Language of Space!"

(English punctuation and phrasing adapted to aUI.

Part V: ENCYCLOPEDIA.

Systematic Thesaurus of Necessary Human Concepts, derived from the 30 Basic Categories of aUI, arranged alphabetically. (Study first Parts I, II, III). (The less important words, which have only to be recognized from aUI into English, but not used actively, are put into brackets or parentheses).

NB. Consider that ultimately these are only examples of the millions of possibilities of creating aUI words. In English, you can call a football also pig-skin or a policeman – copper or flatfoot, according to how you feel about him. In aUI, the attitude or the approach coins the word. E.G. "iron" has the popular aUI name of "wrE" (w-rE = "power" - metal; iron is the metal used for power and strength). But scientifically, we call elements "Ez" (matter-part) by their atomic order number. Iron, Fe(rrum) has the number 26; therefore iron's scientific name is "element 26" or "Ez-26" pronounced "Ez-eA".

Likewise, "hot" is a "fire-quality"; iE = fire, iEm = hot. But, in scientific language one could call it "infra-red", "yk-aim."

You can form many variations of synonyms; e.g. "Ed = medium" could be used for "tool vEd" (v-Ed = active-medium, means by which) or "dEs" = instrument. In English, too, you could call a dentist's drill an instrument, or a means by which he works, or his tool. In aUI you can often use the short general name – like "liquid", – for the special liquid, e.g. water. Instead of saying "He needs much water ("jEn") you could say "He needs much liquid (jE)". Generally, one uses in aUI the shortest expression which is still enough clear. In Highschool we learn "egU", physics, not always "egUw" = "physical science." Besides adding one or two letters for clarification, you can also sometimes transpose letters, e.g. for "od" = food, you can say "do" = victuals, eats, grub. "o-d" means literally "life-means", the "means" by which we "live". "d-o" would mean "medium-life, intermediate-life", as for a stork a frog is a living-being of interest only insofar as it provides a means-by-which he can live. Thus "do" should be used for "food" or "meat", like olives or oysters, which were alive or are alive while we eat them, but not for synthetic jellies. Thus in aUI, you can play with the letters, exchange them and build new words to suit your mood.

Letter "a"

"a" = space; it implies: place, locality, position, distance.
(see: "ad" under "d"; "at" under "t" etc)

"as" = place ("space-thing", "a-s"), a place is a thing in space, as far as space can become a thing and concrete.

"ayn" = point ("a-y-n" = "space – not – quantity"); a point is the smallest space, is space without extension, it has "no-quantity" is just a tiny "dot" in space.

"ayn c´a yb na" ("a point is space without dimension")

"ha c´bu? fu yc iOv bu. bu c´yp fE io, hI?"

"bu c´ha?" ""ab fE ayn ag fE as."" "fu yc iOv bu. fu yc gUv, xa bu c´." ""bu yc wav iOv fu ag yi."" "bu c´yp fE io, hI?" ""bu c´pnEk riOm ag yi Ib yp nam io!""

("Where are you?" ""At this point in this place."" "I (do) not see you. I (do) not know, where you are." ""You can not see me in (the) darkness."" "You are behind this plant, eh?" ""You are most beautiful in (the) darkness and behind a big plant!"")

"am" = spatial ("space-like", space-adjective, space-quality).

av = go ("a-v" = "space-activity," "space-do": as far as one can make space, or do (something with) space, one does this activity by any directed progress, covering distance.
"fu av ad a at fE as" ≡ I go through space to this place.
"fE as cEv am yI ayn ag a" = This place is only a dot in space.

"am e wav cEv yb wU" = Spatial movement can be without power.

vav = send ("v-av" = make-go; send him home = make him go home = "varv" vu at vum uga = "vErv-av" vu at fuga = home = his house. (fuga = fum uga, home = my house; or: your house, bum-uga etc)

NB. (fuga) = as, xa fnu ov, gaf pI as, xa fnu tepAv at o; (home) = the place, where we live, or the place where we came to life. This is an aUI definition into basic compounds. Therefore (fuga) is not an irreplaceable word; it can be replaced by simpler words, and is therefore put in (parenthesis).

(vas) = parcel (va-s = send-thing, a transported thing) Again (vas) is a replaceable word: "(vas) cEv ym Es vapAm yt yf as" (Parcel) is any thing sent from (an) other place. "fu tyvpAv ym Es, vapAm yt fum uga (= yt fuga) yt fum ytu" = fu tyvpAv vas yt-fuga = I got a parcel from home (from my parents). "vapAm yt fum uga" = sent from my house.
(vava) = post-office. "vav-a" = send-space, send-place.
(vava) = uga, at xE nEn Es vayv can iA, Ib yt xE snE vayv at can u, xnu syv snE = (post-office) = house (or: place = "as"), to which many things are-sent all days, and from which they are-sent toward the the people, who (plural) receive them.

(ogav) = walk (og = body, av = go, og-av = body-go, go there bodily)
(ogav = av yb ged, av Ud og, av Ud ogz Ub og, av Ud oged ≐ "walk = go without vehicle, go by-means-of body, go by organs of body, go by (means-of) legs: "fnu wyv ogav; fnu yc bav ged" = we must walk ; we have no(t) vehicle = car.

(nav) = run ("n-a-v" = "much-space-make", n-av = much-go).
(nav) = nem av, nem ev ad a = fast go = (to) fast move through space. "fu nav at vava, yUt fu wyv nem vav vas yt vava at ytu"
"I run to (the) post-office, because I must quickly send (a) parcel from the post-office to (my) parents (in another place = ag yf as).
"fu yc tev ag rUm A. fu c nEm yrOm . hU vava yc vem can A, hI?"
(I (do) not come in good time. I am very sad. Why (is) (the) post-office not active all time, eh?)

bam = near (b-a-m = together-space-quality: if two trees are near, they are "together" in "space".)

"Qg 2 tok cEv bam, snE cEv tab ag a."

(bas = neighborhood; b-as = together-place. bas = can as, xnE c´bam ab fum uga, bam fuga) "fu twUv rIv Ib riOev , yUg fu yc gUv, fum bas UItAv hE at fE" (I will (want to) sing and dance, but I (do) not know, what my neighborhood will say to this (= "my neighborhood will say what to this.")

ybam = far (y-bam = "un-near"). "a-u c´ bam, hI? yr! a-u c´ybam." (u-io-ba = garden: "man-plant-nearspace", a plant-place near a man's home.)" uioba c´as Ub io bam u, vEpAm Ud u." "(A) garden is (a) place of plants near man, made by man." Instead of saying: Your garden is beautiful, you could say: your plants are living beautifully around your house = ag as Ub UIv: bum uioba cEv riOm, bu wav-yEc UIv: pIn bum io cEv riOm ovAm.
"fu UIv at fum bus (neighbor): 'terv at fum uioba. pfa c pIn pnEk riOm io ag can bas.'" (I say to my neighbor: 'Come to my garden. There are the most beautiful plants in all neighborhood'.)

da = way

da.

("d-a" = "through-space": a way is a line through space
(dav) = to travel, d-av = through-go, or da-v = way-make, to make one's way
(dav cEv av ad anam da = to travel is to go through a long way.)
(davev) = to drive: to move "vev" on a way "da" = vev kab da = da-vev.
(ade(v) = (to) journey = "space-through-move" = to (make) move through space
(eda) = road, move-way = e-da; a way we move on.
(ueda) = street, "man-road" = u-eda = man-move-way

ueda c da ge nEn uga. nEn u ogav Ib davev ag ueda Ub nam nuba.
(A) street is a way between many houses. Many men (people) walk and drive in the street(s) of (a) big city. fu dav ek fE da ("I travel over this way") "pI dav cEv ybam av" (The traveling is far going).
"vu Ev ade ek fE eda" He does (makes) a journey over this road.
(How would you express "sentimental journey"? Perhaps: "journey with feelings of the past and of home" = "ade eb yIn O Ub pA Ib Ub fuga."
"fE daiu av eb fu" (This guide goes with me).
(daiu) = guide = way-light-man = a "man" who carries the "light" before me on my "way." "daiu c u, xu av ap fu Ib viOv da at fu"

a : da, ga.

(A guide is a man who goes before me and shows the way (to) me).
"fum daiu, hUd ybam cEv fnum da? fE c anam ade (long journey).
fu c'yrom (sick) . fu yc wav iOv at ha fnu av." - daiu tIv: "fu yc gUv. fa da c ydam, yUg sE Oiv ybam. sE wav cEv , Uf ypAz Ub fE ade cEtAv fnum yo." Try first to translate it yourself, then look it up:

(My guide, how far is our way? This is a long journey. I am sick. I can not see to where (whereto, whither is also "hat") we go." The guide says: "I (do) not know. Here the way is narrow, but it seems far. It can be (possibly = perhaps = twam), that the end of this journey will-be our death.") "rOm ade rUt bu!" (Pleasant journey for you).

dam = wide ("through-space-quality": if there is a "wide" space between, my arrow has to travel long "through space.")
ydam = narrow (y-dam = un-wide, opposite of wide)." cEpAv = pAe
"eda cEpAv yim Ib ydam. ybru tepAv Ib viOpAv vum wyd at fnu. vu tIpAv: 'bnu yc tetAv om yt fa.' (The road was dark and narrow. The enemy came and showed his weapon to us. He said: 'You will not come alive from here). "fnu wav nav. fnu narv!" (We can run. (Let) us run!)
damU = width (wide-concept, wide-ness). "damU c'o an." (width is 5 yeards). How wide is this street? Could your Canary-bird fly (kEdev) "through space" from one side to the other? (fE ueda cEv hUd dam? bum ei-kEos wav-yEc kEdev "ad a" yt a az at pI yf, hI?) The width of this street is only ten meters (yards, units). "damU Ub fE ueda cEv am O an."

ga = inner space.

ga = room ("inside-space = g-a"): a room is a "space inside" e.g. a house. (kU-ga) = church (k-U-ga = high-spirit-room, God-room): In a church should be "room" for the "spirit" up-high (k = above), for God.
(kUga c uga Ub kU; kUga c as, xa fnu Ov a eb, Ib yk, pI kam U, xu cEv rUm, riOm Ib EjUm; kU cEv pI can-rUm , pnEk kam U, xu vEpAv can cU)
(The church is the house of God; The church is the place, where we feel one with, and under, the High Spirit, who is good, beautiful and true; God is the all-good, most high spirit, who made all existence).
"fa, ag fE kUga c ga rUt KU" Here in this church is room for God.
(nArs-ga(v)) = (to) store-(room): "n-A-rs-ga" = "long-time-goods-room"

goods = good-things = rs. In a store-room goods can keep for much-time(n-A).
"ag nArs-ga nEn rUm Es Ib od cEv bApAm Ib vApAm rUt nE A" = In a store-(room) many good things and food are kept and preserved for much time.

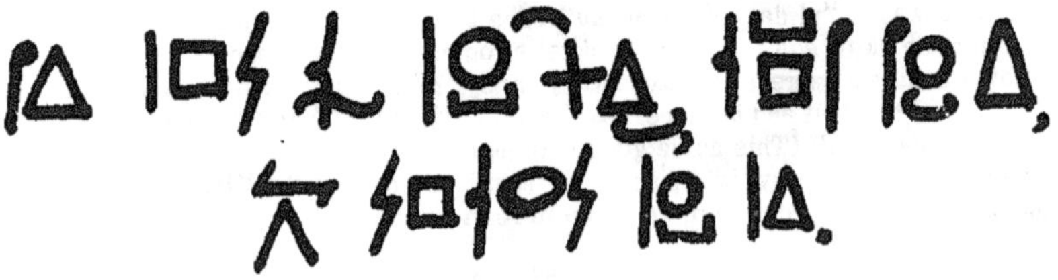

(yr-og-ga) = hospital = bad-body-inside-space = yr-o-ga = bad-life-room, yro = sick, yro-ga = sick-room; y-r = no-good; in a hospital we have no-good life. "yroga c uga, xa u bav yro gaf xa u yov. yIn u Uv, Uf nu wav tyv ro gaf tEv rom ag yroga." (A hospital is a house, where people have sickness or where people die. Some people think that they can get health or become healthy in a hospital. fE c twam = This is possible.
(niOb-ga) = museum = n-iO-,b–ga = much-see-together–room: In a "museum" we "see" lots of things "together." fu iOpAv ag niObga riOm og Ub yvus vEpAm ag wE, Ib bIb jiOvs Ub jEn Ib bEk, Ib yfA yI Es ag mi, xE cEpAv nEm ydim. fu yc wav UIv, hE sE cEpAv. sE cEpAv ycEmUm. (I saw in a museum beautiful bodies of women made in stone, and also pictures of the sea and mountains, and then a thing in color which was very unclear. I can not say what it was. It was abstract (unreal).)
(nuvs-ga) = factory, "plant" = many-men-make-things-room: in a factory, many men make (produce) things. "ag nuvsga, nEn u vEv nEn Es rUt fnu: nEn A Ud fem es. nEn es vEv fUd nEn Es, Uf fnu yc wav dEv can." (In a factory, many men make many things for us: many times by-means-of automatic machines. Many machines make so many things, that we can not use all."
(tebru-ga) = hotel = guest-house = tebru-uga. te-bru = toward-move-- friend, te = come, bru = friend, come-friend = guest = tebru. A friend who comes inside, is a guest. "come-friend-inside-place = tebru-g-a"
uga = house "man-inside-space, the place where a man lives inside."
(ugav(s) = build(ing), house-make = to build; a built thing = a building.)
tugai = window = t-uga-i, toward-house-light: a window lets "light" in "to the "house"
kugaz = roof = k-uga-z = above-house-part
(ugayk = floor, uga-yk = house-under)
(ugayks = mat, floor-thing)
ugta = door (man-into-space: the space through which a man comes into (the house)
(nugta) = gate ("big door")
(yr-uga = prison, yr-u-ga = bad-man-room
yr-uga = bad-house, (yr-Uga = mad-house)
(bad-mind-place, insane-asylum, state-hospital)
"pIn tugai Ub yruga cEv ynam" The windows of a prison are small. "u, xu cEv ag yruga, yc bav wU at av tyg yt tugai. vu yc wav ev yg ugta." (The man who is in prison, not has power to go out from the window. He can not move outside the door, = outdoors.)

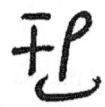

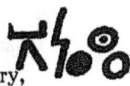

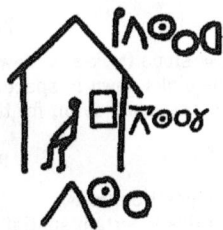

a : ga, ka

"au hIv: hU c fUd nEn u ag yruga, ag yrUga, ag yroga? nu can cEv yrUm, Uyrom, yrom? hI ? kab yf ki fnu yc bav can fE. hU fUd nEn u kab bEn cEv yrUm ? fEn u brOv yrU, hI ? yt hE can fEn yrom u Ib Uyrom u tev? Qg bnu cEv yvrOm at bnum bru, fu iUv , Uf can tEv yrom Ib Uyrom."

(The space-man asks: Why are so many men in prisons, in insane-asylums, in hospitals? Are they all evil, insane, sick? eh? On other stars we (do) not have all this. Why (are) so many men on earth (are) evil? (Do) these men love evil, (eh?). From what all these sick men and insane men come? If you are unkind to your friends, I understand, that all become sick and insane.)

(State-hospital)
Insane-asylum

yrUga

hospital

yroga

(NB. Although "-ga" means "room, space-inside" , in English we use often the word "place" in the same meaning. The word "as", however, is not a place-inside, but signifies "location.")

ka:

tyka = slope (t-yk-a = toward-below-space, tyk = down, tyk-a = down-space, a slope sinks down in space.) uga tepAv tyk, yUt uga ugapAyv kab tyka. (The house came down, for the house was-built on a slope)

ma:

mag = position (m-a-g = "qualified-space-inside" which one is placed; one attains a certain spatial quality by the position, in which one is placed: see "m" for "ma = form."

"ag hEm mag bu brOv at cEv? bu brOv at kav, ykav, gaf Yktav , hI?" (In which position (do) you like to be? (Do) you like to stand, lie or sit?)

na:

na = dimension ("quantity-space, numbered-space, measured-space": we count space in first, second, third, and even "fourth dimension". a̱na = length, a̱nam = long ("one" = a̱, "dimension" = na: a̱-na; what has only one dimension, has only length, the first dimension of the 3-dimensional space. e̱na = flatness, plane; i̱nam = 3-dimensional (ya̱na(m) = short/ness: y-a̱nam = un-long = short, ya̱na = shortness.) (v-a̱na-(v) = stretch = make-long-(verb), lengthen. "nu va̱napAv vum kogz" (They stretched his neck)

a : na

(bana = string = b-ana = together-length: string is a length, a line, used to tie things "together."

anas = line = ana-s = long-thing+)

(wana = cord, rope = "power-length", a strong, long extension, "wom anas")

wanas = rod = strong-long-thing; somehow a rod, which is rigid, seems more of a "thing" than a cord, which seems of indefinite extension.

wanab = band ("power-length-together" = w-ana-b: a strong band binds "together") " fE wanab wom bwanav fnu tab" (This band strongly ties. . .)

(bwana(v) = (to) tie, bind = together-strong-line-(do). "bo bwanav fnu tab rUt zyn o, gaf rUt ybo" (Marriage binds us together for the whole life, or for the divorce. b-o = together-life, wedded life)

(ywanbs = thread = y-w-an-b-s = not-strong-long-together-thing, weak-band)

nanab = canvas (n-ana-b = "many-lines-together" woven, makes canvas)

nanabev = to weave "many-strings-together-move" = to combine strings.

(eana = track = move-line = the line on which things move(d); the tracks of an animal, "eana Ub os," is the way, on which it went so that one still can see its feet in the earth: "c′da, kab xE sE apAv, fUd Uf a tfA wav iOv sEm ykbo ag bEn." (jiOvs = picture, bnUiOvs = print

(sana = row (thing-line, a line in which things are arranged)

rE-ana = wire (metal-line, rE = metal), (rE-n-ana = cable = metal-many-lines)

ana-rE = rail: "length (of) metal", one-dimensional-metal (in one line)

anEs = stick = an-E-s = long-matter-thing

+) True, similar words like "bana, wana, anas" might be confused. But if one interchanges "string, cord, line", it makes less difference than if in English the ear confuses e.g. the similar-sounding words "line, lime, lying". In aUI, if words sound similar, they also mean similar things.

"vus cEpAv kam, kam ag yruga. u yc wapAv tev tyg. vum ga cEpAv ynam Ib yt vum ga at bEn cEpAv ybam, ybam tyk. u cEpAv ag yruga a̲nam A.

pfE vus bapAv rUm yvus, xu brOpAv vu. vum yvus bapAv a̲m brO, Ib ywom ywa̲nbs Ib ba̲na Ib wom wa̲na. yvu iOpAv nam wi̲zos, Ib yvu UpAv, Ib yvu brOpAv Ib yvu bapAv Us:

yvu bwa̲nav ywom ywa̲nbs al nam wi̲zos, Ib davev wi̲zos tak, tak at kam tugai, xa yvum bru cEv. wi̲zos nav tak. ab tugai, vus fev wi̲zos Ib bav ywa̲nbs.

yvu bwa̲nav at ywa̲nbs ba̲na. Ud ywa̲nbs vu vev ba̲na tak at vufU. Ud ba̲na vu fev wa̲na. Ib Ud wa̲na, vu tev tyk, tyk, at vum yvu-bru. nu brOpAv a̲-yf rUt canA."

(pfE = that (man), ywom = weak, wi̲zos = power(ful) insect = beetle, vufU = himself, fev = (to) take, bru = friend, yvu-bru = she-friend, girl, a̲-yf = one-another

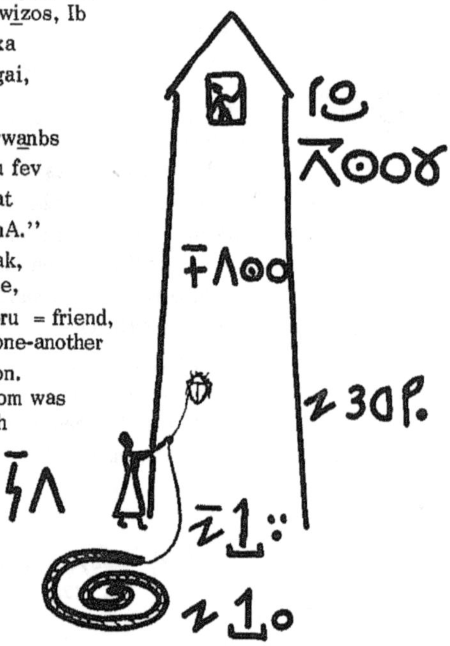

"A man was high, high-up in a prison. The man could not come out. His room was small, and from his room to the earth was far, far down. The man was in the prison long time.

That man had a good woman, who loved him. His woman had only love, and a weak thread, and a string, and a strong rope. She saw a big beetle, and she thought, and she loved and she had an idea:

She ties the weak thread around the big beetle, and drives the beetle up, up toward the high window, where her friend is. The beetle runs up. At the window, the man takes the beetle and has the thread.

She ties to the thread the string. By-means-of the thread, he moves (pulls) the string up to himself. By-means-of the string he takes the rope. And by the rope, he comes down, down to his lady-friend. They loved one-another for all-time. (for-ever)."

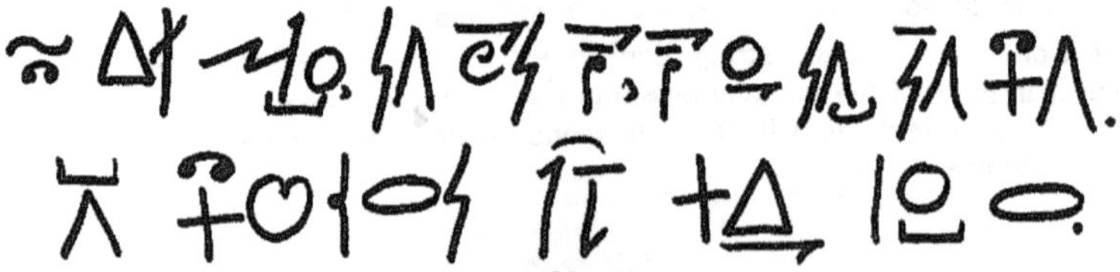

a : na

ge-b-ana = angle = between-(two)-together-lines: an angle lies between (ge) (or "within- two" = g-e) lines, joined together, meeting.

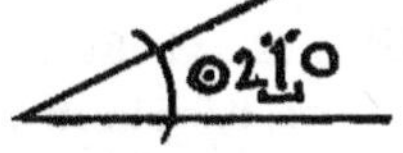

(anan = meter, yard = length-unit could be replaced by "YARD" as proper name)

ena(m) = flat/ness, plane, plain = two-dimension-space (-quality) = two-quantity-space: a plane has length and width.

enas = leaf, sheet, pane = any "flat-thing", not especially a green plant leaf

enaz = field = plain-part, a part of flat surface.

(jena = square = equal (j)-sided-flatness (ena)

(wenas = board = w-enas = strong-sheet, strong-flat-thing = wom enas)

(yn-ena = card = little-flatness; vav-ynena = post-card = send-card

nam = big, large, great (much-space-quality)

ynam = little, small, y-nam = "non-big, ungreat" (slang expression "nym", if no space is stressed)

(For the following see bE, jE, kE under "E")

bEna = land (bEn = earth, bEn-a = earth-space)

jEna = sea (jEn = water, jEn-a = water-space)

kna = heaven, kan = sky, ka = upper-space (slang for sky & heaven)

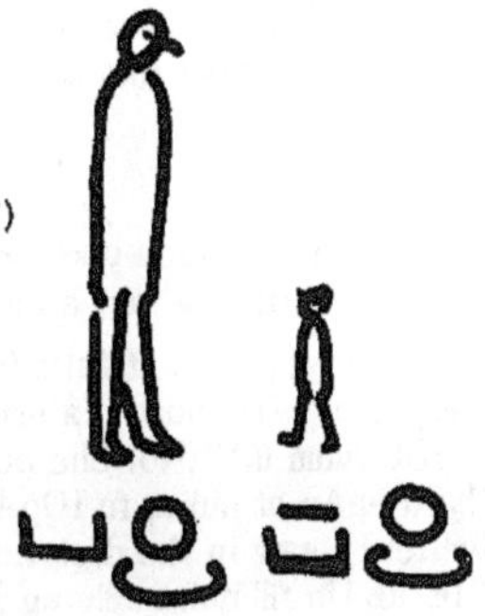

jEgeda = jEged-a = ship-space = harbor

una = country (u-n-a = man-big-space, people-place)

(dova = restaurant, eat-place; ydova = toilet, restroom)

(roga = sanitarium, health-house; yroga = sickhouse, hospital

"Qg bu twUv dov, bu av at dova; Qg bu twUv ydov, bu av at ydova; Qg bu yc wav ydov, bu tev at yroga."
(If you want to eat, you go to a eat-house; if you want to eliminate, you go to the toilet; if you can not excrete, you come to the hospital (sick-house).

a : s

(nase(v) = transport = much-space--thing-move(-do) = n-a--s-e-(v)

"fnu vepAv fnum Es ad anam ytta Ud nam nase" We moved our things (through) a long distance by-means-of-a large transport."

sav = put = s-a-v = "thing-space-make"; if one "makes place" for a "thing" one puts it there; one puts a thing always in some "place," ("as").

a : t

ytta = distance (yt = from, t = to, a = space): distance is the stretch "from" one point in "space" "to" the other.

taz = direction ("toward-space-part"): toward which "" part in space" one moves, determines one's direction.

"yt fE taz aki (sun) tetAv . bu wav iOv, Uf ab fE az i cEv nEk wom, hI ? aki iv yt kan ek bEna Ib jEna." (From this direction the sun will come. You can see, that on this side the light is most strong, (eh?). The sun shines from the sky over land & sea).

a : u,U

ua = dwelling (man-place, human-space) "fE uga c fum ua."

nuba = town, city ("many-men-together-space"): the "space" in which "many people" live "together" is their "town".

(ynuba = village, small town (not-many-people . . .)

gUa = school = knowledge-place = gU-a. The school is a place of knowledge, gU. "gUa ag ynuba cEv riOm . can u gUv a-yf (another). tu tev yt nam ytta at gUa. yUg, tu wav ogav nE." (The school in the village is pretty. All people know each-other. The children come from great distance to the school. But, a child can walk much.)

a : z

az = side = space-part = a-z: this side is "this part" of "space."

taz = direction = az, a av at xE = the side, one goes toward (which).

"bu varv yI ynena at fu!" (you) send a card to me! "vu sav vum anEs bam ugta." (He puts his stick near the door.) "yr! yvu sapAv pI anEs fa rUt yvum u." (No. She put the stick here for her man.)

"yvu apAv at nuba, fu iOpAv xE ag ytta." (She went to the town, (which) I saw in the distance. Literally: I saw which . . .)

"fE az Ub fE nuba cEv ag i, yf az cEv fA ag yi Ub fE bEk." (This side of this town is in the light, the other side is now in the shade of this mountain.) "fnum U syv (receives) gU ag gUa" or: "gU seyv tag fnum U ag gUa." or: "gU sayv tag fnum U ag gUa." (Our mind receives knowledge in school, or: Knowledge is given into our mind in school, or: Knowledge is put into our mind in school.)

"nEn tu yc brOv at av at gUa; num U yc brOv at syv gU. nu brOv at av yt gUa Ib fev anas rUt fev jEos." (Many children (do) not love to go to school; their minds (do) not love to receive knowledge. They love to go from school and take a line for taking (catching) fish.)

a : a = one

a = one: fu EjUrOv Uf am a KU cEv KU = I believe that only one God is God.

am = only = one-ly, one-quality. "yvu brOv am a vus"

an = unit (one-quantity).pI METeR c' an Ub ana ag euROPa.

na = first = number-one = n-a. vu c pI na ag vum bUz = He is the first in his class.

amUm = absolute (am-Um = only-mindquality) Only the mind thinks in absolutes.

abzam = simple (a-bzam = one-fold, see "z" at end of this Part V)

agnUs = case = a-g-n-U-s = one-in-many – mind-thing: a "case" or sample for a scientist, is just "one" among ("in") "many" on which he does research. It is a "mind-thing:", "U-s", concept.

artnU = example = a-r-t-n--U = "one-good-for-many – abstract (or : mind)" If we give as an "example" of charity e.g. the Good Samaritan, this "one" serves as a "good" model "for many" in their "minds."

atek = step = a-t-e-k = "one-toward-move-up": on a step ladder, a "move" "one-up" is a "step", which, like a step in walking leads us nearer "toward" ("t") our goal.

" a atek ag a A, am a atek ag a A!" One step at (in) a (one) time, only one step at a time!

daiuv at cnAm A.

"vu am UIpAv: """yc erv a atek! (He said only: (Do) not move a step!) Qg bnu ev, fu vyotAv bnu." fnu UIpAv:' hU bu yc twUv, Uf fnu tev?' """yUt bnu yc fum bru! bnu cEv fum ybru." 'hU bu Uv fE? hUd bu gUv pfE?' fnu EpAv yrU at bu am a A, hI?' """bnu cEpAv can A yrUm at fu." 'bu serv at fnu a abzam agnUs jOm artnU'. """arv yta (go away!)! fu ybrOv b n u , Ib yc ybrOv am bnum vU.""

Translate this first, then check up by the following translation, and retranslate into aUI, and write this down, and check again, whether this was right:

"He said only: """Don't move a (one) step! If you move, I shall kill you." "We said: 'Why (do) you not want (will), that we come?' """Because you (are) not my friends! You are my enemies.""" 'Why (do) you think this? How (do) you know that? We did harm to you only one time, eh? (=Did we ever do any evil to you?)' """You were (have-been) all time evil to me.""" "(You) give (to) us one simple case as (like an) example.' """Go away! I hate y o u , and (do) not hate only your acts (actions).""" – ybrO yc wyv-bav ytUs gaf ytUw –

– Hate not must-have cause or reason –

(Hate needs no cause or reason, hate does not need cause or reason, hate needs neither cause nor reason . . . and other similar translations.)

 "A"

A = Time

NB. For days (iA), months (ekiA), years (akiA) etc see under "i" below. These time periods and their parts are measured by sun (aki) and moon (eki), and by their light "i": yiA = night, iA = day, iAz = hour.

A = Time; period, epoch, duration, tense etc are implied.

Av = to last (to make time)

vAv = to preserve, keep = v-Av = make-last

A : b

bAv = to keep and hold, hold, (b-A-v = together-time-make). If I keep holding something in my hand, I "make" it stay "together with me" for a "time".

(bav = have is similar: to have and hold = bav Ib bAv, to have for keeps)

A : d

Ad = time-piece, clock or watch (nAd = clock, ynAd = watch) "time-tool"

A : f

fA = now = this-time: Now we shall do it otherwise = fA fnu EtAv sE ag yf mUd = this-time we shall-do it (an) other manner.

kfA = again = k-f-A = (over and) above this time

tfA = still, yet = up to-now, to-this-time = t-f-A, till-now.

yfA = then = y-fA = not-now = yf-A = other-time, maybe later

pfA = then, before-this-time, once upon a time, long ago, "damals"

"fA fnu bav wei, pfA fnu bapAv am wU Ub fnum koged" Now we have electricity, then (at that time) we had only the power of our arms.

fAom = young (this-time-life-quality) Just from this time (born) just "now" (fA) come to "life"; freshly hatched (see pAom under A:o)

iA = day = light-time, the time from light to light is also a day.

fiA = today = this-day = f-iA. serv fnum iAm nod at fnu fiA = give us today. . our daily bread.

pfiA = yesterday = p-fiA = before-today

fiAt = today-toward = to-morrow: today moves "toward tomorrow"

(Other iA-compounds see under "i" below)

Ag = during

jAg = while = same-time-in

A : m

fA(m) = present / time = this-time-quality, as of this time.

pA(m) = past (fore-time, Vorzeit, the time of our "fore-"fathers, pre-time.

tA(m) = future "toward-time" = t-A = the time "toward" which we move.

ka-mA = weather = sky-condition (ka = sky = upper-space); mA = state, condition, see "m" below. m-A = qualified-time = state, status,

A : n

nAm = frequent, often = many-times-quality; ynAm = rare, infrequent

ynA = minute (a little, "minute" time); ynAz = second, (minute-part).

"ynA Ib ynAz c zU Ub iAz, xE c zU Ub iA" = minute and second are parts of the hour, which is part of the day.

A : o

oA = age = "life-time" : one's age is the time one has lived.

fAom = young, now (come to) life, recently born
pAom = old; from the past (pA) still living on (om).

A : r

prAm = early = before-good-time-ly: The early bird was there before = prAm kEos cEpAv pfa Ap.

vrAm = ready = "make-good-time-ly" = "v-r-A-m"; if you make good time or do every thing in good time, you are ready.

A : s

Asev = lend ("time-give" = to give (sev) only for a time (A).

A : v

Uyv(A) = sleep(mind-passive–time = U-yv–A = mind-not-active-time). Sleep should be the time when the mind is at rest.

A : y

ymA = ever (no-quality, i.e. unqualified-time = ym-A) unspecified time.
yA = never (no-time). vu EtAv fE yA: He will-do this never.

SENTENCES:

fnu ov ag A Ib ag a; A cEv nu na Ub a; e cEv a ag A.
We live in time and in space; time is (the) fourth dimension of space; movement is space in time.
vu av nam ytta ag ynam A. He goes (a) great distance in little time.

Ap pI vom-kEbos ItAv eA,
bu UItAv iA:
"fu yc gUv vu" Ul fu.

Before the cock shall crow twice
thou shalt say three-times:
"I know him not" about me.

(kEos = air-animal, bird; bos = domestic-animal; kE-bos = fowl; vom-kEbos = male fowl = cock, rooster. ; Iv = sound, ItAv = will sound, crow. ;
In eA, iA the stress falls upon the underlined nasal vowel. ;

a iA Av hUd anam, hI ? — One day (a day) lasts how long? eh?

a iA wav Av fUd anam hUd o(or:jOm o) = A day may last so long as (how) life, or: like life. ;
A day may last as long as a life.

bu bArv fu ag U ! Urv Ul fu!	Keep me in mind! Think about me!
"fiAt, fiAt, Ib kfA fiAt, ev Ud sEm ynam atek yt iA 't iA." (Ib kfA = and again, 't = at)	To-morrow and tomorrow and tomorrow Creeps with its petty pace from day to day. (Shakespeare's Macbeth)
fA bu cEv tfA fAom;	Now you are still; young;
fiAt bu cEtAv pAom. (Old aUl song)	to-morrow you will be old.
jAg iA Av, u erv!	While the day lasts, man shall move (work).
fnu kfA arv tag u-io-ba!	We again shall go into the garden! (Let us go again into the garden!)
fA pI kamA cEv rUm.	Now the weather is good.
vu nAm av ek fE eda.	He frequently goes over this road.
bu cEv vrAm , hI?	Are you ready, eh?
hE c 'bum oA, fum tu?	What is your age, my child?
"fu yc tu, fu c 'nam vus!", ynvu Ub A akiA UIpAv.	"I am-not (a) child, I am a big man," (the) boy of six years said.
"fu Uv, Uf fu yA iOtAv yI jAe-UI , brOm jOm tok."	"I think that I shall never see a poem lovely as a tree."

(jAe = rhythm =equal-time-movement; rhythm-word = poem). As rhymed couplet:

"fu Uv, Uf am tok cEv pnEk brOm,
Ib jAe-UI yA ctA jOm." ctA = tAc

"bEn ev al sEfU (itself), Ib sE vev a az at aki. ag fE az sE cEv iA;
ag pI az yta yt aki cEv yiA. iA Ib yiA cEv tab eO-u iAz.
a iAz bav AO ynA. ag a ynA cEv AO ynAz.
— ag Ad fnu iOv A. yUg, ag pA , Ib fA (rUt pAom u), aki, Ib yf ki ag yiA, viOv (show) A.
-- bEn ev bIb al aki. fE e Av iAo (365)(= i-Oke--A-O--o) iA; fE cEv a akiA .-- eki ev al bEn ag a ekiA.-- yvus ov Ud A Ub eki, vus ov Ud A Ub aki.

(The) earth moves around itself, and it moves one side to (the) sun. In (on) this side it is day. In the side away from the sun is night. Day and night are together 24 hours. One hour has 60 minutes. In one minute are 60 seconds. In the clock we see the time. But, in the past, and now (for old peoples), the sun, and other stars in (the) night, show the time. --The earth moves also around the sun. This movement lasts 365 days; this is one year. The moon moves around the earth in one month. The woman lives by the time of the moon, the man lives by the time of the sun. –

"b"

"b" denotes "together with", "co-, con-, cum-"

"b : a"

ab = at (a-b = space-together, together in space)
tab = together ("to(-space-)gether"): "fnu cEpAv tab ab uga Ub fnum bru" (We were together at the house of our friend, (= at our friend's house).
ba = nearness ("together-space")
bam = near, ybam = far (not-together-space-quality, un-near)
bamQ = nearly
baz = beside(s), "together-space-part", near-side, by-the-side. (az = side).

"b : A"

bypAm = next ("together-afterward (yp)-time-quality, "together" but "behind" is the next man, close by but a little behind the first man)
bypAv = (to) follow ("next-do, to be the next, next-verb") "bypArv fu!" = follow me! —— "yc bypArv fu" (Do) not follow me.

"b : a"

bav = to join ("together-one-make"); "nu bapAv Ib bypApav vu."
baz = joint ("together-one-part": a joint is a "part" of a structure, in which pieces are united, made "one", come "together.")
Abvana = stitch ("one-together-make——line (ana)": a stitch is a little "line" or thread, which "makes" things hold "together" in "one."
banav = to bind, (together-line-make, make (put) together with a line).
(banapAs = bundle, (banapAm = bound, banapAm-Es = banapAs = bound-thing.)

"b : c"

bcu = companion (together-be-man), the "man" with whom I "am together."
—— fum bcu cEpAv cnA eb fu, yUg fiAt vu cEtAv ybam: fu yc wav bav vu.——
(My companion was always with me, but tomorrow he will be far: I can not join him. "fu yc wav bypAv fum bcu" = I can not follow my buddy)

"b : e"

eb = with (moving-together: if he goes "with" you, you both "move-together"
—— waubos ev eb u : u eb waubos av tab.
(The) dog moves with (the) man: man with dog go together. ——u banav waubos Ud anas, Ut waubos tAv tab eb vu. yUg waubos brOv vum ku, Ib yc twUv av ybam yt vu. ——(The man binds the dog with (= by means of) a line, in-order-that the dog stay together with him. But the dog loves his master, and (does) not want (will) to go far from him.) ——waubos yc ov rUt vu-fU; vu ov rUt vum ku.—— (The) dog (does) not live for himself; he lives for his master.)

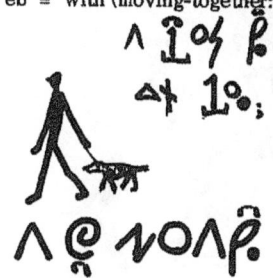

"b:e"

bEtkU, bEtkUv = structure, construct; "together-matter-to-above (=up) - concept": If you construct a structure, you put it "up(ward)" and you put its "material" parts "together," for solidity (bE).

bev = to communicate, bevU = communication. "together-move": if you communicate with somebody, you "move" toward "togetherness" with him.

fnu bav yIn bevU yt a. –– We have communications from space.

bwE = paste, glue; together-power-matter, together-hard (wE): a glue hardens, when both parts are stuck together.

byfEv = to mix, byfE = mixture, byfEm = mixed; "together with-other-matter-(make). –– U Ib drE yc byfEv = Mind and money (do) not mix.

"b:I"

Ib = and; "sound-together": If you say "good and bad", the two concepts are "together" in "word-sound" only, not in mean ing.

bIb = also, too ; together-and: "He went and I, too" –– the "too" strengthens the "and" (Ib).

Ibyf = etc, etcetera, and so on; "and-(the)-other" (other = yf).

"b:j"

(bjOrv(Am) = suit(able) = "together-equal-feeling-good-make, fit(ting)" (If your hat suits or fits (to) your dress, they "make together" the "same good feeling" of harmony)

brUj = agreement, brUjev = to agree (brU = peace). ("together-good-mind-same (move-make)": If you are "together of the same good mind" (and you "make a move", then you both "agree."

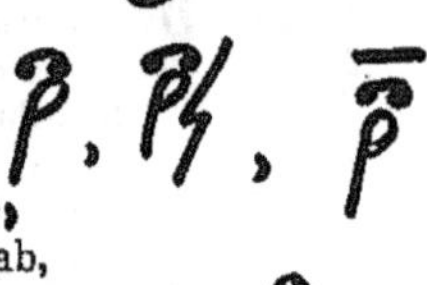

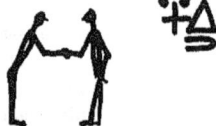

–– fE ca ymA batAv brU, hI ? can u yA brUjetAv. –– (ca = existence-space, world) "Will this world ever have peace, (eh?). All men will never agree."

"b: m, n, o"

bma = configuration, group = "together-form"

ynab = (small) group, "few-space-together" (When few people or things are together in a place, they form a "group."

bo = marriage, wedded life, "together-life

bov = to marry, "make-life-together"

bopAm = married, ybo = divorce

Qg vus Ib yvus ov tab, fE cEv bo. yUg, Qg nu yc wav tab ov, nu vEv ybo.

If a man and a woman live together, this is marriage. But, if they can not live, together, they make divorce.

"b : r, s, t" 

brUvs = adjustment, "together-good-mind-make-thing" (If you adjust yourself to something, you "make up your mind" to get "well along together."
brU = peace "together good spirit", a spirit of good harmony with . . .
ydbrU = war ("against-peace"), "ydbrU Ib brU" Ud ToLSToy.
bydwun = army "together-against (yd) -power-men; bydwum = military.
(An army consists of men who go together against (=yd) a hostile power)
trab = arrangement = "to-good-space-together", "spaced-well (or correctly)"
grab = order = "in good space together" (If things are put in (to) the right space (or place) together, they are orderly arranged.
robU = organization = good-life-together-concept
tab = together : "to-space-with" (see above)
Etbev = touch = "matter-to-with-move-make": If it's "matter", you can touch it, it's no ghost; in touching, you move your finger to it, at it.
EbtAv = to fix = "matter-together——remain (tAv) -make
EbtApAm = fixed (Past-Participle) = Material (made) together-before.
setbav = gather = "things-move-to-gether (in) space-do"

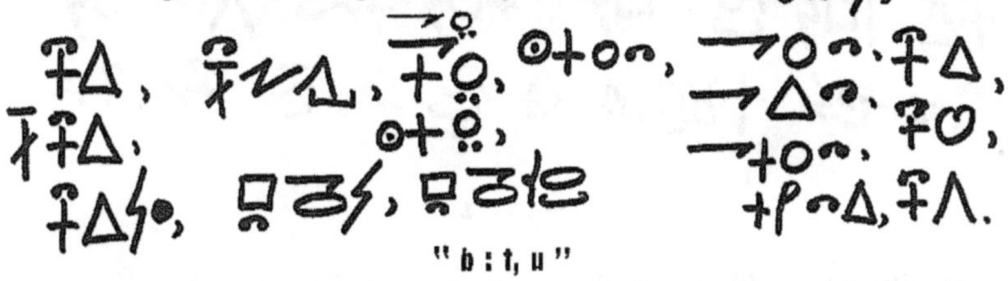

"b : t, u"

tUb = system: "to(for)-mind-together" (In a system, things are put together for our mind.)

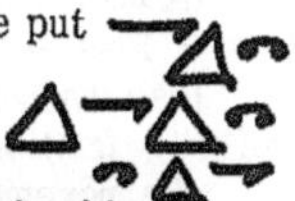

UtUb = theory = mind-system = mental construct
bUt = almost = "together-(in) mind-toward" (This is almost shocking . . means "this is associated (together-in my mind) with a shock" or: my mind moves "toward" a shock.
Ub = of (mentally-together-with) e.g. "The Hamlet of Shakespeare" but also "The Shakespeare of Hamlet" was more mature . . . "
bUvs = connection ("together-mind-make-thing") 
bUm = common = "together (in the) mind quality"; If a tree and a euglena have a green color in common, they are connected (together) in our mind (by this quality).
bav = to have = "together (in) space-verb"; if you have a husband, you are "together" in space (or in the same place) with him.
bavs = property (things that are with me, or that I "have", "have-things"
bavu = owner. He is the owner of this property = vu c bavu Ub fE bavs.
bayv = to belong (to be owned, had; passive of "bav"); bayvs = possession.
——bavu bav fE bavs; sE bayv ag vum bayvs ——
bAv = to keep; sbAv = collect ("things-keep-together-(for a long) time")

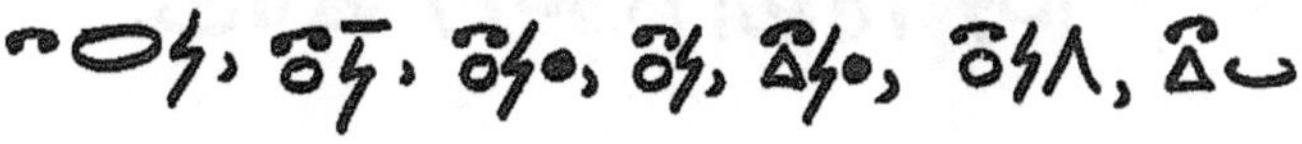

b : w

bwIv = crash = "together-power-noise-make"
bwEm = sticky = "together-force-material-quality", with cohesive force.
bwam = tight (together-power-space-quality): pressed powerfully together in the same space. "ybwam" = loose
bwev = press (together-force-move-make) bew(ev) = grip
bUwev = grasp ("together-mind-power-move") If we grasp an idea, we hold it together in our "mind-power"; bUw = (the) grasp.
bywev = slip = "together without power move" (If two plains slip by each other, they are close "together", but have no cohesive "force": "yw", and so they "move" by (ev).

b : y, z

yb = without "un-with, not-with" — — vus yb yvus cEv kan yb ki — —
(A man without a woman is a sky without a star)
tybse = loss = toward-without-thing-move; tybsev = to lose; (If you lose everything, you "move" toward the "without" —things status.)
ydbe(v) = friction; (rub); "against-together-move": friction hinders the movement of plains close together.
bza = fold: _abzam = simple (one-fold); _ebzam = double (two-fold);
_ibzam = threefold, triple = "three-together-parts-(in one) space-quality.
nUbzam = complex = "many-parts-together-(in one) mind.

— — u yA wav ov yb kEn — — (Man never can live without air = Man can never live without air)
— — bu gUv pI _ibzam ypums Ub a, hI ? — — (ypums = mystery).
(Do you know the threefold mystery of space?)

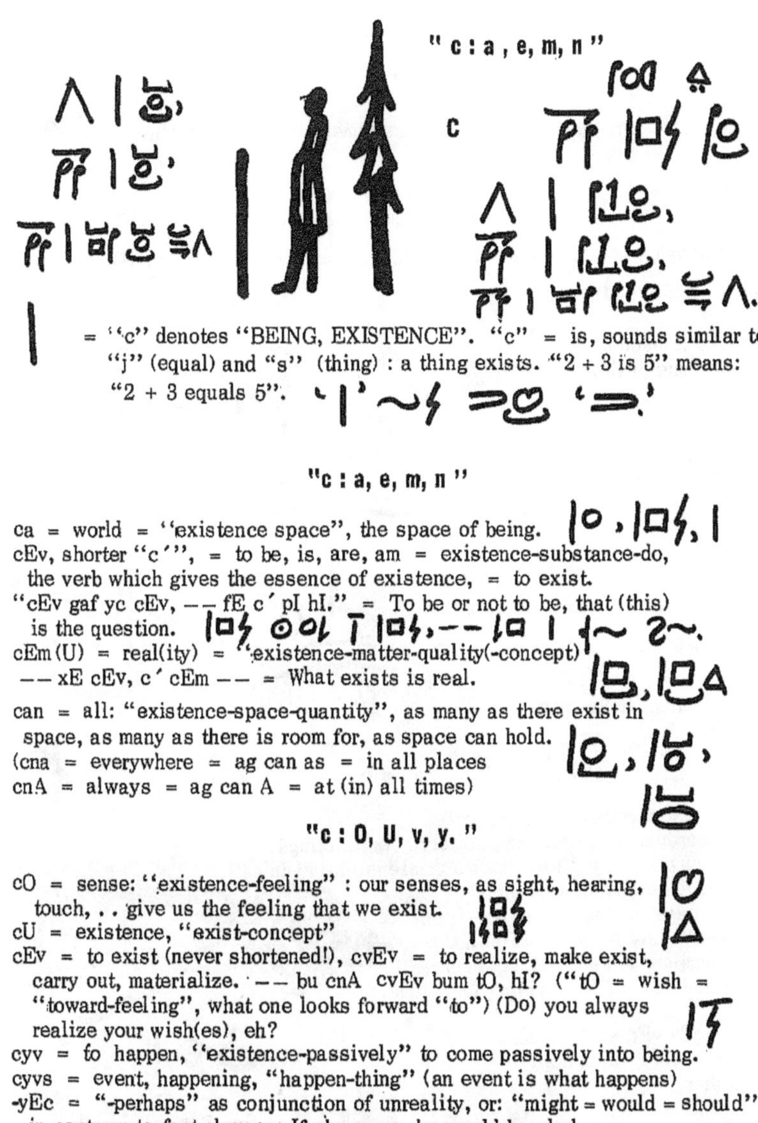

"c : a , e, m, n"

c

= "c" denotes "BEING, EXISTENCE". "c" = is, sounds similar to "j" (equal) and "s" (thing) : a thing exists. "2 + 3 is 5" means: "2 + 3 equals 5".

"c : a, e, m, n"

ca = world = "existence space", the space of being.
cEv, shorter "c'", = to be, is, are, am = existence-substance-do, the verb which gives the essence of existence, = to exist.
"cEv gaf yc cEv, -- fE c' pI hI." = To be or not to be, that (this) is the question.
cEm(U) = real(ity) = "existence-matter-quality(-concept)"
-- xE cEv, c' cEm -- = What exists is real.
can = all: "existence-space-quantity", as many as there exist in space, as many as there is room for, as space can hold.
(cna = everywhere = ag can as = in all places
cnA = always = ag can A = at (in) all times)

"c : O, U, v, y."

cO = sense: "existence-feeling" : our senses, as sight, hearing, touch, . . give us the feeling that we exist.
cU = existence, "exist-concept"
cEv = to exist (never shortened!), cvEv = to realize, make exist, carry out, materialize. -- bu cnA cvEv bum tO, hI? ("tO = wish = "toward-feeling", what one looks forward "to") (Do) you always realize your wish(es), eh?
cyv = to happen, "existence-passively" to come passively into being.
cyvs = event, happening, "happen-thing" (an event is what happens)
-yEc = "-perhaps" as conjunction of unreality, or: "might = would = should" in contrary-to-fact clauses: If she came, he would be glad = Qg yvu tepAv, vu cEv-yEc krOm; more correct: Qg yvu tev-yEc, vu . . .
yc = (is) not = "non-exist"
tycvev = destroy, tycvie = destruction = "toward-non-existence-move" (If you destroy something, you move it toward non-existence, death).
-- bum yta-cEv tyc vev fu ; Qg bu yc cEv-yEc fUd ybam, fu av-yEc at bu. -- (Your away-being (your absence) destroys me; if you were not so far (if you not would-be so far), I should go to you.)

"d"

"d" denotes "through, by (means of), instrumentality, tool, medium.

"d : a"

ad = through = "space-through"

enad = plane (tool), plain-tool

(a plane is used to make (wood) plane or flat --enad vEv tEk enam--

yvu jEv ad anyEd = she drinks through (a) tube (pipe) "straw"

dana = cross ("through-line")

kad = across = "above-through"

Ad = clock, time-piece, "time-tool" instrument for time.

ynAd = watch, little time-piece

"d : b"

bEn = earth (together-matter-plenty)
bEns = earthenware, crockery, pottery, "earth-things"
bEds = apparatus = "together-material-instrument-thing", "together-matter-tool-thing"
bAwd = tongs = "together-time-force-tool", bAv = to hold (for a time) tongs are tools which hold something "forcefully together for a time."

--bAwd cEv vEd xE bAv tab --
(Tongs are tools which hold together

"d : e, E"

kEwed = sail = "air-power-move-tool"
vyevd = brakes = "make--not-move (ye = stop) --tool
Ed = medium = "matter-means (by which)", replaces often the special terms "vEd" = tool, and "dEs" = instrument
dnEm = thick = " through-much-matter-quality" (If you have to cut through a thick slice, you have to cut through-much-matter.)
ydnEm = thin

"d : E"

nyEd = net : "many-holes-tool" (y-E = "non-matter" = hole)
--nyEd c'Ed Ut fev (take) Ib bAv (hold; "take and hold" = catch) jEos. -- A net is a means (medium, tool) in order to take and hold (to catch) fish.
an-yEd = pipe, tube ("long-hole")

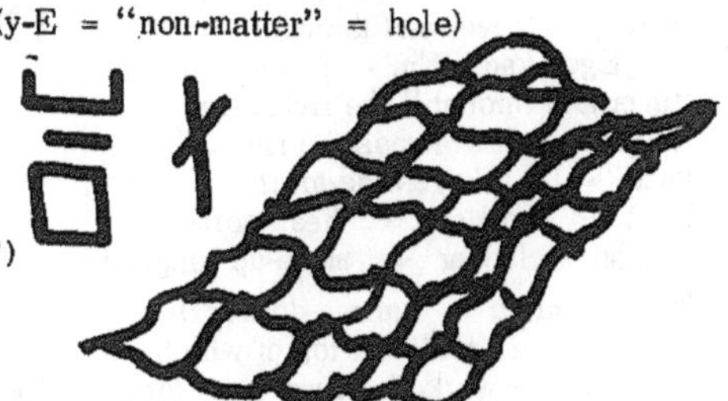

"d : f, g, j"

dyf = (al)though (d-yf = through-other); "although" leads over (through) to something different ("other") from what one expected:
"He w-- strong, although his heart was -- soft."
"vu cEpAv wom, dyf vum gog c'pAv -- ywEm."
fYd = nevertheless
fUd = so : "this-way, this-mind-means", by means of this mental method, thus.
-- bu hUd dEv fE Ed? -- fu fUd dEv sE.-- You how use = How do you use, this tool. -- I thus use it = I use it so.

"d : g, j, i, k"

gad = container = "inside-space-tool" may replace all the following words for "tools" which are hollow for placing something inside.
(sgad = receptacle = "thing-inside-place-tool" (a container need not contain "things" = "s", but can hold liquid).
stag = bag, wanab-stag = basket, ("band-(bound-woven) -bag")
wagd = box, entgad = pan (flat-container), vetgad = drawer = "make-move-toward-inside-space-tool", "make-move-toward-me" = pull, draw.
(jEtgad = cup, yk-jEtgad = saucer ("undercup = under-- liquid-into-place-tool")
odjEgd = pot (soup = food-liquid; soup-inside-tool)
(jEga = basin, "liquid-inside-room", jEgas = vessel, see "j";
jEgad = bucket, "liquid-inside-tool"; jEngad = tub ("n" for "big")
jEg = bottle, ("liquid-inside"), jEd = spoon = "(for) liquid-tool"
jEngad c'nam jEgad, a tub is a big bucket.
-- stag Ib wagd Ib jEtgad: can cEv gad. -- Bags & boxes & cups, are all containers (inside-room-tools). "wagd" = box = strong-container ("w"!)

jEtked = pump = "liquid-to-above--move-tool = liquid (jE) -up (tk) -mover
akjEd = buoy = "above- water-tool", float-above-tool
kajEyd = umbrella = above-space (sky) -water-against (yd): an umbrella protects against water-from-above (kajE = rain)

kiEd = kettle = "above-fire-tool", a kettle hangs above the fire.
kEId = whistle = air (kE)-sound (I) -instrument (d) --xA kiEd Iv sEm kEId, odjE c'vrAm. -- When the kettle sounds its whistle, soup is ready.

d : k

kad = across: "kad c´ek Ib ad." (across is "over and through.") --u jEgev kad ejEn. -- The man swims "over and through" the river, i.e. The man swims across the river.
kazd = lid (above-side-tool).
kogYwd = pillow = "head-soft-tool."
ekanad = ladder = "move-up-length-tool."
kvad = table = "above-do(work)-space-tool (a table is a "tool" on top of which we do things, or work; furniture are "tools" or means of convenience.)
ykavd = bed: ykav = to lie (down-space-verb); bed = lie-down tool.
senkad = tray (things-flat-above-tool: a "flat tool upon" which "things" are carried.)

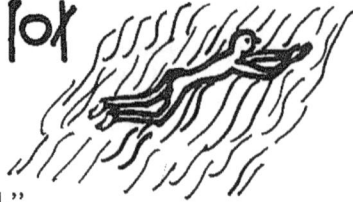

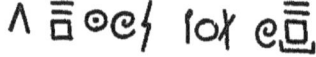

"d : l, m, n"

led = wheel = "round-move-tool."
dam = wide, ydam = narrow; d-a-m = through-space-quality.
"yvu vepAv yI led-ged (a wheel-vehicle) ad yIn dam Ib ydam ueda."
"She pushed (ytwev = push, is here replaced by "drove, moved") a wheel-barrow through streets wide and narrow", a rhyme lost in literal translation. In aUI, rhymes correspond to similar words:

"yvu vepAv ledged ek eda, Ib ytwepAv sE ad ueda." (She drove a wheelcart over the road, and pushed it through the street), or:

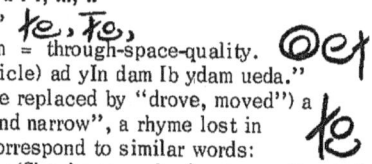

"yvu ledged ek da ytwepAv, Ib sE ad ueda vepAv" or shorter: "yvu ledged vepAv, ek da ytwepAv . . "

nand = brush = "many-long-tool" (a brush has many lengthy bristles).
mi-nand = paint-brush

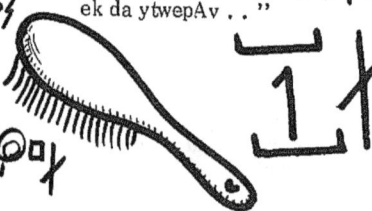

anlEd = pin ("long-round-tool")
yEanlEd = needle: "hole-pin"

"d : r"

brEg(ted)= nail (together-metal-into-move-tool: a nail holds boards "together", when it is "moved into" them. Nail and screw are of metal).

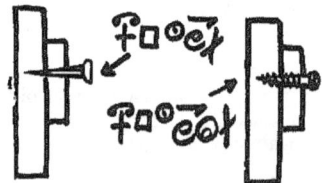

(brElg)
brEgteld = screw = turn-nail, a nail turned around, round = "1"

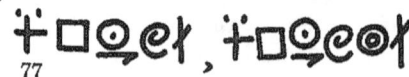

''d: t,u,v''

tagd = key ("to-space-inside--tool"); ytagd = lock (from-space-inside-tool) (a key lets you in, a lock keeps you out, away from the room inside).
vetgad = drawer; "vet" = make-move-toward-(me): pull, draw. "gad" = box, or container. A drawer is a box I pull or draw toward myself.
dU = means by which, "means-concept", instrumentality.
Ud = by means of, by, "with" (the help of). ("with" = in company of = "eb.") "I eat--not with a fork, I eat--with a friend." Do you use your friend to put food into your mouth?--"fu dov --yc Ud tazd, fu dov-- eb bru." bu dEv bum bru rUt sav od tag bum ogta, hI?
fUd = thus, so, in this manner: f-Ud = this-by(means of) = by this means.
vUiOd = pencil = "make-mind-see-tool" = write-tool (vUiOv = write)
jEvUiOd = pen = liquid-write-tool, (ink is a liquid for the pen).
vEd = "tool"; dEv = use: if you "use" a stick to lift a stone, you are "making" the stick a "tool", by which you can raise the stone. (Qg bu dEv anEs Ut vektev·wE, bu vEv anEs at vEd; Ud xE bu wav vektev pI wE: yI vekted (a lever). v-Ed = make-(matter)-instrument.
tedEv = accustom = toward-move-use, getting used.
dEvU = the use, dEvUm = usual; tvUd = device (to-make-mental-tool)
dyv = let, permit: "let is pass" through, passively (yv); dyvU = permission-- "drYv pIn ynam tu tev at fu."--"Let (suffer) the little children (to) come to me."

''d: w,y,z''

wyrtred = whip (for chastizing) = "force-bad-to-good-move-tool"
tytned = whip (for cream) = to (and) fro(m)-much-move-tool.
wyrtrev = to whip = correct forcibly; tytnev = to whip by quick "to & fro".
tykwevd = hammer (down-power-move-make-tool); a hammer comes forcefully down.
bE gwad = frame = "together-in-power-space.
yd = against; wyd = weapon; byd = fight (nIwyd = gun; bydwum = military, bydwun = army, bydwu = soldier
ydbrOv = quarrel (fight); ydbrU = war, ynydbrU(v) = guerilla, little war.
ydwU = resistance = counter-force; yde(v)s = obstruct/ion;
ydyr(ev) = defense (defend); ydwUm = obstinate; ydyb(ev) = insur/anc/e.
anyEd = pipe, tube = "long-hole-tool."
zEvd = knife ("part-make-tool"); bE-zEvd = plough = earth-knife.
zEv-wyd = sword = knife-weapon, cut-weapon. tnEzd = fork
tazd = fork = toward-one-part-tool (the prongs of a fork unite to one).
nEzavd = comb=many-parts-make-tool: a comb divides hair into many parts, (parts the hair)
odz = bit = "live-tool-part", a live tool to make a part = to cut, divide (with live teeth); or: food(od)- part(z): a bit is a part (morcel) of food.

"e"

e = movement, motion -- especially accelerated or irregular, or whirling round.

"e : a, d, g"

ade(v) = journey = "space-through-move", a movement through space.
-ade Ub fnum o Av EO akiA.--(The) journey of our life lasts three-score-and-ten (70) years.

ged = vehicle ("inside-move-tool"), any car or conveyance inside (g) which and "by (d) means of" which we move (e) or travel.
"ged" replaces usually the following:

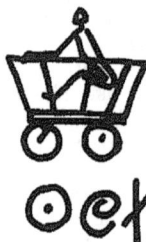

(daged = car = way-vehicle;
a-ged = "space-ship", space-car; anaged = train = "long-vehicle";
jEged = boat = water-vehicle; jEnged = ship = big-boat (big = nam = "n")
jEgeda = harbor, port, haven = "boat-space," place for ships. kEd = wing,
kEged = airplane, air-vehicle; kEwed = air-power-move-tool = sail.
uged = carriage (man-inside-vehicle); wuged = auto = power-carriage.)
e = movement, eU = motion, "move-concept"; em = moving, movable, ev = to move.

--e c´U Ub o, nEn u Uv. yUg, bIb yom Es ev. eki ev (eki = planet, move-star) bIb weiz (electrons, electricity-parts) ev al zEz(zEz = atoms). can ev; can Es ev, yUg ys (nothing) fUd nem ev xUd i. i ev yt ki at ki. U ev yt u at u. a-u ev nEn akiA ad a. au tEv ynam, jOm at to Ub io, xA vu av ad a. - Retranslate: Movement is the spirit of life, many men think. But also inanimated (dead) things move. Planets move, also electrons move around atoms. All move, all things move, but nothing moves as fast as (so fast as) light. Light moves from star to star. The mind moves from man to man. The space-man moves many years through space. The space-man becomes small like (to) the seed of (a) plant, when he goes through space.

tyge(v) = develop/ment = "toward-outside-move/ment", as when a bud unfolds and opens to-the-outside (=t-yg).

e : j, k, m, n.

jAe = rhythm = "equal-time-movement"; jEte (v,m) = current, flow(ing).
skev = carry = "thing-above-move-make", to move something above oneself.
skevu = carrier, porter, carry-man.
atek = step (t-k = toward-above, up), "one-toward-move-up", a step up a ladder.
ate = step (forward), on level ground: ate yAp ate fnu ev at yo. Step after step we move toward death. --iA Ib yiA vEv jAe Ub fnum o.- Day and night make a rhythm of our life.

e : k, m

(v)atkev = r (a) ise = "(make)-up-move, (make)-rise.

etkev = jump, move-up-move; tyke (v) = fall = toward-below (=down)-move.
nem = quick, fast (much movement —within a short time—means speed).
ynem = slow : ynem u ov nEk anam myt (than) nem u, hI? (Does the) slow man live longer than the fast man?

e : r, s, t.

yrytev = flee: "yr" (=evil)-yt (=from)-ev (=move) = move-away-from-evil.
es = machine = move-thing; ves = motor, engine = make-move-thing.
—ves vev es. es fA Ev can, xE wU Ub wom u gaf os EpAv ag pA.—
The engine moves the machine. The machine now does all (everything), which the strength (power) of a strong man or animal did in the past.
—am pI U Ub tA-u dEtAyv rUt uwe.— Only the mind of future-man (the) man of the future) will-be-used (use =dE, tA = future, -yv = passive) for work.
twev = pull: "toward-force-move" (If you pull something, you use force, to get it "toward" yourself).
ytwev = push = "(away) from—force-move, a forceful "away-from" motion.
tytwev = shake = "to(ward and) -fro(m) -force-move = push & pull.
vetev = draw = "make (v)-it-come (tev); move (it)"vev" toward "t"one/self.
vetgad = drawer = move-toward-box. —vetgad cEv jOm at gad (container) gaf wagd (box) yb kazd (lid), veyvAm at bu. vetgad c'sgad, xE veyv tap Ib typ. —A drawer is like (to) a container or box without lid, being moved toward you. A drawer is a receptacle, which is moved forward and backward.

ev = to move, (intransitive, moving oneself) "erv ynE" (move a-little!)
vev = to move (transitive, causative, moving something else), to drive
ves = motor, engine: --ves vev wuged-- A motor moves the automobile.
yev = stop = "non-move-make"; yeyv = to cease: "not-move-passive-make"
yvev = to slide, slip ("passive move make")--yc yverv tyk! (Don't slide down)
yvevAm = sliding, slipping (participle), a passive (yv) involuntary movement: you don't want to slip. --fu c' yvevAm; fu yc twUv yvev.--
Ayev = to rest, Aye = (the) rest: "(for a long) time-no-movement (-make)"
tswev = to strike (a blow) = "toward-thing-force-move-make", to make a forceful move toward something. --tswerv wrE, jAg sE c' iEm! (Strike the iron, while it is hot!)
bwev = to press (together-force-move-make)
ykbowev = to kick (ykbo = foot; wev = force-move-make) "to make a powerful move with your foot" --yvu ykbowev yvum bvu knE nE.-- (She kicks her husband too much--in this marriage: ag fE bo.--)
yem = quiet, motionless, "unmoving", not moving.
(v)yev = (transitive) to stop: --vyerv vu, Ap vu Ev ytre!-- (Stop him, before he does harm!)
yeas = station ("stop-place")
"pI anaged ha yetAv, hI?" -- 'can ged yev ag yeas.'
"fu gUv fE yb bum UIv; yUg sE yetAv ag fE yeas, hI ?"
("Where will the train stop?" 'All vehicles stop in the station(s).'
"I know this without your saying; but will it stop in this station, (eh)?"
--pev nAm c nEk drem myt yev. --Starting often is more easy than stopping. Or: To start is often easier than to stop. Or: Often it is easier to start than to stop. --rUt grtnU, pev at jEv rOjE cEv drem; yUg, yev jEv rOjE c' nEm ydrem rUt nEn u. -- For example, (for instance, e.g. = r.a) starting to drink wine is easy; but stopping to drink wine is very difficult for many men. --pev YdbrU c nEk drem mYt vyev YdbrU.--

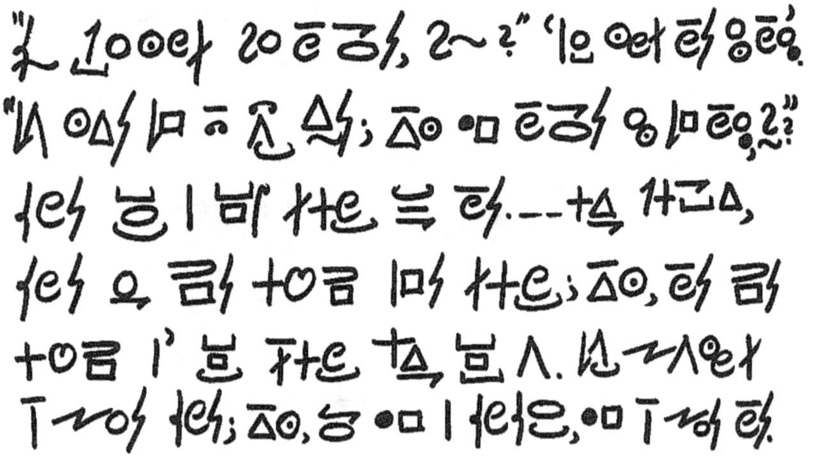

□ "E"

E = matter, implying material, substance, essence, stuff . . .

E : b,d,i.

bE(m) = solid = "together-matter", matter that stays together, does not run or blow apart, is solid. bE is also used for bEn:
bEn = earth, "solid-lots (of)", the most abundant solid is earth.
bibE = chalk = "white-solid" (see "i"); ybibE = coal = "black (ybi)-solid" (bi = white = together-light: all kinds of light are united in white).
bEk = mountain = "earth-high(t)", "earth-above", earth-elevation.
bEnwE = brick = earth- stone; bEns = earthenware, crockery
iOdE = glass = "see(iO)-thru(d)-matter(E)" = transparent-material.
–iOdE cEv E, xE bUt yc iOyv, yUg Oyv, yUt sE cEv wEm, jOm at wE. Qg bu yc iOv enas Ub iOdE, bu Ov sE na-A, yUt bu tswev bum kog yd sE; ne-A, yUt pln zU Ub pl iOdE dzEv bu.–
(Glass is a material, which is almost not seen, but is felt, because it is hard like (to) a stone. If you do not see a pane of glass, you feel it the first-time because you strike your head against it; the second time, because the pieces of the glass cut you.)
–ynam kEos kEdepAv ad kEn. sE OpAv am krO Ub kEdev kad bEn, kad iim nio Ib kad ykam uga. kEos bav·rUm iOz. yUg, kEos yc iOpAv gaf yc iUpAv yI kwE Ub iOdE, xE cEpAv al uioba. kEos am iOpAv nEn riOm riOio. yUg wEm kwE Ub iOdE tswepAv yd sEm kUg Ib zwEpAv sEm kog.–
(A little bird flew through the air. It felt only the joy of flying over the earth, over the green grass and over the low houses. A bird has good eyes. But the bird (did)not see or not understand a wall of glass, which was around a garden. The bird only saw many beautiful flowers. But the hard wall of glass struck against its head and broke its head.) –kEos ykapAv yom yk riOio. (The bird lay dead under flowers).

enaE = paper = sheet-material = flat-matter, 2-dimension-material.
–enaE c'E Ub U. UI Ub U iOyv kab enaE; UI, xE vUiOpAyv twam Ap Oki akiA. –enaE skev Us ad A.– (Paper is the material of the mind. The words of the mind are - seen on paper; the words, which were written perhaps before thousand years (1000 years ago). "vUiOv = make-mind-see.")
ri-anE = silk = "good-light–one-dimension-material = bright-thread"
tEk-YbibE = charcoal = wood-coal

E : j

jE = liquid, often used for water = jEn. j-E = equal (even) matter, since liquid stands naturally horizontal, even, level (of equal height).
jEn = water = liquid (in) plenty, the plentiful liquid
jEna = sea = waterspace; jElbE = island = water-round-earth (literally: "liquid-around-solid", as the liquid water surrounds the earth.

jEuga = bath = "water-house"
jEgev = swim = water-move (to move in the water)
ejE = stream = move-liquid (running-water)
ejEn = river = big stream
gjEm = wet = in-liquid-quality
gjEv = to wet
ygjEm = dry ("inside" a wet rag is liquid, and the rag got wet, when it lay "in" "liquid.")
dakjE = bridge "way above water."
jEk = cloud (water-above)
jEkE = steam (water-air) (liquid-gas).
kajE = rain (sky-water)
jEtkE(v)/m = boil/ing = "liquid-to-gas"
jEle(v) = (to)whirl, eddy(water-round-move)
jElkyk = wave = "water-round-up-down" (waves have a roundish up-down movement), "jEl" symbolizes the long, round, rolling motion; "kyk" the foam spray; "j" is the sound of liquid flowing.
jEwE = ice = water-stone, liquid-stone; cf. jEkE = water-gas = steam.
bikjEwE = snow (white-above-ice), snow is white ice crystals from above.
yitAjE = (morning) dew, thaw, "morning-water" (see "i" for ita = evening)
jEz = drop = liquid-part, the small part of a liquid
jEyte (v) = drain = "water-from-move", to move water away from..= to drain it off.
jEpiv(s) = polish = liquid-front-light-make(thing); (to move liquid about the front (surface) of a solid has a polishing effect.
bijE = milk = white-liquid, also the "milk" of dandelions or coconuts
ybijE = ink = black-liquid
eijE = oil = yellow-liquid
weijE = gasoline, "power-oil", the lighter kind
tyk-weijE = petroleum, heavy oil, "down-gasoline", as it sinks down by weight
jEga = basin = "water-inside-space", a basin is a space where water or other liquid is inside
jEgas = vessel = water-in-space-thing
akjEd = buoy = above-water-tool, it stays above water, floats.

E : k

kE = gas = "above-matter", upper-stuff, since gas is the stuff which rises above other matter, up into space.
kEn = air = "gas (in) -plenty", the gas we have lots of (as long as we do not poison it by atomic radiation), often replaced by "kE", gas.
Just as if a parched man says: "I need liquid", he means water (jEn).
bikE = mist (white-air); ybikE = smoke = black-gas
kEd = wing = "air-tool", air-means (by-which) one masters air;
kEdz = feather = wing-part (z), part of a wing
kEdev = to fly = air-through-move, to move through the air.
kEwe = wind = air-power-movement.
tEk = wood (see tok =tree under "o")
(A tree strives "toward-life-above", and wood is material of the tree, which grows "up" (t-k). Therefore, wood, too, is light and floats in water, rising upward (tak), because it contains air (kE). Thus wood (tEk) is used for buildings erected upward.
–tEk Ub tok, xE ov tak, ev ag jE tak.-
(The wood of the tree, which lives (grows) upward, moves in water upward (tak at kE) up toward the air, which it contains.
ygtEk = cork = outside-wood; bark is outer wood layer, (ygtok = bark).
wygtkEI (v) = (to) sneeze = "force-outside-toward-air-sound-(make)"
(In sneezing, we force air outward ("ygt") with great noise (I).
tYg-okEI = cough

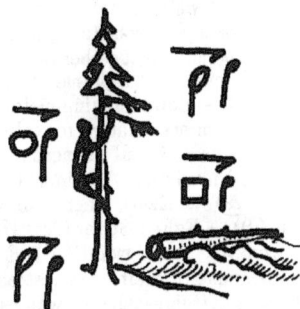

E : m,n,o

Em = material (adjective). En = mass = matter-quantity, matter-amount.
nynwE = sand = many (n)-little (yn)-stones (wE). nynE = powder (many-little-matter-(particles); lighter than powder is: knynE = dust (above-powder)
Eo(m) = natur(al) = matter-life = physical-life (E-o)
kEbio = cotton = air-white-plant; cotton is plant-material, containing much air in its fluffy structure.
noygE = wool; noyg = hair (many--life-outside): the many things which grow outside a living being, are hairs; wool is hair-material.
oygE = leather; oyg = skin = life-outside, the outside of a living being is its skin; leather is oyg-E = skin-material. nosYg = fur
robE = soil, good topsoil; good-life (ro)--earth (bE); earth which is good for life, is soil;
robE-gUw = agriculture =. soil-science (gUw = in-mind-power = science).
Eyo = mineral = matter-without-life (E-y-o), matter-in-animate.
tojE = coffee = "seed-liquid", coffee is a liquid brewed from seeds (beans) of a plant, a seedy liquid. tojE-ybru = coffee-fiend, (actually, the opposite, "coffee-enemy"; tojE-bru = coffee-friend.)

E : p,r

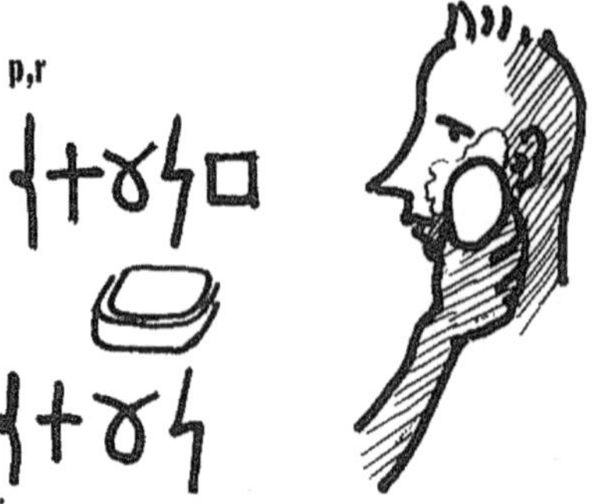

priv = to wash = "front-good-light-make", "front-brighten": if you wash your face, you brighten your front, so as to appear in good light.
privE = soap = wash-material.
"rE" = metal = "positive-matter": metals in electrolysis settle at the positive pole; metals are "good, positive" value, used for money (see "drE" under "r") & coins.
birE = tin = "white-metal"; bikrE = silver = "white-high (grade)-metal";
eirE = copper = yellow-metal; eikrE = gold = yellow-high (precious)-metal;
beirE= brass = (mixed) together (with) copper are "birE" (white-metals);
ekbirE = aluminum = "light-metal" (e-k = move-up, float)-white-metal
tykrE = lead = down (sinking)metal, heavy-metal (rising or floating, and sinking-down are relative to molten liquids in a mixture)
(Besides, we have for all elements their scientific names from their atomic (order) numbers): Aluminum (13) = Ezai; Lead (Pb, 82) = EzIe; Copper (Cu, 29) = EzeU; Magnesium (Mg, 12) = Ezae; Iron (Fe, 26) = EzeA; Gold (Au, 79) = EzEU; Silver (Ag, 47) = EzuE; Uranium (U, 92) = EzUe, etc).
wrE = iron = "power-metal", wErE = steel = hard-metal: iron and steel are used because of their power, strength, or hardness.
bibygrE = salt (table-salt) = white-together (with)-opposite-inside-metal; white-salt, table-salt; bygrE = together (with)-opposite..., because chemically, a salt unites opposites: a base, alcaline, from the metal, and an acid, mixed together. "inside.. (g), since salt is taken inside or in the mouth. (grE = alkaline, ygrE = acid, salt = bygrE)
godz-bibygrE = soda-bicarbonate, "stomach-salt".
–gUw-u nag a-u fUlv can rE, jOm at can yf Ez, Ud sEm zEz-mUn: Eza, Eze,. .
(The scientists among the space-men call each metal, like (to) each other element, by (means-of) its atomic (order)-number: Hydrogen, Helium..)

E : u,v,w,y,z.

UE = substance = mind-matter, substance in a theoretical sense.
vEv = make, Ev = do = essence (of activity)-verb
vEm = elastic = active-matter-quality: elasticity seems an active quality of matter itself
yvEm = plastic = passive (yv)-matter (E)-quality (m): a plastic clay allows itself to be bent and pressed passively.
eiyvE = wax = "yellow-passive-matter" = yellow-plastic

wE = stone, hard-matter, "power-matter"
wEm = hard = "power-matter-quality", hardness as inward power of matter, a cohesive "force."
ywEm = soft = "un-hard"
jE-ywE = jelly = "liquid-soft"; "j EywE" sounds like a jelly, a jelled liquid, becoming a soft solid.
nynwE = sand = many-little-stones, see "E:n", above.
rOwE = jewel, gem = "good-feeling-stone, pleasure-stone", being decked with sparklers, makes you feel good --not me!
krOwE = diamond = high-gem = high-pleasure-stone.

kwE = wall = high-stone (structure), erected, raised high up.

gyE = hole = "inside-no-matter": a hole is a place "inside" material, where there is "no material", nothing is inside a hole.
gyEv = to dig, (make a hole).

–ag fE kwE,	"In this wall
fa cEv gyE;	There is a hole;
ad fE gyE	Through this hole
fnu vetsev drE.–	We bring (what we stole)--the money."
(pAom rI Ub yrfevu)	(An old song of thieves)
	Melody: This old man...came rolling home.

Ez = element = matter-part, each matter can be divided in its elements, which are its parts
Eza = element-one = hydrogen (atomic order-number "1")
Eze = element-two = helium (atomic order-number "2")
Ezi = element-three = lithium (atomic order-number "3")
zEz = atom = element-part: an element itself can only be split up (chemically) into its atoms.

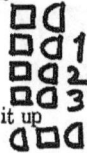

"f"

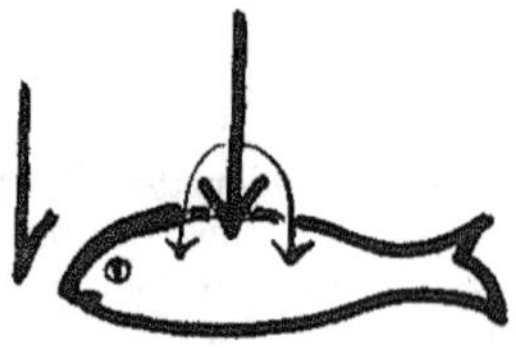

"f" denotes THIS, the arrow of its symbol pointing it out. Likewise the sound of "f" hisses outside toward its object, calling it "this." --I "f" UIv "this", fE. okE (the breath), jOm at kEwe, viOv Ib ev at Es. (The sound "f" says "this" The breath, like (to) a wind, shows and moves to, the thing.)

(I take this fish).

fa = here = this place, this space.
yfa = there = the other place (yf-a)
"yI eiyvE-i fa tev, Ut daiuv bu at ykavd. Ib fa tev yI dzEvs (a cutthing, cutter, hatchet), Ut ayt-dzEv bum kog." (Here comes a candle (wax-light) to light (guide) you to bed. And here comes a hatchet to chop off your head.)
fA = now = this-time; yfA = then (the other time); cf. pfA = then = the before-mentioned time in the past, "damals", that time;
pfa = there, the before-mentioned place; cf. pfE, below.
fAom = young = (from) this-time-living (f-A-o-m), now-liv-ing; (cf: pAom = old, "living" from the "past-time" onward into the present)
fAvm = new = this-time-make-quality; something which is made recently.
-"fAom yvu fA tOv bav fAvm uyg; nu Ap fepAv uyg yt ytyvu," pAom ytvu UIpAv.-- ("Young women now wish (to) have new dresses; they formerly took the dress from mother," the old father said.)
afU(m) = individual = "this-one-mind(-quality)"
dyf = (al)though, see "d" above. fnAn = so often
fnE = so much, fnEn = so many, fnA = so long,

f : e,E,g.

fYd = nevertheless

fev = (to) take = this-move, move to "this" place, to here, to "me" (fu).
fem = automatic = "this (itself) moves", it is automatic, no other (yf) thing is needed to move it.
fE = this = this-matter, this (essentially)
fEn = these = this (-in the)-plural, many-this
pfE(n) = that (those) = before-this, past-this, those-before-(mentioned).
fEm = such = this-quality.
gaf = or = in-place (of)-this, instead (of) this: "bu ferv fu at bum uga, gaf, (or, instead-of-this) terv at fum uga! fE c' jUm (equal, the same) at fu. bu Ib fu, fnu e wyv tev tab." (You take me to your house, or (=instead of this) come to my house! This is the same to me. You and I, we two must come together.)

"f"

— hUd bev eb a-u?
—bevU wav-cEv Ud i, gaf Ud ybal Ib yba-O. (bevU = communication, yba-O = telepathy). bevU eb a-u tfA Oiv (seems) nEm (very) yfam (strange) at U Ub nEn u. (tfA = still, yet). nEn u tfA Uv, Uf yf ki yc bav u.
—pAom (ancient, old) u ag A Ub KoLuMBuS UpAv, Uf yf bEna (aMéRiKa) yc bav u. bEna kab yf az Ub bEn yc wav-bav ("not can-have" = cannot have) u, yUt can fEm u, "ydykbo-u" (Antipodes), tykev-yEc tyk—yt ykaz Ub pI enam bEn; gaf cnA kav-yEc (would-stand) kab kog.; nu UIpAv: "pI bEn cEv jOm at yI kvad; Ib fnu yc sav odjE (soup) byk (underneath) kvad (the table), yUg, bak kvad (upon the table). am fnum az Ub bEn wav-bav u. u yc wav-ov ag yf az Ub jEna" (. . other side of the ocean).
—fA, pAom u Uv: "am fnum ki wav-bav u. u yc wav-ov kab yf az Ub a." —

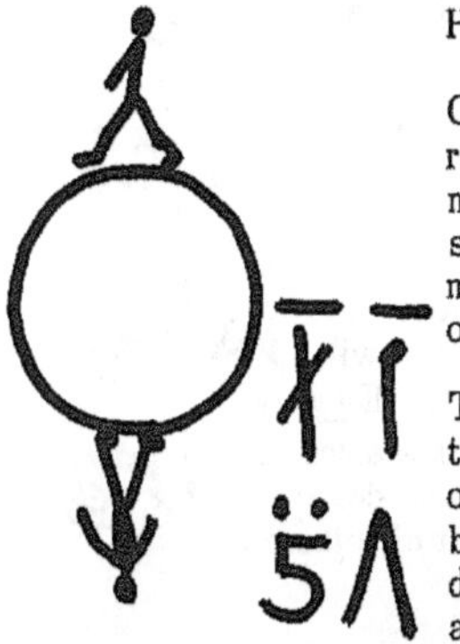

How (to) Communicate with Space-men?

Communication can be by light, or by radio or telepathy ("far-sense"). Communication with the space-man still seems very strange to the mind of many men. Many men still think, that other stars have no(t) men.

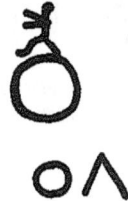

The old people (in) at the time of Columbus thought that another land (America) has no(t) people. A land on the other side of the earth can not have people, because all such people (the Antipodes), would-fall down—from the underside of this flat earth; or always would-stand on (their) heads. They said: "The earth is like (to) a table; and we (do) not put soup underneath the table but upon the table. Only this side of the earth can-have men. Men can not live on the other side of the ocean."
Now the old people think: "Only our star (eki = (planet) can have men. Men can not live on the other side of space."

"f:u"

fu = I = "this (here)-man, at your service", fu = I = me.
fnu = we = us = "this-many-men", these-here-men; fum = my;
fnum = our = we-quality.
—"fnu arv at fnum uga, hI?" (We shall-go to our house = Shall we go home?)
fU = self = "this-mind". —fu c´ fa Ib Uv Ub fU. —(I am here and think of (my) self.) "fum-fU" or "fu-fU" is mostly unnecessary.

"f : U,y"

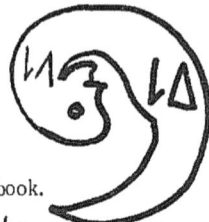

fUs(Um) = subject(ive) = self-thing(-mind-quality)
yfUs(Um) = object(ive) = non-subject . .
fUd = so, thus = (in) this-way (manner, mind); this-mind-through
Uf = that (conjunction) = "mentally-this", e.g.
He thought (that) he was good.
He thought (mentally this:) 'he was good.'
-vu UpAv, Uf vu pAe rUm.
That is your book = This is your book.
(When "that" can be replaced by "this" it is a pronoun (pfE!)
-vu UpAv, Uf pfE uga cpAv rUm.-
(He thought that that house was good)

In aUI, a comma before the "Uf" distinguishes it from "pfE". In English neither comma nor sound distinguishes both "that's".

fUwe(m) = free/dom, liberty = "self-power-move-quality": If one has the "power" to "move oneself" at least at will, one is free: a prisoner in fetters has not this power to move his "self" at will.
--ag fAm anub, u cEv myz fUwem, Uj anam Uj vu Ev fE jam, xE can yf u Ev.
(In present society, man is quite free, as long as he does the same (this same) as (which) every other man does (every body else does).
--fu c fUwem at Ev, xE can yf u Ev. --(I am free to do what all others do).

"f : y"

yf = other = not-this
yfam = strange = "other-space-quality", the quality of another (foreign) land.
yfav = estrange, yfapAm = estranged
tyfyr(v) = (to) trick = "to-other-bad-(do)". If you "trick" a man in mule-trading, you promise him first a good one and show it to him, then you exchange them and lead him "to-another-bad" one, instead.
tyfga(v) = exchange = "to-other-in-place(-do): you move the "other" in(to the) place of the first.
gayfs(ev) = (to) substitute = "in-place (of) -other-thing(-move)" a "sub".
gayfse = substitution.
"pI iOv fnu-fU, jOm at yf u iOv fnu : fE cEv ydrem." (The se(ing) (of) ourselves as (like to) other (men) see us: this is difficult. or: To see ourselves as others see us, is difficult.)
"iOv fnu-fU Uj pIn yf iOv fnu--fE c ydrem."
--yf bEna cnA Oiv yfam at fnu. fnu brOv fnum bEna, yUt fE c bEna, xa fnu tepAv at o, bEna Ub fnum toe Ib tuU. ag fnum bEna fnu brOv fnum ytyvu Ib fnum tuU.--
(Another land always seems strange to us. We love our country, because this is the land where we came to life, the land of our birth and childhood. In our land we love our mother and our childhood.)

 "g"

"g" denotes : inside, within, in, interior, inner. (Guttural "g" is deep "within" the throat. --xÁ fnu vEv pI I "g", fnum gOz (tongue = taste-organ; taste = inside-feeling = g-O) cEv pnEk ybam ag pI ogta (most far inside the mouth, farthest inside . .).
pI I "g" c´ag oIvz (The sound "g" is inside (the) throat)
(o-I-v-z = live-sound-make-organ = throat).

g : a, E, e̲.

ag = in(side) = spatially - within
nag = among = many-within = within a group of many
ga = room = inside-space; gad = container, contain-tool
gav = contain; gayv = be contained, have room inside, "go-in"
sgav = contain things = things-inside-room-make, to make room for things
sgayv = (things) are contained within, they "fit" inside
(sgad = receptacle; --sgad sgav nEn Es--The receptacle contains many things = Many things fit-into the receptacle)
gE = contents = "inside-matter", the material within.
gEm = ful(l), containing (something)
ygEm = empty, without contents
gnEm = full-stuffed, "inside-much-matter"
gyEm = hollow = inside-no-matter-quality
(gyE = hole: gyEm godz gav ys = a hollow belly (stomach) contains nothing, has nothing inside.)
"u eb gnEm godz UIv eb u eb gyEm godz"
(The man with the full-stuffed stomach talks with the man with the hollow belly (stomach).

g̲e = between = be-tween, by-two, within-two, in(midst of) two, inter- . . = e̲ g
g̲ez = interval, between-part, the part between things. ⊙2 = 2⊙

g : O, r

gO = taste = "inside-sense, inside-feeling": to taste something, you put it "inside" your mouth, while you see or hear things outside.
gOrm = tasty, taste-good-quality
grOm = sweet = "inside-good-feeling", sweets make me feel good inside.
(bi-grOd = sugar = white-sweet-food)
ygrOm = bitter = anti-sweet, outside-good-feel, bitter feels better without.
ygrEm = acid, sour: is similar to bitter, but not only a feeling (O), but a chemical quality of matter (E), opposed to:
grEm = alkaline, inside-metal-quality; a "base" contains metal (rE) inside.
bygrEm = sälty; a salt, bygrE, combines "ygrE", acid and "grE", base together ("b").

"g : s, t, w"

sgam = filled (-with-things) (in its room (a); ysgam = empty, vacuous

ugta = door = "man-into-room"; the door lets a man in, into the room.

ogta = mouth, "live-door", "life-into--space" or: "body (og)-toward-space; the place, where food enters (into = g-t) the living organism.

ogtai = lips = mouth-red, life-into--red, the red entrance to the living being.

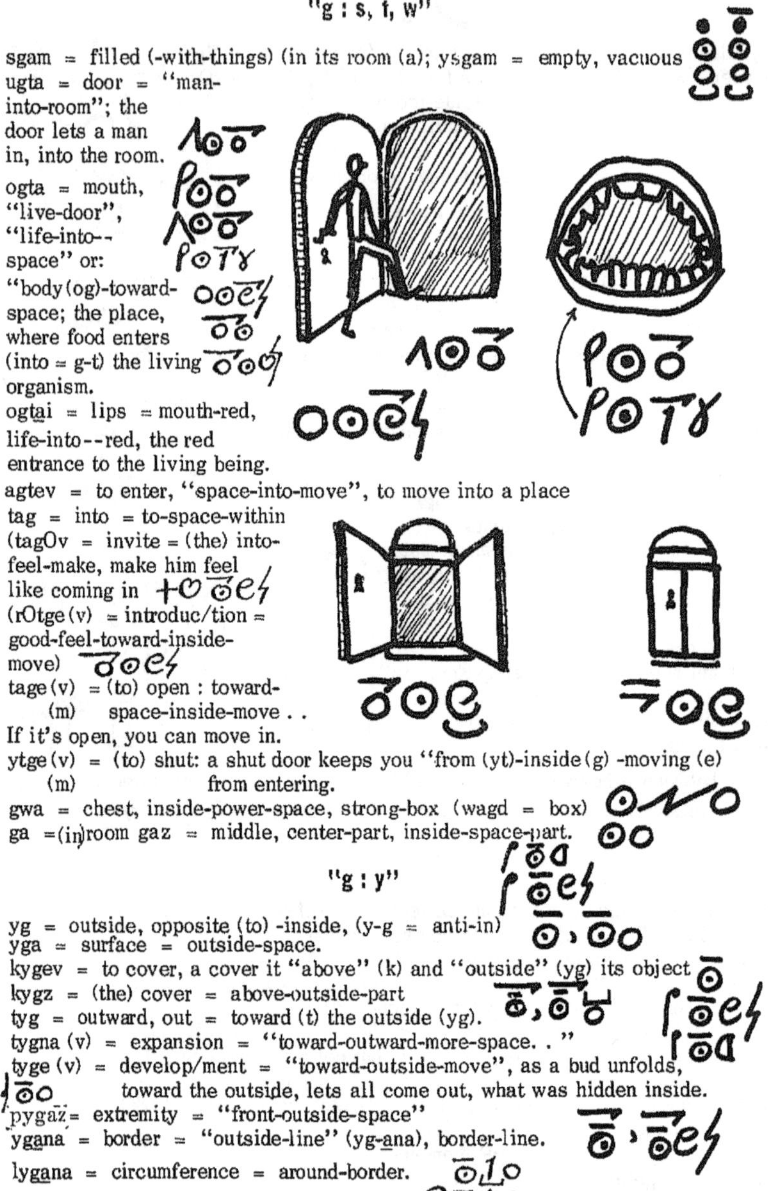

agtev = to enter, "space-into-move", to move into a place

tag = into = to-space-within

(tagOv = invite = (the) into-feel-make, make him feel like coming in

(rOtge (v) = introduc/tion = good-feel-toward-inside-move)

tage (v) = (to) open : toward-
(m) space-inside-move . .

If it's open, you can move in.

ytge (v) = (to) shut: a shut door keeps you "from (yt)-inside (g) -moving (e)
(m) from entering.

gwa = chest, inside-power-space, strong-box (wagd = box)

ga =(in)room gaz = middle, center-part, inside-space-part.

"g : y"

yg = outside, opposite (to) -inside, (y-g = anti-in)

yga = surface = outside-space.

kygev = to cover, a cover it "above" (k) and "outside" (yg) its object

kygz = (the) cover = above-outside-part

tyg = outward, out = toward (t) the outside (yg).

tygna (v) = expansion = "toward-outward-more-space. . "

tyge (v) = develop/ment = "toward-outside-move", as a bud unfolds, toward the outside, lets all come out, what was hidden inside.

pygaz = extremity = "front-outside-space"

ygana = border = "outside-line" (yg-ana), border-line.

lygana = circumference = around-border.

"g : y-- yg"

wEyg = shell = hard-outside, stone-outside, a stony shell is a hard outside, the coat of a snail or mussle; wEyg-kot = nut = shell-treefruit.

"uyg" = human dress:

uyg = apparel, clothes, suit, any form of dress = "human-outside" (Outside "yg" of man "u", we see his dress; it is the outside a human being presents)

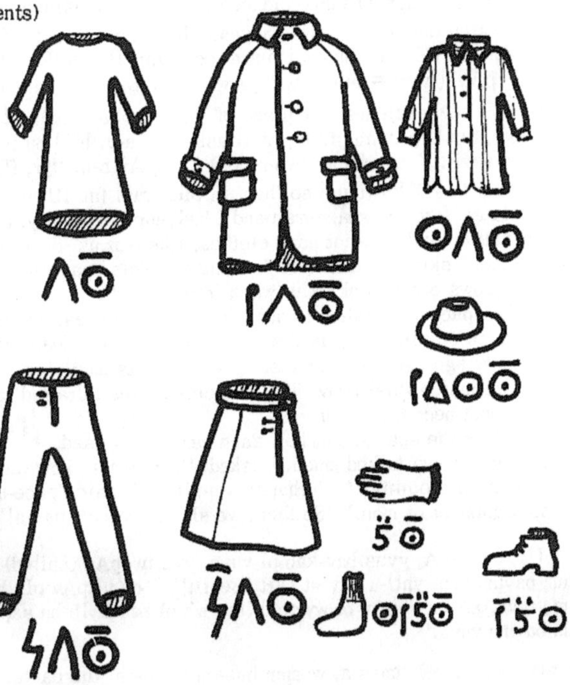

uygE = cloth = dress-material
guyg = shirt = "inside-dress" we wear the shirt.
kuyg = coat = above-dress, upper-dress
yg-kuyg = overcoat, (outer- coat)

kogyg = hat head- (kog)-dress, head-outside (yg).
vuyg = trousers, pants = man-outside, he-apparel, male-dress.
yvuyg = skirt, frock, woman-dress, she-outside, (in spite of the Scotchmen)
gygtev = to dress, put on clothes, "in-outside-come" to come (tev) into one's outer hull.

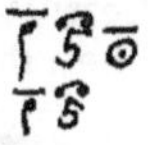

sguygz = pocket, "things-inside-dress-part", the part of the dress, in which one can put things.
boyg = glove = hand-dress, hand (bo)-outside.

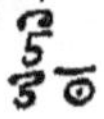

ykboyg = shoe = foot-dress (ykbo = under-hand = foot)
kykboyg = boot = high-shoe
gykboyg = socks = inside-shoe (socks are inside shoes)
oged-yg = stocking = "leg-outside", leggings" (oged = body-move-tool = leg)

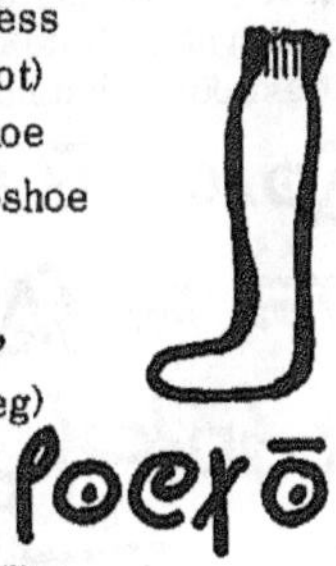

koged-yg = sleeve = upper (k) -stocking, arm-dress; k-oged = arm = upper-body-move-tool.

"yvu bav vuyg, vu yc" (She has pants, he not.)

a-u Ib uyg. The Spaceman and Dress.

--fa a-u Ib fu bapAv nE ydre (much difficulty). a-u --ag num toem bEna (in their native land) yc bav uyg, jOm at fnu. yIn a-u tyjev (change) oyg (life-outside = surface) = skin) jOm gayfs (as substitute) rUt uyg. fE a-u dov (eats) yf od Ib vEv-tnev (grows) yf dnEm (thick) oyg.
--yUg, Qg a-u tOv (wishes = toward-feels, feels-like) at nem tyjev uyg, vu vEv iEm (hot) jE, xE bEyv (which is solidified, "bE" = solid, -yv = passive). fE jE bEyv ag yiE (coldness). a-u dEv (uses) uyg am yd yiE. yf a-u dov trod (medicine), xE vEv ynam iE ag og = (a little fire inside the body). trod vEv yk-aim anai (infra-red rays), Ib a-u tEv riEm.
-fu wyvpAv (wyv = must, wyvpAv = had to) viOv (show) at a-u, hUd can uyg dEyv. (. . . how each dress (= piece of clothing) is used).
--Ul vuyg, fnu UIpAv nE: fu hIpAv (I asked): "a-u, hUd bu fUIv fE uyg?" 'twam : e-anyEd,' (Perhaps: two-pipes) ?, UIpAv a-u. "yr, fE cEv uyg Ub vus." --'fUd, (thus, so then, in this way) fnu fUIrv sE: vuyg!'
(Retranslate: Here the space-man and I had much difficulty. Spacemen, --in their native land (do) not have clothes, like (to) us. Spacemen change (their) skin as substitute for clothes. This spaceman eats other food and grows other thick skin (when it gets cold).
But, if the spaceman wishes to quickly change dresses, he makes hot liquid, which solidifies. This liquid gels in the cold. Spacemen use clothes only against cold. Another spaceman eats medicine, which makes a little fire inside (his) body. The medicine makes infra-red rays, and the spaceman becomes warm.
I had to show the space-man, how each garment is used.
About trousers, we talked much. I asked: "Spaceman, how (do) you call this (piece of) clothing?" 'Perhaps: two-pipes?', said Space-man. "No, this is a garment of men." 'So then, we should call it: pants!" (male-dress)

--"yUg, ag yIn A, yvus bav-kab pI vuyg, yvu twepAv (pulled) xE ayt yt yvum bavum bvu. ynU-u UIv at LIR (Lear):" "bu vEpAv pIn bum tyvu tag bum ytyvu, xA bu sepAv pI wyrtred (the whip) at nu, Ib bu sapAv-tyk bum bavum vuyg."

(But (in) at (some) times a, woman has-on (=wears) the pants, which she pulled off from her own husband. The fool says to Lear: ""Thou madest thy daughters (into) thy mothers, when thou gavest them the rod, and puttest down thine own breeches.""

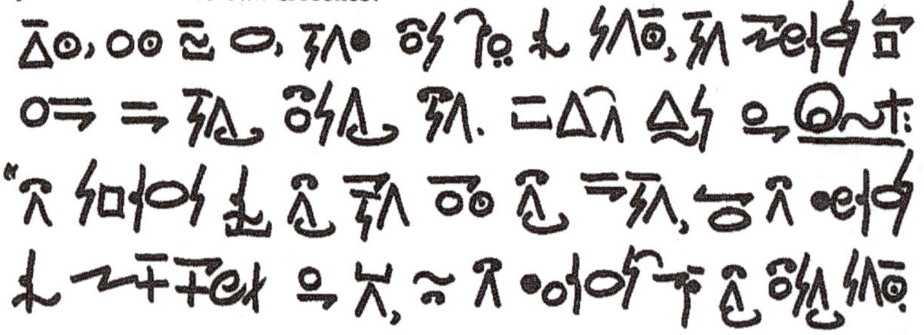

2 "h"

"h" implies Question, Interrogation, doubt, uncertainty: what, how, why?

"h : a, A, E, I, m

ha ? = where? = which place, what space
hA ? = when? = what time, time is in question.
hE ? = what? (what-matter)?
hEm ? = which, what kind of? of what matter?
-hE c´fE ? (What is this?)(What's this?). -fE c´uga. (This is a house).
-hEm uga ? (Which house, what type of house, what material?)
-sE c uga Ub tEk, fE tEk-uga, fu rEtse-pAv xE Ap. (It is the house of wood, this wood-house, (which) I bought (which) before.
(If you don't know that "rEtsev = to buy", you can replace:
-pI uga, fu fepAv xE Ud drE. --(The house, I took (which) by (= for) money.)
hI(v) = (to) question, (to ask) = "question-sound (-make)"
yhI(v) = answer, (to) opposite-(to)-question-sound (-make)
,hI ? = ", eh?" (used at the end of a question, to mark it as question).
--bu c pnEk rUm ykbo-las-rOveu, hI ? -- (You are the best (most-good) foot-ball-player, eh?) or: Are you the best football-player?
"cEv gaf yc cEv, fE cEv pI hI." (To be or not to be, that is the question.)

"h : n, O, u, U, y"

hnEn = hUd nEn = how many; hnE = how much; hEn = what number?
hO = doubt = "question-feeling", uncertainty, a doubter feels questions arising.
yhO(m) = certain/ty, sure/ness = "no-doubt", no-question-feeling.
"vrUpAm yhO, JESUS cEv fum" (Blessed assurance, Jesus is mine.)
hu? = who? = what-man, which man? (In relative clauses, who = xu; e.g. The man who said this, is a liar: u, xu UIpAv fE, cEv yEjUvu.
Most pronouns starting with "h" have corresponding "x" words.
"--hu cEv fE?-- Who is this?" is a clear question. It would be simplest, if one could use "h" whenever a question mark is used.
hU? = why? = (in) what-mind? --hU bu EpAv fE? -(Why did you (do) this?)
"fu yc gUv" --bu Uv, Uf sE cEv rUm, hI?-- 'fu yc gUv, xI sE cpAv rUm." --bIb bu bav ym hO fA, hI ?-- yIn = some
Why did you do this? "I (do) not know." Do you think that it is good? "I do not know, whether (xI) it was good." You, too, have some doubt now, (eh?)
hUm . . ? = What-kind? (In what spirit? quality, essence?)
--What person was he? -- "He was proud." --vu cpAv hUm u--
"vu cpAv yrkOm."
hyt? = why? how-come? for what reason (ytU), "wieso?" (What-(cause) from).
kwyhI(m) = responsib(i)l(ity) = "above-power-answer/able", answerable (yhIm) to a power (w) above (k), to a superior power (kw).

("h" : z)

--hU a-u yc nAm tev at fE bEna, hI? --

(Why don't spacemen come often to this land?)

1)--hE cyv-yEc, Qg a-u iOyv-yEc ag fE una? hUd vu syYv-yEc Ud fnu? 2) vu ha tev-yEc at bEna? 3) a-u twam tev-yEc at NYU-YORK. 4) fnu vrO-UIv-yEc pI a-u, hI? -- 5) yr! yIn ydyrvu fev-yEc pI a-u jOm at yruga-u. 6) nu hIv-yEc pI a-u: "bum agte-dyvU cEv ha?" pI a-u UIv-yEc : 'yc bav.' ('fu yc bav sE.') 7) pIn ydyrvu UIv-yEc: "bu cEv ypnum ybru." 8) a-u yhIv : 'yr! fu cEv bru.' 9) pI ydyrvu hIv : "bru!? bum drE cEv ha?" 10) a-u yhIv : 'fu yc bav drE.' 11) ydyrvu UIv: "fUd bu cEv tOrv-u, Qg bu yc bav drE. 12) bu wyv tAv ag yruga." 13) 'yUg, fu yc wav bav drE. fu yc u Ub fE bEn; fu cEv a-u.' - 14) Qg bu yc cEv u, fUd bu cEv os. bu wyv av tag os-ga, gaf os-yruga.

(Try to translate and understand as much as possible of these aUI - sentences. Figure out what it could mean. Guess and check up!)

15) -- hU fnu wyv etgUv aUI --

(Why must we learn The Language of Space?)

16) --ynam ynvu hIpAv : "a-u hU twUv , Uf fnu etgUv vum nUI? 17) a-u hyt yc vetgUv can vum ApUvs Ib ApUte at fnu? 18) a-u hyt yc vetgUv at fnu, hUd vEv a-ged?" 19) a-u yhIv: 'fu yc gUv bnu. -- bnu cnA dEpAv can bnum ApUvs Ut ydbrU. fu hUd wav-gUv, Uf bnu yc dEtAv fum gU yd fu? 20) Qg trUn bEn-u retgUv fE nUI Ib ytUw, pI aUI, (yb tO at jruts ag drE Ib wU), fu wav cEv yhOm Ib wav rUOv at fEn Uis-u, Ib at yIn num brUje.' --

Notes: 1) cyv-yEc = would happen, iOyv-yEc = would-be-seen, -appear; syv = receive, sy-yv (pronounce: syüv) is passive: be received; syYv-yEc = would-be-received. 3) . . would perhaps come to New York (aUI spells phonetically: U and O are long; the Consonants are capitals anyway in proper nouns and names). 4) vrO = make-good-feeling; vrO-UIv-yEc = would we say a word that makes him feel good = would - we greet? 5) yd-yr-vu = against-bad-men = policeman; yruga-u = prison-man, prisoner. 6) agte-dyvU= entrance-permission = passport. 7) ypnum ybru = secret-enemy = spy. 11) tOrvu = beggar-man, pan-handler 14) os-ga = animal-in-room = stable; os-yruga = animal-jail = cage. 16) etgUv = study, vetgUv = teach; ApUvs Ib ApUte = inventions and discoveries. 18) a-ged = space-vehicle, space-ship 20) retgUv = learn; ytUw = reasoning, logic; jruts = reward : . . without looking for reward rUOv = trust, Uis-u = idea-men, idealists; brUje = agreements.

"h" : z

Why space-men don't come often to this land.

What would happen, if the space-man would appear in this country? How would he be received by us? Where would he land (come-to-land)? Perhaps the space-man would come to New York. Would we greet the space-man? No! The policemen would take the spaceman prisoner. They would ask the space-man: "Where is your passport?" The spaceman would say: 'I have none.' The policemen would say: "You are a spy, a secret agent." The spaceman answers: 'No! I am a friend.' The policeman asks: "Friend?! Then where is your money?" The spaceman says: 'I have no money.' The policeman says: "So you are a vagrant (pan-handler, beggar), if you don't have money. You must stay in jail." -- 'But I can not have money. I am not a man of this earth; I am a spaceman.' "If you are not a man, (so) (then) you are an animal. You must go to a stable or into a cage (animal-jail)."

Why must we study the Language of Space?
(etgUv = to study or to keep learning, while "retgUv" = learning, so that one really knows it well ("r")

A little boy asked: "Why does the spaceman want that we study his language?" Why does the space-man not teach us all his inventions and discoveries (to us)? How-come the spaceman (does) not teach (to) us, how to make space-ships?" The spaceman answers: 'I know you not. You always used your inventions for war. How can I know that you will not use my knowledge against me? -- If enough earthmen learn this language and logic, The Language of Space, (without looking for reward in money and power) I can be sure and trust (to) these idealists and their agreements.'

(Retranslate the above into aUI, and check up whether you did it similar to the preceding text).

"i": a, A, a, b, d, e.

i = Light, suggesting the fields of "Sight, Color, Heat, Electricity. ("i" is the brightest sound, subconsciously associated with "light."

"i: ā, a, A."

anai = ray = "long-light, length-light, light-line" (ana = length)

ia = south = "light-space"

yia = north = un-light-space

ita = west = "light-toward-space" the place toward which the light (the sun) moves

yita = east = opposite (of) west

iA = day = light-time, or: the 24 hours from light to light.

yiA = night, non-day, unlight-time.

itA = evening, light-toward (rest) -time, the light goes toward West (ita) in the evening (itA)

yitA = morning, opposite (of) -evening, when the sun is in the East (yita):

Compare: ia, iA ; ita, itA
yia, yiA ; yita, yitA.

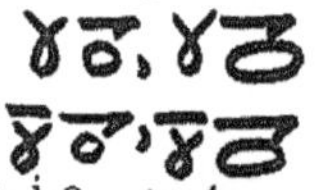

iA = day, fiA = to-day, "this day",

fiAt = to-morrow = today-toward (to-morrow moves), i.e. to-day moves toward to-morrow, to-morrow is the day toward which this day moves.

pfiA = yesterday, before this day.

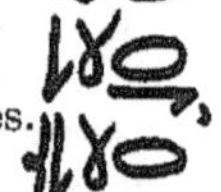

ikA = noon = "high-light-time", high-day, sun stands highest at noon.

iAz = hour = day-part; the day is divided into hours

EiA = week = "seven-days"

i: b

bim = white = "together-light," all kinds of light together, all colors of the rainbow together (b) make white light.

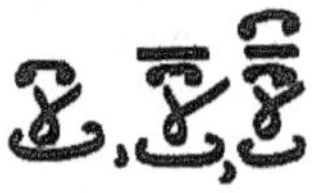

ybim = black = opposite (of) white, "anti-white"

bybim = gray = "together-white (and its) -opposite = b-y-bim = gray = black-and-white mixed, together-opposite-&-white.
b - y - bim.

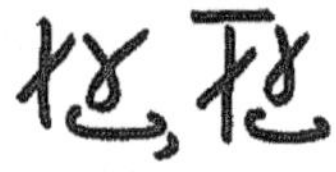

"i: d"

dim = clear = "through-light-quality", when water is clear, light can "go through."

ydim = unclear, dim (strange as it seems) = against-light-quality, opaqueness stops light

Uydim = vague = mentally unclear, mind--against-light . . . , a vague person is against mental light shining into him, does not want to commit himself.

"i: e"

ei = spark = "move-light"; wei(m) = electric/ity = power-spark-power-move-light

wei = move-(drive-) and light power, electricity.

kwei = flash (of lightning) = high-electricity, "high-power-spark"

i : E, j, k

iE = fire, = "light-matter", the material or substance of light is fire.
(v) iEv = to burn = (make) fire (do), (transitive);
iEpAs = a burn (t thing).
kiE = flame, "up-fire", fire burning upward
yniEvs = match = "little fire-make-thing"
iEga = oven, stove, fire-place = "fire-inside space, place in which fire burns
iEtE = ashes = fire-toward-matter, the material to (ward) which the fire leads: fire (material) becomes ashes.
iEm = hot = fire-like, hot "like" fire.
miE = heat = quality (of) fire
riE(m) = warm/th = "good-hot", as long as heat is felt as good, it's
riEmO = warmth as "warm feeling"
ryiEm = cool, "good-cold", agreeably cold
yiEm = cold, = anti-hot, non-fire-quality

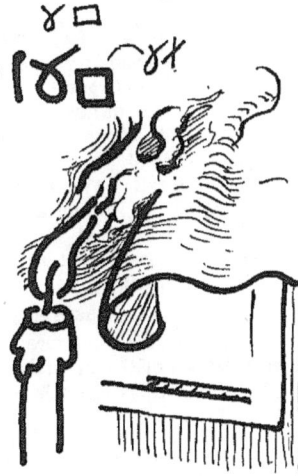

i : j

jiOvs = likeness = "same(-j)-see (iOv) -thing(s)
ijiOvs = photograph = "light-(made)-likeness"

i : k

ki = star = "above-light"; the stars are the "eternal lights" above.
aki = sun = "(number) one-star; the one star most important for us.
akiA = year = sun-time:
pakiA = spring = "front-year", beginning of year
akiAz = season = "year-part"
ypakiA = fall, autumn, "behind-sun-time", late year
akiAnz = calendar = "year-many-parts"
nakiA = summer = much-sun-time
ynakiA = winter = not-much—sun-time.
a calendar divides the sun-year in many parts.
eki = moon = (number) two-high-light, second light, the moon has second hand light from aki, the sun, the first source of light
ekiA = month = "moon-time" moon-period, time measured by the moon
eki = planet = move-star, moving celestial-light
kayrei = lightning = sky-bad-spark, lightning hurts when it burns and kills
kayrOI = thunder = sky-evil-feeling-sound, the fearful sound of the sky.

--yvu: " fu wyv bav drE rUt fAvm aki-kogyg Ib aki-uyg Ib aki-iOd. fnu wyv dav at ia, xa cEv aki." -- vu: 'aki! aki! cnA: aki!! hE c'tsU Ub aki? Ag yiA, sE yc iv . . . Ib Ag iA: sE fem cEv i !' --

i : k; m, n, o

Retranslate:

She: I must have money for a new sun-hat and a sun-dress and sun-glasses. We must go (travel) to the south, where there is sun."

He: 'The sun, the sun! always: the Sun!! What does one get out of the sun? At night it does not shine; and during the day: it's bright anyway!'

(Literally: hE c tsU = What is the purpose . . , the sense of the sun?

-- sE fem cEv i! = It automatically is light = It's light anyway.)

-- "fiAt, fiAt, Ib kfA fiAt ev Ud sEm ynam ate yt iA t'iA." (MaKBeTH, CEiKSPIR)

"To-morrow & to-morrow & tomorrow Creeps with its petty pace from day to day." (Macbeth, Shakespeare)

--fnu ov yt iA at iA, yt akiA at akiA yb gUv: yI tA vetsev (brings) hE?

(. . without knowing: the future brings what = what the future will bring)

fnu trOv, Uf ikA cEtAv nEk rUm myt (more good than = better than) yitA, Ib Uf itA cEtAv nEk rUm myt ikA. (fnu trOv = we hope).

i : m, n, o

mi = color = "qualified light", light of a certain quality (of wave-length, starts usually with the low frequency rays of the rainbow:

1) red , 2) yellow, 3) green, 4) blue, 5) violet =
aim , eim , iim , uim , oim (or: oi, ui . . as nouns)

(("aim" means number -one-light-quality, ei = 2nd light, & etc.)
aUI counts only 5 colors of the rainbow in this way)

aeim = orange-colored = "red-yellow" mixture; aoim = purple etc.

taiv = to blush = to get red = toward-red-do; teiv = to turn yellow, etc.

ykai (m) = infra-red/ness = below-red, (heat-rays)

yraim = brown = "bad-red, dirty-red"

miv(E) = paint, color, dye = color-material

im = bright = light-quality; bim = white

yim = dark = unbright ybim = black

mix black & with to: bybim = gray

iO(v) = sight, (see), "light-sense-verb"

Oiv = seem = feel-shine, we feel it glitters.

i : p, r, u, z .

priv = wash = front-make-light, make the front clean & bright:

prim = clean, yprim = impure, dirty.

--yvus UIpAv at ykwu-ynyvu: "bu prirv pI tugai-iOdE fUd dim, Uf fu yc wav iOv, xI sE c'iOdE gaf kE!" ykwu tvepAv nEn A, yUg yvu yc wapAv vEv jiOvs Ub kE. ag ypAz, ag yvum ytrO, yvu zwEpAv iOdE-enas: sE pAc pI ApUvs Ub pI dim kE-tugai. --

i : r, u, z.

Translate: The woman said to the servant-girl: "(You) wash the window-glass so clear that I can not see, whether it is glass or air!" The servant tried many times, but she could not make the likeness of air. In (the) end, in her despair (ytrO - un-hope, having lost hope), she broke the glass panes: it was the invention of the clear "air-window.")

i : r, U, z.

(raiOm = warm-hearted, good-red-feel-quality, makes our cheeks glow red)
(yraiOm = frigid, un-warm)
Uis = picture, "mind-light-thing", (If I can picture something, my mind gets a ray of light)
evUis = moving-pictures, movie (evUisa = movie-theater, cinema)
rUmti (v) = advertise/ment = good-to-light-make (An "ad" brings the good – qualities of the product – to light)
iv = shine, "light-make", – viv = kindle, make shine, make light, put on . . the light
wei (m) = electric/ity. "power-move-light-quality"
yiz = shade, shadow = dark-part.

What the little boy learned from the Spaceman about light.
—xE ynam ynvu retgUpAv yt a-u Ul i:

—i cEv pnEk nem. i av ad a, yt ki at ki. a-u wav iOv fnu Ud wom iOd: iO-beds. yUg, ybam a-u iOv fnu, jOm fnu cEpAv twam Ap Oke akiA. yUg, a-u bav es (a machine) xE mUnUv pl tA Ub ym cEvs (any beings) Ub ki Ub gUpAm oA. fUd fnum tyge (development) cEv gUm (known) Ud a-u. —a-u UIv: fnum ca cEv ab pl pnEk yg az Ub fnum "bijE-da". Qg fnu tiOv at bijEda, fnu iOv sE, jOm fnu iOv-yEc yl led, gaf enrEs, yt az: fnu iOv am pl ygana-al. Ib sE Oiv at fnu jOm da, gaf ueda. yUg fnu yc iOv "bijEda", xA fnu tiOv at yf az Ub fnum bEn. fE viOv Ib EjUv, Uf fnum bEn cEv am ab a az, ab sEm pnEk-yg yEl. a-u UIv, Uf fE vEv pln bEn-u fUd U-yrom, Uÿgem, Ib tydbrUm. sE Oiv, Uf nu brOv at vyov a-yf. pln cEvs ag gazUb pl bijEda-tygle cEv ag brU eb nu-fU, Ib nu cEv ag gaz Ub rOb. yt yfa, fnum a-u tev. — — fA a-u gUv, Uf fnum ca cEv ag nam tyr. a-u tOv at torv Ib at torv-UIv. yUg, fnu yc iUv aUI.

("i": z)

Retranslate: All about Light = Can Ul i.

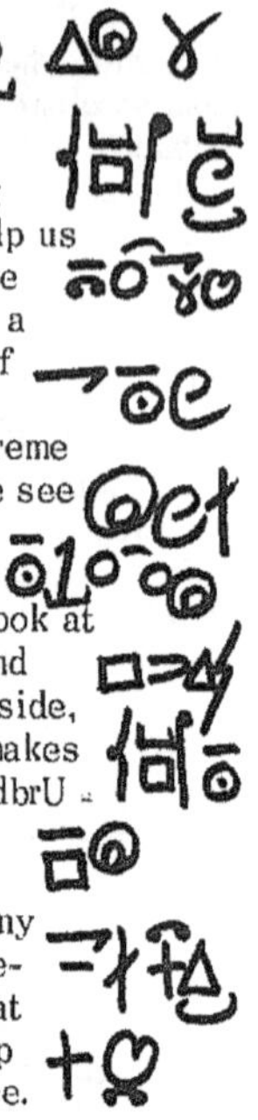

Light is the fastest. (most-fast = pnEk nem). Light goes through space, from star to star. The space-man can see us through strong glasses: see-apparatus. (yba-t-iO = telescope = far-to-see; to help us see far things). But the far (distant) spaceman sees us like (as) we were probably (before) hundred years (ago). But the spaceman has a machine, which figures (counts) the future of any being of a star of known age. Thus our development is known by the spaceman.
—The spaceman says: Our world is at the most outside (at the extreme outside) of our "Milk(y)-Way". When we look at the milky way, we see it (like) as we would-see a wheel, or a plate, from the side:
We see only the border-around (the rim). And it seems to us like a way, or a street. But we (do) not see the "Milky Way", when we look at the other side of our earth. This shows and proves ("makes-see and verifies = makes-true, truth = EjU"), that our earth is only at one side, at its "most outer" (extreme) ring. The spaceman says that this makes the earthmen so insane, extremist (eccentric), and aggressive (t-ydbrU = (inclined) toward-war). It seems that we love to kill one-another (each-other). The beings in the center of the Milky-Way spiral are in (at) peace with themselves, and they are in the middle of harmony (r-O-b = good-feeling-together). (It is) From there (that) our spaceman comes. — — Now the spaceman knows that our world is in great danger. The spaceman wishes to help and to advise (help-say, help through saying). But we (do) not understand The Language of Space.

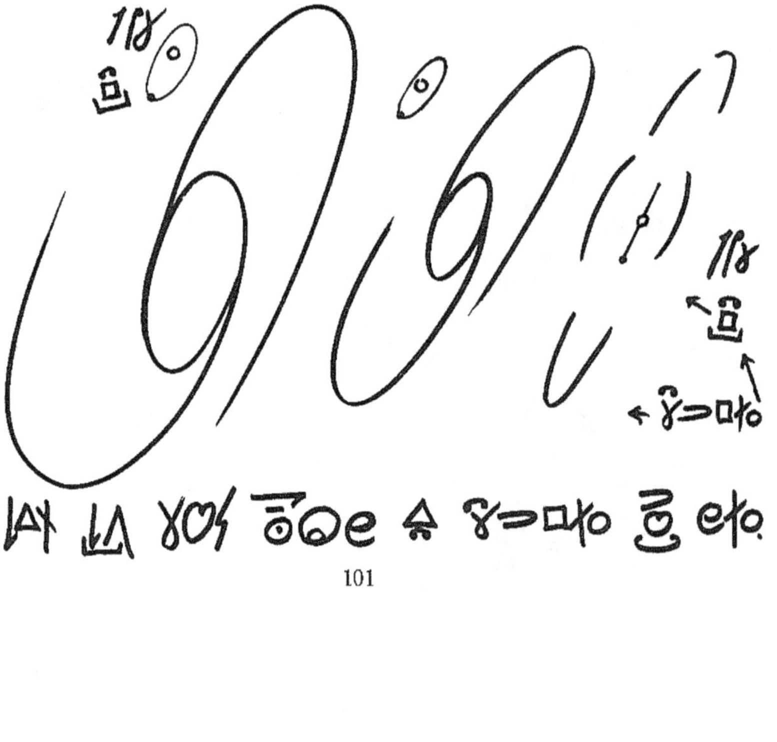

"I" : b, d, j

I = Sound, suggesting: Voice, Word, Language, Acoustics, Hearing . . .
I = sound, Iv = to sound, vIv = to make sound (e.g. play an instrument)
"I" in combinations, short for "UI" (= mind-sound, word, speaking, talk):

yI = "a", indefinite article (rarely used) = "not-sounded", not talked-about (before), "We did not hear a sound (word) of him as yet", as in: "Once upon a time there was a king . . . This king said . . . The king answered . . ." First, when he is introduced as "a king", we have not yet heard of him. y-I = not (before) mentioned; replaced by "a".
yIn = some, several, — —, (plural of indefinite article, left out in English: a king, plural: kings.) As "yI" is replaced by "a," = one,
"yIn" is replaced by "e, i" = 3 or 4 . .

pI (n) = the (plural), definite article = "previously-mentioned":
"I came to an island. I saw a woman. The woman was beauty herself (itself)"
"fu tepAv at yI jElbE. fu iOpAv yI yvus. pI yvus cpAv riO, yvu-fU (sE-fU)."
(First the island is "yI" un-mentioned, "no-sound" has as yet been heard of it; neither of "yI yvus" ("a woman"). But then: "pI yvus", The woman . . .)
Also "pI" (pIn) is used mostly for what "the" can not do: to distinguish singular from plural; otherwise it is omitted.

I : b, d, j.

ybaI = far-sound = radio; yba-uI = telephone = far-voice; (ybatiO = telescope)
(yba-Uti (v) = (to) telegraph = far-write (r) = far-mind-to-light (-bring)
IrEgId = bell = sound-metal — — inside-sound-instrument (= I-rE--g--I-d) = pessle -- inside--bell-mantle
Id = musical instrument. "ytyrApAm Ud IrEgId" = saved by the bell.
jIm = homonymous = same-sound-quality, identically sounding.
yc cEv jI ag aUI (There) are no (t) homonyms in aUI: nor puns!
A boxer bought a fur. He said to the salesman: "It can be cheap fur, for it's for my wife." "You mean skunk!", said the salesman. The man awoke in the hospital. -- (In English "mean" means "low", and also "signify".)
In aUI, there are no such confusions:
--bob-byd-u rEtsepAv yI ygos. (fist-fight-man = fist (bob)-fight-er).
strEvu hIpAv : "hEmosYg?" -- wom-bo-u (strong-hand-man) yhIv: "ym ykdrEm osYg (cheap fur, "low-money outside-animal-thing), yUt sE c' rUt fum byvu (together-woman). pI strEvu hIpAv: "bu EsgUv yr-kEmO-os (bad-smell-beast)" or: "bu cEv ykam yrkEmOos" (EsgUv = to mean, signify; ykam = mean-low). u tEpAv vAm ag yroga. (In aUI he would never have been hit in the first place: ag aUI, vu yA twebepAyv-yEc yt pe (from the start)

I : n, o, O, r.

nIm = loud = "much-sound-adjective; ynIm = soft, low (-sounding) "leise".
oIvz = throat = "life-sound-make-part", life-part = organ: "sound-organ"
IOv = to hear, IO = hearing = sound- feeling; OI = feeling-sound, as in:
tiOI = hallo! "to-see-shout", when I see him, I shout "hallo!"
yrOI = cry = bad-feel-sound; to cry = yrOIv
ka-yrOI = thunder = sky-cry= sky-bad-feel-sound = fearful sky-rumbling

I : r; u,U,y.

yrI = noise, = bad-sound
rI = song, rIv = to sing = good-sound(-make).

I: u,U,y.

uI = voice = man-sound, human-sound
uIves = phonograph = voice-make-machine
UI = word, often replaces: nUI = language
(mind-sound) instead of: many-mind-sounds.
UIv = to say, speak, = mind-sound-make
sUIv = to talk = thing-say = to say something
UIvs = speech = speak-thing
bUI = sentence = together-words (combined)
fUI = name = self-word = the word that means
(stands for) one-self; also: "this"-word:
a name is called instead of pointing: "this!"
yIm = soundless, noiseless, quiet; yImU = quietude, "no-sound-quality".

–IOv yc iUv– (Hearing is not understanding)

--a-u wav IOv fnum ybaI. yUg, a-u yc wav iUv (light-mind-do: (get light (into the) mind = to understand, iUv) fnum UI. a-u Uv, Uf fnum nUI cEv nEm ydrem (very difficult), yUt can I yc bav jam EsgU ag can U'. UI nAm bav nEn EsgU: "MEAN" (MIN), sEfÜ, EsgUv "EsgUv", Ib bIb "gaz" "jnUmz", Ib bIb "ykam" Ub U". "LIKE" (LaiK) EsgUv: "jOm" Ib "brOv". "Light = "i" Ib "cktEm". "Lie = ykav Ib yEjU" "whole" Ib "hole" ("zyn" Ib "gyE") Iv jam. aUI yc bav jIm UI.

Retranslate:

The spaceman can hear our radio. But the spaceman can not understand our words. The spaceman thinks that our language is very difficult, because each sound (does) not have the same meaning in each word. A word frequently has many meanings: "mean" itself means "to signify" and also "middle, average" and also "low of mind, of low mentality." "Like" means "similar or alike" and "to love." Light = (bright) light and "not-heavy." "Lie" = "recline & untruth;" "whole" and "hole" ("entire" and "gap") sound the same. The Language of Space (does) not have homonymous words (homonyms).

"j" :a,b,e,f.

"j" connotes "same, equal, even, level, horizontal (same level), alike . . .

j :a,b,e,f

jam = same, identical = same-space-quality :(If a man occupies always the same space as you do, that man must be you)

jAm = regular = "same-time-adjective"; "regular" means "at equal time intervals"

jAg = while = "same-time-in" : "in (at) the same time as I read this" means "while" I read this . . .

ajnUv(u) = represent(ative) = "one, equal (to) many minds" is one, who represents the cause of many, reflects in his mind the "same" opinion as they, and is thus elected as their representative

jatbem = parallell = same-place-towards–together-moving = j-a-t–bem: If two objects move in two lines "toward the same place together, like two front-wheels of a locomotive, they move on parallel rails.

jE = liquid, jEn = water, the liquid which is "plentiful" (n). liquids are "even-matter", j-E, since they stand even, when at rest.

jEv = to drink, to (take) liquid; jEs = a drink.

–Qg bu bav ys at jEv, pI pnEk rUm jEs Oiv jEn. (If you have nothing to drink, the best drink seems water).

–jE Ib bE Ib kE Ib iE, cEpAv pIn u Ez Ub yIn gUwu Ub pAom A. bEn c' wEm gaf bEm, jEn c jEm, kEn c kEm, Ib iE c 'jOm at wei, yI ma Ub wU. bEm, jEm, kEm–cEv i Ql Ub E. jEn cEv E, xE cEv cnA jEkam, Ub jam kana ag Ql Ub Eo (in the state of nature). jUf (even) pnEk kam jElkyk cEv nEm ykam bEk. (Even the highest wave is a very low hill).

Retranslate: Water (Liquid) and Earth (Solid) and Air (gas) and Fire, were the four elements of the scientists (science-men) of old times. Earth is hard or solid, Water is liquid, Air is gaseous, and Fire is like (to) electricity, a form of energy. Solid, liquid, gaseous, are three conditions (states) of matter. Water is matter, which is always level, (horizontal), of the same height in the state of nature. Even the highest wave is a very low mountain.

jUf = even, adverb: "(in the) same (way, or) spirit (as) this" (which is all the rest); e. g. "Even the richest man must obey the law" i.e. "The richest man, in the same-spirit (j-U) as all these (f) others, must obey . . .

jEkam = level, horizontal = "same-matter–high "(j-E–kam): a horizontal plateau has everywhere the same height

j-yktE(-v) = balance = "equal-burden" (yktEw = burden = down-ward-matter-power

yk- t - E - w

(the powerful down-ward pull of matter).

j : n, o, r, t

jniO(Ed) = scales = "equal-quantity- see(matter-tool)" : By a scale(s) we "see" which "amounts" are "equal,"; we see that things are alike in weight.
jnUrm = normal: "same amount (of) mind-good-quality": If a boy is intellectually normal, he has the "same amount" of "good mental qualities" as the rest.
jnUmz = average = "equal-amount-mind-quality-part: if the average of 2, 4, & 9 is 5, our "mind" divides the "amount" of the sum in "equal parts".
jOm = like, similar "same-feeling-qualified", alike.
jiOs = likeness, "same-see-thing", a-jiOs - map- "space-portrait" (in a likeness, you "see the same" as in the original)
jiOms = copy = "same-see-quality": In a copy you want to see the same quality as in the original. jomz = species
jrute(v) = (to) reward = "equal-good-man-toward-move": What you move, bring, convey "to a good man" is his "reward", "equal" in value to his "good" deed.
jyrte(v) = punish/ment = "equal-evil-toward move" -j-yr-t-e(v): If the same evil is brought (moved) to a man, as he did, this is considered just punishment, jyrte.
jyttUm = mutual = "equal-from-to-mind-quality": If love comes equally "from (and) to" both people, they are mutually in love with each other.

j : U,w,y,z.

Uj = as . . . as: mind-same: as good as true: all the same in the mind.
jUm = equal = same-mind-quality: it is the mind which decides that men are equal, even though the one is great, the other small.
yjUm = different, unequal. (A short, more colloquial term would be "jym" leaving out the "mind-U" (j-y-m-equal-opposite-quality)
EjUm = true = "matter-equal-mind-quality"; if your mind-picture equals the object "matter", you know the truth
EjU = truth; EjUv = to prove, verify, "make-true", show the truth of . . .
yEjUm(s) = false(hood), (mistake)
ygtEjUm = honest, frank = "outward-toward-truth": if you show your inner feeling truly toward the outside, you are honest.
EjUOm = sincere, "true-feeling" tYgOm =
jwUs = law = "equal-power-mind-thing" (j-w-U-s): the thing which rules with equal power in the minds of men, is the law, which should not make differences between rich and poor etc.
jwUr = right, a right. "equal-power-good", a power, equaling a value, or a good, is a right, a good, fair "power"-claim.
jwUsU = justice = law-mind(edness).
jwUsO(m) = loyal/ty = law-sentiment, feeling for lawfulness.
jwyz(ev) = rule: "equal-power-un-part", "equal-power-(for the) whole": a rule is in "force" for the "whole" equally, not just for a part.
t-yje(v) = (to) change: "toward-different(yjUm)-move: if you move into something different, you are changing. jnUz = mean
zEj = proportion: "a part-matter-equal": if the parts are materially equal, or correspond to each other, they are in the same proportion."

Translate:
—pI um Ql Ub knuw cEv ugapAm kab pI Us, Uf can u cEv wUpAm jUm. dyf sE c EjUm, Uf pIn u cEv nEm yjUm ag cEmU, nu Uyv Uj jUm yk jwUs. a-u Uv, Uf pIn u Ub fE bEn cEv nEm yjUm: pIn pnEk rUm Ib nUm u cEv jOm at a-u. yUg, pIn pnEk yrUm Ib ynUm u cEv jOm at yrom os.—

Retranslate into aUI:
The human state (condition) of government is built upon the idea, that all men are created equal. Although it is true that they are very different in reality, they are thought (of) as equal under the law. (Grammatically safer: They think that all men are equal . . .: "nu Uv, Uf can u cEv jUm . . .). The spaceman thinks that the men of this earth are very different: the best and wisest men are like (to) spacemen. But the worst and most stupid men are like (to) sick animals.

(In the melody of "Old Macdonald had a farm, heyi, heyi, ho . . :")

rI Ub jym JiM	The Song of Different Jim.
xA can yf tvu rOvepAv, JiM yc rOvepAv: JiM pAc jym.	When all other boys played, Jim did not play: Jim was different.
xA can yf tvu skepAv kogYg JiM yc skepAv kogYg JiM pAc jym.	When all other sons (boys) wore a hat Jim (did) not wear (carry) a hat Jim was different.
xA can tvu vEpAv nam woz JiM yc vEpAv woz: JiM pAc jym.	When all boys made big muscles Jim made no (t) muscles: Jim was different.
xA can yf tvu brOpAv, JiM yc brOpAv: JiM pAc jym.	When all the other boys loved, Jim (did) not love/d.: Jim was different.
xA can yf u ydbrUpAv, JiM yc ydbrUpAv: JiM pAc jym.	When all other men warred, Jim did not fight: Jim was different.
xA can yf u yopAv, JiM yc yopAv: JiM tfA ov.	When all other men died, Jim did not die: Jim lives still.

(pAc = cEpAv = cpAv -short slang; "jym" slang for "yj(U)m"; tvu = son = boy).

"k" : a,b,d,e;r,s,t

"k" denotes: above, on top, over, upper, superior, high . . . .

k: a,b,d,e

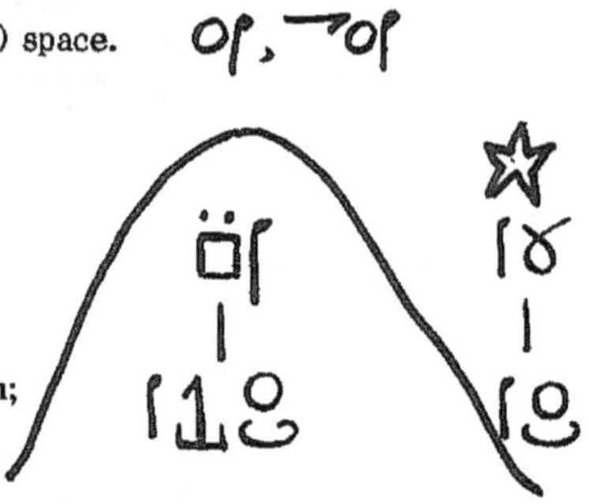

ak = above = "space-above", above (in) space.
tak = up = toward-space-above
kam = high = above-space-quality, spatially—above—adjective
(kam = high-up, high above us;
ki c kam = the star is high)
kanam = high = tall: (rising up)
bEk c kanam = the mountain is high
ykam = low = opposite (of) high.
nykam = deep = much-low, very far-down;
ynykam = shallow = "undeep"
bEk = mountain = earth-height
bak = upon = together-above
kab = on; ab = at, above-at = above and at = on
"On the mountain, way up high" = kab bEk, da tak, kam = kab bEk, (more correct:) ybam tak, kanam
kad = across = above and through.
ek = over = move-above:
"But all the tunes that he could play, was: over the hills and far away."
—yUg can pIn rI, vu wapAv vIv xnE, c'pAv: "ybam ayt Ib ek pIn bEk."
kem = smooth = above-movable: If it is easy to move over something, it must be smooth. 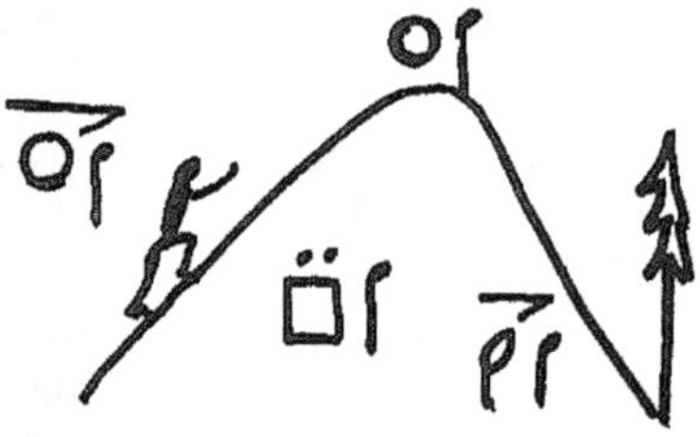
ydkem = rough = against-over-movability:
(a rough surface fights against being passed (or: moved) over.
tEk = wood = toward-matter-above; see: tok = tree, under "o"
(wood contains air, kE, "toward (t)" which the tree grew; see "tak (Em)".
kyfrUm = excellent= above-others-good = good-above (beyond) the rest.

k: r,s,t

rEyka = a mine, mine-shaft = metal-down-space
skev = carry, wear = thing-above-move, = to move (or transport) a thing above oneself, on top of one's head or shoulders, = carry it.
skevu = porter, carrier = carry-man
yksav = deposit, put down = yk (down) + sav (put), or: below thing-space make, make space below for a thing.
tak = up = toward-above. tok tnev tak Ib tEv takEm ag kE. fE tEk tev yt takEm tok. The tree grows up & becomes tall in the air . . .
takEm = tall = "up-matter-quality"; tall means physical, material growth upward.
ektEm = light = "move-up-ward (up-to)-matter"; something light can be easily lifted, moved up; light material floats up.
vektev = to lift = make-upward-move, move-to-above

k: t; v,w,y

tekE = levity, buoyancy = toward-move-up-material (abstract: tekEmU)
tekEm = buoyant, nimble, light-footed = toward-move-up-like = tekQm
tykEm = heavy, grave = toward-below (=down)-matter-like, down-sinking
tykE = weight = down-matter, tykEmU = gravity
yktE(w) = burden, (load) = down-ward-matter (-force), pulling one down
yktEm = burdensome, down-ward-pulling
tykEv = to weigh, press downward (materially)
tykE-an = kilo-gram (weight-unit) (E-an = gram = mass-unit)
katav = to go over, above, transcend (av = go, kat = above-toward)
yktrUm = serious = "down-ward--good-mind-quality", burdened in a good sense
ytkav(Am)= hang(ing) = "from (yt)-above (k)-space (a).." from a place above/ suspended
bytkav(Am) = depend (ent) = "with (together)-hanging from.." (A dependent hangs, like a weight or a fruit from a tree, staying together with his supporter)

k: v,w,y

(Like "ytkav" to hang, also the verbs of "standing, lying, sitting.." lack the element of motion "e").
kav = to stand = "above-space-verb": if one is up in space, he stands
ykav = to lie = "down-space-verb"; if one is down in space, one lies
ykavd = bed = lie-down-tool
vykav = to lay = to make lie down, (causative)
ykta(v) = seat (sit) = "lying-ward-verb", toward lying down; the sitting position is often a preparation for lying down; an in-between state toward lying.
vyktav = to set, to make (v-) sit; setting is a preparation for laying
kwE = wall = above-stone; high-stone: K:
pile stone above stone, high up, and
you have a wall
twEk = pillar = toward-stone-up;
a pillar strives often toward a
stone-rafter above.
(twE)kanas = column = toward-above-stone-line, or pillar-length
(kanas = "column" in a printed vertical row)
(tykwEzev = to crush = down-power-matter-parts-make; to make parts, pieces, out of something hard (wE)
skwEr(v) = support: skev = to carry (something above); support = "thing-above-power-matter-good-make"; power-matter = hard:
a support is "hard, of powerful material & carries something above.
kU = God = above-spirit, the Spirit-above, on high; KU = GOD
kUw = authority = above-mind-power, the mind-power which rules above
ykwu(v) = serv/ant = "the-"under-(somebody else's)-power-man-(serve)
ykwus = service = servant-thing
yk = below (anti-above); ykUm = inferior = undermind-like, underling
tyk = down = toward-below
ykaz = base = under-space-part, under-part
kaz = top = above (space-) part
--KU wUpAv u at vum jiOs Ib jiOms. yUg, u epAv ayt yt kU--
God created man to his image and likeness. But man moved away from God.

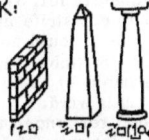

-- fnum bUm nUI -- Our Common Tongue.

-- ag na-A cEpAv pI UI, "ag pe cEpAv a-UI . . . Ib can cEv wUpAm Ud UI . . . "Ib UI cEpAv o-i+)." ag ca-ytU-UIvo 1) Ub pAom kU-O-u 2), fnu pOv gUw-gU Ub tA ag xE 3), fnu IOv, Uf, yUt pIn u, ag yd-ykwevAm 4) yrkO Ub pe-yrUvs 5) Ub "afU-vU", tykepAv ayt yt ca-aU 6) Ub num wUv-KU, nu, yUt-Ub-fE, bIb tykepAv ayt yt can-yf: ag-as-Ub brU Ib brO tepAv ydbrU Ib ydO, yUt "pIn num nUI vEpAyv jym", nu yc wapAv jyttUm 7) iUv, xA nu tvepAv ugav kanam-ugavs 8) Ub BABeL, kam tag kan, Ut viOv; Ib bev num bavum yrkO ag-as-Ub ugav rykOm 9) ki-iO-ugavs, Ut AiOv jwUs Ub KU-ki Ib syv snEm UI.

-- xA u Ub fE eki epAv ayt yt a-UI, UI Ub ca-aU, num bavum nUI zEpAyv tag nEk Ib nEk ynam-nUI ag yrkOm "faU-vU." xA pIn u Ub fE eki yc nEk-A twUpAv bev eb num a-bru, nu yc wapAv iUv can-yf. am u Ib, eb vu, fE bEn, tykepAv ayt yt a-bevU (ybaO), can yf U-cEvs 11) Ub pIn yf ki vApApAv xE.

-- jOm Uj a pyga-ogz, a bo, a boz, Qg dzEpAm ayt yt pI zyn os, zEyv tag ṣEm Ez 12) Ib yov, gaf jOm at pfE nakot, y-vrAm zwEpAm yt tok Ub gU, yt o-jE Ub o-sevAm bevU eb ca, pev zEyv Ib yov, fUd u vu-fU bIb, Qg zayv yt ca, pev zEyv ag vu-fU, Ib yc nEk-A wav iUv vum bavum EsgU.

-- sE c' yb trO, Uf u wav ymA Utev a-yf ag brU Ib brO, Qg nu yc Utev num da typ at can-am 13) aU Ub num ytU. trO yc cEv, Uf u watAv iUv vum bam-u 14) Ud bEn-jOm 15) gebanum UI, Qg vu yc typ-etgUv EjUm UI Ub can-a, aUI.

At the origin was the Logos, "In the beginning was the Word, . . . and all is created by the Word . . and the Word was the light of life+) . . " In the myths 1) of ancient mystics 2), in which 3) we feel-a-foreboding of the knowledge of the science of the future, we hear that because man, in the rebellious 4) pride of original sin 5)), of "individuation", fell away from the cosmic unity 6) of their creator, they consequently fell also away from each other: Instead of peace and harmony, they got strife and dissension, because "their languages were confounded," they could not understand one-another 7), when they tried to build "the tower 8) of Babel high into heaven to broadcast their own pride, instead of a humble 9) observatory-tower to watch the laws of God's stars and receive their word.

When the men of this planet renounced the language of space, the Logos of cosmic unity, their own language fell apart into more and more divided idioms in arrogant individuations. When the men of this planet would no-longer 10) commune with their cosmic friends, they could finally no longer understand each other. Man alone, and with him this earth, fell off from cosmic-communication (telepathy), which all other rational-beings 11) of the other stars had preserved.

Just like a limb, a hand, a finger, if cut off from the whole life-giving-organism, decays 12) and dies, or like that apple, broken unripe from the tree of knowledge, from the sap of life-giving communication with the universe, would rot and die, so man himself, so man him-self, too, if separated from the cosmos, begins to disintegrate in himself, and can no longer understand his own meaning.

It is hopeless that men can ever find one-another in peace and love, unless they find their way back to the cosmic 13) unity of their origin. There is no hope that man shall be able to understand his fellowman 14) in (by) an earthly 15) international tongue, unless he re-learns the true Logos of the universe, The Language of Space.

+)UI = oi, Mind-Sound= Life-Light: If we visualize the primeval Logos who creates, while he speaks words, these creative words must be transparent, they must contain the recipe of creation, as the words of aUI. 1) world-origin-story= myth, 2) God-feel-men, 3) = in them (which), 4) anti-obedient, 5) begin-sin, 6) one-ness, 7) mutually, 8) high-building, 9) good-low-feeling, 10) more-time, 11) mind-being, 12) is-split-into its elements, 13) all-spatial, 14) near-man, 15) earth-like.

"L" : a, b, e, k, m

"L" denotes "Roundness", : circular, spheric, ball, curve, around, about.

L: a, b, e, k, m

la = roundness, "round-space"
al = around, "space-round", round (the) space, around, round
lam = round = round-space-adjective
las = ball, sphere = round-space-thing. (The Pythagorean Ancients considered the round form as symbolic of the perfect good; "l" round, and "r" good are so similar that Chinese and Japanese equate them.)
(ilas = light-bulb = "light-ball") -- las c lam can al. - The ball is round all around.
dlana = axis (as e.g. through the earth) = "through-roundness-(a-) line", an axis is a "one-dimension-space" (ana) a line, stabbing through a round (l) thing, a sphere or a wheel or a circular movement. Where it stabs through, the place, "as" is
dlanas = pole (as is North-Pole).
blams = a knot = "together (tied) -round-thing"; a round thing which keeps (e.g. string) tied together
--anam bana bwanayv ag lam blams.-- (A long string is (being) tied in a round knot.)
blena = button = "together-round-flat": a button is round and flat and it holds "together" e.g. a coat
lena = disk = round-flat (ena)
led = wheel = "round-move-tool" (a wheel is a primitive "means-by which" -d-we move around)
lev = to turn, le = (a) turn
(to) move-round (a corner, e.g.)
lelv = to roll = "round-move-round-make" (round-and-round it rolls)
vel(v) = (to) bend; velpAm = bent. "make-move-round (in a curve)"
--Qg nu "velv" i, nu vEv sE lev. -(If one (they) "bend" light, he makes it turn.)
-- nu dEpAv yEl Ib tEl (rings & hooks) Ap nu ApUpAv (invented) blena-Ib gyE - They (one) used rings and hooks, before they invented button-and-hole. -fA nu dEv blena, Ut bAv uyg tab, Ib Ut bwev (press) Ib bav weim jEte tab. -- Now they use buttons in order to hold the dress together (b) and in order to press and join the electric current together.
yEl = ring = no-matter--round = hole-- round; a ring is something around a hole in the middle, where there is "no matter."
nyElb = chain = "many-rings-together" join to a chain: n-yEl-b.
--Qg bu bwev fE blena, tak-ged yetAv. - If you press this button, the elevator will stop. (tak-ged = up-vehicle, lift). -- tak-ged yetAv ab ne ugayk, Ib yfA etAv tak At kaz Ub uga. -- The elevator will stop at the second floor, and then will move up till (to) the top of the house. -- led lev al, Ib tykE ab yf az ev tyk at ykaz. -- The wheel turns around, and the weight at the other side moves down to the base.

kogel = collar = "neck-move-around"; the collar is a ring (yEl) put (moved) "e" around (l) the neck (kogz) = (above-body-part = k-og-z).
-- kogel c yEl (bwanapAm) al kogz" (tied).
mal = circle = form (ma-) -round (l), qualified-space-round = m-a-l
--mal Ib lena Ib las c lam.

The circle and the disk and the ball are round. -- yUg, mal c lam ana Ub jUm la: fE ana typev tag sE-fU; lena c enam: las c´ inam Es, lam iOpAm yt can az. --
But the circle is a round line of equal roundness: this line returns into itself; the disk is flat (two-dimensional); the sphere is a three-dimensional thing, round seen from all sides.

olE(m) = fat = "life-round-matter" : what makes a "living" thing appear roundish, is its fat. -- ru UIpAv: fum lodbos c lam, yUg fum byvu cEv fum pnEk·olEm bos. - The gentleman said: "My pig is round, but my wife is my most fat (fattest) domestic-animal."
l-od-bos = round-food-beast) ; yolEm = thin, meager
olz = bulb = live-round-thing: -nEn io bav ols Uj ykaz. - Many plants have bulbs as base. volz = gonads, testicles, voz = sex, vom = male.
lypoz = buttocks = round-back-life-part.
tlak = arch, arc, bow = toward-round-space-above: an arch is rounded toward upward: tlak layv tak.-
tlev(s) = curve = toward-turn (-thing), toward-round-move-make; a curve moves toward a turn, toward a round bend
tlevom = flexible = curve-live-quality, toward-round-move-make-living (something flexible seems rather alive, while "stiff, rigid" means dead)
tEl = hook = toward-matter-round: a hook curves toward roundness; it is a material thing, while the circle is abstract space.
takle = spiral, screw-line, coil = upward-round-movement = tak-l-e.
tygle = spiral, snail-line (flat) = toward-outside-round-movement: If you move outside round and round, you get a snail-spiral.
Ul = about = mentally-around: e.g. "we think about her" = "our mind moves around her" : -- fnu Uv Ul yvu. -- = fnum U ev Ul yvu. -
wal = fence = power-space-around = powerful protection around a place.
wyrlev = twist = "force-bad-turn": you force a hen's neck round in an evil way, if you twist it = -- bu vowev yvu-kEbos-kogz al, ag yrUm mUd, Qg bu wyrlev sE. --
ylem = straight = not-round-move = unbending
wylem = stiff = powerfully straight, opposite of rounding, turning (lem)
(y-tlevom = rigid = un-flexible)

"m" : a, A, I, m

"m" denotes "Quality, a kind, sort, type, shape, form.
-m = -qualified, -like, as ending of adjectives & adverbs.

m : a

ma = form = "qualified space"; a form, a shape, is space of a certain quality, of a certain type, e.g. "rounded" or "cubic"
Ama = fashion = "time-form", the form of a certain time or epoch, in which this type e.g. of dress is "fashionable", Amam.
mUma = style = "quality-form", the form of form, in a sense, the form-type; classic style, e.g. is a type of formal attitude
vUma = behavior: "make-mind-form", the mental make-up, the form in which a mind acts, (vU), is its behavior"
vamU = manners, conduct, "act-form-quality"
na-vUma(m) = custom(ary) = much-space (e.g. a whole land, una, has a certain behavior: this behavior is the custom of that land.
nA-Uma = habit = much-time-mind-form: what you do for a "long time" becomes fixed in your mind, a form of behavior, a habit
Uma = character = mind-form
UamA = attitude = mind-space -- situation (see "mA"); the attitude of a man is the situation in which his mind is in space. If a man has an aggressive attitude, that means, his "mind" is at the "time" (A) of a quality, or "state of affairs" in which he approaches dangers, instead of running away, "spatially" speaking.
tUvma = design = toward-mind--form = purpose (tU) -made-form: if an architect shapes, "makes" the form of a building, in his mind, "toward" a certain function, a certain mental idea, he makes the design of this house.
uma = figure = (hu)man-form, shape
mab = configuration, form-together
iO-mab = pattern = "see-form-together": a pattern is a configuration, which is seen together (as pleasing to the eye).
mA = situation, "Zustand", state-of-affairs; can replace "Q" = condition. "qualified time" is a "state": I have a bad time = I'm in a bad state.
(ka-mA = weather = sky-state, the situation in the sky)
(mAg = in the situation, provided that, if = Qg)

m : I, m, U, y.

-Im = -state; shortened ending from
mAI = circumstance; situation "around" somebody; qualified-time-around: If you knew in what circumstances I am, in what "quality" I am at the time, what is happening "around" me, what "time" I have.
-m = adjective or adverb-ending: -ly, -y, -ic, -al, -ous, -ful, -like
mU = quality; -mU = -ism;
mUd = manner, mode, by which; see "vamU" and "vUma" above.
ym = any, i.e. "without qualifications": Give me any food = serv ym od at fu!
(tynUmvU = qualification = "smaller-range (of) quality-make . ."

-- da Ub ki Ib Ub u. --   The Way of the Star and of Man.

--- la c´ ma Ub ki Ib Ub da Ub eki. – Roundness is the shape of the stars and of the path of the planets. -- yUg am pI ana, xE av al ki, azve ge e dlanas, (the line -- half (way) between the two poles -- is the equator), cEv gnUrm (perfect) mal. da Ub eki c´ anapAm (a lengthened, stretched) mal (an ellipsis). eki Oiv at fnu can A jam, yUg u tyjev. ma Ub ki c´lam, yUg ma Ub u tyjev jOm at eki. --- u tyjev mUma Ub vum vUma, ap-can (before-all, foremost, above-all) yvus twUv tyjev Ama can akiA. jUf uma Ub yvus tyjev. (Even the figure of woman changes). yIn-A (some-times) yvu c´ olEm, yIn-A yolEm (non-fat, thin, skinny). rUt u, iOmab Ub vUma c´ nEm pnUrm (very important. Qg a u yjUm Ev, Ib zwEv na-vUma, fE u Oiv U-yrom (mind-sick, insane). na-vUmam mUd Ub vamU Oiv nEk pnUrm myt o. (If one man does (acts) differently, and breaks the custom, this man seems insane. The customary mode (manner) of conduct seems more important than life.)

-- pnEk u yc tlevom. nEn u Uv, Uf nu wav ov am ag a "da-Ub-o". Qg yf u twUv tyjev fE mUd Ub num o, nu cEv vrAm at ydbrU, at yov Ib vyov. (They are ready to war, to die and kill).

"n" : a, A, a, c, e, E, e; j, k, m, n

"n" denotes Quantity, amount, dimension, "lots", plenty, many, much, big, number, size, plural, multitude, crowd.

n : a, A, a, c.

an = size = "space-quantity", how much room something takes, depends on its size. 
nam = big, great: "quantity (of) space-adjective"; ynam = little, small 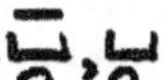
nAm = frequent, "many-times" -adjective, often 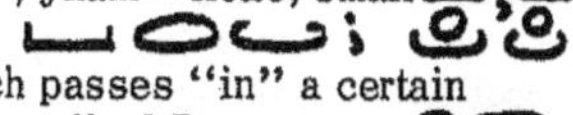
gAn = rate = "in-time-quantity: the amount which passes "in" a certain "time", e.g. in a minute through a pipe, is the "rate" of flow. 
can = all = "existence-space-quantity," the quantity in existence, (all) that exists in space, whatever there is in space. 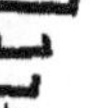 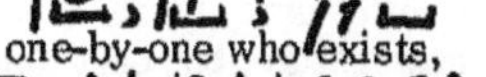
can = every, each = "existing-one-quantity", (each) one-by-one who exists, the number of one and one, whoever there "is". 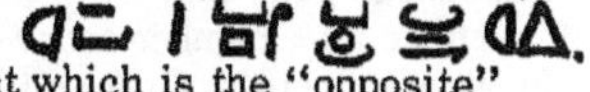
(zyn = whole = part-opposite-quantity, the amount which is the "opposite" of "part", is the "whole")
yn = no(ne), "no amount". 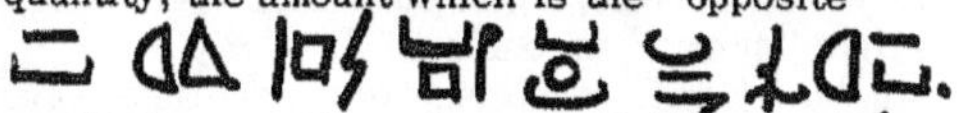
(ana = length = "one-space-quantity" = one dimension, see "a", e.g.:
binanab = linen = "white-many-lines-together" (woven), woven-threads.) 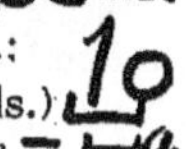
ytna (v) = select/ion = "from-many-one" (take): if you take one out of a choice of many, you are selecting. 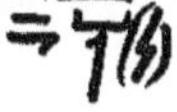

n : b, E.

tebne(v) = add/ition: "toward-move-together-number- (make): if you move some amount to(ward) gether with something else, you are adding together both amounts. 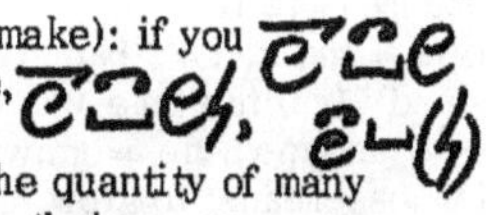
ben (v) = amount = "together-move-quantity(make)"; the quantity of many summands or factors, "moved-together" in their sum, is their "amount", as it were, on a "mountain" heaped together.
En = mass = matter-quantity, the quantity denoted by matter, is its mass; mass is the measurable amount of matter. 
nE = much, nEn = many = quantity-substance; muchness is similar to mass; there is a mass of people = there is much, many; many is the plural of much: nE(n). 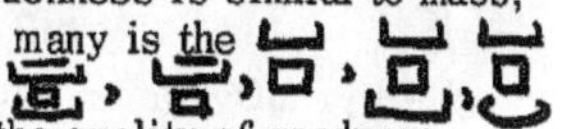
nEm = very: much quality, very good = much of the quality of goodness.
ynE = (a) little, a bit: opposite of much. ynEn = few, not-many.

n : j, k, m, n

jniO (Ed) = scale(s): (Ed = instrument): "same-amount-see--tool": in order to see, whether e.g. a powder has the same quantity as a weight desired, the druggist puts each on either scale. 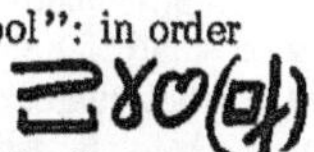
A "scale" is also used in map drawing, for the same distances, the (jn) "same number" of feet to each inch drawn, in order to "see" (iO) the true distance. 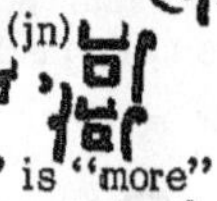
nEk = more: nE = much; "much-above", = "over and above much" is "more"
pnEk = most: "before-more" = most; the most famous man is known before and above (p..k) all the others 
nEke (v) = increase = "more-move-make", to move it toward more, make more.
tnak = limit = "toward (a certain) amount (of) space, above "which one can not go, is the limit "toward" which one can only approach.

"n : k, m; O, p, t, y, z.

tank = degree: "to-one-quantity-up" e.g. raise the temperature one degree = put it "one unit (an) up (tak): t-an-k.

knE = too (much): "above-much" = knE: you drink too much! bu jEv knE!

nUz= quantity: quantity (in the) abstract, in the mind, quantity-concept.

nUmI (v) = account = "quantity-spirit-quality-sound-make": if you give account of how many enemy-soldiers you defeated, you "sound" off about their "number (quantity)" and about the "quality" of your exploits, and about the "spirit" in which you accomplished the mission, about which you "make" your report.

mUn = number = "quality-concept(of)-quantity: a number is the quality of quantity in our mind (U). There are quantities in inanimate nature, but only our "mind" qualifies them by counting.

mUnIv = to count = number-sound-make; to sound or say numbers = to count.

mUnUv = to calculate, figure out = number-mind-make, to make the figuring of the right "number" in one's mind.

n- = -th: nu = four-th, n-4 = number-4; instead of saying: stop at the fourth floor! say: stop at floor number-4: yerv ab nu ugayk!

na = first, ne = second, ni = 3rd, nu = 4th, nOke = 100th. 100=100. 4, 5.

n : O, p, t, y, z.

niOv = measure = quantity-see = n-iOv; let me see (iOv) the amount(n) = let me measure it.

ypnAm = the last = "backward-number-time-quality", the one who comes "behind" (yp) the time (A) of the others, is the "last" number (n)

tnev = to grow; tne = growth = "toward-quantity-- move"; to move to bigness means: to grow.

ytne(v) = (to) decrease, diminish = anti-grow(th); opposite of tne(v).

yn = no (ne) = not-any: I have no time, I have none: fu bav yn A, fu bav yn

But: have you time? No! = bu bav A? hI? -- "yr!" = No!

zyn = whole = part-opposite-quantity, not a part-- but the whole! cf. can!

niO = (The) measure.

-- can gUw wyv niOv! yc am iOv, xI yms cEv nam gaf ynam, nE gaf ynE, nEn gaf ynEn; yUg, gUw wyv gUv, pI trUm nU, pI trUm ben, trUm En, trUm gAn, (Ud xE yI jE nav ad yI anyEd). gUwu bav nEn dEs, Ut niOv pnEk Es Ub Eo. --

All sciences must measure! not only see, whether something is big or small, much or little, many or few; but science must know the correct quantity, the correct amount, the correct mass, the correct rate (by which a liquid runs through a pipe). The scientists have many instruments, in-order-to measure most things of nature.

(gUw = in-mind-power = science; gUw-u = science-man = scientist; wyv = must).

"o" : b

"o" = Life, implying: Animation, vitality of animals, plants, the (human) body and Food.

"o"

o = life; om = alive; ov = to live; os = animal = life-thing, something alive.
o = five, 5 occurs often in living things: original land-vertebrates (e.g. lizards) like cats and man have 5 fingers; nature's rose-family (apple-blossoms, strawberries) have 5 petals. We have 5 vowels.

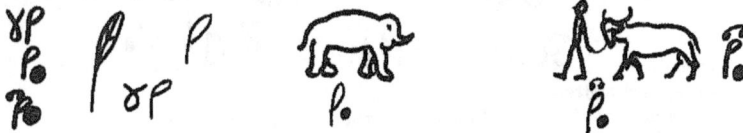

bos = domestic-animal = "together-(with man)-animal", b-os is an animal that lives together with man, in old language, a beast.
bi(jE) bos = cow = milk-beast = white-liquid-beast; bi-bos = white-beast, for short.
ynbi(jE) bos = small-cow = goat
kEos = bird = air-animal
kEbos = chicken = air-domestic-animal, fowl; domestic bird, air-beast
yv-kEbos = hen = female-fowl, she-chick; vom-kEbos = male-fowl = cock
ukbos = horse = man-above-beast, a beast upon which man can ride;
vukbos = stallion, yvukbos = mare; "pAom bybim yvukbos: yvu yc, xE yvu dEvUm cpA" = The old gray mare: she ain't, what she used to be.
(dEvUm cEpA(v) = usuall(y) was.)
yrukbos = donkey, ass = "bad-horse", bad-land-horse, poor-horse.

lodbos = pig, swine = round-food-beast; a porker is round, and we feed on its olE = fat (cf. oleomargarine)
uygbos = sheep = man-outside (=clothing) -beast (for wool)
waubos = dog = "power-space (stronghold, fenced yard) man-together-beast, a watch-dog gives "man the power" of his protection in his yard.
yr-waubos = wolf = bad-dog (-like animal), the wrong kind of dog.
yr-bos = rat = bad-beast, the wrong kind of domestic animal.

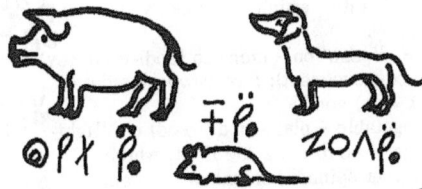

o, o : b: d

bo = hand (sounds as French "bon") = "together-five" (fingers); a hand consists of 5 (o) (fingers) working together.

boz = finger = handpart = together-5-part: a finger is a part of a combination of five.

bozEvz = nail = hand-knife, hand-cutter

(zEvd = knife, part-matter-make-tool, see: "z")

(Many a wife found her "nails" "handy", if she had no other knife to scratch her husband's face = nEn byvu UtepAv yvum bozEvz "bom", Qg yvu yc bapAv yf zEvd, Ut bozEv kup Ub bvu.

bozEv = to scratch

ozevz = claw = 5-part-move-make-part: a claw can move rapidly and rip its victim's skin apart, in 5 parts.

bozvos = cat = nail (claw) -animal as domestic (bos) beast with (man).

kozvos = lion = high-claw-animal; the king of animals is the tallest,

nozvos = tiger = long, big claw-animal; long cat

bowz = thumb: power(w) -finger (boz): the thumb is the strongest finger

ykboz = toe = under (yk) -finger (boz)

ykbo = foot = underhand (yk = under, bo = hand)

o : d

od = food (especially for humans) like "meat" = "life-means" (Lebensmittel) victuals, the "means-by (which) we live"

do = nourishment, eats, "means-to-live" also for animals and plants

dov = to eat, to feed (oneself); dvov = to feed (someone else)

ydov = to excrete, ydos = excrement

(jEv, to drink, could be replaced by "jEtgov" = to imbibe, if one prefers pedantic exactness.)

godz = stomach = inside-food-part; the part of the body "inside" which you stoke your feed is the tummy.

gode(v) = digest/ion = stomach (god)-move (ev), or: inside-food-move(ment): food moves inside.

ygode(v) = (to) vomit

iod = vegetable = plant-food (io-od) or "light-life-means" (i-o-d) : it's the light, which prepares your spinach, or makes it green.

odjE = soup = food-liquid, supposedly nourishing; dishwater won't do.

ei-jE-od = oil (olive or salad-oil), yellow-liquid-food

bi-jE-(od) = milk (-food) =white-liquid(-food); since no other "white-liquid" is so customary, "bi-jE" suffices.

bE-bijE(od) = cheese (-food) = solid-milk (-food), milk-solids

o : d; g

bitei-od = butter = white-to-yellow-food (white milk is beaten into yellow butter.
iojE(od) = tea = plant-liquid (food): tea is made from green plant- leaves
rOjE(od) = wine = good-feeling-liquid (food): the liquid that makes you feel good -- or so they say
nod = bread = plenty-food, the food that is most plentiful or common
tonod = grain = seed (to)-many (n)-food (od) = to-n-od
grO-nod = cake = sweet-bread = inside-good-feel-- bread: the kind of bread that makes you feel good inside
nynzod = meal-flour: "many-little-parts (=powder) -- food (nynz -- od)
osod = meat = animal-food, food made from animals
rodu(v) = cook = good-food-man(do) = r-od-u-(v): a man who makes good food 
odz(ev) = (to) bite = food-part (make) = to cut the food into parts
odzEvz = tooth = food-part-make-part, the "part" of the body which chews the "food" into "parts" a-part, and "makes" it digestible
odzEv = to chew.
bigrO/m(od) = sugar = white-sweet-(food);
grOm = sweet = inside-good-feel (since there no other white sweets important, "-od" is not needed)
eigrO(m-od) = honey = yellow-sweet(-food):
bibygrE(-od) = table-salt = white-salt (-food):
grE = alkaline (in-metal, containing metal)
ygrE = acid (outside metal, opposite of base)
bygrE = salt = together (b) alkaline + acid

o : g

og = BODY/ = life-inside = life-container: life occurs inside a body the body is the container of life.
ogai = blood = body-red, the red liquid inside the living beings
ogE = flesh = body-material
ogwE = bone = body-stone, body-hard the hard matter inside us.
koged = arm = upper-body-move-tool, upper-leg
oged = leg = body-move-tool
oged-baz = knee = leg-joint; baz = joint = together-one-part
gog = heart = inside-body, body-center; "gog" sounds like a heartbeat

"o:g";i

ogz = "organ" = "body-part" (og-z) = life-inside-- part (o-g--z)
jEogz = kidneys = water-organ (jE-ogz) = water -- body-part (jE-og-z)
kEogz = lungs = "air-organ", air-body-part
kazog = shoulder = "top, above-space-part" (of) "body" (kaz-og)
kogz = neck = "above-body-part"
(og) yps = (body) -back, literally: body-behind-thing); more consistent:
(og)ypaz = (body) back-space-part (which expression logical men prefer);
but: "yps" is preferred when you are in a hurry.
ypogz = tail = back-body-part, back-organ; the tail is an organ in the back.
logz = waist = around-body-part, the waist is measured around.
ogta = mouth = body-toward-space (og-t-a), or "life-into-space" (o-gt-a);
the place where things (food) enter, (come-into) the living being.
ogtai = lips = mouth-red, life-into-red, the red gates to life
ubogta(v) = (to) kiss: "human-together-mouth(s)-(make)": if you see
two human mouths joined together, you suspect kissing;
(Qg bu iOv e um ogta, bapAm tab, bu ykUv: ubogtav.)
ogwa = breast = body-strong-space; the strength (w) of the
body (og) seems to lie in its breast or chest (gwa).
yg = outside:
oyg = skin = "life-outside": any living thing is surrounded by skin;
noyg = hair: "many -- life-outside", many --skin: the "many" (things) that
grow on the "outside" (skin) of a living being are not grass, but "hair"
(-- nEn Es, xE tnev kab pl "yg" Ub om cEvs ("oyg"), yc nio, yUg "noyg")
osyg = fur = animal-outside: only animals have furry exteriors.
(gEs = trunk: "inside-matter-thing"; where material things are inside)

o:i

io = PLANT = "light-life": a green plant "lives" by
the "light" of the sun
oii = leaf (green) : "life-green" (thing); ii = green
iod = vegetable = plant-food (od),
"light-food" (i-od)
eliod = beans = "two-round-- vegetable": beans are doubly rounded, kidney-shaped, two spheric
parts united
bEliod = potatoes = earth-round-vegetable (bE-l-iod) 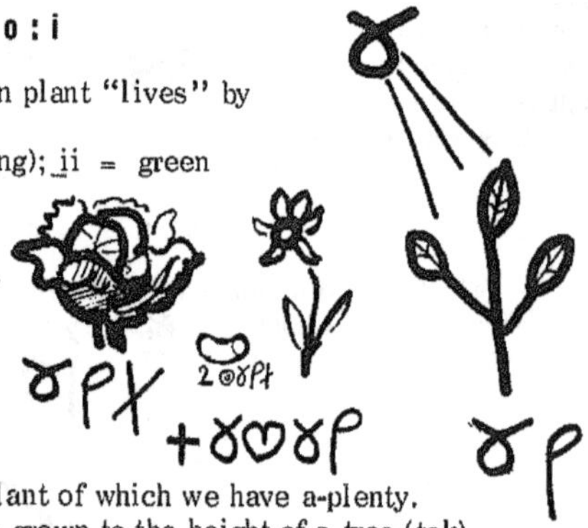
nio = grass = "plenty-plant", the plant of which we have a-plenty.
tok-nio = bamboo = tree-grass: grass grown to the height of a tree (tok)
ykio = moss: "low-plant"
ynios = bacterium = little-plant, micro-plant-thing
riO-io = flower = "beauty-plant" (good-(to) see-plant), the plant we like to see.
io-riO = bloom, blossom = plant-beauty: when a tree is in bloom,
it shows its plant-beauty.

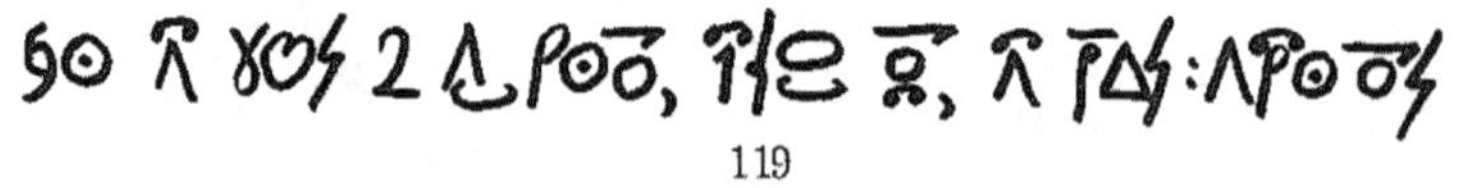

"o : i ; j, k"

tio = sprout = "toward-plant"; a sprout will develop to a plant
cf. "to" = seed = toward-life; tu = child = toward-man.
tio-riO = bud = "towards-(a)-bloom, or: sprout-beauty (t-ioriO, or: tio-riQ)
wanabio = hemp: "power-string-together-plant": hemp-string is used to tie something powerfully together (w-ana-b-io)

o : j, k.

jEos = fish = water-animal; jEoyg = (fish) scales = water-life-outside, fish-skin, water-skin.
kEos = bird, air-animal
(o)kEdz = feather: (kEd = air-tool = wing), wing-part = feather
okE(v) = breath(e) = life-air-(act), breath = the air for life.
tygokEI = cough = toward-outside (tyg) -breath (okE) -sound (I): when you cough, it "sounds" like barking, as you expel "breath out."
tok = tree = toward-life-above: a tree grows to live up high (tak)
(tEk = wood, takEm = high)
yktok = root = "under-tree": the root is under the tree.
tokyt = branch = tree-from (yt): a branch branches out "from the tree"
nAiitok = pinetree: much (-long) -time (nA) -green (ii) -tree (tok): evergreen.
(kup = face = "above-man-front": the face is in front and high up in man,
kupyg = cheek = face-outside: the cheeks are on the outer face.
kUg = head = above-mind-inside: the head is high "up", and "inside" is the intellect, the mind; see under U, u; kog = body-head
gOz = tongue: inside-feeling (= taste) -part (organ), see "O")

o : m, r, s

om = alive: life-adjective; yom = dead = un-living, life-less
ro(m) = health(y) = good-life (-adjective): if you are healthy, your life is good.
yro/m = sick/ness, ill/ness: no-good-life: a sick man has no good life.
trom = medical; trov = to heal, "toward-good-life-lead"; to heal means to bring back the good life of health
trod = medicine = heal-aid, -means; or: t-r --od = toward-good --food
yrod = poison = wrong (yr) -food: nEn trod c yrod (Many medicines are poison)
trogUw = medical science, medicine (as science) = heal-science (gUw)
// os = animal // = live-thing; bos = domestic animal.
(kEos = bird = air-animal; jEos = fish = water-animal, see above, under "o: j,k")
wEyg-jEykos = clam = hard-outside-water-low-animal (ykos)
jEnyEos = sponge = water-many-holes (jE-n-yE)-animal: a sponge has many holes.
izos = insect = 3-part-animal (head-breast-abdomen) see "o: z"
anos = worm = one-dimension (lengthy) animal; nanos = snake = big(n)-worm, big-long
ri-anos = silk worm = shining, bright worm, ri = bright, silk = shining. ri-anE = silk = bright-thread ykos = invertebrate, low-animal (neither vertebr. nor .

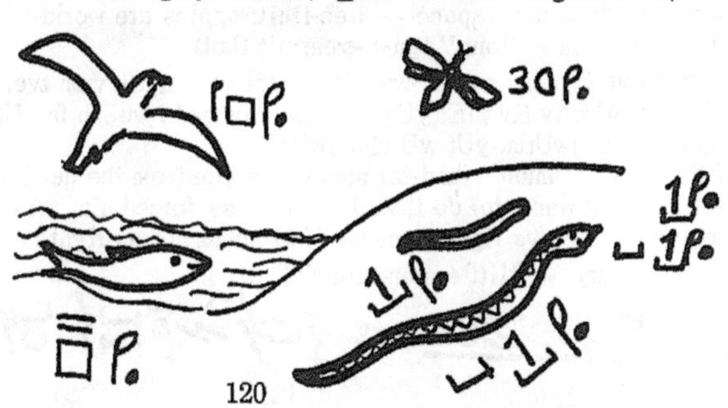

"o:s;t"

arthropod (insect) is a "low-animal" (yk-os), used as description, if no other outstanding feature recommends itself; e.g.:
yneykos = snail, slug; = slow-(yne) -low (yk) -animal (os)
koswyd = horn = "upon (k) -animal (os) -weapon (wyd); a horn is a weapon (wyd = power-against-tool) growing a-top (k) an animal's head.
umos = ape, monkey = human (um)-animal (os), man-like animal
ynos = bacillus = little (yn), micro-animal
(ynios = bacterium = micro-plant)

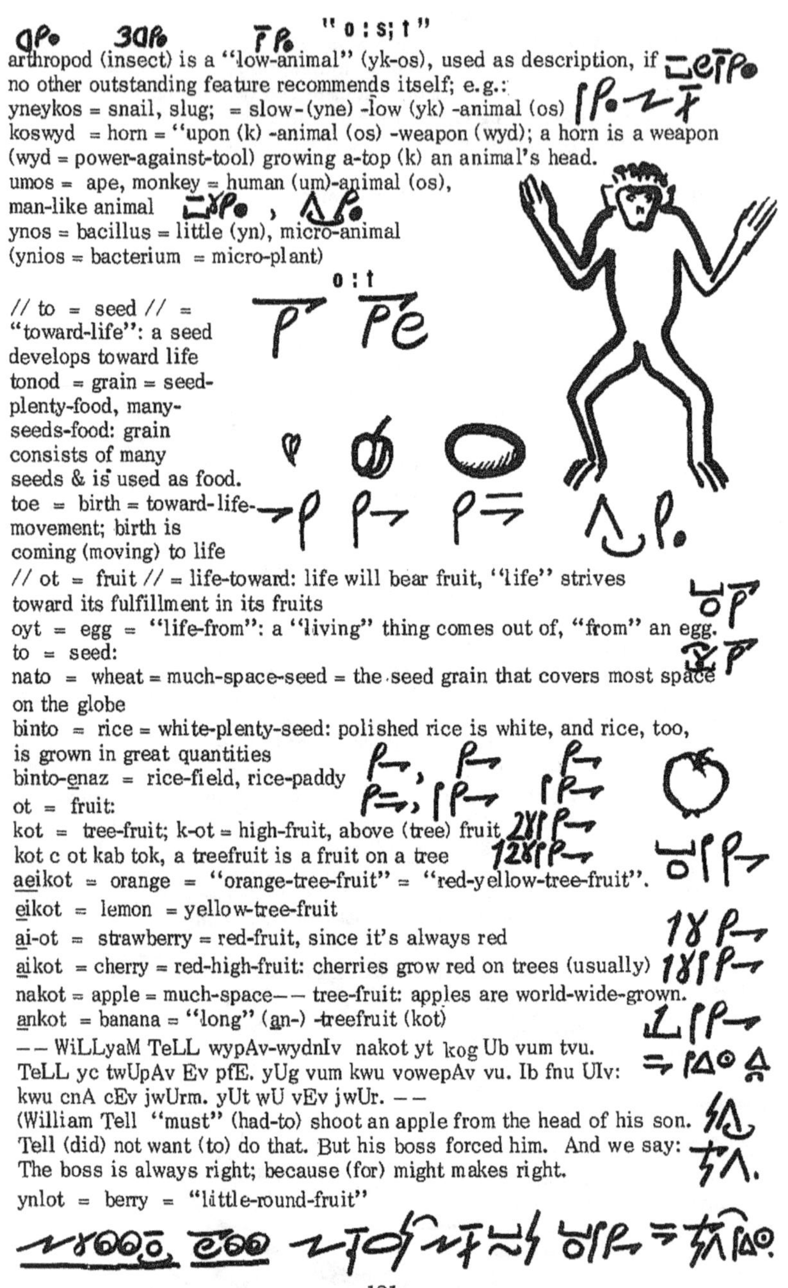

o:t

// to = seed // = "toward-life": a seed develops toward life
tonod = grain = seed-plenty-food, many-seeds-food: grain consists of many seeds & is used as food.
toe = birth = toward-life-movement; birth is coming (moving) to life
// ot = fruit // = life-toward: life will bear fruit, "life" strives toward its fulfillment in its fruits
oyt = egg = "life-from": a "living" thing comes out of, "from" an egg.
to = seed:
nato = wheat = much-space-seed = the seed grain that covers most space on the globe
binto = rice = white-plenty-seed: polished rice is white, and rice, too, is grown in great quantities
binto-enaz = rice-field, rice-paddy
ot = fruit:
kot = tree-fruit; k-ot = high-fruit, above (tree) fruit
kot c ot kab tok, a treefruit is a fruit on a tree
aeikot = orange = "orange-tree-fruit" = "red-yellow-tree-fruit".
eikot = lemon = yellow-tree-fruit
ai-ot = strawberry = red-fruit, since it's always red
aikot = cherry = red-high-fruit: cherries grow red on trees (usually)
nakot = apple = much-space—— tree-fruit: apples are world-wide-grown.
ankot = banana = "long" (an-) -treefruit (kot)
—— WiLLyaM TeLL wypAv-wydnIv nakot yt kog Ub vum tvu.
TeLL yc twUpAv Ev pfE. yUg vum kwu vowepAv vu. Ib fnu UIv:
kwu cnA cEv jwUrm. yUt wU vEv jwUr. ——
(William Tell "must" (had-to) shoot an apple from the head of his son.
Tell (did) not want (to) do that. But his boss forced him. And we say:
The boss is always right; because (for) might makes right.
ynlot = berry = "little-round-fruit"

o : t; U, v, w, y, z.

rOjEot = grapes = wine-fruit; wine = rOjE = good-feeling –– liquid (jE).
(wine makes one feel good, or so they say:
"rOjE vEv u Ov rUm, gaf fUd nu UIv"
wEgkot = peach = stone-inside-fruit: a peach has a stone inside
wEygkot = nut = "hard (wE) -outside (yg) -fruit": a nut has a hard shell outside, and is a tree-fruit (kot).
(cf. wEyg-jEykos = clam = hard-outside –– water-low-animal)

o : U, v, w, y, z.

oUz = brain = life-mind-part: the brain is that part of a living being which represents the mind.
ov = to live = life-verb; ovAm = living, om = alive
vov = procreate = make-live, cause life, engender life
voz = sex = "make-life-part", procreative-part.
volz = gonads, testicles = make-life-round-parts; W. Whitman: "man-balls."
vom = male = active-life-adjective: sexually at least, the male is the active one.
yvom = female = passive (receiving, conceiving) life: the female is sexually passive, receptive;
(vom-to = male-seed = sperm; yvom-oyt = female-egg = ovum)
vnom = fertile = make-much-life-adjective, procreative faculty.
yo(m = dead) = death: "opposite (of) life (adjective)"
"yo, ha c bum dzez?" (Death, where is thy sting?)
yov = to die = no-life-do, the non-life-act;
vyov = to kill = to make-die – = v-yov = make–– non-live = v––y–ov.
woz = muscle = power-life-part = strength-life-part;
wom = strong, wo = strength = power-life-(quality)
anawoz = sinew = one-dimension (lengthy) -strength-life-part (muscle).

oz = cell = life-part; the element (Ez) of life.
ogz = organ = body-part, part of the (human, animal, plant) organism.
odz = (a) bite = food-part, a bit; odzev = to bite (food-part-move)
odzEv = to chew.
izos = insect (3-part-animal): insects are cut, "insected" in head, chest abdomen
zos = arthropode = "jointed animal", parted animal; like insects, e.g. lobsters, too, or spiders, are joined of different parts.

nyEd-zos = "net-arthropod" = spider
(Since insects are the most numerous branch of arthropodes, "fa ykev zos", "here crawls an arthropode" means usually: "here crawls an insect.")
gaizos = mosquito = "inside-red-arthropode (or: insect)"
(when the mosquito drinks blood ogai), it gets red inside).

grizos = bee = inside-good-insect (grOm = sweet!): sweet-insect.
(eigrOm = honey-sweet)
(kE) gizos = the fly = (air) -inside-insect: the fly, flying in the air inside the house, is a "domestic insect" (gizos)
buizos = vermin (flea, bug) = "with-man-insect", vermin lives together with man (b-u): ynbuizos = flea, yrbuizos = bedbug
riOzos = butterfly = beauty-insect, (literally: beauty-arthropode, since no other "zos" is so pretty)
vizos = ant = active-insect because of its industrious activity
(For "ozevz = claw" and "bozvos = cat" see "bo = hand" under "o:b" above!)

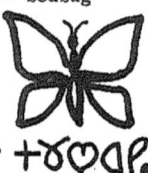

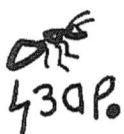

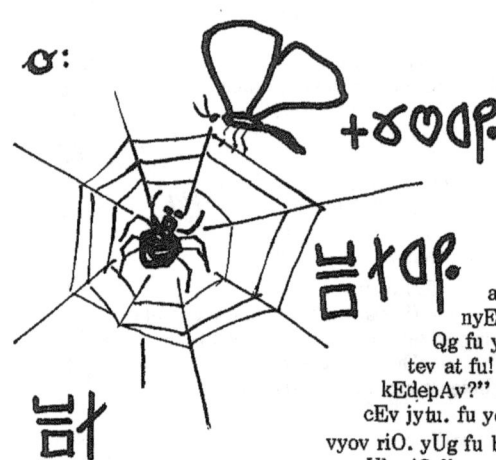

"riOzos kEdepAv tag nyEd Ub nyEd-zos. nyEdzos trApApAv (had waited) nEn iA at fev Ib syv od. fA sE tYvpAv riOzos. riOzos UIpAv: "budrYv kEdev fu yta, nyEdzos. fu c'riOm, Ib fu kEdev ad nEn bEna, kad ejE Ib nio at riOio!"

nyEdzos yhIpAv: "fu yc wav kEdev. fu yc wav tev at riOio. yUg, fu wav vEv nyEd, Ib fu wav trAv. ag ypAz, Qg fu yc wav tev at riOio, riOzos tev at fu! hU bu yc OtepAv, hat bu kEdepAv?" riOzos UIpAv "Ote Ib tyrO cEv jytu. fu yc vyov riOio, yUg bu wav am vyov riO. yUg fu bapAv o yb Ote Ib tyrO, o Ub riO."

(A butterfly flew into the net of a spider. The spider had waited many days to "take and receive" (= "catch") food. Now it got the butterfly. The butterfly said: "(You should) let me fly away, spider. I am beautiful and I fly through many lands, over rivers and grass to the flowers!" The spider answered: "I can not fly. I can not come to the flowers. But I can make a net, and I can wait. In the end, if I can not come to the (pretty) flowers, the (pretty) butterfly comes to me! Why (did) you not (take) care, whither you flew?" The butterfly said: "Care and fear are sisters. I (do) not kill the flower, but you can only kill beauty. But I had a life without care and fear, a life of beauty.") (Retranslate!)

(NB a-u, Eom, yc bav lodbos gaf ukbos gaf kEbos kab vum ki. yUg, a-u wav vEv UI rUt can Es, xE cEv viOpAm at vu . . . rUt artnU, ot, xE cEv cnA aim, cEv fUIpAm (fUIyv) "ai-ot", Ib fUd tap. a-u bIb wav iUv Ib fUIv nEn mEz Ub O (Ud bOg), xnE yc cEv kab vum eki. — — The space-man, naturally, has not a pig or a horse or fowl on his star. But the spaceman can make words for all things that are shown to him . . . For example, the fruit that is always red, is called (is-being-named) "red-fruit" (strawberry), and so forth. The spaceman also can understand and name many sorts of feelings (through empathy), which (do) not exist on his planet.)

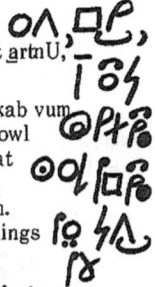

O = FEELING, EMOTION, SENTIMENT, SENS(ATION) etc.

o̲ cO = the five senses

O̲ = ten (We "feel" respect toward the "Ten" Commandments.

10

O : b, c, e, g, i:

EbO (v) = touch, (sense of) touch, "betasten", "matter-together-feeling-(make), "physical-contact-feeling-make"; (b = together, con-: if one feels "con-tact" with a matter, one has the sense of touching it.)

bO = sympathy; (together-feeling). bOm = sympathetic;

(gog) bOm = intimate, (heart-) touching, heart-together-feeling, cordial.

bOg = empathy = together-feeling-within: sympathy as if one lived "inside" or "within" the other fellows skin.

cO = sense: "existence-feeling": the feeling of the existing reality around us, is conveyed to us by our senses, as touch, sight, etc. Without senses we would not know of the existing world of reality around us ("yb pIn fnum cO, fnu yc gUv-yEc pI cEvAm Ea Ub cEmU al fnu".)

Ote(v) = care: "feeling-toward-move": if you move (or direct your feeling toward a person, you care or worry about him

gO = taste "inside-feeling", inside-sense, the sense inside: one must take something "inside" the mouth to taste it, while one "sees" things from the outside.

gOz = tongue: "taste-part, taste-organ", "inside-feel-organ"

tygOm = frank = toward-outside-feeling-quality: If you show your inner feeling toward the outside, you are frank, open.

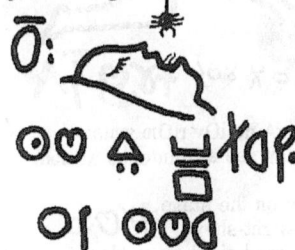

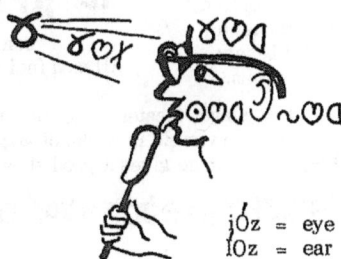

iO = sight = light-feeling, the sense (for) light

iOv = to see (IOv = to hear)

iOd = spectacles, eye-glasses, see-tool

iOz = eye

IOz = ear

O : i, k

bjiOv(U) = compare(-ison) = together-alike-see: if you compare two pictures, you see them together: how far are they alike?

jiOvs = likeness, picture = same-see-make-thing: a likeness makes us "see the same thing" as the original;

ijiOv(s) = photograph = light-picture, -likeness made by light

ijiOv-ad = photo-camera

AiOv = to watch = time-see = look for the time, look a long time; if you watch the clock, you look at it for a (the) time.

atiO = view = "space- - to-sight" the sight out into space, or "the space open to sight" e.g. a mountain-lake-view.

riO(m) = beauty(ful) = "good(-to-) see, good-sight: a beauty is good to look at.

yriO(m) = ugly/ness = "bad(-to) -see, un-pretty"

amriO = ornament = "only-beauty", an ornament is just for beauty, has no other purpose.

riOma(m) = grace(ful) beauty-form, or: beautiful-space-quality

riOe(v) = dance = "beauty-move(ment)", a dancer moves beautifully.

wriOv(Am) = charm(ing) = "power-beauty-make": to charm somebody means to cast a powerful beauty-spell over him.

the man sees the beautiful woman.

vus iOv riOm yvus :

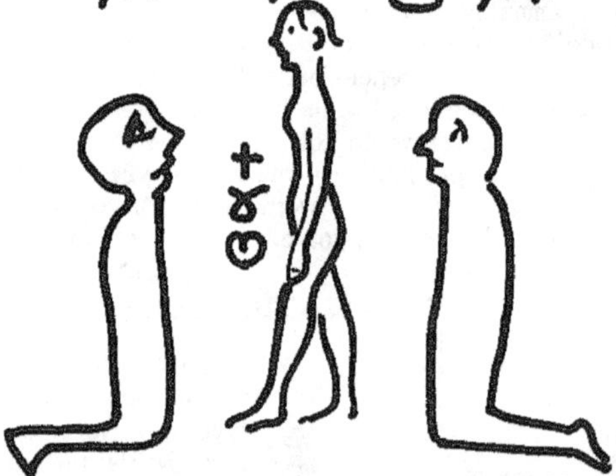

can vus rUm Ov, xA nu iOv riOm yvus:

All men feel good, when they see a beauteous woman.

riOva(v) = stage, theater-stage: beauty-make-place: on the stage, beauty is made visible in works of art; also: "good-sight-show-make-place: a stage gives a good show: r-iO-v-a = good-sight-make-place.

O : i, k, p

UmtiO = test = "mind-quality-to-sight": if you undergo a "test", the "quality of your mind" comes "to sight." If you test a material its quality comes to your mind's sight.

iOv = to see; sight-verb, "light-feel", to sense the light;

(Oiv = to seem = feel-shine-do, feel-light-make: see "i"!)

tiO(v) = (to) look = "toward-see"; you look "to" see, with a view toward seeing.

viOv = to show = make-see: if you show a man your charms, you "make" him "see" them.

viOvs = sign = show-thing, make-see-thing: a sign for danger is something, which makes you see the danger.

viOvsev = to sign, to make a sign.

etviOv(s) = mark = "move-to-sign": a mark is a sign to which a marksman moves his arrow, as a target (at) which he hits.

IviOvs = (a) note, a sound-sign, a sign for a musical tone, "sound-make-see-sign"

iOz = eye = sight-part, see-organ, the organ of sight, sight-sense-part.

IOz = ear = "sound-sense-part": the ear is the part which senses sound.

(Note the difference in accent:

iÓ = sight; ÍO = hearing !)

IOv(Am) = hear(ing, participle):

sound-sense-verb

IOvU = acoustics = hear-mind (science)

IO = hearing (noun or gerund), sound-feeling, the sense of sound.

O : k, p,

Ok̲e̲ = hundred = ten-high-two, zehn-hoch-zwei, 10^2: ten with a high "2"

Ok̲i̲ = thousand = "ten-(with a) -high "3" above, 10^3 = 1000: 3 zeros!

kOm = noble = high-feeling-quality, noble means high-minded.

tukO = respect = to-man-above- — feeling!

you feel respect for a man above you.

kEmO = smell = air(gas) -quality-sense:

you smell the condition of the air

kEmOz = nose = air-quality-sense-part:

the nose feels the type of air:

"What kind of air?"

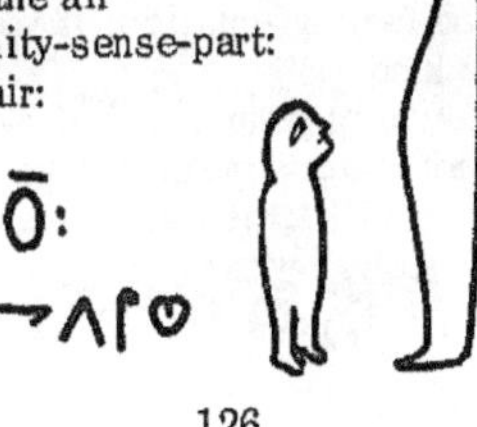

O : k, p, r, s, t

kypO = surprise = "above-not-before-feeling" = "upon-behind-feeling" = "a surprise jumps like a cat "upon" you from "behind," (yp).
pO(v) = anticipat/ion, expect/ation = before-feeling, pre-sentiment, fore-boding.
ypyvU = reserve = "behind--not-active--mind": holding something back ("behind") instead of showing it "actively" (see "U")

O : r, s, t

//rO = pleasure // = "good-feeling" in its widest sense: pleasure in this sense includes joy and even happiness.
rOm = pleasant, "well-feeling", emotionally positive.
vrOv = to please = good-feeling-make, make-(him)-feel-good!
brO(v) = (to) love = "together-good-feeling", you feel good together with somebody you love.
ybrO(v) = (to) dislike = un-love, opposite of love.
brOm = dear: love-quality, beloved and loving, lovely
brOs = pet, favorite-thing, love-thing.
krO = joy = high-pleasure, above-pleasure: joy is above pleasure in intensity and degree.
krOv(U) = enjoy(ment) = joy-make-act = high-good-feel . .
krOm = glad; ykrOm = sad: low-feeling, below-good-feeling.
krOn = delight = high-pleasure-plenty, joy-abundant.
krOI(v) = laugh/ter: (sounds like "crowing") = "joy-sound-(make) = high-good-feel-sound (k-r-O-I): to make the sound of joy is "to laugh."
rOtyg = "smile" = "good-feeling-to-outside" (showing).
UrO(m) = happy/ness = spirit-good-feeling, spiritual pleasure: (rO, krO, UrO are stages of sublimation: pleasure, joy, happiness.)
trUnO = satisfaction; trUn = enough = until-good-quantity;
trUn-O = enough-feeling, the feeling that it is enough good, "to-good-mind-quantity--feeling": when the "mind" feels that it has attained (up "to") the "good (right) quantity (measure) of achievement, it feels "satisfaction".
tUrO(m) = (auspicious) auspices = to-mind-good-feeling (a concept important in Asia), pointing "to(ward) (UrO) happiness': t-UrO.
rOwU = art = good-feeling-power-mind, the "mental power" to make human "feelings" "good", to ennoble them into spiritual happiness, is given to the great artist.
rOve(v) = (to) play = good-feel-make-move: if children "move" about, just because they "feel good", they "play."
rOvU = humor = good-feel-make-mind: if a person has a "mind" able of "making you feel good", he can "humor" you.
vrO(m) = kind/ness: make-good-feeling(-quality): if you "make" somebody "feel good", you are kind.
ynrO(v) = amuse/ment = little(yn) pleasure;
vynrO(v) = entertain/ment = make-amusement, active amusement.
(rIv = sing (good-sound-make): see "I"; riOma(m) = grace(ful): see "O": i)

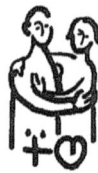

O : t, U, v, w, y, z

yApyrO - regret - "after-bad-feeling"; bad(-yr) -after(yAp): Ap before.
y-Ap - after: if you regret you did it, you feel bad after the deed.
tvOrd - comfort - to-make-feel-good-means: comfort has the purpose of ("toward") making-one-feel-good by "means" of nice words and acts.
tvOrv - to comfort - toward-make-feel-good-do. (see "r": "please").
tvOrU - consolation - to-make-feel-good-concept
tsOb - desire - toward-thing-feeling-together: if you have a desire (-feeling), you long for (strive "toward") being "together" with the object ("thing": s) of your desires;
tsO(v) - yearn/ing, (to) desire - "toward-thing-feeling: you like to strive "toward the thing" you "feel" the yearning for.
tO(v) - wish: toward-feeling: if your "feeling" strives "toward" an event, you are wishing for it.
Ote(v) - (to) care - "feeling-toward-move": if your "feelings move toward" somebody, and you "move", or bestir yourself for him, you care for him.
twOr(v) - (to) entreat: "toward-power-feel-good-make": you entreat usually a "powerful" person, and do it "forcefully", trying to change his mind, his feeling toward" what you deem "as good."
trO - hope - toward-good--feeling": you feel that things will go "toward, to the good" if you are hopeful or optimistic.
tyrO(v) - (to) fear - "toward-bad-feeling": you feel that things will take a turn "toward the bad (yr), if you fear . . .
twyrO - fright, a power (w)-ful fear (t-w-yrO) looking "toward" something strongly (w) bad (yr).
AtyrO - anxiety: "time-to-bad-feeling". (long) "time-fear" (A-tyrO).

O : U, v, w, y, z.

UiO(v) - (to) read/ing - mind-see: you "see" the meaning with your "mind" (cf. U)
rUO - trust: "good-mind-feeling": if you trust somebody, you "feel" that he is good (rU-m) in spirit (U)
UyrO - grief - mind-pain (U-yrO), mental-pain: pain - yrO - bad-feeling.
oyg-yrO - itch - skin-pain - skin-bad-feeling; unpleasant skin-sensations.
Ov - to feel - feel-verb
vOv - to suggest, impress - make-feel, give suggestions (like a hypnotist)
vYrtrO - pardon - bad-make-toward-good-feeling: a pardon converts ("makes") a "bad" sin "toward the good-feeling" of forgiveness.
wO(m) - courage (ous), (brave) - strong-feeling, feeling of strength
wyvO - obligation - must-feeling, (wyv-O); power-passive - bound-by-power. . .
yrwyvO - obsession - evil-obligation, under which I suffer passively (yv).
wyv - must.
yryv - suffer - bad-passive-verb
yrsO - disgust - bad-thing-feeling
nyrvŌ(v) — trouble: many-bad-make-feelings: troubles make me feel bad.
tyiO(v) — (to feel) shame — toward dark--feeling: a boy ashamed flees "into the dark" to hide.
yrO — pain, bad-feeling - anti-pleasure (y-rO)
ydO(v) - hate - against-feeling (yd-O): if I am against him, I hate him.
wydO(m) - ang(e)r(y) - powerful (w) against-feeling, rage
bydwO - shock - together-against-power-feeling: if "shocked", you clash "forcibly together with" something "against which you feel" dismay.
vyrO(m) - cruel/ty: "make-pain (quality)": a cruel man makes us suffer.
Oz - nerve - feeling-part - feel-organ, the organ of feeling.

"p": a, A, e; O, t, U; "Q"

"p" denotes "Front, BEFORE," "fore-" as in: "fore-fathers, for-mer; foremost "pre-" as in: pre-vious, pre-war, prior; ante-rior, proto-zoon; Past.

p : a, A, e

pa = front = "front-space"
ap = before, in front of = space-front, spatially in front of, devant.
pA = past (noun) "Vor-zeit", pre-time; pAm = past (adjective), previous-time-ly
"-pA-", infix of the past, as -ed: "he start-ed" = vu pe-pA-v
Ap = before = time-before, "avant", . . . ago: three years ago = Ap i akiA.
pAvU = preparation, pre-(time-) act, pre-paration, "before (starting) time".
prAm = early = before-good-time-quality; "before" (it's too late), in "good-time" (r-A), goes an "early bird": ag rUm A--prAm kEos av, Ut tyv-fev anos. (in-order-to get-take (=catch) (the) worm(s).)
pe(v) = (to) start, begin; pre-move, fore-move, first-move: he who starts, makes the first move, "before" the others.

p : O, t, U

ypOm = sudden: "no-before-feeling, un-expect-ed: pO = expectation, anti-cipation
kypO = surprise = up (on us from) -behind (yp) -feeling; see O: p.
tap = forward, forth = "toward-space-front", to the (place in) front
(Ib fUd tap = and so forth, etc.)
pUm = principal (adj.); pUms = principle = front-mind-quality-(thing), foremost-(in the) mind.

P : y, z

yp = behind, back, re- (as in re-tro-spect), opposite (of) front
yps = the back (-thing), more correct, since the back is a part, is
ypaz = the back; which is similar in space to:
ypAz = the end = back-time-part: the end of the book is the part to which we come "back in time", later;
ypnAm = last = back-much (back-most) -time-quality
yprAm = late = opposite (of) early (prAm) = "behind-good-time, not-in-good-time.
yAp = after = (opposite of) before (= Ap).
typ = backward, re-, back (come back = re-turn) = toward-behind
typev = return, back-move, come back = typev, tev-typ = come-back.
ypum = secret = behind-man-quality: the secret lies, as it were, "behind" a curtain, protected from the eyes of "man," or behind their back.
ypyv(U) = reserve (-ation) = behind-not-active(-concept); if you hold things in reserve, you keep them "behind" in "inactive" store.

Q : g, l.

Q (pronounced as Q in "wQrd", wOrd) = condition; -Q = in a . . . manner.
Qg = if (condition-in) = on condition, under the condition that . . .
Ql = state, condition, circumstance, "Umstand". (=condition around).
-Q can also be used to make an adverb clearer by the ending:
"namQ" = great-ly, instead of "nam" = great. namQ = in a great manner.

Work and Art -- uwe Ib rOwU. --

--- hU u wyv-yEc (Why would man have-to . .) Ev rOwU gaf gUw? (do art or science, Why should man have anything to do with art or science ?) u wav-yEc cEv am odvu (farmer = food-make-man) gaf uwe-u ag nuvsga. – (Man could be only farmer or work-man in a factory), fE c wyvUm Ut dov, yUg, rOwU yc wyvUm. hyt u c rOwu? (Why is man an artist?) –fE hI bjiOv eb yf hI: hyt u c´u, Ib hUt (=hE-rUt = what-for?) u c´u?-- u yc-yEc u yb rOwU. os dov, Ib fUd c´UrOm. hUt wyv-yEc bEna skev u? --(More correct: – bEna hUt wyv-yEc skev u, hI?) Why should the earth have to carry man? zI´ Ub u cEv oUz. oUz cEv a Ub U. U wUv Ib Uv. fUd u bjiOyv (is compared to . . . = "compares with" (intransitive) God) at kU. --

--- hE cEv nEk prAm: nuvsga gaf odva? Eom, --pI odva! (naturally = EomQ = of course) the farm! --hu c´nEk pAom, odvu gaf rOwu? fa, pnEk u Uv-yEc: EomQ, odvu! yUg, ag wE-gyE ag bEk ab aLTaMIRa fnu Utev (find) jiOvs Ub os, wUpAm (created) Ud nam rOwu. fE rOwu opAv twam 50ooo akiA (= o-O---Oki akiA = fifty-thousand years) Ap fnu = Ap oO–Oki akiA. u c´pAv ad (through, for hundred-thousand years) ad Oke-Oki akiA yI "ot-fev-u" (a fruit-take-man. fruit-picker), Ib os-tyv-fev-u (animal-get-take-man, deer-catcher, hunter) gaf os-vyov-u (deer-killer), -- Ib rOwu, -- Ap vu tEpAv odvu Ib uwe-u. a-u brOv Ib tukOv rOwU Ub u.–

Retranslate: Why should man have anything to do with art or science? Man could be only farmer or worker in a factory. This is necessary in-order-to eat (for-eating), but art is-not necessary. How-come ("wieso") man is an artist? This question compares with another question: Why is man man, and what-for is man man? Man would not be man without art and science. Part of man is his brain. The brain is the seat of the mind. The mind creates and thinks. So man compares with God.

What is earlier: the factory or the farm? Naturally, --the farm! Who is older the farmer or the artist? Here, most men would think: of course, the farmer! But in the caves (stone-holes) in a hill near Altamira we find pictures of animals, created by a great artist. This artist lived perhaps fifty-thousand years before us (= before 50ooo years = 50ooo years ago). Man was through hundred-thousand years a fruit-picker, and deer-catcher or animal-hunter, -- and artist, -- before he became a farmer and worker. The space-man loves and respects (admires) the art of man.

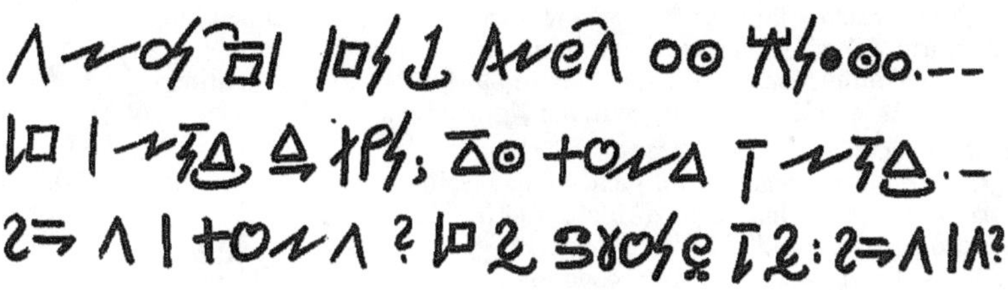

"r" : a, b, c; d, e, E.

"r" denotes "POSITIVE VALUE, GOOD, Well, affirmative . . . "

r : a, b, c

ram = pure = good——only = good——one–quality: if only the good (gold) is therein, this is "pure gold." yram = impure, dirty

brO(v) = (to) love = together-good-feel: if two people feel good together, and would'be sad, if torn apart, they are in love.

bru = friend: together-good-man: a man with whom you are good is your friend.

brU = peace: "together-good-mind (spirit)": if good spirit binds you two together, you are at peace.

brUje(v) = agree/ment = peace-equal-move: if two parties "move in peace on common grounds, they agree on the "same" (j) thing.

brUvs = adjustment = together-good-spirit-make-thing: some "thing" which "makes" a "spirit" of "good togetherness."

carm = complete: "existing space (all)-good-quality."

r : d, e, E.

drem = easy = through-well-move: a field "through which you pass well", is easy terrain; ydrem = difficult.

tre(v) = success, (succeed) = "toward-good-move" is successful.

drE = money = means (of exchange)-, good-material: a man of "means" (d) is a man of money, which buys "material goods." We buy by "means" of money, which was originally metal (rE), or paper through (d) which metal can be exchanged.

drEga = bank, money-place,

drEm = rich, expensive: a moneyed man is a rich man.

yndrEm = poor = little-money; ykdrEm = cheap = low-money (bajo-rato=barrato)

drEts = price, = money-toward-thing = the "money" you need for (toward) purchasing some "thing."

drEv(s) = pay(ment) = money-verb: if he pays the apple, he "moneys" it.

drEseva = market = money-thing-move-make-place, where money & things move.

drEtbe(v) = (to) profit = money-to-together-move: if one profits, money moves "toward" one, is "added" (tebnev); bav = to have.

utgadrE = ticket = man——to-inside-space——money, entrance—— money: a ticket is like money that lets you into the room.

twudrE = tax = to-power-man——money: our taxes are money yielded "to the men in power."

rE = metal = good-matter, positive-matter, used as money, in coins. (metal reacts "positive" electrolytically.)

strE(v) = (sell) sale = thing-to-money (metal) (-make)

rEtse(v) = buy = money-to-thing-move: if you "move" your metal (coins) transferring them (in) to a "thing" you want, you are buying.

stytrE(v) = trade = thing-to-from-money (-make): things are turned into money, and "from" money one buys things in commercial trade.

grEm = alkaline, (basic) = inside-metal-quality: "inside an alkaline substance is metal, e.g. NaOH contains Na, Sodium.

ygrEm = acid, sour = opposite (of) alkaline;

bygrEm = salty = together (b) -acid-(with alkaline): HCl + NaOH = NaCl (salt).

grOm = sweet = "inside-good-(taste) feeling" similar to "grEm", since both are opposites to "sour", ygrEm;

ygrOm = bitter, similar to sour, opposite of sweet, grOm.

Consider the transition: 1) ygrOm,
2) grOm, 4) ygrEm,
3) grEm, 5) bygrEm

r : e; i, j, m, n; o, O

drem = easy = "through-well-move-quality": if you can "well move (breeze) through" a lesson, it is easy, presenting no difficulty (yd) "against" mastering it

ydrem = difficult = "against-well-moving-quality", or: not-easy, or: opposed to-through-mov-ing

tre(v) = success (succeed) = toward-good-move = if one "moves well toward" one's goals, one succeeds.

r : i, j; m, n

prim = clean = "front-good-light-quality" (cf. "dim", clear = "through-light-quality": light shines "through" (d) a "clear" glass or water) "prim" presents a good (r) clean "front," (p).

jnUrm = normal = "equal-quantity-mind-good-quality": for us it is "normal" to have 5 fingers and not 6: in our "mind" we judge it to "good" that all people should have the "same number" (equal quantity) of fingers--otherwise we condemn them as abnormal.

gnUrm = perfect: "in-quantity-spirit--good-quality": "many spiritually good-qual'ties" are "inside" a perfect thing; "perfect" is "inside-valuable" as all values are "inside" perfection.

nUr(m) = value(-able): quantity-spirit-good-quality: value is "good" in our "mind"; it is a quality of "quantity", of "muchness": if a book contains "much good" (spiritually), it is a valuable book.

knUrms = standard = "above-valuable-thing": we set a "standard" of perfection, of what is over and "above" valuable, or superior value.

jwUr(m) = right = "equal-power-mind (spirit)-good": if I have the right on my side, I have a "spiritual" power which would be "equally well" available to all others in the "same" situation;

y-jwUr(m) = wrong = anti-right; jwUs = law, see "j" jruts = reward, jrutev = to reward = "equal-good-man-(to)ward-thing(move)": a just reward "moves toward" (gives) a man the "same good thing" he deserves, an "equivalent" for his "good deed."

trUn = sufficient, enough = "toward-good-mind-quantity": the "amount" which "to our mind" seems just "right" (for the good) is enough.

r : o, O

ogyr = injury = body-harm, body(og) -not-good, body-evil (yr).

tor(v) = (to) help = "toward-life-good-make": torrv fu! (Help me!) means: "bring ("good") "life to" me, "make my life" (into) "good."

tor-UI = advice, counsel = help-word, a word of help, helpful hint.

tOr = please! (por favor) = "to feeling-good": I say 'please', in order "to" make you (and me) "feel good", if you do me a favor: it contributes "to" our "good" fellow "feeling."

ytOr = thanks! = "from-good-feeling": I say 'thanks' "from a good feeling", out of a heart of gratitude.

ytOrv = to thank, ytOrm = thankful: from-feel-good-quality;

tOrv = to beg = "please-do", to say (make) "please."

tOrm = pleasing, (in an officious, submissive sense, trying to please).

(vrOv = to please, "make pleasure, give (true) enjoyment, give joy").

tvOrd (tvOrv) = (to) comfort = "toward-make-feeling-good(tool)" means, instrument: "comfort" is the "means", by which we "make" ourselves "feel good", a comfortable sofa contributes "to our feeling good."

Or = yea

Ur = yes! = mind-positive: if my mind is positive, affirmative, I say: yes!
yr = No! = no-good, that's bad (yrUm = evil); yrm = negative, no-quality.
Urm = positive, affirmative, = yes-quality: mind-good-quality.
rUm = good, rU = goodness = good-spirit, positive spiritually
rUg = well, good-inside, "in" a good way, good-spirit
yrU(m) = evil, harm(ful), anti-good, intentionally bad
rym = bad = positive-opposite-quality, good-opposed, no-good, good-less
rUI(v) = praise = good-word-make: if you say "good words" about me . . .
brUI(v) = approv/al = "together-good-say" (UI): if our minds agree (brUjev) together, and we "say: good!", we approve.
rUtiOs = stamp = "good-mind (value)-to-see--thing": the stamp of approval shows (makes seen) the good value--like a postage stamp.
srUv(U) = recommend(ation) = thing-good-mind-make: if I recommend some-"thing", I foster a "good mind" of acceptance for it.vadrE = postage-stamp
vram = convenient = "make-good-space-quality": make it fit into space.
tyfyr(v) = (to) trick = to-other-bad-(make): a trick does "evil" (yr-U), under the pretext of something else, (other = yf) "to" which it persuades.
yrUv(s) = sin = evil-do(-thing), bad-mind-act: a sin is spiritual.
yrv(s) = (to commit) a crime: evil-act (yr-v) without stress on "mind".
yrvu(m) = criminal, crime-man, evil-doer (without spiritual ethics)
ytyrA(m) = safe/ty = "from-harm-time(-quality)": if you are safe, you are freed "from (yt) evil (yr)" for a "time" (A);
ydyrwa(v) = protect/ion = against-harm-power-space (-make): to "make" a "power-space", strong-place, strong-hold for somebody, means to "protect" him against (yd) harm (yr).
vyre(v) = (to) damage = "harm-move": to move you into harm = to damage you.
tyr(ev) = (to en-)danger = toward-evil (-move): if you are moving "toward-evil (harm)" you are (approaching) danger.
wyrrE = debt = power-bad-money" = " force(-d)-negative-metal (coins): debts are "negative/money" (drE or: rE = positive material-value) with the "power" to enforce payment: wyrrE cause worry!
yrytE = waste = bad-from-matter: the "bad-matter" (yr--E), we throw "away from" us, we call waste.
yrstyg(a) = sewage (plant) = bad-things-to-outside (-place): in sewage, "bad" (useless) things are eliminated "to the outside" (t-yg).
yrfe(v) = theft (steal): "evil-take", a "bad" way of "taking" (fev) something is to steal it.
(-yr- in such combinations means "bad, evil, harmful, negative" in a wide sense; e.g. yr-waubos = wolf = bad-dog, a harmful member of the dog family).

s : a, E, e, t, y.

"s" implies THING, OBJECT, article, item, "it"
Es = thing = matter-thing, material-object
nEs = item = quantity-thing, a thing from a series of many others.
sE = it = thing-matter: the "IT" is not a shaped thing, only the potentiality, the material for a thing.
sEm = its, snE = they (plural of it, e.g. The books are here: I see them)
--pIn Ugs cEv fa: fu iOv snE. --snEm mi c´aim.
snEm = their = they-quality : "Their color is red (The books' color . . .)
sav = to put = thing-space-do = thing-space-verb: putting always needs a "thing" which you put, and a place or "space" where you put it; fu sav fE Es tag fE as = I put this thing into this place.
sev = to give = thing-move-make: whenever you give something, a thing"" is "moved." Thus instead of saying: "Give me an apple" (Give an apple to me = (bu) serv nakot at fu!), you might say: "Move an apple to me!" = (bu) erv nakot at fu!" Even if the verb has apparently no object as "giving is better than receiving", it's things that are given: "Moving things (to somebody else) is better than getting them (having them re-moved) from him."

tsev = to offer = "toward-giving" (t-sev): you make, as it were, a preparation toward giving, if you "offer" something.
Asev = to lend, loan = "(for a) time-giving," give for a time, not for ever.
syv = to receive = "(to get a) thing-passively."
--sevU cEv nEk rUm myt fevU Ib syvU. --"Giving is better than taking and receiving"
(sev-U means really "the give-concept", fevU = the take-idea, etc).
Of course we could simply say: "sev c nEk-rUm myt syv"
(To give is better than to receive).

46:1-11
2.
10.
11.

t: a; b, d, e, E; f, l, m, O.

"t" denotes TOWARD = TO + WARD, FOR, TILL, directed motion, purpose. ("-ward" as in "heaven-ward" = "to heaven" = "t")

t : a

at =to, "space-toward", spatially-toward: if I go to a town, I go in "space toward" it.

At = (un)till = "time-toward": 'Wait until he comes' = 'Wait "toward the time", when he will come.'

trAv(Am) = wait(ing): "toward-good-time-verb": 'I am waiting "toward the time", when it will be "good" to act.

tAv = remain = "toward-time-verb": "tA" = "toward-time", future: What remains, is still there for the future.

tvAv = leave = "make-(it-) remain", causative of 'remain': "v+tAv" "Leave your daughter with me" = Let her remain here = —— (bu) tvArv bum tyvu eb fu!—— = (bu) dyrv yvu, (vErv yvu) tAv fa!——

tAvs = remainder = "toward-future-made-thing": the remaining thing, the lasting thing, is still left for the future.

tAvma = plan = toward-time——make——qualified-space = "tAv = remain"; "ma" = form; tA = future:" (for the) future-made-form: a form, made for the future. The "plan" of an architect is the remaining form; in the "future" the architect will "make" a house of this "form", shaped, or: qualified space.

t : b, d, e, E.

tabwe(v) = attract/ion = "toward-space-together-power-move": an attraction is a "force" which "moves" two objects "toward-together (in) Space."

etdEv(U) = apply (application): "move-toward-use" ("by-means-make" = dEv = use) : to move-toward-using-something = applying it.

te-ytUs = stimulus: "toward-move-cause (ytUs)"; a stimulus is a cause for motion. (ytUs = "from-concept", origin-(from-which), e.g.: "Wine stimulates my desire for that girl" = "Wine is the 'cause' 'from' which my desires "to move toward" that girl, originate "i.e.: ——rOjE teytUv fum tsOb rUt fE ynyvu. = rOjE c ytUs, fum tsOb ytUv yt xE.

tev = come: move-toward, "toward-move-make", Come to me = move toward me! (bu) terv at fu = (bu) erv at fu!

tEv = to become = "toward-matter-verb": If water 'becomes' ice, it is a change "toward" a different form of "matter".

t : f, l, m, O, s.

kyftU(v) = compet/ition = "above-others ——striv/ing (tU)" (tU=toward-mind). We compete with a "mind-toward" getting ahead & on "top (k)" of "others (yf)"

etUl(v) = request: "move-toward-mind-sound(make);" mind-sound = word: a "word" which "moves me to" help you, is your request for help.

myt = than = "quality-from": she is fairer "than" her sister: her sister's beauty is the base-"quality" (m), "from" (yt) which we gauge & compare.

etO(v) = tend/ency = "move-toward-feeling". If he tends "toward" exaggeration, his "feelings" "move him to" exaggerate.

tsUs = result = toward-thing-concept (mind-thing): the result of his labors was a good position, i.e. the "thing" "toward" which he strove.

vetsev = bring = "make-move-toward-thing-move" (sev = give, tev = come): "make-move-toward (v-e-t) -giving": bring me the cat = make that the thing (the cat) move, come, toward me, or give it to me!

tsyv = accept = toward-thing-passive (yv) = toward-receiving (syv).

tyv = get = toward-passively = toward-non-active: if I get angry, I move "toward" anger "passively", driven by a passion.
ytta = distance = "from-to--space", the stretch "from A to B." If you move through the "space" between A & B, you cover the distance A–B.
mytta = range = "quality-distance", gamut: they ranged "from" queen "to" brat(yt-ta) in their qualities (m): "myttapAv yt kyvu at yrtu ag mU."
Ut = (in order) to = mind-toward: I do this "in order to" help you = I do this with a "mind" "toward" helping you.
rUt = for = "good-mind-toward": I brought an apple "for" him = I brought an apple, which is "good" (for him) "to" him. (good = rUm.)
twU(v) = (to) will = toward-power-mind: will-power --a "mind toward" a goal!
tU(v) = effort (to strive) = toward-mind: my "mind strives toward" an aim.
tUs = effect = toward-concept: the "concept toward" which a "thing" tends, is its "effect."
Ute(v) = (to) find = "mind-come" (U-tev): if your "mind comes" upon or moves toward (e,t) an idea, you find it. tUtev = seek
tvev(U) = try, attempt (trial) = "toward-make-move-make": if I try to jump I "make movements toward" jumping. A little bird goes through the "motions" of flying.
twev = pull = "toward-force-move-make": if I pull something "to" me, I "forcefully make it move" toward me, force it to move to me.

t : y.

ytwev = to push = "from-power-move-make": a push is a "power-move" to get something away "from" you.
//yt = from, fro = "opposite(of)-to", implying origin, cause, & away.
yUt = because = opposite(of) "in-order-to" (Ut), opposite (of) mind-to.
ytUs = cause = from-concept: a cause is the "thing" (s) from (yt) which others originate (in the "mind", at least).
ytUw = reason = "from-mind-power": reasoning "power" finds the causes.
tytU = reference, relationship = "to-from-concept": their relationship was love, means: 'love flowed "to & fro" in their "minds" (t-yt-U).
tytUm = relative = relation-quality, with reference to, referential.
yta = away = from-space, yt-a: go away! = go from this space!
ayt = off = space-from, out of this place.
ytev = to leave, depart = "move-(away-) from", yt-ev = from-move (y-tev = anti-come)
vytev = to omit = make-depart, make-from-move-make, make-go-away: Omit it = leave it out, make-it-depart!
tytnev = to whip (e.g. cream) = to-fro(m)-quick-move = t-yt-ne-ev = to-anti-to--much-move (=quick)-make;
tytned = (a) whip = a to-and-fro--quick-move-tool.

"u": a, b; f, g, k

"u" = MAN, PERSON, HUMAN (BEING), PEOPLE (implying "nation", pronouns etc)

-u = -er, -ist; -man: e.g. scient-ist = science-man = gUw-u;
skev-u = carri-er, porter (skev = carry)

u : a, b

nuba = town, city = many-men-together-space: a place where many men are crowded together.
ynuba = village = "few(yn) -men-together-place."
ynab = group: "not-many (in)-space-together": a group = few together.
una = country, land = men-much-space = a big space for people = a land.
unaz = district, prefecture, zone = land-part
una-mi = "country-color" = flag, which bears the country's colors.
bu, bnu = thou, you = together-man, -men: the man with whom I talk "together."
bum, bnum = thy, your(s): you-quality, you-adjective
ub = family, "men-together" (living), people together.
anub = society = space-many-men-together: "society" is used in a general sense, as "Human society be my judge" or in a special sense: "They had tea in a society of friends." Always it's many-men-together.
wanub = league = "power-society": a society joined "together (b)" for "powerful mutual protection;
nub = company "many-men-together".
nulb = club = many-men-round (l)-together: In a club many sit "around" a table.
tube(v) = meet(ing) = "to-men-together-move": men come "to" a gathering.
wynub = committee = power-few-men-together: a committee is a little (yn) company (nub) of people who have special (w-) power together:
—"wynub c ynab (group) Ub u, xnu bav zUm (special = part-mind) wU tab."
bru = friend = "together-good-man", a man "with" whom it is "good" to be together:
byvu = wife: together-woman: the woman with whom you live together, is supposed to be your wife.
bvu = husband = together-man, supposedly similar to "bru."

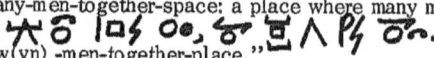

u:f, g, k.

fu(m) = I, me, (my, mine) = this-man-(here) = yours truly, I, myself.
fnu(m) = we, us (our(s): these-men (-quality).
I have my house: fu bav fum uga; fnu bav fnum uga = We have our houses.
Thou hast thy h = bu bav bum uga; bnu bav bnum uga = You have your h
He has his h " = vu bav vum uga; nu bav num uga = They have their h.
ufU = personality = "man-self", "man-this-mind" : fU = self, this-mind.
uyg = dress, clothing, apparel, garment = man-outside, see "g": yg.
(Only "man" wears a "dress" outside, animals have skin and fur:
—am u bav uyg yg, os bav oyg Ibosyg.—
ku = lord, sir = above-man, high-man; kyvu = lady = above-woman, top-dame.
kun = manager, "above-men's-multitude," man-over-many
knu = king = above-many-men = a ruler, set "above many men"; knyvu = queen
kwu = master, boss = above-power-man = top-boss;
ykwu = servant = under-power-man, who stands under somebody's power.
kup = face = "above-(upper) -man (human)-front: the face is in front and above a human body.
kupyk = chin = face-below = under-(the) human-face protrudes the chin
(Most animals, -e.g. worms — have neither face nor chin).

u : m, n; r; t, v, w, y

u : m, n.

um = human = man-quality, man-like

banu = nation = "together-space-many-men". A city = "crowd-place", nuba, is a place ("a") where many men live together; a nation is a group of many men ("nu") who live "together (in) space" (ba). (In aUI, the last part of the word determines the character).

gebanum = international = between-(ge-) nation-al.

nu = they, (num = their) = many-men-(quality); cf. snE = they (=many things)

marbu = secretary = "form-well-together-person": ma = form; "good-together-(wo)man; being on "good" terms "with" the boss (kwu), the secretary concentrates on diplomatic form (ma) & formalities.

pnu(m) = public = "(in) front-(of) -many-men-(quality); before-all-eyes.

ypnum = private = un-public = "behind (the eyes of) -the crowd" (yp-nu), hidden.

u : r

ru = mister, Mr. = (my) good-man, good-Sir, Dear Sir!

ryvu = Mrs, Mistress, Madam = "good-passive-human" (even if she is neither-nor!) (my) good-woman/ artuv = cultivate

aturv(U) = coloniz(ation) = space-for-men-good-make(-ing): to make a ("living-") space "good for human" habitation.

ruwe(v) = work (creative work, as: Dante's Works (labor = uwe!) "good-man-power-move": work is done by good men & is good for men

ruve(m) = busy/ness = "good — — man-act(ive) -move (-like): a busy man "moves actively" for his "good;" (but without creative force "w": ruwe!)

ydyrvu = poli ce(man) = against (yd) -bad (yr) -deed-man: a copper should protect us "against criminals."

u : t, v, w, y.

utUv = educate = "man-to-spirit-(lead) -do", man-to-mind-make: to make a child mind, or to lead man toward the spirit — — is education.

ytu = parent = from-man, yt-u, or: opposite (of-) child = y-tu; parent & child, ytu & tu; "from" the parent comes life "to" the child (t-u).

ytvu = father = from-he = from-male: "from" (yt) him (vu) comes life.

ytyvu = mother: "from-her" we have our life, she bore us: from-she (yt-yvu).

vu = he, him = he-man, active-human; vum = his, yvum = her(s) (possessive).

yvu = she, her = passive-human: at least in sex women are still on the receiving end.

yvus = woman = she-thing, passive-human-thing.

vus = man = he-thing, he-concrete, he-man, active-human-thing.

tu = child = toward-man: developing "toward-man"; or: "to" the child, "t-u", life was given (by the parents, ytu)

tum = child-like

yntu = baby = little-child, infant: not-big-toward-man.

tvu = son = to-he, to(ward) -man: to him life was given, and he will develop "toward-a-man."

tyvu = daughter =to(ward) her.

jytu = sibling, Geschwister, hermanos, brother-&-sister, brethren: "same-parent-person": all persons coming from the "same parents."

jytvu = brother: same-parent-from-man: the man, born from the same parents as I, is my brother.

jytyvu = sister: "same(-parent) -from-woman: my sister is the woman(yvu) who comes from (yt) the same (j) parents.

ytytu = ancestor = from-from-man, fore-father, grandparent = "from-parent."

ytu-jytvu = uncle = parent's brother; ytu-jytyvu = aunt = parent's sister.

ynvu = boy, = little-man, little-he; ynyvu = girl = little woman = little she.

uwe(v) = labor, (mechanical) work = man-power-move: labor is a movement done by man-power. cf. ruwe = work.

knuw(ev) = govern/ment = above (k) -many (n)-men (u) -power (w) -move (ev): to move "many people (by one's) power" ruling "over" them.

unwe(m) = politic/s = "men-multidude (un) -power-move (w-e). politics is the power-game of "moving many people" around as on a chessboard, for the purpose of winning "power."

unwe-rOve = diplomacy = politic-play, power-play. Play = rOve = good-feeling-active-move: the child plays, because to "move" about, to be "active" makes him "feel good." A diplomat wields the "power to move" or maneuver "many people" around, and his "activity" is supposed to create "good feeling."

yu = nobody = no-man = opposite (of) person.
yum = inhuman = no-human-like, like no human being, anti-human.

23:1-6

2.

3.

4.

5.

6.

△ " U " : a, A, b, f; g

U = MIND, MENTALITY, SPIRIT, INTELLECT, abstract thought, idea.
-U = concept: This ending transforms a word into an abstract noun, e. g.
rU-nUm = wise, nUmU = wis-dom; ynUm = stupid, ynUm-U = stupid-ity, -ness.
aturv = colonize, aturv-U = coloniz-ation; u = man, u-U = man-kind.

U : a, A, b, f.

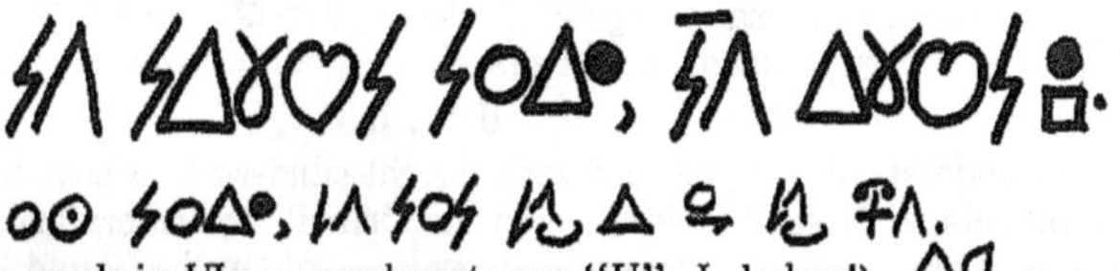

vaUs = letter, epistle = make-space-mind-thing: a letter is a thing (s) which enables the mind (U) to travel through, to "make-space", to make its way through space.
— —ag vaUs, fu vav (send) fum U at fum bru. — — In a letter, I send (vEv av = make-go) my mind to my friend. Letter = "send-thoughts".

— — vu vUiOv vaUs, yvu UiOv sE. — —

He writes . . she reads.

("letter" as part of a word, is UIz = word-part, see "U": I, below!)
Uwa = office = mind-power-space, duty-space: 'You must meet him in his "office"!' means: 'You must meet him in his place, "space", sphere, of (mental) power, in his duty sphere.
ybaUti(v) = telegraph: "far-(yba-)-mind-(U-) -to(t)-light (i): By telegraph, man sends his "mind far" through space by transforming it into"" visible ("light") signs.
yba-uI(v) = telephone = "far-voice" (uI = human-sound: voice). See under "I : u."
AgU = memory = "time-in-mind", "time-knowledge": "in" our memory, "in" this part of our "mind", we hold knowledge (gU) for a long "time."
brU = peace = together-good-mind: When our "minds" get along "well" "together", we are at peace.
("device" tvUd, & c see "d" : U above)
fU = self = this-mind. cf. fu = I, me; myself = me, self = fu-fU; himself = vu-fU, her-self = yvu-fU, themselves = nufU.

U : g.

// gU = knowledge // : "in-mind": knowledge remains "in" my "mind," for keeps.
gUv = to know = "in-mind-verb": what I keep "in mind", I know.
gUa = school = knowledge-place, space (for acquiring) knowledge.
gUOm = conscious = knowledge-feeling-adjective, or: "in-mind-feeling": if one "feels" that one is "in" one's (right) "mind", one is conscious.
gUte(v) = observ/ation = "in-mind-to— —move": What "moves" in-to my "mind", what reaches my mind, I can observe.
EvgUvs = notice = make-know(n)-thing: if I give notice, I make it known.
etgUv = study = "move-to(ward) (=aspire)-know(ledge).
vetgUv = teach = "make (them) move-to-knowledge (v-et-gUv), make-study.
retgUv = learn = "well-study", study-successfully, really learn it.

U : g; i, I

tygU = statement = toward-outside(tyg) — — mind (U): make my mind known to the outside world by my statements.

// gUw = science = "in-mind-power" or "knowledge-power" (gU-w), the power to know.

gUwUm = scientific, science-mind-quality.

(In combinations, gU = knowledge, can often be substituted for gUw = science.)

egUw = physics = motion-science, the science of movements.

egUm = physical

EgUw = chemistry = matter-science, the science of matter, elements;

EgUm = chemic(al)

mUngUw = mathematics, "number-science"; mUngUm = mathematical.

OgUw = psychology = feeling-science, the science of emotions.

OgUm = psychological

trogUw = medicine, medical science = to-good-life- (to health-) science

trogUm = medical

pAgUw = history: past-time; fore-time, -science; pAgUm = historic

Ugs = book = "mind-inside-thing": "inside" a book the "mind" is stored.

Ugz = page = book-part, part of a "mind-inside."

nUgz = chapter = many-pages;

nUgsa = library = many-books-place, a place of many books.

U : i, I.

iUv = understand = light-mind-verb, bright-mind-verb; a bright-mind understands; a "light" is kindled in the "mind" by understanding.

viUv = explain = make-understand, make-light-(in the) -mind by a lucid explanation; viU = explanation.

UiOv = read = mind-see, & vUiOv = write (make-read): see U : O !

iUs = idea = mental picture, image: "light-mind-thing": an idea is a light in the mind, a light-thought, a "bright idea!"

// UI = word // = mind-sound; when your "mind sounds" off, I hear words.

nUI = language = many-words - many-mind-sounds;

nUI-Ugs = dictionary = many-word-book, = language-book

bUI = sentence = "together-words"; words together form a sentence.

abzUI = prose = simple-words: (abz = simple = one-together-part: nUbz (am) "many-parts-together" would be complex, complicated)

jAUI = verse = equal-time-words = rhythm(ic) -words: rhythm in verse consists in equal timing of accent intervals.

fUI = name = self-sound, or: this-word. Instead of pointing: "this" man here!, we say his name: it's John! him-"self" (fU).

pAtUI = record = "past-to-word": one "records" in "words" what has happened before in the "past", which is put "into words".

AvUI = report = "time-make-word", "time-made-word", the time becomes word, even eloquent, in some reports of con"temporaries." Or: "lasting (Av = last) word"; the report lasts, when the action (act = vU) has passed away. "AvU(s) = fact: AvU-I means "fact-sound", make facts sound, facts speak for themselves in a "factual report."

fAvUI, = news: "this-time (news) -made-word"; if "this-time" is put (made) into "words", we have a news-(report).

fAvUIgs = newspaper: "news-inside-thing", something where news are inside.

Yto-rUI = good-bye! = "man-to-move— —good-word": When a man (prepares) to move (away), say a "good word to" him, who is on the "move."

U : I; j, k.

vrO-UI(v) = greet/ing = make-good-feeling-word: greetings make me feel good.
rUI(v) = praise = good-word-(make) : praising = saying nice (good) words.
brUI(v) = approv/al = together (with somebody else) praise: you add your praise to somebody else's plan = you approve.
ydUI(v) = protest: against (yd) -word: say a word against = protest!
ryrUI(v) = argument (argue) = "good-bad(yr) -word (UI)", " positive (r)-negative (yr) -word (UI): if "yes" & "no" fly back – forth, we have an agrument.
tytUI(v) = discuss/ion = "to (and) fro-talk", words flying "towards" (t) and "from" (yt) somebody — — make a discussion.
UIz = letter (as A, B, C) = word-part = a letter is a part of a word.

U : j, k.

E - j - U (-m)

EjU(m) = truth (true): "matter-equal(s) -mind (-quality) "(E-j-U (m-): if you have a "matter-equal" mind, a mental attitude or opinion equal to the material facts of the objective world, you have the truth.
yEjU(m) = untru/th, false/hood: "opposite— —matter—equal—mind", un-true: if you believe or say the "opposite" of (or at least something different from) what "equals" the "material" facts, your mind thinks of expresses untruth or falsehood.
EjUv(s) = prove(proof) = "truth-make", make-it-true (thing), verify, that the facts are the same (j) as your statement about them.
yEjUv = to lie, say or think or feel falsehood, untruth: to live a lie.
yjUtE(v) = err/or = "un-equal— —mind—to—matter (-make): if a man's mind or ideas or opinion (or life) is not equal to (differs from) the material facts, he errs.
EjU-rO(v) = belief (believe): "truth-positive-feel/ing": if you feel "positively" that you are in possession of the "truth", you are a believer; I believe in the Bible = I feel it is true.
nEjUrO(v) = credit: "quantitative-belief": a belief expressed in an "amount" of money, a faith in your solvency is your credit.
jwUr(m) = right, (correct): "equal-power-spirit-positive (-quality)", "equal-power-good": If you have a "right" to a thing you paid for, that means you have the "rightful" (r = good, positive) "power" to hold on to it against an other's claim. But anybody else should have the "same" (j = equal) "power" (w) in the "spirit" (U) of justice, if he bought something. "Right" is a "spiritual" force, which against a robber of brute force calls a
jwUs(u) = law-(yer): "equal-power-concept (-man)". Equality under the law means that all should have "equal-power" (jw).
jwUsku(v) = judge = "law's — —upper-man (-do), the top man of the law-machine: yc jwUskurv Ut yc jwUskuyv! (Judge not, lest ye be judged!)
kU = God = the "above-Spirit", Supreme Spirit, the Spirit above.
kUtU = religiion = God-ward-mind, the mind (turned) toward God.
kUg = head = above— —mind-inside: the head is on "top" & our "mind" is "inside".

U : k; n, O, s.

yktrUm = serious: "burdened-good-mind" (ykt-Em = burdened, ykt = below-ward, down; rU = good-mind); the serious man is bent-down under the burden of his responsiblitities, but has a mind "good" enough to carry them.

tykUiO(v) = (to) list = toward-below (down)-read (UiO) -do(v): something read downward is a list (of names & c), a column etc.

U : n, O, s

nUm(U) = wise (-dom) = much-mind-quality (-concept), great intellect.

ynUm(U) = stupid(ity) = "not-much-intellect-adjective (-concept).

fnUgu = expert = "this--much-mind--man": an expert is a "man" who is "wise" (nU-m) "in(side)", or has applied "much-mind" (n-U) "in" "this" (g,f) (special) field, in which he is expert. Much knowledge (n-gU) of "this" (f) kind is "in" (g) this man (u).

yn-drE-dU(v) = econom-y, (-ize) = "little-money-by--mind": a man who keeps in "mind" to get "by" (by-means-of = "d") with little (yn) money (drE), lives economically.

viOsU(v) = imagine/-ation ="make-see-thing(s) -mind-(verb)." That's just your imagination! means: 'Your "mind makes" you "see" these "things."

UiOv = read ="mind-see": When you can "see" things with your "mind", you are a "mind-reader." Mind-seeing, mental perceiving of its mean-ing, is reading.

vUiOv = write: make (him)-read: if you write for them, you wish you could make (them) read it. Writing is causative of reading.

bnUiO(v) = print/ing ="together-much-read (-make): printed matter is produced in large quantities (much, "n"), together (b) at a time, at one printing. The printing press also presses the print "together" with the paper.

rOkU = virtue = good-feeling-high-mind: if you are virtuous, you "feel good" about it and carry your head, your "kUg" "high" (k). Seriously speaking, virtue should be good (r) emotionally (O) and spiritually (U) and should be directed upward (k(, should make God (kU) feel-good (rO).

EsgU = meaning = "thing(Es)-knowledge(gU)" or: "the matter-thing-- inside-spirit": the "inner-spirit", the essence inside a matter-thing (Es), is its true meaning.

sUgte(v) = experience = "thing-mind-into-move": If you experience horror for the first time, this some-"thing" "moves in-to"(e, -g-t-) or enters, your mind.

Us = thought =mind-thing: as far something intellectual can become a "thing" (concrete), thought is a "mental-thing."

vUtse(v) = decision (decide) = make-mind-to-thing-move: to "make" up one's "mind" to eat an oyster (alive) means to "make" one's "mind move toward" that jelly-"thing."

U : t, U, v, y.

tsU = purpose ="toward-thing-mind": If your "purpose" is marriage, (as Juliet asks Romeo), your "mind" is set "toward that thing."

twU =will: toward-power-mind: the will is the "power" which makes your "mind" move "toward" a certain goal. twUm = willing.

tU = effort, striving "toward" with all your "mind." / design

tUvma =plan= "toward-mind-make-form": When an architect draws a plan, his "mind" looks "toward making" a certain "form." (ma).

OtgU(v) =interest =feeling-toward-know(ing) (know =gU(v)). If you are interested in a girl, you make advances "toward" her, because you "feel" like "knowing" her. ("application" see under: "t" : U)

Ute(v) =find ="mind-toward-move-make", "mind-comes" (U-tev): if your mind hits upon, "comes to" something, you find it.

Ap-Ute(v) =discover/y =(time) before--find: When you find something in time "before" any other mind came to it, it's your discovery.

Ap-Uv(s) =invent(ion) =before-mind-make (thing): if you invent a new machine, your "mind" creates it, "makes" it, "before" anybody else thought (Uv) of it.

wUv = create,
wUvU =creation: "power-spirit-make": the faculty of creation is a "spiritual power to make" new things.
– –kU wUv na u Ib yf wUvU. – –
God creates the first man and the other creation.

Uv = to think, (mind-verb, mind-act)
The doings of your mind are supposed to be: thinking.
UvAm = thinking (participle) as:
UvAm u = the thinking man.

ItUv = suggest, "make-think", make a person think that . . . (whatever you suggest)
utU(v) = educat/ion = man-toward-spirit (-make). If a wife wants to educate her "man", she wants to "make" him over in- "to" (toward) a "spiritual" being. It is easier to lead a child (tu) "toward the spirit."
nuvUs = culture = "many-men-make-mind-thing(s)": the creations of the "many men's minds" in a nation are the "culture" created ("made") by that nation.
Uvo = fiction = the "mind-made life", "life created" by the "mind" of man.

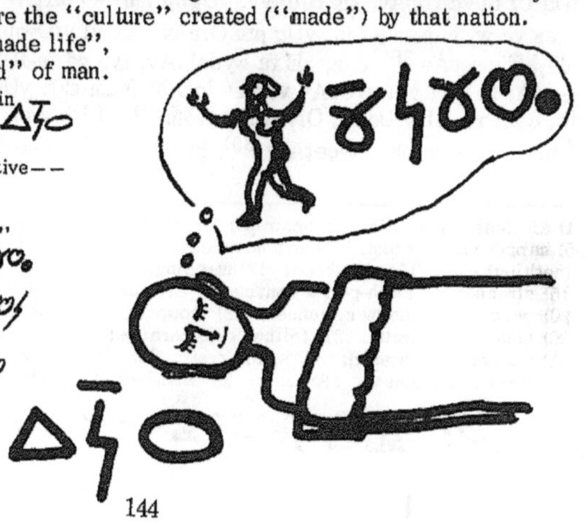

UIvo = story =word-make-life: in a vivid story, mere "words make" people come to "life."
UyvA =sleep = "mind– –in-active– –time": the "time", when the human (conscious, deliberate) "mind" should "not be active" but at (passive) rest.
yiviOs, (yiviOv) =(to) dream = "dark-make-see (things)": the dream makes you see things, while it is dark.
(see i & O)
yUtwO = instinct, drive = "non-intellectual-(irrational) toward-power-feeling": a "powerful feeling" a forceful pull "toward" some goal, which the "intellect" need "not" see through, is a drive.

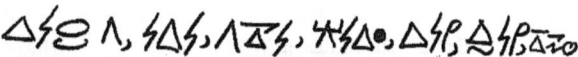

(U : z)

— —kEged-u[1] Ib a-u — —

. . . .

— — — — fa fu ykav fA ag fE yroga[2] Ib trogUwu[3] UIv, Uf fu yApyn[4] yotAv. trogUwu yc gUv, hE cEv fum yro; Ib fu bIb yc gUv, hE cy.pAv.[5] pfE yf Es ag kE Oiv[6] at twUpAv at bev[7] yms at fu. yUg fu am wydnIpAv[8] yd sE. yfA fu OpAv, Uf fu tykepAv Ib tykepAv[9] Ib fu yc gUv yfs.[10]
— —yUg fum AgU kEdev typ at fum tu-oA.[11] xA fu cEpAv ynam tu, Ib bUt tfA yc wapAv UIv fum ytyvu-nUI, cEvs UIpAv at fu:

"etgUrv aUI, Ib vEtAv brU !"

— —fu yc iUpAv EsgU Ub fEn UI; yUg fu OpAv, Uf snE bapAv nykam EsgU.[12] fu etgUpAv nEn nUI ag nEn banu, — — xI[13] a Ub fEn nUI twam[14] cEpAv jOm at pI nUI Ub pfEn yfam[15] UI ? fu dapAv yt bEn-zU[16] at bEnzU; yUg, yn Ub nUI Ub u Ub fE eki cEpAv jOm at I Ub pfEn UI.
— —Ut fu wapAv kEdev ad can bEn, fu tEpAv kEgedu. fu OpAv, Uf ag kana[17] fu cEpAv nEk bam at ytU Ub pfE UI . . . aA[18], xA fu kEdepAv kad PaSiFiK[19] jEnan[20], yfam i kEdepAv ek fnu, Ib fum bo vepAyv at vUiOv:

Ib fu IOpAv I Ub UI ag jam A.

— —yUg, tag bEn tepAv ydbrU, Ib fu tEpAv nIwyd-u[21] Ub nam kEged. ag ypAz, ag twIyg-wyd-kEged, fnu tvykepAv[22] twIyg-wyd[23] bak nuba yb wyd Ib fnu vyopAv nEn Oki u. fu yc vetsepAv[24] brU at fE nuba!
— —ag yf A, nEn kEdevAm lena[25] iOpAyv ak fnum kUg-nuba[26]. yu gUpAv, hE cEpAv fEn lam es. fu kEdepAv tak Ut bypAv[27] yp fE lena, fum nIwyd cEpAv vrAm. fA, yf kE-es tepAv nEk bam at fu, Ut UIv yms at fu. fu IOpAv kfA UI : "vetgUv" Ib "brU". sE twam[28] twUpAv at bev ym nEm pwUrm vavU.[29, 30] yUg, fu [illegible] vpOm[31] twyrOpAm[31] Ud nam wU Ib ne Ub a-es[32] (yUt sE [illegible] cEpAv am kE-es[33]. fUd Uf fu yc iUpAv, xE bepAyv, yUg fu am wydnIpAv yd pfE yfam Es. a-es yc wydnIpAv yd fu, yUg pfa OipAv cEv yI yiOwam[34] ydyrd[35] xE kEtswepAv[36] can, xE fu wydnIpAv, typ yd fu-fU!
— —fA, fu iUv: a-u twUpAv vetsev brU at fnum eki. yUg, fu cEv yovAm, Ib, can, xE UIyv Ud fu, Oiv am U-yrom[37] uI Ub yrom oUz.[38]. fnum eki, fnum bEn, tycetAyv[39], hI ? — — Ib u-U yotAv ag ydbrU?[40]

---

1) airplane-man = pilot; 2) hospital; 3) medicine-man = physician; 4) soon; 5) happened; 6) seems; 7) communicate; 8) shot; 9) fell; 10) other-thing: (nothing) else; 11) childhood; 12) meaning; 13) whether; 14) perhaps; 15) strange; 16) earth-part = continent; 17) heights; 18) once; 19) Pacific 20) ocean; 21) gun-man, gunner; 22) dropped; 23) bombs; 24) brought; 25) disks; 26) head-city, capital; 27) follow; 28) perhaps; 29) 30) important message; 31) suddenly frightened; 32) space-craft; 33) aircraft; 34) 35) invisible shield; 36) threw; 37) insane; 38) brain; 39) will-be-destroyed; 40) war.

"v" : a, A, d, e, f, g; l, p, r, s.

"v" denotes ACT(IVITY): to do, make, create, pro-create, male sex
-v = verb-ending

v : a, d, e, f, g.

vAm = awake: "active-time-adjective": the "awake" time is the time when you are active;
yvAm = asleep = non-active-time-quality: when you are asleep, you are not supposed to be active.
-vAm = -ing (participle ending) = active-time-quality: u c' uwevAm = the man is working.
dvU = process = (by means) through-make-concept": a process is a way, (da) through which one makes something.
dyv = permit, let ="through-non-active", "by-means-—passive"
dyvU = permission = the non-active-means-concept: by his permission I can make the voyage . . . means: somehow "through" him, I can make it, but he is "not actively" helping me, but just passively letting me pass.
vem = active = "active-movement-quality": activity implies motion.
vEm = elastic = "active-material-quality": somehow, elastic material like rubber or steel, seems active, even alive.
kykvEd = spring, (coil) = "up-down-elastic-tool", above-below-make-tool: a (hanging) coil-spring vibrates up and down.
fev = to take = "this-move-active": if I (fu) "move" something to "me, myself (fufU), to "this" man here, to the Ego, . . . I "take" it.
gvU = in-fact, in reality, actual(ly) ="in act(ive-concept)".
tygvEv = produce = "toward-outside-make", "put-out, out-put": if the earth "produces" grass or grain, it "makes" them come "out", "toward the outside," forward, forth.

v : l, p, r, s.

(lt)vU(v) = suggest/ion = "(sound-toward-) act(ion-concept) -make": if one hints something (by word of mouth, by "sound") so that it "makes" the other fellow "act", – if one thus transfers (sound into) action: that is a form of suggestion. Without sound (wordless) thought-transmission is "vUv" alone, and emotional infection: "vOv".
plt vU(v) = propos/ition = "pre-suggest/ion", before-suggest, put something before somebody as a pro-pos-al.
ypev(U) = react(ion) = behind (or: back) -move-act- (concept): ev = to move. If a gun back (yp) -fires, or pushes "back", recoils, it reacts.
yrvU = crime = bad-act = opposite (of) -good—-act—- concept, evil-deed.
nEsvU = industry = "many-matter-things-make-mind-concept": industry "makes (produces) many material things", and still, as the "virtue of industry" (diligence), it is a mind-concept.
wete(v) = impulse (impel) = "powerful-movement-toward-move (doing)": if you have an impulse "toward" kissing a girl, there is a "force" which "drives (moves)" you "toward moving" to the girl and "doing" something to her.

vU = (an) act = do-concept, activity-idea.
AvUs = fact = "time-act-thing": an "act" which happened in "time" (past) is by now a "fact", an actual "thing" of reality.
vUn = operation = "act-multitude"; a complicated act, consisting of "many actions", is called an operation.
vem = active, see: v : e.
-v = verb-ending = "do", for all personal verb forms and the infinitive.
v- = prefix of causatives, & procreative or male properties.
Ev = to do: substance-activity, the essence of activity is "doing"
vEv = to make = active-doing, do-doing, as it were -- almost creative.
yv = to be passive, to receive action, & so oppose
-yv = passive ending, not to be separated: (bum twU)' Eryv! (Thy will) be done! "y" precedes immediately the -v of the active!
yv- = prefix of the receptive, conceptive, conception, conceiving, female.
yvu = she, yvum = her(s).
yryv = to suffer = "evil-passive", to be passive to evil.
vym = passive = active-opposite-quality. (More literally, less popular, you can also form "yvem = passive," in the sense of receptive, receiving action). vym is rather phlegmatically opposed to any action, inactive or receptive.
dyv = to permit, let, allow = instrumentally-passive: if one lets something happen, one is a pipe "through" (d) which the deed flows. but in a passive (yv) sense.
tsyvpA-tiOs = receipt = "toward--thing-passive (syv = receive) -- before-time (pA = past) -- toward-see-thing (t-iO-s); or: to-have-received--show--thing: a "receipt" is a "thing" which shows (toward seeing, t-iO), that one has received (syv) something in a previous time (pA = past).

--jAg bu cEv UyvAm gaf yvAm, bu yc wav Ev yrve. -- vAm u Ev Ib vEv nEn Es. vU Ub nEn u cEv jUm eb y-vEv (un-doing) pI vU Ub vf u. fE y-vEv cEv a ma Ub ydbrU. ydbrU tycvEv (destroys). rOwu, gUwu, wUv (artist and scientist create) Es, xE yc syv nUr yt tycEvU Ub yf Es. rOwu Ib gUwu wav wUv am ag brU.

(Retranslate: While you are sleeping or asleep, you can not do harm. The awake man (Man while awake) does and makes many things. The acts of many men are equal with undoing the acts of other men. This undoing is one form of war. War destroys. The artist and the scientist create things, which (do) not receive their value from the destruction of other things. Artist and Scientist can create only in peace.)

W : a, A, b, d, f, g, i; k, o, O.

"W"

"w" indicates: POWER, FORCE, STRENGTH: ABILITY, POTENCY, POSSIBILITY

w : a, A, b, d, f, g, i.

wam = able, (-ible); wav = can = power-space-(verb or adjective) : if I am able or "can" run away, I have the "power" (strength) and the "space" (room) to dash off (I'm neither lame nor fenced in).

(wOv = may = power-feeling-verb: if I have the feeling of power, I may do something. cf. wav & wOv)

twa = possibility.

twam = possible = "toward-able", toward-can-be, perhaps able, possibly = perhaps (as adverb, before a verb)

twarm = probable = possibility-good-adjective: if something is probable, there is a "good" (r) possibility that it will happen.

--Qg bu bav wom Ib rom oged, bu "wav" av. Qg bum kwu (boss) dyv, bu "wOv" av. yb dyvU, sE yc "twarm", Uf bu atAv, dyf s[illegible] c[illegible] "twam."--

(If you have strong and healthy legs, you "can" go. If your boss permits (lets you), you "may" go. Without permission it is not "probable" that you will go, though it is "possible."

bew (ev) = grip = "together-move-force(move)": a grip is a sort of vice, which has the "force" to "move together." If one "grips" something, one "moves" (drives that grip home).

wyde(v) = attack = "powerful-against-move--(make)": if you attack an enemy, you "move your forces against (yd) him."

tyfwU(v) = influence = "toward-other (yf)-power:" influence is a force flowing in- "to" others."

tygwe(v) = burst: "toward-outside (= outward) -power-move": if a shell bursts, the pieces fly (move forcefully) outward.

wei(m) = electric/ity = "power-movement-light": electricity is the "power" (of) "movement and light": with electro-power you move a motor and light a lamp.

w : k, o, O.

knuw(ev) = govern/ment: above-many-men-power: government exerts "power over many men."

kwev(s) = command = "above-power-move(-make): the commander has the "power" to "move" you from "above" & push you around.

ykwev = obey = "under-power-move": if you obey, you "move under" another man's power or command.

tykwev = conquer = "toward-obey(ing)" "conquest" "forces to obedience" or "under the command" of the conqueror.

ykwuv = to serve = under-power-man-verb.

kwu = boss, master.

kwU(v) = control = above-power(-do) control means "power-over. ."

kwyU = fate =above power-- opposite (to)-mind: Fate is a ruling power, irrational & unintelligible.

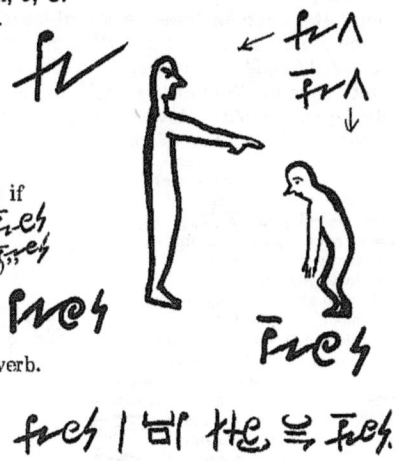

w : o, p, r, t, u, U, v, y.

wo(m) = (strong), strength = "power-life (-quality)": strength is the power of something alive.
ywo(m) = weak/ness, feeble/ness = un-strength, (un-strong).
nyrwo(m) = violent/ce = "much-bad(yr) -strength (wo), evil forcefulness."
yrwo(m) = brutal/ity = bad-power. / shy
rywO(m) = delicate(-cy) = good-non-strength-feeling (-quality): delicacy is a kind of "weakness' viewed as "good" by a feeling of sympathy.

w : p, t, u, U, v, y.

pwUr(m) = important/ce = "before-power-mind-positive (-quality)": if you think something is important, to your "mind" it has a "positive" "power before" other things.
tswe(v) = strike/stroke = "toward-thing-power-move": if you strike some-"thing", you "move forcibly to(ward)" that "thing", — — even if your car strikes a wall.
tweb(ev) = hit = toward-power-move-together (-move): if you hit a target with an arrow, the arrow "moves forcibly toward" and "together" with the target.
tweyd = (a) blow = "toward. power-move-against (yd) - (something)": a blow is always struck "against" something, "toward" which the tool (d) of the blow "moves forcibly."
uwe(v) = work, (labor) = man-power— —move—(make): work is a "power-move" done by man (-power) or for "man", or in a human way. We do not consider a tiger's "powerful motions" for food as work.
wU = power = power-concept, power (in the) abstract;
wUm = power-ful
wUv = create = power-mind-act, the creative act of a powerful mind.
wOv = may (cf. wav = can): "wOv" implies a feeling (O) of permission.
wyv = must = "power-possive": if you "must", you are passively exposed to, or suffer under, a power.
wyvU(m) = necess(ary) -ity = must-concept (-quality): it's necessary = (I) must.
wyvyr = need = "must-evil" = the "bad must": what one must do badly, one needs to do.
vow(ev) = (to) force = active-life-power(-move). Only a "living" being can force somebody, by "actively" applying its "power" on him.
ywe(v) = fail/ure = "un-power-move": if you fail to do something, you do "not" have the "power to move" (in the right direction).
tywe(v)/ -pAm = tire/d = "toward-non-power(impotence)-move: if one tires, one moves toward a state of (powerless) exhaustion.

tywmA = fatigue = the "toward-im-potence-condition (or: state) or: -quality-time— —the time of fatigue.
wyd = weapon = power-against-(tool): the weapon is a tool (d) against (yd) power.
wydnIv = to shoot = weapon- much-sound-make: to make (v) much noise (n-I) with a weapon (wyd) means: to shoot.
nI-wyd = gun = much-noise — —weapon.
twIyg-wyd = bomb = to-power- sound— —outside (yd)-weapon, explosive-weapon: pieces fly "outside" (t- yg) with powerful noise (wI).
twIygna(v) = explo/sion, (-de) = toward-boom-outside-much- space: explosives expand.

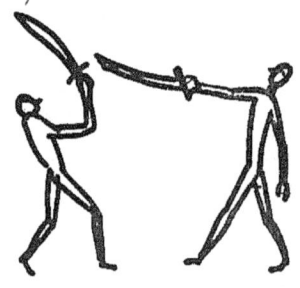

W:

x : a, A, E, I; u, U.

"x" (as in Quixote or Mexico, or "ch" in loch)
implies "RELATION, RELATIVE": "which."
(People who can not pronounce this
snoring "h" -sound, can replace
e.g. xu (who) by "hup" (relative)
and "xa" (where) by "hap."

x : a, A, E, I.

xa = where = which-space, (on) which-place, on the place, where . . .

(ha ? = where ? The differnece between questions and relative clauses, neglected in English, shows in the following sentences:

"Where have you been ?" = "ha bu cpAv ?"
'I was where you found me.' = 'fu cpAv, xa bu UtepAv fu.'

xA = when = which-time, at the time which . . . cf. hA? = when . . . ?
xE(m) = which = which-matter (-quality): the house, which . . = uga, xE

I know in which house he lives = fu gUv, ag xEm uga vu ov.
(Since in aUI, relative and question pronoun are distinguished, it is possible to keep the word-order:
Subject--Verb--Object--adverbials, e.g.
"fu gUv, vu ov ag xEm uga."

xI = whether = which-sound, corresponding to "hI?" (Question-sound)
--fu yc gUv, xI fu arv gaf tArv.-- (I (do) not know, whether I should-go or stay)

xnE(m) = which(plural, Latin quae, Spanish los cuales, German: welche) "which-many-matter (-quality).

. . . . The houses in which I lived = pIn uga, fu opAv ag xnE . . . .
e.g. -- fu AgUv kuga Ib knuga, ag xnE fu opAv. -- If I translate: "I remember the tower and the palace, in which I lived," it remains unclear in English, whether I lived in both, since which has no plural. "xnE" must be translated with ". . in both of which"

xu = who, that, (singular)
xnu = who (plural), e.g. the men, who said this, . . . u, xnu UIpAv fE.
xyvu = who, feminine: the woman, who = yvus, xyvu . . .

xU = relation = "relative-concept."
xUm = relative (tytU = relationship, reference)
xUd = as, how -- referring to "fUd" = so --

y : b, d; c, g; r, s, n, u; v, w, m.
"y"

"y" = OPPOSITE: UN-, NON-, IN-, ANTI-, DIS- . . .
(implies negation, not; as prefix:
cf. in-consistent, dis-honest, un-like)

(In coining new words by prefixing "un-", a musical accent on the "y-" sung high, is advisable. Use hyphen: ỳ-vEv = un-make)

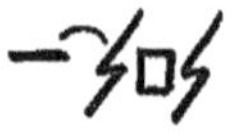

y : b, d.

yb = without = opposite (of) with (eb) = anti-together = y-b. 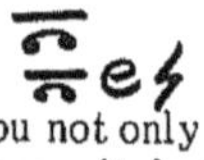
vybev = omit = "without-move" = move (drive) it out, do without.
yd = against = "opposite (of) 'by-means-of', 'by the help of': If you not only offer no help, but even work 'against' me, you are doing just the 'opposite' of a mediator! (medium = dE).
wyde(v) = attack = "power(ful) — —against-move-(make)" 
yde(v) = obstruct/ion = "against-movement— —act": to act against any movement means to obstruct it.

y : g, c.

ygev = avoid = "outside-move": to move outside, around something; get "out of" the way of . . ., cf. ybev! 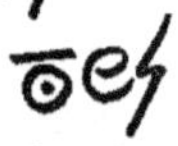
gyE = hole = inside — —no-matter: around a hole, there may be earth, but "inside, within" there is nothing, "no matter". 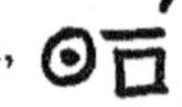
gyEv = to dig: "inside-no-matter-make": to make a hole.  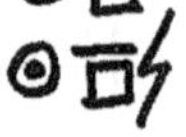
// yc = (is) not: not-is, opposite (of) being.

y : r, s, n, u.

yr ! = no ! ("no-good! evil ! non-positive"); yr, no ! is opposite of Ur! = yes! , and can not be used as adjective (not any). 
yrm = negative, the no-quality.
yn = no(ne) =no-quantity, no amount, none, not any; cf. yr! = no!: "Do you have money?" 'No! I have no money. I have none!' 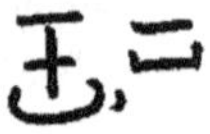
" bu bav drE? hI?" —'yr! fu bav yn drE. fu bav yn!'
ys = nothing = no-thing. 
yu = nobody = no-man, no one, none (as masculine)
yU(m) = /the/ opposite = opposite-mind (-quality), contrast(ing) 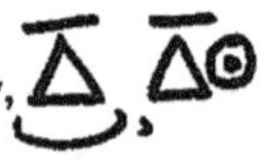
yUg, = but, however = (the) opposite-mind-in: "She was not pretty, but ugly" means: "She was not pretty! 'In-contrast!', the opposite! she was ugly!" yvu yc cpAv riOm, yUg yriOm.. — —

y : v, w, m.

Yv = "opposite-do" to oppose (passively) : Yvev = slip 
wyU = chance = a power, -opposite (to the) mind . the intellect can not fathom Fate (kwyU) nor Chance (wyU).
ym = any = "opposite (to) quality"; "no-qualifications!" Give me any (unqualified) drink! I am dying from thirst! I am not interested in quality. — — serv ym jE at fu! fu yov Ud yjE!— —
— — yc OtgUv mU!

(yI = a(n); yIn = some— —as plural of the indefinite article).

"z" : a, b, d.
" z "

"z" indicates "PART, DIVISION, divide, separate, piece, break; opposite: indivisible, whole.

z : a, b, d.

az = side = space-part: on this side it's cool! means: "On this part of space it is cool"

zam = separate = part--space-quality: if things are "a-part", they are separated.

azve = ½, one-half = "one--division-made(by)--two" = one divided by two; or: one-part-made-two; to make parts, cut a-part = divide.

bza = fold = "together-part-space": if cloth is folded, the "parts" or stripes are (folded) "together" in "space".

abzam = simple, "one-folded" (simplex, ein-fältig);

ebzam = double, "two-fold": two-together-parts (space-adjective); if two parts are folded together, it's double

ibzam = threefold, three-together-parts . . . triple.

buzav(U) = participate,(-ion) = together-man-part-space-make: if I participate in a party, I make(v) myself "part" (z) of it, "together" (b) with other "men" (u) in the same "space (a) "or room".

bUz = class = "together-mind-part"; e.g. a school-class is a "part" of the school, but the "mind" considers many pupils "together" as a class.

zEd = blade = part-matter-tool: a blade is a "tool" which cuts "material" things a- "part."

odz = bit = life-tool-part, life-means--part = food (od) -part (z), since biting cuts the "food" a- "part", and even the "bit" of a borer is originally an imitation of a tooth.

odze(v) = (to) bite = "(to) life-tool-part-move (make)" or: "food-part-move", to "move (make) food (into) parts, cut it a-part."

dzOm = sharp = "tool-part-feeling" or: "through-part--feel-quality": the "part" of a "tool (d)" that cuts "through", "feels sharp."

ydzOm = dull = "not-sharp" or: "not-through . .": a dull tool does not cut through.

ydzem = blunt = "not-through-part-move (quality)" = not-piercing

dzem = piercing, stinging, needle-sharp, pointed "spitzig" = "through-part-move-quality" : what moves "through" most easily, as it "parts" any medium, by the principle of wedge or cone, is

dzez = a sting, prick, "Spitze", point of dagger, spit, thorn, quill: "through-part--move--part"; it is the part which moves through a part, the puncture. (dzev = to sting, prick)

dEz = a cut: "through-matter-part": a cut is a part, "parted" off, cut "through", divided, by a tool (d. .) or "matter, material" divided, or "parted."

zEvd = knife = "part-matter-make-tool": a knife is a "tool" which "makes matter (into) parts", which divides, cuts a- "part."

dzEv = to cut = to "tool-part-matter-make": to divide, take "apart," separate, material by means (d) of a tool (d..) or to move "through" (d) matter (E), "to-cut-through-material."

(All three applications of "d": through, by-means, & tool, are used).

dzEpAm = cut (e.g. "it is cut off"), cloven, Past Participle: taken apart.

kyk-zEvd = (a) saw = "up-down-knife", zig-zag-knife, moved up & down; (cf. jEl-kyk = wave, up-down-wave)

zlEvd = sickle = "part-round-matter-make-tool": a sickle is a "rounded" (l) knife (zEvd): a "rounded tool" (l-d) to cut "matter apart."

tnEz(d) = (road-)fork z : d; E, m, n, o; U, v.

tazd = fork = "to(ward)-one--part-tool": a fork is a "parted tool", whose prongs join in- "to" one (a) handle.

z : E, m, n, o.

Ez = element =matter-part; the fundamental parts of matter are the elements.
Eza = Hydrogen = "element (number) one"; Eze = Helium = element (Nr.) 2;
(In aUI, the scientific names of the elements use their atomic order numbers, although e.g. iron, gold & c have popular names, too. (see "E:z")
zEz = atom = (basic) part (of an) element, still retaining elemental properties.
bzEz = molecule = "together-atoms, atoms joined."
weiz = electron =electricity-part.
zvE = piece: "part-made--matter", material "made" (cut into) parts, or: a part made from matter.
mEz = sort: "quality-matter-part"; I like a sour sort of apples. The 'sour' apples are a "qualified part" from the "material" of all apples.
nazte(v) = distribut/ion = number-one-part-to-move: if in a number of people, you "move to" (give to) each "one part", you are "distributing" the cake.
znEv(U) = divide, (-sion) = "part-number-material-make (-concept)": by dividing, division, one "makes numbered parts" out of "material."
ynaz = detail = "small (no-quantity) side", little (yn) -space-part.
wozam = right = "strong-part-(of) space-quality", "power-life-part-space-quality": the right side of the ("living") body has more "strength". "right or left" are sides (az), "qualities of parts of space."
ywozam = left = weak-part(of) space-quality: the left side is usually weaker.
zomz = race = "part-life-quality-part": a species of animal is "part (of a) qualified type (part) of living (things)." It is, strictly speaking a 'special' (zUm) subdivision, a part of a part. jomz = species

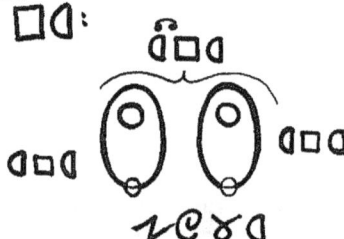

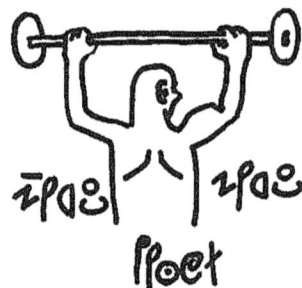

z : U, v, y, z.

zU = part ="part-concept", part (in) abstracto.
zUm = particular, special ="part-concept-quality."
yzUm = general, universal = "opposite(of) special", "un-specified"
azve = ½, one-half ="one-part-make--two" ="one" divided into ("made") "two parts"
izvu = 3/4 = three-fourths, 3 quarters: "3-part-make-4": If you "make" (cut) 4 parts (of a waffle) and take 3 (times) such a part, it's 3/4.

zwEv = break = "part-force-matter-make" or "part- -power-matter (hard-substance) -make": in breaking, one uses no tools (d) as in cutting (dzEv), but usually brute "force" (w) to get (make = v) solid hard material (w-E) a-"part."

zwI(v) = (to) crack = "part-power-sound (-make)": if (one) cracks rocks they break a-"part",-- usually with a "powerful sound". Even the "crack" of a whip cuts through ("parts") the air with strong noise.

wyrzev = to smash = "power(ful) -bad-part-move-make": smashing things up (a-"part") seems useless and "bad" (yr), although one "does" it "forcefully" (w).

zvEz = edge = "part-make-matter-part": an edge is the cutting "part" of a "material" tool (knife); and cutting itself, means cutting a-"part", dividing into parts, "making parts": thus, an edge is the part, making parts.

myz = quite = "quality (of) opposite (of) part": wholly: 'She was quite good' means: 'She was of good "qualities, not (in) parts", but generally (yzUm).

zym = tough = "part-opposed - -quality": if material "opposes" any cutting (dzEv) or breaking (zwEv) a-"part", it must be tough (zym), and stays probably:

zyn = whole = "part-opposite-quantity", the quantity opposite to part is "the Whole."

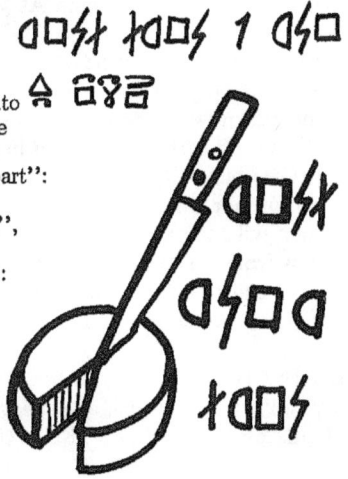

"fu cEv yI zU Ub zU, xE , Ap, pI zyn cEpAv.
fu cEv yI zU Ub yi, xE pI i toepAv."

(pI yrkU : MeFiSTo
The Satan, "evil-god")

("Ich bin ein Teil des Teils, der anfangs alles war.
Ich bin ein Teil der Finsternis, die sich das Licht gebar")
Mephisto, Faust. Goethe.

Literally:
"I am a part of a part, which, formerly, was the whole.
I am a part of Night, who bore herself the Light."

Rhymed:
"I am part of the part which first was all : of Night . . .
And Mother Darkness bore herself the Light." (Goethe's Faust).

In aUI grammar:
"fu c' zU Ub zU, xE Ap c'pAv can: Ub "yi,"
ytyvu yi, xE tvoepAv pl "i".

(In such cosmic dialectic, it is more correct to omit the matter-part of "cEv," to be: cEv = c'; cEpAv = c'pAv . . . without "E".

PART VI. READING.

kUtOr Ub Ku (The Lord's Prayer)

—-fnum ytvu, xu cEv ag kna, bum fUI kUrUryv (tukOryv)! bum knuwa terv! bum twU Eryv kab bEn Uj ag kna! serv fnum iAm nod at fnu fiA! Ib yrvtrOrv pIn fnum ẏrUvs rUt fnu, Uj fnu yrvtrOv rUt pIn fnum yrevu. Ib bu yc daiurv fnu tag yrUm tsOb, yUg, fUwerv fnu tyg yrU! yUt knuwa Ib wU Ib kUO (rUI) cEv bum At ymA Ib can-A. FUd-sE-cErv!

Our Father, who art in heaven, hallowed be Thy name (Thy name be honored = tukOryv, which would be a satisfactory substitute) Thy kingdom come! (knuw = government, would be near enough). Thy will be done (Eryv), on earth as (it is) in heaven! Give us this day our daily bread! (Give our daily bread to us today!) And forgive us our trespasses (and pardon our sins for us) as we forgive our debtors (as we forgive for [the] our evil-doers). And lead us not into temptation (evil-desires), but deliver us from evil (but free us out-of evil). For thine is the kingdom and the power and the glory (and praise is thine) for ever and ever (till ever and all time)! Amen (So-be-it).

–KU vrUrv aMéRiKa, una, fu brOv xE! karv baz sE, Ib daiurv sE, ad yiA Ud i yt ak! yt bEk at ẹna, at jEna bim Ud jElkyk (waves; "foam" would be kEgjE "air-in-water") . . . KU vrUrv aMéRiKa, fum fuga, grOm fuga!

God bless America! Land that I love! Stand beside her (it) and guide her, through the night with (by-means-of) the light from above. From the mountains to the prairie (to the plains) to the oceans (sea) white with (by) foam: God bless America, my home, sweet home!

In rhymes one might translate:

–KU, vrUrv aMERiKa, kUtOr erv tak!
bu karv baz sE,
Ib tArv gaz sE,
varv bum i,
xE ad yi
terv yt ak!
ag dam ẹna,
ad nam jEna,
fu iOv fum banu brOm!
kU vrUrv aMERiKa,
fum fuga, fUd grOm!

THE BEATITUDES.

The Sermon on the Mount.

Seeing the crowds, He went up on the mountain, and when He sat down, His disciples came to Him.
And He opened His mouth and taught them, saying:
"Blessed are the poor in spirit, for theirs is the kingdom of heaven.
Blessed are those who mourn, for they shall be comforted.
Blessed are the meek, for they shall inherit the earth.
Blessed are those who hunger and thirst for righteousness, for they shall be satisfied.
Blessed are the merciful, for they shall obtain mercy.
Blessed are the pure in heart, for they shall see God.
Blessed are the peacemakers, for they shall be called sons of God.
Blessed are those who are persecuted for righteousness' sake, for theirs is the kingdom of heaven.
Blessed are you, when men revile you and persecute you and utter all kinds of evil against you falsely on my account.
Rejoice and be glad, for your reward is great in heaven, for so men persecuted the prophets who were before you.

pIn vrUpAm-rOkU.

kUm-UIvs kab bEk. (Mat. 5)

iOvAm nEn-u, Vu apAv tak kab bEk, Ib xA Vu yktapAv-tyk, pIn Vum U-etgUvu tepAv at Vu.
Ib Vu tagev Vum ogta Ib vetgUv nu, UIvAm:
"vrUpAm cEv pIn yndrEm-u ag U, yUt pI knuwa Ub kna cEv num.
vrUpAm cEv pfEn, xnu ykrOv, yUt nu tvOr-tA-yv.
v r UpAm cEv pIn ywE-rykOm-u, yUt nu stAyv-yt-ytu pI bEn.
vrUpAm cEv pfEn xnu yodev Ib yjEv rUt trU, yUt nu trUnOryv.
vrUpAm cEv pIn kubrOm-u, yUt nu sryv kubrO.
vrUpAm cEv pIn ram-u ag gog, yUt nu iOtAv KU.
vrUpAm cEv pIn brU-vEv-u, yUt nu fUItAyv yIn tvu Ub KU.
vrUpAm cEv pfEn, xnu cEv tyr-bypApAm rUt ytUs Ub trU, yUt num cEv knuwa Ub kna.
vrUpAm cEv bnu, xA pIn u y-rUIv bnu Ib tyrbypAv bnu Ib yt-sev can mEz Ub yrU y.d bnu yEjUmQ yUt fu.
krOrv Ib UrOrv, yUt bnum jruts cEv nam ag kna, yUt fUd pIn u tyr-bypApAv pIn Ap-UI-u, xnu cpAv Ap bnu.

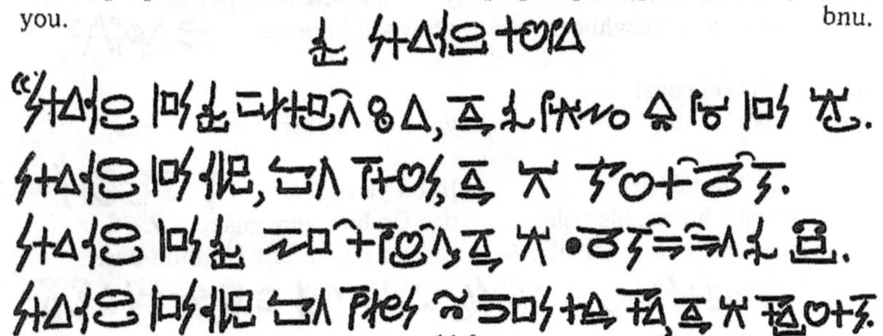

The Ten Commandments (Deut. 5)	pIn 10 (Q) kwevUs.
I am the Lord, your God, who brought you out of the land of Egypt, out of the house of bondage.	fu cEv pI Ku, bnum KU, xu vetsepAv bnu tyg yt pI bEna EGYPT, tyg yt pI yruga Ub y-fUwe.
You shall have no other gods besides me.	bnu yc barv yIn yf kU baz fu.
You shall not make for yourself a graven image . . .	bu yc vErv rUt bu Uiana-jiOs gaf jiOvs . . .
you shall not bow down and serve them.	bu yc velrv-tyk Ib ykwurv nu.
You shall not take the name of the Lord, your God, in vain.	bu yc dErv pI fUI Ub pI Ku, bum KU, yb ytwU.
Observe the Sabbath day, to keep it holy . . .	gUterv pI SaBBaTH-iA. (nE-iA) Ut bAv sE kUrUm . . .
Honor your father and your mother, as the Lord, your God commanded you.	tukOrv bum ytvu Ib bum ytyvu, Uj pI Ku, bum KU kwepAv bu.
That your ways may be prolonged, and that it may go well with you, in the land which the Lord, your God gives you.	Ut bum da vanaryv, Ib Ut sE rUg arv-yEc eb bu, ag pI bEna, pI Ku, bum KU sev at bu.
You shall not kill.	bu yc vyorv.
Neither shall you commit adultery.	yc-Ib bu vorv eb bo-u Ub yf u.
Neither shall you steal.	yc-Ib bu yrferv.
Neither shall you bear false witness against your neighbor.	yc-Ib bu yEjUrv ag jwUskus ytrevAm bum bus.
Neither shall you covet your neighbor's wife;	yc-Ib bu tsOberv byvu Ub bus;
And you shall not desire your neighbor's house, his field . . or anything that is your neighbor's.	Ib bu yc tsOberv uga Ub bus, vum enaz, gaf ym Es, xE cEv Ub bum bus.

The Gospel According to Saint John.	pI rUm-vavU Ud kUrUm JoN.
1. In the beginning was the Word, and the Word was with God, and God was the Word.	1. ag pe cEpAv pI UI, Ib pI UI pAc eb KU, Ib KU cEpAv pI UI.
2. This was in the beginning with God.	2. fE pAc ag pe eb KU.
3. All was made (created) by Him; and without Him was nothing made, that was made (created).	3. can pAc wUpAm Ud vu; Ib yb vu ys vEpAyv, xE wUpAyv.
4. In Him was life; and the life was the light of men.	4. ag vu pAc o; Ib pI o pAc pI i Ub u.
5. And the light shineth in the darkness; and the darkness comprehended it not.	5. Ib pI i iv ag yi; Ib pI yi yc iUpAv sE.
9. That was the true light, which lighteth every man that cometh into the world.	9. pfE pAc pI EjUm i, xE viv can u, xu tev tag Ea.
10. He was in the world, and the world was made by Him, and the world knew Him not.	10. vu pAc ag Ea, Ib Ea vEpAyv Ud vu, Ib Ea yc gUpAv Vu.
11. He came unto His own, and His own received Him not.	11. vu tepAv tag vum bavum, Ib vum bavum yc syvpAv Vu
12. But as many as received Him, to them gave He power to become the sons of God, even to them that believe in His name:	12. yUg, Uj nEn Uj sYvpAv Vu, at nu Vu sepAv wU at tEv tvu Ub KU, myz at nu, xnu EjUrOv tag vum fUI:
13. Which were born, not of blood, nor of the will of the flesh, nor of the will of man, but of God.	13. xnu toepAyv, yc yt ogai, Ib-yc yt twU Ub ogE, yc-Ib yt twU Ub u, yUg yt KU.
14. And the Word was made flesh, and dwelt among us, (and we beheld His glory, the glory as of the only-begotten of the father) full of grace and truth.	14. Ib UI vEpAyv ogE, Ib uapAv nag fnu, (Ib fnu iOpAv vum kUO, pI kUO Uj Ub pI am-vopAm yt ytvu gEm Ub riOma Ib EjU.

– itA - kUtOr. –	Evening Prayer.
Oh fum kU, fum ku,	Oh my God, my master,
pI tes Ub fum tsOb!	The goal of my desire!
fE bum ykwu	This thy servant
tvev at yvAv	seeks to sleep
ag ytyrA Ub bum riOma,	in the shelter of thy grace,
Ib at Ayev	and to repose
yk kugaz Ub bum kubrO,	in the canopy of thy mercy,
tOrvAm bum Ote	imploring thy care
Ib bum ydyrwa.	and thy protection.
yn kU cEv yg bu:	No God is there but Thee:
pI can-wUm,	the all-mighty,
can-tykwAm, (Bahá ù lláh)	all-subduing,
pI yQpAm.	the unconditioned.

Compare an English and an aUI translation of a passage of Bhagavad-Gita:

aUI Bhagavad-Gita: U-kam-u[+]rIpAv:	English Bhagavad-Gita: The Exalted[+]Sang:
–Ud fu fE can-ca c' tygapAm, yUg fu yiOwam[2]cEv fufU.	–By me this universe is spread, but I myself can not be seen[2]
can cEvs cEv ytkavAm[3]bag fu, yUg fu yc cEv fufU ag nu.	The beings all hang[3]within me, but I myself am not in them.
Ib yfA snE yc cEv bag fu: bu yvorv wU Ub ypums fA!	And then they are not inside me: conceive the power of mystery!
fum fU yc uav[4]bag pIn Es, yUg fU skev snE Ib mav snE tyg.	My self dwells[4]not within the things, but carries them and forms them out.
-:-	
–jOm Uj pI kEwe 'g[5]ygEm a, ev ag cạn A at cạn a cnA;	Like as the wind in[5]empty space, moves everywhere in every time;
fUd can pIn cEvs uav ag fu, fum wU lygạnav Ib skwErv can.	thus all the creatures dwell in me, my force surrounds, supports them all.
ag Ea-o-ypAz, can cEvs typ-agtev tag fum pạm ytU[6]	At world-life's end, the creatures all re-enter my primeval womb[6]
Qg fAvm oA petAv Uj cạ, fu wUtAv nu can fAv-m[7]kfA.	If a new age shall start as world, I will create them new[7]again.
-:-	
–kab Eo-ykaz, pạm ytU, fu c' wUvAm can-A tap Ib tap.	–Upon primeval nature's base, am I creative on and on.
pIn QkQ[8]Ub cEvs wUyv tap, ag rOb eb[9]Eo Ub fum twU.	The hosts[8]of beings are born forth, according[9]to my nature's will.
yUg can fEn Ev-U[10], can fEn vU, yc walev fu, yc tnakev fu;	Yet all this doing[10], all these acts, do not confine nor limit me.
yUt fu tAv Ub jUm U can A, yc bytkavAm yt fEn fum vU.--	As I remain of equal mind, depending not on these my deeds.–

(+)spirit-high-person, (2)invisible, (3)are hanging, suspended, (4) dwells, (5)'g for ag = in, (6)origin, (7)two syllables! (8)ten-high-ten, 10^{10} = ten-billions or ten-milliards, (9)in harmony with, (10)do-concept = doings

– fnum jEnged ykapAv ab ykbE-tEl[1] ab jEn-ygana[2] Ub AFRiKa. iA cpAv i-riOm.[3] ryiEvAm[4] kEwe ekEpAv[5] yt jĒna. yUg, ag itA, kamA tyjepAv, Ib tEpAv bwe-iEm.[6] al aki-tyk[7] jEnged-ku[8] tepAv tyg kab jEnged-kygz,[9] Ib nIpAv:[10] "jEugav!"[11] Ib ag a ynA, jEnged-u[12] etkepAv tag jEn, vyktepAv kEwed tag jEn, Ib ag kEwed, trabepAv jEgev-a.[13]

– kab jEnged, eb fnu, e fAoms[14] cEpAv. pIn ynvu, ab na etkepAv tag jEn; yUg, bag[15] kEwed sE cpAv knE walevAm[16] rUt nu; Ib nu fepAv tag num kUg at jEgev ne-kyftU[17] ag tagem jEna. pI a ynvu, ag pe, cpAv ag pa, ap vum cub; yUg, nEk yprAm, tApAv yp. ytvu Ub pI ynvu, pAom nIwyd-bydwuk,[18] kapAv kab jEnged-kygz, Ib tiOpAv rUI-brO[19] at vum ynam tvu. xA tvu pepAv at tAv yp, ytvu unIpAv at vu: "yc serv-tak! vArv-kab at tvev!"

– ypOmQ, yrOI tepAv yt jEnged-kygz: "nyrjEos!" Ib fnu iOpAv ag jEn pI ypaz Ub jEna-nyrcEvs. nyrjEos jEgepAv ylem at ynvu. "typ! terv typ! nyrjEos!", nIwyd-u nIpAv. yUg, pIn fAoms yc IOpAv vu, Ib jEgepAv nEk ybam ayt-- krOIvAm Ib u-nIvAm tfA nEk krO-gEm Ib nIm myt Ap. –

– nIwyd-u, bim jOm binanab, tiOpAv at ynvu.-- jEnged-u vyktepAv yI jEged, etkepAv tag sE, Ib nepAv ayt, Uj nem Uj wapAv at ynvu. yUg, nu tfA cpAv ybam yt nu, xA nyrjEos yc cpAv nEk ybam myt oQ ana-an yt ynvu.

– pIn fAoms, ag pe, yc IOpAv, xE unIpAyv at nu, Ib yc iOpAv nyrjEos. yUg, yfA, a Ub nu tiOpAv al, Ib fnu can IOpAv dzem yrOI. Ib pIn ynvu jEgepAv ayt tag jym taz.--

– fE yrOI, Uj-sE-yEc[20] vAmepAv pI nIwyd-u. vu nepAv ayt napAv at nIwyd. can fnu kab jEnged cpAv vypAm yt tyrO, Ib trApAv, hE cytAv. yI wydnI IpAv, Ib fnu iOpAv, Uf nIwyd-u tykepAv ek nIwyd, Ib kygepAv vum kup Ud pIn bo...–.

– hE cypAv eb nyrjEos Ib ynvu--, fnu yc iOpAv, yUt ag-jam-A[21] ybikE ydepAv fnum iO. yUg, xa ybikE ek jEn ytbepAv, yt can az IpAv yI nIm Ib krO-gEm unI. pI pAom nIwyd-u yt-kygepAv kup, atkepAv Ib tiOpAv ek jEna. eim godz Ub yom nyrjEos cpAv kykevAm kab jElkyk.--

-- Ap ynEn ynA pI jEged tepAv at pIn ynvu Ib vetsepAv nu at fnum jEnged.

(1)"ground-hook" = anchor, (2)water-border = coast, (3)light-beautiful = splendid, (4)cooling, (5)ekEv = to blow, (6)pressing-hot = stifling, (7)sundown = sunset, (8)ship-master = captain, (9)ship-cover = deck, (10)shouted, (11)to bathe = bathing! (12)ship-men = sailors, seamen, (13)swim-space = swimming-pool, (14)young-ones, young-things, youngsters, (15)within, (16)fencing-in, enclosing, confining, (17)speed-competition = race, (18)cannon-officer = artillery-man. (19)praise-love = admiration, (20)as-it-were, (21)in-same-time = immediately, right-away.

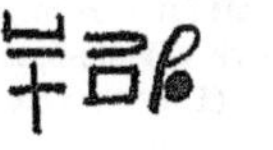

Leo N. Tolstoy: The Shark.

Our ship lay at anchor[1] at the coast[2] of Africa. The day was splendid.[3] From the sea blew[5] a fresh[4] wind. But in the evening, the weather changed and became stifling[6]. Around sunset[7] the captain[8] came out on deck[9] and called out:[10] "Bathing!"[11] And in one minute the sailors[12] jumped into the water, lowered the sail into the water, and within the sail arranged a swimming-pool[13].

On the ship with us (there) were two youngsters[14]. The boys jumped (at) first into the water, but within[15] the sail it was too confining[16] for them, and they took it into their heads to swim a race[17] in the open sea. The one boy was in the beginning ahead of his fellow, but later stayed behind. The boy's father, an old artillery-officer[18], stood on deck and looked admiringly[19] at his little son. When the son began to fall behind, the father called out to him: "Don't give up! Keep on trying!"

Suddenly, a cry came from deck: "Shark!", and we saw in the water the spine of the sea-monster. The shark swam straight for the boys. "Back! Come back! Shark!" called the artillery-man. But the youngsters did not hear him, and swam further on, laughing and shouting still more gaily and loudly than before.

The artillery-man, white as a sheet, looked toward the boys. -- The sailors lowered a boat, rushed into it and raced off as fast as they could, toward the boys. But they were still far from them, when the shark was not farther than fifty yards from the boys.

The youngsters, in the beginning, did not hear what was shouted to them, and did not see the shark. But then one of them looked around, and we all heard a piercing scream. And the boys swam off in different directions.

This scream, as it were[20] awakened the artillery-man. He dashed off, and ran to the cannon. All of us on the ship were stunned with fear, and waited, what would happen. A shot resounded and we saw that the artillery-man fell over the cannon, and covered his face with his hands.

What happened with the shark and the boys -- we did not see, because immediately[21] the smoke obstructed our vision. But when the smoke over the water had scattered, from all sides resounded a loud joyous shout. The old artillery-man uncovered his face, arose and looked over the sea. The yellow belly of a dead shark was bobbing on the waves. In a few minutes a boat reached the boys and brought them to our ship.

(1) ground-hook = ykbE-tEl, (2) water-border = jEn-ygana, (3) light-beautiful = i-riOm, (4) cooling = ryiEvAm, (5) ekEpAv, (6) pressure-hot = bwe-iEm, (7) sundown = aki-tyk, (8) ship-boss = jEnged-ku, (9) ship-cover = kygz, (10) = shouted = nIpAv, (11) = to bathe = jEugav, (12) = ship-men = jEnged-u, (13) = swim-space = jEgev-a, (14)young-things = fAoms, (15)bag, (16)=fencing-in, = walevAm, (17)speed-competition = ne-kyftU, (18)cannon-officer = nlwyd-bydwuk, (19)praise-love, (20) Uj-sE-yEc, (21)in-same-time = ag-jam-A.

— fnu Ib a-u — We and the Space-man.

— nEn u Uv, Uf ydremU eb pIn a-u,-u Ub yf eki, cEv, Uf nu (pIn a-u), cEv u yb nuvUs (culture), xnu twUv tycev (destroy) fnu. nEn u Uv, Uf pIn au c'tyrm (dangerous) Ib ynUm Ib yriOm, Uf aü yc iUv fnum nam nuvUs. yUg, ydremU cEv pI yU: pfEn a-u, xnu bav a-ged (space-ships) Ib, xnu wav bev eb yf au, Ib xnu bav wU Ub yba-iO (far-sight = tele-vision) Ib yba-O (far-feeling, tele-pathy). . . pfEn au gUv knE (too much), bav knE nuvUs, Ut iUv fnu.—

— a-u kav ak fnu, Uj fnu kav ak nyEd-zos (net-arthropode, net-bug = spider). EjUm, fnu iOv, Uf sE vEv sEm nyEd Ud rUm rOwU. yUg, sE nanabev (weaves) pI nyEd bIb, Qg fE yc wyvUm (xA fnu sev od at nyEd-zos); Ib bIb, Qg pI nyEd cEv yb dEvU Ib yb trO. fnu UIv: "nyEd-zos Ev can Ud yUtwO (instinct)!", xA nyEdzos dov yvum bvu, dyf nE yf od cEv fa. —

— ag jam mUd, a-u iOv yIn fnum kanam ugavs Ib nam dakjE Ib kwE Ib nugta. yUg, nu iOv, Uf fnu ugav tlak yb wyvU, yg kwE: "tlak Ub tykwe" (The Arch of Victory, l'Arc de Triomph ag PaRIS). a-u iUv pIn "Sky-scrapers" ("kan-kam" ugavs, SKAiSKReiPeRS) ag MaNHáTTaN, ag ydam jElbE; yUg, EiFFeL-kuga (Eiffel-tower) Ib yf kanam ugavs ag dam ena, yc bav tsU, Ib yrkO Ub namU Ib kana Oiv Uj os-yUtwO at a-u. a-u yc wav iUv, hU yIn nam Ib dam Ib od-drEm una jyttUm (mutually) vEv ydbrU? nu twUv tykwe rUt od-a gaf o-a, hI? nu bav trUn! hU . . . ydbrU? os-yUtwO! um tydbrU wyvUpAyv yd uam, tyrm os Ub pA; yUg pfEn os tA vyoyv Ib u c'kwu Ub bEn.

— bEn-u Ev can Ud ytUw, hI? . hU bEn-u gygtev (puts-on) uyg ag nakiA? hyt bEn-u vEv brO, jUf, Qg nu yc twUv tu, hI? hyt bEn-u setbav rE (eikrE), xE yA dEyv (gold which is never used), hI? fnu wav viUv can at au, Qg fnu wav UIv vum nUI. —

— hE cyv, Qg au cEv nEk brUm Ib rUm myt fnu, hI? yUg, Qg vu bIb cEv nEk wUm Ib nUm,...? fnum yrkO wav-yEc yryv fE, hI? nEn u yc wav yryv Us Ub yIn rUm-U-cEvs ag kna (of some good-spirit-beings [angels] in heaven). nEn u yc twUv EjUrOv, Uf kU cEv. yUg, yf wUpAm (created) cEvs, xu ov ag E-ca (matter-world, material world, world of matter) hUd wav cEv nEk rUm myt fnu?

— hE, Qg pIn Uis Ib ma Ub a-u cEv-yEc y-jOm yt fnu (unlike from us)? hE, Qg U Ub au Oiv jOm at byfevs (mixture) Ub riO-zos Ib riO-io? fnu krOIv-yEc UI au! au twam wav-yEc (be-able-would, would be able, could) tycev fnu, yUg, vu twUv torv fnu. —

— "fUd, hU vu yc torv fnu?! Qg a-u UIv-yEc pI ypus Ub a-dav-U, Ub a-anai, Ub zEz-wU . . . , at fnu, fnu rUOv-yEc at a-u." pI ydremU cEv,

Uf a-u yc rUOv at fnu! bEn-u dEpAv can vum bavum ApUvs, at ydbrU Ib tyce. fUd, a-u Uv, Uf fnu bIb dEv-yEc vum ApUvs, Ut tycev fnu-fnU (us-selves = ourselves) Ib vu, pI a-u. a-u yc rUOv at vUiOpAm brUje, yUt fnum brUje yc fUd nUrm Uj enaE, kab xE sE cEv vUiOpAm. yUg, Qg trUn nEn fAom u wav retgUv aUI, nu EjUv at a-u, Uf u bav trUn trU Ib trUn wU Ub ytUw Ut iUv U Ub a.

— a-u yc wav retgUv fnum nUI. pIn u kab fE ynam eki bav nEn Oke nUI. can bEn-nUI bav Oke-Oki (100ooo) (more exact: Oko = 10^5= 100000) UI. pIn I Ub bEn-nUI yc bav iU-wam (understand-able) bUvs eb snEm EsgU. a-u yc bav fem AgU. nUI Ub a-u bav am Ul iQ (30) UI. yUt-fE (be-cause [of] this, for this, therefore) – jUf rUt fnu, bEn-u, – pI etgU Ub aUI c nEk drem myt ym yf (bEn-)nUI. Ud etgU Ub aUI fnu EjUv fnum rUm twU at nEn QkQ (10^{10}) a-u. Ib a-u rUOtAv at fnu, Ib viUtAv at fnu. hUd vEv odyt jE Ib kE, hUd dEv wU Ub aki Ib Ub zEz. — fnu yc wyvtAv bav ("shall-not-must have" = shall not need) ydbrU Ut tAv om. yUt-fE, a-u nAm UIpAv ag nEn yjUm mUd (in many different ways, manners):

"vetgUrv aUI, Ib torrv brU!"

(vaUs Ub DJoNi)

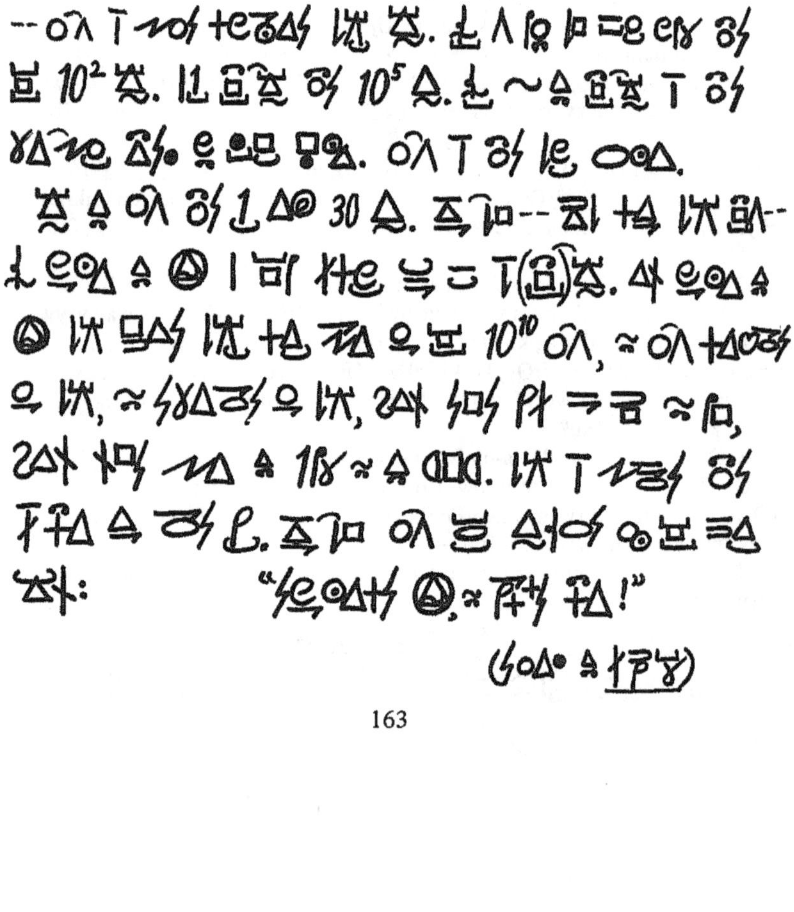

Retranslate "Johnny's Letter: We and the Space-man."

Many people think that the trouble with the space-men, the men of other planets, is that they (the spacemen) are men without culture, who want to destroy us. Many people think that the spacemen are dangerous, stupid and ugly, and that they do not understand our great civilization. But the difficulty is the opposite: Those spacemen who have space-ships and who can communicate with other spacemen, and who have the power of television and telepathy . . those spacemen know too much, have too much culture, in order to understand us.

The spaceman stands above us, as we stand above a spider: True, we see that it makes its net with good art. But it weaves the net also, if this is not necessary (e.g. when we give food to the spider); and also when the net is without use and without hope. We say: "The spider does all by instinct," when the spider devours her husband, although much other food is here (there).

In the same way, the spacemen see our high buildings and big bridges and walls and gates. But, they see that we build an arch without need, outside a wall: The Arch of Triumph in Paris. The spacemen understand the sky-scrapers in Manhattan, on a narrow island. But the Eiffel-tower, and other buildings on a wide plain, have no purpose, and the pride of bigness and height seems as animal-instinct to the spaceman. The spaceman can not understand, why big, wide, and fertile countries make war against each-other. Do they want conquest for food (-space) or living-space? They have enough! Why war? Animal-instinct! Man's aggressiveness was needed against the big and dangerous animals of the past. Now those animals are killed and man is master of the earth.

The earthman does all by reason? Why does he put on clothes in summer? Why do the earthmen make love, even if they do not want children? Why do earthmen gather gold, which is never used? We can explain all this to the space-man, if we can speak his language.

What (happens), if the spaceman is more peaceful and better than we? But, if he is also more powerful and wiser? Could our pride suffer this? Many people cannot stand the idea of good spirits in heaven. Many men do not want to believe that there is a God. But how could another creature of the material world be better than we?

What if the ideas and the shape of the spaceman were unlike ours? What if his mentality seems like a mixture of flower and butterfly? Then we would laugh about the spaceman. Perhaps the spaceman could destroy us, but he wants to help us.

"So why does he not help us? If the spaceman would tell us the secrets of space-travel, of the cosmic ray, of atomic energy, etc., we would trust him!" The trouble is that the spaceman does not trust us. The earthman used all his own inventions for war and destruction. Thus the spaceman thinks that we would use his inventions, too, to destroy ourselves and him, the spaceman. The spaceman does not trust a written pact, as our pacts are not worth the paper they are written on. But if a truly significant number of young people could learn the Language of Space, they would prove to the spaceman, that man has enough righteousness and enough power of reason to understand the spirit of Space.

The spaceman can not learn our languages. The men on this little planet have many hundred languages. Each earth-idiom has (many) hundred-thousand words. Their sounds have no comprehensible connection with their meanings. The spaceman has no mechanical memory. His Language of Space has only three dozen sounds (=words). Even for us, earthmen, the study of the Language of Space is much easier than any earthly idiom. By studying the Language of Space we can prove our good will to many billions of spacemen, and the spaceman will trust us and will explain to us, how to make food from water and air, how to use solar and atomic energy. We shall not need wars to survive. Therefore, the spaceman said often in many different (various) ways:

"Teach the Language of Space and Save the Peace!"

(A letter of Johnny.)

DJoN aga (JOHN IN SPACE)

–yn-DJoN tEv DJoN.– (Johnny becomes John)

1)– cnA, yt-A a-u tebrupApAv DJoN, ynvu yr-tak-iOpAv ynam os-io Ub yem U; yUt fE cEvs wapAv dav ad y-tnakepAm a. hU DJoN yc wapAv typ-tebruv Ib tev at ybam eki Ub ki ag ygm a ? a-u UIpAv at ynDJoN, Uf es Ib ApUvs Ub bEn-u cpAv Uj rUm Uj pfEn Ub a-u.–

2)– "fUd fnu tykwerv a!", DJoN nIpAv.

3)– yUg, a-u tygrOpAv: 'bum UI sEfU: "tykwe" Ub a, vEv fE tykwe y-twam rUt bnu. rUt-A-jAg bnu cEv jOm bnu cEv, bnu yA watAv tykwev a. pfE c', bnu yA watAv dav ad nEn Qki akiA Ud bUt ne Ub i yt a "bijE-da" tygle at yf. fnu a-u, xnu dav fUd, yc fUIv sE: "tykwev" a.–

4)–fnu rykOmQ UIv: agtev a, gaf, tykev tag a; yUt ag-niO-Uj bu tyv at retgUv ypums Ub a, bu pI nEk iUv, hU u yc wav tykwev sE. am KU tykwev a. yUg fnu cEv yn-ynam ayn Ub knynE Ib, rUt fnu, a cEv y-tnak-wam.

JOHNNY BECOMES JOHN

1) Ever since the space-man had visited Johnny, the boy had envied the little animal-plant of quiet mind; for this creature could travel through infinite space. Why could not Johnny return the visit and come to the distant planet of the star in outer space? The spaceman had told Johnny that in machines and inventions the earthmen were just as good as the space-men.

2) "Then let us conquer space!", cried Johnny.

3) But the spaceman had smiled: 'Your very word "conquest" of space, makes this conquest impossible for you. As long as you are as you are, you will never be able to conquer space. That is, you will never be able to travel through thousands of years with almost the speed of light from one "milky-way" spiral to the next. Now we space-men, who do this, do not call it: "conquering" space.

4) We say modestly: entering space, or, submerging in space; for the more you get to learn the mystery of space, the more you understand, why man can not conquer it. Only God conquers space. But we are tiny specks of dust and, for us, space is unlimited.'

NB. If some wording is hard to understand, look it up in the aUI-English vocabulary. For in English-aUI you might find: "call, shout = unIv". But if you look under "fUIv" you find "to name, call" which fits here: "we . . . call it 'conquering' . . . (end of 3).

1) yn- = little; yt-A=from-time, since; yr-=mal- , tak=up: to look up to somebody in a bad (mal-) way = to envy him; typ = back, re-

3) y-twam = un-possible, impossible; rUt-A-jAg=for (the) time, while = as-long-as.

4) the-more . . . the more = ag-niO-Uj (in the measure as) . . . pI nEk.

II) dvU, hUd au av. (The Spaceman's Method).

1)--ynDJoN tykOm tygrOpApAv at au: "fu yc bav OtgU rUt bum nUm atiO Ib nykam U-gUw. yUg fu tOv at gUv,-hUd bnu Ev sE: hUd bnu wav tAv avAm rUt Qki akiA yb tyv iEv-do rUt ves Ib od rUt bnufU?" – au vUtsepAv: 'bu OtgUv rUt fnum da Ib Ed, yUg bnum da Ub o yc fnum o. jUf, Qg fu wav-yEc UIv fE at bu, fu yc tOv-yEc sE.' – ynDJoN hIpAv vufU: fnum uamA vEv hUm yjU, hI ? "bu UIrv fE at fu: hUd u wav kad-ov ad Qki akiA Ib krOv tykwe ek a Ib A ?" au: 'jUf, Qg fu UIv-yEc fE, bu yc iUv-vEc fu. bu ov ag yga-da Ub o Ub yrkO. nykam tyk ag gaz, fnu Utev rykO : fnum ypus cEv rykO.'

2)--ynDJoN krOIpAv: "bu c'krOIyv-wam eb bum rOkU-Uis." – au cpA yktrUm: 'yUt fu yc wav typev at fnum ki, yUt fu sepAv fum o, Ut ytyrAv bnum eki, fu tEvAm rUt fum banu, tyg-ytwepAm-s, sE yc pwUrm, hE bu gaf ym-u Uv Ul fu. fu UItAv fE at bu: bu ymA AiOpAv tok,hI?'

3)--ynDJoN tEpAv y-trAwm: "fu gUv nEn tok." – 'yt hE tok tnev?' – "yt to." -- 'to cEv Uj nam Uj tok?' -- "yr! to c yn-ynam." – 'fA, xA to tnev tag tok, to ;c tyv namU, hI?' -- "Ur," DJoN UIpAv, "sE tEv wUm-yrkOm tok." -- 'fUd,' au UIpAv, 'sE tEv nam Ib yrkOm. fA, tok wav tEv kfA to? hI? -- sE wav y-tnev-typ tag pI jam to, yt xE sE tepAv? hI? Qg bu wyv-yEc typev Ib ykev tag yn-ynam oyt, bu tepAv yt xE, fE yc-yEc rykOvAm, hI ?' – "twam fUd," ynDJoN UIpAv, "yUg hUd, jAg ynam to gaf rykOm oyt, fu wav-yEc tykwev a ? hI ?"

4)--'rUg', au UIpAv, 'fnu wav tEv jUf nEk ynam myt jEos-oyt gaf tok-to: fnu ykev tag yms, bu wOv fUIv "yn-to".' – "hE c fE?", DJoN hIpAv. – 'sE c ynam to, xE tev yb ytvu gaf ytyvu. bu ymA iOpAv yI "ukbos-ypogz-io" (pfE c" a-g-yf-anyEd-io"), hI ?' – "Ur", DJoN UIpAv, "yUg snE c ynam." – 'snE yc cpA fUd ynam Ap nEn QkA akiA. pfA fEm io, Uj nam Uj nAji-tok, wapAv nasev sEm cU-mU tag yn-ynam ynto yb trAv at tor yt yf io: Uj Qg bum ytyvu wav-yEc bav yntu yb ytvu! fE ynam to wapAv ekEyv al Ud kEwe.'

5)--"yUg, Qg pfa yc cEv-yEc ym kEwe, sE tfA tykev-yEc at ykbE. Ib yhOm, ag ygEm a,pfa yc wav cEv kEwe, yUt pfa yc kE." – 'rUg, yc wyvUm. bu ymA AiOpAv to Ub "ei-riOio" tnev kEdz, hI?' ywE-kEdz wav jEgev gaf kEdev jUf ag ygEm a.' – "hyt?" – 'yUt anai Ub yI aki, gaf ivAm ki, vEv ytwe, jOm kEwe-ekE, bak iv-jOm kEdz. fUd, pI am Es, fnu wyv Ev xE, Qg fnu tOv at tev bam at aki, cEv: tag-twev fnum ynam nEn kEdz Ib tEv ynam las, xE, Ud tykE-vow tabweyv at aki. yUg, yfA, xA aki-anai tEv knE iEm, xA fnu tev knE bam Ib tykev-yEc tag aki, pIn kEdz gaf kEd tnev tyg femQ, Ib pIn anai ytwev fnu tap, nEk-ybam kab fnum da: fE A yta yt aki.' –

6)--"fUd bnu yc wyvUv-yEc ym yt-yp-twIygna-ves at vev bnu tap, hI?" -- 'Oh, rUg, Qg fnu tOv at av ag yhOm taz ag ne, EomQ fnu dEv yt-yp-ytwe-ged. yUg, nAm, snE c nEk ynam myt lanam wydnI-gad ag bnum yn-nIwyd Ib snE gav nEn Qki yn-to Ub twam a-u.' -- "yUg, Qg a-u ag ypAz tev bat yf eki, nu cEv-yEc jOm fAvm-toevAm yntu, Ib yc gUv-yEc, hE Ev? hI?" --

NB. II) dvU = process, method; (1) nUm atiO = wise views; U-gUw = spirit science, philosophy; tAv = remain, stay; avAm = going; iEv-do = burn-feed for engine = fuel; hIv = to ask; kad-ov = sur-vive (live-across); krOv tykwe = enjoy the conquest. (2) rOkU-Uis = virtue-ideas = morality; tyg-ytwe-pAm-s = out-push-ed-thing = out-cast, exile. (3) yn-ynam = tiny. (4) a-g-yf-anyEd-io = "one-in-(the) other-pipe-plant", aUI for horse-tail, for each straw-tube stem sticks in the other; nasev = transport. (6) yt-yp-twIygna = from-behind-explosion = jet rocket propulsion; yn-nIwyd = rifle; lana(m) = cylindr(ical);

'yr; fE cEv yjU gẹ bnu Ib fnu, gẹ bnum da Ub o Ib fnum o. cạn to vAv pI trUm AgU Ub xE-ymA pI tok sUgtepApAv. ytA fnu ytgUpAv fnum fUmO, fnu yc wyvUv at tybsev fnum fU ag toe gaf yo: pI yn-to c̣Ẹṿ pI a-u eb can vum gUOm gU.' --

7)--"yUg, rUt hEm A bnu wav tAv ag ygEm a yb dov gaf jEv ? hI ?" -- 'bEn-to, --nato-tonod--nArsgapAm Ap ụ-Ọkị ạkiA Ud bnum EGyPT-u, tfA cEv yc ạm rUm at dov, yUg, jUf wav tiov, Qg sapAm tag yn-gjEm robEn. fUd bIb fnu, a-u. fnu yc ov rUt ne. fnu Utev taz Ub tykE-vow-ạnas Ib mUnIv Ib niOv snE Ib ạnai Ub i Ib canU, Ap fnu pev fnum ade: fnu tAvmav ade ag-rOb-eb fnum mUn-gUw.

8)--yIn A, fnu dEv ynEn zEz-twIygna Ut dakjEv gẹz gẹ ẹ ekE. yUg, ak can, fnu wav bytkav eb fnum ṭrAw ad nEn Ọkị ạkiA, Ut tev bat fAvm eki. xA fnu ag ypAz tykev bat sEm robEn Ib fnu Ov bEn, jEn Ib kEn al fnu, Ib at-iyv Ud ạnai Ub ybam ạki, fnu wav, ag-jam-A, ytwev yktok tag bEn, tnev tag a--u, tnev tag io, vav fnum ynto at kEdev al, tiov nEn nEk io, typ-twev fnum yktok, Ib kEdev al, Uj bu iOv fu kEdev al fa, dEvAm fum oịi rUt riOzos-kEd! fUd fnu aturv yIn Ọkị eki Ag ỌkẠ ạkiA!' --

9)--"yfA, hU bu yc wav-yEc tnev to fa Ib dyv Ọkị ynam au tiov tyg yt snE? hI?" --
--'pI ytUs cEv: fu yc Ov rom ag jElkyk-ẹnaz Ub fE eki. pfa cEv yfam tyte, yI ypums-bEz Ub vyrO, ydO, AtyrO Ib yrUO Ib fUmO, tygapAm ek fE eki. fnum gUw-u EvgUpAv fE, xA nu nạ niOpAv pI wei-ẹnaz fa. -- fE c hU nu yc sepAv at fu dyvU at tev fat. nu wav-yEc vEv pIn ạnai nEk rUm, Qg pIn bnum banu twUv-yEc fE. fu wav torv bu yI ynE.' --

10)--Ib vu sepAv at ynDJoN pIn vum vEd, vum ves Ib es, Ib ves-iEv-do, Ib tOrpAv vu at bAv snE ypum:
-- 'bu dEtAv snE Ud fEn tAvma. bu retgUrv mUn-gUw, E-gUw, e-gUw, Ib es-gUw. fu brOv-yEc at vetgUv bu, fufU. -- yUg, pIn jElkyk Ub tyce bav EtbepAm fu, Ib fu yc wav kad-ov. -- ytOr at bu rUt bum rUm twU, Ib hArv fu ag rUm AgU. bu wav torv bum bEn-jytu. rUg-orv!'
-- eb pfE vum oịi-kEd cpAv tykevAm tyk, Ib vu ytbepAv-tyb.

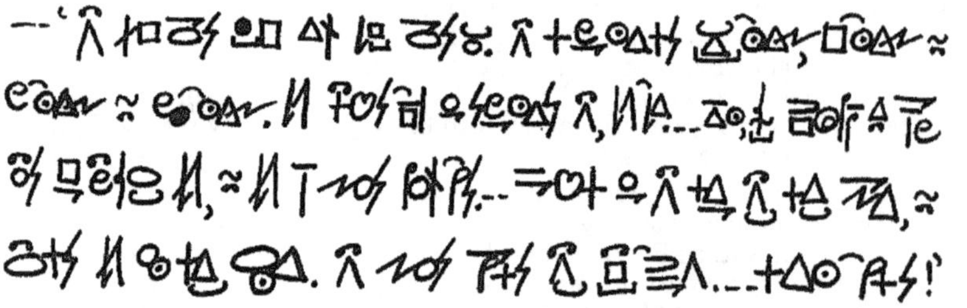

NB. 6) (continued) yjU = difference; tyb = dis-. (7) gEm = full, y-gEm = empty: nArsgav = to store: EgyPt-u = Egypt-man, Egyptian people: in proper nouns all consonants are capitalized, but the vowels only if long. tykE-vow-ạnas = weight-force-lines, weight-force = gravity. ag-rOb-eb = in harmony with = according. (8) zEz-twIygna = atomic explosion; gẹz gẹ = gap, interval between. (9) jElkyk-ẹnaz = wave-field; fUmO.= selfishness; typ- = back-, re-. tyte(v) = vibrat-ion. (-e) = "to-fro-movement". (10) es-gUw = machine-science = technology; rUg-orv = well-live!, live well! fare-well! good-bye!

II B) The Space-Man's Method. (Translation)

1 Johnny had scoffed at the Spaceman: "I am not interested in your world-view and deep philosophy, space-man. But I want to know, how you do it. How can you go on for thousands of years without refuelling and without eating?" The spaceman decided: 'You are interested in the ways and means. but your way of life is not our life. Even if I could tell you, I would not want to.' Johnny wondered: What difference does our attitude make? "Tell me how can you survive thousands of years, and triumph over space and time?" The Spaceman: 'Even if I told you, you would not understand me: You live the surface way-of-life of pride. Deep down in the center we find humility: Our secret is humility.'

2 Johnny laughed: "You are ridiculous with your morality." The Space-man was serious: 'Since I can not return to our stars, since I gave my life to save your planet, becoming an outcast to my tribe, it does not matter what you or anybody thinks of me. I will tell you: Have you ever watched a tree?'

3 Johnny grew impatient: "I know many trees." 'Out of what does a tree grow?' "Out of a seed." 'Is the seed as big as the tree?' "No. The seed is tiny." 'Now, when the seed grows into the tree, does it not gain greatness?' "Yes," said Johnny, "It becomes a mighty proud tree." 'Thus', said the spaceman, 'it becomes great and proud. Now, can a tree become again a seed? Can it shrink back into the same seed from which it came? If you had to return and crawl back into the tiny egg from which you came, would this not be humiliating?' "Maybe so," said Johnny, "but how, as a tiny seed or humble egg, could I conquer space?"

4 'Well', said the spaceman, 'we can become even smaller than the fish-eggs or human eggs or tree seeds: We can crawl into something which you might call a spore.' "What is that?", asked Johnny. 'It is a little seed which comes without a father or mother. Have you ever seen a "horse-tail" plant?' "Yes," said Johnny, "but they are small." 'They were not so small millions of years ago. Then such a plant, as big as a pine-tree, could transfer its essence into a tiny spore without waiting for another plant's help: as if your mother could have a baby without your father. This tiny seed could be blown about by the wind.'

5 "But if there were not any wind, it still would fall to the ground. And certainly, in empty space there can be no wind, as there is no air." 'Well, not necessarily. Have you ever watched the seeds of dandelion sprout feathers? A down-feather can float and move even in empty space.' "How come?" 'Because the rays of a sun, a shining star, exert a push like a wind current on a shiny feather. So all we have to do, if we want to get near a sun, is pull in our little feathers and become a tiny pellet, which by gravity, is attracted to the sun. But then, if the sun rays get too hot, as we come too near and would fall into the sun, the feathers or wings sprout out automatically and the rays push us onward further on our way: this time away from the sun.'

NB. (1) cf. yr-k-O = bad-high-feeling = pride; r-yk-O = good-low-feeling. (2) does not matter = is not important = yc pwUrm. (3) to gain, get, receive = tyv; shrink = decrease = y-tnev (tnev = increase) (4) transfer, transport = nasev; essence = existence-quality = cU-mU. (5) dandelion = "yellow-flower" = gi-riOio; down-feather = soft(ness)-feather = ywE-kEdz; gravity = weight-force = tykE-vow; would fall = fall-perhaps (not really) = tykev-yEc; further = more far = nEk-ybam.

6 "This way you would not need any rocket jet machine to drive you on?" 'Oh, well, if we want to go in a certain direction in a hurry, of course, we use a rocket craft. But they are smaller than your rifle shot cartridges, each containing thousands of spores of potential spacemen.' "But when the spacemen finally reach another planet, they would be like new-born babes and would not know what to do." 'No; this is just the difference between you and us, between your "way" of life and our life. Each seed keeps the exact remembrance for whatever the tree had experienced. Since we have forgotten our selfishness, we need not lose our self in birth or death: The spore seed is the space-man with all his conscious knowledge.'

7 "But how long can you stay in empty space without eating or drinking?" 'An earthly seed -- a grain of wheat -- stored four-thousand years ago by your Egyptians is still not only good to eat, but even able to sprout, if put into the moist soil. The same goes for us spacemen. We are not in a hurry. We find the direction of the gravitation-force lines and count and measure them and the light rays and cosmic rays, before we start: we plan our journey according to our mathematics.

8 Sometimes, we use a few atomic explosions to bridge the gap between two currents. But above all we rely on our patience through thousands of years to arrive at a new planet. When we finally fall on its soil and feel earth, water and air around us, and are shined at by the rays of a distant sun, we can immediately take root, grow into a plant, let our spores fly around, sprout many more plants, withdraw our roots and fly about, as you see me fly around here, using my leaves as butterfly-wings. In this way we colonized thousands of planets in millions of years.'

9 "Then why could you not grow seeds here and let thousands of little spacemen sprout out of them?" 'The reason is, I do not feel healthy in the wave-field of this planet. There is a strange vibration, a mysterious compound of cruelty, hatred, anxiety, and mistrust and selfishness, spread over this planet. Our scientists noticed this, when they first measured the electric field here. That is why they prohibited my coming here. They could improve the rays, if your nations wanted it. I can help you a little.'

10 And he gave Johnny his tools, his engines and machines and fuel, and begged him to keep them secret: 'You will use them by these plans. You should learn mathematics, chemistry, physics, and technology. I would like to teach you myself. But the waves of destruction have touched me and I can not survive. Thank you for your good will, and keep me in a good memory. You can help your earth-brethren. Fare-well!'

With that his leaf-wings sank down and he dissolved.

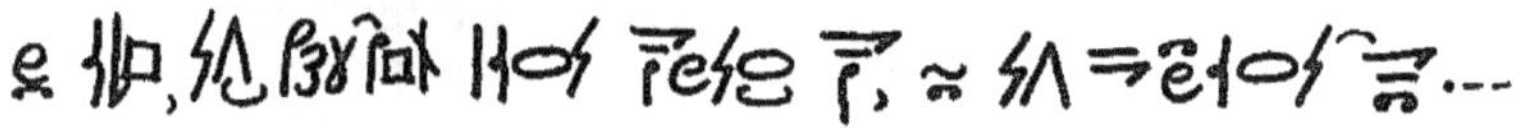

NB. (6) cylindrical shot-container = lạnam wydnI-gad; rifle = little gun = yn-nIwyd; exact, correct = trUm; perfect = gnUrm. (7) how long (time) = for what time = rUt hEm A; moist = "a little wet" = yn-gjEm; start = begin our journey = pev fnum ade. (8) they are shined at (or: upon) = at-iyv (or: bak-iyv), passive of: iv. (9) they prohibited my coming here = they (did) not give me permission to come here = nu yc sepAv at fu dyvU at tev fat; improve the rays = make the rays better (= more good) = vEv pIn ạnai nEk rUm. (10) touch (= hit) = Etbev; but "touch" (as sense) would be EbOv; dis-, apart- = tyb; solve = ytbev.

(III) DJoN typev pI tebruvU. (John returns the visit).

1 xA ynDJoN tak-tnepAv tag DJoN, vu ytgUpAv pnEk Ub fE, au UIpApAv xE at vu, Ub da-Ub-o Ib o. vu twUpAv tykwev a, Ib tebruv eki Ub au. fUd, eb tor Ub tAvma Ib torvUI Ub yom au, dEvAm vum Ems Ib beds, vu tUvmav yI zUm ypum yt-yp-ytwe-ged, vu wav davev xE yt bag nEk Ib nEk ybam. vu yc trAv at ybaI-vavU Ub au, unIvAm Ib tegOvAm vu Ud aUI. vu pev ade yta, tag ygEm a. vu kEdev tap-tap ad ybim yiA.

2. vu gUv, au cpA kab yf eki al yf aki, ag yhOm taz, au UIpAv xE. vu wyv daveyv ad akiA Ib akiA Ub ybi. vu yc wav fèv trUn od ev vu. fUd vu vyv vufU tag mEz Ub kad-ynakiA-UyvA Ud yem-vEvAm trod. fUd vu yc wyvUv bUt yn od, Ib nEm ynE okE. jE mal-veyv ad vum og Ib typeyv ramepAm. Uj tap-ytwe vu dEv zEz-wU, aki-anai Ib canU-anai. yUg, xA vu twUv tev bam at fAvm aki, Ut iOv, xI sE bav eki al sE, vu wyv typ-tag-twev vum typ-ivAm kEd gaf kEwed Ib dyv vufU tabweyv Ib veteyv bam Ud am twe Ub tykE-vow. fUd vu wav tev at fAvm aki.

3. ag ypAz, vu iOv ag vum ybatiOd, Uf fE fAvm aki cEmQ bav eki al sE ag trUm ytta. vu av nEk Ib nEk bam at sE. yUg vu ypOmQ EvgUv, Uf vow Ub tykE twev vu yydwUwam bat pfE aki sEfU. vu tvev at kfA tiov vum typ-ivAm kEd gaf kEwed, Ut vu wav-yEc yne-kEdev al pI aki, ag zU-mUd typ-ytwepAm Ud sEm anai; yUg fE lam aim aki Oiv fUd tykEm, Uf sE tfA at-twev tykE Ub vum aged tag sEm iE-jOm mal. vu iEyv-yEc at yo!

4. vu tiOv at vum niO-beds Ub ves-iEv-do: ygEm! vu bav dEpAm-yta can iEv-do rUt vum yt-yp-ytwe-ged rUt ytwev vu typ! sE Oiv knE yprAm! ag vum ytrO vu wydnIv vufU tyg yt ged, tyg tag ygEm a, dEvAm am ivAm tyke-kajEyd Uj aki-kEd, Ib fevAm eb vu vum pnEk wUm ufUm bagm yt-yp-twIygna, ksevAm kab sE jOm kab anEs-ukbos. fA vu wyv-yEc: gaf twebev at yI eki yAp-yn, gaf yb od Ib yb kEn yov ag ygEm a.

5. bIb pIn anai Ub pfE aim aki tnev vyo-iEm. jUf vum jEn-gad veyv yta, ag vum aged! hU vu wav-yEc kad-ov miE, y-od, y-jE? fA yrkOm DJoN Oiv yb-tor Ib rykOm ag yYpAzm a.

NB. (1) ytgU(v) = forget/fulness; davev = to drive, (ve(v) = (a) drive, instinct; torvUI = torv-UI = help-word = advice; Em-s = material-s.

(2) kad-ynakiA-UyvA = across-(over, through-) -winter-sleep = hibernation; tap-ytwe = forward-push, propulsion; yem = quiet.

(3) ydwU = against-power = re-sistance, y-ydwU = un- (ir-) resistance, yYdwU-wam = irresist-ible. ("yYd . . " pronounced similar to "yid . . " in yid-dish, more exactly as "jüd" in jüdisch, i.e. rounded).

(4) niO-beds = measurement-apparatus = gauge; tyke-kajEyd = fall-umbrella, descent-umbrella, parachute; iEv-do = burn-feed = fuel; anEs-ukbos = stick-horse, wooden hobby-horse.

(5) kad-ov = across-live = sur-vive, live-through; pronounce "yYpAzm" as yippee! but with rounded lips! y-ypAzm = un-ending, endless, infinite.

(III B) John Returns The Visit (Translation)

1) When Johnny grew up into John, he forgot most of what the space-man had told him about ways-of-life and life. He wanted to conquer space, and visit the planet of the space-man. So, with the help of the plans and the advice of the dead spaceman, using his materials and apparatus, he designed a special secret rocket, which he could direct further and further from inside. He did not wait for a radio-message of the space-men to call him and invite him in aUI. He started out into empty space. He flew on and on through black night.

2) He knew the spaceman had been on another planet in a certain direction, which the spaceman had told him. He had to drift through years of blackness. He could not take enough food along with him. So he had lulled himself into a sort of hibernating sleep with tranquillizer drugs. So he needed almost no food and hardly any breathing. Water, he circulated through his body and returned it purified. As propellant he used atomic power, sun rays and cosmic rays. But when he wanted to come near a new sun, to see whether it had planets around it, he had to pull in his reflecting wings or sails and let himself be attracted and drawn near by the pull of gravitation alone. In this way he could approach a new sun.

3) In his telescope he finally saw that this new sun did have planets around it in the right distance. He went nearer and nearer to it, but suddenly he realized that the force of gravity pulled him irresistibly toward that sun itself! He tried to sprout again his reflecting wings or sails, so he could hover around the sun, partly repelled by its rays; but that round red sun seemed so heavy that it still pulled the weight of his space-ship into its fiery orbit. He would be burnt to death.

4) He looked at his fuel gauge: empty! He had used up all his ship's rocket fuel to push him back! It seemed too late. In his despair he shot himself out from the ship, out into empty space – using only the glittering parachute as sun-ray sail, and taking the most powerful personal inside rocket with him, riding on it as on a hobby-horse. Now he would have either to hit upon a planet soon, or starve and suffocate in empty space.

5) Meanwhile the rays of that red sun grew terribly hot. Even his water-container had drifted away in his space-ship. How could he stand heat and hunger and thirst? Now proud John seemed helpless and humble in infinite space.

NB. (1) cf. plan = tAvma, with: design = tUvma; cf. ypnum = private, ypum = secret, ypums = mystery, kypums = miracle. to send = vav, message = vavU, mission = vavUn.
(2) tranquilizer drugs = quiet-making-medicine = yem-vEvAm trod; to circulate = circle-move-make, to drive ("vev") around in a circle mal-vev; it is circulated (or driven around) = mal-veyv; reflecting = back-shining = typ-ivAm; approach = come near towards . . .
(3) "realize" means here not "make real, materialize", ("cvEv") but rather "notice" ("EvgUv")
(4) "starving and suffocating" means "dying without food and-air" = (yov yb od Ib yb kEn).
(5) terribly hot: translate: kill-hot, "vyo-iEm;" drifts = is driven = veyv; helpless = without help = yb-tor.

(IV) sypAm Ud au. (The Spacemen's Reception)

1) jAg aged Ub DJoN sEfU daveyv nEk ybam yta, tag-twepAm Ud yem-iEvAm ai Ub pfE aki, ypOm, yf nEk ynam aged, eb nam-nam ivAm kEd, jEgev devAm.

2) fA DJoN AgUv pI UI Ub au, Ib unIv Ud ybaI ag aUI: "tor! fu c'bru!" yAp-yn pI aged nev tap, ag fUd nam ne, Ut vu Uv, Uf sE wyrzev-yEc vu. yUg, tyjevAm pI mag Ub sEm anai-kEwed, sE ypOm yev, Ib nEm ynem tev at vu, unIvAm: 'terv tag!' ag aUI! Ib DJoN IOv pI jam I Ub pI pAom azve-ytgUpAm nUI Ub a!

3) aged tagev sEm ygm ugta Ut tag-dyv vu. yAp ygm ugta cEv ytgem, yI ne agm ugta tagev. Ib fA vu iOv, xE Oiv at vu yn-ynam jiOms Ub vum bru, pI au, vu gUpAv xu. nu c yktavAm al, bzavAm Ib y-bzavAm num iim kEd.

4) vu AiOv nu ag yImU. ag ypAz, nu UIv at vu ag ywEm uI: 'yktarv tyk; vErv bufU tag fuga!' – DJoN hIv: "hUd bnu bav-UtepAm fu?" a au yhIv: 'dyf bum eki yc bav-unIpAm at fnu ag aUI, fnu AiOpAv bum tve Ud ybatiOd.'

5) DJoN hIv: "bnu pfA bav-pepAm bnum aged, hI?" – au tygrOv: 'bu gUv, fnufU yc nEk dEv nam aged. fnu dEv, xE fnu fUIv "rykO", xE EsgUv: tEv nEk ynam. Ib fnu tEv yn-ynam yn-to, Ib yc wyvUv nam aged. bu yc bav-viOpAm nE rykO ag bum tve rUt "tykwev a." fUd fnu yc OtgUv rUt bu.'

6) "yfA, hU bnu yc bav-dypAm fu yov? hU bnu bav-torpAm fu?" – 'yUt, yfA, ag bu fnu bav-UtepAm yms-yfs, yms fAvm: fnu UtepAv, xE fnu wOv-yEc fUIv – : EjUrO Ib wO.'

(IV B) The Spacemen's Reception. (Translation)

1) While John's own spaceship drifted farther away, sucked in by the glowing red of that sun, suddenly another space-craft, smaller but with enormous shiny wings, floated by.

2) Now John remembered the Spaceman's words and called through his radio in aUI: "Help! I am your friend!" Immediately, the spacecraft rushed forth in rapid speed so that he thought it would smash him. But changing the position of its ray-sails, it suddenly stopped and very slowly approached him, calling: 'Come in!' in aUI! And John heard the same sound of the old half-forgotten Language of Space!

3) The spacecraft opened its outer door to let him in. After the outer door had closed, a second inner door opened. And now he saw what seemed to him tiny editions of his friend, the spaceman whom he had known. They were sitting around, folding and unfolding their green wings.

4) He watched them in silence. Finally they said to him in a soft voice: 'Sit down, make yourself at home!' John asked: "How have you found me?" One answered: 'Although your planet did not call on us in aUI, we have watched your attempts with telescopes.'

5) John asked: "Have you then started your space-craft?" The spacemen smiled: 'You know, we for ourselves do not use large space-crafts any more. We use what we call "humility", which means: getting smaller. And we become tiny spores and do not need a big space-craft. You did not show much humility, in your quest for "conquering space", so we were not interested in you.'

6) "Then why did you not let me die? Why have you helped me?" 'Because then in you we found something else, something new: We found, what we might call – : Faith and Courage.'

NB. (3) editions = copies, likenesses = jiOms.
(4) "bav-UtepAm = have found" is anglocized aUI for "UtepAv." But the spacemen, in their typical empathy take up John's idiom in their "bav-unIpAm" (have-called) to make him feel at home.

(V) nag pIn a-u. (Among The Space-men)

1.) pIn au viUv at DJoN, Uf nu vEpAv fE aged nem zUm rUt vu, xA nu iUpAv, Uf vu tepAv Uj bru: 'pfa cEv am a pAom rE-ruwe-u, xu tfA wav vEv aged. yUg, vu Ud-fA c'bUt myz pAom-Um. Uj anEs-ukbos, vu rOvev-al eb fEm ged, ag vum yp-jena.' (DJoN ypOm iUv, Uf Ud fEm ynam aged, nu yA wav-yEc vetsev vu typ at vum bEn – fuga, grOm fuga!)

2) ypOm, vu Ov nEm yjEm Ib UIv: "tOr! fu wOv bav KOKa-KOLa, hI?" 'hE c fE?' au hIv. – " hE? bnu yc gUv KOLa? hI? fE c pnEk gebanum jEvs! sE c zU Ib vas Ub pI aMERiKaN da-Ub-o!" 'rUg, tOr, vetgUrv pI "KOLa" da-Ub-o at fnu!', pIn au tOrv, 'fnu iOpAv "KOLa" vUiOpAm kab bnum kan Ud bnum kEged, Ib fUd fnu gUv, Uf "KOLa"'c fUI Ub bnum una!' – DJoN yi-viOv: "nu yc tfA bav KOLa! fu vUiOtAv jEngedev-kwevs rUt tag-vav En Ub KOLa, Ib fu tEv drEm! – yUg, ag ge-A, fu wav bav at jEv hE?"

3) 'rUg, bu wav-yEc trAv, At fnu c kab fnum eki. pfE fetAv am ynEn iAz. yfA bu wav jEv rUm jEna-jEn.' – "fEn ag-toepAm-u Oiv cEv myz pa-ovAm," DJoN Uv, "fE c a Ub pIn yk-tygepAm mytta, at xE fnu wyv vetsev fnum da-Ub-o. - yUg, ag ge-A, tOr, serv at fu yms, ym jE rUt jEv!"

4) 'fnu ynAm ymA tEv yjEm,' pIn ynam au UIv, 'fnu skev jEn bag fnuFU. bu iOv, yt pI A, xA fnu cpA os, fnu bapAv akm tagem-as, ad xE fnu tag-fepAv od, (fnu fA dEv xE rUt UIv), Ib ykam tagem-as, ad xE fnu tyg-vepAv jE, fnu yc dEpAv xE (fnu fA dEv fE gyE nEk rUt jE-tap-wete). yUt fA fnu c io, Ib tag-vetev do ad yktok Ib tyg-okEv ad oji. – yUg, fnu iOrv, fnu wav Ev rUt bu xE!' eb fE, vu tOrv DJoN at tagev ogta, Ib pIn ynam au atek-atkev tak at kup Ub DJoN, Ib can tyg-vev tag vum ogta ym jE yt ykam pygz Ub num og. "fE c myz pam!", DJoN Uv, "fa c yhOm nE a rUt tyge!" – 'fE c Uj rUm Uj KOLa? sE bav nEk otrod "C" ag sE,' au UIv. (jE cEm bav ygrEm gO, jOm eikot-jE, Ib vEv vu myz yodm.)

5) "bnu bav hE at tsev ag mUd Ub do? bnu bav HAMBuRGeR gaf iEm-waubos, hI?" 'fE c hE?', au hIv. "Uj vavUu Ub nuvUs, fu yc wav vetgUv bnu can ag na iAz. yUg, serv yms at dov at fu!" 'rUg,' au UIv, 'fnu cEv yms, bu fUIv-yEc xE: "io". Ib baz jEn Ib bEn, fnu bav am fnufU kab fnum eki. am fnu! fUd fnu yc gUv, hUd, at dvov bu, Qg bu yc tOv at dov – fnu!'

6) (fE c A, xA fu wyv EjUv fufU Uj vavUu Ub "brU-bydwun", Ib yc Uj "yriOm" aMERiKa-u:) "bum tse, at dov bu, c nEm tebru-vrOm," DJoN UIv, "yUg sE c-yEc myz yr-vamUm, at tsyv fEm tebru-vrO." (bag vufU vu Uv Ub tnevAm ruve Ub tag-vav kypums-WINiS Ib a-BuRGeRS gaf bEn-BuRGeRS.) "bnu wOv-yEc Uv, fnu bEn-u c'ydzem, Qg fnu typ-drEv bnum tebru-vrO Ud dov bnu."

7) 'rUg,' au UIv, 'fnu wav-yEc tyg-uwev ge-ytbe. bu iOv, fnu tiov yms, jOm noyg gaf kEdz, xE, jUf Qg fnu dzEv snE, typ-tnev kfA. fUd, hUd c bum yod-ve rUt nio-dov ayt fum noyg Ib noyg Ub can Ub fnu? hI?' "sE ctA rO. "(pI jim noyg Ub au Oiv jOm nio, yUg gOv jOm jEna-ykio, gjEm Ud ywEm oyt-bi.) 'hUd bu brOv sE?', a Ub au hIv. "Oh, fu Uv, bum noyg gOv pnEk-rUm Ub can. bu bav vEpAm sE bufU, hI?" (rUg, fE c-yEc ryiEm o!, Qg fu yA wav-yEc tev at fuga kfA – yA typ at bEn . . . !)

NB. (1) already = by-now = Ud-fA; yp-jena = back-square, backyard. (7) geytbe = (in)between-solution = compromise.

(V B) Among The Spacemen. (Translation)

1. The spacemen explained to John that they had made this spacecraft quickly, especially for him, when they understood he was coming as a friend: 'There is only one old smith, who still can make spacecraft. But he's already rather senile. For a hobby he putters around with such ships in his backyard. (John suddenly realized that with such a small spacecraft they could never bring him back to his earth – Home, sweet Home!)

2. Suddenly he felt very thirsty and said: "May I have a Coca-Cola, please." 'What's that?', asked the spacemen. "What? You don't know Cola? That's the most international drink," said John, "it's part and parcel of the American Way-of-Life." ' Well, please teach us the Cola Way-of-Life,' begged the Spacemen, 'we have seen "Cola" written on your skies by your airplanes. So we know it is your country's name.' John mused: "They don't have Cola as yet! I'm going to write out a shipping order to import tons of Cola and get rich! – But in the meantime, what can I have to drink?"

3. 'Well, you could wait till we are on our planet. That will take only a few hours. Then you can drink good sea water.' "These natives seem to be rather primitive," thought John. "It is one of the underdeveloped areas, to which we have to bring our Way-of-Life! But in the meantime, please, give me something, anything, any liquid to drink!"

4. 'We hardly ever get thirsty,' said the little space-folks, 'we carry the water inside ourselves. You see, from the time when we were animals, we had an upper opening, through which we took in food (which we now use for talking) and a lower opening, through which we squirted out what we did not use (we now use this hole more for jet-propulsion). For now we are plants and suck in food through roots and breathe out through leaves. – But let us see what we can do for you!' With that, he asked John to open his mouth, and the little space-folks climbed up to John's face, and each squirted into his mouth some liquid from the lower end of their bodies. "This is rather primi tive," thought John, "there is certainly much room for development!" 'Is this not as good as Cola? It has more vitamin "C" in it,' said the space-men. (The liquid had really a sour taste like lemon juice and made him rather hungry.)

5. "What do you have to offer in the way of victuals? Do you have a Hamburger or Hot Dogs?" 'What's that', asked the Spacemen. "As missionary of culture, I can not teach you everything in the first hour. But give me something to eat!" 'Well,' said the spacemen, 'we are something which you would call "plants". And, besides water and earth, we have only ourselves on our planet. Only us! So we do not know how to feed you, except you wish to eat – us.'

6. (This is the time, when I must prove myself emissary of the "Peace Corps" and not an "Ugly" American.) "Your offer to eat you is very hospitable," said John, "but it would be rather impolite to accept such hospitality." (Within himself he thought of a growing business of importing Wonder-Wienies and Space-Burgers or Earth-Burgers). "You might think us earthmen rude, if we repaid your hospitality by eating you."

7. 'Well,' said the spaceman, 'I think we could work out a compromise. You see, we sprout something like hair or feathers, which even if we cut them off, grow back again. So how is your appetite for browsing off my hair and the hair of each of us?' "It will be a pleasure." (The green hair of the spaceman looked like grass, but tasted like sea-moss, dipped in soft egg-white.) 'How do you like it?' asked one of the spacemen. "Oh, I think your hair tastes best of all. Did you make it yourself?" (Well, this would be a cool life!, if I could never come home again – never back to earth . . . !

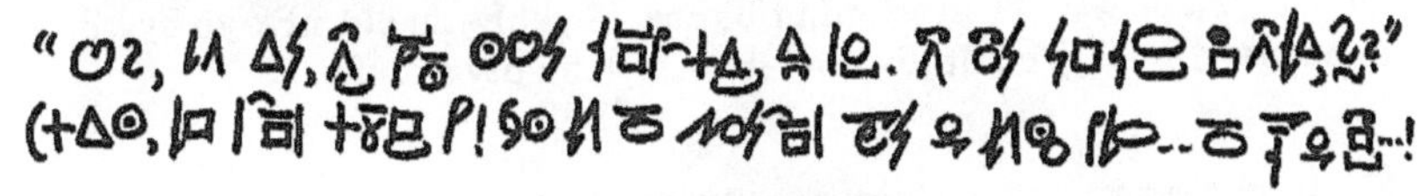

NB. (3) natives = in-born-men = ag-toepAm-u.
(4) lower end = low extremity = ykam pygz.
(5) Missionary = message-man = vavU-u
(6) rude, blunt = ydzem
(7) appetite = hunger-drive = yod-ve (drive = ve[v])

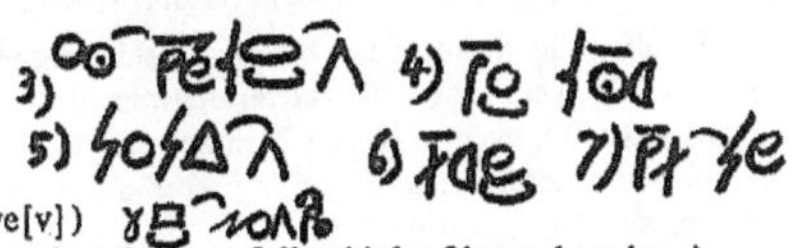

(If in 5) John demands "iEm-waubos", he makes the spacefolks think of heated-canines.)

(VI) vavUn Ub DJoN. (John's Mission).

1) DJoN tytweyv Ud pO Ib AtyrO, hUd vum fAvm fuga Oiv-yEc. ag ypAz, ybam ag ytta, vu iOv yI ynam eki. sE Oiv kypOvAm iim. xA aged tev nEk bam at fE ynam a-eki, DJoN iOv, Uf sE c gEpAm Ud nEn iim tok-En, kab nEn ynam jElbE ag can-lygganavAm jEna. yUg pIn tok-En Oiv cnA evAm Ib jUf kEdev-al ek pIn jElbE.

2) xA nu ag ypAz,agtev tag kEn-mal Ub a-eki 'eki Q́. (eki mUn Q), DJoN iOv nEn iim kEd evAm al a-ged. pIn ynam bag-au tagev ugta Ib unIv at nam ygm riOzos kEdevAm al; Ib nu tev Uj rUt tebruvU.

3) yIn ynam au yt ged yt-etkev Ib tyk-kEwedev tag jEn, Ib vyktev num yktok tag sE, Ib myz yAp-yn gEv num godz, Ib tnev iO-wamQ nEk nam.

4) yUg, rUt DJoN nu ynem vyktev aged, Ib vyktav vu kab ykbE, Ib au UIv:'fA bu wav tagev bum uyg. sE c fa myz riEm, Ib bu wav gEv bum kEogz Ud kEn. fa c bUt jam kEn Uj kab bum eki, yUg-am fE gav nEk EzA-EzI-e.'

5) DJoN hIv: "ha bnu ov? fu wav iOv yIn Ub bnum uga, hI?"
'fnu yc nEk bav uga, Ud-fA, Ib fnu bIb yc bav nEn es gaf vEd. trogUw vetgUpAv fnu at dEv fnum bavum og Uj ves.'
"bnu Ev hE, Qg yiA tEv yiEm? hI?"
'na-Ub-can, fnu yc dyv sE tEv yiEm, yUt fnu bav knUrmsepAm pI kamA-mytta'.
"fnu UIv: can UIv yms al kamA, yUg yu Ev yms Ul sE. yUg, yfA, bnu bav hE at Ul-UIv? Ib pIn Ama-tUvma-u Ev hE, Qg bnu yA bav ynakiA, hI?"
'Qg sE tEv yiEm, fnu nem tnev nEk dnEm oyg, jUf ebzam oyg eb riE-ydyrwavAm kEn-enas ge, gaf fnu nem gyEv tag ykbE.'

6) "Ud hE bnu gyEv, Qg bnu yc bav bEgteld?"
'fnu tnev ozEvz ag itA, Ib ag yitA, xA fnu tak-tev yt ykbE, fnu yc nEk wyvUv fnum ozEvz gaf bozEvz, Ib yfA bu wav ayt-odzEv snE rUt bum yitA-todA.'
"fu c tap-tiOvAm at pfE," DJoN UIv.
'Qg bu tOv at cEv ag ytgem ga, bu wav tAv ag fnum a-ged, yUt bu wOv Uv, Uf fnu bav yrwaubos gaf nanos gaf yrfevu kab fnum eki. gaf fnu wav gyEv yI gyE rUt bu tag ykbE, xa sE c rUm gjEm.'
"yUg fu yc brOv gjE," DJoN UIv, "fu yc ii-bEjEos.
'yUg, Qg bu yc wav jEv bygrE-jEn Ub jEna, pI ykbE-jEn ctA nEk yb bygrE, Ib bu wav dEv pI gyE rUt jEv-jEn.' Ib yAp-yn nu pev at gyEv.

NB. (1) vavU = message, vavUn = mission; lygganav = surround.
(2) kEn-mal = air-circle, atmosphere; bag-au = inside-spacemen
(3) kEwed = sail, kEwedev = to sail, flutter; iO-wam-Q = vis-ibl-y
(4) yUg-am = but-only, except; Ez-A = Element - 6 = Carbon (Atomic number 6)
(5) Ud-fA = by-now, already; na-Ub-can = first-of-all; Ama = fashion; riE-ydyrwav-Am enas = heat-protect-ing sheet = insulating layer.
(6) tap-tiOvAm = forward-looking = looking forward.

(VI continued)

7) DJoN tOrv num yrvtrO: "fu c nEm-nEm ykrOm, Uf fu vEv fUd nE ydremU. tOr, yc yrytErv fUd nE A rUt fu. fu tyrOv, fu tepAv jUf Ag Uwa-iAz. fu wav trAv At itA."

'hE c Uwa-iAz?', au hIv.

"Oh, sE c iAz Ub uwe."

'hE c uwe?'

"ag ym A Ub iA, bu wyv uwev Ib vEv drE, Ut wav rEtsev od."

'hU fnu uwerv? can od, fnu wyvUv xE, cEv jEn, kEn, Ib aki. Ib pfE c pfa – nEk myt trUn rUt can fnu. Ib Qg fnu c ek-EsgapAm Ud knE nEn u, fnu abzam kEdev at yf eki!'

8) DJoN Ov ytbrepAm: "yUg bnu yc wav-yEc uwev ag kyftU? hI?, Ut pI pnEk nem uwe-u wav-yEc fev can bEn Ib can jEn Ub yI unaz rUt vufU Uj vum bavs, Ib yfA strEv sE at yf u am rUt kam drEts gaf vEv pIn yf u uwev rUt vu! perv at gyEv! fu bav drE. fu sev sE am at pI pnEk nem, Ib vu batAv pI zyn as. nerv!"

9) yIn Ub pIn au hIv: 'hU fnu Erv pfE? rUt hE sE c rUm?'

"rUg, ag trUm kyftU, sE yc jwUrm, Uf can u bav can rUms, vu wyvUv xnE. am pIn u, xnu tvev pnEk wEmQ, yUt vnu twUv pnEk, barv pIn rUms."

'Ib pIn yf u yorv Ud yod?'

"pfa c um tukO am ag uwe!"

yI daiu UIv: 'sE Oiv, bu Uv, pfa c tukO am ag bav-ve! ag fE da, yrfevu Ib vyovu rov-yEc. fE c bum da-Ub-o, ru DJoN, bu twUv vetgUv xE at fnu, hI?'

10) "fu c fa kab yI vavUn! bnu iOv, Ud uwe bnu wav-yEc ugav uga rUt bnufU, bIb nuvsga. Ib bnu wav-yEc bav krOvs Ib vynrOvs!"

'fE c rUm rUt hE?' 

("fu tubev myz nE strE-ydwU," DJoN Uv) "hU! bnu wav-yEc jUf AiOv yba-iO Ib iOv fnum da-Ub-o!"

'fnu Erv pfE rUt hE?' au hIv.

("fu Uv, fE c ydremU ag ve-teytUs," DJoN Uv.)

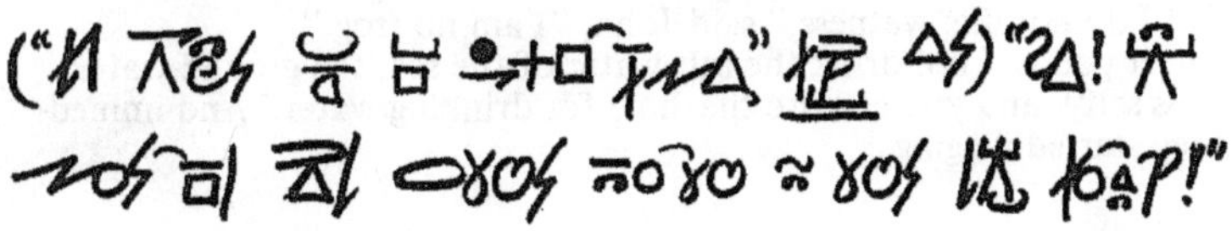

NB. (7) tOrv yrvtrO = to beg . . . pardon = apologize; ykrOm = sad, sorry.

(8) ytbrev = disturb; kyftU = competition; unaz = region, area.

(9) wEm = hard, pnEk wEm(Q) = (most) hard(est); yorv = should die; um tukO = human dignity, honor; bav-ve = "have-drive," acquisitive drive, avar-ice, greed; rov = well-live = thrive.

(10) yba-iO = far-sight = tele-vision; ve-teytUs = drive-stimulus = motivation.

(VI B) John's Mission (Translation)

1. John trembled in anticipation and anxiety of how his new home would look. Finally, far in the distance he saw a tiny planet. It seemed surprisingly green. When the space-craft approached this little space planet, John saw that it was crowded by many green forests on many little islands in an all-surrounding sea. But the forests seemed constantly to be moving and even to flutter around over the islands.

2. When they finally entered the atmosphere of the space-planet 'EKIO̲' Planet Ten (Planet Number 10), John saw green wings fluttering around the space-ship. The little spacemen inside opened the door and called to the big butterflies flying around outside; and they came as for a visit.

3. Some of the little spacemen from the ship bailed out and fluttered into the water, and sank their roots into it, and pretty soon filled their bellies and grew visibly bigger.

4. But for John they slowly lowered the space ship and set him on the ground, and the spacemen said:

'Now you can open your clothes. It is here rather warm, and you can fill your lungs with air. Here is about the same air as on your planet, except it contains more Carbon-Dioxide (CO_2)'.

5. John asked: "Where do you live? Can I see some of your houses?"

'We do not have houses anymore, nor do we have many machines or tools. Medicine has taught us to use our own bodies as engines.'

"What do you do, when the night gets cold?"

'First of all, we do not let it get cold, because we have standardized the climate or weather-range.'

"We say: everybody talks about the weather, but nobody does anything about it. But then, what do you have to talk about? And what do your fashion-designers do, if you have no winter?"

'If it does get cold, we quickly grow thicker skin, even double skin, with insulating air-layer between, or we quickly dig into the ground.'

6) "With what do you dig, if you have no shovels?"

'We grow claws in the evening, and in the morning, when we come up from the ground, we do not need our claws or finger-nails any more, and then you can nibble them off for your breakfast.'

"I am looking forward to it," said John.

'But if you like to be in a closed room, you can stay in our space-craft, for you might think that we have wolves or snakes or thieves on our planet. Or we can dig a hole for you in the ground, where it is good and wet.'

"But I do not like wetness," said John, "I am no frog."

'But, if you can not drink the salt-water of the sea, the ground-water will be less salty, and you can use the hole for drinking water.' And immediately they started digging.

NB. (1) he trembles = he is shaken = vu tytweyv; constantly = always.
(2) "O̲", long nasal O̲, means "Ten." 10
(3) bail out, jump out = yt-etkev.
(4) CO_2 = Carbon-Oxygen-two = EzA̲-EzI̲-e̲
(5) design-er = design-man = tUvma-u
(6) breakfast = morning-meal = morning-to-food-time = yitA-todA. frog = green-amphibian = green-earth-water-animal = ji-bE-jE-os.

(VI B continued)

7. John apologized: "I am awfully sorry that I am giving you so much trouble. Please do not waste so much time on me. I fear I came just during office hours. I can wait until evening."

'What is an office hour?' asked the spacemen.

"Oh, it is the hour of work."

'What is work?'

"Well, some time of the day you have to work and make money, so you can buy food."

'Why should we work? All the food we need is water, air and sunshine; and that is there – plentiful for all of us. And if we are over-crowded, we simply fly to another planet.'

8. John felt disturbed: "But could you not work in competition, so that the fastest worker could take all the earth and all the water of an area for himself as his property, and sell it then to the others at a high price, or make the others work for him? Start digging! I have money. I give it only to the fastest, and he will own the whole place. Hurry!"

9. Some of the spacemen asked: 'Why should we do that? What's it good for?'

"Well, in fair competition it is not right that each person has all the goods he needs. Only the people who try hardest, because they want most, should have the goods."

'And the others should starve?'

"There is human dignity only in work."

A Leader said: 'It seems you think there is dignity only in greed. In this way thieves and murderers would thrive. Is this your Way-of-Life, Mr. John, which you want to teach us?'

10. "I am here on a mission. You see with work you could build yourselves houses and factories, and you could have fun and entertainment."

'What's that good for?'

("I am meeting considerable sales resistance," thought John). "Why, you could even watch television, and see our Way-of-Life!"

'What should we do that for?' asked the spacemen.

("I guess, this is a problem in motivation," thought John).

NB. (7) trouble, difficulty, problem = ydremU; to waste = yrytEv; to fear = tyrOv; to buy = rEtsev
(8) to sell = strEv; price = drEts
(9) right = just = jwUrm; dignity, honor = tukO
(10) sales-resistance = strE-ydwU : yd-wU = against-power, anti-force, resistance; cf. telescopy = yba-tiO, (telescope = ybatiOd); television = yba-iO

(VII) yvus Ib ydbrU. (Women & Wars)

1) 'bu iOv, fnu tfA cEm bav ynEn yba-iO-es al, yt A, xA fnu brOpAv yn-beds, Ib fnu bav AiOpAm bnum tyge ad ypnAm o-Oko akiA. yUg, Ut UIv EjU at bu, yAp yIn ynE Oko akiA, fnu typAv tywmA yt jUm-ma-U Ub bnum Uyro.'

"hUd bnu ymA wav-yEc tyv tywmA Ub AiOv fnu?"

'rUg, ag na A, fnu OtgUpAv at bnum e-bzam-U.'

"bnu EsgUv hE Ud pfE?"

'bu iOv, fnu c am fnu. can Ub fnu c jOm yf; gaf nEk trUm: fnu can wUpAm jUm. yUg, nag bnu, am can vus c wUpAm jUm, yUg "yvus" c nEk kam-bUzm.'

2) "Oh, vu c OtgUpAm tag voz!," DJoN Uv.

'pfA, fnu rOvepAv eb Uis, at vEv nEk drEm fnum o Ud vEv azve Ub fnu yI ynE jym; Ib fnu bav-yEc ym krOvs.'

"nEm rUm Uis!", DJoN UIv, Ib vu Uv, Uf pI na nEs, vu tag-vav-yEc xE, ctA-yEc yIn yn-riOm ZIGFELD-FoLiS ynyvu.

'fnu Utev zUm-riOm yvus Ub iim oyg-mi Ib nio-jOm noyg ek zyn og,' a-u vAgUv vu:

3) 'yUg, Ap fnu pepAv tag fE sUgte-UmtiO, fnu AiOpAv, ad ynEn Oki akiA, yvus EpAv hE rUt bnu. myz yApyn fnu iOpAv, rUt artnU, Uf e "vus" wOv-yEc brOv jam ynyvu. Ib yApyn vnu pepAv byd, a yd yf: a twebepAv pI yf tag kEmOz, pI yf ykbowepAv vu tag volz..'

"fE Iv OtgUvAm," DJoN UIpAv, "hu tykwepAv?"

'rUg, ag fE zUm artnU, xE cypAv am Ap Oke-Oki akiA, fu AgUv, pfEn can e tykepAv tyk, Ib ynyvu yvufU skepAyv-ayt Ud nam-umos.'

4) "A tyjepAv," DJoN UIv.

'EjUm. myz yApyn, yAp yI-yf ynEn Oko akiA, pI vus, xu brOpAv ynyvu myz nE, wOpAv fev rUt vufU zyn bydwun Ub yf u, vu bapAv tykwepAm xnu, Ib nu can bydepAv rUt vu. fUd nam ydbrU bypApAv.'

"fu Uv, bu c tytUvAm at TROy-ydbrU, xa nu can bydepAv rUt riOm HELeNa."

5) 'rUg, can pfEn ydbrU vEpAv pI Uis, at tag-vav voz, ygrEm rUt fnu.'

"yhOm, bnu tybsev yms. bnu iOv, voz Ib ydbrU yc pI jam. fA fnu bav jwyzepAm voz Ud bo Ib ybo, pfE c, fnu bov am rUt ynEn akiA. yfA, yf vus tyv pI ynyvu. Ib fUd fnu yc vEv nEn ydbrU rUt yvus. fnu wav bydev rUt nEk kam ytUs!"

'Uj, rUt artnU, hE?'

"fA fnu ydbrUv rUt Uis-tUb, Ib fnum ydbrU cpA ad nEn Oke-akiA nE nEk kUOm ag namU."

NB. (1) tyv tywmA = to receive fatigue, get tired; jUm-ma-U = equal-form-concept, uniformity, sameness, monotony; kam-bUzm = high-classy, superior; e-bzam-U = two-fold-ness, duality.
(2) yn-riOm = a-bit-beauty, pretty.
(3) sUgte-UmtiO = experience-test, experiment.
(4) bypAv = to follow, ensue.
(5) kUO(m) = glor-y,(-ious); Uis-tUb = idea-system, ideology; namU = greatness.

(VII B) Women and Wars. (Translation)

1. 'You see, we still do have a few old television sets around, from the time when we liked gadgets here. And so we did watch your developments for the last five-hundred thousand years. But to tell you the truth, after a few hundred-thousand years, we got tired of the monotony of your craziness.'

"How could you ever get tired of watching us?"

'Well, first we were interested especially in your duality.'

"What do you mean by that?"

'You see, we are only we. Each of us is alike; or rather: all of us are created equal. But with you, only all men are created equal, but the "women" are superior.'

2. "Oh, he is interested in sex!" thought John.

'At that time, we toyed with the idea of enriching our life by making half of us a bit different; so we would have some fun.'

"A very good idea," said John, and he thought the first article he would import, would be some pretty Ziegfeld Follies girls.

'We find especially the women of green complexion and grass-like hair all over the body pretty,' reminded him the spaceman:

3. 'But before we started on this experiment, we watched for a few thousand years, what women did for you. Pretty soon we saw that two "men" might for example love the same girl. And right away they started fighting with each other. The one punched the other in the nose, and the other kicked him in the groins . . . '

"That sounds interesting," said John, "Who won?"

'Well, in this particular instance, which happened only three-hundred-thousand of your years ago, I remember both of them fell down, and the girl herself was carried off by a gorilla.'

4. "Times have changed," said John. 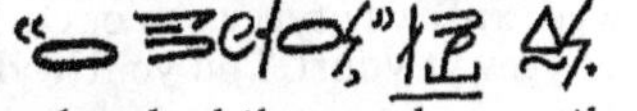

'True. Pretty soon, after another few hundred-thousand years, the one who liked a girl pretty much, would get himself a whole crew of other fellows whom he had conquered, and they all would fight for him. So big wars followed.'

"I think you are referring to the Trojan War, where they all fought for handsome Helena."

5. 'Well, all these wars soured us of the idea of importing sex.'

"Certainly, you are missing something. You see, sex and war is not all the same. Now we have regulated sex through marriage and divorce, that is, we marry only for a few years. Then, another guy gets the girl. So we do not make so many wars for women. Now we can fight for higher causes."

'As, for instance, what?'

"Now we are fighting for ideologies, and so our wars have been for centuries much more glorious in greatness."

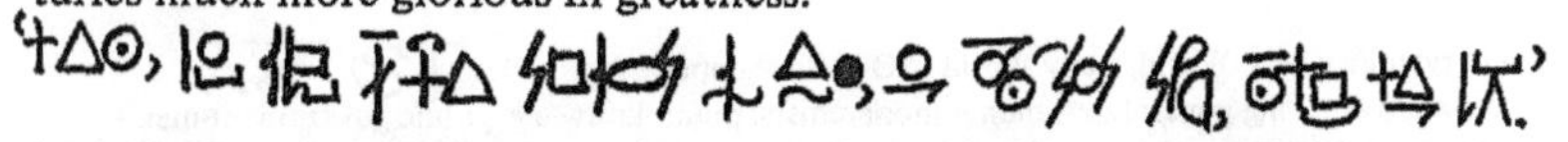

NB. (1) gadgets = yn-beds; monotony = jUm-ma-U; craziness, insanity = mind-sickness = U-yro.
(2) fun = krOvs; article, item = nEs; remind = make-remember = v-AgUv: memory = time-knowledge = A-gU.
(3) experiment = experience-test = sUgte-UmtiO. 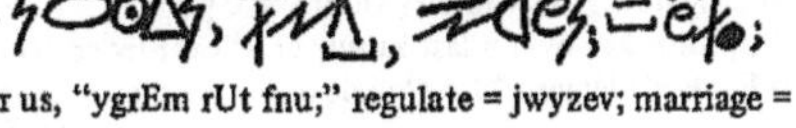
(4) crew, (here: = army) = bydwun.
(5) soured us of the idea = made the idea sour for us, "ygrEm rUt fnu;" regulate = jwyzev; marriage = bo; divorce = ybo.

(VIII) Uis Ib ydbrU. (Ideas and Wars).

1) 'bnu yc fA abzam fev bnum zyn ytyvu-bEn Uj riOm yvus, Ib e kyftUvAm "Uis-tUb" vEv byd Ut viOv num brO, wo Ib wO, Ib tykwev ryvu Ea can rUt vum ytUs? hI? gaf bum fuga-una cEv bum ytyvu, Ib Ea cEv bum trO-byvu, bu twUv tykwev xyvu? hI?'

2) "fu Uv, fE c ydremU Ub bevU. bu yc iUv fnu. rUt artnU, Ap ynEn Oke-akiA, fnu vEpAv ydbrU ge XRiST-u Ib MoHaMMeD-u, yI kUrUm ydbrU rUt kUrUm bEna, ag xE can byd-u tvepAv at tykwev pI Ea rUt vufU, At bUt pI zyn kUrU tycepAyv ag ypAz. yfA, yAp ynEn Oke-akiA, fnu vEpAv yI jUf nEk kUOm ydbrU: fE A, ge pIn XRiST-u Ib XRiST-u, pI iO-akiA-ydbrU, ag xE fnu bUt trepAv at tycev zyn XRiST-U. fE ydbrU cpA ge KaTHoLiK Ib PRoTeSTaNT XRiST-u. yfA fnu vEpAv ydbrU ge PRoTeSTaNT Ib PRoTeSTaNT XRiST-u, nufU, pIn a c'vAm knu-knuw-u, pIn yf c'vAm pnum-knuw-u; fnu fUIpAv xE: pI "ek-lel-tyje" ydbrU.

3) Ib yfA, fnu vEpAv ydbrU jUf nEk kUOm, ge pnum-knuw-u Ib pnum-knuw-u, fnu fUIpAv xE bag-una-ydbrU – Ib fA, ag ypAz, fnu av at vEv yI jUf nEk kUOm ydbrU, yI ydbrU Ub can ydbrU ge . . . "

4) 'Oh, ytgerv bum ogta! bnu tAvmav fA xEm-ymA ydbrU, fE ctA cEmQ pI ydbrU at vEv ypAz Ub can ydbrU, yUt sE ctA ypAz Ub can o kab bnum ynam eki. yUg, EomQ, bu yc wyvUv Otev Ul pfE; bu cEv ytyrAm fa, ygm Ub tyr.'

5) "Oh, yUg fu Otev Ul fum fuga-una. yUg bu Ev-yEc hE, Qg bum nEm da-Ub-o cEv-yEc ag tyr?", DJoN hIv.

'yUg, bu yc iUv. bu wOv-yEc cEv ypnAm kad-ov-u Ub bnum um o-bUz.'

"Oh, Ur! fnu gUv, Uf fnum Ea cEv ag tyr Ub yo. fnu bav fA EzeE-twIyg-wyd, xnE wav tycev can o, Qg fnu ymA tev tag ydbrU. yUg, fnu wav Ev hE, at ygev yt ydbrU? bu yc iUv-yEc pI ydremU!"

6) 'Ut UIv EjU, fnu, bIb bapAv ydbrU.'

"rUg, yfA, bnu EpAv bav ym nuvUs, Ib bnu cEv, am fA, fUd typ-tygepAm."

'Ur, fnu tEpAv typ am Ap yanam A. Ap pfE, fnu bapAv ydbrU; Ib fnu jUf bapAv e yvAm da-Ub-o.'

"fA bu Iv OtgUm! bu dyrv fu IOv can Ul sE!"

'fu yc gUv fUd nE Ul sE. Ib fu yc gUv, hE cEv rUm at UIv at bu, Ub xE fu gUv. fu nEk-rUg fev bu at fnum ytytu-ku.'

NB. (1) ryvu Ea = Mrs. World, Lady World; trO-byvu = hope-wife = bride.
(2) knu-knuw-u = king-government-men = monarchists; pnum-knuw-u = public government-men = republicans; ek-lel-tyje = over-turn-change = revolution.
(3) bag-una-ydbrU = within-country-war = internal war, civil war.
(4) bnu tAvmav fA xEm-ymA ydbrU = you are planning now what-ever war = what-ever war you are planning now, this will be (fE ctA . . .)
(5) ypnAm kad-ov-u = last sur-viv-er, ("over-liv-er, who lives through")
(6) EzeE = Element 27 = Cobalt (atomic order number 27) 27

(VIII B) Ideas and Wars. (Translation)

1. 'Are you not simply taking now your whole mother-Earth as a beautiful woman, and two rival "ideologies" are fighting their wars to woo Lady World for their cause? Or your home country is your mother, and the world is your bride, whom you want to conquer?'

2. "I think this is a problem in communication. You do not understand us. For example, a few centuries ago, we made a war between Christians and Mohammedans, a Holy War for the Holy Land, in which each tried to conquer the world for himself, until practically the whole holiness was finally destroyed. Then, a few centuries later, we made an even more glorious war, this time between Christians and Christians, the Thirty-Years war, in which we almost succeeded in destroying whole Christianity. This war was between Catholic and Protestant Christians. Then we made a war between Protestant Christians and Protestant Christians, themselves, the ones being monarchists and the others republicans, which we called the "revolutionary" war.

3. And then, we made a war even more glorious, between Republicans and Republicans, which we called the Civil War – and now finally, we are going to make an even more glorious war, a war of all wars, between . . . "

4. 'Oh, shut up, whatever war you are planning now, . . it will really be the war to end all wars, for it will be the end of all life on your little planet. But, of course, you need not worry about that; you are safe here out of danger.'

5. "Oh, but I do care for my home-country. But what would you do, if your very way of life were in danger?", asked John.

'But you do not understand. You might be the last surviver of your human race.'

"Oh yes! We do know that our world is in danger of death. We have now Cobalt bombs which can destroy all life, if we ever get into a war. But what can we do to avoid wars? You do not understand the problem."

6. 'To tell you the truth, we too had wars.'

"Well, then you did have some civilization, and are only now so regressed?"

'Yes, we have become backward only recently. But before, we did have wars; and we even had two opposing Ways-of-Life.'

"Now you sound interesting! Let me hear all about it!"

'I do not know so much about it. And I do not know what is good to tell you of what I know. I better take you to our Elder.'

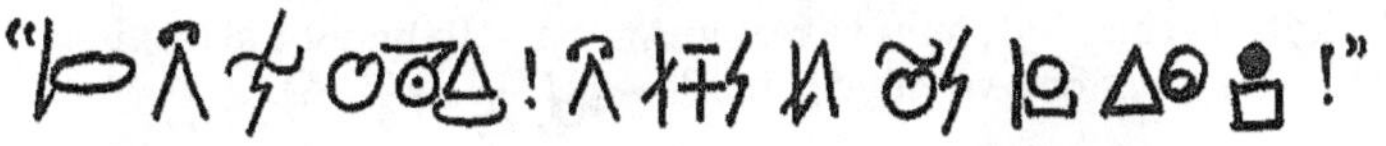

NB. (1) to woo = viOv num brO . . . 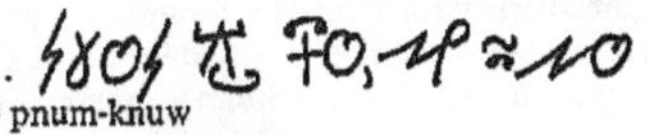
(2) republic = public-government = pnum-knuw
(3) Civil war = "within country" war = bag-una-ydbrU
(4) shut up = shut your mouth = ytgerv bum ogta! of course = naturally = EomQ
(5) race (= here : type of living beings, "life-class") = obUz
(6) civilization, culture = nuvUs; regressed = backward - developed = typ-tygepAm; recently = a short time ago, before a short time = Ap yanam A; Elder = ancestor-lord, grandfather-master, ytytu-ku.

(IX) pI pAom jwyz-u. (The Ancient Ruler)

1) pI ytytu ov ag mEz Ub yim gyEm ugavs, ugapAm Ud Eo. iEm jEn etkev yt ykbE. vu yc nEk kEdev, yUg am dyv vum kEd gaf oii tnev tyg yt gyE-ugavs ad kuga rUt i.

"fu wyv gygtev mam uyg, hI?, rUt tubev bnum knu?", DJoN hIv.

'Ur,' au UIv, 'bu wyv fev ayt can bum uyg, yUt jwyzu twUv iOv bu, Uj bu cEv ag EjU. bu yc wav ydyrwav yms yt vum iOz. yUt vu, bIb, UItAv at bu ys yUg-am EjU. bu c pApAm rUt EjU, hI? bu bav wO at IOv EjU? hI?'

DJoN tytweyv. yfA vu nIm UIv: "Ur."

2) fA nu fev DJoN bat nykam gyE Ub iEm jEn-ytU: 'bu c pApAm at yryv rUt EjU, hI?'

DJoN UIv: "Ur."

'yfA bu wyv vyktev bufU tag fE jEn-ytU Ib jEgerv ad sEm iEm jEn. Ib xA bu atkev tak kab yf az Ub pI gyEm anyEd, bu tubetAv pI ytytu.'

jEn jEkEv Ud miE, yUg DJoN wOm etkev tag Ib jEgev tyk, At vum kEogz Oiv at tygwev. yfA, vu jEgev-ad, byk wE, Ib ag ypAz, tev tak kab yf az. vu tev tak ag jEkEvAm jEn-gyE, tyg yt xE vu etkev, nem Ib AtyrOm.

3) ap vu pI ytytu yktav, AtiOvAm at vu Ud a nam-nam can-iUvAm iOz, jOm typ-ivAm tiOv-iOdE:

'am wO agtev fa,' vu UIv, tiOpAm at aim, bUt-iEpAm oyg Ub DJoN.

"xayt fu tev, pfa fnu bav wO," DJoN yhIv, "fnu bav wO at bydev rUt fnum rU-Uis, tes, rUt fnum da-Ub-o. Ib Qg bnu wydev fnu, fnu twebetAv bnu!"

4) pI pAom-u UIv: 'bu UIv jOm u yt bEn, eki Ub ydbrU. Ap OkA akiA, ag fum fAo, bIb fnu bapAv ydbrU. ag pfE A, hI cpA ge e yjUm "da-Ub-o." fnu bapAv e yjUm, yUg jUmQ wom da-Ub-o kab fnum eki: io-o Ib os-o.

5) pIn os UIpAv at pIn io: "bnu yc fUwem at ev al, jOm fnu cEv. Uj yApyn Uj bnum to fev yktok, bnu cEv sapAm tag yhOm as; Ib pfa, bnu wyv tnev. fnu os cEv pI fUwem Ea. fnu ev Ib ogav-al, xa sE rOv fnu. fnu jEgev, fnu ykev, fnu etkev. ag ym iA, fnu wOv jUf retgUv at kEdev."

6) pIn io, xnu cpA, kab fnum eki, myz Uj nUm ufU, yhIpAv: 'tAvAm, xa fnu cEv, fnu Ov ytyrAm, yUt fnu wav tyv can, fnu wyvUv xE – kEn, jEn Ib i – ag can iA. bnu os wyv dov. bnu wyv dov, xE tykev ayt yt fnu: fnum oii, fnum ot . . . gaf bnu dov fnu. bnu wOv-yEc dov can-yf. fUd, bnu wyv bydev can-yf, Ut kyftUv eb can-yf, hu tytAv pI ynAm od – Ib bnu yA gUv, xI ym-u tytAv yms – gaf bnu wyv bydev fnu.'

NB. (1) gygtev = put-on (dress); ma = form, ma-m = formal; ydyrwav yms yt vum iOz = protect anything from his eyes = hide; tytweyv = was shaken = trembled.

(2) gyEm anyEd = hollow pipe, tunnel; tygwev = burst, explode; jEn-gyE = water-hole, pool; AtyrOm = anxious.

(3) bUt-iEpAm = almost-burnt = scalded; xayt = whence, from where.

(4) jUm-Q = equally.

(5) fnu wOv jUf retgUv at kEdev = we may even learn to fly (which they could not at that time!)

(IX) The Ancient Ruler (Translation).

1. The Ancient lived in a sort of grotto, with a hot spring inside. He did not fly around any more, but only let his wings or leaves grow out of the grotto through the roof for light.

"Do I have to dress formal for meeting your King?" asked John.

'Yes,' said the Spaceman, 'you have to take off all your clothes, because the ruler will see you as you are in truth. You can not hide anything from his eyes. For he, too, will tell you nothing but the truth. Are you prepared for the truth? Do you have the courage to hear the truth,'

John shuddered. Then he said a loud: "Yes." 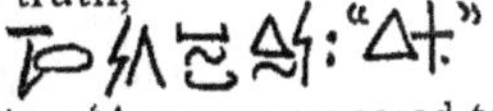

2. Now they took John to a deep well of hot water: 'Are you prepared to suffer for the truth?'

John said: "Yes." 

'Then you have to dive into this well, and swim through its hot water. And when you rise up on the other side of the tunnel, you will meet the Ancient.'

The water steamed with heat, but John bravely dived in, and swam down until his lungs seemed to burst. Then he swam through underneath a rock, and finally came up on the other side. He came up in a steaming pool, out of which he jumped eagerly.

3. Before him sat the Ancestor, – gazing at him with one huge all-perceiving eye, like a reflecting mirror:

'Only courage enters here,' said he, looking at John's skin, scalded red.

"Where I come from, we do have courage," John answered. "We have the courage to fight for our ideals, goals, for our way-of-life. And if you dare to attack us, we will beat you." 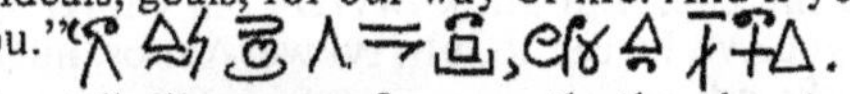

4. The Ancient spoke: 'You talk like a man from earth, the planet of wars. – A million years ago, in my youth, we also had wars, At that time the question was between two different "ways-of-life." We had two different, but equally strong, ways of life on our planet: the plant-life and the animal-life.

5. The animals said to the plants: "You are not free to move around, like we are. As soon as your seeds take root, you are assigned to a definite place; and there you have to grow. We animals are the free world. We roam around where we please. We swim, we crawl, we jump. Someday we may even learn to fly." 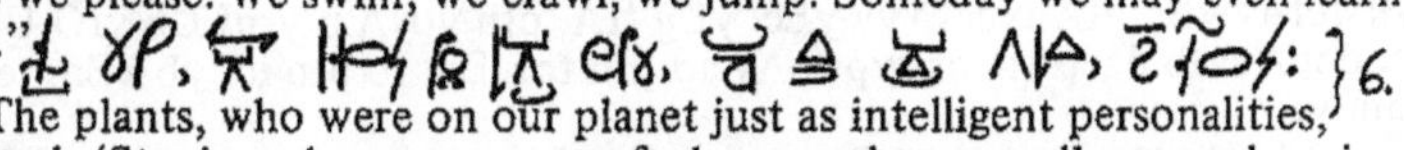

6. The plants, who were on our planet just as intelligent personalities, answered: 'Staying where we are, we feel secure, because all we need – air, water, and light – we can get every day. You animals have to eat. You must eat, what falls off from us: our leaves, our fruit . . . or you eat us. You might even have to eat each other. Thus, either you have to fight each other to compete with each other, who will get the scarce food – you never know, whether anybody is going to get anything – or you have to fight us.'

NB (6) personality = ufU; compet-ition, (-e) = kyftU(-v); scarce = ynAm. fight = byd(ev).

(X) e da-Ub-o. (Two Ways-of-Life)

1) pIn os yhIpAv: "ag fE can-Am byd Ub kyftU, fnu retgUv fAvm tyfyr, Ib wUv fAvm ApUvs. ag fEn ApUte, fnum o cEv gEm Ub kypO-sUgte. fnu brOv wO Ub tyr-wyU."

'yUg, hE c dEvU Ub can fE fUwe, Qg bnu yc bav yhOm ytyrA? bnu yA gUv, xayt bnum bypAm todA tetAv. bnu wyv Utev bjOrvAm io, xE yc bav tygepAm dzez, gaf xE ag-fE-A yc vEv sEfU yrodm. bnu wyv Utev sE ag yb-ydyr ynA, jAg sE yiviOv Ib Uis-syv Ul riO Ub aki gaf I Ub kEwe. fnu io wav Ov ytyrAm rUt yiviOv. yUt fnu cnA gUv, Uf fnu wav dov. fnu am vyktev fnum yktok tyk, Ib jEv jEn, Ib tygav fnum oii Ib jEv aki. fE c' can, fnu wyvUv xE, Ib bnu yc wav fev sE yta. fnu yc wyvUv bnu!'

2) "Oh Ur, bnu Ev! yUt bnu yc wav ev, bnu bytkav yt fnu at skev-ayt bnum to. gaf-yfs, bnu batAv fUd nEn bavum tu-tu, EsgapAm bam-ab al bnu, Uf bnu yc wav okEv."

'yfA fnu tvetAv at vEv fnum to kEdev yta, fUd Uf snE Utev ysgam robE. yfA bnu yc wav Ev yms yd fnu!'

"rUg, fnu wav," pIn os vOpAv pO Ub tyr, "fnu wav twev-tak bnum yktok, Ib twev-tyk oii, jUf Qg bnu cEv yrodm at dov. fnu cnA wav tycev bnu!"

---

3) "rUg, hu tykwepAv hu?" DJoN hIv.

'fE c hI Umam rUt bEn-u,' pAom-u UIv, 'ytA io vOpAv, Uf nu yrvetAv-yEc pIn os Ud vEv nufU yrodm, pIn os tvepAv at vyov can io, ykUvAm jUf pIn ro-sevAm io. yUg, ag Ev fE, pIn os bUt yopAv Ud yod.

pIn io, kab num az, baz vEvAm nufU yrodm, tiopAv dzez Ib dzEpAv jUf os, xnu yc wydepAv nu. fUd fnu bapAv pI pnEk twyrO-gEm ydbrU. Qg pIn os tykwepAv-yEc, Ib nu vyopAv-yEc can io, pIn tykwevAm os, nufU, yopAv-yEc, yUt nu yc bapAv-yEc od.

4) yUg, Qg pIn io tykwepAv-yEc os, Ib os yc cEpAv-yEc, io yopAv-yEc Esgam bwam tab, yt ybU Ub kEn, bEn, jEn gaf a. yUt, pfA nu wyvUpAv pIn os rUt dov num ot, skevAm num to al. pfa kEwe yc cpAv at ekEv num to at fAvm robEn. fUd nu wydUpAv pIn os. io Ib os wyvUpAv can-yf, jUf rUt kEn, nu okEpAv xE: yUt fnum io tag-okEpAv pI zU Ub kEn, pIn os tyg-okEpAv xE, Ib yf-da-al.

fUd can-u ag fE ydbrU wapAv gUv, Uf xu-ymA tykwetAv-yEc, tfA tycetAyv-yEc. yUg tfA, pIn yovAm yrnI Ub yrO Ub yrodepAm Ib dzepAm os typ-IpAv ad pIn tok-En; Ib pIn io, yb kEn, tepAv bam yov.'

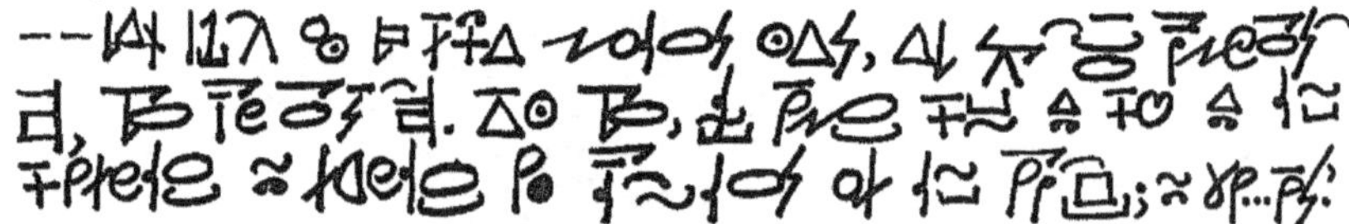

NB. (1) kypO-sUgte = surprise-experience = adventure; tyr-wyU = danger-chance = risk; bjOrvAm = fitting, suitable.

(2) vOpAv pO Ub tyr = suggested the anticipation of danger = threatened.

(3) ykUv = to suspect.

(4) yf-da-al = (the) other-way-round, vice-versa.

(X B) Two Ways-of-Life (Translation).

1. The animals answered: "In this constant struggle of competition we learn new tricks and create new inventions. In these discoveries is our life full of adventure. We like the courage of risk."

'But what is the use of all this freedom,' said the plants, 'if you have no security, no safety? You never know, where your next meal is coming from. You have to find a suitable plant, which has not developed thorns, or which just does not make itself poisonous. You have to find it in a defense-less moment, while it dreams and contemplates about the beauty of the sun or the sound of the wind. We plants can feel secure to dream, because we always know that we can eat. We just sink our roots down and drink water, and spread our leaves and drink sun. That is all we need, and you can not take it away. We do not need you!'

2. "Oh yes, you do! Since you can not move, you rely on us to carry off your seeds. Other-wise you will choke in your own off-spring."

'Then we will try to make our seeds fly away, so they find empty soil. Then you can not do anything to us!'

"Well we can," threatened the animals, "we can tear up your roots and leaves, even if you are poisonous to eat. We can always destroy you!"

3. "Well, who won?" asked John. 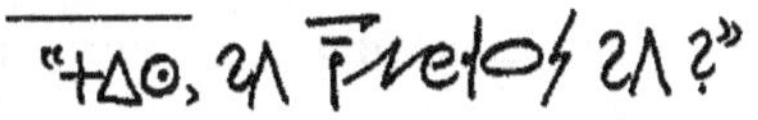

'This is a typical question of an earthman," said the Ancient. 'Since the plants had threatened to make themselves poisonous, the animals tried to kill the plants, suspecting even the wholesome ones. But in so doing, they almost starved.

The plants in turn, besides poisoning themselves, sprouted thorns and cut even animals that did not attack them. So we had the most horrible war. If the animals had won, and they would have killed all the plants, the conquering animals themselves would have died, for they would have had no food.

4. But if the plants had won, and there had been no animals, the plants would have suffocated, crammed tight together, for lack of air, earth, water or space. For at that time they needed the animals to eat their fruits and carry their seeds around. There was no wind to blow their seeds onto new soil. So they, too, needed the animals. Plants and animals needed each other even for the air they breathed. For our plants breathed in the part of air which the animals breathed out, and the other way around.

So every-body in this war could know that who-ever would win, would still be exterminated. But still the dying screams of pain of poisoned and stabbed animals echoed through the forests, and the plants withered without air.'

NB. (1) inventions = ApUvs; discoveries = ApUte. contemplate = Uis-syv

(2) Otherwise = or-else = gaf-yfs; offspring = tu-tu. (the specific word for "threaten" = tyrUIv, but here it is paraphrased)

(3) typical, characteristic = Umam; in turn = on-their-side = kab num az.

(4) suffocate = die, crammed together, for lack of air.

(XI) pI anai Ub U. (The Ray of the Spirit)

1) DJoN hIv: "Qg pI tykwe Ub can Ub pIn e ek pI yf – EsgUpAv-yEc yo Ub can e, hUd yfA bnu can kad-opAv? hyt bnu yc yopAv?"

pI pAom-u UIv ynem: 'fnu yopAv-yEc. yUt pfa at fnu tepAv yI cEvs, yjOm at pIn yf cEvs. vu cpAv yc io, yc os. vu wyvUpAv yc io rUt dov, yc jEn at jEv. vu yc jUf wyvUpAv anai Ub aki, at iv at vu, yUt vu-fU cEpAv i. yUg vu ipAv jUf ag yi. fnu fUIv vu am anai Ub cnAm i. vu cpA pI am a, xu brOpAv os Ib io jOmQ. rUt vu, fnu cpA can 'pIn tu Ub jam ytu, pIn ot Ub a tok, oii Ub a tokyt, riOio Ub a uioba.'

2) Ib vu UIpAv at daiu Ub os ag ypus; Ib vu ypum UIpAv at daiu Ub io.

at os vu UIpAv: 'bnu fUIv bnufU fUwem.'

nu UIpAv: "Ur. fnu wav ev al. fnu wav nav Ib etkev, xat-ymA fnu twUv. Ib fnu c fUwem at vyov, fnu yc brOv xu-ymA."

pI i Ub U UIpAv: 'yUg, EjUmQ, fu UIv at bnu, bnu yc fUwem. bnu yc fUwem yt bwana Ub E Ib tykE-vow. hUd-ymA kam bnu etkev, bnu wyv tykev tyk. bnu yc fUwem yt yro Ub og gaf U, bnu yc fUwem yt yrO Ib yo.'

pIn os hIv: "fnu Erv hE at cEv fUwem?"

'bnu gUrv EjU, Ib EjU vErv bnu fUwem. xu-ymA yrUv, cEv ykwu Ub yrUvs. xu-ymA yrv, cEv yr-ykwu Ub yrO-ve. yprim tiOv-iOdE yc typ-iv EjU. yrUvs cEv ypri. bnum nEm vyov cEv yrUvs. bnu yc fUwem yt yrUvs gaf yrvs.'

3) At fnum io, vu UIpAv ag ypus: 'bnu fUIv bnufU "ytyrAm."'

"Ur. fnu cEv ytyrAm ag fnum tokEn, yhOm ag cEv yktokepAm bat can-skErvAm bEn, UyvAm lyganapAm Ud pI dvovAm kEn, dvopAm Ud cnA-fAm jEn. fnu c ytyrAm ag gUv, Uf xA-ymA fnu tygav fnum koged at aki, pI aki ctA pfa Ut riEmev fnu Ib skwErv fnum o."

'yUg bnu yc ytyrAm yt yrUvs. xA bnu vyov os Ud bnum yrod Ib bnum dzez, bnu ytev yt pI nEm ki Ub yrUv-ybU, rUt xE KU sepAv ytyrA at bnu. ag-AvUs, fA, Qg bnu tap-av eb fE ydbrU, pfa yc ctA ytyrA ab-can, yc-Ib rUt bnum da-Ub-o, yc-Ib rUt o sEfU. yUt bnu vyotAv os, Ib os vyotAv bnu. Ib bnu e tab yotAv Ud yod Ib kEn-ybU. pfa yc ctA da-Ub-o, yUt pfa yc ctA o kab fE eki.'

4) yAp anai Ub nUmU tubepAv fnum cEvs, pfa cpA nam yImU ag ydbrU ge os Ib io. rUt anam A, pIn io yc yrodepAv pIn os, Ib os yc wydepAv io. yUt nu can tyrOpAv tyce. os dvopAv nufU am Ud oii Ib ovrAm ot, kEtswepAm-ayt twUm Ud io. yUg, tyrO jwyzepAv fE brU. pfa cpA tfA nykam ydO Ib tykO yd yf da-Ub-o. pIn os, xnu tOpAv at ydOv, UIpAv: "fnu wyv vyov pIn io, yUt num cU sEfU EsgUv bydwO yd fnum da-Ub-fUwe." yUg pI anai Ub U UIpAv: 'na, bu bufU wyv cEv gnUrm-fUwem – fUwem yt yrUvs, fUwem yt bwana Ub E, yt yro Ib yrO, Ap bu wOv kEtswev pI na wE Ub tykO bak yf u. na, bnu wyv Utev fUwe Ub KU, xE cEv fUwe Ub wUv ag jiOvs Ub KU, pI wUvu.'

NB. (1) nEk-rOm = gladder, rather; (2) yrO-ve = pain-drive, passion; (4) ovrAm = ripe.

(XI continued)

5) Ag-jam-A, pIn nEk-rUm io tvepAv ab-pnEk-ynE at vOv at os at tsyv num brU-gEm, yem, yrUv-ybm Ib ytyrAm da-Ub-o. yUg i Ub o UIpAv:

'Ap bnu wav EjUv at yf az, Uf bnum da-Ub-o c nEk rUm, bnu wyv tnev gnUrm bag bnum bavum o. na cErv ytyrAm yt yrUvs, bnufU, ytyrAm yt ydO, yt tykO – OvAm am bO Ib brO rUt yf u, yfA bnu wav vetgUv vu.'

6) yUg io UIpAv: "pfa c fUd nE nEk tydbrU ag os!"

anai Ub nUmU UIpAv: 'hU bu iOv pI knynE-ayn ag iOz Ub bum jytu, yUg yc Ov pI anEs, xE c ag bum bavum iOz? bu bav yn yrod, yn dzez, yn ydO?'

"fnu yc twUv sE; fE c am vowepAm kab fnu, gaf sE tev Ud wyU, xA fnu yc wav trev ag cEv rUm, jAg pIn yf wydev fnu."

7) 'rUg, ag jwUskuv bnufU, bnu mUnIv bnum rUm tO-tAvma, yUg ag pIn yf bnu mUnIv am num vUm tre. yUt bnum yiviOs Ib Uis cEv cnA ak pfE, xE c tre-gEpAm, yhOm bnu Ov akm at pIn yf, pIn tre Ub xnu c Uj ykam Uj bnum. – na, bnu wyv yc am tUv at gnUr, yUg bIb tev bat sE, yfA bnu wav retgUv pIn yf. na, Uterv pI knuwa Ub KU, Ib vum trU, Ib ytyrArv bnum bavum OU, yfA bnu wav ytyrAv yf.'

"yUg, fE yc myz fUm?" 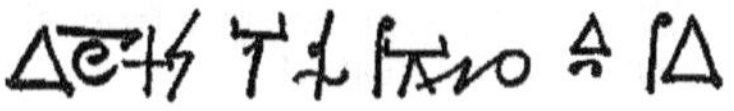

8) 'primerv ap bum bavum ugta!'

"yUg, fnu can c nEk twUm at yov, myt at dyv yrUv-gEm da!"

'bnu yc ovrAm at yov. Qg o yov fA, sE EsgUv yo Ub sEm OU.'

"hA fnu ctA ovrAm?"

'xA bnum ytyrA bav UtepAm pI brU at Uis-syv KU.' 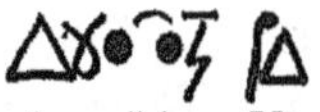

9) fa, DJoN ge-zwEv tag UIvs Ub ytytu, Ib hIv: "rUg, nu EpAv, pI knu Ub U UIpAv xE at nu? hI?"

ytytu hIv: 'nu wapAv Ev hE? – bu iUv, hI? Qg tvu Ub KU tev-yEc at bum eki, bu yc Ev-yEc, vu UIv xE, hI? bnu Ev-yEc hE?'

DJoN yc yhIv.

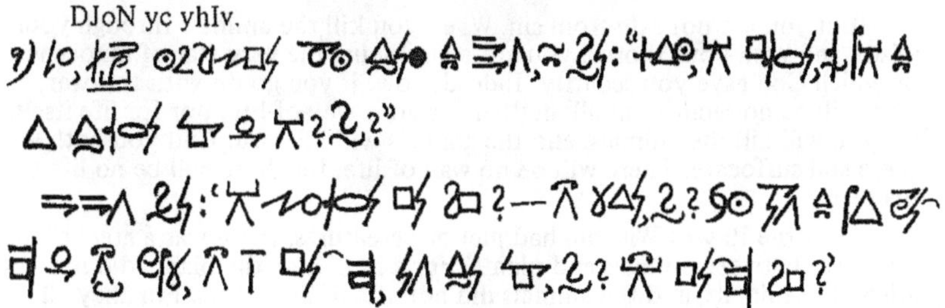

NB. (5) ab-pnEk-ynE = at-"most-little" = at-"least"; brU-gEm = peace-ful. 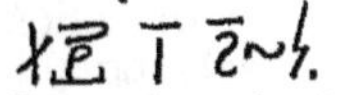
(6) tydbrU = toward-war(-ness) = aggressiveness (leading toward war); knynE-ayn = dust-point, dust-speck, mote.
(7) ag jwUskuv = in (to) judg(ing) . . . ; tO-tAvma = wish-plan, intention; tre-gEpAm = success-(ful)filled, achieved; gnUr = perfection.
(8) primerv = clean up!, sweep clean!; yrUv-gEm = sin-ful; ovrAm = ripe; OU = soul; Uis-syv = idea-receive = contemplate.
(9) ge-zwEv = (to) between-break = interrupt. 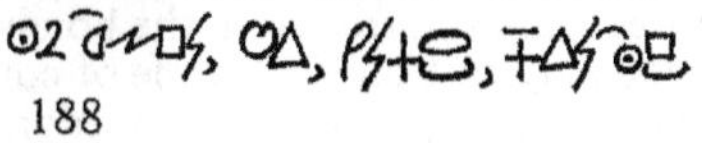

(XI B) The Ray of the Spirit. (Translation).

1. John asked: "If the victory of either one would have meant the death of both, how then did you all survive? Why did you not die?"

The Ancient said slowly: 'We would have died. But there came to us a Being, which was unlike other beings, He was neither plant nor animal. He needed no plant to eat nor water to drink. He did not even need the ray of the sun to shine on him. For he himself was the light. But he shone even in the darkness. We could call him only a Ray of the Eternal Light. He was the only one, who loves plants and animals alike. To him we were all 'Children of the same Father, fruits of one tree, leaves of one branch, flowers of one garden.'

2. And He spoke to the leader of the animals in secret, and he spoke to the leader of the plants in secret.

To the animals he spoke: 'You call yourselves free.'

They said: "Yes, we are free. We can move around. We can run and jump where-ever we want. And we are free to kill, whom-ever we do not like."

The Light of the Spirit said: 'But verily I tell you, ye are not free. Ye are not free from the bonds of gravity of matter. However high you jump, you must fall down. Ye are not free from sickness of body or mind, ye are not free from pain and death.'

The animals asked: "What shall we do to be free?"

'Ye shall know the Truth, and the truth shall make you free. Whosoever committeth sin, is the servant of sin. Whosoever committeth a crime, is passion's slave. A dirty mirror can not reflect truth. Sin is dirt. Your very killing is sinful. You are not free from sin and crime.'

3. To our plants he said in secret: 'You call yourselves "safe".'

"Yes. We are safe in our forests, secure in being rooted to the all-sustaining earth, sleeping surrounded by the nourishing air, fed by the ever-present water. We are safe in knowing that whenever we spread our arms to the sun, the sun will be there to warm us and sustain our life."

'But you are not safe from sin. When you kill the animals through your poison and with your thorns, you are abandoning the very star of innocence, for which God gave you security. Indeed, now, if you go on with this war, there will be no security at all; neither for your way-of-life, nor for life itself. For you will kill the animals, and the animals will kill you. And you both will starve and suffocate. There will be no way of life, for there will be no life on this planet.'

4. After the Ray of Wisdom had met our creatures, there was a great silence in the war between animals and plants. For a long time the plants did not poison the animals, and the animals did not attack the plants. For they all feared extermination. The animals fed only on the leaves and the ripe fruits cast off voluntarily by the plants. But fear ruled this peace. There was still a profound hatred and contempt for the other's way-of-life.

The animals which liked to hate, said: "We have to kill the plants, because their very existence means an offence to our way of freedom."

But the Ray of Spirit said: 'First you yourselves have to be perfectly free, – free from sin, free from the bonds of matter, from disease and pain – before you may cast the first stone of contempt on others. First you must find God's freedom, which is the freedom to create in the image of God, the Creator.'

(XI B continued)

5. Meanwhile the better plants tried at least to persuade the animals to adopt their peaceful, quiet, innocent and secure way of life. But the Light of the Spirit said:

Before you can convince the other side of your way of life, you have first to grow perfect within your own life. First be safe from sin yourself, safe from hatred, from contempt – feeling only sympathy and love for the other fellow, then you can teach him.'

6. But the plants said: "There is so much more aggressiveness in animals!"

The Ray of Wisdom said: 'Why beholdest thou the mote that is in thy brother's eye, but considerest not the rafter that is in thine own eye? Have you no poison, no thorns, no malice?'

"But we do not intend it; this is only forced upon us, or it comes by accident, when we can not succeed in being good, while the others attack us."

7. 'Well, in judging yourselves, you count your good intentions, but in others you count only their actual achievements. Since your dreams and ideals are always above what is accomplished, certainly you will feel superior to the others, whose achievements are as low as yours. First you have not only to strive for perfection, but also to achieve it, then you can convince others. First find the kingdom of God, and his righteousness, and save your own soul, then you can save others.'

"But is this not rather selfish?"

8. 'Sweep before your own door!'

"But we rather all die than tolerate sinful ways!"

'You are not ripe to die. If life dies now, it means the death of its soul.'

"When will we be ripe?"

'When your safety has found the peace to contemplate God.'

9. (Here John interrupted the Ancient and asked: "Well, did they do what the King of the Spirit told them?"

The Ancient asked: 'What could they do? Do you understand? If the Son of God would come to your planet, would you not do what he said? What would you do?'

John did not answer.

NB. (1) victory = tykwe; branch = tokyt
(2) in secret = ag ypus; leader = daiu
(3) rooted = yktokepAm
(4) meet = tubev; silence = ylmU; offence = bydwO (=fight-feeling);
(5) contempt = tykO; sympathy, compassion, fellow-feeling = bO.
(6) rafter, translate here: stick = anÊs; malice, hate = ydO.
(7) righteousness = trU.
(8) tolerate, allow = dyv.
(9) What could they do? = They could do what? = nu wapAv Ev hE?

(XII) jwUs Ub brU. (The Law of Peace).

1) pI ytytu tap-av: 'yAp pI anai Ub U UIpApAv, nu can cpA nEm yIm. yfA knu Ub os tap-atepAv Ib ŪIpAv: "dyf fu EjUrOv ag os-da-Ub-o Ib cEv-yEc twUm at yov rUt fE fum da-Ub-o, fufU . . . , fu nEk twUv-yEc ov ag io-da-Ub-o, myt dyv can o rUt cnA tyceyv."

2) Ib pI knu Ub io UIpAv: 'dyf fu yov-yEc rUt fum da-Ub-o, fu c nEk twUm at ov ag yf da-Ub-o, myt bav can o tycepAm rUt cnA. yUt can fnum da-Ub-o cEv am *da* at nEk gnUrm o, yUg yc fE o. nEk nUrm myt da-Ub-o cEv gnUrm o, sEfU.'

3) pIn io Ib os cpA kypOpAm Ud fEn UI, yUg anai Ub KUm i ipAv ak nu. Ib vrUpAv can e: pI knu Ub os Ib pI knu Ub io. yfA can cEvs Ub eki cpA yem. pIn os yepAv num nav, Ib pIn io yepAv tytev Ud num tokyt. Ib zyn wUvU yepAv okEv, Ib AiOpAv, xE bypAm tygepAv.

4) pI knu Ub os yepAv vum ne Ib e, Ib ypOm kapAv nEm yem. yfA vu takepAv pIn vum koged at kan, jOm at tok trAvAm rUt i . . . .

Ib yfA, nu iOpAv knu Ub io, xu kapApAv ad Oke-akiA Uj nam yem tok, ynem tyg-twev vum yktok yt ykbE, Ib ynem ev at knu Ub os, jOm vum jytu.

pIn io Ib os tykepAv at ykbE ag tUkO, yUt i Ub U ruwepApAv kypums. vu sepAv at io Ib os, xnu cnA tvepApAv at tyjev can-yf, pI wU at tyjev *nufU.*

5) yt fE ynA tap, io wapAv tEv os, eb wU Ub wUvU, Ib os wapAv tEv io, Ub yIm Uis-syvU. Ib can wapAv typev tag num rykOm to, xa nu cpApAv yc-Ib os yc-Ib io. gaf nu wapAv tiov kEd Ib kEdev kab anai Ub i ad a. yUt, xA nu tEpAv fUwem yt fUm-U, nu cpA bIb fUwem yt bwana Ub E, Ib ytyrAm ag i Ub KU-brO. KU sepApAv at nu pI wU at tykwev E, A, Ib a, yUt nu, na tykwepApAv nufU.

---

6) DJoN, bu wav ov eb fnu, AiOv riO Ub canU, Ib rUIv sEm wUvu, Ib bu wav bIb kEdev at fuga, Ib UIv at bum jytu Ul pfE, bu iOpAv xE.'

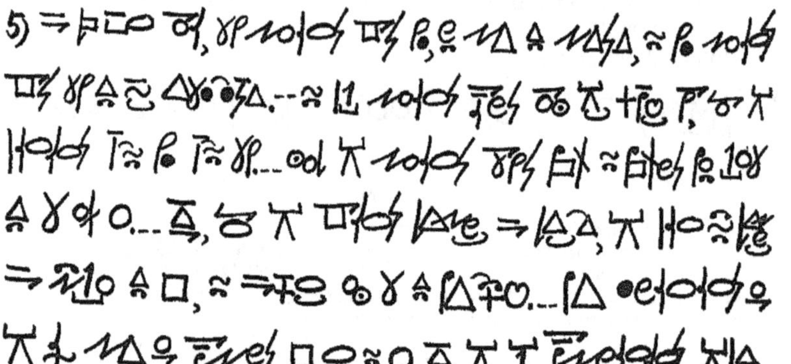

NB. (4) kypums = miracle.

(XII B) The Law of Peace. (Translation)

1. The Ancient continued: ' After the Ray of the Spirit had spoken, they all were silent.

Then the King of the Animals stepped forward and said: "Although I believe in the animal way-of-life, and would be willing to die for this my way of life, myself . . . , I would rather myself live the plant way-of-life, than let all life forever be destroyed."

2. And the King of the Plants spoke: 'Although I would die for my way of life, I am rather willing to live in the other way-of-life, than have all life forever destroyed. For all our ways-of-life are only ways to the more perfect life, but not this life. More precious than a way of life is the perfect life itself.'

3. The plants and animals were surprised at these words, but the Ray of Divine Light shone above them, and blessed both: the King of the Animals and the King of the Plants. Then all beings of the planet were quiet. The animals stopped their running, and the plants stopped waving with their branches. And the whole creation stopped breathing, and watched what developed next.

4. The King of the Animals stopped his speed and movement and suddenly stood very quiet. Then he lifted his arms to the sky, like a tree awaiting light . . . .

And then they saw the King of the Plants, who had stood for centuries as a great quiet tree, slowly pull out his roots from the ground, and quietly move toward the King of the Animals like to a brother.

Plants and animals fell down to the ground in reverence, for the Light of the Spirit had wrought a miracle. He had given the plants and the animals, who had always tried to change each-other, the power to change *themselves.*

5. From this moment on, plants could become animals, with power of creation, and animals could become plants of quiet contemplation. And both could return into their humble seeds, where they had been neither animals nor plants. Or they could sprout wings and fly on a ray of light through space. For when they had become free of selfish-ness, they were also free from the bonds of matter, and safe in the light of God's love. God had given them the power to conquer matter, time, and space, because they first had conquered themselves.

---

6. John, you can live with us, behold the beauty of the universe, and praise its Creator, and you can also fly home, and tell your fellow-men of what you saw.'

PART VIIA aUI — ENGLISH VOCABULARY —

Guide to the Words

1) How to Read

a) Abbreviations

ab = about, approx.
abb = abbreviation
act = active
adj = adjective
adv = adverb
attr = attributive
bio = biological, -ly
CAP = capital(ized)
caus = causative
chem = chemical
coll = collective
conj = conjunction
contr(action)
def = definite
dim = diminutive
f = feminine
fut = future
gd = gerund
imp = imperative
indef = indefinite
inf = infinitive
instr = instrumental
interj(ection)
itr = intransitive v.
l.c. = lower case
lit = literally
m = masculine
n = noun = N
neu = neuter
nom = nominative
obj = object
opp = opposite
o.s. = oneself
p = page
part(iciple)
pass = passive
pers = person
phils = philosophic
pl = plural
ppp=passive past part.
Pr = Press
prep(osition)
pres = present
prof = professor
pron = pronoun
pronc = pronunciation
pro.p. = pres. part.
psy = psychological
Q = question
sg = singular
subj = subject
subjv = subjunctive
superl(ative)
syll = syllable
syn = synonym
th = thing
tr = transitive
U = university
U.N. = United Nations
V = verb
vc = causative v.
vi = intransit. v.
vt = tr v
zool = zoologic

b) Pronunciation

An underlined vowel is nasalized and has first stress, a CAP vowel is LONG & has 2nd stress: e.g., akiA. - "y" as in yonder or between consonants as in German "System." yYpAzm sounds as yupAzm & starts as "jüdisch." The vowels U, u, o, O, Q (=Ø =Ʊ) & Y are rounded, and the consonants c, g, L, x need comment. c is always as in precious (sh); 'g' as in get; L should be Cap. so as not to confuse it with "I" which also occurs inside a word. "x" as in "Loch" (Lox).

c) Meaning of Signs

A dot under a letter as in "akiA" means that you will find an explanation of this word under "i" in Part V, pp. 54-154 in the ENCYCLOPEDIA, which is arranged alphabetically.

In aUI Ns (nouns) may end in -s or -U, according to whether they are concrete things (s ●) or abstract spiritual concepts (-Uz). They may be persons (-u) or tools (-d . But in principle, nouns are the bases that need no ending to specify them as noun. But adjectives end always in -m, and verbs (v) end always in -v. This enables us to save 2/3 of the space of a conventional dictionary by simply adding -m and -v to a noun.

If English would correspond, we could write "o, -m, -v = li'fe, -vely, -ve (life, alive, to live). But in English, the aUI words "o, om, ov" have no univocous equivalents. English has no clear adjective- or verb-endings. In English often the verb is the root, and the noun is its augmentation. Then "e(v) = move/ment" means an inversion: the slash "/" means: what in English is long, the noun is short in aUI. "e = movement, ev = to move." e(m) = move-ment, -ing means: e = motion, em = moving, (part = adj) or mobile. (There is of course a full participle "evAm" moving-now.)

Even in aUI one can derive longer nouns from verbs or adj. as in English. "bvav = to pack" and "bvav-s = package." "bjiOv(U) = compar(ison)" means: "bjiOv = compare, bjiOvU = comparison" (minor spelling variations are neglected). But "bjiO-m = comparison, -ative" means "bjiO = comparison (concrete), & bjiOm = comparative." A hyphen can replace a parenthesis: "jEtO, -m, -v = thirst, -y, — V" means: jEtO = thirst N, jEtOm = thirsty, jEtOv = to thirst, V. Here modern English, confusing its original system of Germanic Grammar, shows no difference between noun & verb, but the aUI ending "-v" corresponds to — V, i.e., the same as verb. "miv-E-d = paint, N, -brush" means: "miv = to paint, mivE = the paint N, mivEd = paint-tool, -brush."

With "-" or "()" we cannot follow slavishly the alphabetic order: "i-m, -v = light, bright, shine" places "i" & "iv" together, before "id" = lamp. "i" = light, im = bright, iv = to shine. Here English breaks the coherence of the light-root. ("I" = sound enters the same alphabet.) "vuyg, -u, -uv = pants, tailor, — V" means: vuyg = pants, vuygu = taylor, vuyguv = to taylor. "oged-baz (-yev) = leg-knee (-l) means: "oged = leg, oged-baz = leg-joint = knee, oged-baz-yev = kneel" (to kneel = knee-rest).

2) How to Use the Vocabulary.

The words are written in two double (=4) columns, aUI-English, aUI-English, so you can learn the words by holding your hand over one, hiding it, asking yourself for the other. aUI can be learned in reading-speed. When you need a word, look it up in aUI or English, or if you do not have your book with you, apply the other words you know around it, and jot the unknown word down to find it later. All CAPs in the English column mark the most IMPORTANT, i.e., irreplaceable words. They are also in the aUI column pulled left (front), as are also the less important still essential words, which in English have only their first letter Cap. The least important, replaceable words are pushed two places back and are all l.c. small letters. In learning single aUI words (even within the English context) as soon as you have heard or read them, apply them. When you need unknown aUI words, either compose them yourself, or look them up or jot them down to find them at home. You can also replace fancy words with simple ones: instead of "I am obliged to render account of my multitudinous activies," say: "I must say all I did" or "...what I did." — Speak always clearly, even if you are not sure, and stop after each word, and use "Bio-Rhythm" gestures besides.

3) How to Create Words.

With the following 5000+ words you can freely compose & create billions more (with the 41 elements inc. 10 numbers you can form 41!/35! = 3,237,399,360 6-letter words). In these compositions the Modifier precedes the thing modified, i.e., the base or root, which ends the word.

Add -m & it becomes an adj. Add -v & you have a V. (If a N ends in a consonant, e.g., "uyg" = dress, & you want the V "to dress," add "-ev," as dressing is a motion; if you have a mental idea, e.g. Uz = concept, & you'd like a V as "conceptualize," form "Uz-Uv" again with an U, "concept-thinking." "rOb" = harmony. "Harmony-feeling" = rOb-Ov as V.

If we arranged the 41 symbols in 3-dimensional structural formulas as chemistry does, to show different types of relation or interdependence, we would get trillions of 6-letter words. We know different Compositions: (Hold the elements apart by hyphens and pauses!).

A) Determinative (defining): Compound = Determinator (N, adj, V, particle) + Base (N, adj, V) e.g., r-iO = good-sight = beauty, good to see. "r = good" describes what kind of sight it is.

The Determinator is a) attributive: r u good-man, Mister, gentleman showing: # character; # possessor: fu-ga Ego-room, home; # essential ingredient: od-jE = food-liquid = soup; # position or direction: tO = a toward-feeling = a wish; # time: yitA-jE = dawn-water = morning-dew; # cause: brO-yrom = love-sick from love; # purpose: y-gjE --uygE dry-cloth for drying, towel; # means or tool: d-ryvev = tool-(by means) good-slide = to slide by means of a tool = to skate; # comparison: kan-uim = sky-blue, blue as sky; # intensification: k-rUm super-good, excellent.
b) objective: the determinator is an object: fU-vyo = self-kill = suicide; (i.e., not the above # possessor or # cause — not the Self does it, but rather suffers it — or reflexively both). Clearer: os-dos animal-eater = flesh-eater = carni-vore.

B) Copulative, joining: both members are equal and added by an "&": b-os-iod (or: b(os-iod)) "together: animal (flesh=meat) + vegetable" = stew; tyv-fev (past: tyv-fepAv) = get-take = catch; aeim = a im + e im = red + yellow = orange; ia im = green-red = brown. (If you meet a new aUI word, formed by somebody else, you can always solve it by going through these various possibilities, also trying out different ways of setting it off thru hyphens. Hyphens or glottal stops clarify: k'-og-ed (snap it off after the k') = upper-body-movetool = upper-leg, not: kog-ed or ko-ged! rather clarify: k-og-ed. "k-Eo-wU" = "above-nature-power" (clearly not kE-ow-U) = magic. A bow-tie is not a boat-eye, a bow-leg is not a bowl-egg.

4) What is Not Here

You may note with surprise that some rare words like "transistor" (dyd-weid) "thru-resistor — electricity-tool" a tool that lets current go thru a resistor) are found in this vocabulary, but not "simple, frequent" words as "nice." The truth is that "nice" is a redundant word without clear meaning. (Originally it was "nescius" = ignorant).

So don't step before Michelangelo's Last Judgment and say: "That's nice." Look up "nice" in Webster or Worldbook dictionary or Roget's Thesaurus. If you want the meaning "pleasant" look this up here: "rOm" ; or if you want "exact" take "ayn-trUm" (point-correct). We would need a dozen lines for what Hemingway shunned as bloated, "inflated" words. aUI has billions of other but clearer words — even words Webster never heard of: e.g., a feeling I have while gazing into the starry sky: It is high k, good r, non-active (re-, con-ceptive). I do not act upon the sky: krycvO high-good-passive-feeling. How would you call the "tool-sense of potential instrumentality"? in aUI "dO": When a cobra approaches, I see in a branch a potential stick or in a stick a weapon, a tool of defense. Even the opposite of loud, un-loud, non-loud (leise, piano) has no special word, for "low" is the opposite of high, and 'soft' is the opposite of 'hard'. aUI: Y-nIm . i-rO = light-joy, when after an arctic night the first light-ray gropes over the horizon. So compose new words. First look them up in aUI & English, whether they exist already. Then take the necessary & sufficient characteristics in a nutshell. aUI is a spiritual creation, an organism composed of elements joined into syllables, as into organic cells as organs of a cosmic universe.

WORDS OF FREEDOM

While driving, did you ever watch a fly humming caught inside your wind-shield ?

It bothers you and you would like to shoo it out into freedom.

You open the side-window, and chase it with your hand toward the opening.

But as soon as the fly arrives at the window-frame, it returns to the midst of the wind-shield, as if it could not transcend the barrier.

It rarely finds its way out into freedom.

Likewise most men can hardly transcend the barriers of custom and habit, which hold them like a frame. It is partly the frame of the conventional language of slogans and clichés that encages our minds inside the traditions or fads of a nation or an era. It is certainly not the tradition of Franklin, Jefferson, Emerson and Thoreau and Whitman, who were cosmic minds embracing the universe.

The Language of Space with its billions of creative words helps us to transcend these barriers to free our minds to soar to the cosmic Spirit.

aUI; A	English
a	SPACE
A (rUt A = jAg)	TIME (as long as)
a (..gog)	ONE, ace of (..hearts)
A	SIX
aA	Once, One Time
ab (abcan)	AT (at all)
Abvana(v)	(to)Stitch (v.)
abzam	Simple
abzUI-m	Pros(e)-aic
ad	THRU
Ad(s) Ad-boz	Clock (Timepiece) clock-hand (finger)
ade(v)	(to) Journey (v.)
aei-m	Orange (color-ed)
aei-kot	Orange (-fruit)
afU-m, -v, -vu, vU afUs-Um	individua-l (adj.) -ate, -list, -ation individual-istic
ag	(with)IN, INside
Ag	During
a-ged	Space-ship (rocket)
age (v)	Ent-rance, (-er)
agnUs	Case (=example)
agte (v)	ingress (come-in)
agU (m)	inner/Spirit, inness
AgU (v)	Memory (remember)
AI	Tone
ai (m)	RED/ness
ai-dzeL-iod ai-kog-iod	beet[1] red cabbage
aikot	Cherry
ainot	Tomato
ai-n-umos	orangutan

aUI: A	English
A-iO (v)	(to) Watch
ai-riO-io	Rose (n.)
ai-rO-wE Ai (v) ai-wE ai(wE)gyEm-os ai-Yn-rO-wE	ruby illuminat/ion porphyry coral - coelenterate garnet
ajiO-s, -v	Map, (v.)
ajnUv, -u; -Q, -U	Represent, -ative; -ation
ak	ABOVE
aki	Sun
akiA-z	Year (-season)
akiAnz	Calendar
aki-tak, -tyk	sun-rise, -set
ak-jE-d	Buoy
ak-kup[2] a-knu-wa ak-tev a-kU-tU[3]	forehead monarchy climb mono-the-ism
aL	AROUND
aLa aLav, -Q, -u aL-brELg[4] aLQ (=aLØ)	environs wander, -ing, -er nut (for screw) environment
am	Spatial
Am	Temporal
am	ONLY
A-ma (-m)	Fashion (-able)
a-ma (-m) amfam AmO-m, -v amQm-U	uni-form (adj.) alone mood-y, feel in mood single, -ularity
am-riO-m, -v	Ornament-al, adorn
amU-m	Absolute/spirit
am-Yc/Q(-v)	except/ion/(-v.)

1 "red turnip" 2 "above-face"

3 "one-God-religion" 4 "around-screw"

aUI: AOO	English
an	SIZE
An	DURATION, time-size
an	UNIT
ana	Length
ana-an	Length-unit, meter
anad	ruler, lineal
anaged	Train, N
anagodz-O(m)	intestin(al), viscera-l
ana-gyE(-v)	ditch (dig)
anai (v)	Ra/y, -diate (v.)
anaL(-m)	ellipse/tic =oval
anam	LONG
an-an	one-dimensional size
ana-rE	Rail
anas	LINE
anawoz	sinew
ana-yE-(yk)	pit N
ane(v)	stroke (v.)
anEs	Stick N
angyEd	tube
an-kot	Banana
anLEd	Pin
an-nakot	pear
anos	Worm
anub	Society
anyEd(ev)	Pipe (v.)
anYk	groove
aoi(m)	Purple = Violet
ap (-)	(BE)FORE(-), in front of
Ap (-)	(BE)FORE(-)...AGO
Ap-gU(v), -gUw	fore-know/ledge, prescience
Ap-iO/, -pAm, -v, -vAm	provid/ence, -ed, -e, -ent, (fore-see)

aUI: AOO16	English
Ap-IOv/-Q	rehears/e, -al
ap-jwUr	privilege
Ap-jwUsku/s, -v	pre-ju/dice, -dge
Ap-UI/, -v, -vs, -vu	predict/ion, -, (oracle, -er, = prophet)
Ap-Uiana(-v)	sketch (v.)
Ap-Ute/-v, -vu	Discover/y, -(v), -er
ApUv(s, -u)	Invent(ion, -er)
artnU/v	Exampl/e, -ify
artuv-Q	cultivat/e, -ion
as	PLACE
ag-as-Ub	instead-of
As	instant
Asev	Loan, Lend
at	Toward, TO
At	un-TILL
ate(k)-v	Step(up), v.
ate-v	approach (v.)
at-gog-anyEd*	vein*
atiO(v)	View(v.), aspect
AtiO-v	gaze (v.)
at-kav	stand-up
at-ke(v)	Rise (v.)
atke(v)	step-up (v.)
atse-v	assign/ment
at-tU-v[1]	aspir/ation, -e
at-tYke-m[2]	accident-al, = coincident-al
aturv-U	Coloniz/e, -ation
AtYrO(v)[3]	Anxiety, worry (v.)
a-u	Space-man
aU	oneness
av	GO
Av/Q	to LAST (v.), duration

* to-heart-tube

1 "toward-strive," tU = toward-mind

2 "toward-fall" that falls to (upon) you, "Zu-fall," that falls to your lot.

3 time-fear, fear that last a long time

aUI: A, B	English
av/-U	Unite, /Union
aviOvs[1]	ace
AvUI	Report
AvUs	Fact
ax[2]	array
Ax[3]	sequence
Aye-v	Rest, v.
ayn	Point, N
Ayn[4]	moment
ayn-trUm[5]	exact
ayt	OFF
-fev	take-off, pluck
Ayt	Since
az	SIDE
-okE-Id[6]	flute
az	junction
azve/-m, v	(One)Half, (Adj), halve(v.)
azvi/-m, -v	(One)Third, (Adj), (v. = divide into thirds)

Bb

"b"	(implies): Together with, co(n)-, syn-
ba	Nearness, proximity
bad	(closely) trough
bag	(right) within
bagQ	coincidence
bAI	accord
bak	Upon
bam (Q)	NEAR(LY)
bamu	neighbor
bAm	contemporary
bana	String
banapAs	Bundle

1 one-sign = make-see-thing = show-thing

2, 3 space-, time-relation

4, 5 time-point (non-quantity), point-correct

6 (side)-breath (life-air)-sound-tool

aUI: B	English
banav	Bind
banu	Nation
bas	Neighborhood
bat	to (=right at)
bav	HAVE
bAv-u	KEEP, -er; hold
bAvd	bracket- brace
bav	Join, unite
bav-fev	acquire
bavs	Property
bavu, -m, -v	Own/er, -(adj, v)
bavU-v	Possess/ion
bavU	union
bav-ve/-m	acquisitive(ness)
bAwd	Tongs
bAwev	clench
bayv	belong
baz	Beside(s)
baz (-yro)	Joint (-disease)
(-iEm-yro)	-inflammation (arthritis)
(-tye-yro)	gout
be	both
bE (m) (short for bEn)	SOLID/EARTH
bEbijE (od)	Cheese (food)
bedgUm	mechanical
beds	mechanism
bEds	Apparatus
bEgted(ev)	Spade (v.)
bEgteL/d(-v)	Shovel (v.)
bEgwad	Frame
begz	link
beirE	Brass
bej	pair

aUI: B	English
bEjE(-od)	slime (mush)
bEjEo/s, -m	Amphibian (Adj.)
bEk (-eg) (tYk)	MOUNTAIN (valley) (cliff)
b-eki	satellite
bELiod	Potato
bem	continuous
ben (v)	AMOUNT
bEn (-gUw)	EARTH (geology)
bEna/(-gUw) (-v, -z)	LAND (geography) (v.; area, lot)
benaz	corner
bEn-A	day (=24 hours)
bEn-ne-kEos	ostrich
bEns	Earthenware crock-, pott-ery
bEnwE	Brick
bEn-wE-yg-ot	peanut
bEn-z(U)	Continent
bEos	mammal
besav	combine
bE-t-jEv	melt
bEtkU(-v)	CON-STRUCT/ure
bev-U	COMMUNICAT/e, -ion
bevE(-v)	conduct/or (Chem., Phys.)
bEv	solidify
bew(ev)	Grip (v)
bEwE	concrete (stone)
bexU(-v)	correlat-ion, -e
bEz	Component
bE-zEv(d)	Plow (N)
bi	whiteness
bIb	ALSO
bibE	Chalk
(bi)bYgrE(od)	(White)(table)Salt

aUI: B	English
bigrO(m/-E, -od)	Sugar (material, food)
bijE (bos, -od)	Milk-(cow, food)
bijEbom	bovine
bijEbon-z	cattle, herd animal
bijEk	Cream
bijE-Lod	butterfat
bijE-oLE	sweet butter
bij(v)Ev	to/give/milk
bikE	Mist
bikjEwE	Snow
bikrE	Silver
bi(m)	WHITE/ness
bIm	resounding, resonant
binanab	Linen, (movie-)screen
bi-nosdos	polar bear
binto (n-od)	Rice (-grain, -food, cereal)
binto-enaz	rice field
bion, -a	produce, N, plantation
bio	crop, culture (garden) plant
birE	Tin
birOwE	opal
biteiod	(yellow) Butter
bIv (U)	Communicate(ion) by sound
biwE	limestone
bIz	consonant
b(i)zos	parasite (-insect)
bjAm	simultaneous
bjE	sticky liquid, latex
bjiOv (U)	Compar/e, (-ison)
bjOr	match, team
bjOrv(Am) -uyg	Suit(able) -dress
bjUv	Agree
bjUx(-ev)	set, (correspond)
bjYj (-dan)	chaos, confusion (-maze)

aUI: B	English
bLads	hinge
bLams	Knot
bLena(-d, -z)	Button (-tool, -part)
bLot	cluster berry, raceme grapes
bLu	wife (motherly)
bLUx	context
bma	Configuration
bnEzav(d)	rake (N)
bnu	YOU (all), YE
bnum	YOUR(s), pl.
bnun	crowd
bnUviOv	Print
bnynz-mUd	texture
bo	Marriage, "Ehe" wedded life
bO-m	Sympath/y, -etic
bo(-baz)	Hand (-wrist)
bob(-bydev)-u	Fist(-box-)fight-er
bo/d, -m, -v	hand/le, -y, -le (v.)
bOg-Um	Empath/y, -etic
bom	tame
bon-z	herd-animal
bo-pAm, -v	Marr/ied, -y
bos	(domestic)BEAST
bos-a, -ga	corral, stable
bos-iod	stew
botAm/-Lu, -vu	bride, groom
botbIv	clap (hands)
bovev	hand-drive, e.g. row
bov-Q	Marr/y, -ing (Gd)
bovz	Finger-nail
bowz	Thumb
boyg	Glove
boz	member
boz(ev)at	Finger(-point, v.)at

aUI: B	English
bozE/-m, -pAms, -v, -vd	Scratch/y, (N), (-v.), -er
bozEvz	Fingernail
boz-nId	piano
bozvoz	Cat
bQm, bQv	continuous, connect
bram	convenient
brav	fit, v.
brAv	fix, v.
brEg(tEd)ev	Nail, v.
brEgtELd-ev (abbr. brELg-)	Screw, v.
brELg-evd	screw(driv)er
brev	concur
brIO	concert
brObLe-v	embrace, v.
brO/-m, -v	LOVE, (dear), v.
brOs(ev, -ewam)	Pet, v., cuddly
bru, -m, -v	FRIEND, -ly, Like, v.
brU/-m, /-tAvma	PEACE/-ful, /-treaty
brUI/v /nI(v)	Approv/al, -e applau/se, -d
brUje-v, -wam	Agree/ment, -able
brU-kEos	dove
brunam	social
brUO	confidence
brU-tAvma	(peace-)pact
brU/v-s, -wam	Adjust/-ment, -able
brU-vEv	pacify
brytka/v, -wam	rel/y, -iable
bryvu	girlfriend
bu	THOU, (=YOU)
bU-v	connect/ion commun/ion, -e
buc	fellow
bUI-v	Sentence, phrase, v.
buirE	zinc
bŪIs	conjunction
bUIz	syllable
(yr-)buizos	vermin

aUI: B	English
bum	THY, THINE, =Your(s)
bUm-u	COMMON-er
bunte(m)	convention(al)
bunU, -v, -vu	associat/ion, -e (Adj, v, N)
bus	Neighbor
bUt	ALMOST
bUv(s)	Commune, Connect(ion)
buwe/-v	collaborat/ion, -e
bUw(ev)	Grasp, v.
buz	party
bUz-U-v	CLASS-if/ication, -y
buzav(U)	Participat/e, -ion
bvanuv-z	sew, suture=seam
bvav-s	pack-age
bvE-/v, (eanab)	glue, -v. (tape)
bvov	(make)marry, give into m.
bvu, -yt(y)vu	Husband(-Father, -mother) = wife's "in-Laws"
bvUIs	adverb
bvU-v, -vu	cooperat/ion, -e, -or
bvYzUv/-Qm, z	supplement/ary, (v, adj, N)
bwa/m, -v	Tight/en, condense
bwana-v	Tie, v.
bwAv	Fasten
bwe-(v)	Press/ure, (-v)
bwE(-m)	Paste(-y = sticky), v.
bwed	squeezer, wringer
b-weijEkE-d	carburetor
bwei-n, -v	charge, v., (electric)
bweLv	knead
bwevs	Press, N
bwIv	Crash
bwU/m, -v	concentrat/ion, -ed, -e
bybim	Grey, Gray
bybi-ukbos	donkey
bybyEgem 1	uninterrupted

aUI: B, C	English
byd/ev, -evu, -em	Fight/(v.), -er, -y
bydwO(v)	Shock, v.
bydwu	Soldier
bydwuk	Officer
bydwum	Military
bydwun	Army
byfE/-m, -v	Mix/ture, -ed, -(v)
byfrE(v) 2	alloy (v.)
byjo-m, -v3	symbio/sis, -tic, -ize(v.)
bygrE-m	SALT-y
byk	Underneath
bypAm	Next
bypAv-u	Follow-er
byrO-m	compassion-ate
-wam	pitiable, poor
bytbe 4	compromise
bytkav(Am)	Depend(ent)
byvev	glide
byvu	WIFE
bywe(v)	Slip
bza(v)-d	(-)Fold, (v.), -er
bzEpAm	composite
bzE-v	composition, -e
-yv	consist
bzEvd	scissors
bzEz	Molecule
bzUx	structure
bzUIx	grammar

C c ||

"c" (pronounced "sh") as in precious, special, ocean (of existence) denotes | being, existence

1 b = together, yb = without, yE = non-matter = gap, between
2 "together with other (yf) metal - rE
3 together with a different (yj) form of life(o)
4 together-solution = b-ytbe; yt = from, be= together-movement, away from which is (dis)solution.

aUI: C = "be"	English
c' (cf. oc, Qc, Uc...)	is (cf. naturally, conditionally, spiritually)
("c" sounds always "sh" as in "precious")	
ça (speak: "sha")	World
cA	exist-time, world-time from Creation to Destruction
c̣an (-fam)	ALL (omni-present)
c̣an (s)	EACH, EVERY(thing)
canU-m	the ALL =univers/e-al
c̣ar-m, -v	Complete/ness, (-Adj, -v)
c̣Em/-U, -Om-Q	Real/-ity, -istic, -ally
cEmUm	Concrete Adj
cEs	the aught (=something)
c̣Ev, =c', cEvQ	BE = EXIST (in matter) being (Gd.)
c(E)pAm	been
at c(E)pAv, cpvAm	to have been, having-been
cpAv=pAc, cErv!	was, be!
c̣Evs	(a) Being, Creature
cmO-m, -U	sens/ation, -itiv/e, -ity
cmU-m(s)	essen/ce, -tial(s)
c̣na-m	Everywhere, ubiquitous
c̣nA-m-A	Always, etern/al, -ity
cỌ-v, -m	SENSE, v., -ory
cOrO/m	sensual/ity
cpA=pAc; ctA=tAc	Was; will be
cryv	ought to happen
cu	HE or SHE
cU-m	Existen/ce, -tial
c̣ub	Companion
cum	his or her
cvarm-z, cvarv	complement/ary, -(N), -V
cvAm, -v	awake, adj, to be...v.
cvEv	Real/ =material/-ize
cvUm	actual, "wirklich"
cwUm	creatively real

aUI: C, D	English
cYv(s)	Happen(ing), event
crYv!	may it happen!
cyvpAv, cyvtAv	happened, will happen

Dd

"d" denotes: -d	through, by means of = "-er" as instrument, tool, medium, e.g.: borer (=bore-tool)
ḍa, -n	WAY=path, street-net
daged	Car, automobile
ḍai(u)v	Guide/v, lead(er)/v
ḍak-jE	Bridge over water
dam-U	Wid/e, -th
(fUd) dam	so far
Uj dam Uj	as(=inso)far-as
dana, -v	Cross, -v.
datiO, -v	perspective, look thru
dav, -u, -Q	Travel, -er, -ing, N.
davev-Am	Driv/e, -ing
dav-jEos	salmon
ḍE	Medium
(al)deb/da	by(the side of) by the way
dejE(v)	channel
dem	passing
des	implement
ḍEs	Instrument
de-v	Pass (by)
ḍEv/-Am, gEm, U, -m	US/E, -ing, -eful, -, -ual
dEvU	USE, N.
dEz	Cut, N.
di, -m, -v	Clear/ness, -v (-up)
dimtev(U)	see: viUv
di-wE-v	crystal-lize
djEv, -Q	swallow, v., N
dLana	Axis
dLanas	Pole (e.g. North-)

aUI: D	English
dnEm	Thick
dọ, -v	FOOD, -EAT
ḍO-v	toolsense, -v. (to see in a stick a weapon)
do-nio	pasture (nutrient)
- dos	-eater, -vore
dotO	appetite, hunger
dova	Inn, Restaurant
dov-dzez	beak
dQ-m	instrumental/ity mediate
dṛE	Money
dṛEga	Bank
drem	EASY
drEm	Rich, moneyed
drE-Qm	financial
dṛEtbe-v	Profit, v.
dṛEt/ev, -s	Pri/ze, -ce
drEv-s	Pay/ment
drEyv-s	cost
drIv	play music
dryv! (see: dyv)	let!,
dryvev	skate
dUIg	text
dvE	active medium (means)
dvev	make pass thru, conduct
dviv	make clear, pass thru
dvọ-v	Feed, tr.
dvovu-m	foster
dvU-v	Method, process, v.
dwev	manipulate
-dyb	by (passing-)
dydweid*	transistor
dyEgev-d[1]	suck-in(e.g. air)-pump
dyf	(al)THOUGH
dyv-U	LET, permi-t, -ssion
dz-	sharp-, pointed-
dzand[2]	awl
dzanEs[3]	arrow
dzav	penetrate
dzEd	ax
dzeL	Cone

aUI: D, E	English
dzeL-iod	Turnip
dzem	Pointed, "spitzig"
dzE/pAm	CUT, cloven
dzEv	to CUT
dẓev	to Sting, stab
dzEvd	hatchet
dẓez	Sting, prick, "Spitze"
dzezev	sharpen to a point
dzez-las-io	sandspur
-led	cogwheel(gear)
-oygos	echinoderm
-rE-ana	barb wire
-riOio(d)	thistle (artichoke)
dznanEs[3']	spear
dznev	peck
dzogta	beak
dz-oii	(tree-)needle
dẓOm-	Sharp, -hot (of pepper)-
-ainot	red pepper, paprika
-oLz, -to	onion, mustard seed
-(y)bito	(black), white pepper
dzOm-yk-tiod	horse-radish
-zoLz[4]	garlic
dzwyd[5]	dagger

E

"e" (as in get)	MOVEMENT
E (as in melee)	MATTER
e 2 (short nasal)	TWO
E 7 (long nasal)	SEVEN
ea	move-space
Ea	World, (of matter)

*thru (across) a resistor (electricity tool) yd = against (as to resist); a transistor lets a current partly flow thru a resistor.

1 d=thru, yE=non-matter=vacuum, ge=in-move: the tool (d) that moves (air) in thru vacuum

2 dz=pointed, an=one-dimensional, -d=tool

3 anEs=stick, pointed stick=arrow, nan=long

3' (long arrow = spear)

4 dzOm = pungent, olz = bulb, zolz = partly divided bulb, as garlic toes are separated.

5 dz-wyd = piercing weapon = dagger w-yd = power-against = weapon, which we use powerfully (violently against a man.

aUI: E	English
eA	Twice
E-an	Matter-unit, gram
e-ana	Track
eana	tape, =ribbon
eb	WITH
EbO-v	Touch, v, (tasten=feel)
EbtA/v-pAm	Fix-ed
ebzam	double, twofold
Ec	is (by material) e.g.: wood
ed	thru (moving)
Ed	(Medium)means by which
eda	Road
edQ	transition
eg/-i	Between-, inter-; twi-light
egU/m, -w	Physic/al, -s
EgU/m, -w	Chemi/cal, -stry
ei	Spark
EiA	Week
ei-aniod	squash
eidzeLiod	Carrot
eigrO(m-od)	Honey(food)
eijE(od)-kot/-tok	Oil(food), olive/tree
eikEos	Canary-bird
eikot	Lemon
eikrE	Gold
ei-m	YELLOW
eirE	Copper
eiriOio	Dandelion
ei-wEgkot	apricot
eirOjE(-tonod)	beer, (-barley)
eiyvE	Wax
ejE/-n, -v	Stream, river, flow

aUI: E	English
ej(L)u	(female)twin
EjU-m	TRU/th, e
EjUrO-v	Belie/f, -ve
-wyvs	dogma
EjUv(-s)	Prove, (proof)
EjUO-m, -v	Sincer/ity, -e, feel-
ejvu	boy-twin
ek (-)	OVER(-), sur-
ek-a	over-space (e.g. in tunnel)
ek-av	over-go, surmount
ekanad	Ladder
ekatiO(s)	overview, (chart)
ekbirE	Aluminum
ek(jE)da	over-pass, (bridge) viaduct
ekdrEm	expensive
ekE(v)	Air-current; blow=v.
ekfUI	title
eki	Planet
eki	Moon
ekiA	Month
eki-A	planet-time
eki-a;-e (etc.)	planet 1; 2, near sun, etc.
ekrE	magnesium
ektE/m, -v	Light(=not heavy), -en
ektev	overcome
ekzUm-Q	especial-ly
e-Led	Two-wheel, Bicycle
eL	(moving) around
eLiod(-to)	Beans (seed)
em	MOV-ing, -able
Em-Um	Material-istic
En	MASS (of Matter)
ena-m	Flat/ness, Plane

aUI: E	English
enad	Plane (tool)
enaE	PAPER
ena(grO)mod	(sweet)pancake
enan	area
en-anos	platyhelminthes
enas	Leaf=sheet, pane
enaz	Field
enEs	layer, slab
engad	pan
EniO(d)	Scale(s) (=tool)
EniO-v	(mass-)weigh
enrEs	Plate
en(t)gad	Pan
eO	emotion
Eo-m	Natur-al
Eo-na	landscape
Ers	goods, wares
es (-vUiOv)	MACHINE(type-write)
Es	THING (a material thing that can be put in a bag)
-vU-v	reif/ication, -y
Esga(m)	Full/ness(crammed)
EsgU/-v	Mean/ing
/-vo	myth
et-	(move-)toward, ad-, ap-
etbav	acquire
Etbe(v)	(to)Touch="berühren", contact
etdE/v, -d, -U	Appl/y, -iance, -ication
etgU-v	STUDY
etkev, etkEv	Jump; spring
EtkE-v	evaporat/ion, -e
etkos	rabbit
etO-v	tend/ency
et-UI-v	Request
et-viOv-id	beacon
et-viOv(s)	Mark

aUI: E, F	English
etviOv sev	beckon
etvU-v	inten/tion, -d
etwOv	take heart
E-tyf-gav-Q	metabolism [1]
eU-z	MOTION
ev	MOVE, intr.
Ev	DO
EvgUv(s)	Notice
evUis-a	Movie-theater
Evyjed	catalyst
ew	Energy
Eyje	matter-change
Eyo-m(see yomE)	Inorganic Mineral
EZ	ELEMENT
Eza	Hydrogen, H
EzA-jEn	Carbo(n)-hydrate
Eze	Helium, He

= Element Atomic No. 2 = e 2

EzE	Nitrogen, N
EzE-oz-E	protein [2]
EzeA	Iron, Fe, (At.No.26)
EzI	Oxygen,), (At.No.8)

F f

"f" indicates: pointing gesture — "This" (finger and lips)

fa, -m	Here, present
fA, -m	Now, present
fAg:...	now happening:... (after e.g. past story)
fam	unique
fAo/m	You/th, -ng
fajU/m	unique identity
fat	Hither, here to
faU(m) (see:afU(m)	Individual

[1] "Stoff-wechsel," matter exchange

[2] nitrogen-cell-matter

aUI: F	English
fAvm	New
fAvUI/gs	News/-paper
fayt	Hence, herefrom
fE, -n	THIS, THESE
fEbyf	Miscellany
fem, -vU -v	Automat/ic, -ion, -ize
fEm	Such
fev	TAKE
fiA	Today
fiAt	To-morrow
fIz	vowel
fmUma	personal life style
fnAm	modern
fnu-m	WE = US, OUR
fnuga-brO	home-love, patriotism
fnUgu	Expert
fnUI, -m	fam/e, -ous
fOvAm	aware
frAvm	fresh
fu, -m	I = ME, MY = mine
fufU	Myself
fUma	self-style of life
-fU-m	-SELF, -concerned
fUd	SO
fuga	Home
fUI	NAME
-drE(v)	check(-pay)
-mUz	denominator
fUIs	pronoun
fUjU(m), -v	identi-ty, (-cal), -fy V
fUmO-m	self conscious/ness
fUs(Um)	Subject(ive)
fU-tyb-zO	dissociation
fUvyo-v	suicide, v.
fUwe/-m, -v	Free/dom, -v.
fyd	nevertheless
fyfbrU-v	compromise

aUI: F, G	English
fyrtyfve	projection (psy.)
fyrUI-v	confess/ion
fyrvO	guilt-feeling
fyrvU-m	guilt-y
fyrvUIv	accuse
fyt-YrzwYvO	phobia

Gg

"g" as in go, gut, get)

"g" indicates	"(with)—IN(side)"
-g (e.g. rU-g)	adv.-ending, e.g. well
ga	ROOM
gad	Container
gaf (-gaf)	OR (either—or)
gaizos	Mosquito
gak	Ceiling
gam-U	interior-ity
gAn	rate
gav	Contain
gayf, -Qm	instead of, vicarious
gayfs/-e, -ev	Substitut/e, -ion, -e, v.
gayk/-uygE	floor/-carpet
/-kygz	covering
gaz/-ayn	MIDDLE, center
ge(-v)	Ent/rance, -er, v.
gE	CONTENTS
ge (-) -vu(-v)	BETWEEN, inter-mediat/or, -e
gebana	Angle
(-mUn)gUw	trigonometry
gebanu/m	International/al
gebena	(inner)corner, 'Ecke)
gebwe/-v	pinch
ged	Vehicle, CAR
gegUa	high school
gEm-U	Full-ness
gEs	Trunk (suitcase)

aUI: G	English
gEtok	Stem
gE-tyv	absorb
gEv	Fill
gEz	nucleus
gez	Interval, gap
ge-zwE/v	interrupt/ion
gIO, gIU	insight, intellect
(kE)gizos	Housefly
gjE	sap
gjEkE	froth
gjEL	blister
gjEm-Q	Wet-ness
gjEv	moisten, dip
gLa/d, -v	bowl, confine
gLaned	piston
gLIjEv	gargle, v.[1]
gnam	inwardly spacious
gnEm	full-stuffed
gnub/as, -Q	institut/e, -ion
gnUr-m	Perfect/ion
gO, -v	TASTE, -v.
gode(v)	Digest/ion
god-jE	stomach juice
godz	Stomach
-ana	guts (intestine)
-bibygrE	(bicarbonate) soda
-kE-v	belch, burp, v.
gog/-ev	Heart, throb
/-bOm	Intimate
gOke	% per cent
gOki	‰ per mill
gOrm	Tasty
gOz/-ev	Tongue, lick
gQ/m-Q	inward/ness, -ly
grA-m	punctual/ity
grab/-ev, -em	Order, -v., -ly
-Ax-mQ	corresponding time order, respective /ness, -ly
grav	fit-in

aUI: G	English
grEm/ev	Alkali/ne, -ze
grizos	Bee
grO-m	Sweet/ness
grOjE-tok	syrup-tree(=maple)
grOms	Candy
grOnod	Cake
grOtrOkEv-Q	ferment, -ation[2]
grO(trOkE)yio	yeast
grU-m	integr/ity, -ous (inner good/-ness)
gu	inhabitant
gU-m, -v	KNOW/ledge, -ing, -v.
gUfu-m, -s	special/ist, -ic/-ty
guga-s	interior-, furniture
gUa	School
gU-hUte-v	research, -v.
gUO-m	Conscious/ness
gU-pnUI-v	lecture
gUru-m	sage
gUse-v	inform/ation
gUte-v	Observ/ation
gutve(v)	motiv(at)e
gUv	KNOW
gUviv	enlighten
gUvu	phil. doctor=Ph.D.
gUv-UmtiO	examination
(-) gUw/-u, -Um	(-)Scien/ce, -tist, -tific
gUw-tve/-as	experiment/-lab
gUw-tvem	experimental
-tUvma	diagram
guygs	Shirt
gvav	fill
gvU	In fact
gvuyg	underpants

[1] inner-round-sounding-liquid that makes noise inside (the mouth) by being rolled around

[2] sugar-to-wine + gas (CO_2)

[3] fungus = ynyio

aUI : G, H	English
gwad	Chest = box
gwUtrO-m, -v	enthus/iasm, -iastic, -e
gwUvu-m	geni/us, -al
gybwe, -UyrQ	stress, neurosis
gyde-v	inhibit/ion, -e
gyE, -v	Hole, dig
gyE-d	digger = tool
gyEga	cave
gyEL, -da	hollow sphere, tunnel
gyELd	drill = tool
gyELzam	concave
gyEm/-os	Hollow/coelenterate
gygev	throb
gygtev	Put-on (dress)
gykboyg	Sock(s)
gyrvYgUyro [1]	paranoia
gyrytev [2]	desert, v.
gytwe, -v [3]	Strain, V

Hh

"h" denotes	"Question"
ha ?	WHERE
had ?	wherethru ?
hat ?	Where to, whither ?
ha(te)v	seek, (where it is)
hA ?	WHEN ?
hayt ?	Wherefrom, whence ?
hE ?	WHAT ?
hEm	which(thing), what kind?
hE-Qg	suppose..., what if...
hEn ?	which things ?

hI ? . . . , hI? Question, . . . , eh ?
ends sentence with normal order: bu dov, hI? "You eat, eh ? = Do you eat ?"

hiOv	gaze = gape
hIv	Ask
hLu ?	what woman ?
hnA ?	how much time? how long ?
hnAn ?	how often ?
hnE ?	how much ?
hnEn ?	how many ?

aUI : H, I	English
hO(v), -m	Doubt, v., -ful
hQ ?	under what conditions ?
hu - n ?	WHO ?, which people ?
hU ?	WHY ?
hUd ?	HOW ?
hUm ?	What kind of ?
hUt ?	What for ?
hUtev	search for
hUtO-m	curio/sity, -us
hvu ?	what man
hUv-O	wonder (-feeling)
hyt ?	What from, why ? how come, "wieso ?"
hytbe-v	problem-put
hytkav-O-v	suspense-feel, (-ing)
hytUv-Q	investigat/e, -ion

Ii

"i"	LIGHT = bright
I	SOUND (heard)
i	THREE
I	EIGHT
ia-m	South-erly
i-an	photon (=light unit)
iA - m, - Ugs	DAY, -ly, -book=diary
iaigrO-m, -v	chocolat/e, -y, V.
iai-m	brown/ness
iau(-m)	Southman, Tropian = Negro
iAz - em, - ev	HOUR-ly, -- do
id	Lamp
Id	Music instrument

[1] g-yr=inner evil, v-yg=make outward; paranoia = outward projection of inner destructive drives, consciously denied.

[2] g-yr = in-bad, yt-ev = from-go, away from friend in-a-bad (situation)

[3] g=inside, yt=away from, we = power-move = thrust: in strain we try (inwardly) to flee, but are tied on as by a rubber-band.

aUI: I	English
I-da	sound-channel
idE-m	translucent/material
idU-m	intellect-ual
iE -	FIRE
- as	-place
-bEk	volcano
iEd	lighter (fire-tool)
iEdE-m	combustible, fuel
iEga	Stove
iEm, -U	Hot, Heat
iEm/-an	calory
/-gad	oven
/-iod	(hot) vegetables
iEpAs	a Burn, N.
iEtE	ashes
iEv/	Burn, V.
-ayn	focus
-do	fuel
i-gebana-m	triang/le, -ular
I-gUw	sound science, acoustics
ii-m	Green/ness
iianiot	cucumber
iibEjEos	Frog
iimoLE-dzeL-ot	avocado
IirOwE	emerald
ijiO(va)d	Camera
ijiOv(s)-u	Photograph, N.-er
ikA-do	Noon-lunch
ilas	Lightbulb
im	Bright
Im	Sounding
inam	3-dimensional, stereo
In-an	volume
I-nanab-ev	braid, V.
I-ne-krO-z	scherzo
io-m, -v	PLANT-like, live as P.
iO, -v	SIGHT, SEE
IO-v	HEAR/ing
iod	Vegetables

aUI: I	English
iOd	Eyeglasses
-nanos	cobra
IOd	hear-aid
iOdE-m	Glass-y, transparent
iodos	herbivore
iodz	salad
I-oged(-os)	octopus (animal)
io-gUw	botany
iO-gUw	optics
io-ii(mE)	chlorophyll
io-jEod	(herb) Tea
iO-mab	Pattern
ioriO-v	Bloom
iot [1]	vegetable-fruit
iOvu	beholder
IOvu, -n	hearer, audience
IOvU	Acoustics
iO-vUv	visualize
io-wanoz [2]	plant-fiber
io-wygE [3]	cellulose
io-yk	root
iOz/-jE, -v	EYE-tear/weep
iOz-yg	eye-shade
IOz/-jE	EAR-wax
IOz-yg	ear-muffs
IrEg(Id)	Bell (sound tool)
iriO-m	Splend/or, -id
i-rO [4]	light-joy (photo-esthetics ?)
I-rO [5]	sound-joy (phon-esthetics ?)
is	light-spot

1 io = plant (light-life), ot = fruit, kot = tree fruit. iot are e.g. cucumbers, kot e.g. cherries

2 "plant-tendon" wanoz = tendon (c.f. fiber)

3 plant-powerful(w) outward (yg) wall-matter(E)

4 Webster knows no such concept. We become aware of "irO" (light-joy) e.g. after a long arctic night, when the first light-ray like a groping finger, reaches across the horzon.

5 "IrO" Sound-joy, e.g. the first bird's voices at dawn after a long silent night.

aUI : I, J	English
ita	West
itA-do	Evening-supper
(It)vU-v	Suggest/ion by sound
iU/s	Idea
iUv	Comprehend
iv	Shine
i-ves	light machine, generator
I (v)	(to) SOUND
IviOvs	(Music-)Note
Iwyd	rifle
iyi(v)	twinkle
iyiOv	blink
iyO-m	blind/ness
IyO-m	deaf/ness
izodos	insectivore
(i)zos	Insect
(zos =	arthropod=spider, crab &c)
izos	firefly

Jj

"j" denotes:	'Same, Equal, even, horizontal, (liquid)
jAe	Rhythm
jAg	WHILE
jam	SAME
jAm	Regular(ly timed) (at same time)
jamAg	immediately
jamev	imitate
jamtazU-m	consisten/cy, -t
janav	allign
japIz-ev	alliterat/ion, -e
jatbem	Parallel
jA-UI	Verse
jA-vUIgs	periodical (journal)
jazQ-m	symmetr/y, ic
jE-m	LIQUID, (water)
jEbE-na	goo, -swamp
jEbE-v	smear, V.
jEd	Spoon

aUI: J	English
jEda	channel
jEdak	aqueduct-bridge
jEdev-u	Swim-mer (thru water)
jEg	Bottle
jEg-(nam)-iot	(big) gourd
jEga	Basin
jEgad	Bucket
jEgas-yt	Vessel -- tank
jEged-a	Boat-harbor
(jEged-)bove/-v	row, V
-d	oar
jEgev	Swim (in water)
jEgnos	Odontoceti (toothwhale)
jEk	Cloud
jEka-m	LEVEL, horizontal
jEkaz	(river)bank
jEkda	bridge
jEkE	Steam
jEkEbos	tame duck
jEkEos	Duck, N.
jEkev-d	float, (-N.)
jE-ki,	comet,
-os	seastar(fish)
jEkyt	spring, N., well
jELbE	Island
jELe-v	Whirl
jELkyk	Wave
jem	steady
jEn	WATER
jEna/	Sea
-kEos	-gull
-u	-man
jEn-bydwu	marine (-sailor)
-bydwuk	navy officer
na-, ne-, ni-. . 1, 2	1st(=admiral), 2nd (=captain). . .
jEnbydwun	navy

aUI: J	English
jEn-Ez	hydrogen
jena	Square
jEngad	Tub
jEnged	Ship
jEnkE(b)os	(tame) Goose
-jEnos	-big fish
jE-n-vogz[1]	liver [1]
(jE-)priv	wash (with water)
jEnyEos	Sponge
(jE-)nynyE/yv	seep
-gEtyv-Q[2]	osmosis
jEn-ygana	Coast, (water-border)
jEn-yt	well, N.
jEogz	Kidney
jEonos	Whale
jEos	FISH
jEoyg	(fish-)Scales
jEpiv(s)	Polish, N.
(jE)priv	wash
jErE-m	mercur/y, -ial
jEroii	tea plant
jEs	(a) Drink, N.
jEsgU/-m, -s	Synonym/y, -ous, --
jEtbEv	freeze (solid)
jEte-v	Current, -- flow
jEtgad	Cup
jEtgo-v	(Im-)bib/ation, -e
jEtked	Pump
jEtkE-m, -v	Boil/ing, -V.
jEtO-v	thirst
jEtwEv	freeze (hard)
jEtyg	fount
jEtyk	waterfall
(jE)tykyvev	to sink
jEuga	Bath
jEv (-s)	DRINK, N.

aUI: J	English
jEvogz[1]	gland
(jE-)vUtiOd	(ink-)Pen
jEvyt(ev)	spout
jEwE/(-d)-ryvev	Ice/-slide, (-skate)
jE-waubos	sea/l (-dog)
jE-ygte-v	Drain
jEyt	font
jE-yte-v	outflow
jEywE/-gyEmos	Jelly/fish(=coelenterate)
jEz-ev	Drop, -drip
jI/m-UI	Homonym/-y, -ous, --
jimaL-m	equator-ial
jina	cube
jIOd	mirror
jiOm/-ev, -s	Look-alike, Copy, N.
jiOs	Likeness (by nature)
jiOv-s	Represent="darstellen" de/pict(ure)
jLA-m	periodic(ity)
jLo = L5	Lagrange, (same distance from all gravities)
jnA-do(-v)	diet, V.
jniO-/Ed, -v	Weigh/t-scales, -V.
jnoz	tissue (bio.)
jnUm, (-v, -z)	Average, (V., N.)
jnUrm	Normal
jnUz/-gUw	the mean, (statistics)
/-mUnUv	stat. calculate
jOm (-ev)at	LIKE (to), (simulate)
-jOm	-oid
jOv	resemble
jomz	Bio-type:
na-jomz, ne-, ni-,	kingdom, phylum, class

1 jE-n-vogz = big(gest) gland
jEvogz = gland (liquid-/secreting active life-inside part (body part)
n = big-(gest)

2 gEtyv = absorb
nynyE-gEtyv = seep-absorb = osmose

aUI: J	English
nu-, no-, nA, nE-, nI-jomz	order, family, genus, species, race
jQm	constant
jrut/-ev, -s	Reward, N.
jrutryv, -s	deserve; merit
jrutryv-wam	worthy
jrutyv	earn (=be rewarded)
jUc	is (=equals)
jUf	Even (e.g. even, if) conj.
(yr-)jUIv	equivocate
jU-m, -v	EQUAL/ity, -V.
jUma-m	typ/e, -cal
jumos	chimpanzee
jUx-Um	logic-al
jvEv	Give to drink, 'tränken"
jvOv	similarize
jvOxU-m, -v	analog/y, -ous, -ize
jvUv-Q	equat/e, -ion
jwUm-U	just-ice
jwUr, -m, -U	(moral-)RIGHT, Adj, righteousness
jwUr-bram	appropriate
-vyov	execute
jwUs, -ev, -Q	Law, -sue, -suit
jwUs/(-fUwe)-dyvQ	license
jwUskas	court of law
jwUsku/-s, -v	judge/ment, -V.
jwUsOm	Loyal
jwUsu	Lawyer
jwUsU(-m)	Justice (legal)
jwUs-vyov	execute (legally)
jwU-vUv	justify
jwyz/-ev, -Qm, /-u	Rule, -V., regular Ruler
jyfev-u	imitate, -r
jyktev	teeter
jyktE/-v /-w	Balance equilibrium
jym ('slang')	Different
jypAz(ev)	rime, V= rhyme

aUI: J, K	English
jyrted	rod (punish)
jyrtedrE	penal-fine
jyrtev	Punish
jyrts	Punishment
jytLu	(motherly) sister
jyttUm	Mutual
jytu	Sibling, Brethren
jytU	brotherhood
jytvu	Brother
jytyvu	Sister

Kk

"k" denotes:	"Above, over, high up
k- (prefix)	superior, supreme"
kab	On
kad(-)	Across, (sur-)
kadav	go across
kad-ov	Survive
kag	in & above (as God)
kajE-yd	Rain (-umbrella)
kam; -A -gnubas	HIGH (e.g. star), weather academy
kam-gU/a, -vu	college, professor
kamQ	climate
kan-t, -yt	Sky,-ward, -from
kana-m	Height, high (e.g.) mount
kan/as, -Es	Column, Post (pillar)
kaniod	asparagus
katav	go over
kav/-ayn	Stand/-point
kayrei-v	Lightning, -strikes
kayrOI-v	Thunder, V.
kaz-ev	Top, -V.
kazd-ev	Lid, -cover, V.
kazog	Shoulder

aUI: K	English
kcangUa	university
kE-m	GAS (e.g. Air), -eous
keb	upon (moving)
kE-binto	puff rice
kEbio	Cotton
kEbnos	turkey
kEbos	Fowl, Chicken
Ked	Trans-, over-
kEd-ev	Wing, -fly
ked-vuyg-ev	disguise
kEdvev	cast, hurl, shoot
kEdynbos	bat
kEdz-Em	Feather-y, fluffy
kEgev	fly (e.g. balloon)
kE-ged	Airplane
kEgEv-Q	inflat/e, -ion
kEgjE/m, -n	Bubble(s)/y, -foam
kei	meteor
kEId	Whistle
kEjE/-v	fog, distill
kELas	balloon
kELdvev	fling
kEL-tswed	sling (whirl-)
kem	Smooth
kEm	Gaseous
kEma	atmosphere
kEmO-v	Smell, (sense)
kEmO-z	Nose
-nos	elephant
kEmOz-(kos) -wyd(-nos)	rhinoceros
kEn-Om	AIR-y
kEnId	(pipe-) organ(music)
-kEnos	-big bird
kEoga(-s)	nest (-place)
kE-ogz/-yro	Lung/s, (-pneumo/nia)
kEom	aerobic
kEos	BIRD
k-Eo-w/U, -u	magic/-ian
ke-rE	magnesium
k-etgUvu	grad-student
kE-tmO/-v	sniff, -V.
kEtO-v	thirst V. (for air, gasp)
kEtswe/(-d), -v	Throw, (sling), -V.
kev	soar
kEv	become air, gasify
kEwe, -d	Wind, Sail
kfA /, -v, -vQ	again; repe/at, -tition
-IyIv-u	stutter-er
ki	STAR
k-iE-v	Flame, V.
kiE(gLa)d	(round) Kettle
kiE(n)id	Candle (Torch)
kiE-wam	flammable
ki-gUw-u, -v	astronom/y, -er, -ize
kin-tygle	galaxy
kLanas	(round) column
kLĒz	lump
-klot	-round tree fruit
kLuga	dome
kLyg/ed, -ev	envelop, wrap
kna-m	Heaven-ly, -great
knand-ev	broom, -sweep
knāu	angel
kne-m	super-speed, -quick
knE-v	Too (much) do
-uwev, -vEv	over-work, -do
knev-s	gain, N., win
knE-viOv	exaggerate
kni-v, knIv	glare, din
knO, -m, -v	exuberan/ce, -t, -feel-
knot	big tree fruit
knu, -v	King, reign
knuga	Palace
knu-kEos	eagle
knUr, -m	worth, -precious
knUrms	Standard
knuwa	Kingdom

aUI : K ...	English
knuw-ev	GOVERN/ment
knuwz	(Political) Party
knuyg	mantle, cloak
knynE	Dust
knyr-ykeos	dragon
kO	sublime-feeling
	Queen
kog	Head (of body)
k-oged	Arm
koged-yg	Sleeve
kogzeL	Collar
kogiod-	cabbage
kog-(n)oged	cephalopod, (squid)
-riOrio, -trioriO	cauliflower, broccoli
kog(e)z	Neck
kog-wyg	helmet
kog-yg	hat
kog-ywd	pillow
kom-u	noble-man
kOm	Noble (feeling)
k(os)wyd	Horn
-kot	-tree fruit
kOtev	regard (highly)
kozvos	Lion
kQm	boom-(=high state)
kra	elysium
kraz	peak
-krE	-noble-metal (gold)
krI-kEos	lark
(k)riOv	admire
krO-m	Joy-ful, glad
krO-I (v)	Laugh/ter
krO-iA-v	holiday, celebrate
krO-Las	pearl
krOn	Delight
krOv-U	Enjoy-ment
(k)rOvs	Fun
krOwE	Diamond

aUI: K ...	English
krQ	hausse
krU-m, -v	excel/lence, -lent, -V.
kryfa	Eden
krypnU-m	arcan/um, -e
kryvO	conceptivity for sublime (starry sky)
ksev-u	Ride-r, (horseman)
ku	Lord, Sir
kU, KU	god, GOD
kubrO	Mercy
KU-brO	God's grace
kUg-u	Head-man
kuga	Tower
kUga	Church, Temple
-u; -knu	minister, priest; Pope
kugaz	Roof
kUgjEv	baptize
kUgs	gospel
kUgyg	Crown
kUI, -v -u	Logos, preach-er
kUiO-v -u	contemplat/ion, -e, -er (= mystic)
kUit-u-m	ideal, -ist, -ic
kU-krO	bliss
kU-kvad	altar
k U-ma(- m)	ritual (- adj)
kUm/Ugs	Holy/Book = Bible
kUm-UI/-v-u	sermon/-preacher
kun-ev	Manage/r
kUO-v	Glor/y, -ify
kup, -ev	Face, V.
kupyg	Cheek
kupyk	Chin
kUr-eijE/v	Anoint, -oil
kUriA-v	holiday, -celebrate
kUrO	virtue
kUru	saint
kUrUI-v	oath-swear
kUrUI-vo	legend

aUI: K ...	English
kUrU/m, -s	Hol/iness, -y, shrine
kUrUv	hallow
kU-tak, -iA	Resurrection, Easter
kU-t-kna-iA	Ascension day
kUtoe, -iA	Nativity, Christmas
kUtOr-v	Pray/er
kUtU-m	Religio/n, -us
kU-tvu	Godson, Christ
kUvrO	Piety
kUw	Authority
kuyg ('bvuyg)	Coat (suit o'clothes)
kUz	Head (spiritual)
kvad	Table
kve	victory
kvei	lightning
kvEmO-v	fragra/nce, -te, emit smell
kvetgUv-u	professor
kvEv	give air, ventilate
kvu(v)	direct/or, V/N.
kvypOv	surprise, V.
kwE-v	WALL, V.
kwei	(lightning) Flash
kwev-s	Command, (-N)
kwQ-v	mastery
kwu	Powerman, boss
kwU-m	Control, (N), main, adj.
kwuga	castle
kwUIv	persuade
kwuv-Q	dominat-ion
kwU-v	Control
kwyd-os	horn-animal (bull, stag)
kwyhI, -m	Responsib/ility, -le
kwyU	Fate
kwyvU	obligation
kyb	beyond

aUI: K, L	English
kybA-m	timeless
kybe/-m, -v	transcend/ence, -ent, -V.
k(yb)rUm, kyfrUm	Excellent (beyond, above others)
kydaz	Bottleneck
kyfa-kEos	paradise-bird
kyftU-v	compet/ition, -e
(kyf see kyb)	
kyfwO, -U	triumph, sway
kyge-d, -v	Cover, V.
kyg-nUr/-m, -v	digni/ty, -fied, -fy
kygus	Mantle
kyg-wyvQ-m	luxur/y, -ious
kygz	Cover (-part)
kykboyg	Boot
kyke-v	Bob up & down/movement
kyktad	throne
kykvE/m, -s	Spring/y, (elastic), --
kykzEv-d	Saw, (-tool)
kypO/-v	surprise (-feel)
kypOwyU	adventure
kypums	Miracle
kyUw-ev	Destin/y, -e
kyvu	Lady

L

"L" (to avoid confusion of l with I) denotes: "Roundness, around"

La-m	ROUND/ness
LafUsUI/n	essay, treatise
Lamz	knob
Lana-m	Cylind/er, -ric
LanE/s, -v, -wyd	-club, v., weapon
Las	Ball
Le	Turn, N.
Led, -yg	Wheel, -tire

aUI: L	English
LeL-(d)ryve/d/v[1]	roller-skate/s
LeL-v	Roll/er
Lem	Turning
Lena	Disk
LEs	bullet
Le-v	Turn
Lid	lamp (bulb)
LiOdE	lens
Lod, -Em	Bacon, -fat, adj.
Lodbos-	Pig-, Pork-
-woged	-ham
LodjEbE	gravy
Lom	female
Logana	belt (around body)
Logz	Waist
LQ	circumstance
Lu(s)	She (woman)
Luga	-igloo
LUv, -Am, -Q	consider/ing, -ation
LybE-v	insulat/ion, -e
LydyrE-v	insulate against danger
LyEs	hollow sphere
Lyg - ev	bulge, N, V
Lygaz	rim, margin
Lygana-v	Circumference, surround
Lygena	wide belt, girdle
Lygev	surround
LygEv	wrap
Lyiz-	spot
-ozvos	leopard
Lynos	coccus
Lyntok	round bush
Lypoz	Buttocks
Lyps	hump
Lyp-ukbos	camel
Lyz, -m	whole, -adj.

[1] LeL = roller, LeLv = to roll, yvev = to slide or slip, ryvev = to slide-well (r) d-ryvev = to slide with a tool, tool-slide, e.g. to skate, LeL-dryvev = to roller-skate; LeL-dryved = the roller-skate-tool, the skates.

aUI: M ... Mm	English
"m" denotes:	Quality, type, kind of
-m	-qualified, -ious, Adj. ending
ma, -m, -v	FORM, -al, — V
mA	SITUATION
mab	Configuration
mag	POSITION
mAg=Qg=	provided that, if
maL-v	CIRC/LE, -ulate
mAL	Circumstance
-maLg	situation in which I am
marbu	Secretary
mayvE	plastic
mEz	Sort
mi-m	COLOR-ed
miE	HEAT
miv, -E, -d	Paint, N, -brush
mO, -m	sensitiv/ity, -e
mOz	trait
mQ-tnak-ev	determin/ant, -e
mQ-v	defin/ition, -e
mQ-vU-v	qualif/ication, -y
-mu	-ist
mU(z)	QUALITY
mUd	Manner, Mode, way
mUIs	adjective
mUma	Style
mUn	NUMBER
mUn-gUw	Mathematics
mUnI v	to Count
mUnU/v	Calculat/ion, -e, figure out
mUv-U	Descri/be, -ption
mUz	kind, N

aUI: M,N	English
myt	THAN
mytta	Range, Scope, Gamut
myz	Quite, just

———— N n ————

"n" denotes: Quantity, "lots," plenty, big, many, much, multi-, plural

-n — Collective, many together (e.g. u-n = many persons together, "people")

n- (e.g. no5) - th (e.g. fifth) (used for ranks & classifications, e.g. na-jomz = first-group = kingdom; ne-, ni-, nu-, no-, nA-, nE ... jomz = phylums, class, order, family, genus, species 1,2,3,4,5,6,7

nabydwyk — first officer=general

na — DIMENSION

-na e.g. Eng(Li)na — -land, e.g. England

na- — macro-, big-
nA — long-time

na, nA — First; Sixth

nA-brO — faithful love

nAd(s) — (Big) Clock

na-ekiA — First month: January

nag — AMONG

na-iA — No. 1 day = Sunday

nA-litok — Pine tree

nA-jomz — genus
na-jomz — (bio)kingdom
nAjQ — fidelity
nA-jvU/-m, -v — persever/ance, -ant, -e

nakiA — Summer

nakot — Apple

nam — Big, large

nam-dzogta-kEos — toucan

nAm-Q — Frequent-ly

namiot — pumpkin

aUI: N ... 2	English
namLot	melon
namto	corn
nAm-Um	Usual

nAn — often
nan — km, kilometer
nan- — long-

nanab — Canvas, -

nanabE-v — Weave, V

nan-bEjEos — salamander

nand-ev — Brush — V

nan-jEos — eel
(nan)kEmOz-nos — elephant
(nan)kogz-jEn-kEos — swan
(nan)kogz-kEos — crane (bird)
(nan)kogz-nes — giraffe
nanod — noodle
nan-dzogta-kEos — stork
(taim)nan-oged-kEos — flamingo

nanos — Snake

nan-vekted — crane (tool)
nArs — supply

nArsga — Store

nase-v — Transport

nA-tedEv — accustom
natek-da — stair-way
nA-tiO-v — gaze

nato — Wheat

nA-Uma — Habit

nav-Q — Run, N

navUma-m — Custom-ary

nA-wo — stamina
nA-ydO, /m, v — resent/ment, -ful, -V
naz — region

naz-tsev — Distribut/ion, -e

ne, -v — SPEED, hurry

nE — MUCH

ne — second = 2d
ne-jomz — phylum

aUI : N...	English
ne-ekiA	February
nE-ekiA	July (No. 7 month)
nE-ged	truck
ne-iA	Monday
nE-iA	Saturday
nE-jomz	species
nEjUrO	Credit
nEk	MORE
UjnEk...UjnEk	the more...the more
nEkbrO-v	prefer/ence
nEke-v	Increase
nEk-mUn	majority
nEk-rOg	rather
nEk-rU- tvEv	improve
ne-kyftU-v	speed-race
nem	Quick = FAST
nEm	VERY
nEn	MANY
nEn-kog(gyEmos)	hydra(coelenterate)
nEnoged(gyEmos)	polyp(coelenterate)
nEn(v)ev	multiply (tr)
nEruwem	diligent
nEs	Item
nEsgU, -m	ambigu/-ity, -ous
nEsyU-m	Industr/y, -ious
ne-tnO-m	eager/ness
nEv	augment
nEzavd	Comb
ni	brightness
nI	loudness
ni, nI	Third, Eighth
nia-m	tropic/s, -al
nia-tok	palm tree
-nId	big music instrument
nidU-m	intelligen/ce,-t
niEm-an	calory (kg-)
ni-, nI-jomz	(bio) class, -race
nim, nIm	Brilliant, Loud
nio-dov	Grass, graze

aUI : N...	English
niO-d	Measure-tool
nio-ba	park (garden)
niObga	museum
nio-etkizos	grasshopper
niO-v	Measure, v.
nioz	hay
niv	shine brightly, glare
nI-v	Loudly roar, shout
nI-(tyk)zwEv	crunch
nIwyd	Gun, cannon
nO	ardor
nod-E	BREAD-dough
nodEL	dumpling
nodzEvz	molar
no-ekiA	May
n-ogta	snout
noiA	Thursday
noii-od	lettuce
no-jomz	(bio-)family
nosdos	bear
nosyg	fur
-not	big fruit
noyg-/E-bos	HAIR/-wool, -sheep
noyg-buizos	louse
-zvE-d;v	shave/s, —V
nozvos	Tiger
nQ	plenty
e.g. (Brit-)nu(m)	(britain-(-)nation-al
nu-m	THEY (them)- their
nU see: nUz	
nu	fourth
nub-u	Compan/y, -ion
nuba-u	TOWN-, Citizen
nube/v	conven/tion, -e
nu-brOpAm	popular
nUbza/m, -w	Complex, Adj., N
nu-ekiA	April
nuga	hall
nuged	bus
nUgsa	Library

aUI: N ...	English
nugta	Gate
nUgz	Chapter
nUI, -v	Language, -talk-much
nu-iA	Wednesday
nUIvo	Novel, Story
nu-jomz	(bio-)order
nu-kwu	demagog
nuLb	Club (Social)
num	THEIR
(rU)nUm	Wise (good)
numI-v	Account
numos	gorilla
nunba	city
nUr/-m, -Ov	Valu/e, -able (-worthy) to value V
nUrs	treasure
nUrUm	sage
nUrv	be valid, gelten
nutga	Gate
nuvrU-m	mor/es, -al
nuvUs-Um	Cultur/e, -al
nuwa-z	state(=nation), county
nuwe/-m	Politic/s, -al
-brUje	treaty
nuvsga	Factory
nUz-Qm	Quanti/ty, -tative
nybikEd	cigar
nybikEos	raven
nyEd	NET
nyEdzos	Spider
nyELb	Chain
nyje/v, -wam	var/y, -iable (math)
nykam	Deep
nykIv	groan
nym(=ynam)	(slang for) Tiny

aUI: N, O	English
nyn	many-little
nyne-v	swarm
nynE-v	Powder
nynjE-v	sweat
nyn-oikLot	mulberry
nynto-aikot	pomegranate
nyntod	cereal
nyntokot	fig
nyntoz	meal-flour
nyntygvav	strew
nynwE-z	Sand-grain
nynyE/d, -v, -yv	sieve, strain/er, -V, seep
nynzEv	crumble, disintegrate
nynzod	Flour
nyrcEvs	Monster
nyrtcyvs	disaster
nyrjEos	Shark
nyrO-	agony
-kyUw	the tragic
-UIviO	tragedy
nyrvO-v	Trouble
nyrwo /m, -v	Viol/ence, -ent, -ate
nyz	whole N
nyzgrUvQ	integrati/ng (on)
nyzUm	entire

O o	
o	LIFE
o	FEELING
o, o 5, 10	FIVE, TEN
oa	living space
oA	Age
o-bUzU	bio-classifications (e.g. phylum, genus) taxonomy
oc	'is' (by nature) "grass 'is' green"
o-cEvs	living being
od	FOOD
odgev	Dine, v
odjE-v	Soup, sup

aUI : O	English
odjEbE	sauce
odjEgd	Pot
odLena	Dish
odva-u (see voda-u)	Farmer
o-dyv	tolerate
odz(ev)	Bit(e)
odzevz	incisors
odzEv	Chew
odzEvz	Tooth
Oe	Excitement
Ofuz	ego
og	BODY
oga-v	Walk
ogai/-anyEd	Blood/-vessel
ogE	Flesh
oged, -baz (-yev)	LEG, -knee-(l)
oged-yg	Stocking
ogev	gait
oge-wam-U	skill-(full-ness)
ogiE	fever
ogta/-jE-v	Mouth/-saliva-te
(ogta-jE-)tyg-vev	spit
ogtai	Lips
ogtrew-ev	gymnastics(-do-)
ogU	mind
ogu-u, Um	biolog/y, -ist, -ic
OgUw-Um	Psycholog/y, -ist, -ic
ogwa	Breast
(og)yps	Back (of body)
ogyr	Injury
Ogyr	trauma
ogz	ORGAN (of body)
Oh!	Oh! ?

aUI : O	English
oI	animal voice
oim	Violet (color)
oi i	(plant) LEAF
oii-gEz-iod	leaf-stalk, -celery
oiijE	green tea
oi i-od	spinach
oi-riOio	violet (flower)
Oiv/-Q	SEEM/, Appear/ance
oIv	vocalize
oIvz	Throat
okE/-v	Breath/-e
-Id	flute
okEz	oxygen
Oke = 10^2	Hundred
Oki, Oku = 10^3, 10^4	1000; 10,000
oLE/-m	FAT, adj.
-kot	avocado
-roduv	fat-fry
oLs, oLz	Bulb (plant-)
om, Om	ALIVE, FEELING
Om	decimal
onU	wit
Or, -m	yea, feeling yes, positive
o-ruwe	lifework, profession
os	ANIMAL
osdos	carnivore
OsEz	Id
osga	stable
osgUw/-u,-Um	zoolog/y, -ist, -ic cf. jomz bio-classif.
osLana	sausage
osod	Meat
osyg	fur
osyrga	cage
ot-fev/Q	FRUIT-harvest
Otbe-v	concern
Ote-v	Care, V
Otve(-v)	motiv(at)e

aUI : O	English
OtgU-m, v	INTEREST/-ing, be-ed
Otkev	come = be aroused
otrod	Vitamin
otybe-v	rot
otyg-ev	peel
O-tyge-v	expression
O-tytwe-v	thrill
oU	mind
OU-v-Q	Soul, meditat/e, -ion
OU-typ-oge	re-incarnation
o-uwe	occupation
OU-ytbe-v -vu	psycho-analy/sis, -se, -st
oUz	Brain
ov-Am	LIV/E, -ing partc.
Ov	FEEL
ovrAm	ripe
o-vyjed	enzyme
ow	strength
OwEm	severe
oyg	Skin
oygE	Leather
ogy-Id-ev-u	drum, -V, -er
oyg-mi	complexion
oygyr/O-m	Rash/Itch-y
oygz	skin/-seales
oygzyr/-v, -wam	wound, -V, vulnerable
oyt	EGG
/bi(mE)	albumine
-E	egg-proteins
-ei	yolk
oz	CELL
Oz/-m, -ybyem	NERV/E, -ous
ozev	rip
ozEv-z	Claw
Oz-typve	nerve-reflect
ozvos	Feline, wildcats

aUI: P	Pp English
"p" denotes:	front, before, pre-, ante-, pro-
pa	FRONT
pA, -pA-	PAST; -past in verbs (-ed)
pAc	was, "formerly"
pAg:	introduces verbs in present form but past meaning
-pa(m)	primeval, "Ur-"
pA-gUw, -u, Um	histor/y, -ian, -ic
pakiA	Spring
pa-kog	forehead
pA(m)	Past, 'fore-time'
panEs	ledge
paom	primitive
pAom	Old
pat	forward, ahead
pAtUI	Record (chronicle)
pArtA-m	tradition-al
pav	Precede
pAv-U	Prepar-e, -ation
paz	front-part = tip
paz-tvykav	to tip, tilt
pe-v	Start = begin
pe-bUI	premise
pfa	There
pfA	Then = at that time past, 'damaLs'
pfat	Thereto, thither
pfayt	Thence, Therefrom
pfE-n	THAT, -Those (pron.)
pfiA	yesterday
pfrUI-v	promise (personal)
pfu	that person (he or she)
pI, -n	THE, (-plural)

aUI: P	English
pio	alga(-e)
pItvU-v	Propos/al, -e
piv	glisten
pLev	turn ahead
pma-v	model = mold
pnEk/-ev	MOST, maximize
-mUn	maximum
-kte	platinum
pnEn (pl.)	most people
pne-v	gain, win
pnUIv-Q	propaga/te, -nda
pnum-vEvQ	Public/-ity
-knuw	republic
pnuv/-u	publish-er
pO-v	Expect/ation
podzevz/-os	(front) incisor rodent
pOi-rUI(v)	phony-praise = flattery
prAm	Early
prAv-u	pioneer
prav-u	lead-er
prev	advance
prim-d	CLEAN-er (thing)
priv-u	Clean-er (man)
(jE)priv, -s	Wash, laundry
privE	Soap
prO-v	prospect
prQz	advantage
prUIv	promise
psUIs	article
pU	prinzip = principle
pu	principal N
pUI	preface
pUis	vorbild, = model
pUIs	preposition
pUm-s	Principal adj, -ple
pun-az	prefect-ure
pvev	launch
pwaubos	wolf (timber-)
pwev	prevail
pwu	president
pwUm	predominant
pwUr/(v), -m	Importan/ce (emphasize), -t

aUI: P, Q	English
pydev	prevent, hinder
pygaz	façade
pygnUr	showy rank, = distinction
pyg-ogz	Limb
pygUI-v	pronounce/iation,
pyg-vEv	fake
pyg-(v)Oi-d, v	pre/-text, -tend
pygz	Extremity
pykaz-ev	found/ation
-mQ	basically
(at)pynEk	(at)least
prykO-m, -v	vanity, vain, be —
pyrO-v	premonition -feel
pyrUI-v	warn/-ing

Q

"Q" (sounds Ø, Ö as O in wOrd, 'wQrd' but rounded as in Wörter, Ør, Öhr, coeur) denotes: 'Condition, if', a (transient) state

-Q can replace -U, -Uz e.g. nQ 'plenty' is transient Quantity. nUz; wQ = transient wU = power

(m)-Q	after adj = adverb ending: nem-Q = quickly
(v)-Q	after V = gerund ending: ev-Q = 'the' moving = the motion
Qc	happens to be, 'is' under condition, if
kvad Qc iim =	(the) table is green (if, or while it is painted), but:
nio oc iim =	grass is green (by nature).
Qg	If
Qg-hI	Whether
QL	State = Condition, Circumstance-s around, Umstand
Qm	Conditional
Qv	to work, function & be under conditions

aUI: R Rr..	English
"r"	denotes Positive, Good, Well
-r-(v): Erv!	Imperative: Do! (doing is good)
rA	right time, kairos
raiO-m	rosy-warm (hearted)
ram/-ev; -jEn -riOio	Pur/e, -ify; fresh water lily
rA/m-v	due, time well
raO-m	tact-full
re, -v	Function, V. to f.
rE - m	METAL-lic
rE-ana, -v	Wire, to w.
rE-gad, -ev	can N., to c.
rem	functional
rE-nana	Cable
rEjUrO-(gE)m	faith-ful
rEseva	market
retgUv, -u	Learn, scholar
rEtse-v	Buy
re-v	(to) function
rEv/-a, -u	forge, smith/-y —
rEyk/a, -ev, u	a mine, to —, -r
rEz	proton
ri, rI	gleam, song
riA	feast
rian/E, -os	Silk, -worm
riE/-iv, -m, -v	Warm/th, glow, —,—,
riE/-brOsev	cuddle
riE-jEos*	tuna
rI-izos	cricket
rIkEos	thrush
riO-m -gO	Beaut/y, -iful art-taste
rIO	euphony
rioba	eden
riO-brO	love for beauty
riO-e(v)	Dance, V

aUI : R..	English
riOio/-yEL	Flower/wreath
/-gyEmos	sea-anemone
riO-kEos	peacock
rIO-kEos	nightingale
riO-kogz(-kEos)	swan
rioL	garland
riOma-m	Grace-ful
riO(na)vUma	ceremony
riO(k)rO	(joy) pleasure in beauty
(k)riOv	admire
riOva-v	Stage, to —
riOvga	theater
riOw/U, -u	visual art/ist
rIOw/U, -u	Music, composer
riO-ynkEos	hummingbird
riOzos	Butterfly
ri-v	gleam
rI, -v	Song, sing
ri-yEjU-v	flatter/y
ro, -m, -v	Health, -y, thrive
rO/-m, -v	Pleas/ure, -ant, enjoy
rOb, ag-eb	Harmony, according to
-robE-	organic matter
robEgUw	Agriculture
robEn	Soil
robEnU	troll
rObI	melody
robU, -m, -s, -v	Organi/zation, -c, -sm, -ze
rodu/ga, -v	Cook, Kitchen — V
rOg	gladly, like to
roga	sanitarium
rOiAm	festival
rO-Iv	jubilate, jubeln
rOjE/(Lot)bLot-od /-vkE-m	Wine (berry)grape, food alcohol-ic

* 'warm-fish': the tuna has warming veins.

aUI : R ...	English
rojE-ygrE	vinegar
rOkEmO	perfume
rO-knE-viO-v-u	caricature, V, -ist
rOkU	Virtue
rOm-ybra/m -v, -vu	clown/ish, -V, -N
rO-nI-v	joy whoop,
rOtge-v	Introduc/tion, -e
rov	Thrive
rOv	Enjoy
rOve, -s, -v	Play, -thing, -V
rOvdv/s, -U	Toy, game
rOvs	fun
rOv/-u, -U	Humor/ist, —
rOwE	Gem
rOwU-gUw	esthetics
rOw/U-u, -Uv	Art/ist, —, create —
rOw/um, Um	artistic, esthetic
rQ	good occasion
rQg	luckily
rQL	opportunity
rQm	lucky
ru-m	Mister, gentlemanlike
rU	Goodness = G.
rU-brO	virtue (love for G.)
rUg	well
rU-gEv-Q	fulfil-ment
rUgO	virtue (taste for G.)
rUg-te/rv!-/pAm	welcome! Adj.
rUgUw	ethics
rUI-v-s	Praise, V, Compliment
rUi-m	ideal
rU-m	GOOD
rUmti-v	Ad(vertise/ment)
rUnU-m	wis/e, -dom
rUO-v	Trust
rUrO	virtue (pleasure in G.)

aUI : R ...	English
rUt/-A-jAg	FOR prp.; as long as
rUtiOs	Stamp (of approval)
rUv-s	Do good, Benefit V.
rU-vavU	evangel
ruve-m	Bus/iness, -y
ruwe-v	Work
rUwO/-m, -u	hero/ism, ic, —
rUz	asset-s
-rv	imperative ending
ry-aiOm	Cool(-headed)/ness
rybO-v	detach/ment
ryb-wo-v	relax/ation
rydbe-v	massage
ry-dnEm	fine
rydzOm	mild
ryiEm	Cool
rykneos	lizard
rykO-m, -v	Hum/ility, -ble, feel h.
ryktwUm	earnest
rym (slang)= yrUm	BAD
rynwUm	subtle/-ty
rypav	succe/ed, -ssion
rypn/um, -U/m	priva/te, -cy, arcane
ryrO-v	Conscience, feel —
ryrUI-v, -wam	Argu/ment, -e, -able
ryrU-m	conscientious/ness
rytna/m, mu, v	elite, — N, select
ryve, -dE-v	slide, lubrica/nt, -te
ryve-ged	sled
ryvev	to slide
ryve-wenas	ski (-board)
(k)ryvO-v	conce/ptivity, -ive (feel the starry sky)
ryvu	Mrs., Madam
ryvU	acquiescence
rywE-m	mild/ness
rywo-m	Delica/cy, -te
rywO-m	shy/ness
rywQ-m	gentle/ness
ryxiU	wit

aUI : S ●…●+ English

Ss●

aUI	English
"s" denotes	a thing, object, it, put in a bag
sana	Row, Series
sav	PUT
sbAv	collect
sbev	contribute
sE-m	IT-s
sefUrkU/, -v /yvs	sacrifice, V, victim
senkad	Tray
setbav	Gather
sev, (-s), -u	GIVE, (gift), -r
sEz	article = item
sgad	Receptacle
sga/m, -v	Filled, contain
sguygz-/	Pocket
-oś	marsupial
-netkos	kangaroo
sgvav	cram
skenad	tray
skenEs	shelf = ledge
ske-noygE-bos	llama
ske-v	CARRY
skev-bag	brief case
-bang	suitcase
skevu	Carrier, Porter
skwenas	(book) shelf
skwEr-v /kanas	Support pillar
snE	THEY, THEM (=pl. of It)
snEm	THEIR (of things)
sno-m	they (animals), their
so	it (alive)
sO-v	realization = apperception, -e
srUv-U	Recommend-ation
sryv! sryYv!	receive! be received!

aUI : S, T●⌐ English

aUI	English
stag	Bag
strE-v, -va	Sale, sell, mart
strEs	Goods = merchandise
stvyrO-v	threat-en
styrO-v	dread
stytrE, -v, -m	Trade, V, commercial
sU (=sE)	(spiritual) it
sUgte/-v	Experience
-twU	will to Exp.,
-ve	adventure drive
sUI-v	Say, Talk
sUIs	noun
svUv	operate
sybtev	get lost
syv	Receive
(sryv, sryYv,	receive, be received
syvpAyv	was received
syvpA/m-, -v	received, PPP., P.
syvpvAm	having received
syvtAv	will receive

Tt⌐

"t" denotes (the gesture of) "to(wards)" (un-)to, e.g. sky-ward

aUI	English
t-	'toward' as 'nearly'
e.g. t-riO	near-beauty = pretty
tA-m, -	FUTURE
tA-(v)	verbending: will, shall
tab	TOGETHER
tabtLypev	knit
tA-b(y)vu	fiance, (-e)
tabwe-v, -d	Attract/ion, magnet
tAc	will be
tag	INTO
tAg :	introduces futures, although verb forms stay present.
tagbwev	impress
tag/d, -em, -ev	Key, Open, V.

aUI	English
tag-dyv	admit
tagjEv	suck-in
tag-okEv	inhale
-sev	invest
-vav	import
-viov	implant, graft
t-aim	pink
taim-dav-jEos*	salmon
taiv	Blush
tak	UP (ward)
take-v	Elevation, rise
takEm	Tall
takem	light = buoyant
tak-ged	Elevator, lift
takLe-	Spiral (upward)
-kEged	helicopter
tak-sev	give up, yield
tAm	Future, adj.
tanam	lengthy
tank, -Q	Degree, rank
tap	FOR/WARD, -th
tape-v	proceed
tapLe-v	coil
tap-ne	course
tap-nIv	challenge
tap-re-v	progress
-tswev	project
-we-v, -d	prop/ulsion, -el, -ler
tAv	REMAIN, STAY
tAvma	Plan, adj.
tazem, -ev-	Direct/ion, steer
-evu	helmsman
taz/-d, em	rudder
tazd (see tnEzd)	fork
taz-iO	aspect
taz-tabwed	mariner's compass
tcev	entstehn, arise, come to be
teb	toward together
tebAv	attach
tebev	reach
tebOv	grope

* pink-travel-fish

aUI	English
tebgUvs	seminar
tebne(v)	Add/ition
tebru/v, -vQ, vu /-ga, -m, -mU	Guest, visit, -N, -or hotel, hospit/able, -ality
tedEv	Accustom
teg —	Intro —
-brav	-inter-mesh
tegO-v	Invite
tegrO/v	introduc/tion, -e
tegUv	recognize
tek-	upward
tekam	vertical
tekEm	levity, light, adj.
tEk-/	WOOD-
-Id	xylophone
tek-ved, -vev	lever (jack-) to lift
tEk-vu	carpenter
-ybibE	charcoal
tEL, -d	Hook, angle
-anEs	(fishing) rod
tEL-Lyp-ev	crochet
teL-ev	spin, — V
tes, -ev	Goal, aim V
tev	COME
tEv	BECOME
tew-ev	motiv/ate
teyt-U/s, -v	Stimul/us, -ate
tfA	Yet, Still
thyr/O, -wO	risk; anxiety; adventure
-rOve	gamble
-vyhOd-e	bet
tiA	dawn
tio	Sprout
tiO-/v; iOdE	Look, -ing glass
tIO-v	listen/ing
tIOI-v	Hallo, to hale
tiorIO	Bud
tIrv	chirp
tiv	brighten

aUI: T γ... ʊ	English
tiyiv	beckon
tLak/-wyd	ARC(h), Bow
tLam	roundish
tLe-v/-om	CURVE, Flexible
tLom	lithe
tLyp	loop
tLyrO-m	dizz/-iness, -y
tnak/ev, -O	Limit, V, moderation
tnev, (tnEkev)	Grow-th
-jEvogz	thyroid
tneLg-ev, -yro	swell/ing; tumor
tnEz(-d)	Fork (-tool)
tnOv	wish = want
tnusev	dispense = distribute
tnybev	scatter
to	SEED
tov	SEED, to sow V
tO/-v, -m	WISH-(v), -ful
tOb-ev	Desire
toe-v	Birth, - come to -
tOge-m	introver/sion, -ted
tOiv-Q	appear/-ance
tojE	Coffee
tok-/	TREE
/dzne-kEos	woodpecker
-En = tonk	forest
-grOjE	maple syrup
-jE	sap
-nio	bamboo
-podzevos	squirrel*
-yg	bark
-yk	root
tok-yt	Branch
-zvE	log
tonk/-os	forest/-deer
ton-od	Grain-food = cereal
-jE-(bE)	gruel (mush)
tOr !	Please!

aUI: T ʊ... ∓	English
tOr/-m, -v	Pleasing, beg
tor-v/,-UI-v	Help, /advice, -se
tos	animal-child
tovev	bear = give birth
trab-ev	Arrange/ment
trAv-Am	Wait-ing
trAw-m	Patien/ce, -t
traz	bearings (direction)
tre/, -m, -v	Succe/ss, -ssful, -ed
trebe-v	achieve/ment
trew-ev	Exercise, to train
triOm	pretty
tro/, -d, -m, -v	Cure, medicine, -al, heal
trO/-m, -v	Hope-, ful, — V
trod/gagUw, -u	Pharmac/y, —, ist
trogUw/	Medical-Science,
/u	physician
troL/-d, -Lu (v)	pill, nurse
trOtvyce-v	disappoint
trOtyce, -v	disappointment, be disappointed
trov-U	Heal, therapy
troyvAmu/	patient
tro/dzEv/-Q, -u	surg/ic operation/-eon
trU-/	Righteousness
trU-bO	confidence
trUI-v	counsel
tru-kO	honor
trUm-U	Righteous, correctness
trUn-O	Enough, satisfaction
trUn-zUm	specific
trUv-U	Correct-ion
truwe	task
tryrUIv	apologize

* tree-rodent

aUI: T•...T		English
tse-v		Offer
tsOb/-ev -ve(v)		Desire tempt/ation
tsU-v		Purpose, intend
tsUs		Result
tswe/, -v/d		Blow, to strike, mallet
tswU-v		o.s. exert/ion (oneself)
tsyy-U		Accept-ance
tu/-m /-wyr-fev-u		CHILD-like kidnapper
tU-v		Effort, Strive
tUb		SYSTEM
tube-v		Meet/ing
tugai		Window
tUgi-v tUIv tukbos		inspir/ation, -e tell mule
tukO-v		Respect
tUkO-v		Revere/nce
tum		Childlike
tUrO-m		Auspic/-es, -ious
tUs-ev-Am		EFFECT, (V), -ive
tUte, -v		search, seek
tUv		STRIVE
tUvma		Design
tUwe-v tvaiv -(t)vAm, e.g. wU-tvAm		endeavor embarrass* -ive (e.g. creative)
tvAv t(v)az/ev-d		Leave = let remain direct/ing, compass
tve-v		Attempt, TRY
(tvev)tyv'os tvevU-v tvEvQ tviov tviOv		hunt trial, make a —, treat-ment make sprout hint

aUI: T...T		English
tvoev		bear, give birth
tvOr-v, -m		COMFORT-ing
tvOrd-Qm		Comfort-able (material)
tvov tvOv		to sow V affect
tvu		SON
tvU/d, -v		Devi/ce, -se
tvUk tvyc/d, -ev tvykav		victory erase/r to tip
tvykev		Drop, V
tvykOv tvyktev tvyrev tvyrO, -v, -u		debase subjugate endanger terror, frighten, terrorist
twam, -Q -U-m		Possibl/e, -y = Perhaps -bility, potential Adj.
twarm-Q, -U		Probabl/e, -y, -ility
twarQ twaubos		opportunity jackal
tweb(-ev at) -Las -nI-v twed(ev)		Hit (aim at) baseball knock trigger
twEk(ana)		Pillar (column)
twev-d -nId (tweyd) twI-v		PULL-ey harp (blow) crash, V
twIygna, -v, -wam		Explo-sion, -de, -sive
twIyg-wyd-ev		Bomb, V
twok twO-v		oak dare
twOr-v		Entreat/-y
twU-, m, -v		WILL, -ing, to want
twudrE		taxes

* make blush (red)

aUI: T...	English
twUIv	demand
twukv/e, -O	ambition, -feel
twUs	goal
twydO-v	annoy/ance
twyrQ-v	Fright-en
twyte-v	tremble
tyb(-)	DIS -, DYS-, apart
tyb(n)-av	disperse
tybe-v	seclude o.s.
tybfev	pluck apart
tybiOv	disregard
tybjEv	spray
tybnev	subtract
tybOv	to miss (V), want N, want
tybse-v	LOS/s, -e
tybtage-v	yawn
tybtonod	oats
tybtwe-v	distract/ion
tybtyke-v	decay, to
tyc/ev, Ev	perish
tyc-v-e-v	Destr/uct/ion, -oy
tyc-jwUskuv	condemn
tydbrU-m	Aggressive/ness
tyd-Um-u	fool/ish
tye-ytev	to quit
tyfev	to alter V
tyfga-v	Exchange, V
tyf-nUIv	translate
tyfrO	witz, joke
tyfwU-v	Influence
tyfyr-v	Trick
tyg	OUTward
tyg(v)a(v) /EjUm	(to) Spread (tr) outspoken
tyg-ejE-v	outflow
tyge-v	Develop/ment
tygLe/-v,	SPIRAL, V.
-ga, -os	snail/house, —

aUI: T ...	English
tygna-v	Expan/sion, -d
tygokEI-v	Cough
tygO, -m, v	Frank/ness, be f.
tygrO, -v, -m	Smile, to —, -ing
tyg-sev	spend
tyg-te	exit
tygU-v	State/ment
tyg-UIv	profess
tygvav	spread (tr)
tygvev	emit
tygvE-v	Produc/-t, -e
tygwe-v	Burst
tyiA	dusk
tyiQ	Shame
tyje-v	Change
tyjewamgUw-tUwma	variable design graph
tyj-mag(ev)	shift (v = verschieben)
tyk	DOWN, sub-
tyka-v, -m	Slope, oblique
tykad	seat (as folding chair)
tykbrO	charity
tykbwe-v	suppress/ion
tykE-an	Kilogram
tykEm	Heavy
tyke-v	FALL
tykE-v	WEIGH/T
tykE(vo)w	Gravity
tykena	Curtain
tyketazm	steep
tykjEv	submerge
tykLeL-v	revol/ution,-ve
tykLev	to bow, V. intr.
tykQ-v	Contempt, despise
tykrE	Lead (metal)

aUI: T	English
tykrOIv	deride
tyksav	suppose
tykUiO-v	List
tykvLev	bow down, tr.
tykvev	subdue
tykw-Am	subjugating
tykweijE	petroleum
tykwe-v	Conque/st, -r
tykwevd	Hammer
tykweyvd	anvil
tykyve-v	slide down (sink)
tykzwEv	Crush
tyngyEv-d	funnel
tynev	shrink
tynmUv-U	qualify, -ication (restrict)
typ (-)	BACKWARD, RE-
typ-bwe-v	re-press/ion
typev	Return
typE-v	(mechanic)react(ion)
typ(gUv, -iUv)	recognize
typ/-i(v;-Iv	Reflect/ion; Echo
typO-m	shy/ness
typ-re-v	repair
typ-take-v	re-surrect/ion
typ-twe-v	withdraw
typviU/v	feedback
typ-vU-v	reaction
typ-we-v	restrain
tyr'-m	Dangerous
-bypav	persecute
tyrev	Endanger
tyrhQ	crisis
tyr-/omOmu	hypochondria'-c
tyrO-v, -m	Fear, — , -ful
tyrUI-v	warn /-ing
tyr/ve-v	ruin
-vyjUv	discriminat/ion, -e
tyr-yn-Um	foolish
tyt	To & Fro

aUI: T, U	English
tyt/ana, -m	Breadth, broad
-bUI-v	convers/ation, -e
tyte-v	Vibrat/-ion, -e
tytLe(v)-d, -s	swing, V, N; pendulum
tytne-d, -v	Whip (e.g. cream)
tytnyrO/v	vacillat/ion, -e
tytO-v	hesitat/ion, -e
tytUI-v	Discuss/ion
tytU, -m, -v	Refer/ence, -ential
tytwe-v	Shake
tyv; (os)	GET (hunt)
tyv-fev	Catch
tyvos	game (-deer)
tyvu	Daughter
tywe-v(-pAm)	Tire-d
tywmA -v	Fatique, v.
tywO-m	timid/ity

U u

u-m	human, person
-u	-er, -or
U	SPIRIT
-U(z)	Concept
u, U = 4, 9 49	Four, Nine
ua-v	Dwell/ing
UamA	Attitude
ub, -Q, -m	Famil/y, -iarity, -iar
uba	town
Ub	OF
ubogta-v	Kiss
UcO-v	perce/ption, -ive
Ud	BY (means of)

aUI: U...	English
Ud-fA	BY now, Already
U-diO-v	diagnos/is, -e
UE-m	Substanc/e, -tial
ueda	Street
Uf	THAT = conj.
ufU-m, -v	Person/ality, -al, -ify
(u)ga, -k	House-Roof
ugakyk	rug
uga-pyg	balcony
Uga-v	institute
(v)ugav-s	Building
(u)gayk	Floor
uged	Carriage
Ugs-jiOvs	BOOK-illustration
-mUv	-review
-tygsev-Q	-edit, -ion
ugta	Door
ugU	Opinion
UgO	inner sense, taste
UgrO(m)	content/ment
UgUw	Philosophy
Ugz	Page
UhO-m	Skeptic/ism
uI	Voice
Ui-v	understanding
Ui-ana-v	Draw/ing
UI-m	WORD, literal
UI-kEos	parrot
UI-mav	formulate
UI-n	vocabulary
UI-nz	idiom
ui-m	Blue/ness
ui-kot	plum
UI-(k)rOvs	joke, -v
uioba	Garden

aUI: U...	English
UiOv	READ, to —
ui-rOwE	saphire
UIrOves	pun
Uis	IDEA, picture
Uiv	Understand
UIv	SAY, Speak
uIves	Phonograph
UIviO	Drama
UIvo	Story
UIv/-Q, -s	Speech
UIwUv, -u, -s	Poet/ise, poem
UIz/,	letter (a,b...z),
-ev	spell
-mUngUw	algebra
Uj...Uj	As...As
Uj nEk... Uj nEk	the more...the more
Uj sE yEc	as it were...
ujEgos	dolphin
U-jwUsku-v	critic-ize
Uk-Q	sur-, super-iority
ukbos	Horse
ukcEwu	wizard
UkrO	bliss
UL	ABOUT
um	HUMAN
-Um	-Minded
uma, -m	Figure, shapely
Uma	Character
umjEgos	porpoise
umos	Ape
UmtiO-v	Test, — V
un	people, demo—
una	COUNTRY
U-nam	great

aUI: U	English
una-mi	Flag
unaz	District
(un-En-)-viOvQ	(mass-)demonstration
unIv	Call out
unwe-rOv/e-m, -u	Diploma/cy, -tic, -t
UO-v	Intuit/ion
Ur!	Yes!
Uogz	cerebrum
UriA-m	pentecost-al
Urm	Positive = affirmative
U-ro/m	San/ity, -e
UrO-m	Happi/ness
Us-gEm	THOUGHT-ful
Ut	In-order-to
Ute, -v	Find, -v
U-tEv-U	spiritualiz/-e, -ation
Ut-fev/-U	assum/e, -ption
utga-	(outer)door
-baz	-hinge
-drE	-ticket
UtiO-z	world-view, aspect
UtrUv-Q	conver/t, -sion
Utse-v	trend
Utsyv-Q	hypothes/ize, -is
UtrogUw-u	psychiatr/y, -ist
Utrov/-u, U	psychotherap/ist, -y
UtUb-u, -uv	Theor/y, -ist, -ize
utUv-u, U	Educat/e, -er, -ion
Utve, -v	attention, pay —
Utyge-v	Express/ion
uU	Mankind
Uv-Am	THINK-ing (Part.)
uv-(EpAm)	artificial — (manmade)
uv-tok	artific. tree
UviO(-v)	(en-)vision
U-viOvs	symbol
Uvo-v	Fiction, write —

aUI: U, V	English
UvO-v	illusion, to imagine
UvO-Uyro	psychosis
U-vytUv	derive, deduce
Uwa-m, -u	Offic/e, -ial, N
-kwu, -wU	bureaucra/t, -cy
U-wam-U	talent/ed
uwe/v	Labor, — V
/vye-v	-strike, V
Uydim	Vague
uyg-ev	CLOTHE
uygbos	Sheep
uygE-zvE	CLOTH-rag
U-ygem-u	Extrem-ist
U-ypnAm	ultimate
U-yro-m	mental disease, insane
-v	behave crazily
UyrO(-m), v	Grie/f-, (Sad,)-ve
Uyr-UvO	hallucination
Uyt	for = because
Uytbe-v	analys/is, -e
-Uz	concept
e.g. n-Uz	quantity (-concept)

Vv

"v" denotes:	"Active, DO, MAKE, Procreative, male
-v	Verb-ending
-v(e)- shows a	causative, transitive V.V.
vadrE(viOv)s	postage (stamp)
v(AgUv)s	Rem/ind, (-ember)-er
vAm-ev	Awake-n
vamU-m	Manners, polite
vanaiv	radiate tr.
vana-v	Stretch
vas	Parcel
vatke-v	Raise
vaUs	epistle
vav (av)	SEND (GO)

aUI: V	English
vAv	Preserve, keep
vava	Post office
vavas	Address
vavU, -v	Message, convey
vavUn	Mission
vavUs	Letter = epistle
vav-ynena	Postcard
vayvs	missile
ve-bjyjO-v	confus/ion, -e
(ve-cvAv	awaken (tr.))
vEd	TOOL
ved-	motor
ved-gU/-m, w	techn(olog)ic, -y
vejE-/gad	jug
vejEv	pour
vej(Evogz)-Ed	adrenal (gland)-in
vEjUrO, -v	convi/ction, -ince
vEjUv/-u, -d	witness, –, certificate
vekEv	to blow (tr.)
vekted	Lever
vekte/s, -v	(Elevator), Lift, —V
veL-v, -pAm	Ben/d, -t
vem	ACTIVE
vEm-E	Elastic, Rubber
venav	flatten
ves-gUw	Engine-science
vEsgUv-Q	interpret-ation
vEs-ev/Q, -u	manufactur/ing, -er
vetev	Draw = pull
vetgad	Drawer
vetgU/(bUI), v	Teach/ing (doctrine); —v
-kwU, -z	discipline, lesson
vetkev	(make) skip
vetsev-	Bring
-wanab	conveyor belt
vetwOv	encourage
vetwov	strengthen

aUI: V	English
ve-v	DRIVE, (make) move
vEv (-)	MAKE- (causative)
-vEvd	producer-tool, (...generator)
vevO	drive-feeling
vEvz	factor
vid	flashlight
viE/-d, -v	match, kindle
viEvd	lighter (tool)
viOsU-m, -v	Imagin/ation, -ary, -e
viov	to plant
viO-v	Show
viOv-d	pen (cil)
viOv-e(v)	gesture (V)
viOvs(ev)	(to) Sign
viU-v	Explan/ation
viv	(make) Light
vIv	Play (sounds) music
vizos	Ant
vLe/-v, (d)	(make) turn(-er)
vLybE-v	insulat/ion, -e
vma-v	sculpture
vne-v	chase, v
vno/-m, -v, -vE	Fertil/ity, -e, -ize, -r
(v)nu, -m	They, their (masc.)
vnUr-v	to value, appreciate
vnynzEv	grind
vnyrOv-Q	torture
vo(-)	male-(animal), he
vo-b(ijEboz)	bull (of bovine)
vod-a, (-u)-uv	farm, (peasant), to f.
vOe-v	excite/ment
vogz	gonads
vOiv	pretend
voLz	Testes
vom, -to	Male, sperm
vOm	manly
v-OtgUv	interest tr.
vOtke-v	arous-al, -e V
vov	Procreate
vOv	Impress

aUI: V	English
vO-w	suggestion-power
vow(-ev)	(to) Force
voz-Lanad	SEX - phallus
vQ-m, -v -vQ	condition-ing, — V -ification, -ing
vram	Convenient
vrAm, -U	READY, -ness
vrav vre/m, -v vriO-v, -m vriOd vrOkU vrom	allocate practic/al, -ice beautify, cosmetic cosmetic N morale wholesome
vrO-m	Kind/ness
vrOUI-v vrov-U	greet/ing(s) cure
vrOv	Please = bring joy
vrUIv	(to) Bless (by word)
vrUv	Bless = make good
vrUma vr-ytU-v -vu	reform rationalis/ation, -e -er, -or
vu (-m)	HE, him (his)
vU-g	ACT-ually
-vU vUd vugav-u vUIc	-fication device build-er predicate
vUiOv/ -es	Write typewriter
vUiOd	Pen(cil)
vUIs vUIvu vUIv vukbos vUm vuma	verb speaker elucidate stallion creative statue
vUma	BEHAVIOR
(-)vUn	Operation, -ry
vus	MAN

aUI: V	English
vUtse, -v	Deci/sion, -de
vUv-Q -vUz vUviOv vUvu	act (creatively)-ion -ify, -al, -ize symbolize actor
vuyg/u-v	Trousers, tailor,—V
v-UyvA-riOio -to vUyvAv vUyvA-yrtrod vUz-iO vybev v-yb-tUs-O-v vybyfev vyce-v vydEjUv v-y-dvev-d vyd vydyrov-Q vyEd vyEjUv vyeme/-d, -v	poppy-flower -seed hypnotize opium scene omit frustrat/ion, -e sever, isolate destr/uction, -oy lie (against truth) make-non conduct-or make hate vaccinate, -ion gouge falsify transquillize/er, -e
vyev-d	(make) Stop, Brake
vygav vygem vyhOv, -d vyiOv vyi-v vyI-vyov vyjUv	exclude eccentric guarantee, pawn to hide eclipse, darken hush-kill distinguish
vykav	to LAY
vykev vyktav	to subdue to seat
vyktev	to Lower, put down
vykwu(-v)	(to) boss
vym (slang!)	Passive
vynpwUrm	pedantic
vynrOv-s	Entertain/ment
vyOiv vyokEv vyotnevs	dissemble choke cancer
vyov	KILL
vyOv vypAv vypev vyprAv	to numb, V to finish terminate delay

aUI: V, W	English
vypriv	to dirty
vyrav	to pollute
vyrdanav	to crucify
vyre-v	Harm
vyrkEm/Ov, -os	stink, skunk
vyrkrOiv	ridicule
vyrLev-Q	perver/t, V, -sion
vyrmaL	vicious circle
vyrO, -m, -v	cruelty, hurt
vyros	virus
vyrtEv	spoil tr.
vyrtrOv	forgive
vyrUIv	condemn
vyrUm	corrupt Adj.
vyrUv	worsen, corrupt
vyrwUIv	curse
vyrwyvU-v	comp/ulsion, -el
vyrydnub-Uyro	psychopathy
vyte-v	Omi/ssion, -t
vytkav-Ov	hang (tr), — suspen/se, -d
vytne-v	decrease
vytUv-u	(to) Cause, author
vytyr-v-u	rescue-er
vyy	Stun
vYv	annul
vyz	defect
vyzbyU	complement

Ww

"w" denotes: Power, Force, Energy Strength, Hardness

aUI: W	English
wagd	Box
waIv	to bark
waL-ev	Fence-in, confine
waLg	Enclosure
(-) wam-U	(-)able, Ability
wana	Cord, Rope
wanab	Band
wanabio	Hemp
wanab-stag	Basket
wanas	Rod
wanOb	bond
wanoz	tendon
wanub	League
waubos	Dog
wav	CAN = be able
wE	STONE
webjanai	laser-ray*
wEbvE	Cement = Concrete
wed	power tool
wEg-kot	Peach
(-)wei-d	electric(ity)-device
weijE; weijE	Benzol; gasoline
wei-m	Electric/ity
wein	elect. intensity
wei-tabwe/d, -m	electro-magnet/ic
weitwam-U	voltage, el. potential
wei-vd	battery
-vEvd	elec. generator
wE-jiOvs	(stone-) sculpture
wEk	high rock, cliff
weLv	warp
wELyg	crust
wEL-zos	crab
wE/m, -v	HARD-en
wenaE	card-board
(wenas-)ryvev	(board)Ski-ing
wenEs	sheet = plate
wErE	Steel
wEs	a stone, rock
wete/-pAm, -v	Imp/ulse, -ive, -el
wE-uma	statue
we-v	thrust
wEyg/-jEykos	Shell/-fish, = clam
weygknot	coco-nut
wEyg(k)ot	(tree) Nut

*powerful-move-together-equal-ray

aUI: W	English
wEyg-os	turtle
wEzos	lobster
wiozE	starch
wI-v	roar
wizos	Beetle
woged	thigh
wo-m	Str/ength, -ong
wO-m	Courag/e, -ous
wOtgU-m, -v	fascinat/ing, -e
wOv	May (=might)
woz	muscle
wozam	Right (side)
wrak!	quack!
wrE-gad	Iron-kettle
wreiz	positron
wriO	charm
wryv-U	should = ought, duty
wU-m	POWER-ful
wu-ga	powerman, castle
wuged	Automobile
wuIv-Q	vot/e, -ing
wUI, -v	slogan, -persuade
wUIzev'-Q	to (cast) spell
wUkO-m	power-pr/ide, -oud
w(u)riO(-v)	(to) Charm (V)
wUv-u	Creat/or, -e
wuyg-(-ged)	armor (-car)
wUyvs	creature
wyd	WEAPON
wyde(-v)	(to) Attack
wydE-v, -	to arm
wydnI-v, yvs	Sho(o)t, what is shot
wydO-m	Ang/er, -ry
wyg-z	crust
wygtkEI	Sneeze
(wygwev)	(burst)

aUI: W, X	English
wyktev	subdue
wyLem	Stiff
wynd	weaponry
wynub	Committee
wyrfev-u	rob-ber
wyrLe'-v, -d	Twist, wrench
wyrLu	witch
wyrrE	Debt
wyrtred	Whip, Scourge
wyrUI-v	curse
wyr-vyev-d	trap
(w)yryd-ev	offen/ce, -d
wyrykU	demon
wyrzev	Smash
wytnav-Q	election
wytte-v	quake
wytyrA-d, -m	pawn = secur/ity, -e
wyU, -rOve, -tev	Chance, -lottery, -guess
-v-Q	-venture V, N
-viOvs	-signs = code
-ytna-v	-lottery-play
wyv	MUST
wyvO	Obligation
wyvU, -m, -v	Necess/ity, -ary, need
wyvU-Uyr	compulsion (neurosis)
wyvyr	a need
wyzbEm	tenacious
wyzEm	tough

X x

"x" denotes	RELATI/VE, -on
xa, xA	, Where, When
xat, xayt	, whither, whence
xE(m)	, Which
(Qg)xI	, Whether
xLu	, who f.
xnE-m	, Which, that pl. things

aUI: X, Y	English
xno-m (-adj)	, which, that, pl. animals
xnu-m	, who pl. persons
xo	, which (of animals)
x-Q	introducing a relative pron. object e.g. 'u, 'xQ' bu iOpAv xu, tev" the man 'where' you saw whom (=him), is coming" = the man whom you saw..." which contradicts 'Subject-verb-object rule.
xQ	,'Where' = which condition
xrObca-m	-cosm/os, -ic
xrUI	Logos
xu-m	,Who, ,Whose
xU(z)	RELATION (concept)
xUd	As, How
xUm	RELATIVE adj.
xUv	relate
xvu	, Who m.
xyvu	, Who f.

Yy

'y" indicates: opposite 'un-', 'anti-' negative, 'in-', 'non-' (the bar covers all that is denied as a minus — (...) before a parenthesis (= yb-i = without light, = y-bi - anti-white = black). l.c. "y" before vowels (even before Capital Y), means un-, not-, since vowels have no opposites, e.g. yo (as in British yonder) means 'non-life' death, not anti-life. But before the consonant-concepts, Y, vowel Ü, means anti-, e.g. Yk Strictly, ỹ = consonant, Y = vowel —, yY - sounds near 'yield,' rather 'jüdisch. Both y & Y are rounded.

y-; Y-	un-; anti-
Y; e.g. Y-O	Zero, 0; null-feeling

aUI: Y	English
ya; yA	Nowhere; Never
yana-m	Short/ness
yana-Ui/s, -v	abbreviat/ion, -e
yAp	AFTER
yAp-Yn	Soon
yAp-YrO	Regret
Yb (-)	WITHOUT, (-less)
Yb-...	un-..., in-...a-, ab-
Yba	Absence
YbaI	Radio
Yba-iO	Tele-vision
Ybam	Far
Yba-O	Tele-pathy
Yba-tiO-d	Telescop/y
Yba-uI	Telephone
Yba-Uti-v	Telegraph
Ybav-Q	to lack, -N
YbdQm	direct
Ybev	seclude o.s.
YbevE-v	non-conduct/or
Ybgez	immediately
YbibE	Coal (bituminous)
Ybib-ukbos	zebra
YbijE	Ink
YbikE, -v, -d	Smoke, V, Cigaret
Ybim	BLACK
Yb-iOg	un-seen, regardless
YbirIkEos	blackbird
Ybi-u	Negro
YbiwE	anthracite, -coal
Yb-kE-om	an-aerobic
(-)Ybm	(-)Less
Yb(-nub-cEm)	schizophren/-ia,
-Uyro-m	-ic
Yb-o-bE	inorganic matter

aUI: Y ... English

Ybo-m Divorced

YbO-m, -v want, deprived, miss V
YbQ lack

YbrO-v Dislike-Loathe V

Ybru, -v Enemy-dislike V

Ybtonz straw
Yb-tUs-O, -m frustrat/ion, -ed
Yb-UIm mute

YbU-v Lack

Ybum wild (= untamed)
YbuygQ-m naked/ness

Y-bwam-ev Loose-n

Ybydyr defenseless
YbyfQ-m; -v solit/ude, -ary, seclude o.s.
YbygsQ-m bare/ness
Y-bYrOm; ruthless;
Yb-YrOm painless
YbYrU/m innocen/ce, -t
YbYrvem harmless
YbytkavA-m independen/ce, -t

Yc (IS) NOT

Yc(Ib)...Yc(Ib) Neither...Nor

YcEm unreal

YcEmUm Abstract

YctLevom rigid
Yc-UI-v negat/ion, -e
Yc-vUm -inactive, idle

Yd (-) AGAINST, anti-

Yda/m, -z NARROW, Waist

Ydam-wuyg strait jacket
Yd-atke-v rebel/lion, V

Yd-be, -v Friction, rub

Yd-brO-v aversion, detest
Yd-bru-v foe, oppose

YdbrU-v WAR, — V

Ydbwlv clash
Yded valve (door)
Y-dEm-Q immediate-ly

Ydev-s, -Q Obstruct, -ion, Abstr.

aUI: Y ... English

(yr) YdIv grumble

Ydkem Rough

Yd-krOIv ridicule
Ydku-m, -v rebel-lious, -l V
Ydkwe-v infringe/ment

YdnEm THIN

Yd-nynyE-d, -v screen, V

Ydova Toilet

Y-dov, -s Excre-te, -ment

Yd-O-v Hate, V

Ydrem-U Difficult-y

YdrO-Iv mock
Yd-tybsa, -v, -vQ insur/ance Co, -e, -ance
YdU-v oppos/ite, -e

YdUI-v Protest, to —

Yd-um in-human
YdvEv undo
Ydvu opponent
YdvU-v oppose (actively)

Ydwe-v Attack

YdwO shock
YdwQd resistor

YdwU-v Resist/ance

YdwUm Obstinate

Ydybe-v Secur/ity, -e

Yd-(y)kwev disobey

YdYr-d Shield

Yd-yro-m, -v immun/e, -ize

Yd-yr-v Defen/ce, -d

Yd-Yrvu-k Police-officer

YdYrwa-v Protect/ion

Ydzem Blunt

YdzOm Dull

yE void, vacuum

aUI: Y □····⊙	English
yEanLEd	Needle
yeas	station
(-)yEc	'WOULD' contrary to fact
yed	stopper
yEd	hollow drill
yejE; -n	pool; lake
yEjU, -m, -v	Lie, false, Lie V
yEjUms	Mistake
yEL-ev	Ring, V
yem, -U	Quiet, N
ye-mA(-drE)	pension (money)
yE-primd	vacuum-cleaner
ye-tO-v	linger-wish
ye, -v	Stop, V
(ye)Yk-YrO	neurotic depression
yeYv	Cease
Yf	OTHER
Yfa, YfA	THERE, THEN
Yf-am	Strange
Y-fam -Um	absent-minded
Yfa-rO, -m, -v *	drollness, funny, joke
Yfa-v, -pAm	Estrange-d
Yf-bwUm	other-concentrated
Yf-da-al	The other way around
yfQ	otherwise
Yfs	Else, other thing
Yf-taz-m	inverse
YfUd	other way
YfU-m	unselfish
YfUs-Um	Object-ive
Y-fUwe, -m	bondage, unfree
Yf-yt(y)vu	step-fa(mo)ther
Yg	OUTside

*Strange-pleasure-make

aUI: Y ⊙····γ	English
Yga	Surface
Ygana	Border
(v-)Ygav	exclude o.s. (tr.)
Ygaz	(the) outside N
Yg-bo-brO	Extra-marital love
YgEm	Empty
Ygev	Avoid
YgjE-m	Dry/ness
-roduv	-bake
-uygE	-towel
Ygkuyg	Overcoat
Ygm-Q	out-er, -ward-ly
Ygode-v	(to) Vomit
Yg-ogz	limb
YgrEm	ACID
Y-grizos	wasp
YgrO-m	Bitter
-jEvogz	-gall (gland)
YgtEjUm	Honest
YgtEk	Cork
Ygtok	Bark (tree)
YgU-v	Ignor/ance, -e
Yguyg	overall
YgyEjU	sham
YgyrkO-m	vanity, vain
Ygz-ev	peel
YgzEv-d	scrape-r
Y-hI-v	Answer, V
YhO, -m, -v	CERTAIN/ty, be c.
yI	a(n)
yia, -kwydos	north, -reindeer
yiA, -kEos	NIGHT, -owl
yibeirE	bronze
yiEm	COLD

aUI: Y	English
yikA	midnight
yi-m	DARK/ness
yIm-U	Soundless-ness
yImA	quietude
yIn-A	SEVERAL, some-times
yio	mushroom
Y-iO(-vA)m =	Blind, unseeing
yiOwam	Invisible
yIs	something
yita	East
yitA-do-v -jE	Morning-breakfast -dew
yi-to yiU-v yiv yIv	rye conjecture, V is-dark = light off be silent
yiviOs	Dream
yiz-ev	SHADE, v
Yje-v, -wam	var/iation, -y, -iable
YjE-m	Thirst-y
Yj-ogav	limp V
YjU, -m, -v	Diffe/-rence, -rent, -r
YjUtE-v	Err/or
YjwUr-m	Wrong
Yk	Under, BELOW
Ykai(m)	Infra-red, hot
Ykam	LOW
Ykana-v	underline
Ykav, -d	Lie, Bed
Ykaz	Base, underside
YkbE(-tEL)	Ground (anchor)
YkbELiod	Potato

aUI: Y	English
Ykbo, -baz	FOOT, -ankle
-(we)v	Kick, V
-Yg	Shoe
Ykboz	Toe
YkdrEm	Cheap
Ykenas	Mat
Yke-v, -m	Crawl-y
-os	Reptile
Ykio	Moss
Ykioz	Root
(ykjEtgad=) =YkLena	('under-cup') Saucer
Ykna YknanabE Ykneos Ykog YkOm Ykos YkQ-m	underworld rug lizard abdomen ignoble, = cheap invertebrate inferior/ity
YkrO-m, -v	Depression, Sad, mourn
Yksa-v	Deposit, V
Ykta, -v	a Seat, to Sit
Yktad	Chair
Yktev	descend
YktE-m	Burden-some
YktE/v, -w	to, a Load
(YktEje-v	to balance)
Yktio, -d	root, radish
Yktok	(tree-) Root
YktrUm	Serious
YkU Ykuga	Hades (god) basement
YkU-m	Inferior (spirit)
Yk-Uv, -Am, -u	to Susp/ect, -icious, -er

aUI: Y	English
YkU-yvu	the suspect
Ykwev-Q	Obe/y, -diance
Ykwu-v	Serv/ant, -e
Ykwus	Service
YLem	Straight
Ym	ANY
YmA	Ever
Yms	Anything
Ymu	anybody
Yn	No(one), None
Yn-	Little-, Micro-, -i.e. diminutive
YnA	Minute (1/60 hour)
Ynab	Group
Yn-Ad	Watch (timepiece)
YnakiA	Winter
Ynam	Small
YnAm	Rare
yn(an)os	bacillus
Ynaz	Detail
YnAz	a Second (1/60Minute)
Yn-banu-m	trib/e, -al
YnbijEbos	Goat
Ynbizos	flea
Ynbos	mouse
YndrE/dU-v /gUw	Econom/y, -ize -ics
YndrEm	Poor
YnE, -k	a LITTLE, -less, minus
Yne-m	SLOW/ness
YnEn	FEW

aUI: Y	English
Ynena	Card
YnenEs	flakes
YnEsvUm	lazy
Yne-tok-os	sloth (animal)
YnEv	reduce
Yne-Ykos	slug (snail)
Yn-grO-nod	cooky
YniEvs	Matches (to kindle)
YniOd	microscope
Ynios	Bacteri/um, -a
YnIwYd	handgun
-YnkLot	-tree berry
Yn-kn/u, -yvu	prince/, -ss
Yn-kog-iod	Brussels sprouts
YnLiod	pea(s)
Ynos, Abbr. Yn(an)os)	Bacillus
ynpo	protista
YnrO-v	Amuse/ment
Yntok	bush
Yntos	animal-baby
Yntu, -gUa	Baby, -nursery
(yn-)tvycevd	eraser
Ynu	Dwarf
Ynub	community
Ynuba	Village
YnUm	Stupid
Yn-uma	Doll
Ynumos	monkey
Ynvu-m	Boy-ish
YnvUiOs	article (=essay)
YnvUm	idle
Yn-walv	yelp
YnwUm	Subtle
YnYdbrU	Guerilla-war
YnyEd	Sieve
YnyejE	puddle

aUI: Y...	English
YnyEjUv	mistake V
Yn-yio(s)	fungus (mold)
Yn-Ykam	Shallow
Yn-(Yr)bos	(pest-) mouse
YnYr-izos	Louse
YnYrzos	mite
Ynytgev(iOz-kazd)	blink (eye-lids)
YnYtQv-d	relay-trigger
YnYvu	Girl
Ynz	detail
yo-m, -v	Dea/th, -d, Die
yo-bEna	desert
yod (-O)	Hunger (-feeling)
yod-Ov, -Q	starv-e, -ation
yo-dos	hyena
yo-enaz	cemetery
yog-as	morgue
yog-wad	corpse, coffin
yogU-v	ghost, haunt
yo-gyE-v	grave, -dig
yo-kEos	vulture
yokEv	choke
y-oLEm	lean
yom-E, -u	Dead-matter, cadaver
yOm-U	insensitiv-e, -ity
yOtev	neglect
yo-tnevs	carcinoma
Yp	BEHIND
YpakiA	Autumn
Ypav, YpAv	Follow; (in time)
Ypaz	Back
YpAz, -ev	END, to —
Y-pev	terminate
YpLev	turn-back (-left)
YpnAm	LAST, latest
Ypnum	Private
YpO-m	Sudden/ness

aUI: Y...	English
Yp-og-wE/,-z	spine, vertebra
Yp-og-z	Tail
Y-prA-m, -v	Late, come l.
Y-prim-, -E, -s	Dir/ty, -t, -t-things
Ypriv	become dirty
YprQz	draw-back
Yp(z)	BACK (side)
Yp-U-gUw-Um	metaphysic-s, -ical
Ypu/m, -s	Secret, — N
-ms-U	mystery
Yp-Ytwe	rocket-propulsion
YpYvU-m, -v	Reserve, -d, — V
yQm	unconditioned
Y-Q	opposition
Yr!	NO! (not: Yes)
Yr-	Mal-, ill-, bad-
Yraim	Brown
Y-raiOm	Frigid
Yram	Impure
Yr-bav-ve-m	greed-y
Yr-bEjE	mud
Yr-bio	plant-parasite (vine)
Yr-bizos	bed-bug
Yr-bos	Rat
Yr-bov	mishandle
Yr-bwav-Q	cramp V, spasm N
yr-bwev	oppress
yr-bzos	vermin
yr-djEv	'mis-swallow' = wrong way
yrdwev	(bad) manipulate
Yr-E	(bad) dirt
Y-re(v)	Mal-function (V)
Yr-fe(v, -vu)	Theft, steal, thief
Yr-fUmO	selfishness
Yr-ga, (v)	cage, (confine)
Yr-g-O-tYg-og(Q)	conversion-neurosis
YrI-v	Noise, V = make —,
YriO-m	Ugli/ness

aUI: Y	English
Yr-ios	weed
Yr-izos	bug
YrjUI-v	equivocat/ion, -e
Yr-ked-ge(v)	infringe/ment)
Yr-kEm	foul
Yr-kEmO-m, -v	stench, stinky, sense st.
YrkQ-m, -v	Pride, proud, be pr. —V
YrkU', -hIv -Q, -u	Satan, -inqui/re, -sit/ion, -sit/ion, -or
YrkU'-is (-viOvs)	idol (symbol)
Yr-kwu	tyrant
Yrm	NEGATIVE
Yr-mam	mis-shapen
Yr-mi-v-s	Stain, V, -spot
Yr-nI(v)	(to) Scream
Yr-nu/daiu, -kwu	demagog
Yro-m, -v	Disease-d, ILL-/ness, be —
YrQ, -m, -v	PAIN, -ful, hurt itr.
Yrod	POISON
Yrod-zos	scorpion
Yrogga	Hospital
Yr-og-u	cripple
YrOI(v)	(to) Cry
YrO-jEv	weep
Yros-ga	cage
YrO-tok	willow
YrO-ve	Passion
Yrow	fury
(YrozEv-a	Wound, -N)
YrQg	unfortunately
YrQm	unlucky
YrsQ-v	Disgust, V
Yrstyg(a)	Sewage (-plant)
yrtabwev-d	bait, N
yrt-cyvs	accident (bad)

aUI: Y	English
yrte	damage
yrtE-v	spoil V
YrtneLg-ev	tumor-grow
Yr-tnev, -s	grow (-wrong), mal-growth
Yr-tnevu	freak (grown-person)
Yr-trod	bad-drug
Yr-trUnOm	smug
YrtsObve	temptation
Yrtu	Brat (bad child)
YrtUIv	scold
YrtukO-v	envy, - V
YrtUvma	plot, intrigue
Yr-tybsev	lose
Yr-(tyb)-twev	distort
Yrtyf-brO-m	Jealous/y
Yr-tyf-rO-m	Envy, -ious
Yr-tyg-UI, -v	treason, betray/al
Yr-tyrom-O	hypochondria
Yr-tyrv	revenge
Yr-uga	Prison
Yr-U-ga	Madhouse, (state hospital
yrUI-v	invective, revile
Yrukbos	Ass, jackass
YrU-m	Evil, -Adj.
YrUv(-s)	to, (a) Sin
YrUz	defect N
Yrv	Commit a Crime
Yr-vamU-m	impolite/ness
Yrv-danav	crucify
Yrve(-v)	(to) Harm
Yrv/s, -u-m	Crim/e, inal, -Adj.
YrvtrO-v	Pardon, V.
YrvU-z	Crim/-e, Abtr.-inality
Yr(v)yEjU-v	fraud, deceive
Yr-vytka-v	hang (for crime)
Yrvz	fault
Yrwanub	gang (bad—)
Yrwaubos	Wolf (big, bad —)

aUI: Y	English
Yrwo-m	Brutal/ity
YrwOm	rash/ness
YrwyvO-v	Obsess/ion
YrybO-m, -v	alienat/ion, -ed, feel — -ed
YrydEjUI-v	slander
Yryde-v	offen/ce, -d
YrydI-v	growl, N, V
Yrye-m	lame/ness
Yr-Yg-bo-brO-v -u, yvu	Adulter/y, -er, -ess
Yr-yiE/m, -yro-m	cold, -sick (head)
Yr-ykna-m, -u	hell/ish, -folk
Yr-Ykwu-m, -v	slav/e, -ish, V
YrYte-v-u	Fl/ight, -ee, fugitive
YrYtE-v-u	Waste, to — V, -er
YrYtO	fugue
YrYv-s	Suffer, victim
Yrz	draw-back
Y s	NOTHING
Ys-Evu	bum
Ysgam	Empty (of things)
Y t	FROM
Yta	AWAY
YtA	Since
Ytag/d, -ev	Lock, V
Ytbe-v	(Dis)Sol/ution, -ve
Ytbre-v	Disturb/ance
YtE-s	source (material) matrix
Yte-v	Leave, to —, Depart/ -ure
YtEjU-v	fallacy, V = be in...
Yte rUI	Goodbye
Ytge/m, -v	Shut, Adj, V

aUI: Y	English
YtgoganyEd	artery
YtgU-v	Forget/-ting
Ytkav, -Am	Hang-ing
Yt-kygev, -u, -v	Uncover, detect/ive
YtLu	mother
Yt-na-v	Select/ion, cho/ice, -ose
-twUm	arbitrary
Y-tne-v	Decrease
Yt-og-jE-v	urinate
(v)Yt-Oiv	disappear, dis-illusion (tr)
ytO r / - m, -v; -tO	THANK, -ful, to — V congratulation(s)
Yt-pA-gU	tradition
Y-tre, -m	Ill/-success/, un...ful
Y-trO, -v	Despair, V
Yt-se-v	spend
Ytta-m, v	Distan/ce, -t, — o.s.
Yt-tedEv	to wean, disaccustom
(v)Yt-trOv	(be)disappoint-ed o.s. (tr.)
Yt-tygav	stray off
Ytu	PARENT
YtU-g -m -v -vu	Origin/-ally -al -ate -ator = author
Ytu-jYtvu	Uncle
Ytu-jYt/Lu, -Yvu	Aunt
YtUs	CAUSE
Ytu-sev, -s	bequeathe, inheritance
YtUw-am	REASON-able
Yt-uygev	undress
Ytvev	remove
Ytvu	FATHER

aUI: Y	English
Yṭwe-v	Push, — V
YtwO	drive-feeling
YtẉU	Logical Necessity
(Ytyptwlygna	rocket explosive propulsion)
(Yt)Ypwe -ged	rocket propulsion -vehicle
YtYṛA, -m, -v-u	Safe/ty, save, -ior
YtyrAv/U Ytyre-v Ytyrv, -u, -U Yt-YtLu	salvation escape rescue, -er, — N grandmother
Yt-Ytụ/	Anceṣtor(s), grandparent
/-sYv-Q	-inherit-ance
YtYtvu YtYtyvu	Grandfather Grandmother (as spouse)
Yt-Yvụ	MOTHER
yụ	NOBODY
y Ug	BUT = however
yUg-am	But-only = except
y U, - m, - v	OPPOS(it)E, N, Adj, V
Y-UIv Y-UIv	contradict babble
yum	Inhuman, brute
yUI-tu	infant
y Uṭ	BECAUSE
yUtev	guess
yUṭ-fE	Therefore
yUtwO	Instinct
Ỵv	Oppose (passive resistance)
-Yv-	female-, passive = conceptive
YṿAv, -Am	to Slumber, asleep
Yvem	passive
YṿE, -m, -v	Plastic, Adj, be p. —

aUI: Y	English
YvE-mav	to mold (= form) V
Yṿe(-v-Am)	(to)Slip/ping = Part.
Yv-kEbọs	Hen
YvO-m Yvogz	langu/or, -id womb
Yṿom -	FEMALE
Yv(om)oyt	ovum
Yṿov	Conceive
-Yvs (e.g. se-yvs	something — -ed; -en something given = a gift)
Y v ụ	SHE
Y-vugav Yv-ukbos YvUm	'unbuild' = dismantle mare passive, conceptive
Y v ụ s	WOMAN
Yvụyg	Skirt, Frock
Yw- Y-wam	weak-, soft- unable
Ywanbs	Thread
Y w Ẹ - m	SOFT/matter
YwEd	cushion
Yẉe-v	Fail/ure
YwEmos	mollusk
Yẉo-m, -v	Weak/ness, -en
YwO-m YwQ-UyrO	timi/dity, -d asthenia
Y w ọ z (a m)	LEFT/side
YwUm Y(x)a Y-yo-wam yYpAzm	impotent nowhere immortal infinite, unending
Y ẓ U - m, - v	GENERAL/ity, -ize

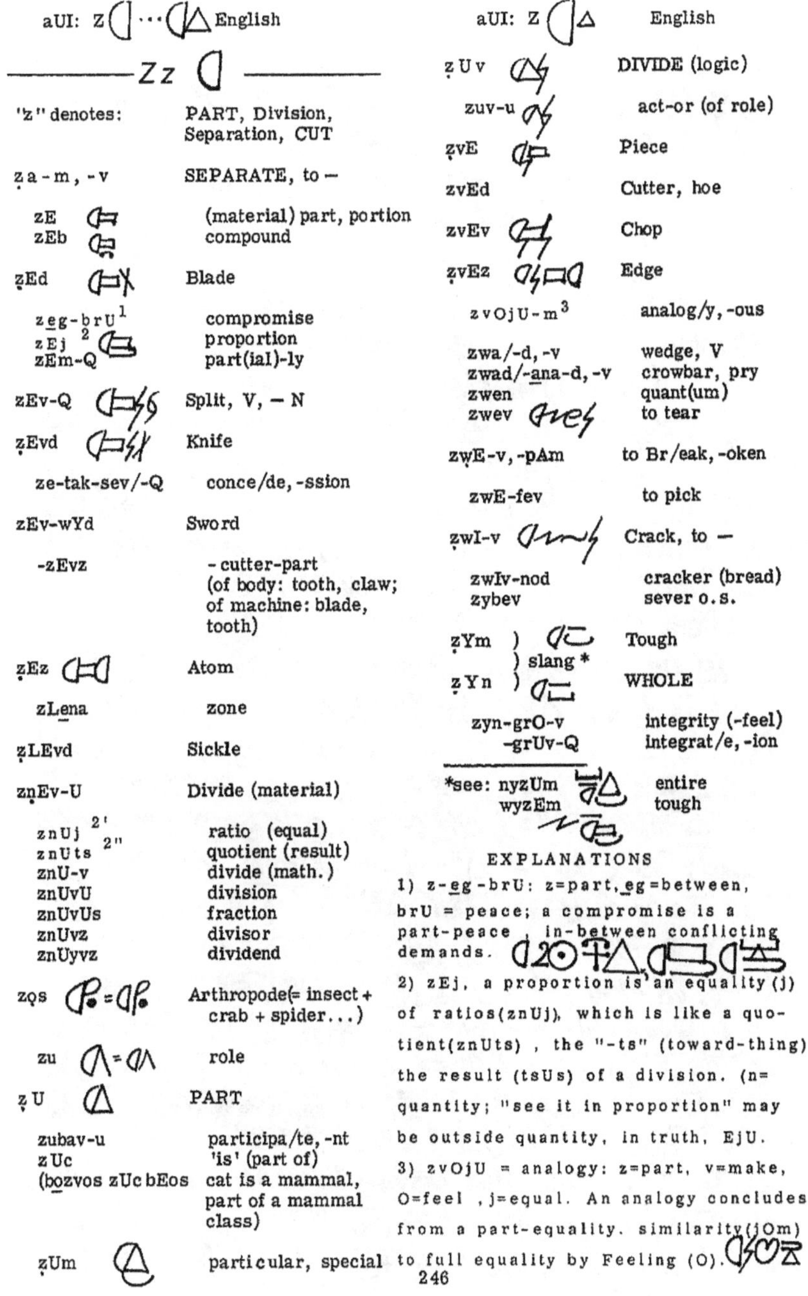

aUI: Z ···	English
Zz	
"z" denotes:	PART, Division, Separation, CUT
ẓa-m, -v	SEPARATE, to —
zE	(material) part, portion
zEb	compound
ẓEd	Blade
zeg-brU[1]	compromise
zEj[2]	proportion
zEm-Q	part(ial)-ly
zEv-Q	Split, V, — N
ẓEvd	Knife
ze-tak-sev/-Q	conce/de, -ssion
zEv-wYd	Sword
-zEvz	- cutter-part (of body: tooth, claw; of machine: blade, tooth)
ẓEz	Atom
zLena	zone
ẓLEvd	Sickle
ẓnEv-U	Divide (material)
znUj[2']	ratio (equal)
znUts[2"]	quotient (result)
znU-v	divide (math.)
znUvU	division
znUvUs	fraction
znUvz	divisor
znUyvz	dividend
zọs	Arthropode(= insect + crab + spider...)
zu	role
ẓU	PART
zubav-u	participa/te, -nt
zUc	'is' (part of)
(bozvos zUc bEos	cat is a mammal, part of a mammal class)
ẓUm	particular, special

aUI: Z	English
ẓUv	DIVIDE (logic)
zuv-u	act-or (of role)
ẓvE	Piece
zvEd	Cutter, hoe
zvEv	Chop
ẓvEz	Edge
zvOjU-m[3]	analog/y, -ous
zwa/-d, -v	wedge, V
zwad/-ana-d, -v	crowbar, pry
zwen	quant(um)
zwev	to tear
zẉE-v, -pAm	to Br/eak, -oken
zwE-fev	to pick
ẓwI-v	Crack, to —
zwIv-nod	cracker (bread)
zybev	sever o.s.
ẓYm)	Tough
) slang *	
ẓYn)	WHOLE
zyn-grO-v	integrity (-feel)
-grUv-Q	integrat/e, -ion

*see: nyzUm — entire
wyzEm — tough

EXPLANATIONS

1) z-eg-brU: z=part, eg=between, brU = peace; a compromise is a part-peace, in-between conflicting demands.

2) zEj, a proportion is an equality (j) of ratios(znUj), which is like a quotient(znUts), the "-ts" (toward-thing) the result (tsUs) of a division. (n= quantity; "see it in proportion" may be outside quantity, in truth, EjU.

3) zvOjU = analogy: z=part, v=make, O=feel, j=equal. An analogy concludes from a part-equality, similarity(jOm) to full equality by Feeling (O).

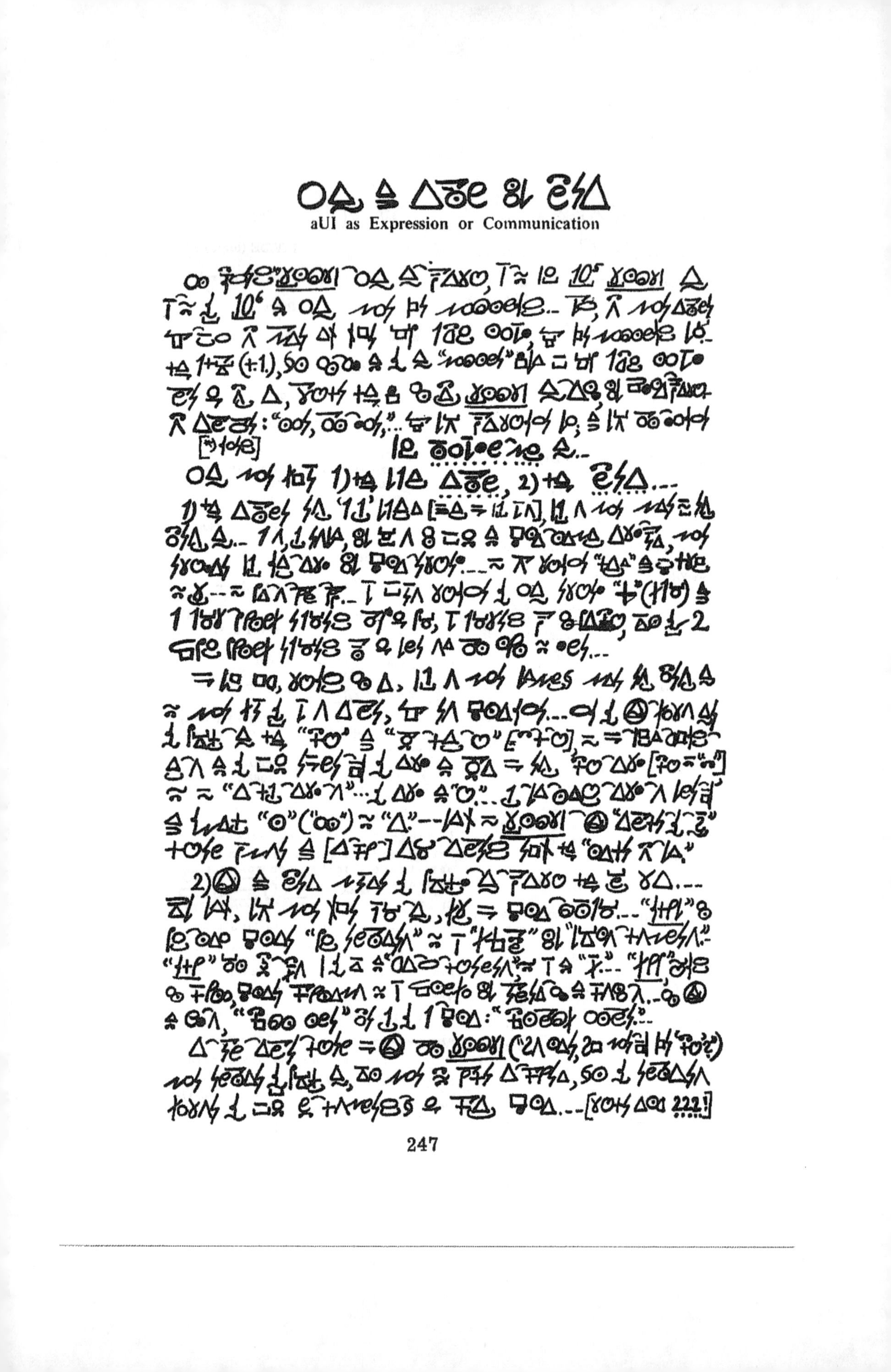

aUI as Expression or Communication

aUI as Expression or Communication

In the following English-aUI vocabulary neither all hundred-thousands of English words nor the millions of aUI words can be included. Still, you can express whatever you like by using simpler substitutes, which are included here. E.g. if for the very word "include" no simpler replacement comes to your mind, look it up in a common English dictionary or synonym list. You will find: enclose; contain, put-in (=gav, tag-sav), which we listed here as we included (put-in) all *irreplaceable* words.

aUI can be used 1) for individual expression, 2) for communication.

1) For expressing his unique individuality, each man can create his own words. Alone or in a group of Semantic Meditation he can first envisage each category or symbol. A child saw "goodness" as something warm and bright—a Christmas tree. Another girl saw the aUI symbol of the cross as one ray-arm reaching upward to heaven, another radiating down in mercy, but the two horizontal arms reaching out to embrace and give.

Out of these visualized elements each can freely create his own words and can let others guess what he meant. Before the aUI leader tells the standard word for "love" as "together-good-feeling": (=b-r-O), a schizothymic of the group would omit the idea of togetherness from his love-concept, and a puritan—the idea of feeling. Autistic idealists would stress "g" (inside) and "U" (spirit). Thus an English-aUI guessing game serves as diagnostic tool to "know thyself."

The more he is understood by others, the better he is adjusted to the group.

2) aUI as *communication* needs the standard vocabulary for quick understanding. Even so, we can use abbreviations, clear from the context. "Prof" in a college means "professor", not profit or professional. "Pro" among boxers is the opposite of amateur, not of "con(-tra)." "Doc", heard in a hospital is no "dock" for ships or prisoners. In mechanics' aUI, "brElg gev" means univocally "a screw enters."

Guessing games from aUI into English ("Who knows what 'brO' could be?") can teach the standard words, but can also help psychotherapy, if the teacher leads the group cooperatively to the right meaning.

In psycho-counseling a Nazi, who had the obsession to "die for the glory of the Leader," we analyzed "glory", and developed "kUO" as "god-feeling." Finally he himself wondered: "Why should I die so that Hitler could feel like God?"

PART VII B

Vocabulary: English — aUI

Not all the 400,000 words of the English language, nor the billions of words of aUI, can be here. If you don't find a word, look it up in Worldbook dictionary and use its definition, or in Roget's Thesaurus, and use its synonyms. Or simply say it in shorter words: He 'abandoned' his girl = he went away from her when she needed him ('went' you find in Webster dictionary as Past of 'go'). He abandoned his land = he yielded or gave it up — forever (cnA-ytev).

NB, A dot under a letter indicates the basic category, under which a word is explained in Part V, Encyclopedia, E.g. UL look up 'L.' Verbs end in -v, adjectives in -m. Add/ition = tebne(v) or tebne-v means: addition = tebne, to add = tebnev, thus the aUI verb is longer. In aUI the noun is mostly short & basic. (Alphabetic sequence may be a few places modified.) CAPITALS in English mark the most important IRREPLACEABLE concepts. Capital first letter means still important words included in 3rd edition; small letter (l.c.) set in to right marks less essential additions. In aUI Capitals mean LONG vowels, also L is Capital, for l looks like I. Footnotes show how to define & replace with smaller words. "/-" marks stem-end: yana/-v, UIs = yanav, yanaUIs.

associat/ion, -e, =N, adj ‖ buna, -v-u, -m means: association = buna,
V: associate = bunav, V
=N: associate = bunavu
= adj: associate = bunam

If English & aUI correspond, ' sets off root from ending: predominan/ce, -t = pwU-m means pwU=N, pwUm = adj. If part of aUI is in parenthesis, LIFE(guard) = (jE)ytyrvu, = (water) rescuer, the full word is used first, & once he is known "ytyrvu" = rescuer, is enough.

English & aUI correspond in same sequence: BE(ing); is, conditionally ‖ =cEv(s), c', Qc means to BE = cEv, a Being = cEvs; is = c', is conditionally = Qc.

English, as French & Chinese, has thousands of homonyms; Shakespeare warned: "equivocation will be our undoing." So miss (N; v) = r(yn)yvu; ybOv means: Miss Noun, Ms = ryvu (or, little miss, girl = rynyvu); or: miss, verb feel the lack of = yb-Ov, the feeling of without. Since aUI makes the meaning clear, no explanation should be needed, if the reader savors each aUI element. The redundant meanings are ignored for: 'I missed the target"; we say, 'I did not hit it." I missed my rendevous: I did not find him there.

Aa

"A"

English	aUI
A (article)	yI
abbot	am-kUtu-kwu
abbreviat/-e, ion	yana/v, -UIs,
abdomen	yk-og
ability	wam-U
(-)Able	(-)wam
ABOUT	UL
ABOVE (-inside)	ak, (kag) (as God)
absent	Y-fam
Absolute	am-Um
absorb	gEtyv
Abstract, adj	Y-cEmUm
(Abstracta end in	-U
academy	kam-gnubas
accelerate	(tnEk-)v-nev
accent (=main tone)	kwUm-AI
Accept	tsyv
accident (ce-incidence)	yr-tcyvs, (at-tyke)
accomplish	vrEv
accord, -V	rOb, -ev
According to	ag-rOb-eb
Account, -v	nUmI-v
accuse	fyr-vUIv
Accustom	(nA-)tedEv
ace (-of hearts)	a-viOvs (a-gog)
achieve-ment	treve/v
ACID, -adj	Y grEm
Acoustics	IOvU
acquiescence	rYvU
acquire	bav-fev, et-bav
acquisitive/-ness	bav-ve(-m)
ACROSS	kad
ACT/-ion, -or	yU/-v-Q, -vu
to act (on stage), -or	zuv-u
ACTIVE	vem
actual/, -ity;-ly	cvUm, cvU; vUg
ADD/ition	tebne(v)
addict/, -ion	yr-wyv-u, -U
to be ___ -ed	yr-wyvwUv
address N (place)	vavas
adequate (adj)	jrUm
Adjectives end in:	"-m"
adjective	mUIs
Adjust-ment	brUv-s
admiral	najEn-byd-wu
admir/e, -ation	(k)riOv, -Q
admi/-t, -ssion	tag-dyv, /-Q
adrenal-in	ve-jEvogz-Ed
Adulter/-y, V	(Yr-)yg-bo-brO-v
advance/ment	pre/v
advantage	prQz
adventure	(thyr-)wO(-vU)
Adverbs end in:	"-mQ" or "-g"
adverb	bvUIs
Advertise/ment	rUmti-v
Advi/ce, -se	torvUI, -v
aerob/e, -ic	kE-io/ms, -m
affect	tvOv
AFTER	yAp
Again	kfA
AGAINST	Y d
Age	oA
Aggressive/ness	tydbrU-m
Agree/ment	brUje-v; bjU-v
Agricultur/e(-al)	robE-gUw(-Qm)
ahead	pat
aim, V	tes, -ev

English: Air	aUI
AIR-y	kE(n)/, kE(nQ)m '(kE = gas)
Airplane	kEged
albumin	oyt-bimE
alcohol	rOjE-v-kE
algebra-ic	UIz-mUn-gU/w, -m
alienat/e/d, -ion	(v-) yrybO/-m, -v
alike	jOm
ALIVE	om
Alkal/ic, -ine	grEm
ALL	can
allergy, (have —)	og-yr-typ-e(v)
allign	janav
alliterat/e, -ion	j-Ap-Iz(-ev)
allocate	vrav
Allow, is — ed	dYv, (pass.) dyYv
alloy	byf-rE
allure	yr-tabwe-v
ALMOST	bUt
alone	amfam
alphabet (ABC—)	UIz-tUb (ABC-Ax)
Already (by-now)	Ud-fA
ALSO	bIb
altar	kU-kvad
alter	tyfev
although	dyf
Aluminum	ekbirE
Always	cnA
ambiguous/, -ity	nEsgU-m
ambitio/n, -us	kyftO-m, twuk-ve-m
AMONG	nag
AMOUNT	ben-v
Amphibian	bEjEos
Amuse/ment	yn-rO(-v)
analog/y, -ous	jyOxU, -m
analys/e, -is	U-ytbe/-v
Ancestor	ytytu

English: Arc	aUI
Anchor	yk-bE-tEL
AND	Ib
angel	kna-u
Ang/er, -ry	wydO-m
ANGLE	gebana
to angle (fish)	tELev (jEos)
ANIMAL, (big —)	os, -nos
Animate	(U-)vov
ankle	yk-bo-baz
annoy/-ance	v(-yn-)twydO-v
annul	vYv
Anoint	(kUr)eijEv
ANSWER (v)	Y-hI (v)
Ant	vizos
Anticipat/ion, -e	pO-v
antithesis	yd-U-sav-Q
anvil	tyk-weyvd
Anxiety (feel —)	AtyrO(v), thyrO(-v)
ANY (-body, -thing) -way	Ym (-u, -s) -hUd
Apart	tyb
APPARATUS	beds
APPAREL	uyg
appeal	vOe-v
appear-ance	(t)Oiv-Q
appetite (have —)	dotO-v
applau/de, -se	brUI/-nIv, -nI
Apple	nakot
Appl-y, -ication	etdEv, -U
appreciat/e, -ion	vrOnUrv-Q
approach	ate-v
appropriate	jwUr-bram
approv/e, -al	brUI-v
apricot	ei-wEg-kot
aqueduct	jEdak
arbitrary	ytna-twUm
arcan/e, -um	(k)ryp-nUm-s

English: A r	aUI
Arch	tLak
architect/ure	vuga/-vu, -gUw
ardor	nO
area	bEnaz, enan
Argu/ment, -able	ryrUI, -v, -wam
arise, come to be	at-kav, tcev
Arm	k-oged
Arm/ament, — v	wyd-Ev
armor	wuyg
Army	bydwun
AROUND (-moving)	aL, (eL)
arouse	vOtkev
ARRANGE/ment	trab-ev
array	-ax
arrow	dz-anEs
ART-ist, visual —	rOw/U-u, riOv/U, -u
artery	yt-gog-anyEd
arthritis	baz-iEm-yro
arthropod	zos
artichoke	dzez-riOiod
Article [1](a, the), [2](essay), [3]item	[1]psUIs; [2] yn-vUiOs, [3]sEz
artif/icial, -act	uv-(EpAm), -s
AS (...AS)	Uj (...Uj)
as for (me)	Uj rUt (fu)
(=LIKE	jOm)
(=while, when	jAg)
as-it-were	Uj-sE-yEc
ascend	tak-av
ashamed	tyiOm
Ashes	iEtE,
Ask	hIv
Asleep	(U-)yvAvAm
asparagus	kaniod
aspect	atiO: UtiO

English: A w	aUI
aspir/ation, -e	atU, -v
Ass, donkey	yr-ukbos, bybi-ukbos
asset(-s)	rUz
assign	at-sev
associat/ion, -e, =N	buna, -v, -u
assume	Ut-sav
a-sthenia	y-wQ (-Uyro)
AT (-all)	ab (-can)
atmosphere	kEma
Atom	zEz
attach(ment)	te-bAv(s)
Attack	wyde-v, yd-wev
ATTEMPT	tvev
Attention	Utve
Attitude	UamA
Attract/ion	tab-we(v)
audience	IOvu
augment	nEv
Aunt	ytu-jyt/Lu, -yvu
Auspic/es, -ious	tUrO-m
author (=creator)	vytu, (v)ytUvu wUvu
Authority	kUw
AUTOMAT/IC-ally -on	fem-Q fem-es
Auto(mobile)	wuged
AUTUMN	yp-akiA
Average	jnUmz
avocado	(iim)bLE(dzeL)-kot
Avoid	ygev
Awake(n) (tr)	vAm(-ev)
aware	gUOm
AWAY	yta

English	aUI
awl	dzand
Ax	dzEd
Axis	dLana

Bb

English	aUI
Baby; animal —	yntu; yntos
BACK—(of body)	Yp(s), Ypaz; (Ypoz)
-bone	yp-og-wE
(-ward)	typ
Bacillus	yn(an)os
Bacon	Lod(bos-Lod)
Bacterium	ynios
BAD (= evil)	rym, (yrUm)
BAG	stag
bait, — V	yr-tabwev, -d
bake-r	nod-vu, ygjE-roduv-u
Balance, -V	jyktE-v
balcony	uga-pyg
BALL, -oon	Las, kE-Las
Bamboo	tok-nio
Banana	ankot
Band (to bind), music	wanab, v-rIO-b
Bank (money), river—	drEga, jE-kaz
baptiz/e, -m	kU-gjE/-v(-Q)
barb-wire	dzez-rEana
bare/ness	yb-ygz-Qm
Bark (tree-)	tok-yg
barley	ei-rOjE-to
BASE (=basis)	ykaz
-ball	tweb-Las
(adj = vile, gross) base(-ness)	yr-yk-Em(-U)
basic-ally	(p)ykaz-m, -Q
Basin	jEga

English	aUI
Basket	wanab-stag
bat (animal)	kEd-ynbos
Bath-e	jEuga-v
battery (electr.)	weivd
BE(-ing); is;	cEv(-s); c';
condition ally,	Qc;
naturally, partly,	oc, zQc,
spiritually	Uc
= equals	jEc
beacon	et-viOv-id
beak	dz-ogta
Bean(s)	eLiod
Bear (give birth);	(tvoev);
carry,	skev,
(carnivore)	nosdos
beard	kup-yk-noyg
bearings (direction)	traz
Beat, (strik	tweb-ev, (tswev)
BEAUTI(FUL), -fy	riO(m), v-riOv
BECAUSE (of)	yUt, Uyt
beckon	tiyiv, et-viOvsev
BECOME	tEv
Bed	y-kavd
-bug	yr-buizos
Bee	grizos
been, having —	cEpAm, cEpAvQ
Beer	ei-rO-jE
beet(s)	ai-dzeL-iod
Beetle	wizos
BEFORE, in front	Ap, ap
Beg	tOrv
Begin/ning	pe-v
BEHAVIOR	vUma
BEHIND, N	Yp, Lypogz
Being = N, Part, grnd	cEvs, cEvAm, cEvQ

English: Bel	aUI
Belie-f, -ve	EjUrO-v
Bell	IrEg (-Id)
belly (stomach)	pLyk-og, (godz-Lyg)
Belong	ba(r)yv, cErv
BELOW	Yk
belt: (body-), wide	Log-ana, Lyg-ena
BEND, bent PP; =warp	veLv, veLpAm; weLv
Benefit, V; -N	rUv;-s
Benzol	weijE
bequeath	ytu-sev
Berry, (tree-), cluster	yn-(k)Lot, bLot
BESIDE(S)	baz
bet	thyr-vyhOd-ev
betray/al	yr-tyg-UI(v)
BETWEEN	ge, eg
beyond	kyb
Bible	kUm-Ugs
Bicycle	e-Led
BIG	nam
Bind	banav
bio-logy (kingdom, phylum, class, order, family, genus, species = 7th clasif.)	o-gUw (na-jomz, ne-, ni-, nu-, no-, nA-, nE-jomz)
BIRD, (big —)	kE(n)os
Birth (bear)	toe(v)
BIT-e, (—v)	odz-e (-v)
Bitter	Y-grOm
BLACK (-bird)	ybim, (ybi-rI-kEos)
BLADE	zEd
Bless (verbal)	vrU(I)v
Blind, v	iyOm, viyOv

English: Boy	aUI
blink	iyiOv
bliss	UkrO
blister	gjEL
Blood	ogai
Blo(ss)om	iorio
Blow, a —; to — (v)	tswe; (v)ekEv
BLUE (adj.)	ui(m)
Blunt	y-dzem
Blush	taiv
Board	wenas
BOAT	jEged
bob (up & down)	kykev
BODY	o-g
(to)Boil, boiling (adj)	jEtkEv, jEtkEm
bolt & nut	brELg-aL-brELg
Bomb	twIyg-wyd
bond	wanob
bondaged	y-fUw/e(m)
BONE	og-wE
Book (-review)	Ugs(-mUvU)
boom, (high crest)	kQ, krQ
Boot	kyk-boyg
Border	yg-ana
bosom	pL-ogwa
boss	kwu
botany (see biolog.)	io-gUw
(any plant can be identified with 7 figures)	
both	be
Bottle	jEg
Bow; (tr.)v— down	tLak; tyk(v)Lev
bowl	gLad
Box; -er	gwad; bob-bydev-u
Boy	yn-vu

English: Bra	aUI
brace = bracket	bAvd
Brain	o-Uz
Brake(-s)	vyev(-d)
Branch	tok-yt
Brass	beirE
Brat	yr-ty
Brave	wOm
BREAD	nod
Breadth	tytana
(to)break (& enter)	zwEv, (teg-zwE-v)
breakfast	yitA-do[1]
Breast	ogwa
Breath-e	okE-v
Brick	bEn-wE
Bridge	jEk-da
briefcase	ske-gad
BRIGHT, -en	im, tiv
brilliant	nim
Bring	vetsev
Broad	tytanam
broccoli	kogiod-tioriO[2]
Broken	zwEpAm
broom (-sweep) bronze	knand(ev) yi-beirE
Brother (-hood) — &sister = siblings)	jytvu, jytU (jytu)
Brown; dirty —, (adj)	i'a'i(m): yr-ai(m)
Brush, (v.) (paint —)	nand(-ev), mi- —, mivEd
brussels sprouts	yn-kog-iod
Brutal/-ity	yr-wo(-m)
brute (-matter)	yum-s, yom-E

English: BY	aUI
Bubble	kEgjE
Bucket	jEgad
Bud	tio-riO
bug	yr-izos
Build(ing)	ugav(s)
Bulb, (plant-part)	oLs, oLz
bulge, (v) bull bullet bum	Lyg(-ev) vob-(ijE-bonz) LEs Ys-Ev-u[3]
Bundle	banapAs
Buoy, -ant (light)	akjEd, takem
Burden-some	yktE(w)-m
bureaucra/cy, -tic	uwa-wU, -m
to BURN, a —	iEv, iEpAs
burp, — v	godz-kE-I-(v)
Burst	tygwe(v)
bus bush	nu-ged (L)yntok
Bus/y, -iness	ruve-m
BUT (= however)	yUg
Butter	bijE-Lod
Butterfly	riOzos
Buttocks	Lypoz
Button	bLena
Buy	rEtsev
BY (means of) -the side of -the way of passing-by	Ud deb deb-da dyb

---

[1] morning food

[2] head vegetable = cabbage buds (toward plant-beauty)

[3] nothing-doer

Cc

English	aUI
cabbage	kog-iod
Cable	rE-ana
cage	yr-os-ga
Cake	grO-nod
Calculat/e(-or), -er(man),-ion	munU/-v, -d, -vu, -vU
Calendar	akiAnz
CALL (out); (=name)	unIv; fUIv
(C)calory	(n)iEm-an
camel	Lyp-uk-bos
Camera	i-jiOvad
CAN (be able),	wav, P. wapAv
can N	rE-gad
Canary-bird	ei-kEos
cancer (-disease)_ous	yr-tneg(-yro)-Qm
candidate for —	Ut- —
Candle (wax-light)	kiE-id, (ei-yvE-id)
Candy	grOms
Cannon	nI-wyd
canopy	kugaz
Canvas	nanab
capture	wyr-fe(v)
CAR	(da)ged
carbohydrate	Ez-A-jEn
Carbon	EzA
carburetor	b-weijE-kE-d
CARD	yn-ena
Care	Ote-v
caricature, -v	(rO-)knE-viO-v
carnivore	osdos
carpet	gayk-uygE
carpent/er, -ry	tEk/-vu, -vUn
Carriage	u-ged
Carrot	ei-dzeL(-iod)
CARRY	skev
Cart	aged
Case, (e.g.: in — of)	agnUs
cast (=hurl, shot)	kEdvev
Castle, (King's —)	(k)wuga, (knuga)
Cat	bozvos
Catch	tyv-fev
cattle	bijE-bonz
cauliflower	kogiod-riOio
(causatives start with:)	v(e)— -v
CAUSE, -ative	YtUs, -vUm
to Cause, -ing	vytUv, -Am
Cave	gyEga
Cease	yeyv
Ceiling	gak
celebrate	kU-riA-v, krO-iAv
celery	oii-gEz-iod
Cell (bio-)	oz
cellar	yk-uga
cellulose	io-wyg-E
Cement	wE-b-vE
cemetery	yo-enaz
Center	gaz
cephalopod	k(og-)oged (ywEmos)
cereal	nyn-tod
cerebrum	U-ogz
ceremony	riO-(na-)vUma
CERTAIN/-ty	yhO-m
certif/y, -icate	vEjUv,-d
Chain	nyELb
Chair	yktad
Chalk	bibE

English: Cha	aUI
challenge	tap-nIv
Chance	wyU
Change	tyje-v
channel; sound-chaos	jEda; I-da)-v) bjyj
Chapter	nUgz
Character	Uma
Charcoal	tEk-ybibE
charge, V, N (electr.)	bwei-v, -n
charisma-tic	brO-wU-m
charity	tyk-brO
Charm-ing	wriO-v-Am
chart	ek-atiO
chase	v-ne(v)
CHEAP	yk-drEm
cheat (-man)	Yr-yEjU(v-u)
check (-pay)	fUI-drE(-v)
Cheek	kupyg
Cheese (-food)	bEbijE(od)
CHEMI-cal, -stry	EgU-m, -w
Cherry	ai-kot
Chest	gwa
Chew	odzEv
Chicken	kEbos
Chief; adj.	pu; pUm
CHILD-ish, animal —	tu-m, tos
chimpanzee	jumos
Chin	kup-yk
chirp	tIrv
chlorophyll	o-i i(-mE)
chocolate	iai-grOs
choke (tr)	(v)-yokE-v
choice, (choose)	ytnav
Chop	zvEv
Christ(-ian), anointed	Xrist(-u), kUr-eijE-pAm

English: Coc	aUI
Christmas (-day)	kU-toe(-iA)
Church	kUga
cigar/et	(n)ybikEd
Cinema/play	evUis(a)
CIRCLE, -ulate	maL-ev
Circumference	Lygana
Circumstance	mAL, LQ
citizen	nubu
City	nuba
clam	wEyg-jE-ykos
clap, v	botbI(v)
clash	yd-bwIv
CLASS; bio —	bUz; ni-jomz
Claw	ozEvz
clay	ywEb E
CLEAN, v, -er(means)	prim, -ev, -d
CLEAR	dim(-ev)
clench	bAwev
cliché	Yg-jwyz-wUI
cliff	bEk-tyk
climate	kamQ
climb	aktev
cloak	knuyg
CLOCK	n-Ad
close	ytgev
CLOTH	uygE
CLOTHE(S)	uyg
Cloud-y	jEk-Qm
clown; (V,N), -ish	rOm-ybrav, -u-m
Club: social; stick	nuLb, LanEs
Coal	ybibE
Coast	jEn-ygana
Coat	kuyg
cobra	iOd-nanos
coccus	Lynos

English: Coc	aUI
Cock	vom-kEbọs
coco-nut	wEyg-knot
code (rule; signs)	jwyz; wyU-viOv(s)
coelenterate	gyEmos
Coffee	tọ-jE
coffin	yo-gwad
cog-wheel	dzez-Led
coil (long, high)	tap-Le(v), tak-Le-v
coincidence	bagQ
COLD (-sick[ness])	(yr-)y ị E m (-yro/m)
collaborate, -or	b-uwev-u
Collar	kogzeL
collect, -ive	sbA/v, -pA-ms
college	kam-gUa
Coloniz-e, -ation	artụv, -U
COLOR, v	mị-v Ev
Column	(twE-)ḳ (L)anas
co(m)-...	b-, tab-, teb-...
Comb	nEẓavd
combin-e, -ation	besa-v, -vQ(-pAs)
combustible	iEdE-m
COME, (sex)	ṭev, (Otkev)
comet	jEki
Comfort, N, V, -able	tvOr-d; -v, -wam
(a)Command	kẉev(s)
COMMANDS end in:	"-rv"!
commerc/e, -ial	stytrE/m
Committee	wynub
COMMON	ḅUm
Communicat(ion), sound -	bev(U), bIv(U)
commun/-ion, -e	bU/-v-Q
community	ynub
Compan/ion; -y	cụb, nubu; nub
Compar/e, -ison	bịiOv, -U

English: Con	aUI
compass (mar.-)	taz(-tabwe)d = tvazd
compasses	maL-d
compassion, felt —	byrO, -v
Compet/ition	ḳyftU-v
complement	cvarmz
Complete/ness	caṛm, car(v)
Complex/ity;/—psych.	nUḅza, -m;-w
complexion	oyg-mi
complicate V.	nUbzav
compliment	(t-)rUIs
component	bEz
compose; -r(music)	bzEv; rIO-wUv-u, -U
composite	bzEpAm
composition; (music)	bzE; (rIO-)wUvU
COMPOUND	zEb
compromise	fyf-brU(v)
compulsion, (neurosis)	wyvU(-Uyr), (tyf-Yr-zwyvO)
co(n)-..., (toward)	b-, tab-; teb
concave	gyELzam
concede	ze-tak-sev
Conceive	yỵov
concentrat-ion, -e	bwU, -v
concentric	maL-aL-maL-m, jagaz
(-)concept	(-)Uz
conceptivity (sense for spirit)	ryvO
concern, -v	Ot-be-v
concert	brIO
conclude/-sion	U-v-ytU(-v)
Concrete, adj, N	çEmUm, bEwE
concur/rence	bre-v
condemn, -ation	(yr-,)tyc-jwUsk/uv, -U
condens/e, -ation	bwav, Q
CONDITION; v tr	Q(=Ö), mA; vQv
under what conditions?	hQ?
Conduct: (behave); let thru (electr.)	vUma(-v); dvev
Cone	dẓeL
confess/ion	f-yr-UI(v)

English: Con-	aUI
confide/nce	trUO-v
Configuration	mab
confine/ment	yr-g(L)av-Q, g(L)ytgev
conform/ism	bUj-ma(m)
confus (vtr)	ve-bjyjOv
confus/ion, (feel —ed)	bjyjO(-v)
congratulat/-e, -ions	rU-tO(v), ytOr-tO(v)
conjecture (v)	yiU(v)
conjunction	bUIs
CONNECT-ION	bUv-s, bQv-Q
Conque-st, (-r)	tykwe(-v)
conscience (feel), know	(ryrO), grU-gU
conscientious/ness	ryrU-m
Conscious-ness	gUOm-U
consider-ation	LUv-Q
consist of	bzE-yv Ud
consistency: (character; material)	jam-taz-U; bzE-w
Consol/ation, (-e)	tvOr(v)
consonant	bIz
constant, -cy	jQm-Q
Construct/ion	bEtkU-v
CONTAIN(-ER)	gav, (gad)-, (s)gav
contemplate-r	kU-iOv-u
contemporary	bAm
Contempt-uous	tykO-m
content adj.	UgrOm
CONTENTS	gE
context	bLUx
Continent	bEn-zU
Continue, -ing	tap-av, -Am
continuous, (uninter.)	bQm, (bybyEgem)
contradict	Y-UIv
contrast, v	byU-v
contribute, -ion	sbev-Q
Control, v	kwU-v

English: Cov	aUI
Convenient, (-ce)	bram(s), vram(s)
conven/tion-al, -e	bunte-m, -v
conversation, -e	tyt-bUI, -v
conversion: rel, ; - neurosis	U-trUvQ; (YrgO-)tyg-ogQ
convey-or, -belt	vetsev-wanab
convi-ction, -nce	vEjUrO-v
(to) Cook, -y	rodu(v), yn-grOnod
(to) Cool	ryiE/m (-v)
cooperat/-ion	bvU-v
cope	jwQv
Copper	eirE
Copy, (N)—, to —(v)	jiOm-s, -ev
coral	ai-(wE)gyEmos
Cord	wana
Cork	yg-tEk
corn	nam-to
corner	bena
corpse	yomu, yog
corral	bosa
Correct; -ion, -ness (= adequate)	trU/m, -v; vU, -mU (jrUm)
correlat(-e), ion	bexU, (-v)
correspond(ence)	bjUx/ev
corrupt, adj	v-yrU-v, pAm
cosm-ic, -os	xrOb-ca/m, -cu, -cU
cost	drEyv
Cotton	kE-bio
Cough	tyg-okE-I
council	trUIvub
counsel, -or	trUIv-u
Count	mUnIv
COUNTRY	una
county	nuwaz
Courage(ous)	wO(m)
course	tapne
court (of law)	jwUsk-as
COVER, V	kyg-z, -ev

English: Cow	aUI
Cow	bijE-bos
crab	wELzos
Crack(-v), er	zwI(v)-nod
cram, -med	sgvav, Esga(pA)m
cramp, — v	Yr-bwamQ-v
crane: bird,	nan-kogz-kEos,
lift —	nan-vekted
Crash, (-together)	twIv, (bwIv)
Crawl	ykev
Cream	bijEk
Creat/e, -ive, -or; act	wUv, -Am, -u; vUv...
Creature	çEvs, wUyvs
Credit	nEjUrO-v
cricket	rI-izos
Crime; commit a —	yrv-s; yrv
Criminal	yrv-u
cripple, (v)	yrogu, (v-)yrtnev(-u)
crisis	tyr-hQ
crochet	tLyp-ev
crocodile	nyr-ykeos
crop (produce)	bio(s)
Cross	dana-v
crow(-bar)	ybi-kEos, (zwad-anad)
crowd	bnun
crown	kUg-yg
crucify, -ixion	vyr-danav-Q
Cruel-ty	vyrO/m-Q
crumble	nyn-zEv
crunch	nI-tyk-zwEv
Crush	tyk-zwE(v)
crust	w(E)yg
Cry	yrOIv
crystal	diwE
cub; cube	ynbos; jina
cucumber	ii-aniod
cuddle	(riE-)brOs/-ev,
-y	-wam
cultivate	artuv
Culture	nuvUs

English: C, D	aUI
Cup	jEtgad
cure	vrov
curi/osity, -ous	hUtO, -m
Current	jEte
curse, —v	wyr-UI, -v
Curtain	tykena
CURVE, v	tLe, -v
Cushion (head; tool)	kog-ywd; ywEd
Custom-ary	navUma-m
a Cut	dEz
to CUT (split)	dzEv, (zEv)
(P.P.) been cut	dzEpAm
Cutter (-part), -man	zvEd, (zEvz), dzEvu
cycle	mQL
Cylind/er, -rical	Lana, -m

Dd

dagger	dzwyd
dainty/ness	rywo-m
dam	yd-ejE -wE
DAMAGE (vtr)	(v)yrte(-v)
Dance, V	riOe-v
Dandelion	ei-riOio
Danger-ous	tyr-m
dare	twOv
DARK/ness	yi-m(U)
DAUGHTER	tyvu, (tLu)
dawn	tiA
DAY, (24 hrs.)	iA, (bEnA)
DEAD	yom
deaf	IyOm
DEAR	brOm
Death	yo

English: Deb	aUI
debase	tvykOv
Debt	wyrrE
decay, v	tyb-tyke, -v
dece/ive, -ption	yr-yEjU-v(Q)
decimal	Om 10
Deci/de, -sion, -sive	vUtse-v, —, -m
decode	tyg-vUviOv
Decrease (tr)	(v)y-tne(v)
de-duce	U-vytUv
DEEP	nykam
deer (see stag)	tonk-os
defect N; made —	yrUz; vyrz
Defen/d, -se; -less	ydyr-v, yb-ydyr
defin-e, -ite, -ion	mQ-v, pAm; mQ
Degree	tank
delay	vyprA-v
Delica/te, -cy	rywo-m
Delight	krOn, -v
demagog	yr-nu-/daiu, -kwu
demand	twUI-v
democracy	nu-knuw
democratic (majority-ruled)	nEk-mUn-knuwem
demon	w(yr)ykU
demonstrat/ion (mass-)	(un-En-)viOv-Q
denominator	fUI-mUn
den'y/-ial	yc-UI(v)
department	gUz U
Depend, -able, -ent	bytka-v, -wam, -vAm
Deposit	yksa(v)
depression; psy.	ykQ; (ye)ykyrO
deride	tyk-rOIv
descend	ytkev
describe	mUv
desert v, (leave)	g-yr-ytev
desert N	yo-bEna, YbjE-na
Deserve (=should be rewarded) (-t)	jrut-r-yv(-s)
Design, — v	tUvma-v
Desire, — v	t(s)Ob(ev)

English: Din	aUI
desolate	y-bOm
Despair (-ing)	y-trO-v, (-m)
Despise	tykOv
destin/-ation, -e, -y	kyUw/-taz, /ev, —
Destr/uct/ion, (-oy)	tyce(v), (t)vyce(v)
detachment (psy.)	rybO
Detail	yn(a)z
detect-ive	yt-kygev-u(-v)
determin/e, -ant	mQ-tnak-ev
Develop/ment	tyg-e(v)
Device, -se	(t)vU-d, -v
Devil	yr-kU
devour	zyn-(yr-)djEv
Dew (-drop)	yitA-jE(z)
diagnos/e, -is	U-diO-v
diagram	gUw-tUvma
Diamond	krOwE
diary	iA-Ugs
Dictionary	nUI-Ugs
DIE (death	yo-v
diet, — v.	jnA-do(v)
DIFFER-EN/T, ce	Y-jU(m, v), "jym"
Difficult, -y	ydrem, -U
Digger; (tool)	gyE'/-v-u;(-d)
Digest/ion	gode-v
dignity	kyg-nUr
diligent/, -ce	nE-ruwe-m(U)
Dim	y-dim
(-)DIMENSION	(-) n a
Dimin/ish, -ution	ynEv, y-tne(v)
(Diminutives begin:	yn-) yn-am
din, v	knI (v)

English: Din	aUI
Din/-e, -ner	ọdge-v
dip	gjEv
Diplomacy	un-ẉe-rOve
direct adj	y-dEm, yb-dQm
Direct/ion, -ly	t(v)az(ev)-emQ
direct/or	kvu(v)
Dirt/y, — v	(v-)y-pṛi/m-E, -v; yrE
Dis-, Dys-	tyb-, yt-
disappoint/ment	tyb-trO-v
disaster (strikes)	nyr-tcyv/s
discipline	vetgU-kwU
discord	y-rOḅ
Discover/-y	AṗUte-v
discrepancy (is)	tyjU(-v)
discriminate	(tyr-)vyjUv
Discuss/ion	tyt-UI-v
DISEASE	y ro
disguise	ked-vuyg-ev
Disgust	yr-sO
Dish (food-sort)	od-Lena, do-mEz
dis-illusion	(v)yt-Oiv
dis-integrate	(tyb-) nynzEv
Disk	Lena
Dislike	y-brỌ(v)
disobe/y, -dience	yd-ykwe-v
dispens/e, -ation	t-nu-sev-Q
disperse	tyb-(n)av
disregard	tyk-iOv
dissemble	vyOiv
dissociation (psy.)	fU-tyb-zO
Dissol/-ution, -ve	ytbe, -v
DISTANCE, v	yttạ-v
distill	kEjEv
distin/guish, -ction	vyjU-v
distort	yr-twev
distract/ion	tyb-twe-v
Distribut-ion	tnu-sev-Q

English: Dra	aUI
District	unaz
Disturb/ance	yt-bṛe(v)
ditch	ana-yE
DIVI/DE;-sion(math)	ẓ (n) Ev- U;znUv-U
divi/dend, -sor	znUyvz, znUvz
divine: v, adj	UOv, kUm
Divorce	ybo-v
dizzy/ness	tLyr-O(m)
DO (omit as auxiliary)	E v
(do) not be sad!	yc cErv UyrOm!
doctor	gUvu, gUwu
doctrine	vetgU-bUI
document	Uwam-pAtUI
Dog	waubos
dogma	EjUrO-wyvs
Doll	yn-u-ma
dolphin (porpoise)	u-jE(g)os
dome	kLuga
Domestic Animal	bos
domina/te, -nt	kwuv, -Am
donat/e, -ion	brO-sev, -Q
donkey	bybi-ykbos
Door; valve	ugta; yded
Double	ebzam
Doubt, v	hO-v
dough	nod-E
dove	brU-kEos
DOWN	t y ḳ
dragon	knyr-ykeos
Drain	jẸygte-v
Drama	UIviỌ
Draw: pull; picture	veṭev; Ui-anav
draw-back	yrẓ

English: D, E	aUI
Drawer	vetgad
Drawing	Uiana
dread	styrO-v
Dream, — v	yiviO-s, -v
DRESS, v	uyg (ev)
drill (a hole)	gyELd, yEd-ev
DRINK, (N); imbibe	jEv(s); jEtgo-v
drip (v)	jEze(v)
Drive (psy); v	ve(vO), (da)vev
drop N	jEz
to Drop, let-fall	tvykev
drug (bad —)	(yr-)trod
drum	oyg-Id
Dry, v	ygjE-m, -v
Duck (down, v)	jE-kEos (tykLev)
due	(wyv)rAm
Dull; senses	y-dzOm; yOm
dumpling	nodEL
duration	AvQ
During	Ag
dusk	tyiA
Dust	knynE
Duty	wryvU
Dwarf	ynu
Dwell/ing	ua(v)

Ee

English: D, E	aUI
Each	can
eagle	knu-kEos
EAR (-muffs)	IOz (-yg)
EARLY	prAm
earn (=be rewarded)	jrut-yv

English: Ele	aUI
earnest	yk-twU(m)
EARTH-(quake)	bEn, bE-wytte
Earthen-ware	bEns
EAST; -er	yita; kU-tak-iA
EASY	drem
EAT (dine)	dov, (odgev)
eccentric (man)	ygaz-m(u)
echinoderm	dzez-oyg(-os)
Echo	typ-I(v)
Econom-y(-ize)	yn-drEdU(v)
eden	rioba
Edge	zvEz
(book-) edit(-ion)	(Ugs-)tyg-sev(-Q)
Educat-ion	utUv-U
eel	nan-jEos
EFFECT-ive	tUs-rUm
Effort	tU
e.g. (=for example)	rUt artnU = r.a.
EGG	oyt
ego	O-fu-z
Eight, 8	I = 8
Either (both; each)	be; can
not — either	yc — bIb
Either — or	gaf — gaf
ELASTIC	(kyk-)vem
elect	r-ytnav
ELECTRIC/ity	wei-m
(-)electric device	(-)weid
electro-magnet	wei-tabwed
Electron	weiz
ELEMENT	Ez
Element H, He, Li (atomic numbers 1, 2, 3)	Eza, Eze, Ezi

English: Ele	aUI
elephant	(nan)kEmOz-nos
Elevat-ion(-e)	take(v)
Elevator	tak-ged
eliminate	vytev
elite (-man)	rytnam-u
ellipse	anal
Else	yfs
elucidate	vUiv
embarrass	tvaiv
embrace	brObLev
emerald	ii-rOwE
emit	tyg-vev
emotion	eO
Empathy	bOg
emphasis, -ize	pwUre-v
employ/er	vykwu-v
Empty (of things)	ygEm(ys-gam)
Enclos(ur)e	waLg/ev
encode	tag-vUviOv
encourage	ve-twOv
End-ing (= end-sound)	y-pev, ypAz, -v yp-I
Endanger	t(v)yrev
endeavor	tUwe
Enemy	ybru
Energy	ew
Engine	ves
Enjoy-ment	(k)rO-vU
enlighten/ment	gU-vi(v)
Enough	trUn
Enter/-ance	(at-)ge-v
Entertain(ment)	vynrOv(s)
enthus-e, -iasm;-iastic	gwU-trO-v, —, -m
entire/ty	nyz-Um
Entreat(y)	twOrv(U)

English: Ex	aUI
(letter) envelop (v), -e N	(vavUs-)kLyge (-v), -d
environment	aLQ
Env-y(ious); (status)	yr-tyf-rO(m); yr-tukO(m)
enzyme	o-vyjed
EQUAL/ity	jU(m)
equat-e, -ion	jUv-Q
equator(-ial)	ji-maL(m)
equilibrium	jyktew
equivocate	Yr-jUIv
erase-r	(yn-)tvyc-ev, -d
Err/or	Y-jUtE(v)
escape (v)	yt-yr-e(v)
especial-ly	ek-zUm-Q
essay (treatise)	afUs-UIn
essen/ce, -tial	cmU-m
esthetic-s, -al	riO-gUw-Um
Estrange, -d	yfa-v, -pAm
Etc.	Ibyf
Eternal	cnAm
ethic-s, -al	rU-gUw-Um
euphon-y, -ous	rIO-m
evangel	rU-vavU
evaporate	EtkEv
Even: level; even He!	jEkam; jUf(adv)
EVENING	itA
Event	cyvs
(-)Ever	(-)ymA
EVERY	can
Evil (adj)	yrU-m
(bio-)evol/ution, (ve)	(o-)tyg-ne(-v)
exact(-ly)	ayn-trUm(Q)
exaggerate-d	knE-viOv, -m
Exalted (-one)	U-kam-u
examin/ation	gUv-UmtiO-v
Example (ify)	artnU(v)

English: Exc	aUI	English: Fee	aUI
Excell/ent, -ence	k(yf)rU/-v, -m, —		
Except = but (only); = only-not, v	yUg(am); am-yc(-Qv); yUg-Qv	façade	pygaz
exceptional	yg-yf-Qm	Face (v)	kup(ev)
Exchange	tyf-gav	Fact	AvUs
Excite/ment	Oe-v	factor	vEvz
exclude	vygav	Factory	nuvsga
Excre/ment, -te	ydo-s, -v	Fail/ure (v)	ywe(v)
excuse	tryr-UIv	faith-ful (relig.)	rEjUrO(wa)m
execute	jwUs-vyov	fake	(yr-)pyg-vEv
Exercise (v)	trew-ev	FALL	tyke(v)
exert/-ion	tswU-v	fallacy	(yr)yt-EjU
EXIST/, ence	cEv, cU	FALSE/hood, -ify	yEjU(m), v-yEjUv
Expan-sion, -d	tygna-v	fame, -ous	fnUI-m
EXPECT/ation	pO-v	FAMIL/Y, -iar; bio-	ub-Om; no-jomz
expens(ive)	ek-drE(m)	FAR; as far as, insof.	y-bam; Uj dam Uj
Experience	sUgte(v)	Farm-er, —v	vod-a, -u(-v)
experiment (v)	gUw-tve(v)	fascinate	wOt gUv
Expert	gUfu	Fashion	Ama
Expla(i)n/ation, (v)	viU(-v)	FAST (=quick)	nem
Explo-sion, (-de)	twIygna(-v)	Fasten	bwAv
Express/ion	U-, O-tyge(v)	FAT (adj); (food)	oLE(m): Lod(Em)
extr-a, -eme	kyg-Qm	Fate-ful	kwyU-m
Extremist	U-ygem(-u)	FATHER	ytvu
Extremity	pygz	Fatigue	tywmA
extro-ver'sion, -t	tyg-O'-vu, -m	fault	yrvz
exuberance, -t ful —	knO-m, -v		
EYE (shade, vizor)	iOz, -ydyr, -yg	FEAR (v)	tyrO(-v)
		feast-day	riA
		Feather-y	(o-)kEdz-Em
		Feeble(-minded)	ywom-Um.

English: Feed	aUI
Feed;-back	dvov; typ-viU
FEEL-/ing "deprived"	O-v; Yb-Ov
feign	pyg-vOiv
fellow	buc
FEMALE (conceptive) (childbearing)	yvom, Lom
Fence (-in)	waL(ev)
ferment-ation	grO-t-rO-kEv-Q
Fertile, -ize/r	vnom-vE(v)
festival	rO-iA
fever	og-iE
FEW	ynEn
fiancé(e)	tA-b(y)vu
fiber	io-wanos
-fication	-vU
Fiction	Uvo
fidelity (love)	nA (-brO)-jQ
FIELD	enaz
fig (-fruit)	nyn-to-kot
Fight (quarrel)	byd-ev, (yd-brO-v)
Figure (human); (number)	(u)ma; mUn-ma
Filial-devosion (Asia)	tutkQ
FILL (cram, tr)	gEv, (sgav, gvav)
Find	Ute(v)
fine (thin; penal)	r-ydnEm, jyrte-drE
Finger	boz
finish	vypAv
FIRE (make F.)	(v)iE(v)
-fly; -place	izos; iE-as
FIRST	na
FISH (big –)	jE(n)os
catch—	tyv-fev(tELev)jEos
Fist (-fight)	bob (-bydev)

English: Foot	aUI
fit (-in)	brav (grav)
FIVE	o 5
Fix	EbtAv, brAv
Flag	unami
flake (y)	yn-enEz(-wam)
Flame, v, -able	kiE, -v, -wam
Flash (-light)	kvei, (vid)
FLATness	ena(m)
flatten	venav
flatter/-y	pri-yEjU(v)
flat-worm	en-anos
flea	yn-b(etk)izos
Flee	yr-ytev
FLESH	ogE
Flexible	tLevom
Flight	yryte
float	jEkev
Floor	(u)gayk
flour	nyntoz
flow	ejE(v)
Flower	riOio
fluffy	kEdz-Em
(side-)flute	(az-)okE-Id
fly; N, V to —	(kE)gizos, kEdev
Foam	kE-g-jE
focus	iEv-ay'n
fog	kEjE
Fold (V)	bza(v)
Follow	bypav
font	jEyt
FOOD, nutrient	od, do
Fool/ish	tyr-ynUm, tydUm-u
FOOT	yk-bo

English	aUI
FOR: prp; conj =because	rUt; yUt
Force, v	vow, -ev
forebode	pyrUIv, pOv
forehead, lit.	ak-kup, pa-kog
Forest	tonk
forge: iron	rEv; (yr)-vyEj-Uv
(documents)	(Uwa-pAtUI)
Forget/ting	ytgU-v
forgive/ness	vyrtrO(v)
Fork: road (tool)	tnEz (d)
FORM, (V), -al	ma, (-v), -m
former-ly	pA-m, -g
formula(-te)	mUn-ma(v)
forsake	gyr-ytev
fortress	wuga
FOR-th, -ward	tap
foster (-parent)	dvov(-ytu)
foul	yr-kEm
found/ation	pykaz-ev
fount	jEtyg
FOUR = 4	u 4
Fowl	kEbos
fraction	znUvUs
fragrate	kvEmOv
Frame (v)	bEgwad(ev)
Frank/-ness	tygO(m)
fraud, do —	yr-yEjU(-v)
freak; animal, man	yrtnev-(o)s, -u
FREE/dom	fUwe-m
freeze (hard)	jEt-bEv, -wEv
Frequent-ly	nAm
fresh; new, pure; disrespect(ful)	frAvm, ram, ydkum/Q
FRICTION	ydbe
Friday	nA-iA
FRIEND, (fem)	bru, (bryvu)
Fright(en) (ful)	tw-, tv-yrO-(v) (-gEm)
frigid	Y-raiOm
Frog	ii-bEjEos
FROM	yt, Yt
FRONT; in F. of	pa; ap
froth	kEgjE
FRUIT, big, -round, -tree—; round tree fruit	ot, n-, L-, k- kL-ot
frustrat/ion, -e, -ed	yb-tUsO, -v, -m
fry	oLE-roduv
Fuel	iE-dE
fugue (psy.)	yr-yt-O
FULL-ness	gEm-U
with things, matter	(E)sga/m, gnE/m
fulfil-ment	rU-gEv-Q
Fun;-ny	(k)rOvs;yfa-rOvsUm
Function, (v), -al	re, (-v), -m
fundament(al)	pyk-az(-m)
fungus	Yn-yio
funnel (v)	t-yn-yE(-d), (-v)
Fur	(n-)os-yg
furniture	g-uga-s
fury, -ious	yrow, -Om
FUTURE (adj)	tA(-m)
what follows, is F:	tAg:

Gg

English	aUI
gain: win; profit	knev(s), pne(v)
galaxie	kin-tygle
gall	ygrOm-ogz
game (hunt)	rOvevU(feyvos)
gang	yr-wanub
Gap	gez
gape (eyes)	gezav, (hiOv)

English: Gar	aUI
Garden (v)	uioba(v), nioba
gargle (v)	gLI-jE(v)
garland	rioL
garlic	dzOz-oLz
GAS(eous), -ify	KE(m), v
Gasoline	weijE
gasp	kEtO-v
Gate, (barrier)	nugta, (yded)
Gather-ing	setbav(-s)
gaze; wonder	AtiOv; hiOv
gear (=cogwheel)	dzez-Led
gelatin-ous	o-jEywE-m
Gem	rO-wE
GENERAL, (-ize)	yzU-m(-v)
N (army)	na-bydwuk
generator	wei-vEvd
genius(-ial)	gwUvu(m)
gentle/-ness	rywQ(m)
Gentleman	ru
genus	nA-jomz
Geography (phys.)	una-gUw, (bEna-)
geology, (earth)	bEn-gUw
"Geschwister" = siblings	jytu
gesture, v	viOve-v
GET = receive!	tyv, imp: tryv!
2) = become	2) tEv
ghost	yogU
gift	sevs
giraffe	(nan-)kogz-nos
Girl	yn-yvu
GIVE (-up=yield)	(tak-)sev
glad(-ly)	rO-m, (-g)
gland(-ular)	jE-vogz-om
glare, v	kni-v
Gla-ss(adj), -ze	iOdE(-m), -v
gleam	ri(v)

English: Gra	aUI
glide, v	byve-v
glisten	niv
glitter	piv
Glory	kUO
glottis	uIvz
Glove	boyg
glow, v	ri-Ei-v
glue (latex), -c	bvE(bjE)-v
GO (-across)	(kad-) av
over	ek-av
Goal (:aim; will-)	tes, twUs
Goat	yn-bijE-bos
GOD(-son), god/dess	kU(-tvu), k/yv/U
Gold	ei-krE
gonads	vogz
goo	jEbE
GOOD, (-s)	rUm, (Ers)
-bye; fare-well	yte-rUI; rUg-orv!
Goose (tame)	jEn-kE(b)os
Go-over	kat-av, kad-, ek-av
gorilla	n-um-os
gospel	kUgs
gouge	vyEd
gourd	jEg-nam-iot
GOVERN/ment, (v)	knuw(ev)
Grace-ful	riOma-m
Grade (degree)	tnak (tank-)
gradual	tank-Qm
graduate student	k-etgUvu
graft (=implant);	tag-viov;
=bribe	drE-vyrU(v)
GRAIN: food; sand	tonod; nynwEz
Gram(me)	Ean
grammar	bzUIx
grand	Q-nam
grand-daughter	tu-tyvu
Grand-father	yt-ytvu

English: Gr . . . Gu	aUI
Grand-mother	yt-ytLu
Grand-parent	yt-ytu
grand-son	tu-tvu
Grape (raceme)	rO-jE-ot (bLot)
graph	(tyjewam-)tUwma
Grasp (v)	bUw(ev)
GRASS (-hopper)	nio (-etk-izos)
grave (-digger) adj	yo-gyE(v-u) U-tykEm
Gravity	tykE-vow
gravy	L-od-jE
graze	nio-dov
GREAT	(k-)nam, U-nam
greed(-y)	yr-bav-ve(-m)
GREEN	iim
Greet/ings (v)	vrO-UI(v)
Grey, gray (adj.)	bybi(m)
Grief, -ve;-vous	-U-yr-O, -v; v— m
grind	v-nyn-zEv
Grip (v)	bew(ev)
(pain-)groan	(O)nyk-Iv
groove	anyk
grope	tEbOv
Ground, N	ykbE
Group, v (configuration)	ynab(ev) (mab)
growl (v)	yr-yd-I(v)
Grow/th	tne(v)
gruel	ton-jE
guarantee (-v)	vyhO-v
Guerilla	yn-yd-brU
guess	(w)yUte-v
Guest (visit)	tebru(-v)

English: G, Har	aUI
Guide-(man), v	dai(u)-v
guilt (-feeling)	fyrv-U, (-O)
GUN(-v)	nI-wyd(ev)
guts	godz-ana
gymnastics (— do)	og-trew(ev)

Hh

Habit	nAUma
hail (=ice)	jE-wE-k
HAIR (-locks)	noyg(-z)
HALF	azve
hall	nuga
Hallo (o)!	tIOI
Hallow	kUrUv
hallucinat/-ion	(U)yr-UvO(v)
hallway	utga(-da)
ham	(Lod-bos-)woged
Hammer (-v)	tyk-wevd(-ev)
HAND (of clock)	bo (Ad-boz)
hand-drive (e.g. row)	bov-ev
handle	bod(ev), bov
handsome	triOm
handy	bom
Hang(-ing)(tr)	(v)ytkav(Am)
— for crime (tr.)	yr-(v-)ytkav
Happen(-ed), to be, P.	cyv(-pAv); Qc, QpAc
Happy	UrOm
Harbor	jE-ged-a
HARD-en	wEm-ev
HARM (, v)	yrve(-v), vyre(-v),
-ful	(-gE)m
-less	yb-yrvem
Harmony (music) (-ize)	rOb(-I)v rObIv
harp	twe-Id
harvest (v)	ot-fe(v)

English: Hat	aUI
Hat	kog-yg
Hatchet	dzEvd
Hate, (make —)	(v-)ydO-v
hay	nioz
HAVE	bav
HE (-or-she)	vu (cu)
HEAD-man; body-	kUg-u; kog
HEALTH-y	ro-m
HEAR/ing	IO-v
HEART	gog
HEAT	iEmU
Heaven	kna
HEAVY	tykEm
HEIGHT: star, mountain	kamU, kana
helicopter	takLe(-kE-)-ged
Helium (El. 2)	Eze
hell	(yr)ykna
helmet	kog-wyg
HELP v	tor-v
hemo-globin (Fe-N)	ogai-EzeA-E
Hemp	wanabio
Hen	yv-kEbos
Hence	fayt
HER (poss.) (conceptive; motherly L)	yvu(m); Lu(m)
herbivor/e, -ous	iodo-s, -m
herd (-animal)	bon(-z)
HERE (-to)	fa(-t)
hero/-ic	rU-wOm-u
heroic fortitude	rUwO
HER-self	yvu-fU, Lu-fU

English: Hos	aUI
hesitate	tytOv, yetOv
hide	vyOiv
HIGH: star; wall	kam; kanam
high school	ge-gUa
HIM, (HIS)	vu(m)
hinder	pydev
hinge (door-)	bLadz, ugta-baz
hint	tviOv
his-or-her	cum
History	pA-gUw
Hit (v)	tweb (-ev)
Hither	fat
hoe	zvEd
Hold	bAv
HOLE (dig a —)	gyE(v)
holiday (make —)	(kU)riA(v)
HOLLOW (-ball)	gyEm (gyEL)
Holy-/iness	kUrU-m
Home, -y, -love	fuga-m, f(n)uga-brO
home-land, -less	fnuga, yb-f(n)uga
Homonym(ous)	jI(m)
Honest (-frank)/-y	yg-t-EjU-m
Honey (-ed) food	eigrO(-m)od
Honor, (=virtue)	t(r)ukO, (rOkU)
HOOK (v)	tEL(-ev)
HOPE(v)-ful;-less	trQ(-v)-m; yb-
Horizon(tal)	jEka(m)
Horn (-animal)	k(os)wyd, kwyd-os
horr-ible/-or	tvyrO-m
Horse (-radish)	ukbos, (dzOm-yk-tiod)
hospita/-ble, -lity	tebrum-O

English: Hos	aUI
Hospital	yrog(g)a
hostil/ity	Y-brO(m)
HOT (infrared)	iEm, (ykaim)
Hotel	tebruga
HOUR-ly, do –	iAz-em, -ev
HOUSE, v	uga-v
HOW?, rel.	hUd?, xUd
however; =nevertheless	hUdymA; fyd
How many?, rel.	hnEn?, xnEn
HUMAN, -being	um, u
Hum/ble, -ility	rykO-m
hummingbird	(ne)riO-ynkEos
humor-ous	rOvU-m
hump	Lyps
HUNDRED	Oke
Hunger (famine)v	yod-Q, -O(v)
= appetite	dotO
hunt (animals), (N)	(os-)tvev-tyv(Q)
hurl	kEdvev
Hurry	ne(v) (-O)
Hurt; tr.	yrO(v); vyrO(v)
Husband	bvu
hush (-kill)	vyI(-vyo)v
hydr/a(-oid) (coelenterate)	nEn-kog(gyEmos)
Hydrogen	Ez-a
hyena	yod-os
hypno/sis(tize)	vUyvA(v) [1]
hypochondria(c/al)	(Yr-)yro-tyrO(m)u [2]
hypothesi/s, -ze	U-tsyv-Q [3]

---

1 v-UyvA-v make sleep

2 (bad) sickness – fear

3 mind-accepting

English: Imp	aUI
II	
I (myself)	fu, (fufU)
-ic, -ical, -ish	-m
Ice	jEwE
Id	O-sE
Idea (thought, image)	iUs, Uis
ideal, -ist	rUi(m), kUit-u
identi-ty, (-cal)	fUjU(m)
idiom	UIn
idle, (do nothing)	yn-vUm, ys-vUm
idol, (symbol)	yrkUis, (yrkUviOvs)
IF	Qg (=Ög)(Ø as in 'wOrd')
(=whether)	(Qg-hI)
-ification, -ify (v)	-vQ, -vQv
igloo	Luga
ignoble (cheap)	y-kOm(yryk-cEm)
Ignore	y-gUv
ILL/ness; be, make I.	yro-m; -v, v-v
illuminat/ion	Ai-v
illusion, (have – -ary	UvO(v), -m
illustrat/e, (-ion)	Ugs-jiOv(-s)
image	Uis
Imagin/ation	viOsU(v)
imitate, (others)	jamev, (jyfev)
immediate(ly)	yb-dQm(Q), (jamAg)
immune, (-ize)	(v-)yd-yro/-m, (-v)
impel	wetev
(Imperatives end in:	-rv!)
implement	des
impl/ication, (-y)	t-EsgU(v)
impolite	yr-vamUm
import, v	tag-va, -v
Importan/ce, -t	pwUr, -m
impoten/ce, (-t) (non-erect/ion)	y-wU(m) y-take(-m)
impress/-ion	vOv/Q, tag-bwev/Q

English: Imp	aUI	English: Inv	aUI
improve/ment tr	nEk-rU/-tE(v), -vE(v)	Inside, right —	ag, bag
Im-pulse (-pel), -ive	wete(-v), -pAm	insight (spirit)	gIO (giU)
Impure(-ness)	y-ram(-U)	insofar-as	Uj-dam-Uj
IN (order to)	a g(Ut)	inspect/-or, -ion	tiOgt/u-v, /U
inactive	yc-vUm	inspir/ation, (e)	tUgi(v)
incisor	p-od-zevz	instant	As
Increase, (v)	nEke(v)	instead	gayf
index (v)	(ABC-)tykUiO(v)	Instinct	yUtwO
Individual, -adj.	afU/s, -m	institute	Uga
Industr-y, (-ious)	nEsvU(m)	institution	gnubas
In-fact	gvU	INSTRUMENT: tool; musical I; I—ality	dEs: vEd; Id; dQ
infant	y-UI-tu	insulat/ion (-e) V	LydyrE(v)
Inferior	ykUm	Insur-ance, -(e)	Ydybse(-v)
infinit-e, -y	yYpAz-m, -Q	integrity	zyngrO
inflat-e, -ion	kEgEv-Q	integra/te, -tion, -l	nyz-grU/v, -Q, -b
Influence (v)	tyf-wU(v)	intellect(-ual)	idU(m)
inform/ation, -er	gUse(v)-u	intelligen/ce (-t)	nidU(m)
infringe-ment (v)	yr-ked-ge(v)	intens/e, -ity	gytwe(m);
(-ing: Part; gernd	-vAm; vQ = vØ	-ity (electr.)	-n; wein
inhabit-/ant (v)	gu(v)	inten/tion, (-d)-al	etvU(-v)-m
inhale	tag-okEv	inter-	eg-, ge-
inherit(ance)	yt-ytu-syv(Q)	(tr)INTEREST, (v)	(v-)OtgU (-v)
inhibit/ion	g-yde(-v)	interior	gam
In-human	y(d)um	inter-mesh	teg-bre(v)
Injur-y, (-ious)	ogyr(m)	International	gebanum
Ink	ybi-jE	interpret-er, -ation	vEgUv-u, -U
inner (sense), spirit	agU/m; UgO	interrupt	ge-zwEv
innocen/ce, (t)	yb-fyrU(m)	Interval	gez
inorganic matter	yb-o-bE	intestin/e, (-al)	ana-godz(om)
inquisit/ion, -or	yr-kU-hIv/Q, -u	Intimate	gogbOm
inquisitive/ness	hUt(v)O-m	INTO (motion)	tag, (teg-)
Insane/ity (adj)	Uyro(m)	intrigue	yr-tUvma
INSECT (-arthropode)	izos(-zos)	Intro-duc/tion, (-e)	tegrO(v)
insectivore	izo-doz	introver-sion, (-t'ed)	tOge'(-m), -vu
insensitive	yOm	Intuit/ion, (-e)	UO(-v)
		inva/de, -sion	wyr-teg-e(-v)
		inve/ctive, (-igh)	yrUI-m, (-v)

English: I, J	aUI
Invent(ion)	ApUv(s)
inver/se; -t;-ted	yf-taz/;-ev;-epAm
invertebrate, (adj)	yk-os, (yb-yp-ogwEm)
invest	tag-sev
investigate, (-ion)	hytUv(-Q)
Invisible	yiO-wam
Invit/ation, (-e)	tegO(v)
inward, -ly	teg, tOg; gQm-Q
iodine (El. I 53)	Ez-o'i
ion (free charge)	e-bweiz
Iron (El. Fe 26)	wrE (Ez-e'A)
irony (oppos-humor)	yd-EsgU;yU-rOvU
(Irrealis attaches	-yEc)
irresponsible	Y-kwyhIm
is (condition, equals, naturally, partly, spiritually)	c, cEv (Qc, jUc, oc, zUc, Uc)
(-ish	-m)
Island	jELbE
-ism, -ist; -istic	-(m)U, -(m)u; (m-)Um
isolat/ion, -ed	v-y-bev, -Q-m
isotope	Yf-En-jEz
IT(s), (spiritual)	sE(m), (sU-m)
Itch-y (v)	(yw-)byg-yrO(v)-m
Item	nEs
-ive (future)	-(t)vAm
-ize	-vUv

J j

English	aUI
jackal	twaubos
January	na'-ekiA
Jealous/y (adj)	yr-tyf-brO(m)
Jelly(-fish) (coelenterate)	jEywE, (-gyEmos)
jest	rO-UI
Jewel	rO-wE

English: J, K i n	aUI
JOIN(T)-disease	ba-v, (-z)-yro
joke (disharmony without harm)	UI-krOvs (y-rOb yb yr-ve)
journal	jA-vUIgs
Journey, V	ade, -v
Joy	krO
jubilate	rOIv
Judge (v)	jwUsku-v
Judgment	jwUskus
jug	vejE-gad
Jump (v)	etke(v)
junction	(t)az
Just/ice, N(adj)	jwUsU(m)
just: (=right), =only, =quite; =even)	jwUm; am; myz; jUf
just-if/ication, (-y)	jwUm-vQ(v)

K k

English	aUI
kangaroo	sguygz-netkos
KEEP(-er):hold; preserve	bAv(-u); vAv
Kettle	kiEgLad, wrEgad
Key	tagd
Kick (v)	ykbowe(v)
kid	yn-tos
Kidney	jEogz
KILL-er (v)	vyo(v)-u
Kilogram	tykE-an
KIND/ness (adj.)	vrO(-m)
Kind: quality; sort	mU(z): mEz
KINDLE (make light)	viEv, (viv)
King, -dom, bio. —	knu, -wa; na-jomz

English: K, L	aUI
Kiss (v)	ubogta(v)
kitten, (=cub)	yn-bozvos, yn-tos
knead	bweLv
Knee, -l (v)	oged-baz, -(-yev)
Knife	zEvd
knit (v)	tab-tLyp(-ev)
knob	Lamz
knock	tweb-nI(v)
Knot	bLamz
KNOW/ledge (v)	gU (v)

L l

English	aUI
Labor (v)	uwe(v)
laboratory	gUtvas
Lack (v), feel —;	bU(v), ybO(v)
not have, condit.	ybav, ybQ
Ladder	ekanad
lake	yejEn
lame/ness	yr-ye(m)
Lamp	(L)id
(-)LAND, -	bEna; -na
e.g. Scot-land	SCoT-na
LANGUAGE (-word)	nUI, -UI
e.g. English	eNGL-UI
languor	yvO
LARGE	nam, tyt-nam
lark	krI-kEos
laser (ray)	web-j(-anai)
LAST; adj, ; v	ypnAm; Av
Late	yprAm
latex	bjE
Laugh/ter, (v) at	krOI(v) yd
launch	pvev
laundry, (place)	priv(a)s
Law(-yer), -suit	jwUs(-u), -dvU

English: Lib	aUI
fa-(mo-)ther-in-law	b(y)vu-yt(y)vu
LAY (v); -er	vykav; enEs
laz/y, -ness	y-n(Es)vU(m)
Lead, (-er), v	dai(-u), -v
LEAF: green; sheet	oii, enas
League	wanub
Learn/ing (gnd)	retgU(v)
(at)least	(at)pynEk
Leather	oygE
LEAVE: depart; tr, -(it)	ytev; tvAv(sE)
lecture	gU-pnUIv(s)
ledge	panEs
LEFT (side)	ywoza-m
gone; remained	ytepAm; tvApAm
LEG	oged
legal	jwUsUm
legend	kUrUm UIvo
Lemon	eikot
Lend	Asev
LENGTH-y	ana, t-ana-m
lens	LiOdE
leopard	Lyiz-ozvos
(-)less	yb-..., -ybm
Less (=minus)	ynEk
lesson	vetgUz
LET, let! let's go!	dyv, dryv" fnuarv!"
Letter: (A, B, C); sent	UIz; va(v)Us
lettuce	noiiod
Level (N, adj, v)	jEka(-m), -v
Lever, jack-screw	vekted, tek-ved
levity	tekQ
L 5 (lagrange)	5 jLo
Liberty	fUwe

English: Lib	aUI
Library	nUgsa
license (permit)(N)	jwUs-dyv(-Q)
lick (tongue)	gOzev
Lid (= cover)	kazd, kygz
LIE (down, false)(v)	ykav; (yr-)Y(d)EjU(v)
LIFE(-guard)	o, (jE)ytyrvu
Lift (N, v)	vekte-s, -v, tek-vev
LIGHT: N, v; adj	i viv; ektEm
= lamp	i(s)(v)id
buoyant-light	tekEm, takEm
turn off the light!	vyirv!
lighter (tool)	viEd
Lightning	kayrei, kvei
(-)LIKE (similar)	(-)j Om
to Like (love)	bruv, (brOv)
Likeness	jiOs
lily	ram-riOio
Limb	yg-ogz
Limit (to –)	tnak(ev)
limp V	yj-ogav
LINE	anas
Linen	bi-nanab
linger	yetOv
link	begz
Lion	kozvos
Lip	ogtai
LIQUID (adj)	jE(m)
List (V)	tyk-UiO(v)
listen	tIOv
Liter, -re	jE-an
literature	nUI-gUw, UIvon
lithe	tLom
LITTLE: adv; small	ynE; ynam='nym'

English: Ly	aUI
LIVE	ov
liver	jEn-vogz
lizard	(r)ykneos
llama	ske-noygE-bos
Load	yktEw
loathe	ybrOv
Loan	A-se(v)
lobster	wEzos
Lock, (v)	ytag-d, (-ev)
log	tok-zvE
logic(-al)	jUx(-Um)
Logos	xrUI, kUI
LONG, (time)	anam, (nA)
how long? (time)	hanam? (hnA?)
as long as	rUt-A-jAg
Look; -alike	tiO-v; jiOm
looking-glass	tiOv-iOdE
(he) looks (healthy)	(vu) Oiv (rom)
loop	tLyp
Loose	y-bwam
Lord	ku
LOSS, lose V; forfeit	sybte(v), tybse(v)
lot	Enaz
lottery (play –)	wyU-ytna(v)
Loud	nIm
Louse	yn-yrizos
LOVE (ly), v	brO(m), -v
Loyal(ly)	jwUsOm(Q)
LOW, -er (v)	ykam; vyktev
lubrica/nt, (-te)	ryve-dE(-v)
luck(il-)y	rQ-(-g)-m
lump	kLEz
Lungs	kE-ogz
luxury(ious)	kyg-wyvQ(m)
-ly (adverb)	-m(Q), -jOm

Mm

English	aUI
MACHINE	es
macro-	na-
Mad-house	yr-U-ga
magic-ian	k-Eo-w/-U(m), -u
magnesium(Mg 12)	kerE, (Ez-O'e)
magnet, -ism, -ic	tab-wed, -Q, -m
main	kwUm
majority	nEk-mUn
MAKE	v E v
Mal-	yr-
MALE	vom
mallet	tswed
mammal	bE-os
MAN, he-	u, vus
Manage/r	kun-(ev)
manipulate	(yr-)dwev, -bov
Mankind	u-U
manly	vOm
man-made-	u-v(EpAm)-
MANNER, (s)	mUd, (vamU)
manufactur(ing)	vEsev(Q)
MANY (-little, /e.g.sand)	nEn, (nyn-/wE)
Map	a-jiOs
maple (-syrup)	grOjE-tok (tok-grOjE)
mare	yv-ukbos
margin	Lyg-az
Mark, v; N	etviOv, -s
Market	rEseva
Marr/iage, (-y), tr.	bo(-v), bvov
marsupial	sguygz-os
mart	strEva
Masculine	vom
MASS (weight), -es (people) (rel. service)	En, un-En (kU-ykwus)

English	aUI
massage (v)	r-ydbe(-v)
Master(-y)	kwu (kwQ)
Mat	(yn-)ykenas
Match, V; -es (fire–)	bjOrv; (yn-)viEd
MATERIAL-is/t-ic,/-m	E-m-Um/-u; -U
Mathematics	mUn-gUw
matrix	ytE
MATTER	E
mattress	k-ykavd-vEmE
maxim-um, -ize	pnEk(mUn), -ev
may; is allowed	wOv; dyYv
May	no-ekiA
maze	bjYjO-dan
Meal: (flour; -time)	nyn-z-od: nyntoz; todA
MEAN: average; signify	j n Uz; EsgU(v)
=base; MEANS (by which)	ykEm; Ed
mean-time	eg-A
Measure: N, V	niO-d, -v
Meat	osod
Mechanic, -al -ics, -isation, -ism	bedgU/vu, -m bedgU, -vQ; beds
mediat/e, (-or)	gev(-u)
Medical	trom
MEDICINE: pill; art	t r o d; tro-gUw
meditat/e, -ion	OUv-Q
MEDI/UM, (-al) spiritist.	d E, (m); vavU-tyvu
Meet/ing	tube(v)
melody	rObI
melon	nam-Lot
melt	bEt-jEv
member	boz

English: Mem	aUI
Memory (have in —)	AgU(v)
mend	trQv
mental, (-disease) -disharmony	ogUm, U-yro U-y-rOb
Merchandise	strEs
mercury, Hg 80	jErE, EzIO
Mercy	kU-brO
merit, (N)	jrutryv(s)
Message	vavU
metabolic, -ism	E-tyfga/m, -vQ
METAL	rE
metaphysics	yp(e)gUw
meteor, -ology, -ist	kei; kamA-gUw, -u
Meter	ana-an
Method	dvU
micro- (scope)	Yn-(iOd)
Mid-(dle); mid-East	gaz-; gaz-yita
mid-night	yikA
might, v; N	wOv-yEc; wUn
migrat/ory, -e	jIAm-ade/m, -v
mild	ry-dzOm, -wEm
mile	Oki-ate
Military, adj, N	byd'-wum, -wun
Milk(-food) v, give M.	bijE(-od)v, bijvEv
MIND (-ed)	(og)U(-m)
Mine: (my; ore-)-er	fum; rE-yka(v-)u
MINERAL	Eyo
Minus	ayt, ynEk
Minute (1/60 hr.)	ynA
Miracle	kypums
mirror, v	jiOd, -ev
mis-	yr-
Miscellany	fEbyf
miss: N; v (say: "hot-hit, -meet"	r(yn)yvu; (t)ybOv yc-tweb(ev), tube(v))

English: Mor	aUI
missile	vayv-wyd
Mission	vavUn
mis-lead	yr-daiv
mis-shapen	yr-mam
Mist	bikE
Mistake, (v)	yEjUms, yn-yEjU(v)
Mister, Mr, Mrs.	ru; ryvu
mite (vermin	yn-yr-zos
Mix(-ture);-ed	byf-Ev(s);-Em
mock	vyr-krOIv
model (sculpt)	yvEmav
(exemplar); ideal	pma(v); kUit
moderat/ion, (-e)	tnakO(-m), -v
modern	fnAm
modest	fU-tnakOvAm
moist(-en)	gjE-m(-v)
molar	nodzEvz
mold 1(model) 2 (fungus)	pma(v), yvEmav 1 2yn-yio
Molecule	bzEz
mollusk	ywEm-os
moment	Ayn
monarch(-y)	a-knu(-wa)
Monday	ne-iA
MONEY	drE
monk	am-kU-tu
Monkey	(yn-)umos
monotheis-m, t(ic)	a-kU-tU(m-)u
Monst(e)r(-ous)	nyr-cEvs(-Om)
Month-ly (N)	ekiA-m, (-s)
May = 5th mo.	no-ekiA
mood	AmO
Moon	eki
moral - adj	nu-vrU-m
morale	vrOw
MORE:	nEk;
the M... the M	Uj nEk...Uj nEk
MORNING	yitA

English: Mor	aUI
morgue mortal	yo-ga yo-wam
Mosquito	gaizos
Moss	ykio
MOST; pl. men	pnEk; pnEn
MOTHER (conceivg.)	ytLu, (ytyvu)
Motion	eU(z)
motiv(ate)	tew(ev)
Motor, (tool)	ves, ved
MOUNTAIN	bEk
mourn	ykrOv
Mouse	yn-bos
MOUTH	ogta
MOVE/MENT; tr., -ing	e(v); vev, -em
Movie (theater)	evUis(a)
Mr., Mrs.	ru, ryvu
MUCH	nE
Mud(dy)	bE-ypri(m), yr-bE(m)
mulberry mule multiply, (tr) murmur (v, (N)	nyn-oi-kLot t-uk-bos nEn(v)ev ydimUIv-(Q)
Muscle	woz
Museum	niOb-ga
(cereal) mush mushroom	(ton-)bEjEod yios
Music(-art)ian	rIO(-wU)vu
MUST, P	wyv, wyvpAv
mute	yb-UIm
Mutual-ly	jyttUm-Q
MY, -self	fum, fufU
Myster/y, (-ious) (metaphysic)	ypums(-Um) (yp-U(m))

English: M, Nex	aUI
mystic(-al), -ism	kU-iOv-u, (-Am), -U

Nn

English: M, Nex	aUI
Nail (iron; finger)	brEg(tEd); bozEvz(bovz)
naked/ness	yb(u)ygzQ(m)
NAME (v)	fUI (v)
NARROW	y'-dam
Nation-al	banu-m
nativity (Xmas)	kU-toe(-iA)
Natur-e, (-al)	Eo(m)
navy, -al	jEn-bydwu/n, -m
NEAR-ly; -ness	bam-Q; ba
Necess-ity, (-ary)	wyvU(-m)
Neck; (bottle-)	kog(e)z; kydaz
Need: N, (v) is (was) needed	wyv-yr, wyvU(v) wyv(-pAv)
Needle (tree-)	yE-anLEd, (dz-oii)
NEGAT-ive, -ion	yrm, yc-UI(m)
neglect (v)	y-Ote(v)
Negro; Tropi-an, -c	ybi-u(m); iau(m)
Neighbor, -hood	bus; bas; bam-u, -a
Neither — nor	yc(Ib) — yc(Ib)
Nerv'e, (-ous, -ness)	Oz (-yb-ye-m)
nest	kEo-ga
NET	nyEd
neuro'sis, (-tic)	gybwe-UyrQ(m)
Never; -the-less	yA; fyd
New(-s)	fAv-m(-UI)
Newspaper	fAvUIgs
Next	bypAm

English: Nig	aUI
NIGHT	yiA-
nightingale	(-)rIO-kEos
NINE	U 9
nitrogen, N7	EzE
No! No(ne)	yr!; yn
(soul=)noble(-man)	kOm(kom-u)
NOBODY	yu
Nois-e, -y	yrI-m
noodle	nanod
Noon	ikA
Normal	jnUrm
North	yia
NOSE	kEmOz
NOT = is not	yc
Note (music);	I-vi Ovs
NOTHING	ys
Notice, (N)	EvgUv(s)
noun	sUIs
(make nouns by adding: e.g. the conscious (N)	-s, -z; -U, -Uz, u pI gU Om-z
Novel (story)	nUIvo
NOW	fA
nowhere	y-xa
nucle-us, -ar	gEz, -Um
numb, (v)	yOm, (vyOv)
NUMBERs: 1, 2, 3, 4,5,6	m Un: a, e, i, u, o; A...
nurse	troLu
nursery	yntu-gUa
Nut; (screw)	wEyg-ot; aL-brELg
nut-&-bolt	brELg-aL-brELg

English: One	aUI
Oo	
oak	twok
(boat-) oar	(jEged-)bovevd
oat(s)	ukbos-to
oath (holy-)	kUrUI
Obe/dience, (-y)	ykwe(v)
Object(ive)	yfUs(Um)
Obligation	wyvO, kwyvU
oblique	tykam
Observ/ation	gUte(v)
Obsess-ion, tr. v. be obsessed = must	yr-wyv-O, vyr-wyv yr-wyv
Obstinate	yd-wUm
Obstruct/ion	ydev/s
occasion (good)	rQL
occupation	o-uwe
octopus	I-oged
OF; OFF (=minus)	Ub; ayt
offen/ce, (-d)	(w)yryd(-ev)
Offer, to — v	tse, -v
Offic'e, -ial	Uwa(-u)m
Officer	bydwuk
Often, how o.?	nAn, hnAn?
Oh!	Oh!
-oid (human-oid)	-jOm (u-jOm)
Oil (food)	(od)eijE
olive (-tree)	eijE-kot, (-tok)
Old	pAom
Omi-ssion, (-t)	vyte(v), vybe(v)
ON	kab
ONCE	aA
ONE, -ness	a, -U

English: O n	aUI	English: O, P a	aUI
onion	dzOm-oLz	OUR-selves	fnum, fnufU
ONLY	am	outer	ygm
		outflow	tyg-ejE
opal	bi-rO-wE	OUTward	tyg
Open, to -(v)	tage-m, (-v)	OUTside, (N), adj	yg(-az)
Operat/e, -ion (surgic.)	svUv, (s)vUn; tro-dzEv(Q)	outspoken	tyg-EjUm
Opin-ion, -e v	ugU-v	Oven	iE(m)ga(d)
opium-drug	vUyvA(-yrtrod)	OVER	ek
opponent	ydvu		
opportun'ity, (-e)	twar-Q(m)	over-all	yg-uyg
Oppo'se; (passively, actively)	Yv-, Yd-vUv	overcoat	yg-kuyg, knuyg
		over-come	ek-tev
		over-do	knE-vEv
		over-view	ek-a-tiO
OPPOSITE-, adj-	Y-, Y-U(m)	overwork	knE-uwe(v)
-ion	Y-Q	owe	drEr-v
oppress	yr-bwev	owl	yiA-kEos
OR; -or	gaf; -vu	Own-, v (adj), -er	bav-, (um), -u
oracle (-decision)	(kU-ApUIvs, (-vUtse)	oxygen, (O, 8)	okEz, EzI
Orange (-fruit) adj.	a'ei-(kot)m 128	**Pp**	
orang-utan	ai-numos	pacify	brU-vEv
ORDER; bio.-;	grab, nujomz	pack	bvav
in order to	Ut	pact	brU-tAvma
(Ordinals 1st 2nd 3d	na, ne, ni ... 1, 2, 3	Page	Ugz
ORGAN (of body)	ogz	PAIN-, v; -ful	yrO, -v; -m
organic	robUm	Paint/: v, N;-er, -brush	miv/, -E; -u, -d
Organiz-ation, (-e)	robU(v)	painting	mivpAs
organism	robUs	pair	bej 2
(pipe)organ	kE-nId	Palace	knuga
Origin(-ate), -al(ly)	ytU(-v);-m, (-g)	palm	nia-tok
Ornament	am-riO	Pan (-cake)	engad; en-grOmod
osmosis *	(jE-nyn-yEyv) - gE-tyv-Q	Pane	enas 2
ostrich	bEn-ne-kEos	panther	Lyiz-ozvos
OTHER-wise,	yf-Q	Pant-s (-y)	(Yn-)vuyg
-thing (else)	yfs	PAPER	ena-E 2
other-way(-around)	Yf-Ud, yf-da(-al)		
Ought-to	-r-; wryv		
(he) ought-to-go	(vu)arv=wryv-av		

* (seep-)absorption

English: Pa	aUI
paprika	ai-dzOm-ot
paradise(-bird)	kyfa(-kEos)
parodox(ical)	fU-yUI(m)
Parallel	jatbem
paranoi'-a, -d	gyrvyg(-Uyro)u, -m
parasite, -ic	byros-Qm
Parcel	vas
PARENT	ytu
Pardon (v)	vyrtrO(-v)
park	nioba
parrot	UI-kEos
PART;(-ial)-ly; v	zU, zE; zEm-Q;zUv
Participat/-ion, -er	zU-bav-U, -u
Particular	zUm
Part/ing, (leave)	yte(v)
partner	zUbav-u
Party (polit.; social)	knuwz; buz
Pass(ing)	dev(Am)
Passion	yrOve
PASSIVE: inactive	y-vem, "vym"
receptive	yvUm
(Passive V. ends in:	-yv)
PAST (-V, -ending)	-pA-(m)
(from now on all in past:... pAg:...)	
Past = after	yAp
Paste	bwE
pasture	do-niov
patent	ApUvs-ydyrwa-d
path	yn-da
Patien/ce, -t	trAw-Om
patient (sick)	tro-yv-Am-u
Pattern	(p)iOmab
pawn	vyhUd
PAY-ment	drEv-s

English: Pet	aUI
pea	yn-Liod
PEACE	brU
Peach	wEg-kot
peacock	riO-kEos
peak	kraz
peanut	bEn-wEygkot
pear	an-nakot
pear-shape(d)	jEz-ma(m)
pearl	krO-Las
peasant	vodu
peck	dznev
peculiar-ity	fUzUm-U
pedantic	v-yn-pwUrm
peel	ot-yg(-z)-ev
pelt	os-yg
Pen	(jE)vUiOd
Pencil	v(U)iOd
pendulum/ v	tyt-Lev-s
penetrat/e, -ing	dza'v, -m
pension (pay) v	yem-A(drE)v
Pentecost	U-r-iA
People (collect)	nu, (un)
pepper: black-,	dzOm/-ybi-to,
red-	/-ainot
percent	gOke
perce/pti/on, -ive	UcO/, -v, -m
Perfect, v	gnUr-m, -v
perform-ance	pnuv, -IvQ
perfume (v)	rO-kE-mO(-v)
Perhaps	twam(Q)
perish	tycEv
period-ic(al)	jLA-m(s)
Permi/t, -ssion	dyv, -U
persecut-ion	tyr-bypAv-Q
persever/an/ce, -t,-e	nA-jvU/, -m, -v
persist/-en/ce, -t, --V	bjAwU, -m, -v
PERSON (-ality, -ze)	u (-fU-v)
persua/de, -sion	wUIv-Q
perver't, -sion	vyrLev-'u, -Q
Pet (v)	brOs(-ev)
(heavy) Petroleum	(tykw-)oijE

English	aUI
phallus	voz-Lanad
Philosophy	U-gUw
phobia	fytyr(zwyv)O
Phonograph	uIves
phony	(yr-)pOi(-yg)
phosphorus P 15	Eza'o
Photograph (N)-er	ijiOv(s)-u
photon	in
phrase (v)	(yn-)bUI(v)
phylum	ne-jomz
PHYSIC-/al, (-s); = material	egU/m, (-w); Em
Physician	trogUwu
physiolog-y, (-ic)	og-gUw-(Um)
piano	boz-nId
pick N; v	dze-tykwevd; zwE-fev
Picture: likeness; idea	jiOvs; Uis
Piece	zvE
Pierc'e, -ing	dz'av, -ev; dz-am, -em
pi'ety, (-ous)	kU-g'O (m)
Pig	Lodbos
pill	troLd
Pillar; support	twEk; skwEr(-kanas)
(head-)pillow	(kog)yw(E)d
Pin	anLEd
pinch	ge-bwev
Pine-tree	nA-ii-tok
pink	taim
pioneer, v (N)	prAv(-u)
Pipe; smoke — P.; (flute-)	an-yEd: ybikE-a.; an-yEd(-kE-)Id
piston	gLaned
pit'y, -iable	byrO(wa)m
pituitary	bjEvogz
PLACE	as

English	aUI
Plan	tAvma
Plane (-tool)	ena(d)
Planet	eki
PLANT, (cultured); v. -ation	io, (bio); viov biona
Plastic (adj)	(ma)yvE(m)
Plate (metal-) (food-) dishes	wenEs, en-rEs (od-Lena
platinum (Pt 78)	pnE-krE (EzE'I)
platyhelminthes	en-anos
PLAY, (v) music	rOve(v), drI(v)
PLEASE! (-ing)	tOr ! (-m)
to please v	vrOv
PLEASURE, - ant	rO - m
plenty	nQ
plot: intrigue; lot	yr-tUvma; enaz
Plough V, (N)	bEzEv(d)
pluck: apart, (off)	tyb-, (ayt-)fev
plum	ui-kot
(Plural '-n' in articles:	pIn, yIn, fEn)
plural	nEk-mUn
plus +, (=more)	Urm, (nEk)
pneumo'nia (-coccus)	kEogz/-yro (-Lynos)
Pocket	sguygz
(verse)poem(creation)	(jA-) UI-[vUvs]
Poet (word-creator)	UI-vUvu
Point; (of spear)	ayn (dzez)
Poison	yrod
polar-bear	bi-nosdos
Pole (e.g. North-)	dLanas (yia-)
Police	yd-yrv-u
Polish (N)	jEpiv(s)
polite/ness	vramU(m)

English: Pol	aUI
Politic(al)s, -ian	nu-we(m), -u
pollute/d, -ion(v)	v-yram-e(v), vypriv
polyp(-coelenterate)	nEn-oged(-gyEmos)
poly-sem-e, -ous	n-EsgU/I, -m
pomegranate	nyn-to-aikot
pool	(yn-)yejE
POOR	yndrEm
Pope	kUga-knu
poppy(-seed)-flower	vUyvA(to)-riOrio
popular	nu-brO(pA)m
porpoise	um-jEgos
Port	jEgeda
Porter	skevu
portion	zE
POSITION	mag
POSITIVE (emot.)	Urm, Orm
positron	wreiz
Possessi/on, -ve	bavs, bavU-m
POSSIB-le, -ility	twam, -U
post (pole); send	kanEs; vav
postage	vadrE
Post-office	vava
Post-card	vav-ynena
Pot	(rE-)glad; odjEgd
potassium, K, 19	EzaU
Potato	bELiod
potential (adj.)	twamQ-(m)
pour	vejEv
Powder	nynE
POWER-ful	wU-m
practic'-e, -al, (N, V)	vre, -m, -v
Praise, (v)	rUI(v)
Pray(er)/v	kUtOr/v
preach-er	kUIv-u

English: Pri	aUI
Precede, -nt	pav, A-pavAms
Precious	(k)nUrm
predestin-ation, (-e)	Ap-kyUw, (ev)
predicate, v	vUIc, -ev
predict-ion, v	Ap-UI, -v
predominan'ce, -t	pwU-m(Q)
preface, v	pUI-v
Prefect'-ure (Asian)	pun-az
prefer/ence (v)	nEk-brO(-v), -tO(v)
prejudice,'-d	Ap-jwUsku-'s, -m
premise	pe-bUI
premonition	pyrO(-v)
Prepar-e, -ation	pAv, -Q, -U
preposition	pUIs
prescience, -t(v)	Ap-gU, 'm, v
PRESENT; here; N, V; in the P:	fA(m);fam; sevs, tsev; fAg:
Preserve	vAv
president	pwu
Press (N)	bwev(s)
PRESSURE	bwe
pret'end, -ext	(p)vOiv-d
Pretty	triOm
prevail	pwev
prevent	pydev
Price	drEts
Prick, v	dze-z, -v
Pride	yrkO
priest	kUga-u
Primeval(-), (=Ur-)	pa(m)
primitive (N)	pasom-u
prince-ss	yn-knu(-knyvu)
Princip'al, adj, N;-le	pUm, pu; pU(ms)
Print, v	bnUiO(v)
Prison	yr-uga

English: Pri	aUI
Priva'te, -cy	(r)ypnum, -U
privilege	ap-jwUr
Probab'le, -ility	twarm-U
problem-atic	hytbe-m
proceed	tap-ev
PROCESS	dvU
PROCREATE	vov
Produc't, -e, -tion	tygvE, -v, -vU
produce N (crop)	bion
profess	tyg -UIv
profess-ion-al	o-ruwe-m
professor, master	kam-gUvu, kvetgUvu
Profit-(e)er	drEtbe-v-u, (yr-. . .)
program (play)	vU-(rOve-)tAvma
progress (v)	tap-re(v)
prohibit/ion	pydUI-v
project -V, N	tap-tswev, (tap)tUvma
-ion (psych.)	fyrtyfve(v)
promise [1]personal	[1]pf rUI-v
[2] hopeful	[2]prUI-v
pronoun	fUIs
pron(o)unciation, -e	pyg-UI-v
Proof	EjUvs
propaga'-nda, -te	pnUI-v
prop/ulsion(-el)ler	tap-we(-v)-d
Property	bavs
prophe-cy, -size, -t	ApUI, '-v, -u
Proportion-ate	zEj-Um
Propos-al	pItvUv-s
Pros-e, -aic	abzUI-m
prospect, v	prO, -v
Protect/ion	ydyrwa(v)
protein (egg-stuff)	EzE-ozE(oytE)
Protest, v, -er	yd-UI-v-u
protist(a)	yn-po
proton	rEz
Proud, (-of power)	yrkOm, (wUkOm)

English: Pyr	aUI
Prove	EjUv(iOv)
provide-n'ce, -t	Ap-'iOv, iO;iOvAm
pry, (=peek)	zwad-anav, (eg-tiOv)
psychiatr'-y, -ist, -ic	U-trogUw'-u-m
psychoanalys-is, -e	OUytbe'-v
-ist, -ic	-u, '-m
psychogram	OU-viOvs
Psycholog'y, ist, ic	OgUw-u, -m
psychopath/y,	vyrydnub(Uyro),
-ic	-u, -m
psycho'sis, -tic	UvO-Uyro, -m
psychotherap'y, -ist	Utrov, -U, -u
PUBLI'C, -ation, -sher	pnu '-m, -vU, -vu
puddle	yn-yejE
puff	tyg-wekE(v)
PULL-ey	twev-d
pulsate	gogev
pumpkin	nam-iot
Pump V	jEtke-d, -v
pun	UI-rOves
Punish/ment	jyrte-v
punctual/ity	grA-m
Pure, -ify	ram-ev
Purple	aoim
Purpose	tsU
Push	ytwe-v
PUT	sav
put on dress	gygtev
pyriform (adj)	jEż-ma(m)

Qq

quake V — wytte-v
QUALITY — mU
qualify — mQvU-v
Qualification limit — tyn-mUv
QUANTITY — nUz
quantum — zwen
Quarrel (bitter —) — yn-ydbrU yd-brO(v)
Queen — knyvu
QUESTION, v — hI (v)
QUICK — nem
Quiet: motionless; soundless — yem yIm
quince — tnakot
quit(s) — (t-ye)-yte(v)
Quite — myz
quote — vUIv
quotient — znU(v)ts(Us)

Rr

Rabbit — etkos
race: [1]speed, [2] species — [1]ne-kyftU-v; [2]nI-jomz
raceme — bLot
radiate — (v)anaiv
radical (root-ish) — iotyk-Um, pUm
in principle, essential — pUm, cmUm
Radio — ybaI
radish — ykt-iod
rag — uygE-zvE
Rail — ana-rE
Rain, (-bow) — kajE, (ka-tLak)
Raise — vatkev, tak-vev
rake — bnEzavd
Range — mytta
rank — tankQ
Rare — ynAm
rash/ness — yr-wO(m)
Rat — yr-bos
Rate — gAn
rather — nEk-rOg
ratio-n, v — znUj-e(v)
rationaliz-ation, -e — vrytU-v
raven — n-ybi-kEos
Ray — anai
(re- (= back) — typ-)
reach V — tebe-v
React/ion — typ-vU(v), -Ev
READ/ing — UiO-v
READY-ness — vrAm-U
REAL-ity; actual-ity — çEm-U ;cvUm, -U
"Wirklich" creative — cwUm-U
Realize (make real) — cvEv (-U):
=apperceive — sOv(-U)
REASON, (v)-able — ytUw, (-ev), -am
rebel/lion, N, v — yd-atke(v-u)
Receipt (-slip) — tsyvpA-tiOs
RECEIVE — sYv
Pass: is being r—ed — syYv(Past)sYv-pAv
Pass.P. was r—ed — sYvpAyv, f. syvtAv
Imp. receive! be r—ed! — srYv!(Pass.)sryYv!
Receptacle — sgad
recognize (merit) — typ-gUv; (nUr-Uiv)
Recommend/ation — srUv/U
Record (sound —) — (I-)pAtUI
RED (adj) — ai(m)
red-cabbage — ai-kogiod
reduc'e(lessen)-tion — (v)ynEv-Q

English: Re	aUI
Refer/ence	tytU-v
Reflect/ion; think	typ-i(v); LUv
reflex (psy.)	Oz-typvU(v)
reform, (-er)	(v)rU-ma(v)
regard, V	kOte-v
regardless	yb-iOg
region	naz
Regret, v	yAp-yrO-v
Regular: time, rule	jAm; jwyzQm
rehears'al, (-e)	Ap-IO(-v)
reifi-cation, (-y)	Es-vU(v)
reign, -N	knuv-Q
reincarna-t'ion, (-e)	OU-typ-og-e(v)
rein-deer	yia - kwyd-os
reject/ion	typ-ytwe(v)
relate	xUv
RELATI'on, -ve	xU - m
relax/ation	ryb-wo-v
relay (v)	yn-ytQ(-v)
Religi-on, (-ous)	kU-tU(m)
rel'y, -iable	br-yt-ka-v, -wam
REMAIN-der	tAv- s
Rememb'rance, -er	AgU-v
Remind(-er)	v-AgU-v(s)
remove, (v)	yt-ve(v)
repair v	typ-re(v)
repe'at, -titive -tition	kfA-v, -m, -vQ
Report (v)	AvUI(v)
Represent-ative; -ation	ajnUv-u; -Q
repress-ion	typ-bwev-Q
Reptile	ykeos
republic	pnum-knuw
Request	etUIv
rescue, N, -er	(v)ytyrv-U, -u
research (v)	gU-hUte(v)
resembl'e, -ance	jOv-Q
resent/ment	nA-ydO(-v)

English: Rig	aUI
Reserve (v = be re—d); (=keep)	yp-yv-U(-v); yp-bAv
resign(ation)	typ-twev-sev(Q)
Resist/ance, -or	yd-wU(v); ydwQd
resound-ing	bI'v, -m
Respect; -ful	tukO, -v; -m
respectively	grab-Ax(-Q)
respond	kyhIv
Responsibil-ility, (-le)	kwyhI(m)
Rest, (-well)	(r)Ayev
Restaurant	dova
restrain/t v	typwe(v)
restrict/ion	tyn-mU(v)
RESULT, —v	tsUs-ev
resurrection (day)	(typ)kU-take-iA
be re—ed, resurrect(t.)	typ-tak-(v)ev
Return v	type-v
(spirit) reve'al, -lation(v)	(U)ytkyge(v)
revenge, v	yrtyr(v)
Revere/nce	tUkO-v
review; book —	typ-tiO; Ugs-mUv(U)
revile	yr-UIv
revol'ution, (-ve)	tyk-LeL(-v)
Reward v	jruts-ev
rhinoceros	kEmOz-kwyd-os
Rhythm	jAe
Rice (field)	binto (enaz)
Rich	drEm
Ride	ksev
riddle (secret —)	(ypumsUm)hytbe
rifle	Iwyd
RIGHT (morally)	jwUr(m)
— moment; — place	rA; ra
— side	woza(m)

Righteous/ness (-correct/)	jwUrU(m) (trUm)
rigid-ity	yc-tLevom-U
rim	Lygaz
rime (rhyme)	j-ypAz(ev)
rind (tree bark)	wygz, (tok-ygz)
RING, N, v	yEL, vIv
Ripe/ness, -n	o-vrA-m, -v
Rise	atke-v, takev
risk v	thyr-ev
ritual (adj)	kU-ma(m)
River	ejEn
Road	eda
roar, v	wI, -v
rob(-ber)	wyr-fev(-u)
robin	ai-gwa-kEos
rock (piece); high —	wE-s, (-z); wEk
rocket - explosion	yt-yp-twIygna
- propulsion	yt-yp-we
- vehicle	yt-yp-we-ged
Rod, (punish)	wanas (jyrted)
rodent	podzevos
roe	(yn-)nE-kwyd-os
role	zu
Roll, v; list; bread	LeL(v); viO-LeL yn(-LeL-)nod
roller (skate), N	LeL-(d)ryve'-v, -d
Roof	kugaz
ROOM	ga
Root (tree-)	iotyk, (yk-tok)
Rope	wana
Rose	ai-riO-io
rosy (-warm-feel)	rai(O)m
rot (v)	o-tyb-e(v)
Rough-ness	yd-kem-U
ROUND/ness v	La-m, v
Row (line)	sana
to row (a boat)	bovev (jEged)

Rub, (-ber)	ydbe(v); vEmE
ruby	ai-rOwE
rudder	tazd
rug	gayk-uygE
ruin	tyc-ve(v)
Rule(-r); (line-straight)	jwyz'-ev, (-u); (anad)
Run	nav, nev
ruth-less-/ness	Y-byrO(m)
-ry (carpent-ry)	-vUn
rye	yi-ton(od)

Ss

SACK	stag
Sacrifice (v: to —)	se-fUrkU(-v)
SAD/ness, (-den, v) -den, v	(v-)Y-k(r)O'm, U-yrO'm, -v
SAFE/ty	ytyrA-m
sage	gUru, nUrUm
Sail, -or	kEwed, jEn(bydw)u
to sail (by ship)	-jEnged-ev
saint	kUru
salad	iodz
salamander	nan-bEjEos
Sale	strE
saliva	ogta-jE
salmon (pink)	(taim)dav-jEos
SALT-y; v	bygrE-m, -v
(table-salt)	(bi-)bygrE
salvation	ytyrAv-U
SAME	jam
Sand	nynwE
San'e, -itarium	U-rom, roga
(tree-)sap	(tok-)gjE
saphire	ui-rOwE
Satan	yrkU
satellite	b-eki

English: Sat	aUI
Satisf'act'ion, -ory, -y	trUnO-m, -v
Saturday	nE-iA
sauce	odjEbE
Saucer	(yk-)Lena
sausage	osod-Lana
Save	ytyrAv
Saw (tool)	kyk-zEvd
SAY	UIv, sUIv
Scale(s) (mass-measure space-measure (fish-) scales	jniO(-Ed) En-iOd) a-niOd) (jE)oygz
Scale v	ek-tev
scare, (v) scatter scene	tvyrO(-v) tnybe-v vUz-iO
Sceptic/ism	UhO-m
scherzo schizo-phrenic (psychosis) schola'r, -stic	I-ne-krOvz yb-nub-cEm(-u) (Uyro) retgUvu, -m
SCHOOL (-adj) v	gUa (-m)-v
SCIEN'CE, -tific	gUw-Um
Scissors	bzEvd
scold	yr-tUIv
Scope	mytta
scorpion scrap e(-r)	yrod-zos yg-zEv(-d)
Scratch	bozEv
Scream (v)	yr-nI(v)
screen	nyn-yE'-d, v
Screw (Abbr.) -driver —	brEgtELd, (brELg)-ev -vLev(d)
sculpt/(ure) 1(portrait) 2(abstract)	1 wEjiOv(-s) 2 wEma-v

English: Sep	aUI
SEA, -anemone -gull	jEna; riOio-gyEmos jEna-kEos
seal seam search	jE-waubos bvanavz hUte(v)
Season	akiAz
Seat (chair)	ykta, (tykad)
(to)Seat vtr.	vyktav
SECOND (time) 2nd	ynAz ne
Secret,(adj)	ypus, (ypum)
Secretary	marbu
secur'e: adj, v; -ity N	wytyrA'-m, -v;-d
SEE	iOv
SEED	to
seek; where?	tUtev; ha(te)v
SEEM	Oiv
seep	nynyEyv
Sell/ing	StrE-v-Q
(good-)Select/ion	(r)ytna(v)
self-conscious/ness	fU(yr)gUO(m)
(-)SELF(ish/ness)	(yr-)FU(-m/O)
seminar	teb-gUvs
SEND	vav
sensation-al	cmO-m
SENSE, v	cO, -v
to sense stench sense-less (without purpose) sense-less (unconscious) sensitiv'ity, -e sensual/ity	yr-kEmO-v yb-tsUm yb-gUOm mO-m, cOvAm cOrO-m
SENTENCE N: V to	bUI: jwUskuv at
SEPARATE, v	zam, zav

English: Sep	aUI
September (9th mo.)	nU-ekiA
sequence	Ax
Serious/ness	yktrU(m)
Serv'ant, -e, -ice	ykwu, -v, -s
Set: v; (N)	vyktav (bjOr)
SEVEN 7	E
sever; — parts	(v)ybev, (tybzav)
SEVERAL	yIn
severe	OwEm
sew	bvanav
Sewage (-plant)	yrstyg(-a)
SEX	voz
shack	yn-uga
SHADE, shadow	yiz, syiz
Shake v	tytwe-v
SHALL (=future) go = ought to (go)	-tA-: a-tA-v -r-: a-r-v = wryv av
Shallow	yn-ykam
sham, v	yg-yEjU, pyg-vEv
Shame	tyiO
share	bzU-v
Shark	nyrjEos
Sharp(-en); =hot, edge make pointed	dzOm-(ev); dzenav dzemev
shave	(no)yg-dzEv
SHE	yvu, Lu
Sheep	uyg bos
sheet: metal, linen	wenrEs, binanab(-ena)
shelf	skenEs
Shell	wEyg
Shield	ydyrd

English: Sie	aUI
shift, v	tyj-mag-(ev)
SHINE v, N	iv, (r)in
Ship	jEnged
Shirt	guygs
Shock (-v)	(b-)ydwO-v
Shoe	yk-bo-yg
Shoot, a shot; arrow	wydnI(v): kEdvev
Shop: [1] handicraft-place [2] small store [3] v; (try) to buy	bo-vEv-as yn-nArsga t-rEtsev
Short (-hand)	yana-m(viOvs)
shot (arrow--)	wydnI(vQ); kEdve(vQ)
Should 1(=command) 2(=ought to) 3(=perhaps will (if I should die)	1 -r- 2 wryv(-yEc) 3 -yEc (Qg fu yov-yEc)
Shoulder	kazog
Shout,	nI-v
shove v	ytwe-v
Shovel (=digger	bEgteLd gyEd)
SHOW (V)	viO-v
shrine	kUrUvs
shrink	t(v)ynev
Shut v	ytgev
shut-in v	g(L)ytgev
Shut adj	ytgem
shy/ness 1(timid) 2(reserved)	1 rywO-m 2 typO-m
SIBLINGS	jytu
Sick/ness	yro-m
Sickle	zLEvd
SIDE	az
Sieve, sift	nynyE'd, -v

English: Sig	aUI
SIGHT	iọ
Sign v	viQvs-ev
Silen't, -ce; be s— t	yIm-U; yIv
Silk (-worm)	rian'-E, -os
Silver	bikrẸ
Similar, be, make s.	jOm, jOv, jvOv
Simple	abẓam
simulat/e, -ion	jOmev-Q
simultaneous	bjAm
Sin (N)	yṛUv(s)
Since, (prp.)	ytA (Ayt)
Sincere	EjUỌm
Sinew	anawọz
Sing-er	rIv-u
single	amQm
singular n(=unique)	a-mUn (fam)
sink v, (outflow)n	tyk-yvev(jE-yte)n
Sir	kụ
Sister (motherly)	jytyvụ, (jytLu)
SIT	yḳtav
Situation (Zustand)	ṃA
SIX 6	A 6
SIZE	aṇ
(ice)skate, N	(jEwE-)dryvev, ryved
skeleton	b-ogwE-n
sketch v	p-Ui-ana-v
ski N	(ryve-) wenas
V	(wenas-)dryvev
skill-ful (-ness)	oge-wam(-U)
SKIN	ọyg
skip (tr: make jump)	(v)etkev
Skirt, -motherly	yvuyg; Luyg
skunk	vyr-kEmos

English: S no	aUI
SKY	kạn
(lie)slander(,v)	yryd(Ej)UI, -v
slave	yr-ykwu, -v
sled	ryve-ged
Sleep (N)	Uyv(-A)
Sleeve	kogeyg
Slide, v — down	ryve, -v; tyk-yvev
slime	bEjE
1(whirl) sling	1(kEL-)tswed
2 loop-band	2 tLyp-wanab
Slip v, — by	(yr-)yve-v; bywev
slippery	(b)ywe-wam
slogan-ize	wUI-v
SLOPE	tyḳa
SLOW/ness, v	ynẹ'm, -v
sloth (bio.)	yne-tok-os
slug (=snail)	yb-ygw-yneykos
SMALL/ness	yṇa(m)
Smash	wyrẓe-v
(bad-)smear, v	(yr-)jEbE, -v
SMELL (sense)	kEmO-v
emit S.	kvEmOv
Smile v, N	tygrO-v
smith, -y	rEv-u, -as
Smoke v	ybikẸ-v
Smooth	kẹm
smug	yr-trUnOm
Snail (-house)	yne-ykos (tygLe-ga)
Snake	nanọs
snare	vyr-bwanav
Sneeze, v	wygt-kẸI, -v
sniff v	kEtmO-v
snout	nogta

English: Sno	aUI	English: Spo	aUI
Snow	bikjEwE	(to) sow v, sow N	tvov yv-Lodbos
SO (long a time) (so much; so well)	f Ud, f'- (f'nA) (fnE; frUg)	SPACE; to s.	a; vyttav
Soap	privE	spacious	gnam
soar(ing light)	kev; tekEm	Spade	bEgted
Social	b(r)unam	Spark(-le)	ei-v, (eiyi-v)
Society	anub	sparrow spasm spatial	na-ynkEos yr-bwavQ. am
Sock(s)	gykboyg		
Soda (bicarbonate)	godz-bibygrE	Speak	UIv
SOFT	ywEm	spear	dzanEs
Soil	robEn	SPECIAL, -ist	zUm; fnUgu
Soldier	bydwu	specific	zU-trUm
SOLID, (adj)-ify	bE(-m), -v	Species	(nE-)jomz
Sol-ution, -ve	ytbe-v	Spectacles	iOd
SOME 1(several,); 2 =any, 3 =a, an (neglected)	1 yIn; 2 ym, 3 yI	Speech	UIv-s, -Q
		Speed, v	ne-v
some-body; -thing; -time	yI-u; yms, yIs; yInA	(magic)' spell spend sperm sphere, hollow — spice	(w)UIze'-v-Q yt'-sev vom-to Las, LyEs dzOm-Ed
SON	tvu		
Song	rI	Spider	nyEd-zos
Soon	yAp-yn	spin, V spinach spin'e, (-al)	teL,-ev oi iod Yp-og-wE(-m)
soothe	brUvEv		
Sort	mEz	Spiral: coil; flat	takLe; tygLe
sorrow	y-krO	SPIRIT-ual, -iz-ation	U-m, U-tEv-'U
Soul	OU	spit (saliva) (=spear)	(ogta-)jE-vytev dzanEs
SOUND, v; make s.	I (v); vIv		
Soundless-ness	yIm-U	Splendor, (-id)	i-riO, (-m)
Soup-y	odjE-m	Split, (N)	zEv (-Q)
Sour/ness (adj)	y-grE(m)	spoil (tr.)	(v)yrtEv
source	ytEs	Sponge	jE-nyE-os
South-ern	ia-m	spot	Lyiz

English: Spo	aUI
SPOON, (v)	jEd, (-dov)
spout, v	jEvyt-ev
Spread (tr.)-v	tyg(v)a-v
Spring: 1 jump, 2 elastic, 3 season, 4 well	1 et-ke-v, 2 kykvEd,. 3 pakiA, 4 jE(k)yt
Sprout; tr.	tio(v); tvio(v)
Square, -ish	jena, -m
squash	ei-aniod
squid (mollusk)	kog-n-oged (ywEmos)
squirrel	tok-(podze)vos
Stab v	dze-v
stable	bos-ga
stag	nE-kwyd-vos
Stage v	riO-va-v
Stain, v	yr-mi, -v
stair (-way)	n-atek(-da)
stallion	v-ukbos
stamina	nA-wo
Stamp (of approval)	rU-tiQs
postage —, v	vadrE-v
STAND; — up	kav; at-kav
— point	(kav-ayn,)atiO-ayn
Standard, -ize	knUrms, -ev
STAR-ry, -like	ki-m, -jOm
starch	wio-zE
starfish	jE-ki-m-os
START, v	pe-v
starv-e, -ation	y-od-O-v, '-Q
STATE 1(condition) 2 = nation	1QL (ŎL) 2 nuwa
statesman	nuwa-wu
State/ment	tygU-v
statistic's, do — -ian, a s...c	jnUz-mUn'U, -v ...U-vu, ...U-s

English: Sto	aUI
Station	ye-as
statue (stone-,metal)	wE-, (rE-)-vuma
Stay	tAv
steady	a-taz-m, jem
Steal (v)	yr-fe(v)
Steam	jEkE
Steel	wErE
steep	tyke(taz)m
steer v	tazev
Stem	gEtok
stench (sense —)	yr-kEmO(v)
Step (-up), v	ate(k), atkev
step-fa(-mo-)ther	yf-yt(y)vu
stew	b-os-iod
a Stick N	anEs
(to)Stick, -y	bwE'(-v), -m
Stiff	wyLem
Still (yet); more, = silent, quiet	tfA; nEk ylm; yem
Stimulus	te-ytUs
Sting, to —	dzez, dzev
stink, (v)	v-yrkEmO(v)
stir	tyt-vev
Stitch, v	Abvana(v)
Stocking	ogedyg
Stomach	godz
STONE, a —	wE(-s)-z
Stop, v, (tr-)	(v-) ye-v
stopper	yed
Store v	nArsga-v
stork	nan-oged-kEos
Story	UIvo

English: Str	aUI
Straight	yLem
1(stress)Strain v; 2(sift)	1 gytwe-v; 2 (nyn-yE-v)
strait-jacket	(ydam)wuyg
Strange-r	yfam-u
straw (sans seeds)	yb-to-n-z
Strawberry	aiot
stray	yt-tygav
Stream	ejE
Street	ueda
Strength-en	wo-v(v-)ow-ev
stress	gybwe-v
Stretch v	v-ana-v
strew	nyn-tyg-vav
String	bana
Strike /a blow work-stop	tswe-v uwe-(v)ye
Striv-e/-ing	tU-v
(caress)Stroke v; (apoplexy) N	(r)ane-v; oUz-vye
STRONG	wom
STRUCTURE	bEtkU, bzUx
(grad-) student	(k)etgUvu
Study N, (v) -place	etgU(v)-as
(to) Stun, v	vyv
stupid/ity stutter-er	yn-U(m) kfA-IyIv-u
(personal)Styl'e, -ize	(f)mUma-v, fUma
Subdu-e, -ing	vykev, tykvev; tykwAm
Subject(ive)	fUs (Um)
subjugate	(t) vyktev
Sublime; sense for the —	k(yb)Um, kOm; k(yb)O

English: Sur	aUI
submerge submit o.s.	tykgjEv f-yktev
Substance	UE
Substitut-e N, V;-ion	gayfs, -ev; -e
Subtle/ty	rynwU-m
subtract-ion	tybnev-Q
Succeed; (=follow)	trev; (ypav)
Success; (-ion)	tre; (rypa-vQ)
SUCH; such a long time	fEm; f'...:f'nA
suck (-in); (air)	tag-jEv;(dyEgev)
Sudden/ness	ypO-m
sue v	jwUsev
Suffer (hurt)	yryv(yrOv)
Sufficient	trUn
Sugar, (y)-food	bigrO, (m)-od
Suggest(-ible)/ion; v (power) of -ion suicide, V	(It)vU-v(wam);vOv vO(-w) fU-vyo-v
Suit (able)	bjOrv(Am)
suitcase suit (of clothes)	skev-gad kuyg-bvuyg
Summer	nakiA
SUN, -rise, (-set)	aki, -tak (-tyk)
Sun-(-first)-day	na-iA
super, -iority	k-, Uk, -Q
Superior: place; status	akm; kQm
supplement, v, N(ary) supply, V	bvyzUv-z(Qm) nArs, -ev
Support (v)	skwEr(v)
suppose; ... (suppose! you fall!)	tyk-sav; hE, Qg... hE, Qg bu tykev!
suppress-ion	tyk-bwev-Q
Sure-ly	yhOm-Q
Sureness	yhO

English	aUI
Surface	yga
surge'on, -ry	tro-dzEv'-u, -Q
Surprise v	kypQ-v
Surround/ing	Lygana-v, Lyge-v
Surviv'e/-al	kado-v (Q)
Suspect v, N	yk-Uv, yk-Uyvu
suspicious	ykUvAm
suspense (-feel)	hytkavO(-v)
suture v,(N)	(oyg-)bvanav(z)
swallow N	kEg-izo-dos
v: (wrong way —)	djEv, (yr-djEv)
swamp	jE-bEna
swan, (poet.)	nan-kogz-jE-kEos, (riO-kogz)
swarm (v)	nyn-e(v)
sway, v	kyf-wU, -v
swear, (curse)	kUrUIv, (wyrUIv)
sweat (v) (skin-)	nyn-(oyg-)jE(-v)
sweep (v)	knand-e(-v)
SWEET/ness, (-bread)	grO'-m (-od)
swell, v	tneLg, -ev
Swim, -v (duck-)	jEge-v, (jEde-v, ek-jEdev)
swine	Lodbos
swing, v (tool)	tyt-Le'-v, (-d)
Sword	zEv-wyd
syllable	bUIz
symbio'sis, -tic, v	byjo-m, -v
symbol, /-ize (tr.)	(v-)U-viOv(s)
symmetr-y, (-ic)	jazQ(-m)
Sympath'y, -etic; (pity)	bQ-m; byrO-m
symphony	byU-brIOn
sym, sy(n)— . . . , (=equal-)	b-, eb-, tab-; j-. .
Synonym'-ous;-y	j-EsgU'-s, -m; —'
synthesi'ze, (-s)	bU-sav-(Q)
Syrup, (sugar-)	(bi-) grOjE
SYSTEM	tUb

T t

English	aUI
Table	kvad
tact; (rhythm)	rA-O; (jAe)
Tail	yp-ogz
tailor, v	vuygu, -v
TAKE, -out	fev, yg-fev
talent (-ed)	U-wamU (-m)
Talk, v; — much	sUI(v); nUIv
Tall, (high)	takEm, (kanam)
tame, v	bom, -ev
tank, (armor-)	gad, wuyg-ged
tap (liquid)	jE-gayt
tape, v	e'ana-v
task	truwe
TASTE, (-y);art —	gO (-rm);rUgO
Tax	twudrE
taxonomy	o-bUzU
Tea; green —	io-jE, oii-jE
teaplant	jE-io
Teach/ing, (-er)	vetgU-v(-u)
team	bjOr
tear(-drop); v	iOz-jE(z); zwev
technique	dvU
technolog-y, -ic	ved-gU'-w, -m
Telegraph	yba-Uti(v)
Telepathy	yba-O
Telephone	ybauI(v)
Telescope/y	ybatiO(d)
Television	yba-iO
tell	tUIv
temptation	tsOb-ve(v)
TEN 10	o 10
tenaci'ous, -ty	wyzbEm-U, nA-(c)Ev

English: Ten	aUI
Tend/ency	etO-v
tens'ion, -e	tybwe-m
Tent	nanab-uga
Tenth	nO
term'-inate	ypAmQ; (v-)ypev
Terr'ible/,or-ist	twyrO'-(gE)m, vu
Test, v	UmtiO, -v
Testicles	voLz
text	dUIg
texture	bnynz-mUd
-th, (fif-th)	n- (no)
THAN	myt
THANK,'-ful, v	ytOr'-m,-v
THAT, (those)	pfE(n)
(which)	xE (hEp)
(he said)that (he)	(vu UlpAv), Uf(vu)
in order that	Ut
THE, (plural)	pI (n)
the more...the more	Uj nEk... Uj nEk
theater	riOv-ga
THEIR, (of things);	num, snEm;
of animals	nom
THEM (things)	nu, (snE)
(of animals)	no
theme	pfUs
THEN, (past)	yfA, (pfA)
Thence	pfayt
Theory	UtUb
therapy	trovU
THERE	yfa, pfa
Therefore	yUt-fE
Therefrom	pfayt
Thereto	pfat

English: Thr	aUI
THESE	fEn
thesis	U-sav-Q
THEY, (of things);	nu, (snE);
(of animals)	no
THICK	dnEm
thief	yr-fevu
thigh	woged
THIN	y- dnEm
THING; concept	Es; Uz
THINK	Uv
THIRD	ni
Thirst(y); (for air)	yjE(m);jEtOv;
	(kEtOv, m)
THIS	fE
thistle	dzez-riOio
Thither	pfat
Thorn	dzez
thorough	druwem
THOSE	pfEn
THOUGH,(-nevertheless)	dyf, (fyd)
THOUGHT	Us
THOUSAND	Oki 10^3=1000
Thread	ywanbs
threat(en)	stvyrO(v)
THREE-dimension'al	i-na'-m
thrill, v	O-tytwe, (v)
Thrive	rov
Throat	oIvz
throb	gygev
throne	kyktad
THROUGH	ad, ed
Throw, v	kEtswe, -v

English: Thr	aUI
thrush	rI-kEos
thrust, v	we, -v
Thumb	bowz
Thunder	kayrOI
Thursday	no-iA
thyroid	tne-jEvogz
Ticket	utga-drE
tickle, v	rO-yw-ane, -v
Tie, v	bwana-v
Tiger	nozvos
Tight-en	bwa'-m, -v
TILL (until)	At
(top-)Tilt (tr.)	(paz-)t(v)yka-v
TIME(s), v to T	A; rAv
T. of existence	cA
how much T?	hnA?
time-less	kyb-Am
time-piece	nAd
timid/ity	(t)ywO-m
Tin	birE
tip, trV = to tilt	paz, paz-tvykav
Tire, N, v -ed	Led-yg; tywe'v, -pAm
tissue (bio)	jnoz
title	ek-fUI
TO, (right at)	at, t', (bat)
to & fro	tyt
Tobacco	ybikE-io
Today	fiA
Toe	ykboz
TOGETHER, (moving)	tab, (teb)
Toilet	ydova
tolerate	o-dyv
Tomato	ainot
To-morrow	fiAt
Tone	AI

English: Tra	aUI
Tongs	bAwd
TONGUE	gOz
TOO: also; too much	bIb; knE
TOOL	vEd
Tooth; on wheel	odzEvz; dzez
Top	kaz
Torch	kiE-nid
torture, N	vnyrOv, -Q
Touch: sense; hit, v	EbO-v; Etbe-v
TOUGH	'zym' = wyzEm
TOWARD	at
Towel	ygjE-uygE
Tower	kuga
TOWN (big)	(n)uba
Toy, v	rOve-s, -v
Track	e-ana
Trade, v	stytrE, -v
tradition-al	pArtA'-vQ, -m
trag-edy,	nyrO'-UIviO,
-ic	-kyU'w, m
(Loco-)Train N;	anaged;
V (teach)	trewev
traitor (secret)	yr-tyg-UIvu;
(turncoat)	t-ydbru(-ked-evu)
tranquilize-r	vyemev-d
Trans-, (=beyond)	ked-, (kyb-)
transcend-ent	kybe-v, -m
transistor	dydweid
transit	ked-ev
transition	edQ
(Transitive, causative prefix)	v-
transitive	kedvUm
translat'e/ion	tyfnUI-v
translucent/ (material)	idE-m

English: Tra	aUI
transparent (m)	diOm, iOdE(m)
Transport, v	nase-v
trap (catch); N	(wyr-)tyvfev, -d
(hold), N	(wyr-)bwAv, -d
trash	yrytE
trauma-tic	O-vyrO-m
Travel, N	dav-Q
Tray	senkad
tread (step)	ogev, (ate-v)
treason	yr-tygUI, tydbru-e
treasure	nUrs
treat-ment, -ise	tvEv'-Q, -UI
(peace-)treaty;	brU-tAvma;
state —	nuwa-brUje
TREE: -fruit; (big, round; tree berry)	tok, k'-: k-ot (knot, kLot; yn-kLot)
tremble, v	twyte, -v
Trial (law —)	tvevU, (jwUs —)
triang'le, -ular	igebana-m
tribe	yn-banu
Trick, v	tyfyr-v
trigger, v	twed, -ev
trigonometry	gebana-(mUn)-gUw
triumph	kyfwO
troll	robEnU
Tropian (=Negro)	iau-m
tropic/s	nia-m
Trouble (to suffer) v,	nyrvO-v
=difficulty	ydremU
Trousers	vuyg
truck	nE-ged
Tru'e/, th	EjU-m
Trunk	gEs
Trust, v	rUO-v
Try; tr. (a man)	tve-v; tvevUv(u)
Tub	jEn-gad
tube	(L)angyEd
Tuesday = 3rd day	ni-iA

English: T, Und	aUI
tug-boat	twe-jEged
tumor	yr-tneLg
tuna-fish	riEm-jEos
tunnel	gyE-da
turkey	kEbnos
Turn, v; — ahead	Le, -v; p-Lev
— back	yp-Lev
Turnip	dzeL-iod
turtle; turtle-dove	wEygos; brO-kEos
Twice	eA
twilight	egi
twin: male, fem.	eju: ejvu, ejLu
twinkle, (sparkle)	yiti-v, (iyi-v)
Twist, v	wyrLe, -v
TWO	e 2
Typ'e, (-ical)	(j)Uma(-m)
type v	es-vUiOv; es-viOv
type-writer	vUiOv-es
tyrant	yr-kwu

Uu

English	aUI
Ugly/ness	yriO-m
ultimate	U-ypnAm
Ultra—: above, beyond	k, kyb-
ultra-violet	k-oim
Umbrella	ka-jE-yd
[1]UN, -([2]anti; [3]without; [4]against; [5]non-; [6]zero-)	[1]y-, [2]Y-, [3]yb-, [4]yd-, [5]yc-, [6]Y-
Uncle	ytu-jytvu
un-clothed	yb-uygQm
unconditioned, -al	yQm
Uncover	yt-kygev
UNDER(-), toward-	yk(-); tyk—
under-line, v	yk-ana, -v
Under-neath	byk
underpants	gvuyg

English	aUI
UNDERSTAND/ing:	
1(comprehend)	1 (iU-v)
2 perceive	2 Ui-v
undo	yd-vEv, tyc-vEv
undress	yuygev, tyb-uygev
unfortunately	yrQg
unfree	y-fUwem
uni-form (adj)	a-ma(-m)
un-interrupted	yb-yE-gem
union, (together)	(b)avu
unique	fam
UNIT	an
Unit'e, -y (tr); join N	(v)av-U; b(v)av-U
Univers-e, -al	canU-m
university	kcan-gUa
un-natural	yd-Eom
Unseeing	yc-iOvAm, iyOvAm
Unselfish (altruistic)	y-fUm, (yf-Um)
UP (-ward)	tak (tek)
uphold	tak-bAv
Upon (motion)	bak, (keb, bek), kab
upward	tek
urge(nt)	wyv-ne'v(-m)
urin(at)e; drain	yt-og-jE(v); jEytE(v)
USE, (N)-ful	dEv'(-U), -gEm
Usual	dEvUm

V v

English	aUI
vaccinat'e, -ion	v-yd-yro-v'-Q
vacilat'e/ion	tytO-v
vacuum, -cleaner	yE, -privd
Vague-ness	U-ydim-U
valid;be v.='gelten'	rom, wom;nUrv, c'nUrm
Valley	bEk-eg
VALU'E, (-able); to v.	nUr(m); vnUrv
valve (liquid –)	(jE-)yded
vanity (vain)	yg-yrkO(m)

English	aUI
(tr)var'y, -able, -iation	(v-)yje'v, -wam-s; -vQ, -vU
VEGETABLE-s(-fruit)	iod, (iot)
VEHICLE	ged
veil (face -)	diOm(kup)uygE
/blood/Vein (toward heart)	(at-gog)/ogai/ angyEd
venture, (v)	vU-wyU(-v)
verb	vUIs
(Verbs end in:	-v) (tr.v, causatives begin: v-)
vermin (bad -)	(yr-)bizos
Verse	jAUI
vertebra'-te	yp-og-wE'z, -os
vertical	tekam
[1]VERY, 2=same, 3= self, 4= even	1nEm, 2jam 3 -fU(sEfU, vufU), 4 jUf
VESSEL	jEgas
viaduct (water-)	ek(jE)da
Vibrat'-ion(-e) v	tyte(v)
vicarious	gas(yf-)Um
Vice-versa	yf-da-aL
vicious/ness; -circle	vyr(yd)U(m); vyrmaL
victim	yv-yrs
victory (conquest)	tvUk, (tykwe)
View, v	atiO, -v
Village	yn-uba
vinegar	rojE-ygrE
Violen-ce, -t	nyrwo, -m
VIOLET: color, flower	oi(m), oi-riOio
Virtu'e, (-ous) (taste for goodness)	(v)rOkU, kUrO, rU(b)rO(m) (rUgO), grU-m

English	aUI
virus	vyroz
viscera(l)	(ana-)godzO(m), yk-og(m)
vision, v	UviO-v
Visit/or V, N	tebru', -v, -vU
visual; — art	iOwam; riOwU
visualize	iOvEv, iOvUv
Vitamin	otrod
vizor (eye-shade)	iOz-ydyr
vocab'ul/-ary (le)	UIn(-z)
vocalize	oIv
VOICE, v	uI, -v
void	yE, Yg
volcano	iE-bEk
volume	inan
Vomit	ygodev
vote V, N	wytnav, wuI
vowel	fIz
vulture	yo-kEos

Ww

English	aUI
Waist	Logz, ydaz
Wait	trAv
wake =to be awake	cvAv
Walk	ogav, ogev
WALL	kwE
wander	aLav
want; wish, lack	twUv; t(n)Ov, ybOv
WAR	yd-brU
Warlike	tyd-brUm
Warm/th, v	riE-m, riEv
warn	tyrUIv, pyrUIv
warp	weLv
was	pAc
WASH	(jE-)priv
wasp	y-grizos
Waste, v	yrytE-v

English	aUI
Watch: v; timepiece	AiO-v; yn-Ads
WATER, (=liquid)	jEn (jE)
waterfall	jE-tyk
Wave; to w. v	jEL(kyk);tytev
Wax	eiyvE
WAY, (manner)	da, (mUd)
W.C.	ydova
WE	fnu
WEAK/ness, (-ly)	(t)ywo-m;v-ywov
wealth	drEmU
wean	yt-tedEv
WEAPON	wyd
Weather	kamA
Weave	nanabev
wedge	zwad
Wednesday	nu-iA
weed	yr-ios
Week-ly	EiA-m
weep-ing, V, N	iOz(yrO)jEv-Q
WEIGH/T, mass-w.	tykE-v, E-niOv
welcome	(rUg-)terv
Well (good)	rUg, rUmQ
= spring	jEn-yt
West	ita
Wet	gjEm
Whale: 1 baleen	1 jEonos
2 tooth —	2 jEgnos
WHAT ?;...what (rel)	hE ?;...xE; xE; xQ...xE *

*xQ ("where") can introduce a relative pronoun object, which follows after the verb in aUI (as Subject-Verb-Object is the rule): "u, xQ fu gUv xu, tev" = "the man, where I know him, comes" = "the man, whom I know, is coming." Also "which, what..."

English: Wha	aUI
What-kind (of...)	hUm ?...,xUm
Wheat	nato
Wheel	Led
WHEN ?; when	hA ?;...xA
Whence	hayt, xayt
WHERE ? rel. where	ha ?...,xa (relative) xQ....*
where-in ? where-on ? where-to ?	hag? xag hak? xak? hat? xat?
Whether	QgxI, QghI
WHICH (pron.) adjective	hE ?...xE, xQ.*..xE hEm ?(rel.)...xEm
WHILE conj.	jAg
Whip (scourge) v (for cream)	wyrtre'd, -v tvytne'-d, -v
Whirl v	jELe-v
Whistle	kEI-d, -v
WHITE/ness	bi-m
Whither ?, whither	hat ?...,xat
WHO ?;rel. who, pl. fem.	hu ? hnu ? xu, xnu, nhvu ? hnyvu ? xyvu, xnyvu
WHOLE (adj), -some	'zyn', nyz(-Um);vrom
whom ?;...whom whom do you know = you know whom ?	hu ?; xQ...xu bu gUv hu ?
whoop (joy) whose ? whose fem:	rO-nIv Ub hu ? xum, xnum Ub hLu ?xyvum, xnyvum
WHY ?; how come ?	hU ?; hyt ?
Wide, width	dam, -U
WIFE	byvu
wild; sans-restraint	ybom, ybum; yb-typwe-m

English: Wor	aUI
WILL, to w., -ing; —	twU,-v;-m;yc-yd
will-be; will go willful willow	tAc; a-tA-v twU-gEm yrOI-tok
(N, V, N)win-ner	pne'v-u
Wind	kEwe
Window	tugai
Wine	rOjE
WING	kEd
WINTER	yn-akiA
Wire	rEana
Wis/e, -dom;-wise e.g. length-wise	rUnU/m;-Q(-g) anam-Q, ana-g
Wish v, -ful	tO'-v, (-gE)m
wit-ty	OnU, ryxiU, tyfrO-m
witch	wyrLu
WITH	eb
withdraw	typ-twev
Within	bag
Without, (=outside)	yb; yg
witness, V, N wizard-ry	vEjU-v-u Uk-cEw'u; U
Wolf	p-waubos
WOMAN, (motherly)	yvus, Lus
womb (shelter) wonder, V, N	(L)yvogs hUv-O(s)
WOOD- -pecker	tEk tok-dzne-kEos
Wool-ly	noygE-m
WORD (for word)	UI (-mQ)
WORK (creative) v	(r)uwe-v
worker wood-worker (carpenter)	uwevu, -vu tEk-vu

* (see previous page)

English: W, X, Y	aUI
World (-view)	Ea-, ca-;-UtiO
Worm-y	anos-om
worry, v	yn-yrvO, -v
wors'e, (-t)	(p)nEk-rym, -yrUm
worth-y	nUr-m, trUn—m
'Would'=after verb:	"-yEc"
Wound, skin — (v)	oyg-zyr(v)
wrap, V, N	kLyge-v;-d
wreath, (flower)	rioL (riOio-yEL)
wrench, v	wyrLe'd, v
wrist	bo-baz
WRITE	vUiOv
writing-brush	mi-nand
Wrong; adj, v	y-jwUr, -m, -v

X x

xeno-phobe	yfau-ydbru
X-ray, v; picture	d-anai-v-;-s
xylo-phone	tEk-Id

Y y

Yah-weh	KcU
yang	vin-pUz
Yard: 1 meter, 2 court	1 t-ana-an, 2 waLg-enaz
yawn v	tyb-tage(v)
yea (emotional)	Or
Year-ly	akiA-m
yeast	grO(-t-rO-kE)yio
YELLOW	ei(m)
yelp, v	yn-waI-v
YES, (emotional)	Ur, (Or)
Yesterday	pfiA
YET, (=more)	tfA, (nEk)
yield (v)	tak-se(v)

English: Y, Z	aUI
Yin	yin-pUz
yolk	oyt-ei
YOU(R); pl.	bu(m); bnu(m)
Young, Youth	fAom, fAo

Z z

zebra	ybibi-ukbos
zen	OUw
Zero	Y
zinc (Zn, 30)	bui-rE (Ez i O)
zone	zLena
zoo	nosba
zoolog'y, -ic	os-gU'w, -m

If man by cosmic soul possessed
received in symbols truth's bequest
and lives by Spirit's task-behest:
on this earth is he cursed or blessed?

BIBLIOGRAPHY

Alpers, B. 1944, Anti-social tendencies after hypothalamic destruction, Psychosomatic Medicine, 2:286.

Aquinas, see Thomas

Augustinus, A. De mendacio, Ch. IV; De trinitate; (Opera); Confessiones.

Babbage, S.B., The Mark of Cain, Stud. in Lit. & Theol., Grand Rapids, 1966, Eerdmans.

Bach, G.R. & R.M. Deutsch, 1974, Pairing, How to achieve genuine intimacy, NY: Avon.

Beecher, M & W, The Mark of Cain, 1971, Harper & Row, N.Y.

Bhagavad-Gita, tr. Schroeder, L., Jena 1955, E. Diederichs.

Binswanger, L., 1942, Grundformen und Erkenntnis menschlichen Daseins, Zürich, Max Niehans

Black, M. 1963, Models & Metaphors, St. i. Lang. & Phils. Ithaca, Cornell U. Pr.

-----, 1968, The Labyrinth of Language, N.Y., Praeger

Bloomfield, L., 1933, Language. N.Y., Holt.

Brown, R.W. 1970, Psycholinguistics, N.Y., Free Press

Buber, Ma. Ich und Du (I and Thou), Leipzig, Inselverg, 1923.

-----, Distance & Relation, Psychiatry, May 1957, vol. 20, no. II.

Buren, P.M. van, The Edges of Language, 1972, N.Y., Macmillan.

Carnap, R. The Logical Syntax of Language, London 1949, Rutledge & Paul.

Chase, St. 1938, The Tyranny of Words, N.Y., Harcourt, Brace & Co.

Cherry, C. 1957, On Human Communication. N.Y., Wiley.

Chomsky, Noam. 1965, Aspects of the Theory of Syntax, Cambridge, M.I.T.

Clemens, see Mark.

Comenius, J.A. 1938, The Way of Light, (Via Lucis) XIX, 9, Liverpool, U.P.

DeSaussure, Ferd. Cours de Linguistique générale, Lausanne, 1916.

DeLaguna, G.A. 1927, Speech – Its Function & Development, New Haven, Yale U.P.

Dollard, J. & Miller, N.E. 1950, Personality & Psychotherapy, N.Y., McGraw-Hill.

East-West Journal, Feb. 1979, Zumberge, R. Jr: The Language of Space, p. 80-85.

Eisenson, J., Auer, J.J., Irwin, J.V. 1963, Psychology of Communication, N.Y., Appleton, Century & Crofts.

Eliot, T.S. On Poetry & Poets. N.Y. 1957, Farrar, Straus.

----, Burnt Norton, 1936, Harcourt, Brace, N.Y.

Emerson, R.W. Essays, Nr. X "Circles" (quotes Augustine: God is a circle... cf. good = R, similar to: round = L) 1903-4, Houghton-Mifflin, Boston, MA.

--------, Language, in Nature IV. Complete Works.

Frankl, V.E., 1969, Man's Search for Meaning, Washington Press.

Franklin, B. The Complete Works, London 1806, Longman Hurst.

Freud, S. 1912, The Interpretation of Dreams, N.Y., MacMillan.

Fries, C.C., 1952, The Structure of English, N.Y., Harcourt, Brace

Fuller, B. (R.B.), 1969, Ideas & Integrities, pp. 39, 47, 117. N.Y. Macmillan, Collier.

Goethe, J.W., Faust, I,1, & Etymologie, v.I, p. 898, Stuttgart, Cotta ed. 1959

Goldstein, K. 1948, Language & Language Disturbances. N.Y. Grune-Stratton.

Habsburg, Otto v. 1959, Social Order of Tomorrow. 1964, Word & Revelation, Westminster, MD, Christian Classics

Hammarskjöld, D. Markings, N.Y. 1964, Knopf.

Hanson, R.S. 1968, The Psalms in Modern Speech, Philadelphia, Fortress Press.

Harris, Z.S. 1963. Structural Linguistics, U. Chicago P.

Hayakawa, S.I. 1963. Symbol, Status & Personality. N.Y., Harcourt, Brace & World.

Heffner, R.M.S. 1949, General Phonetics, Madison U. Wisc. Pr.

Hertzler, J.O 1965, Sociology of Language, N.Y. Random House.

Hockett, Ch. 1958, A Course in Modern Linguistics, N.Y., Macmillan.

Humboldt, W. 1884, Uber den National-Character der Sprache, IV, Berlin, Dümmler

Huxley, T.H. & J. 1947, Touchstone for Ethics, N.Y., Harper.

------, A. 1945, The Perennial Philosophy (Not I, but God in me), Harper.

IPA, International Phonetic Assn., 1949, IPA Alphabet, Dept. Phonetics, University College, London, W.C.I.

Jack, A. The Language of Space & Cosmic Elements of Meaning, Scross, East-West Jl, Ap. 1977, p. 86.

James, W. ed. 1955, Principles of Psychology, Chicago, Encycl. Brit., p. 282.

Jaynes, J. The Origin of Consciousness in the Breakdown of the Bicameral Mind. Princeton 1974, Houghton Mifflin, Boston 1977.

Jefferson, Th., Autobiography of, Putnams, 1959 ed. N.Y.

Jesperson, O. 1928. Language, its Nature, Development & Origin. N.Y., Holt, Rinehart, Winston. (p. 402, 442) (cf. "i" for "quick," "ah" for "large": "An idea language would express the same thing by the same means... Sound & Sense would be in perfect harmony.")

Jones, D. 1962. An Outline of English Phonetics, 9th ed. Cambridge, Engl. Heffer & Sons.

-----, 1966, The Pronunciation of English, Cambridge U.P.

Kainz, Fri. 1941-69, Psychologie der Sprache, Stuttgart, Ferd. Enke, vols. I, II, III, IV, V, Va.

-----, Introduction to: aUI, Language of S pace, p. v. See Weilgart, W.J., "Language of Learning Psychology & Logotheraphy."

-----, Über die Sprachverführung des Denkens, 1972, Berline, Dunker & Humbolt.

Kant, I. Kritik der reinen Vernunft — (Critique of Pure Reason, WW.) Reclams Universal Bibl. Leipzig. (Ding an sich, Thing in itself)

Katz, J., 1966, Philosophy of Language, N.Y., Harper.

Korzybski, A., 1949, General Semantics, Self-publication.

Ladefoged, F. 1962, Elements of Acuostic Phonetics, U. Chicago P, p. 92, 102.

Laotzu, Tao Te Ching, tr. Gia-Fu-Feng, & J. English, Vintage, N.Y. 1972.

Leibniz, G.W. 1666, Dissertatio de Arte Combinatoria, Leipzig, Fick Seubold, 1927 ed.

Linsky, L. 1952, Semantics & the Philosophy of Language, Urbana U. Ill. Press.

Lorenz, K.Z. 1966a Er redete mit dem Vieh, den Vögeln & Fischen, p. 88. Glenview, Ill. Scott-Foresman. (Solomon's Ring.) "Interjections."

------, 1966b. On Aggression (Das sogenannte Böse). N.Y. Harcourt, Brace, World.

------, 1965. Evolution & Modification of Behavior, Univ. of Chicago Press.

Maerth, O.K. 1971, Der Anfang war das Ende, Dusseldorf-Wien, Econ. p. 168f.

Mark Twain (Samuel Clemens), "The Family Mark Twain," ed. 1935, N.Y. Harper, p. 1143 & 1163, on German & French... 1206 misuse of words.

Mann, Th. 1924, Der Zauberberg (Magic Mountain), Ch. 7, Frankfurt, Fischer.

Matthias, J. 1969, Learning Speed Comparisons with the Language of Space. Decorah, Luther College Lab, Cosmic Communication Co., Decorah, Iowa.

Mao-Tse-Tung, 1969, in: Essential Works of Chinese Communism, ed. Chai, W. N.Y. Bantam Matrix Bks., p. 97-100, II, 7: "On Contradiction."

Mauthner, F. Beiträge zu einer Kritik der Sprache, 3 v. 1923, Leipzig, Meiner.

May, Rollo. 1958, Existence. N.Y. Basic Books, p. 71 "ahA experience."

Menninger, K. 1968, The Crime of Punishment, see "Jargon," Viking Pr., N.Y.

Musil, R. 1965. The Man without Qualities. N.Y. Capricorn Books.

-----, Five Women, 1966, N.Y. Delta Books, p. 84: "Talk was not the medium for thought, but something like jewelry to impress others."

Neihardt, J.G. 1961. Black Elk Speaks. Lincoln, U. Pr. of Nebraska.

Ochs, S. 1965. The Elements of Neurophysiology. N.Y., J. Wiley.

O'Neill, G. The High Frontier, human colonies in space, 1977, Wm. Morrow, N.Y.

Osgood, C.E., Sebeok, T.A., Diebold, R. 1965, Psycholinguistics. Bloomington, IN U. Press.

Paget, R. 1930, Human Speech. N.Y., Harcourt, Brace & World.

Peirce, C.S. Collected Papers, 1931-35, Signs, vol. II. Cambridge, MA.

Piaget, J. 1971, The Language & Thought of the Child, N.Y., World Publishing.

Plato's Republic, V, 473, Platonis Opera, 5 vol, Oxonii, Clarendon Pr. (Euthyphro Laches, Euthydeums, Gorgias, Protagoras).

Ray, J. 1862 (Sept. 27, Oct. 4 & 11). Polynesian Language, The Polynesian, Honolulu, Hawaii. (Lips, tongues, cheeks resemble objects of the visible world.)

Razran, G. 1961. The Observable Unconscious, Psychology Review 68.

------, 1939, A quantitative study of meaning by semantic conditioning. Science 90, p. 89f.

Russell, B. 1957. Mysticism and Logic, Garden City, N.Y., Doubleday-Anchor Books, p. 129, 207.

Shakespeare, W. Com of Err, III, 1, 75; Hamlet II, 2, 139; V, 1, 148; Othello I, 3, 46; K. John III, 1, 63; 12th Night, III, 1, 24 (on language). cf. "Shakespeare Psychognostic" by W.J. Wellgart.

Solzhenitsyn, A. Nobel Prize Acceptance Speech, in TIME, Spt. 4, 1972, N.Y.

Spinoza, B. Ethica, ed. 1882, Amsterdam, ed. van Vloten, Part II, definitio 6.

Steiger, B. Revelation, the Divine Fire, 1973, pp. 167-172 on Language of Space.

------, Mysteries of Time & Space, 1974 – both Prentice Hall, N.J. Englewood Cliffs.

Steiner, R. Anthroposophie, 1924, Rudolf Steiner Verlag, Dornach, Basel, Switzerland.

------, Eurythmie als sichtbare Sprache, 1924, Dornach, Basel, Switzerland.

Swedenborg, E. Arcana Coelestia, 8 vol, London 1749-58, Swedenborg Society.

Talleyrand, Ch. M. in: Memoires de Barere, 1842, in: Büchmann: Geflügelte Worte, 1950: "language serves to hide one's thoughts."

Thomas Aquinas: Summa Theologiae, De Natura materiae (Opera).

Thomas, C.K. 1958, An introduction to the Phonetics of American English. N.Y., Ronald Press.

Tillich, P. 1944, Existential Philosophy, Jl. of History of Ideas, 5:1.

------, Kairos, Darmstadt, Reichl, 1926 (Courage to exist).

Tolstoy, L. Horse Strider, in: Short Stories, Modern Library 1964, N.Y.

Trubetzkoy, N.S. 1969, Principles of Phonology, tr. Baltaxe, C.A.M. Berkeley & L.A., U. Cal. Pr. p. 98f, 66f, 273, 298.

Tylor, E.B. 1903, Primitive Culture, N.Y. vol. I, p. 220: ch. v, vl, 1977.

-----, Anthropology, 1881, p. 128. ("puf" = a blowing imitation...)

Vendler, Z., 1967, Linguistics in Philosophy, Ithaca, N.Y., Cornell U. Press.

Vischer, F.T. 1879, Auch Einer, 1904 Volksausgabe. (Tücke des Objekts)

-------, 1846-57, 1922-3, Aesthetik – Wissenschaft des Schönen, 6 vols.

Waldheim, K., 1973, Austrian Example. N.Y., Macmillan.

Weilgart, W.J. 1937, Gedichte — Traumgesichte (Dream Poems), Vienna, Concordia.

-------, Kunts & Mystik, 1939 (Creation & Contemplation), Bibl. p. 419. (Dissertation, Univ. Vienna) Name: Weixlgärtner, Johann Wolfgang.

-------, 1946, Macbeth — Demon & Bourgeois, New Orleans, N.O. Shakespeare Soc.

-------, 1947, March, No. 3: Creative Tensions, Monatshefte, 39th yr, Madison, Wisc., Univ. Wisc. Monthly.

-------, Peace Education, Education, 67th yr, N.Y.

-------, Peace Philosophy, in: Personalist, 28th yr, Jan, Univ. S. Calif, L.A.

-------, 1950, Who Is Peaceful? N.Y. Exposition Press or: Cosmic Communication, Decorah, Iowa. New ed. "Peace thru People, 1973.

-------, 1952, Shakespeare Psychognostic, Character Evolution & Transformation, Bibl. pp. 239-276., Tokyo, Hokuseido. (Reviewed in Nippon Times)

-------, 1954, July: Fredens Etik (Ethics of Peace) in: Världs Horisont, United Nations Journal, p. 23. Göteborg, Sweden.

-------, 1954/55, La psychologie de la paix et la chrétienté, Psyché, Paris, 96/97.

-------, 1955, June: Heilung eines Waschzwanges, in: Traumerleben im prapsychot. St, with Jost, F., & Sinn, W. Wienr Archiv für Psychologie, Psychiatrie & Neurologie, pp. 101-115 (Cure of Compulsion Neurses)

-------, 1956, Versuch zu einer selbstgelenkten Kindertherapie, (Self-directed child therapy) Der Psychologe, VIII, v. 8, Bern, Swiss Psy.

-------, 1957, Was ist Normal — im Schatten der Atombombe? (a Psychology of Aggression) Vienna, Gerold & Co.

-------, (1957, Feb. Reviewed in: Världs Horisont (World Horison, U.N. Jl.))

-------, 1957, Was ist Normal ? Kind & Jugend in der Gemeinschaft (Child & Youth in Society), Vienna, Austrian State Publication on Education.

-------, 1956, Oct. with Jost, F. Alkoholismus & Zoophilie (Hypno-semantic therapy) in: Heilkunst, 69th yr, X., Univ. Munich Therapy Journal.

-------, 1958, April, aUI, a psycho-symbolic Language of Semantic Therapy, in: International Language Review.

-------, 1966, Spring. WERT (Weilgart-Ethos-Rhyme-Test) vol. 8, no. 1, International Mental Health Research, New York.

Weilgart, W.J. 1968, aUI, the Language of Space, New Delhi, Delhi, Bombay, Calcutta, Madras: Chand & Co; & Cosmic Communication Co., Decorah, IA 52101, U.S.A. (Reviewed in London Times Lit. Sup.) 4th edition, 1979, Cosmic Com. Co. Tape Cassette aUI Sounds; Cosmic Cards.

-------, 1970. The Language of Space — Peace through Understanding. Decorah, Iowa, Cosmic Communication Co.

-------, 1970a.a. aUI — Bio Rhythms of Communication. Decorah, IA, Cosmic Communication Co.

-------, 1971, July, Communication: Logic or Command. Cosmic Communication Co. & in: Papers in Linguistics, Linguistic Research Inc., p. 127-68. University of Illinois, Champaign, Ill. & U. Alberta, Edmonton. (Also through Cosmic Communication Co., Decorah, Iowa 52101.)

-------, 1971a, Cosmic Dreams in Healing Words (Poems in aUI & English), Cosmic Communication Co., Decorah, Iowa 52101.

-------, 1972, Cosmic Christ (Poem with Picture, in aUI), Cosmic Communication Co., Decorah, IA 52101

-------, 1975, Cosmic Communication in Elements of Essence. Cosmic Communication Co., 100 Elm Ct., Decorah, IA 52101

-------, 1976, Cosmic Elements of Meaning, Symbols of the Spirit's Life. Cosmic Communication Co., Decorah, IA 52101.

-------, 1977, Cosmic Logotherapy with aUI, the Language of Space. Cosmic Communication Co., Decorah, IA 52101.

(About W.J. Weilgart's "aUI, Language of Space" & "Cosmic Elements of Meaning": LONDON's TIMES, Chicago Sun Times, Whole Earth Catalog, Steiger, B. "Revelation, the Divine Fix," Kainz, F. "Language of Learning Psychology & Logotherapy," A. Jack: "Language of Space" in Scroll, East West Journal, April 1977: "masterful...marvelous," Rev. Prof. R.S. Hanson: "to understand reality & learn to think"; L. Griffiths, N.E. Iowa: "a cosmic man," Zumberge, R.: "aUI words...for my deepest feelings & highest thoughts...simple yet profound." (East-West Jl. Feb. 1979, pp. 80-85).)

Weinrich, H. 1966. Linguistik der Lüge, Heidelberg, Lambert Schneider.

Weldon, T.D. Vocabulary of Politics, 1953, Baltimore, Penguin Books.

Westermann, D. 1937. Laut & Sinn in einigen West-Afrikanischen Sprachen. Archiv für vergleichende Phonetik, 7: 154-93.

-----------, 1907, Grammatik der Ewe Sprache. Pp. 83ff. (here sounds are symbolic of meaning, e.g. "i" means "bright & quick.")

Whorf, B.L. Four Articles on Metalinguistics, 1950, Washington, D.C. Foreign Inst. Dept. of State.

Wiener, N. 1965, Cybernetics: Control of Communication. Cambridge: MIT Press.

Wittgenstein, L. Tractatus Logico-philosophicus; 1922, & Philsophic Investigations, 1953, Blackwell, Oxford.

World Book Dictionary, 1967. Chicago, Field Corp.

Wundt, W. Völkerpsychologie. 1904. vol. 1, pp. 116, 126, 136, 332.

Yudovich, Ia, Luria, A.R. 1968, Speech and the Development of Mental Processes in the Child. London: Staples Publ. Co.

Ziff, P. 1960, Semantic Analysis. Ithaca, Cornell U. Press.

Zipf, G.K. 1935, The Psychology of Language. N.Y. Houghton-Mifflin.

Zumberge, R. Jr. The Language of Space...Dr. Weilgart's book...East-West Jl., Feb. 1979, pp. 80-85.

U.P. = University Press. Univ. = University. U.N. = United Nations.

Publications by Prof. Dr. Dr. W. John Weilgart

Weilgart, W. J.: Kunst & Mystik (Psychology of Creation & Contemplation) Bibl. p. 419, Wien, University of Vienna 1939 (Weixlgärtner)

———, Creative Tensions, Monatshefte, 39th year, Mr. 1947, No. 3, University of Wisconsin Monthly, Madison, Wisc.

———, Peace Education, in: Education, 67th year, New York, N.Y.

———, Peace Philosophy, in: The Personalist, 28th year, Jan. (Periodical of Philosophy Dept., U. of S. Cal., Los Angeles)

———, Who is Peaceful? Exposition Pr. N.Y. 1950

———, Fredens Etik (Ethics of Peace), in: Världs Horisont, (World Horizon) United Nations J1., J1. 1954, Göteborg, Sweden

———, Was ist normal (What is normal?), Rev. in: Världs Horisont, U.N. J1, Feb. 1957, p. 23

———, Was ist normal im Schatten der Atombombe? (Psychology of the Aggression drive), 1957, Vienna, Gerold & Co., Wien

———, Shakespeare Psychognostic, Character Evolution & Transformation, Bibliogr. pp. 239-276, Hokuseido Publ., Tokyo, 1952

———, (Weilgart, Wolf): Macbeth: Demon & Bourgeois, in: N.O. Shakespeare Society Publ., 1946

———, Heilung eines Waschzwanges, in: Zum Traumerleben im präpsychotischen Stadium, Jost, F., Weilgart, W. J., Sinn, W., in: Wiener Archiv fur Psychologie, Psychiatrie & Neurologie, June 1955, pp. 101-115 (Cure of compulsion neurosis, with prepsychotic dreams)

———, La psychologie de la paix et la chretienté, (Psychology of peace and christianity,) in: Psyche, Paris, 1954/55, No. 96/97.

———, Gedichte—Traumgesichte (Dream Poems), Concordia Publ., Vienna

———, Versuch zu einer selbstgelenkten Kindertherapie, (Self-directed child-therapy) in: Der Psychologe, VIII, v. 8, Bern 1956 (Swiss P. J1)

———, Was ist normal: Kind und Jugend in der Gemeinschaft (Child & Youth in society) Austrian State Publications on Education, Vienna 1957

———, & Jost, F., M.D., Alkoholismus und Zoophilie (Hypnotic semantic therapy of alcoholic zoophiliac) in: Heilkunst, 69th year, Heft X, Oct., 1956, University of Munich Therapy journal

———, WERT (Weilgart-Ethos-Rhyme-Test), Wert Diagnosis for Prophylaxis & therapy, Spring 1966, v. VIII, No. 1 (International Mental Health Research) New York

———, aUI, a psychosymbolic language of semantic therapy, in: International language review, April 1958

———, aUI, The Language of Space, (John W. Weilgart) (c) 1968, Chand & Co., New Delhi, Delhi, Bombay, Calcutta, Madras, Hyderabad &c. & Cosmic Communication Co., Decorah, Iowa 52101, in USA.

———, The Language of Space, Peace through Understanding, 1970, Decorah, Ia.

———, aUI, BioRhythms of Communication, 1970, Decorah, Cosmic Communication Company, Decorah, Iowa

———, The Sounding Cave of Wind & Wave, Cosmic Communication Co.

———, Communication: Logic or Command, Papers in Linguistics, Linguistic Research Inc., Universities of Illinois & Alberta vol. 1971. pp. 127-168

———, aUI, The Language of Space, 1974, 3rd enriched edition, Cosmic Communication Co., Decorah, Iowa 52101, & Chand, Delhi, India

———, Cosmic Communication in Elements of Essence, 1975, Cosmic Communication Co., Decorah, Iowa 52101

———, 1971, Cosmic Dreams in Healing Words (aUI & English), Cosmic Communication Co., Decorah, Iowa

———, Cosmic Cards for plays with fate. 1970

———, Toward a Scientific Language (for Academy of Science). 1976

———, Cosmic Elements of Meaning, Symbols of the Spirit's Life (Cosmic Communication Co., Decorah, Iowa 52101. USA) 1976

---- Peace thru People, a philosophy of survival for the pan-atomic age, 1977

---- Cosmic Logotherapy with aUI, the Language of Space: Health thru Harmony, Creation & Truth, 1978

---- aUI, the Language of Space, Pentecostal Logos of Love & Peace, 4th ed. 1979

www.ingramcontent.com/pod-product-compliance
Lightning Source LLC
Chambersburg PA
CBHW080324270326
41927CB00014B/3090

* 9 7 8 0 9 1 2 0 3 8 0 8 7 *